IBSEN: THE CRITICAL HERITAGE

THE CRITICAL HERITAGE SERIES

GENERAL EDITOR: B. C. SOUTHAM, M.A., B.LITT. (OXON)
Formerly Department of English, Westfield College, University of London

For list of books in the series see back end paper

IBSEN

THE CRITICAL HERITAGE

Edited by
MICHAEL EGAN
Department of English, University of Lancaster

ROUTLEDGE AND KEGAN PAUL LONDON AND BOSTON

First published 1972
by Routledge & Kegan Paul Ltd
Broadway House, 68–74 Carter Lane
London EC4V 5EL and
9 Park Street,
Boston, Mass. 02108, U.S.A.
© Michael Egan 1972
No part of this book may be reproduced in
any form without permission from the
publisher, except for the quotation of brief
passages in criticism

First published as a paperback in 1985
ISBN 0-7102-0592-9

Printed in Great Britain
by W & J Mackay Limited, Chatham

FOR JANE

General Editor's Preface

The reception given to a writer by his contemporaries and near-contemporaries is evidence of considerable value to the student of literature. On one side we learn a great deal about the state of criticism at large and in particular about the development of critical attitudes towards a single writer; at the same time, through private comments in letters, journals or marginalia, we gain an insight upon the tastes and literary thought of individual readers of the period. Evidence of this kind helps us to understand the writer's historical situation, the nature of his immediate reading-public, and his response to these pressures.

The separate volumes in the *Critical Heritage Series* present a record of this early criticism. Clearly, for many of the highly productive and lengthily reviewed nineteenth- and twentieth-century writers, there exists an enormous body of material; and in these cases the volume editors have made a selection of the most important views, significant for their intrinsic critical worth or for their representative quality—perhaps even registering incomprehension!

For earlier writers, notably pre-eighteenth century, the materials are much scarcer and the historical period has been extended, sometimes far beyond the writer's lifetime, in order to show the inception and growth of critical views which were initially slow to appear.

In each volume the documents are headed by an Introduction, discussing the material assembled and relating the early stages of the author's reception to what we have come to identify as the critical tradition. The volumes will make available much material which would otherwise be difficult of access and it is hoped that the modern reader will be thereby helped towards an informed understanding of the ways in which literature has been read and judged.

B.C.S.

Contents

ix

CONTENTS

Preface

This volume in the *Critical Heritage* series is the only one so far to deal with an author whose language was not English. Ibsen's impact, however, was felt throughout the English-speaking world in his lifetime owing to the speed and efficiency of translation, and to this extent he functioned in effect as a contemporary English and American playwright. There is little evidence to suggest that Ibsen was ever influenced by critical reaction to his work in England or the United States; but this does not minimize the intrinsic interest and value which that response has for ourselves.

ACKNOWLEDGMENTS

I wish to thank the following for permission to reprint copyright extracts or complete items from the sources printed below:

Mrs Elinor Finley for theatre notices, reviews and articles by William Archer; Miss Jennifer Gosse for articles by Sir Edmund Gosse in *Fortnightly Review* and from *The Prose Dramas of Henrik Ibsen*; the *Spectator* for two unsigned articles by Sir Edmund Gosse and for a review of *A Doll's House* and *The Master Builder*; the Society of Authors on behalf of the Bernard Shaw Estate, as the literary representative of the Estate of James Joyce and as the literary representative of the Estate of Havelock Ellis, for all quotations from Bernard Shaw, James Joyce and Havelock Ellis; the *Observer* for reviews of *The Lady from the Sea*, *Hedda Gabler* and the satirical poem by William Hardinge; the *Evening News* for four theatre reviews; the *Evening Standard* for two theatre reviews and from the report of a murder trial; *The Times* for seven theatre reviews; the *Sunday Times* for four theatre reviews; John Farquharson Ltd, for the letters from Henry James to Edmund Gosse; Mr J. C. Medley of Field, Fisher and Co. for George Moore's 'Note on Ghosts' in *Impressions and Opinions*; the Estate of the late Max Beerbohm and the *Saturday Review* for all extracts by Max Beerbohm; the *Daily Telegraph* for theatre reviews by Clement Scott and two unsigned reviews; the *Illustrated London News* for a theatre review by Clement Scott; Odhams Newspapers Ltd for two reviews from the *People*; the *New York Times* for three theatre reviews, 1889, 1894, 1898.

I would also like to acknowledge my gratitude to Dr David Craig and Dr Anne Wright of the English Department, Lancaster University, and to Mr Eric Homberger of the School of English and American Studies, University of East Anglia, who all read my Introduction and made valuable suggestions.

Introduction

That major innovating talents are frequently received with hostility is a commonplace in literary history; yet to point this out is only partly to account for the uniquely bitter and vicious antagonisms which characterized Ibsen's contemporary reception in Europe and the United States. It was almost as if the future of civilization itself was felt to be at stake; throughout the Western world literary and political establishments reacted sharply, and polarized in extreme positions, over his name and work. Ibsen became a symbol. In Sweden during the 1880s, for instance, conflicting passions ran so high over *A Doll's House* that even to mention it in polite society was to risk a breach of decorum. On one occasion a well-known hostess, mindful both of this and of the success of her party, wrote tactfully across her luncheon invitations: 'You are politely requested not to discuss Ibsen's new play.' In the Anglo-Saxon world—the area dealt with specifically in this book—he was to some (the 'Ibsen-phobiacs' as William Archer was later to call them) one of the chief manifestations of contemporary evil and corruption: unquestionably a sexual degenerate, an advocate of free love and votes for women and, worse still, a socialist; to others (the 'Ibsen-maniacs') he was something only slightly less than *salvator mundi*, the champion of and spokesman for all progress, a fighter in the vanguard for feminine emancipation and, better still, a socialist.

A curious self-consciousness infuses the writings of Ibsen's contemporaries when we read them now. They were aware that the clash over his name, and what it came to represent, was somehow pivotal; that future generations would judge them in its light. So acutely did Ibsen appear to challenge or confirm their values that even as they reacted—part of the history of that response itself—came the recognition that its direction and quality were intrinsically important, a reflection of and a comment on the period. As early as April 1891, William Archer, one of Ibsen's chief defenders in England, satirically but bitterly proposed the compilation of a volume modelled on Wagner's *Schimpflexicon*, a dictionary of abuse, in which to record the hysterical obloquy levelled at the author of *Ghosts*. In what is probably the most famous short piece of polemic to come out of the Ibsen controversy (No. 72) Archer made a start on his 'Manual of Malediction', his 'Baedecker to Billingsgate', and simply listed the howls of abuse and execration which appeared in the national press following the London première of *Ghosts*.[1] The impact of this tactic on Ibsen's opponents was so profound, so chastening, that two years later Archer made use of it again (see 'The Mausoleum of Ibsen', No. 114). Shocked perhaps at the cumulative violence of their reaction—'a loathesome sore unbandaged; a dirty act done publicly . . . Revoltingly suggestive . . . Merely dull dirt long drawn out . . . Garbage and offal . . . putrid . . . foul and filthy . . .', etc.—the critics thereafter modified their tone; posterity, after all, was watching.

The story of the battle over Ibsen in this country is a curious one. It is easy to mock his critics for their blindness and cultural Toryism, and praise his defenders for their courage and percipience: there is undoubtedly an exhilarating David-and-Goliath quality in the spectacle of a handful of intellectuals and actresses slowly taking apart the Victorian establishment. And yet a strangely English spirit pervaded the whole debate—which is not to say that it was not bitterly or even bitchily conducted. But it was possible for the defenders to claim that a low blow had been struck—as Archer did when he compiled his *Schimpflexicon*—and for the attackers to agree. Again, satire became a formidable weapon—but a snobby, very Victorian kind of satire, with each side, but more characteristically Ibsen's critics, attempting to affect a careless, upper-class insouciance. Repeated efforts were made to have him laughed out of the theatre—'How We Found Gibsen' (No. 71) and some of the press reactions to *Ghosts* and *Rosmersholm* (Nos 45, 46, 49, 51, 53, 65, 66) are excellent examples. A flurry of uneasy, tight-lipped satirical verses accompanied these efforts (see, for instance, No. 104). When they failed, Ibsen's antagonists mocked him on stage, and a rash of crude parodies—one of the earliest, in May 1891, was by the young James Barrie, his first play (No. 92)—poked fun, to the accompanying applause of the press, at the improbabilities of his plots. An anonymous commentator in the *Saturday Review* announced gleefully in March 1891:

Ibsen is to be burlesqued, and great is the indignation thereat in the Ibsenite camp. *Bogies* will turn into ridicule the 'sacred drama of *Ghosts*' and *Goats*; *Go-a-Hedda Gabler* will make fun—if it can?—of *Hedda Gabler*. The burlesques in question are to be published shortly, and are the production of Mr Henry Gibson. *Apropos* of Ibsen, it may be some consolation to those who do not bow down and worship before this latest golden calf of the Freethinking community, that in Rome *La Casa della Bambola* fell to pieces like a card house never to rise again.[2]

Ibsen's supporters, for their part, took care on the whole to place themselves culturally and aesthetically upwind—their tone was loftier, more detached. If they felt indignant over Ibsen's treatment in the West End they were careful not to show it. Instead they ridiculed his opponents' philistinism and mocked their inconsistencies: how, they queried, could Ibsen be both too improbable and yet too nastily true to life, too immoral and yet only too tediously moralizing? 'When we find Mr. Clement Scott and the critic of the *Daily Telegraph* [i.e. Clement Scott] flatly contradicting each other, chaos seems to have come again,' wrote Archer in April 1891.

The whole acrid dispute was, in its way, a struggle over Ibsen's respectability—the inevitable terms, perhaps, in which an argument of this nature would present itself in Victorian England. '*The Pillars of Society* may excite Scandinavian audiences,' wrote the theatre columnist of the *Sunday Times* with coy prurience, 'but it must be adapted to English theatrical conditions lest it chance to suggest the pillows of society.'[3] When, in 1891, Elizabeth Robins and Marion Lea were able to stage the first London production of *Hedda Gabler* at the Vaudeville, and when, two years later, Beerbohm Tree himself played Dr Stockmann at the Haymarket, the battle was virtually over. Ibsen had become fashionable.

Despite its scope and intensity, then, the Ibsen wrangle was of relatively short duration. This is something worth bearing in mind when we consider the later years of his reception in England, 1895 to 1900, for there is more than a touch of gratuitous heroics in the tone adopted by some commentators—Bernard Shaw for one—at this time. For three or four years, say between June 1889 and June 1893, the argument was genuinely bitter and in the balance. Thereafter, following the triumph of Beerbohm Tree's *An Enemy of the People*, it died gradually away until by the turn of the century Ibsen's genius was universally acknowledged. Ironically, it was even exaggerated. When his inferior, bombastic Norse sagas were produced in London for the first time—*The Vikings at Helgeland* in 1903, *Lady Inger of Östraat* in 1906—they were treated as major theatrical occasions, such was his prestige. Even the waspish Clement Scott, Ibsen's bitterest antagonist, conceded defeat as early as 1899 when he published his memoirs:

The Ibsen reaction, with its unloveliness, its want of faith; its hopeless, despairing creed; its worship of the ugly in art; its grim and repulsive reaction, regret it as we will, is a solemn and resistless fact. At the outset some of us, conscientiously and in the interests of the art we loved and had followed with such persistency, tried to laugh it out of court. But the time came when the laugh was on the other side. I own it; I admit it.[4]

EARLY REACTIONS AND TRANSLATIONS

The Ibsen explosion, for all its vivid intensity, and for all the reputations which it made and sundered, bore little relation to the sequence in which his dramas were published, or to the vigorous campaigning attempts made to bring his name before the public. Born in 1828 he was already an old man, with few years of creativity remaining him, by the time general attention was paid to his work in this country. Why this was so is difficult to say. Edmund Gosse, an acute and sensitive critic, had held a militant public brief for him since the early 1870s (see Nos 1, 2, 3, 14) following a visit to Norway. During the mid-1880s adaptations of *A Doll's House* and *The Pillars of Society*, consciously trivialized and denatured for English consumption, were performed in London under the titles *Breaking a Butterfly* and *Quicksands* (Nos 5, 17). Yet neither these efforts nor the campaigns of Gosse and, later, Archer aroused much interest. Not even the availability of what were, under the circumstances, quite reasonable translations, made much of an impact—it was an age in which the reading of a play was considered to require as much expertise as the reading of a musical score. Not until the early 1890s were British dramatists, led by Henry James (recently humiliated as a failed playwright), to publish their work as literature—designed to be read. It was to result in the emergence of a new genre: the Shavian play-novel, complete with preface and extended directions.

Emperor and Galilean, translated and introduced by Catherine Ray, was published by Samuel Tinsley in 1876—the earliest complete Ibsen drama to appear in English (see No. 4). Three years previously Edmund Gosse had translated and published substantial portions of *Love's Comedy* in the *Fortnightly Review*, and a year before that, in 1872, a slim volume called *Norwegian and Swedish Poems*, containing a translation of Ibsen's *Terje Vigen*, was privately published in Bergen by Johan A. Dahl; but Gosse's version was incomplete and only part of an article on Ibsen (No. 3), and Dahl's volume was hardly noticed. The importance of Miss Ray's text is therefore central; and it is ironic that of the translator herself almost nothing is known other than that she later wrote some weak novels with a Norwegian orientation. *Emperor and Galilean* itself was almost universally ignored, and another four years were to pass before anything else appeared in English.[5] In 1880, however, the unfortunate T. Weber, subsequently pilloried by Archer in an article called 'Ibsen as He is Translated' (No. 35), published in Copenhagen a tortured rendering of *A Doll's House*. Luckily this version of the play, translated into a painful pidgin, attracted no attention whatsoever. Two years later, in 1882, Mrs Henrietta Frances Lord, a genial crank who believed in a Christianized version of metempsychosis (No. 40), published a marginally superior translation entitled *Nora*. Her chief reason for doing so appears to have been the opportunity it provided to furnish a long preface on the subject of marriage (No. 8). Three years later she produced a version of *Ghosts*, published in three successive numbers of the socialist journal *Today* (January, February and March 1885) and subsequently made into a book with an introduction by the translator suggesting that Mrs Alving might have overcome many of her difficulties had she only practised a little Christian Science on Oswald (No. 40). Finally, in 1888, the young Havelock Ellis edited for Walter Scott Ltd, in their *Camelot Series*, the first serious collection of Ibsen's plays. It contained two translations by William Archer, *The Pillars of Society* and *Ghosts*, the latter being an extensively revised version of Mrs Lord's rendering, and a translation from the German of *An Enemy of Society* [sic] by Karl Marx's daughter Eleanor.[6]

'A DOLL'S HOUSE' AND 'THE PILLARS OF SOCIETY'

Nevertheless, as we have seen, neither the availability of translations nor the enthusiasm of Gosse and his friends did much for Ibsen in England. Rather, and more predictably perhaps, it was the staging of local productions in, as it were, unsterilized versions, which initially aroused widespread attention. The first of these was *A Doll's House*. Janet Achurch's Nora, played at the Novelty Theatre on 7 June 1889, marked the first decisive moment in the history of Ibsen's contemporary reception in this country. Overnight, literally, he became a famous man. As Archer noted in the *Fortnightly Review* barely four weeks later: 'If we may measure fame by mileage of newspaper comment, Henrik Ibsen has for the past month been the most famous man in the English literary world.'[7] His presumed commitment to women's rights and other revolutionary notions, and his rumoured sexual depravity, did more in a week to bring his name before the public than all Gosse's books and articles had done in nearly twenty years.

The ironies implicit in all this began to caricature themselves almost immediately. Press reactions to *A Doll's House*, centring as they did on particular, local issues, set the tone and direction of Ibsen criticism for decades to come. For years—in some quarters even today—it was impossible to discuss Ibsen without referring to the position of women in society, although the playwright himself repeatedly stressed that he was less concerned with questions of marriage and suffrage than with the plight of the repressed individual in Victorian society. It is quite probable that the course taken by Ibsen's reception in England, and thus thinking about his drama in later years, would have been markedly different had London's first taste of his unexpurgated work been, say, *An Enemy of the People* or *The Pillars of Society*. As it was, his critics, both for and against, chose to do battle over the issue of women's rights; and in particular over the specific event of Nora's having deserted her children. The slamming of the Helmers's front door re-echoed in the Victorian and Edwardian mind for nearly a quarter of a century.

At first the press were inclined to dismiss Nora's decision, along with the rest of the play, as improbable. Clement Scott was particularly contemptuous: 'How it could ever be possible for any woman with the maternal instinct fully developed to desert her children because her pride has been wounded, are points that may be very clear to the Ibsenites, but they require a considerable amount of argument to convince the commonsense playgoer.'8 Note how Scott distorts Ibsen's intent by caricaturing Nora's complex series of insights ('her pride has been wounded'), shifting the drama's emphases until they accord with a scale of values he can deal with. It is precisely because Nora's 'maternal instincts' are fully developed, because she cares about her children's future and her own, that she leaves home. Yet Scott resolutely adopts Helmer's position; not from malice but because this is the only view of the action that appears comprehensible. This was later to become an almost universal tendency among Ibsen's critics. *Hedda Gabler* was condemned because, they said, the stage ran with blood and mounds of corpses blocked the view. *Rosmersholm* presented nymphomania to the public gaze and *Ghosts* advocated suicide, incest and other sexual indecencies. The substantive moral issues Ibsen raised were characteristically ignored or caricatured.

In the majority of cases this was not done deliberately. Ibsen's critics viewed his plays through the eyes of Manders, Brack, Helmer because, broadly speaking, of a coincidence of values. People—and dramatists—simply didn't do such things. The *Daily News*, for example, observed of Nora in a review: 'In spite of Ibsen or any other theorist, it may be confidently asserted that no women who ever breathed would do any such thing.'[9] Krogstad alone emerged relatively unscathed—he, at least, declared *Truth*, behaved (in the end) like a gentleman.[10]

But of course, as the presumed implications of *A Doll's House* made themselves felt, the tone soon changed from a mild refusal to suspend disbelief to a bitter antagonism. Nora's departure, presented with the dramatist's approbation and as the apparent moral of the play, was viewed by a shocked public as a direct attack on the institution of marriage. Nora became a monster, an unnatural woman, a Victorian Medea capable of deserting home, husband and children in search of a specious ideal—the indulgence of self. What particularly stuck in contemporary throats was her remark, 'We have been married eight years, and we are strangers. I have borne three children—to a stranger. I cannot remain any longer under the roof of a strange man.' The hostility—and the adjectives—spilt over on those audiences who applauded, or who at least failed to condemn, these sentiments. They were unnatural-looking women, long-haired men, a socially and sexually perverse collection of atheists, socialists and positivists who had assembled to gloat over Ibsen's revolting ideas. The London press was filled with this sort of abuse. The Earl of Jersey, Governor of Australia, took his cue from the British papers when Janet Achurch arrived in Sydney with her production of *A Doll's House*. He and his wife 'sternly refused' to attend the play and the Countess, according to a report in the *Era*, a London stage journal, 'wrote a letter in which she said that she had heard too much about Ibsen's plays to wish to see one of them, and that she did not think that any actress who would appear in them could be considered a lady. Miss Achurch,' the *Era* concluded tartly, 'is bearing up wonderfully.'[11]

Wonderfully, perhaps, but also somewhat ambiguously. On the eve of her departure for Australia she was interviewed by the *Pall Mall Gazette* about her attitude to the part.[12] It is a measure of public opinion at the time that she was able to offer only the weakest of rationalizations in Nora's defence. Yes, she agreed, Nora had done wrong to abandon her children, but on the other hand she did not believe that her example would tend 'as some say' to easier divorce and the reckless abandonment of home. 'What it ought to do is make [women] much less reckless about marrying . . .' Miss Achurch added that she thought Nora would probably return after some years, but that the marriage would fail again. Helmer was 'impossible, utterly impossible'.

Throughout Europe the dispute over Nora's return and the consequences of her departure had become a key issue in the Ibsen debate. Few doubted that return she would; and if you were of the pro-Ibsen camp you would show how, the miracle of miracles having occurred, her decision to leave is vindicated. Indeed in Germany public pressure on this point was so strong that Ibsen was compelled to write, and sanction for production, a 'happy' ending along these lines. In England this version was fortunately never used, although as we shall see it formed the basis for early adaptations of the play in the United States. Instead, public argument centred on the consequences of her going, Ibsen's supporters adopting the approach I have just mentioned, his detractors suggesting vehemently that the effects of her actions must be disastrous. The most influential statement of this view came from Walter Besant, the novelist, who, in January 1890, published a seminal piece in the *English Illustrated Magazine* which provoked a minor storm in the literary world. Besant's object was to demonstrate the folly and criminality of Nora's ideas by examining their consequences—not for herself, for she is irredeemably lost, but for her family. Nora, now a novelist of notorious reputation, returns after many years to find Helmer a lonely drunk, and her children in various stages of delinquency and despair. Complete social disgrace has come upon the family. This pitiable state of affairs turns tragic when Krogstad, now manager of the bank and one of the pillars of the community, refuses his permission to allow Emmy, Nora's daughter, to marry one of his dazzlingly successful sons. In despair Emmy drowns herself. But Nora, that unnatural woman, is unmoved. As she leaves town the bier carrying Emmy's corpse goes slowly by and she almost feels a spark of motherly care and love. But she controls herself and remarks coldly: 'What have I to do with a strange man and his dead child?' It is left to Mrs Linde, accompanying Nora to the station, to speak the moral: 'Nora,' said Christine, 'you will never—never—never—forget this scene. Go! You will be haunted forever with the destruction of your own children by your own hand.'

This splendidly melodramatic effort, presented with all the skill of a professional writer, provoked a series of equally splendid retorts. Bernard Shaw, for example, was fond of telling his friends that Besant's story so enraged him that he immediately sat down to compose a reply, 'Still After the Doll's House' (*Time*, February 1890) in dramatic form. He was so impressed with the result, said Shaw, that he realized he was a born playwright; and from that day forward made the theatre his career. Eleanor Marx also composed a retort to Besant's tale, and others appeared in Germany, Scandinavia and the United States. The most notable of these, perhaps, was 'Nora's Return: A Sequel to *The Doll's House* by Henry Ibsen', written by a formidable American lady, Mrs Ednah Dow Littledale Cheney. The gist of her account is that Nora, after many years spent in good works, returns home to nurse Helmer back to health when a cholera epidemic strikes the town. Over the years he has come to understand the error of his ways and has, in addition, begun to notice with increasing frequency Nora's uncanny resemblance to Michelangelo's Virgin of the Pietà, Raphael's Madonna and St Joan of Arc. As a result of these events the long-awaited miracle occurs and the pair are joyfully reunited. Nora's earlier decision has been vindicated.

While these sequels were being composed Ibsen's supporters—that small band of critics, translators and actresses—were following up the *succès de scandale* of *A Doll's House* with a second play. We can only speculate, of course, about the processes of choice, why and how one play was selected rather than another; yet one does feel that the final selection, *The Pillars of Society*, surely not one of Ibsen's best or most representative plays, was an odd one. But public opinion may have compelled it; possibly the Ibsenites wanted to cool matters by offering the least provocative, which is to say most conventional, of his social dramas; or possibly they wished to show that he was not wholly obsessed with venereal disease and the question of women's rights. In any event the play was staged at the Opéra Comique on 17 July 1889, with Genevieve Ward as Lona Hessel and W. H. Vernon as Consul Bernick. The producers, sensitive to the charge that they were capitalizing on smut and fashion, offered only a single, mid-week matinée and announced beforehand that the proceeds would be donated to Vera Beringer, the child actress who appeared as Olaf.

Attitudes to Ibsen, both public and private, had however already formed and hardened. He was the Ibscene dramatist, spearhead of the insidious attack on traditional morality. Two months earlier *The Pillars of Society* might have been received with comparative warmth; for years the London stage had been awaiting a conqueror. Now the critics were merely disposed to find fault at every turn. Reading through the press reviews one cannot fail to be struck by their surprise at the play's inoffensiveness; to this extent the calculations of Ibsen's supporters proved to be correct. But the fear and hostility aroused by *A Doll's House* were not to be easily dissipated. If that play was the English

9

Hernani its successor was not to be allowed to pass unmolested. *The Pillars of Society*, inoffensive, even orthodox, was dismissed—with a cataclysmic public yawn. Tedious and prolix, drawled the critics; what a ghastly bore. Still, they had to admit the audience received it with enthusiasm, though one could not forbear to add sourly that 'expressions of weariness at the prosiness of many of the speeches were not unfrequent'.[13]

The Pillars of Society achieved little, and it certainly failed to convince the critical establishment that Ibsen was a serious and competent dramatist with no morbid interest in hereditary disorders or socialism. The intransigence of the prejudice confronting Ibsen's admirers was clearly very disheartening and left them with this choice: quit or fight back. For nearly two years they did nothing. Throughout the rest of 1889 and the whole of 1890 no attempt was made to produce another Ibsen play in London; stray articles appeared, letters were exchanged— such as Gosse's vigorous attempt to win Henry James's public support (Nos 41, 74)—and Besant's story was taken up from time to time. But the Ibsenites were too demoralized to risk another massive public censure and it was not until the early months of 1891 that they were able to seize the initiative once again. Then, by a coincidence of accident and design four of Ibsen's finest and most powerful dramas were produced in rapid succession on the London stage.

THE CENTRAL PHASE

Between the end of February and the beginning of May 1891, a matter of ten weeks, *Rosmersholm*, *Ghosts*, *Hedda Gabler* and *The Lady from the Sea* were all premièred. The uproar and the acrimony ('A loathesome sore unbandaged' etc.) were unprecedented. By the time *The Lady from the Sea* was produced in May, London was glutted with Ibsen and the arguments over his merits and demerits; but—and this was obviously more important—it was also clear by this time to all but his most vociferous opponents that he was a major talent and no passing fashion. The spring of 1891 was perhaps the most momentous period in the history of the modern British theatre.

Rosmersholm was given a single matinée performance at the Vaudeville on 23 February 1891. Florence Farr, a hitherto unknown actress, played Rebecca; F. R. Benson appeared as Rosmer. By all accounts, even the most hostile, they gave a splendid performance. But bewilderment and anger greeted the play itself. 'What is this?' demanded the *Evening News and Post*, echoing Rosmer's words at the conclusion of Act I. 'An Ibsen service . . .' answered the *Daily News*, 'at once indecent and absurd.' The *Era* went further. Recalling a private reading of *Ghosts* which Dr Edward Aveling, the socialist propagandist, had given a week earlier, it went on to demand that the full authority of the Lord Chamberlain's office be brought to bear on the Ibsen movement. The public censor become a focus for reaction. 'The followers of "the master" who would invite ladies to a reading of *Ghosts* and a discussion thereon would stick at nothing,' the *Era* warned. *Rosmersholm* was a disgusting portrayal of nymphomania and should be forbidden the public stage. Others supported this call. *Truth* attacked Ibsen as a 'crazy fanatic, and determined socialist', and the *Queen* dismissed the play as 'weird and gloomy'. Even Beerbohm Tree, who was later to do so much for Ibsen's reputation in this country, warned the members of the Dramatic and Musical Benevolent Fund campaign that 'we are approaching an epoch when love as it has hitherto been used for stage purposes will be banished, the heroine be a protoplasm and the heavy villain a piece of bacillus'.

On the other hand, one or two reviewers greeted the play with moderation and even approval. Clement Scott wrote a surprisingly balanced piece, deploring Ibsen's values and attitudes of course but acknowledging that his dialogue was 'incisive, pure, and at times unquestionably poetic'. He added: 'Say what we will about Ibsen, he unquestionably possesses a great power of fascination.'[14] *Black and White* hailed the occasion as an epoch-making event and Justin McCarthy remarked unequivocally in the *Hawk*: '*Rosmersholm* is to my thinking a very great play. It is certainly one of the most remarkable plays that has ever been placed on the London stage' (No. 57).

But the Ibsen faction was no longer naive, nor was it inclined to take further chances. The existence of a public censor made a prosecution for obscenity by no means unlikely; at the very least it was quite probable that permission for future productions would be refused. A shrewd stratagem was therefore adopted. Following the analogy of Antoine's Parisian *Théâtre Libre*, an enterprising Dutch journalist called J. T. Grein established in London an Independent Theatre. Its purpose, he announced at the conclusion of the first performance of *Ghosts*, was to regenerate the English theatre by making it possible to bring before the public plays that might suffer at the hands of the censor or the box office. The law was circumvented by issuing tickets to subscribers only —no money was taken at the doors. Ibsen's admirers enthusiastically supported the venture.

The Independent Theatre's first and most notable production was *Ghosts*, undertaken at the Royalty Theatre on 13 March 1891—less than three weeks after *Rosmersholm*. The hysteria and abuse which greeted this production has already been referred to. *Truth* called for the immediate prosecution of the theatre management; the *Daily Telegraph*, in a wild-eyed editorial, demanded that existing legislation be altered so that the loophole which Grein had discovered be closed forever. No summary can adequately convey the quality of fear which gripped the national press on 14 March; the reader may turn to the relevant pages of this book to judge for himself.

The extremity of London's response compels us to look for explanations beyond the undoubted outraging of Victorian social convention which the play contains—for in what sense was *Ghosts* more terrible than *The Cenci*, *The Duchess of Malfi*, *Lear*? How more appalling than the *Agamemnon*, *Titus Andronicus* and *Edward II*, or more cruel and sexual than *The Bacchae*, *Phaedra* or *Oedipus Tyrannos*? A clue to the answer lies, I think, in a casual remark thrown out by an American reviewer of the play: 'It is possible to stomach incest as a dramatic theme when it is treated classically as in *Oedipus* and *Phaedra*, or poetically as in *The Cenci*, but with nineteenth century surroundings it is asking too much.'[15]

Ibsen had energized the banal settings of the Victorian bourgeois farce; he dared to write drawing-room tragedies. His generic antecedents were not Shakespeare or Racine; they were Scribe and Sardou—remorselessly, frighteningly modern. Ibsen, for the first time, portrayed on the stage a contemporary, tragic middle class. As Henry James perceived, he accomplished in the theatre what had already been achieved in the novel. This is what was meant by Ibsen's 'realism'—that he dealt uncompromisingly with a recognizable modern world, a world dominated throughout the nineteenth century by a thrusting, ambitious, self-confident social class. His heroes were not distanced from bourgeois audiences by time, costume or social degree, and were therefore, in their travail, profoundly disturbing. They opposed, or were opposed by, a modern world; in Ibsen society replaced Nemesis as the tragic force crushing individual expression. His protagonists did not move, as the pastiche heroes and heroines of Romantic tragedy moved, in an obsolete feudal world. He broke free from the traditional tragic mode, a mode unable even to conceive of the genre without a prince at its centre, by liberating it from the supremacy of Attic, Elizabethan and neo-classic drama. Or rather, he broke into it by mining the auriferous vein of

European social comedy and transforming its emphases; he created the tragedy of manners.

But during the nineties all this was by no means clear. Ibsen was confusion and chaos. He was 'gloomy' because where levity was anticipated he was serious, 'boring' because where action was wanted he analysed, 'obscene' because where titillation was customary he judged. Arthur Symons and Ibsen's other defenders in England were compelled to remind his attackers what they already well knew: that Ibsen 'paints ordinary life; his people are . . . the people one meets in the City, one's lawyer, one's banker, the men one hears discussing stocks and shares . . .'[16] Symons's catalogue is of course revealing in its ingenuousness; but it illustrates sufficiently the point I am making. Speaking of the years 1884 to 1915 Hannah Arendt, in *The Burden of our Times*, calls them the era of the political emancipation of the bourgeoisie, the triple decade during which the Victorian middle class was reaching for an imperial analogy to its established social predominance—seeking, in its demand for colonial markets, to influence British foreign policy.[17] And it was precisely at this moment of vaulting ambition that Ibsen, instead of affirming the values and institutions of the middle class, called them radically into question. The theatre of Scribe and Sardou, of Augier, Labiche and Dumas *fils*, whatever mild challenges it offered to Victorian sensibility, always comfortingly reasserted its prejudices in conclusion: what James called 'the time-honoured bread sauce of the happy ending'. The stock situations of the *pièce bien faite* expected and received stock responses. Ibsen, working within the genre, posed instead disturbing questions and demanded a troubled response; it was in this way that he made possible the writing of contemporary theatrical tragedy.

It is this, to my mind, which underlies the fear experienced by many of Ibsen's contemporaries, which accounts for what I described earlier as their apprehension that the future of civilization itself might be at stake. He appeared to threaten the destiny of their modern bourgeois world by challenging its central ideologies and institutions. This is why he was repeatedly accused of socialism. 'The middle class,' noted an acute reviewer in the *Athenaeum* in 1896, 'embraces its prejudices and loves not argument.' The even more cynical W. L. Courtney, a critic and academic of considerable standing, but by no means an Ibsenite, advised British playwrights in the pages of the same journal: 'There must be a little psychological analysis but not too much; a little girding at social conventions, but social conventions must ultimately prevail;

there must not be too much logic, but there must be romance and sentiment.' In such a climate the resolutions offered to the quite conventional and even stock predicaments posed in plays like *A Doll's House* and *Rosmersholm* could not fail to provoke an uproar. It was hardly the sexuality and frankness of Ibsen's plays which appalled; nothing which his dramas contained could match in overt prurience and titillation nudge-and-winkers such as Sardou's *Divorçons!* which enjoyed popular West End runs. But Sardou and his contemporaries projected their themes lightly, humorously, reassuringly: they were, the audience was constantly reminded, not serious, not dangerous, not *real*. In this connection Francisque Sarcey, the French drama critic, once reproved an actress for portraying too realistically her distress at the prospect of her lover's execution.

Dear Lady [he wrote in his review], pray do not be so anxious. You are in M. Scribe's hands; he is a fine fellow and he won't let you down. In the last act he will restore your handsome lover and see that you are married. Your young man pretends to put his head on the block and we pretend to believe that he may lose it. You must pretend to be anxious because courtesy demands it, but if you are more than reasonably anxious you embarrass both the author and all of us. The emotion that you show must bear some relation to the truth of the situation—and the truth is that none of this is really true: it has never happened.[18]

It must also be remembered that middle-class participation in the theatre—both as creative artists and as audiences—was, in 1890, a comparatively recent thing, spanning not more than fifteen or twenty years. From the time of Waterloo to the mid-1870s audiences had been drawn almost wholly from the working class, and the entertainment offered reflected their taste: burlesques, extravaganzas and melodramas. As far as literature was concerned, the middle class concerned itself with the novel. Its attitude to the stage was predictably hostile (on his twenty-third birthday Gladstone noted in his diary that the theatre was to him as sinful as the race-course) and of course not without class animus. But during the last quarter of the century, and largely as a result of dedicated Shakespearians such as Irving, whose Hamlet was the sensation of 1874, the wealthier classes were gradually lured back. By the latter half of the seventies white tie and tails were compulsory in the stalls, the working-class audiences were pushed into the galleries or the pit, and in most theatres 'dress circles' were established. Following the remorseless logic of Johnsonian economics, whereby the drama's patrons are given what they pay for, managers increasingly provided respectable, which was to say middle-class, entertainment. A campaign for the 'revival' of the British theatre was begun and 'literary gentlemen', that is, novelists, were urged to try their hand. Starting times were altered to accord with the dining habits of the bourgeoisie, the curtain-raiser was abandoned and anglicized versions of Scribe and Sardou, or indigenous variants on the same lines, became standard. There was thus no precedent for Ibsen when he emerged between 1889 and 1891; and the London theatre-goer, together with his critic, could only respond with hostility to what appeared to be a monstrous affront.

But *Ghosts* marked both a climax and a turning point. Following Archer's attack in the *Pall Mall Gazette* the critics lowered their voices a little; at least they stopped calling for the public prosecutor. Further, the corpus of Ibsen's work was increasingly impressive, the weight of his achievement and the consistency of his point of view undeniable. Surveying the whole *Ghosts* affair in 1906 Robert Ross commented:

Of *Ghosts* you can say nothing which has not been better said by Mr William Archer and Mr Bernard Shaw. Since *Hernani* no play has produced such results on the drama of Europe. It taught French dramatists that psychology does not entirely centre on a wife's infidelity; it taught English playwrights that truth and probability are not strange, but quite as romantic and dramatic as middle-class fictions and false sentiments forming the staple and sewerage of the English stage. It killed Clement Scott.[19]

Ross overstates things a little here—Scott did not of course die until after the turn of the century. But the point he is making is valid enough: it became very clear soon after *Ghosts* that the attitude Scott typified and led had been defeated. Within five weeks of the Independent Theatre's inaugural venture *Hedda Gabler* was given its London première; three weeks later *The Lady from the Sea* was staged. In retrospect it is obvious that the struggle to suppress Ibsen, although by no means abandoned, had been lost.

Hedda Gabler, produced at the Vaudeville on 20 April, was greeted with predictable disapproval but also with respect. *The Times*, which until then had ignored the whole furore, at last consented to notice an Ibsen première (No. 75). *Hedda Gabler*, it thought, was 'in some respects' the most acceptable of its author's dramas. The play 'was not disfigured, like some of his earlier pieces, by shallow and untenable views of heredity', but was instead a careful investigation into epileptic lunacy. To make up for the potential dullness of this inquiry, the paper continued, there were in addition a number of brilliantly portrayed minor characters. The *Sunday Times*, while deploring the grimness of the plot, nevertheless hailed the piece as 'Ibsen's latest and greatest drama . . . one of the most notable events in the history of the modern stage . . . a wonderful work of art' (No. 80). The *Observer*, a little more cautious, remarked that it 'can hardly by any stretch of critical courtesy be called a pleasant play, but it certainly came as a pleasant surprise to many of its hearers at the Vaudeville the other day' (No. 81). Others such as A. B. Walkley praised the play as 'a masterpiece of piquant subtlety, delicate observation, and tragic intensity'. On the other hand, many of Ibsen's bitterest opponents were unmoved. Clement Scott published one of his customary acetic attacks in the *Daily Telegraph*, and followed this up a few days later with a vicious article in the *Illustrated London News* (No. 79) in which he denounced not only Ibsen for his diseased preoccupation with corruption and filth but also his translators for having misled the public as to the true nature of the play's degeneracy by suppressing many of the more notorious passages in the original. This was of course nonsense, but it stuck; and it may be the origin of the widespread and persistent belief that in the Norwegian text Brack refers specifically to the groin when speaking of Lövborg's death. W. L. Courtney in the *Quarterly Review*, Oswald Crawfurd in the *Fortnightly Review* and anonymous contributors to the *Saturday Review*, the *People*, *Temple Bar* and *Truth* all published bitter notices of the play.

HENRY JAMES AND IBSEN

The last word in the squabbling over *Hedda Gabler* was spoken, unexpectedly, by Henry James. In June 1891, he published a long and carefully thought out commentary which effectively silenced all opposition (No. 84). This article was extremely important. First and most immediately, it marked the emergence on Ibsen's side of a formidable and widely-respected new champion who, as a close friend of both Elizabeth Robins and Edmund Gosse, was to be drawn increasingly into the public debate. Secondly, 'On the Occasion of *Hedda Gabler*' marked a moment of creative departure in James's own career. Until this time, despite the stream of books, articles and translations sent to him by Gosse, he had found himself rather embarrassingly siding with Ibsen's critics. It was not that he shared Scott's prejudices and responses; on the contrary, he could see the seriousness of Ibsen's intent and understood his strong moral convictions; but he felt that Ibsen lacked dramatic verve, that he was at odds with his form—in a word, mediocre. James expressed these doubts in a fascinating series of letters to Gosse which are reproduced here for the first time (see Nos 15, 41, 74). Through them one can plot the course of his early response to Ibsen: how, his attention caught by one of Gosse's campaigning articles in the *Fortnightly Review* (No. 14), he read everything about the Norwegian he could lay his hands on; then the bewilderment and confusion as he encountered a style of drama wholly new and unexpected. Later, as he began to grasp the implications of Ibsen's innovations and as, in particular, he found opportunities to see the plays in performance, his doubts gradually disappeared. By the summer of 1891, after careful research, he was prepared to declare himself publicly an Ibsen supporter; by mid-1892, as Elizabeth Robins testified, he was an enthusiastic convert. It was soon after this that he made a small but significant attempt to learn Norwegian; thereafter, too impatient to attend on the efforts of Archer and Gosse, he used regularly to visit Miss Robins, who spoke the language, to have Ibsen's latest play translated. Finally, his total involvement in the Ibsen movement: attending the rehearsals for *The Master Builder* and almost every performance, appearing repeatedly in the journals of the day to speak out on Ibsen's behalf.[20]

From this time onwards Ibsen's example was increasingly to affect his work. By 1893, the year in which *The Master Builder* was first performed, James was wholly committed to carving out a new career for himself as a dramatist. Late in 1889 he had put into effect his long-deferred plan to write for the stage. It was a period of low ebb in his career. *The Tragic Muse*, his novel of the theatre, had been coolly received; he was lionized but seldom read, a man of letters who had lost his audience. It was in this context that he turned hopefully towards the reviving middle-class theatre, and at first it seemed his ambitions were to be realized. Armed with a detailed knowledge of the Paris stage, the technique of which, he assured William, he had in his pocket, he scored a modest but encouraging success in September 1891 with a dramatization of *The American*. Yet even this, James knew, was a hollow victory; the play would almost certainly have failed had not the Prince of Wales unexpectedly attended a performance and, on rising, been overheard to say that he had liked it. Nevertheless James persisted; he knew he lacked experience and had given himself five years in which to succeed. He turned out several scenarios and five full dramas in just over three years, but found it impossible to get them staged. Actor-managers were crying out for new contemporary plays but James's prolix, heavy-handed comedies were unactable. Burning to succeed he sought to make his plays conform to the tastes of the London public; increasingly, then, he began to imitate Ibsen. Throughout the West End indigenous drama was beginning to follow Ibsen's lead. Shaw, Pinero, Jones, Carton and Grundy were all turning out plays marked to a greater or lesser extent by Ibsen. In 1893, the year James sketched out *The Other House*, a morbid tragedy modelled quite explicitly on *Hedda Gabler* and *Rosmersholm*, Pinero (to take only one example) produced *The Second Mrs Tanqueray*, a play hailed as the British answer to Scandinavia. Finally, in 1895, James succeeded in getting one of his dramas performed: the ill-fated *Guy Domville*, an uneasy amalgam of Ibsen and Sardou. The story of its disastrous first night is well known: how the whole venture fell apart in Act II during an absurd drinking scene (later deleted); how the gallery began to sing 'Where did you get that hat?' when the leading lady entered in a ridiculous creation; and how, finally, someone shouted out 'It's a bloody good thing you are!' when George Alexander, playing Guy, announced: 'I am the last, my lord, of the Domvilles.' At the end of the play, in response to sarcastic calls for the author, the unsuspecting James, who had kept away through sheer nerves, was led on by Alexander. It was later said that he turned white, and nearly fainted, when instead of applause he was greeted with jeers and cries of derision.

But even after 1895, when James had returned with some relief to the 'other ink' of narrative prose, Ibsen continued to exert a formative pressure on his work. Significantly, he began to turn his dramatic ideas into novels. The play analogy was foremost in his mind during these years—almost as if he felt impelled to justify his venture by rescuing something from the debris. Repeatedly his novels and tales took a direction quite consciously modelled on the drama: *The Other House* was immediately turned into a novel and *The Spoils of Poynton*, his next effort, was conceived from start to finish as a kind of extended prompt-book, with dialogue cast on theatrical lines and the action broken up into acts and scenes. It is usually forgotten however that at this time it was the drama of Ibsen, and not that of the *pièce bien faite*, for which James had developed a deep contempt, which proffered the really fruitful analogies. One might argue that it was James's encounter with Ibsen which made possible novels like *What Maisie Knew*, *The Awkward Age* and *The Turn of the Screw*, those sombre explorations of domestic depravity and threatened innocence, as well as the more explicitly derivative *The Other House*, *The Spoils of Poynton*, *Covering End* and *The Wings of the Dove*.

INTERLUDE

Meanwhile the storm over *Hedda Gabler* and Ibsen had subsided. *The Lady from the Sea* was performed in May 1891, but evoked little excitement (Nos 85, 86, 87). For the rest of the year, and indeed throughout the whole of 1892, both sides allowed matters to lie dormant. *Peer Gynt* appeared in a translation by William and Charles Archer, and a few review-articles were published, on the whole favourable and exegetical, dealing both with this play and Ibsen's other cumbersome verse dramas, *Brand* and *Emperor and Galilean*, but there were no performances. Later in the year the well-known Dante scholar, Philip H. Wicksteed, produced an excellent little volume called *Four Lectures on Henrik Ibsen* which was very favourably received. Wicksteed's 'lectures', originally published in the *Contemporary Review*, dealt mostly with *Brand, Peer Gynt* and Ibsen's poetry. The author was one of Ibsen's most enthusiastic admirers in England and, according to Halvorsen, even took quotations from *Peer Gynt* as the text for the sermons he delivered as a Unitarian minister.

In the spring of 1892 *A Doll's House* was briefly revived at the Avenue, and one or two indigenous dramas, written as direct commentaries on Ibsen, were staged in London. The most interesting of these was a curious full-length melodrama by Austin Fryers called *Rosmer of Rosmersholm* (but produced under the title *Beata*) which was performed at the Globe on 19 April 1892. This play had an odd history. Shortly after the première of *Rosmersholm* Fryers had taken part in a correspondence printed in the *Era* in which he suggested that Ibsen's play contained all the elements of an excellent drama—if only he had used them. The real play in *Rosmersholm*, Fryers argued, lay in the events leading up to Beata's suicide, and thus *Rosmer of Rosmersholm* is the play which, in Fryers's opinion, Ibsen ought to have written. It was not particularly well received, but the reviewers were by no means hostile.

'THE MASTER BUILDER'

Towards the end of 1892 *The Master Builder* was published in Copenhagen. In literary circles in England, as Elizabeth Robins vividly describes in *Theatre and Friendship*, the atmosphere suddenly grew very tense. The galleys from the Norwegian publisher arrived 'in small, in very small, violently agitating spurts—or as one might say, in volts, projected across the North Sea in a series of electric shocks'. Ibsen's critics were apprehensive, his supporters very excited: 'Mrs Hugh Bell . . . wrote from Yorkshire on [November] 9th: "What, oh what of Gewirriwiggs?"—the name we rejoiced in giving the play before Ibsen had taught us to say "The Master Builder".'[21] Gosse and Archer collaborated on a translation and the play, with Miss Robins as Hilda, went into rehearsal. On 20 February 1893, the curtain went up on the first performance.

Appropriately enough, its first public defence was undertaken by Henry James, who on 17 February published an intelligent and perceptive discussion of the drama and its intricate symbolic manner (No. 96). He had spent the winter of 1892-3 reading through the original with Elizabeth Robins, and it is an index of his assessment of the play and public opinion at the time, that he felt a defence was called for before anyone had even seen it performed.[22] The morning after the première the critics, as usual, were deeply hostile but the terms of their abuse had changed—the outcry over *Ghosts* and the respect accorded *Hedda Gabler* had assured that. The *Gentlewoman*, whose tone to date had been hardly soft, gentle and low, went so far as to extend it a warm welcome, confessing that their critic had been converted to Ibsen by the original production of *Hedda Gabler*. The rest of the press remained unconverted; but they also ceased to be shrill. Almost without exception they decided, instead, that Ibsen must be insane. If he was neither evil nor pornographic then madness alone accounted for his bewildering productions. As for *The Master Builder* itself, it was most charitably seen as a study in lunacy: Solness was mad, Hilda crazy and Mrs Solness, with her obsession over the nine dolls, positively psychotic. 'Hitherto,' announced the *Evening News*, 'his characters have been only eccentric . . . But in *The Master Builder* . . . Ibsen has given himself a free hand, and instead of one mad character presents us with a trio . . .' (No. 98). Clement Scott consigned to an asylum everyone associated with the venture: 'a play written, rehearsed, and acted by lunatics.' The *Stage* found it 'three acts of gibberish', and the *Morning Post* 'simply blasphemous'. *Black and White*, having dropped Justin McCarthy as their regular reviewer, uncharacteristically poked fun at the play: 'Are you conscious of the troll within you? How is your troll since last we met? will supersede the weather as an afternoon-tea topic, I fancy.' Even the *Pall Mall Gazette*, which had on the whole supported the Ibsen faction, declared the play a disaster. It granted that Ibsen was a great man; granted even that the play was, as Gosse and Archer argued in their preface, an allegory of his life; but it found theatrical allegory tedious and uninteresting. To have even staged it at all was a blunder; it was playing into the hands of the philistines (No. 101). The *Spectator*, the *Saturday Review* and the *Hawk* all published unfavourable reviews. Hardly a critic found a kind word to say.

Yet it is possible to view the response to *The Master Builder* as a necessary prelude to the rave reviews which were accorded Beerbohm Tree's production of *An Enemy of the People* later in the year. Ibsen's critics, when confronted with *The Master Builder*, abandoned mere abuse, on the whole, and did try, even if unsuccessfully, to understand him. That they could not led them to conclude that he was simply insane. When *An Enemy of the People* was staged on 14 June 1893, however, it was almost universally acclaimed in the press. *The Times*'s reviewer was pleasantly surprised at its accessibility (No. 109); the *Daily Chronicle* welcomed its accord with the progressive spirit of the age (No. 111); and even the hitherto curmudgeonly Clement Scott paid tribute to its power and virility (No. 110). It was, in its own way, a famous victory; and indeed, this crack in the monolith of Victorian prejudice proved decisive. Four years later the Archbishop of Canterbury and the Queen herself, as part of her Jubilee celebrations, attended a performance of *Ghosts*: a neat symbol, as Bernard Shaw was quick to see (No. 151), of Ibsen's final triumph.[23]

The importance of Shaw's own role in the Ibsen controversy has been greatly exaggerated—not least so by himself. Through successive editions of *The Quintessence of Ibsenism* (1891, 1913, 1921) and in his letters, prefaces and journalism, he built up the myth—in this case as in many others—of the overwhelming significance of his own contribution. As a defender of Ibsen in the early nineties, however, he was far less important than Archer, Gosse or even Philip Wicksteed, although in later years, his position enhanced by his reputation as a playwright, he was better placed to call attention to his own contribution. *The Quintessence of Ibsenism*, unquestionably, was a fine, lively and intelligent book; it was most timely in its appearance and it remains a readable account of Shaw's own intellectual development. He seized on Ibsen as a banner—the definition of Ibsenism implicitly offered (a literary campaign for moral reform through the exposure of middle-class hypocrisy) was the quintessence of Shavianism. It tells us more about Shaw and the way in which he used and misunderstood Ibsen than it tells us about the complexities of, say, *Hedda Gabler* or *Little Eyolf*. Furthermore, it did little to make Ibsen acceptable to his detractors, or help his supporters to expound the intricacies of his stylistic innovations.

(In 1913 Shaw added a section to the *Quintessence* in which he declared that Ibsen's major technical discovery was 'the discussion'.) One can test this by looking for traces of the book's impact on Shaw's contemporaries in quotation or allusion in support of an argument. They are not to be found.

Apart from *The Quintessence of Ibsenism*, which appeared, admittedly, at the height of the Ibsen controversy in June 1891, Shaw was not nearly so vociferous in Ibsen's defence as he later made out. Throughout the crucial period 1892–4 he was virtually silent and it was not until 1897— a good two-and-a-half to three years after the battle had been won— that he published his first important review (No. 149). Even when he joined the *Saturday Review* as theatre critic in 1895 he waited more than a year before speaking out. Thereafter, in a series of biting articles he helped turn the defeat into a rout. It was not until 1898, however, the year in which Scott retired from the *Daily Telegraph*, that he produced *The Philanderer*, the play in which he satirized both sides involved in the Ibsen argument and, in the figure of Cuthbertson, Clement Scott in particular.

In June 1893, following the success of Tree's *An Enemy of the People*, much of the bitterness went out of the Ibsen debate. When Heinemann issued a collection of parodies by 'F. Anstey' (the novelist Thomas Anstey Guthrie), even Ibsen's supporters saw the joke. *Mr Punch's Pocket Ibsen* (Guthrie's witty parodies had first appeared in *Punch*) was well received everywhere and even translated into Norwegian (*Punch's Lomme-Ibsen*, Christiania, 1893). The most amusing was Guthrie's parody of *The Master Builder*. Hilda has fallen in love with Dr Herdal, the world's greatest pill-roller. Unfortunately he is no longer able to swallow his own pills. She urges him: 'But you rolled them, you took them, and I want to see you stand once more free and high and great, swallowing your own preparations. . . . At last! Now I see him in there, great and free again, mixing the powder in a spoon—with jam! Now he raises the spoon. Higher—higher still! (A gulp is audible from within.) There! Didn't you hear a harp in the air?'

THE LATER PERIOD

The major theatrical events of 1894, 1896 and 1897 were all Ibsen premières: *The Wild Duck* in May 1894, *Little Eyolf* in November 1896 and *John Gabriel Borkman* in May 1897. The reader may trace for himself the pattern of their contemporary reception; it is enough to note here that while reactions were mixed (Clement Scott, for example, hung on to the bitter end) they never again plumbed the depths of the early nineties. In 1895 Max Nordau's *Degeneration* (*Entartung*) appeared in English and briefly revived the flagging resistance to Ibsen. In his chapter on the Norwegian playwright Nordau sought to show that he was the archetype of contemporary degeneracy. These assertions were developed at length and supported by specious scientific evidence and reasoning. In the following year, however, A. E. Hake published an anonymous retort entitled *Regeneration* (London: Constable, 1896) and the affair was forgotten. Following the production of *John Gabriel Borkman* in 1897 the whole Ibsen dispute suddenly ceased.

For the next six years the English literary world appeared virtually to forget about Ibsen. A few books, such as *Ibsen on his Merits*, by Sir Edward Russell and P. C. Standing, consolidated the favourable climate of opinion, and a handful of new editions and reissues appeared in 1898, 1899 and 1900; but, judging from the dullness of the reviews, no one seemed particularly interested. In marked contrast on Ibsen's seventieth birthday in 1898 the rest of Europe celebrated extravagantly. In Norway especially the opportunity was taken to honour a great man: in Christiania a lush ceremony was held during which young ladies, dressed as Ibsen heroines, presented him in turn with a single rose. England alone failed to rise to the occasion and her 'delicate compliment to Ibsen' was seized upon by Shaw as an opportunity to get discussion going again. Yet this too failed and when *When We Dead Awaken* was published two years later it was hardly noticed. Not even James Joyce's excited review in the *Fortnightly Review* (No. 153) attracted much attention to it. In 1901 *The Pillars of Society* was revived and in 1902 *The Lady from the Sea* was given a second chance; but only the politest regard was paid to these efforts. Consolidation characterizes the years between *John Gabriel Borkman* and the première of *When We Dead Awaken* in 1903; Ibsen was being absorbed into the establishment.

His last play was received with puzzlement and bewilderment, but also with the most cautious, careful respect. He had become a genius, and due obeisance had to be made. 'There is always this to be said about Ibsen—' wrote *The Times* uneasily, 'whether you clearly understand him or not, he gives you a thrill which no one else can give you.' With equal circumspection the *Daily Chronicle*, clearly at a loss, suggested that 'the strength of the play is its inconsistency, combined with the air of mysticism marking nearly all the plays written by Ibsen during the past decade.' Even the *Daily Telegraph*, now no longer embarrassed by the presence of Clement Scott and eager to redeem itself, was able only to squeeze out ambiguities of this sort: 'But we do not for a moment believe that *When We Dead Awaken* is either a good specimen of the author's powers or a good play in itself. Except that it is more fully charged with possibly allegorical meanings, there is little or no change from, or advance on, previous work.' Max Beerbohm, having taken over from Shaw on the *Saturday Review*, found both its symbolism and meaning facile, and the *Academy* called it 'a welter of dark utterances, vague symbolisms and mysterious figures of speech'.

Some of the smaller journals almost succeeded in recreating the spirit of 1891: 'Deplorably dull' was the judgment of the *Referee*; 'A work more dreary in theme or more contrary to real life cannot be imagined,' complained *Lloyd's Weekly News*. But the decade had gone, the century had turned; Ibsen had come to stay and everybody knew it. When, later in the year, *The Vikings at Helgeland* was staged at the Imperial under the direction of Gordon Craig, the *Daily Chronicle* greeted the event with banner headlines over three columns and two large illustrations in the text. Comparable treatment, in spirit if not in space, was accorded the play elsewhere.

All this time Ibsen himself was dying. A severe stroke in 1901 left him paralysed and speechless. The critics treated this fact with sympathy, of course, but considered his work posthumously: his *œuvre* was complete. In 1904 his *Collected Letters*, edited by Halvdan Koht and Julius Elias, were published in Copenhagen and Christiania and the following year an English edition was prepared by John Laurvik and Mary Morison (London: Hodder & Stoughton; New York: Fox, Duffield & Co., 1905). In England it was reviewed by William Archer (No. 169). In the same year *The Wild Duck* and *An Enemy of the People* were revived. Of particular interest in the many press notices and reports following these performances was Keir Hardie's characteristic response to *An Enemy of the People*. An enterprising young journalist spotted him in the audience, along with other parliamentary figures including Winston Churchill, and had the wit after the show to ask his opinion. Hardie's tart comments, turning the occasion to political advantage, are reprinted in this volume (No. 173).

The following year, in 1906, Ibsen died. All the major journals carried obituaries fulsome in their praise and thorough in their commentaries—Archer in the *Monthly Review*, Dowden in the *Contemporary Review*, Symons in the *Quarterly Review* and so on. Yet, oddly, the most perceptive obituaries appeared in American magazines. The

English, as Henry James foresaw in 1891, never took Ibsen to their hearts. They learned to respect and even to admire him; but they never loved him.

II

IBSEN IN AMERICA

In the United States contrasting immigrant traditions, complicated by language and locale, produced a situation which, in its extremities, caricatured the polarities in England. In the mid-west a large Norwegian population, clannish, literate and proud of its national heritage, in many ways pioneered sympathetic attitudes to Ibsen in the Western world; on the east coast a British-oriented and English-speaking community, with strongly Puritan habits of mind, took its cue (now negative, now positive) from the London journals. There were respectable exceptions to this—William Morton Payne and W. D. Howells to name two—but on the whole the derivative nature of much east coast comment makes it extremely difficult to get at the heart of the genuinely local response to Ibsen. The problem is further complicated by the fact that many New England journals frequently reprinted wholesale the campaigning articles by Gosse and Archer (or, in translation, their equivalents in France and Germany). It is important to bear these factors in mind when tracing the pattern of American response towards the turn of the century.

These two communities, with their cultural, linguistic and geographic differences, overlapped only slightly; we are dealing with two histories, not one. Yet where they did come into contact the effect was crucial. Eastern hostility to Ibsen was tempered at important junctures by the sensitive and informed early criticism of Rasmus B. Anderson, then Professor of Scandinavian Languages at Wisconsin, and later by that of Hjalmar Hjorth Boyesen, a Professor at Columbia.[24] On the other hand, it is probable that Anderson's subsequent *volte face* over Ibsen, which led him in later years to condemn what he took to be the improprieties rampant in the prose tragedies, was affected by his contact with the eastern Puritan tradition in the criticism of men such as William Winter, theatre reviewer on Greeley's *Tribune*. Equipped with an acute intellect and an even sharper tongue, Winter was to Boston and New York what Scott had been to Manchester and London. He was at the height of his powers in the nineties and continued to exercise considerable influence until his retirement in 1909.[25]

Contact between these two communities, then, though never decisive in determining the direction of Ibsen's reception, led to key individuals changing sides or declaring their loyalties. Anderson and W. D. Howells are contrasting cases in point. Howells in particular, ultimately one of Ibsen's prominent defenders in America, did little on his behalf until 1894, the year Boyesen published his *Commentary on the Works of Ibsen*. Following the New York production of *Ghosts* in that year Howells at last spoke out, declaring the occasion 'a great theatrical event—the very greatest I have ever known'. As Henry James's friend and supporter he was associated with James's conversion to Ibsen. Howells subsequently published the longest and most perceptive obituary Ibsen was to receive in the Anglo-Saxon world (No. 178).

The austere ethical milieu of New England was mitigated further by a variety of factors which, acting singly and in conjunction, assured Ibsen a readier reception in the United States than almost anywhere else in the Western world. At the turn of the century commentators such as Archibald Henderson were inclined to account for this by gesturing towards the perfections of American society: Ibsen was 'hammering at an open door' etc. There is something in this, but much more important was American deference to Europe—the complex fate, as James called it, of the New Englander's superstitious over-evaluation of all things European. This operated on a multiplicity of levels, from a reluctance to attack Ibsen to a willingness to accept Europe's favourable verdict on him. Then, the fact that the Ibsen debate in America took place both before (in the mid-west) and slightly after (in the east) the controversy in England greatly softened his reception in New York and Boston. All the ground had been covered before and self-conscious New Englanders were unwilling to appear to be lagging behind in appreciation of the Scandinavian genius. Their Norwegian-speaking compatriots in the mid-west had settled their differences and were unanimous in Ibsen's support; and Archer and Gosse appeared to have carried the day in London. Finally, two incalculable factors. First, the fact that the United States lacked an institutionalized censoring body. It is probable that the absence of such an institution, which in England and elsewhere had acted as a focus for hostility, eased even further such tensions as were produced. Secondly, the fact that in the commercial 1890s few were willing to gamble on a box-office flop. This meant that Ibsen was introduced gradually, over a matter of twenty years. New York experienced nothing like those ten explosive weeks in London in 1891.

NORWEGIAN–AMERICAN REACTION

Until about 1870 most Norwegian-Americans,[26] like most Scandinavians, paid little attention to Ibsen. Indeed attitudes towards his work in the mid-west closely followed those in Norway. He was known, of course, and undoubtedly read by some, but on the whole his work was discounted and regarded as vastly inferior to Björnson's—as indeed it was until the late 1860s. Yet even at this time one or two people recognized his potential and began to clear the way for him. This was especially so at Luther College, an ethnic school for immigrants' children founded in 1861, where Lyder Siewers and Laurens Larsen, two teachers, ensured that copies of his early plays were to be found in the library. Both men had known Ibsen in Christiania and, where possible, used his plays in their language classes—Paulson notes that one of their text-books contained six scenes from *Haermaendene paa Helgeland* (*The Vikings at Helgeland*). Nevertheless, until the early seventies the name of Ibsen aroused little excitement in Milwaukee. Even *Brand* and *Peer Gynt*, subsequently the pillars of Ibsen's reputation as a poet throughout the Norwegian-speaking world, were largely ignored when they first appeared in 1866 and 1867.

But in 1871 Ibsen at last began to make a name for himself as a serious writer. In that year he published his *Digte* in Copenhagen, and for the first time the Norwegian-American press sat up and took notice. *Skandinaven* published a favourable report and, in the following year, reprinted three poems from the collection together with a Norwegian summary of Gosse's enthusiastic review of *The Pretenders* (*Academy*, 1 August 1872). *Brand* and *Peer Gynt* began to receive the attention they deserved, and in the course of the next three or four years many Norwegian-Americans began to speak of Ibsen as Björnson's chief rival as Norway's greatest living writer. In 1875 Throud Bothne, an Ibsen enthusiast, joined the staff of the now influential Luther College. He quickly introduced the study of *Peer Gynt* and *Brand* into his language classes and as a result became the most popular teacher in the school. An added consequence was that his opinion of Ibsen, placing him far above Björnson, began to spread in the community. By the late seventies many people, including the Rev. Erik L. Petersen, an influential critic, were saying that Ibsen had surpassed Björnson.

No one had yet attempted to stage one of Ibsen's dramas. *Brand* and *Peer Gynt* were read for their poetry; as plays they were beyond the resources of Milwaukee while Ibsen's more actable dramas, *The*

League of Youth and *The Pillars of Society*, had only just appeared. The demand for his work was therefore met (and encouraged) by the bookstores, which began increasingly to stock his works and advertise them. One of the more enterprising stockists, a man called Relling, took over *Norden*, a small local paper, and began to print reviews of Ibsen's plays in order to stimulate both discussion and sales. In the same commercial spirit he gave prominence in 1880 to a dull and artificially extended debate on *A Doll's House* between a well-known critic named P. P. Iverslie and Ole S. Hervin, a bright young man who wrote under the pseudonym Herman Wang. The earliest known piece on Ibsen in America is thus to be found in Relling's journal which, on 2 January 1879, published a review of *The Pillars of Society*. Paulson is probably right in describing this as a piece of covert advertising; the writer, P. P. Iverslie, does little else than encourage his readers to buy the play:

I strongly urge everyone to purchase the work that he may see how Consul Bernick, the 'Pillar of Society' founded upon a three-fold lie, eventually becomes so shaken that he fully acknowledges his misdeeds; and I wish that everyone might recognise, if he has not done so already, that 'the spirit of truth and the spirit of freedom' are the true 'Pillars of Society'. *The Pillars of Society* is much better than *The League of Youth*, another drama by the same author.

About the same time that this review was published Ibsen was produced in America for the first time. According to *Budstikken* (5 February 1879) *The Pillars of Society* was staged in German at the Stadtheater, Milwaukee, towards the end of January or early February 1879 (the exact date is unclear). This performance was ignored by the Norwegian community, however, and it was not until three years later, when *A Doll's House* was produced in Milwaukee, that a wide and enthusiastic press was accorded one of Ibsen's plays. Unfortunately *The Child Wife*—so it was renamed—bore little resemblance to Ibsen's original. William Laurence, who adapted the play, made use of the happy 'German' ending and introduced, for comic relief, an Irish widow and, in the second act, songs for the children. His innovations proved so successful that at one point the show was stopped and one pretty little ditty given an encore. In the following year, 1883, Helena Modjeska, the Polish actress, appeared in yet another adaptation of the play, *Thora*, in Louisville, Kentucky. This production was also well received.

By the early 1880s Ibsen was a dramatist of international importance and Norwegian-Americans were justifiably proud of him. They received his work, with some exceptions, very warmly, though now, as in Norway, they began to view him as a radical rather than as the conservative he had originally appeared to be. A mark of their pride is the surprising fact that *Ghosts* was given its world première, in Norwegian, in Chicago in 1882. Admittedly it was not especially well received—*Skandinaven* expressed the general view when it described the play as at once Ibsen's gloomiest drama and the most revolutionary work in Norse literature. But thereafter successive works were greeted with enthusiasm. *An Enemy of the People*, Ibsen's next play, was reviewed everywhere at length, and the fact that he was commenting directly on the outcry which greeted *Ghosts* was not lost on his American reviewers. Interestingly, whereas in England most commentators took up Stockmann's aphorism 'the strongest man is he who stands most alone', in the mid-west virtually every reviewer built his comments round the statement, 'the majority is always wrong'. The English response perhaps reflects the interest in the Nietzschean *Ubermensch* in educated circles at this time; the mid-western reaction suggests the ambivalence of an immigrant's relationship to the vaunted ideals of American democracy. In both cases we can see how Ibsen's contemporaries unconsciously used his plays as a means of self-definition.

With the appearance of *The Wild Duck* in 1884 Ibsen's reputation among Scandinavian peoples as Norway's greatest living writer was assured. In America the play was received with great excitement and Iverslie, in *Norden*, praised it lavishly. Yet Ibsen's next two dramas, *Rosmersholm* and *The Lady from the Sea*, were virtually ignored; it is impossible to say precisely why. He was extremely popular and widely read; and at Luther College, now one of the centres of the community's intellectual life, Bothne was conducting 'open forums' on his work which were very well attended. Fortunately, none of Ibsen's subsequent dramas was overlooked in this way. In a long editorial on 5 February 1890, *Skandinaven* publicly acknowledged his superiority to Björnson. Throughout the nineties *Hedda Gabler*, *The Master Builder*, *Little Eyolf*, *John Gabriel Borkman*, and *When We Dead Awaken* were all received with favour and acclaim, though without much critical insight. The only important dissenter was Professor Anderson who, as a close friend of Björnson's, consistently took his part in the inevitable comparisons that were made. Eventually, however, Anderson began to attack even Björnson, thus destroying his own reputation as a serious critic.

THE NEW ENGLAND RESPONSE

In New England there was greater opposition to Ibsen than elsewhere in America. The cycle of dramas and the pattern of reaction imitated the English response, just as the Norwegian-Americans had kept an eye on what was happening in Norway. The first important production was in 1889 when, on 21 December, Beatrice Cameron played Nora in *A Doll's House* at Palmer's Theatre, New York. Five months earlier Janet Achurch had created the part in London and had received a hostile press. The New York papers appeared to take their cue from this and treated the play with scorn: 'A psycho-metaphysical harangue' (*World*); 'Silly, illogical, tedious' (*Evening Post*); 'More weariness than satisfaction . . . Henry Ibsen does not write plays in the least suitable for the stage' (*Sun*). The *New York Dramatic Mirror* was particularly virulent: 'Nora, the heroine, is a mixture of Frou-Frou and Feather-brain . . . she is a freak rather than a type, and freaks are not welcome in the dramatic world . . . The dialogue is wearisome—an arid desert without oases . . . It is a dose that will make even the Ibsen cranks quail.' Only the *New York Times* kept its sense of balance:

Like most of Henrik Ibsen's plays *A Doll's House*, as the name is translated from the Norwegian for the American stage, or *Nora* as it is called in the German, is before everything a play to be read. It abounds in subtle strokes that need very dextrous acting to bring them into just enough relief and no more. It is also full of long passages into which action is hard to force. But what more than anything else makes it a play to read rather than see or hear is the difficulty an average audience experiences to see what the playwright means—what Ibsen is driving at.

For an audience composed of persons who think deeply on such questions as the position of the married woman in the family, and on the finer shades of the problem how women should be educated for the responsibilities of marriage, few plays can be more attractive. Those who have read the play beforehand are also able to grasp the whole effort that Ibsen has made and appreciate the literary art as point succeeds point in the characters of husband and wife. But for those who go to the theatre to while away a couple of hours and to be amused *A Doll's House* is not the play they want.[27]

Confronted with such caution, such hostility, the cold commercial climate of the American nineties grew positively arctic around Ibsen. When his plays failed in London this judgment was confirmed. Nothing further was produced professionally for another five years, although one or two amateur productions were attempted, and only the occasional long study appeared in the intellectual journals: Ernest Tissot in the *Chautauquan* (October 1892)—a translation of an article originally published in *La Nouvelle Revue*; Maurice Francis Egan in *Lippincott's*; a series of intelligent pieces in the *Dial* and elsewhere by William Morton Payne and Hjalmar Hjorth Boyesen (No. 116); and the odd book reacting to what was going on in London, such as Mrs Cheney's riposte to Walter Besant.

In 1894 an English theatre company arrived in New York with a production of *Ghosts*. As in London, it was this play which aroused the greatest antagonism. The response was quite genuine—Ibsen was now a resistless fact in England—and reflected the play's outraging of Puritan convention. With Courtenay Thorpe as Oswald and Ida Jeffreys Goodfriend as Mrs Alving, it opened at the Berkeley Lyceum on 5 January to the familiar, dispiriting reception: 'A more hideous or depressing story could scarcely be imagined' (*Evening News*); 'Powerful, unsavoury drama' (*New York Herald*); 'The dramatisation of a scene in a dissecting room' (*World*). Most other papers took a similar view, though the *New York Press* ('Most revolting drama ever played before an American audience') was under the impression that Oswald goes mad because he cannot marry his sister. Their critic described this lamentable predicament with such horror that he forgot to say anything more about the play.

More than a touch of *parti pris* is detectable in these reviews. They were written in defiance of prevailing European winds, out of a sense of deep prejudice. As the *New York Times* noted, many people went along to the opening night to be seen rather than to see; and others stayed away in protest. This became a common occurrence as the play toured the east coast. In Boston the Governor of the State refused a box when the company visited the town in May, and the local preacher, who even resented the fact that his church was on the same block as the theatre in which the play was performed, delivered a hell-fire sermon denouncing it and everyone who had anything to do with it (see No. 118). Subsequent revivals of the play in Boston encountered similar reactions. As late as 1935 the city's mayor was capable of describing a recent production as 'abhorrent' and 'revolting'.

Undoubtedly the most memorable production of *Ghosts* in America was Mary Shaw's version which opened to a lukewarm reception at the Manhattan Theatre, New York, in 1903. Throughout the latter half of that year and through most of 1904 she and her company toured courageously through what was still a comparatively wild west. 'Playing

Ibsen in the Badlands' is one of the most amusing pieces in this volume, as well as one of the most evocative. Joseph Dannenburg's account of that remarkable journey (No. 180) sticks in the mind with welcome persistence, though perhaps not so persistently—if one is searching for the most quintessentially American response to Ibsen—as P. T. Barnum's immortal telegram sent to the playwright on his seventy-fifth birthday: 'How Many Thousand Dollars do you want per Evening?'

The squabble over the 1894 production of *Ghosts* in New York and Boston, mild as it was when compared with the hysteria which seized London, turned out to be the high point in the controversy over Ibsen in America. Since the tour had not done particularly well no further productions were attempted for a while, and thus the dust was allowed to settle quietly. Furthermore, it became clear in the latter half of 1894 that Ibsen's genius was now acknowledged everywhere else: in the mid-west, in England, and indeed throughout the rest of Europe. Boyesen's *Commentary* was winning golden opinions at home and abroad and the mood was capped—the moment appropriately seized— by Beerbohm Tree's arrival in the city with his successful London production of *An Enemy of the People*. The play opened at Abbey's Theatre on 8 April 1895: only the third of Ibsen's plays to be seen in six years. In England no fewer than eight of his dramas had been staged in the same period.

The critics were both genuinely pleased with *An Enemy of the People* and, at the same time, unwilling to appear less appreciative than their British and Norwegian-American colleagues. They gave it an almost universally good press—with, I think, something like relief—and hopefully scribbled *finis* over the whole affair. The *Evening Post* summed up the general view when it commented that the play 'introduces the Norwegian playwright in a new and more agreeable light as a political satirist'. Some papers went even further. The *New York Herald* proclaimed Ibsen 'incomparably the most profound thinker who writes for the modern stage'. The struggle, such as it had been, was over; henceforth Ibsen's new plays were to be given at intervals but received, with one or two exceptions, without passion. Unfortunately it is also true—and perhaps these points are related—that most American comment at this time was of a comparatively low standard: a combination of erratic judgment and mediocre expression which has made it difficult to justify including much of it in this volume.

Between 1895 and Ibsen's death in 1906 most of his dramas were produced in the United States although *Brand* was not staged in its entirety until 1928 (the Yale production celebrating Ibsen's centenary) and *The Wild Duck* was not seen in English until Nazimova played Hedvig in 1918. Nevertheless, in the years before his death and in those immediately afterwards *John Gabriel Borkman, Hedda Gabler, The Master Builder, Rosmersholm, Little Eyolf, When We Dead Awaken* and *Peer Gynt* were all given their American premières. Looking through the contemporary reviews I was struck by their inconsistency, their failure to form a coherent pattern: what, after all, distinguishes Ibsen criticism before this time, and in England up to the First World War, are the clear lines and almost predictable relations into which the elements fall. But in America after 1895 the picture slowly dissolves: each play is received as it comes; few critics make an effort to see Ibsen in a wider context or relate their judgments to any consistent point of view. One can only explain this by suggesting that Ibsen had ceased to be a symbol, a rallying point for partisans of change or repose. What we are left with after 1895 is simply a catalogue of theatre notices.

John Gabriel Borkman was given its American première at Hoyt's Theatre on 18 November 1897, just seven months after the first London production. The reviews it received, although considerably more genial and even-tempered than many published in London, are notably superficial in comparison. 'The Norwegian has his faults, God wot!' wrote the *New York Press*. 'Who is free? . . . He is the John Knox of the drama.' But, continued their reviewer, Hilary Bell, *John Gabriel Borkman* 'is a play which searches the innermost recesses of human character'. The *Evening Post* was equally facile and even more ambiguous: 'it is a strong . . . and true study of certain phases of human nature', but 'considered as a whole it is narrow, gloomy and morbid.' To the *New York Herald* it was 'a gloomy drama well played', but to Anna de Koven in the *Sunday World* 'in Henrik Ibsen the North has brought forth a faithful interpreter, a voice of elemental force and fire . . . if climate makes man, and man makes literature, there never was a more brilliant exponent of this causation than Ibsen.'

Early in the spring of the following year Elizabeth Robins arrived in New York with her by now classic production of *Hedda Gabler*. This was to be the first of many productions of the play, which has almost always been well received in that city. The company opened at the Fifth Avenue Theatre on 30 March 1898, to a warm reception, many reviewers praising the play for its ingenuity. 'A strange drama, ingenious in its development of character, strong in situation and uninterruptedly interesting' (*World*); 'Like most of Ibsen's dramas . . . constructed with admirable simplicity, compactness, clearness and ingenuity,' leading to 'a tragic climax' (*Evening Post*); 'A drama of abnormal life' (*New York Herald*). Only Hilary Bell in the *New York Press* was severe: the play 'brought no joy to the Ibsenites, nor any recruits from the ranks of the non-believers'. It was a little late in the day for this kind of remark, especially as the reviewer overlooked that he had praised Ibsen in the same paper only a few months before. Unfortunately, this sort of inconsistency, praising one production, damning the next, was common among many New York critics at this time. More useful were the judgments on Hedda herself. To the critic of the *Evening Post* she was 'essentially unreal'; in the *World* she was interestingly compared to Iago, and in the *New York Herald* she became 'an intellectual devil'.

In 1900 Florence Khan appeared at the Carnegie Lyceum, New York, as Hilda in *The Master Builder*. The text used was what was called an 'acting version' by Charles Henry Meltzer, and the production was not well received—whether because of the performance, the adaptation or the play itself is difficult to say. Whatever the reason *The Master Builder* was given the worst press an Ibsen play had received since *Ghosts*. The *New York Herald* was particularly scathing, attacking the plot as 'simply stupid' and going on to describe the rest of the play as 'this wildest of Ibsen's dramas . . . essentially a study of some very occult idea in Ibsen's mind . . . It suggests opium smoking and heavy doses of bromo-seltzer in the morning.'

Others were equally obscure and dismissive. The *Sun*, for instance, commented sourly: 'An attempt at symbolism . . . one of the poorer examples of Henrik Ibsen's dramatic composition.' Undismayed, the acting profession continued to offer Ibsen productions. Later in the same year the popular *Hedda Gabler* was revived by Blanche Bates and in 1903 it was revived again by Mrs Fiske and yet again, on two separate occasions in 1904, by Mary Shaw and Nance O'Neill. In that same year the tireless Miss Shaw, as I have already mentioned, toured the 'badlands' with her 1903 revival of *Ghosts*, and in March 1904, Florence Khan opened at the Princess Theatre in *Rosmersholm*. On this occasion the press were fairly evenly divided. The *Globe and Commercial Advertiser* published a brief but very enthusiastic comment in which the play was described as 'short, swift and terse . . . closely articulated, logically ordered and skilfully wrought'. On the other hand the *Evening Post* felt that it had 'far less dramatic movement than either [*A Doll's House* or *Ghosts*] . . . and a full measure of the pessimism that infects almost all of Ibsen's inventions'. The paper went on to add the acid comment that nevertheless *Rosmersholm* was 'an example of Ibsen's method nearly at its best'. The *New York Dramatic Mirror* was wholly ambiguous: '*Rosmersholm* is at once one of the deepest and—in the printed pages— one of the clearest of Ibsen's plays', but 'the joy of anticipation was the only joy experienced by the auditors. The presentation was in almost every respect a disappointment.' The *World*, for its part, pointedly ignored the production and the *Sun* and the *New York Herald* both found it a gloomy and depressing play although, added the *Herald* unhelpfully, 'it provokes thought'.

On 25 February 1907, Richard Mansfield appeared in his famous production of *Peer Gynt* at the New Amsterdam—the first performance of the play in English. This production, omitting Act IV, was the same as that performed in Chicago a few months earlier. Contrary to popular belief, it was not at all well received, although Mansfield himself scored a tremendous personal triumph. The *Evening Post* was typical, praising Mansfield's acting and wittily describing Peer as 'a sort of Norse Rip Van Winkle . . . among the Catskill gnomes', but dismissing the play itself as an effort which 'rises but at a few points to the level of a masterpiece'. Other papers gave equally mixed reviews. 'The performance promised well in the first act but thereafter interest waned until by the end it took on dreariness' (*New York Press*); 'though vague and puzzling at times, and always sordid in its view of man's baser nature, it is nevertheless wondrous in its scope and variety' (*World*). Only the *Sun* gave *Peer Gynt* a completely warm reception. Under the headline 'Mansfield Rides the Pig', it lavishly praised his performance and the play as 'a creation of extraordinary variety and vitality and good humour'.

Two months later, in May 1907, Madame Oda made her New York debut in *Little Eyolf* at the Carnegie Lyceum. But again, although the star was well received, the critics were unimpressed with the play itself. The *New York Press* printed a short, cool notice and the *Globe and Commercial Advertiser*, clearly willing to be kind, was able only to say that 'while the play is morbid and philosophical, it is peculiarly interesting'. To the *Evening Post* it was 'mystical, morbid, melancholy and exceedingly unpleasant'; to the *Herald* the characters and situations were 'imperfectly realised . . . peace comes to the troubled hero through the fire of suffering'. But the *New York Dramatic Mirror* liked it: 'While on the surface it appears as little more than a study of opposing temperaments, it has a greater depth of poetry and a far more subtle motive than the better known of his modern plays.'

DEATH AND POSTHUMOUS REPUTATION

When Ibsen died, most American newspapers and journals, from Chicago to Minneapolis, carried leaders and obituaries paying tribute to his stature as a man and as a dramatist. The *Boston Evening Transcript* scored something of a triumph with a long appreciation by the French actor-manager Lugne-Poe; the *Minneapolis Tribune* carried an obituary by Wilhelm Pettersen, Professor of Norwegian Literature at the Augsburg Seminary; and the *Cincinnati Tribune* published an article by Montgomery Phister. All mourned the passing of 'the Scandinavian Shakespeare', and in the *Independent* George Brandes and Edwin Slosson published simultaneously acute assessments of Ibsen's life and its impact. 'Ibsen as an Interpreter of American Life' (No. 179), Slosson's article, is a particularly interesting piece.

The intellectual periodicals, with more space at their disposal, printed lengthy studies: Edmund Gosse in the *Atlantic Monthly*, for example, and W. D. Howells in the *North American Review* (No. 178) wrote booklet-length appreciations of up to ten thousand words. But these were obituaries only in the most technical sense; Ibsen's creative life had ended more than five years earlier. What they were doing was clearing the ground for what Archibald Henderson later called 'the Ibsen harvest': that extraordinary crop of books and pamphlets which has been a feature of Ibsen studies since his death. In the English-speaking world alone a major contribution has appeared almost every year since 1906; the number of smaller items—chapters in books, articles, reviews and public lectures—is enormous.

At no point since his death has Ibsen's standing as a major dramatist been seriously questioned—with the possible exception of Spengler's harsh assessment in *The Decline of the West* (1923). On the contrary, his reputation has advanced with each decade. Since the publication of Francis Fergusson's *The Idea of a Theatre* in 1949, and Professor Ellis-Fermor's 'Ibsen and Shakespeare as Dramatic Artists' in 1956, it has been common to compare him favourably with the greatest tragedians. Kenneth Muir's *Last Periods of Shakespeare, Racine and Ibsen* (1961), John Northam's *Dividing Worlds* (1965) and David Grene's *Reality and the Heroic Pattern: Last Plays of Ibsen, Shakespeare and Sophocles* (1968) are all notable contributions to this aspect of his posthumous reputation.

Twentieth-century assessments of Ibsen have tended to fall into five broad categories. Critical biography is the first and by far the largest of these groups. Into it comes Edmund Gosse's *Ibsen* (1908), Haldane Macfall's *Ibsen: The Man, his Art, and his Significance* (1907), and Montrose Moses's excellent *Henrik Ibsen: The Man and his Plays* (1908). Other notable general surveys include Otto Heller's *Henrik Ibsen: Plays and Problems* (1912), Hermann Weigand's *The Modern Ibsen* (1926) and A. E. Zucker's *Ibsen, the Master Builder* (1930).

The second broad category is what one might term 'figure-in-the-carpet' criticism—studies which claim to have discovered the key to Ibsen. An important book in this group is Jenette Lee's *The Ibsen Secret* (1907). Others are *Henrik Ibsen: A Critical Study* (1912) by R. Ellis Roberts and *Ibsen and His Creation* (1921) by Janko Lavrin.

The third and fourth groups attempt to place Ibsen in an intellectual or historical context. The first of these one can loosely describe as Ibsen and his critics. The present volume is an instance—others are noted in the bibliography. Group four views Ibsen primarily as a Scandinavian, and notable work in this connection has been done by Muriel Bradbrook in *Ibsen the Norwegian* (1947) and Brian Downs in *Ibsen: The Intellectual Background* (1946).

Fifth and last are those studies which have advanced our understanding of Ibsen's technical achievement. John Northam's *Ibsen's Dramatic Method* (1953) and P. F. D. Tennant's *Ibsen's Dramatic Technique* (1948) are both excellent representatives of this group.

The reader will have noticed that each of these categories has tended to mark a phase in contemporary Ibsen criticism—the general surveys, on the whole, appear earlier than considerations of his dramatic method. This reflects the increasing sophistication of Ibsen studies, and one is grateful for the insights afforded us. But on the other hand, the growing expertise of Ibsen's critics marks his alienation from contemporary audiences. As early as 1913 Shaw noted this situation with alarm; the dramatist who stirred Victorian audiences to a passion was being silenced by acceptance. This is, unfortunately, very much the situation today. Ibsen, that most accessible of modern writers, is read only in the universities. He has become the preserve of the academics.

REFERENCES

1 *The Quintessence of Ibsenism* by George Bernard Shaw (London, 1891) is of course the best-known long defence of Ibsen in England. It is notable that

Shaw quotes Archer's attack in this book; Henry James also referred to it with approval.

2 The *Saturday Review*, 21 March 1891, p. 356. Henry Gibson—Henrik Ibsen. Cf. William Archer, 'Ibsen as He is Translated' (No. 35).

3 *Sunday Times*, 21 July 1889, p. 7.

4 *The Drama of Yesterday and Today*, by Clement Scott (London: Macmillan, 1899), p. x. Scott was the doyen of London theatre critics. As regular reviewer for the *Daily Telegraph*, then Britain's largest paper, and as editor of the *Theatre* and sporadic contributor to *Truth*, he was single-handedly responsible for a great amount of the vituperation levelled at Ibsen.

5 At some time between 1876 and 1880 an undated volume called *Translations from the Norse* was published in London. It contained a bad version of *Catalina*, Act I, and *Terje Vigen*. Bibliographers are divided over the date of publication: Hollander gives 1876, the B.M. Catalogue 1880, and Halvorsen 1878 and, in amended versions, 1876. My own view is that it was nearer 1880. The author was anonymously described as a BSS, i.e. a member of the British Scandinavian Society. He was later identified as one A. Johnstone.

6 The fact that, as the press saw it, Ibsen was taken up by the socialists as a castigator of bourgeois hypocrisies, ensured that they paid him as little attention as possible. But see Engels's letter to Ernst (*Selected Correspondence of Marx and Engels*, F.L.P.H. Moscow, 1953: letter of 5 June 1890). Eleanor (Tussy) Marx was an active socialist. A tragic figure, she later poisoned herself after a miserable affair with the propagandist Dr Edward Aveling.

7 'Ibsen and English Criticism', by William Archer, *Fortnightly Review*, 1 July 1889.

8 *Daily Telegraph*, 8 June 1889, p. 3.

9 *Daily News*, 8 June 1889, p. 6.

10 'Ibsen's "Dolls" in Archer's "Doll's House"', by *Scrutator*, *Truth*, 13 June 1889, pp. 1127–8.

11 *Era*, 29 August 1891, p. 8.

12 *Pall Mall Gazette*, 5 July 1889, pp. 1–2.

13 *Queen*, 27 July 1889, p. 140.

14 This moderate review, so different in tone from that published in *Truth*, must call into question Archer's subsequent claim in *The Mausoleum of Ibsen* (q.v.) that Scott was the anonymous waspish reviewer in this journal.

15 *World*, 6 January 1894.

16 *Universal Review*, April 1889.

17 I am also indebted in this connection to E. J. Hobsbawm's *Industry and Empire* (London: Weidenfeld and Nicolson, 1968).

18 I have taken this quotation from Martin Lamm's *Modern Drama* (Blackwell, 1953).

19 'En Revenant de la Revue', *Academy*, 17 March 1906, p. 262.

20 Readers interested in following up these remarks should consult my own *Henry James: The Ibsen Years* (Vision Press, 1972) and Elizabeth Robins's

Theatre and Friendship (London, 1932) which is a carefully and thoroughly annotated collection of letters from James to herself. They reveal the intensity of his interest in Ibsen, which at times was obsessive, while her own commentary provides a series of insights into James's work at this time. It is worth remarking that her observations, together with the letters to Gosse referred to above, make it clear that, contrary to Allan Wade's speculations in *The Scenic Art*, James did not attend the original perform-ances of *A Doll's House*, *Rosmersholm* or *Ghosts*. This is a point of some importance as his attitude to Ibsen underwent revision as soon as he saw the plays performed.

21 *Theatre and Friendship*, p. 78.

22 James was obviously pleased with his essay and subsequently republished it, together with his earlier piece on *Hedda Gabler* as a single chapter in *Essays in London and Elsewhere* (London, 1893).

23 'Ghosts at the Jubilee', *Saturday Review*, 3 July 1897.

24 Anderson wrote the first English-language article on Ibsen to be published in the United States (*American*, 15 April 1882, pp. 8–9). He was also involved in the first English-language performance of *A Doll's House* staged at Milwaukee in 1882, and was for many years prominent in the Ibsen camp. Hjalmar Hjorth Boyesen is well known for his excellent *Commentary on the Works of Henrik Ibsen* (London: Heinemann; New York: Macmillan, 1894) which enjoyed a high reputation throughout the English-speaking world.

25 In the late 1890s Anderson became extremely reactionary. He began to oppose the progressive causes in religion and the arts which he had previously espoused, joined the Norwegian Synod and bought the Norwegian-language paper *Amerika* with the express purpose of attacking contemporary immorality. The tone of his changed attitude to Ibsen can be gauged from the following extract from his autobiography, *Life Story* (Wisconsin, 1915), p. 487: 'I have no sympathy with [Ibsen's] so-called social dramas, begin-ning with *A Doll's House* and [ending with] *When We Dead Awaken*. Aside from the improprieties and offense against good morals that are found in them, they seem to me mere twaddle and all the symbolism which they are said to contain I regard as a mere opinion of his readers and admiring critics.'

26 I am indebted for this term, and for most of the information contained in the next few pages, to A. C. Paulson's *The Norwegian-American Reaction to Ibsen and Björnson, 1850–1900* (St Olaf College Press, 1937). Outside specialist libraries this book is available, so far as I know, only in the New York public library. I have also found useful, but occasionally inaccurate, Einar Haugen's 'Ibsen in America' (*Norwegian-American Studies and Records*, vol. XX, 1959, pp. 26–43).

27 *New York Times*, 22 December 1889, p. 11.

The materials printed in this volume follow the original texts in all important respects. Lengthy extracts from the plays of Ibsen have been omitted whenever they are quoted merely to illustrate the work in question. These omissions are clearly indicated in the text. Typographical errors in the originals have been silently corrected, but where Ibsen's critics have made a significant mistake this has been left.

1. Edmund Gosse on Ibsen's poetry

1872

'Ibsen's New Poems', an unsigned review of *Digte* (Copenhagen, 1871) by Edmund Gosse, *Spectator* (16 March 1872), xlv, 344–5 (not 22 April 1872, as given in *The Letters of Henrik Ibsen* (New York, 1905), trans. John Laurvik and Mary Morison, p. 230n. Sir Edmund W. Gosse (1849–1928), the well-known critic and essayist, first became interested in Ibsen after a visit to Norway. This piece is his first published article on Ibsen and the first mention of Ibsen in England. On 2 April 1872, Ibsen wrote to Gosse: 'I could not wish a better or more laudable introduction to a foreign nation than you have given me in your excellent review, nor is there any nation to whose reading public I should feel it a greater honour to be made known than yours. If it can be done through your friendly and capable intervention, I shall be ever lastingly indebted to you.' The full text, and Ibsen's other letters to Gosse, are in Laurvik's and Morison's edition.

The distinguished Norwegian writer whose name stands at the head of this article has won his laurels almost exclusively in dramatic literature. His plays are highly esteemed among his countrymen, and have gained him a place in their estimation second to none of his contemporaries. At last he has gathered together the lyrical poems of his later years in the little volume now under review, and they are found to possess all the grace and vigour that his earlier work would lead one to expect. It is rarely that an excellent dramatist is without the singing gift, the merely lyrical faculty; for one Massinger there are ten Jonsons and Deckers; and the genius of the Danish language tends so naturally to the ballad and folk-song, that it would be a matter for wonder if so eminent a poet should write in it without exhibiting this tendency. Still there are signs here to show that Ibsen feels himself to be master of another style, and not wholly at home in this.

These poems consist of short songs of irregular measure, after the fashion of Heine's *Lieder*, of political and festival poems, of verses of society, and of easy epistles to friends. They are the work of the leisure hours of a man of letters. The thoughts are rather fantastic than profound, and there is much that is only of passing local interest; but there are high excellencies of structure and workmanship, and over almost all there is thrown a mist of dreamy pathos and pensive feeling that is very charming, and highly characteristic of the nation. The Norwegians are a courtly, dignified, somewhat melancholy people; their mirth is harsh and their humour bitter, but it is in their quiet meditative moods that they have most attraction, when they seem to retire into a sphere of thought, and lose all sense of worldly things in a sort of half-sad Nirwana. This pensiveness is well reflected in such verses of Ibsen's as *En fuglevise* ('A Bird's Song') and the exquisite *Med en vandlilje* ('With a Water-lily'). He is peculiarly happy, at least to an Englishman's fancy, when he takes some scene or custom of his own picturesque land as the subject of his musings; but he is not always to be persuaded to look kindly at the actualities of his fatherland. With true Norse instinct, he gazes longingly at the South, and would fain write of palm-groves and desert fountains. Now and then the wildness of Norwegian scenery rouses him to a grotesque indignation:—

> Stene har vort Norge nok af;
> Vilddyr har vi og en flok af!

> Stones our Norway has enough of,
> Wild-beasts too we have a troop of,

he cries, with Hudibrastic force, in an ungracious little poem of this collection.

It may be well to glance at the literary influences which have been brought to bear on this man's life. A poet is not a solitary thinker; he is moulded always by the bias of his age. To read a poet's character fully, we must know who his teachers and who his friends have been. Henrick Ibsen was born in 1828 at Skien, an ancient town near the lowest of the great chain of lakes that run up to the Hardanger Fjeld. Here, among the glorious pinewoods and large spaces of gloomy water, the boy took in his first experiences of life.

It was a stirring time in Norsk history. The Danish yoke had been thrown off for fourteen years, and the energies of the nation, so long palsied, were quickening into vigorous life. A school of literature was in the very act of creation. Just twenty years before had been born in the two great western ports two children whose writings were to raise Norway to a fair station in the world of European letters. The one,

Wergeland, was a poet full of ardour and fire, eccentric, outrageous, republican, an innovator by the very conditions of his existence, as full of clear light and sharp piercing air as is the atmosphere of his country; the other, Welhaven, was gracile and polished, delicate in taste, correct in execution, a satirist, a critic, a Pope and a Wordsworth in one. Wergeland was the first to usher in the new epoch in the most startling fashion possible. In 1830 he published his *Skabelsen* ('The Creation'), a colossal drama to which our own Bailey's *Festus* is child's-play. This portentous poem was but the first of the multitudinous writings of a volcanic author, whose genius, perhaps, culminated in his *Svalen* ('The Swallow'), a summer-morning story for mothers who have lost children, a poem full of brilliant audacities and ringing with aerial melody, a work worthy of him who sang upon the Euganean Hills. In 1841 *Svalen* was published, our Ibsen being then a school-boy. Meanwhile the large brain of Welhaven had not been idle. The extravagances of Wergeland were the subject-matter of his earliest writings; with exquisite keenness and sagacity he exposed the faults of the brother-poet, not so keen, alas! to appreciate his beauties. Soon he became known as himself a poet. In 1834 appeared his *Norges Dæmring* ('Norway's Twilight'), a brilliant satire in sonnets, sparkling with wit and polemical zeal. The dilettante patriotism of the young men, the exuberance of the poets, the vanity of the great cities were trenchantly attacked in this delightful poem. He had drawn a hornets' nest about his ears. Wild was the discussion, frantic the indignation roused; but the satire struck home to the heart of the nation, and a new epoch began. This great struggle occupied the boyhood of H. Ibsen. When he reached manhood Wergeland was dead, and Welhaven was beginning to rest upon his oars. The crown of poetry was round the head of Andreas Munch, the lady-lover and pourer-forth of gentle rose-coloured *pensées*. But two young men were growing up in whose minds the seeds of new and advanced thought were springing into blossom,— Henrik Ibsen, the founder of the Norwegian drama, and Björnstjerne Björnson, the first Norsk novelist.

Ibsen, originally an apothecary, found himself full of enthusiasm for literature, and threw off the bondage of his profession for a student's life at Bergen. The deplorable state of the stage interested him from the first, and as early as 1851 he became director of the theatre at Bergen. In 1856 his first important drama was published, *Gildet paa Solhoug* ('The Feast at Solhoug'), and at once obtained him an audience. In consequence he threw up his position in favour of Björnson and came to

Christiania. From that time forth his success was assured, and when in 1864 he produced his medieval drama of *Kongs-Emnerne* ('The Pretenders'), he rose at once in popular estimation to the highest rank among living writers. Since 1864 he has been a traveller in the South of Europe and Egypt, as some of these lyrics testify, and is lastly, with B. Björnson, the recipient of a grant of money from the Storthing, answering, in some measure, to that attendant on our own Laureateship.

The poet is remarkable above his predecessors for his desire to preserve and restore in an artistic form the Norsk language or dialect. He is not content to write in the Danish of Copenhagen, but he studiously introduces the words common among the people and the idioms of the earlier original Norse tongue. In his hands the Norsk differs very markedly from Danish. It will be interesting to watch whether this innovation will prove to be a mere affectation of the moment, or whether a chasm between the two literatures will absolutely be formed. We fancy the labours of Ibsen and his fellow poets are in vain; we notice that Copenhagen is every year attracting the Norwegian poets as a place of publication more and more, and we fear this movement will suffer the fate of that formerly made to separate the literature of Scotland from our own.

2. Edmund Gosse on *Peer Gynt*

1872

'A Norwegian Drama', an unsigned review of *Peer Gynt* (Copenhagen, 1867) by Edmund Gosse, *Spectator* (20 July 1872), xlv,
922–3. Gosse followed this up with a long, signed article,
'Norwegian Poetry Since 1814', in *Fraser's Magazine* (October
1872), n.s. vi, xxxiv, 435–50, in which he included about two and
a half pages on Ibsen, 'the name which stands highest among the
poets of the new school, a star that is still in the ascendant'.

It is not too much to say that within the green covers of this book the
Norwegian language received a fuller and more splendid expression
than in any previous work. It comes from the hand of Henrik Ibsen,
a poet who is fast gaining for himself that European fame which nothing but the remoteness of his mother-tongue has hitherto denied him;
his *Brand*, published in 1866, produced a great sensation in Scandinavia,
and paved the way for this later drama, which surpasses it in vigour and
fire, if it does not rival its spiritual sweetness.

Peer Gynt takes its name from its hero, and the germ of him is to be
found in an old legend preserved by Asbjörnsen. Peer Gynt was an idle
fellow, whose aim was to live his own life, and whose chief characteristics were a knack for story-telling and a dominant passion for lies.
Out of this legendary waif Ibsen has evolved a character of wonderful
subtlety and liveliness, and hung round it draperies of allegorical satire.
Peer Gynt is an epigram on the Norway of today; it satirises, as in a
nutshell, everything vapid, or maudlin, or febrile in the temper of the
nation; in sparkling verse it lashes the extravagances of the various
parties that divide the social world. It is the opposite of its predecessor,
Brand, for while that poem strove to wake the nation into earnestness
by holding up before it an ideal of stainless nobility, *Peer Gynt* idealises
in the character of its hero the selfishness and mean cunning of the worst
of ambitious men. In form, the poem is indebted to *Faust*; but the style

and execution are original and masterly: it is written in a variety of lyrical measures, in short rhyming lines. With such a prelude, we proceed to examine it.

The first act opens with a briskness worthy of the famous opening scene in the *Alchemist*. Peer Gynt, a strong, lazy young peasant, is in high dispute with his mother, Aase, a credulous, irritable, affectionate little woman, whose character is finely drawn throughout the piece. Peer Gynt's nature is one that needs the spur of ambition, or the pleasure of sinning, to rouse it from inaction. In this first scene, it is not till his mother, in the course of her angry rhetoric, tells him that Ingrid, an old flame of his, is going to be married, that he shakes off his sloth. He determines to stop the wedding at all events, and with that object goes off to the bride's home, leaving his enraged mother on the top of the quern, where he has lifted her in a fit of droll mischief. He breaks in, an unwelcome guest, among the feasting and dancing, and manages at last to snatch up Ingrid, and dashes up the mountain-side with her. But not before Solvejg, a gipsy-girl, has seen and fallen in love with him. So far the first act. To say that Ibsen describes scenery in his plays would be to do his judgment and taste a great wrong; but it is one of his greatest powers, and a manifest mark of genius, that by small and imperceptible touches he enables the reader to see the surroundings of his dialogues, and gather a distinct and lovely impression. In this act it is strikingly so; the narrow green valley, the buttresses of pine, the cloudy mountain-ridges, are never distinctly alluded to, and yet one is fully conscious of their presence; in this act, too, the simple humour of the dialogue is not interrupted or overlaid by any allegorical writing.

It is not so with the second act. Peer, outlawed for his treatment of Ingrid, whom he had immediately deserted, lives in the hollows of the mountains, and adversity makes for him strange companions. For he slips into an atmosphere of the supernatural, and holds intercourse with trolls and phantom-girls. The finest scene in the act is one of trenchant satire. He rides into the cave of the Old Man of the Mountain, King of the Trolls, a person averse to anything foreign or modern; he is hospitably received, on condition that he conforms himself wholly to the ways of the mountain-people. There is a benighted party in Norway whose one cry is monopoly,—Isolation is their gospel; that an article is made at home is the same thing as saying it is good. They are the Trolls! These people bring Peer some mead. Ugh! it is sour. Never mind, it was brewed in the mountain! Everything must be old-fashioned, home-made, national; and Peer Gynt at first is attracted by their volubility and arguments, but soon he is shrewd enough to perceive how unnatural and constrained it all is, and in pure selfishness he does what others have done from patriotism,—he leaves the Trolls for a wider, free sphere. Before getting rid of them, however, he has a deadly battle in the dark with Böjgen, the spirit of sounding gloom, in whose name we may trace the origin of our old nursery foe, Bogey.

In the next act, Peer is living all alone in the forest, tormented with spiritual and physical afflictions. In this down-hearted condition, hunted by day and plagued by night, we almost forget his selfish cunning in pity, even as the woes of Caliban soften our hearts. In the midst of all this, Solvejg, the brave gipsy-girl, comes up into the forest to be with him, having left all for his sake. But the happiness of her love is not for him; the spirits plague him sevenfold, and he flies from her and them. Poor old Aase has become a pauper, and lives, as Norwegian paupers mostly do, as the charge of a farmer. Peer comes to see her at dead of night, and the meeting forms one of the most powerful passages in this strange book. Old Aase lies in bed alone; at her feet her old black cat lies coiled; the wasted fire is burning low on the hearth. While she yearns for her son, the door opens and he is with her, awed and subdued by suffering. They play one of the old baby-games together, that Aase taught Peer so many years ago; but strange sounds ring in her ears, strange lights flash in her eyes; the fire burns down, the cat has slunk away; there is silence, and Peer is alone with his mother's dead body. With one kiss of the dear dead lips he is away to sea. All this evolves itself in short lines, alternately rhyming, a wild, ghostly metre; it is the death-scene of all sentiment and goodness in Peer; henceforth he cares only to live his own life and in his own way.

The fourth act takes us on twenty years, and reveals Peer as a middle-aged gentleman of fortune, who, having given up his business in America, that of sending heathen-gods to China and negro-slaves to Cuba, is enjoying himself with a few friends on the coast of Morocco. The friends, however, sail off with his yacht, and are blown up with all his property. Once more he is alone and penniless. He starts east, announces himself as the Prophet in an oasis of Sahara, is hailed as such by a choir of ecstatic girls in a magnificent lyrical passage; passes through a variety of grotesque adventures, clothed in dialogue of the most brilliant sarcasm on political and social matters; and finally is discovered in Egypt, conversing with the statue of Memnon, and meeting with the most extraordinary personages. The advent of each gives occasion to a separate lampoon. We will describe one, to give an idea

of the poet's manner. At Cairo he is introduced to a melancholy shadow
that has travelled from Malabar. Everything is going wrong in Malabar.
Of old, four hundred years ago, only orang-outangs lived in the woods;
and all their language was shrieking and whining. But the Dutch came,
and settled; and now the Malabarese, degenerate folk, use human
language, and forget the apes. But the Shadow and his friends have
made a league for the restoration of whining and shrieking; they have
proved the people's right to scream; they have screamed themselves, to
point out its use in folk-song-making; but alas! the people will not
have them. The meaning of all this is plain. It is a harsh, but surely half-
merited attack on the voluble party who are striving to divide the
language of Norway from that of Denmark by the construction of a
new-old tongue on the foundation of Aasen's Norwegian *Peasant
Grammar.* These men—Mr. Kristoffer Janson is the most talented of
them—write poems and edit newspapers in a dialect crude and ugly
enough to deserve Ibsen's cruel taunt about the orang-outangs. Peer
Gynt suggests that the Shadows should go west, a hint perhaps to the
folk-poets to try a new field in the prairies of Minnesota.

In the fifth act two scenes of peculiar excellence stand out. One is the
first, in which Peer, after twenty years more of hard work in California,
returns to Norway with a new fortune. The mountain-peaks, swathed
with lurid storm-cloud, lie ahead of them, and as the scene proceeds, a
tempest drives the ship against the rocks, and no one but Peer is saved.
The feeling of the storm is rendered magnificently. The other is a
funeral sermon preached by a village-priest over an old man who has
been the opposite of Peer, living honestly in a narrow sphere, without
ambition. The rest of this act is too allegorical, too metaphysical, for
pure beauty. It closes with the final salvation of Peer, through the love
and faith of Solvejg, who, as a momentary glimpse of her in the fourth
act led us to expect, has waited for him with patient longing. To her he
is driven by the mocking ghosts of his better thoughts and aspirations.

Peer Gynt is the incarnation of that cowardly egotism that lives only
for itself, and sneers at all exalted sentiment,—a vice that may be
considered the special growth of our own time. Against this selfishness
the poem is a powerful protest, and in spite of the author's too-obvious
pessimism, there can be no doubt that it will have a purifying influence
on the youth of his only too-sensitive nation. Whether Norway needs
the rebuke more than England may be open to doubt. Against one
thing we would protest, the flippant judgment some Scandinavian
critics have passed on Ibsen as a merely 'negative' satirist. A man who

pours out the vials of scorn upon vice, and recommends virtue with such winning sweetness as does the author of *Peer Gynt* and *Brand*, is anything rather than negative.

We have said enough to show that this is a great and powerful work. It would be rash to pronounce anything impossible to the author of the third act of *Peer Gynt*, but it would seem that his very power and fluency are dangerous to him; the book is not without marks of haste, and there is a general sense of incongruity and disjointedness. The African act exemplifies this mixture of brilliant and crude elements; one is alternately delighted and scandalised. It is to be hoped that Ibsen will not be so led away in future by the perilous sweetness of the Lyaean god as to neglect to give his work its due elaboration and polish, for it is obvious the less a polemical writer is open to criticism himself, the more will his strictures have weight with his readers.

3. Edmund Gosse on Ibsen's elaborate irony

1873

From 'Ibsen, the Norwegian Satirist', by Edmund Gosse, *Fortnightly Review* (1 January 1873), xix, 74–88 (same article, *Every Saturday* (1 February 1873), xiv, 133ff.). This very long article discusses *Love's Comedy*, *Brand* and *Peer Gynt*, but the last two are dealt with in less detail than the first and chiefly involve descriptions of the plots. A major feature of the piece is Gosse's extended translations of scenes from *Love's Comedy*: these constitute the play's first appearance in English and the earliest translation of any Ibsen play to be published in England. The brief comments below, which indicate the direction and scope of Gosse's argument, are taken from the final pages of the article.

The whole poem—its very title of *Love's Comedy*—is a piece of elaborate irony. We may believe that it is rather Svanhild than the extravagant Falk who really speaks the poet's mind. It is impossible to express in brief quotations the perfection of faultless verse, the epigrammatic lancet-thrusts of wit, the boundless riot of mirth that make a lyrical saturnalia in this astonishing drama. A complete translation alone could give a shadow of the force of the original.

[Gosse goes on to describe *Brand* and *Peer Gynt* (cf. No. 2). He concludes:]

Love's Comedy, *Brand*, and *Peer Gynt*, despite their varied plots, form a great satiric trilogy—perhaps for sustained vigour of expression, for affluence of execution, and for brilliance of dialogue, the greatest of modern times. They form, at present, Ibsen's principal and foremost claim to immortality; their influence over thought in the North has been boundless, and, sooner or later, they will win for their author the homage of Europe. It was a white day with me when I first took *Brand* into my hands in the languor of a summer's day at Trondhjem, and I may trust that some competent translator will one day set these books before my countrymen in an English dress.

4. Catherine Ray on the conflict in Ibsen's work

1876

From Catherine Ray's Introduction to her translation of *Keyser og Galilæer* (*Emperor and Galilean*, London: Samuel Tinsley, 1876). Miss Ray has the distinction of being Ibsen's first English translator. The first section of her Introduction gives an account of Ibsen's life and career to date.

Ibsen belongs to the class of authors who cannot be driven to produce by the force of outward circumstances; even the want of the bare means of existence failed to urge him when the spur of transient inspiration had ceased to stimulate. He exercised moreover a degree of self-criticism, which caused him to alter and reject, not only plots, outlines, and imperfect works, but larger finished productions which on a colder, more mature consideration did not satisfy his fastidious taste. Two romantic plays acted at Bergen, and much applauded by the public, were nevertheless withheld by him from the press. It also often happened that a work begun in prose like the *Comedy of Love* (*Kjærlighedens Komedie*) was transposed later into verse; while the *Heroes of Helgeland* (*Hærmændene paa Helgeland*) begun in verse, was subsequently executed in prose.

The attention which Ibsen has attracted almost exclusively in his capacity of poet during the last twenty years, and which has coupled his name with Björnson in all studies of Norwegian literature, is based upon two very different styles of production. The historical dramas form the first group, and among these the most celebrated are *Hærmændene paa Helgeland*, and *Kongsemnerne*. In the second may be reckoned *Kjærlighedens Komedie, Brand*, and *Per Gynt*. The difference between the two groups is great enough to warrant the supposition that they could scarcely be written by the same person.

The beautiful ruling idea of the poem [says a critic of *Catalina*] is the sharply defined contrast between morality and the immutable power of the principle

51

involved in it, and the inexplicable hankering after independence in the individual, which, although springing from an almost demoniacal corruption of this moral principle, has, in its enthusiasm for freedom, its warm love for the past, and even its opposition to the depravity from whence it arose, an appearance of right, an outward approach to rectitude.

This feature runs through all Ibsen's works, and in none is it more apparent than in *Keyser og Galilæer*. It has been expressed in various ways according to the different phases of life impressed on the mind of the poet. A single man at war with inherited right, social prejudices, and established law, determines, in endeavouring to reach his aim in life, to follow another rule than that which his conscience approves, and prudence might dictate; and although predestined to fail, follows his path with a consistency, perseverance, and determination, that compel admiration. The contrast is well seen in *Kongsemnerne*. Haakon Haakon-son has success on his side, because he has right also; the happy consciousness of going on 'a great errand', has given him the 'real kingly mind', so that it is said of him, 'blood and the axe even seem sources of fruitfulness wherever he goes, crops grow where he has trodden them down, it is as if heavenly powers are swift to wipe away guilt from behind him'. On the other hand, Duke Skule so much more richly endowed by nature, with the qualities of a leader and recognised as such by other men, finds it all the more difficult to bow to Haakon, in whose kingly dignity he sees only an accident, and nothing of the anointing, before which all must bow.

Brand tells the story of a man who believes the voice within him is the only thing he has a right to listen to, and he listens so long to its tempting talk about the power of the individual will to free itself from all outward consideration that he remains deaf to the earthly calling and the social ties among which he has been placed. He storms on recklessly after his religious and moral ideal, which at last can be found nowhere, except in his ever narrowing mind, and to which he is willing to sacrifice himself and those dearest to him. The strong tendency to religious enthusiasm always latent in the Norwegian peasant, is finely brought out in some of the minor characters of this play, and contrasted with the narrow, businesslike self-seeking, which is its frequent concomitant.

In *Kjærlighedens Komedie*, the conflict lies between the individual and society, in matters of love. The poet Falk, a spoiled nature as to disposition and self-consciousness, is frightened back by the irrelevant things which he cannot confine within his own boundaries. Ibsen here presents a comical gallery of portraits, whose ludicrous conviction that life consists only of constant change and intercourse with the outer world, is in perpetual conflict with the idiosyncracies of the solitary lover, who like Skule and Brand fails at last because he has no solid scheme for building up the new ideas, though ready enough to pull down the old ones that stood in his way.

Per Gynt is a sketch of a purely egotistical man. Readers of *Brand* and *Falk* might have supposed them intended to represent martyrs of an ideal. No man is a martyr when he falls in consequence of his obstinacy and errors. He only deserves the martyr's crown who loses his own individuality and offers himself for the general good. In the conflicts painted in the characters named, as in life itself, the undivided right is not for all time on one side. He who is in the right, is always he who has most that is positive to offer, but he loses his title to it, so that it goes over to his adversaries if he drive on his work by means which pull down more than he can build up again when he has reached his aim. He is in the wrong when, his mission fulfilled, he thinks the full measure of development is reached, and that which he has built must stand as the boundary line for that which shall come after.

Ibsen in no way intended his heroes to be patterns for imitation. This is clearest in *Per Gynt*, who, in following out the determination to 'be himself' by almost too unconditional measures is checkmated at last, by death coming and breaking up all.

A well-known Swedish author, Almquist, has somewhere said 'that he did not write to demonstrate this or that truth, to inculcate this or that rule of life, but because it amused him to write as he did, and for no other reason'. At one time it seemed as if Ibsen had chosen the same motto. In early days he tried to establish the modern balance-system between good and evil, and finished his work, not with the triumph of virtue and the punishment of vice, but with one counter-balancing the other. If in this way a poem gains in reality, there is danger in a drama of a poet losing command over the mass of material, and leaving a cloudy impression on the reader. This rock, Ibsen has not quite steered clear of in *Brand* and *Per Gynt*.

He seems to have forgotten the old proverb, *ernst ist das Leben, heiter ist die Kunst*. The poet without a tendency, amusing himself by opening the door to an endless prospect, filled with strange figures and characters for his readers to contemplate, withdrawing into the shade with his individual opinions about men and things, leaving them even uncertain if he have any, can point to nothing but a cloudy future, as he pulls down one belief after another, more in irritation than in the hope of bettering them in their reconstruction.

Ibsen by no means sins in the excess of idealization, a temptation too often leading others to sacrifice truth. With an inexorable determination which becomes almost savage, he drags out every feature and fault in a character. His apprehension of physiological peculiarities is extremely sharp, not only in normal types, but in the analysis of exceptions where a man seems divided against himself. In expressing the observations he has made, he possesses a mastership of language, which leads him on until his diction becomes sometimes a trick instead of a work of art. It may be said of those of his dramatic works intended for representation on the stage, that a rare skill is manifest in them of bringing events together, so as to sustain interest, and more and more enchain the spectators' attention to the end. His early poems are of varying excellence, some of the earliest are mere studies, yet collected they contain more poetry than has been brought together by one individual in Scandinavia, since the time of Welhaven and Wergeland.

In his dramas, Ibsen allows himself a superfluity of detail good enough in itself, but not always favourable to the effect of the whole. In his lyric poems where the boundaries are closely drawn, the firmness and decision of his style is apparent, and the impression left is far clearer and pleasanter.*

* These critiques, as well as the biographical details, were mainly taken from the *Skilling Magazin* of January, 1868; and the *Ny Illustreret Tidende*, of 1874; both published in Christiania.

5. Quicksands (The Pillars of Society)

1881

An unsigned notice, *Theatre* (1 February 1881), iii, 105, of William Archer's adaptation of *The Pillars of Society*. The play was well received by the audience. A Danish correspondent reported to his Copenhagen paper that the enthusiastic public called loudly for the author, 'a request which was readily met, without any reserve or trace of embarrassment by Mr. Archer, the English translator'. This was the very first of Ibsen's dramas to be performed in England and it excited little interest. It was staged at the Gaiety Theatre on 15 December 1880. The cast was as follows:

Consul Karsten Bernick	Mr W. H. Vernon	Krupp	..	Mr G. Raiemond
Sansted	Mr Vincent ..	Hausen	..	Mr A. C. Hatton
Astrup	Mr Girardot ..	Olaf	..	Master Arnold
Nilson	Mr Freeman ..	Mrs Bernick ..		Miss M. A. Gifford
Johan Hessel	Mr Arthur Dacre ..	Martha	..	Miss Fanny Addison
Hilman Hessel	Mr G. Canninge ..	Lona Hessel ..		Mrs Billington
Dr Borck	Mr T. Balfour ..	Dina Dorf	..	Miss Cissey Grahame

The characters, described in the original title as 'pillars of society', are the leading merchants in a small Norwegian town, which prides itself upon its freedom from the commercial vices of 'great communities', such as England and America. At the head of the little band of self-righteous vestrymen is Consul Bernick, who is worshipped by his wife and sister, as well as respected by his neighbours. At a moment when Bernick has, as he says, need of all his reputation in order to carry his scheme of a local railway in the teeth of opposition, he is troubled by the return from America of his brother-in-law, Johan Hessel, whose name is in the worst odour in consequence of his misconduct before his exile, fifteen years ago. The crime for which Hessel has thus paid informal penalty was in reality Bernick's; and Bernick is terribly distressed to find that the reports which he has set about concerning the absent Johan are by no means forgotten. He cannot stop the stone which he has set rolling, and he lacks the moral courage to clear his brother-in-law's character. Just when his social danger is at its worst, a way of escape suggests itself. Johan expresses his intention of leaving Norway for a period of three months, at the expiration of which he will come back to demand the rehabilitation of his good name. He is going in the Florida, a vessel which Bernick knows to be a coffin-ship, almost certain to founder; and Bernick lets him go, without a word of warning. The crime, independently of the treachery towards a self-denying friend, is a terrible one, and for a while it seems as though it were to be terribly punished. On the eve of the presentation of a testimonial from his admiring fellow-townsmen, Bernick discovers that his little boy Olaf was on board the Florida when she sailed, and it is not until after a spell of agonising suspense that Bernick hears of his son's escape, and of the Florida's detention in port. On this he humbles himself in a speech addressed to the astonished deputation of admirers, and proclaims his intention of forthwith commencing a better life in a new country; but Bernick's cold-blooded villainy appears somewhat inadequately punished.

In this play, tentatively produced and fairly successful, Mr. W. H. Vernon, Mrs. Billington, Mr. Arthur Dacre, and Miss Cissey Grahame, specially distinguished themselves.

6. Rasmus B. Anderson on Ibsen's genius

1882

From 'Henrik Ibsen', an article by Rasmus B. Anderson, *American* (15 April 1882), iv, 8–9. This is the earliest known discussion in English of Ibsen in America. Some scholars cite Anderson's review of *Brand* in the *Literary World* (7 October 1882), xiii, 325–6, but this is obviously wrong. Anderson (1846–1936) was at this time Professor of Scandinavian Languages at Wisconsin and a prominent Ibsen supporter. In the late 1890s, however, he changed sides and began to attack the Ibsen movement (see Introduction).

Since the publication of this work [*Emperor and Galilean*] Ibsen has written *Samfundets Stötter* (*The Pillars of Society*) 1877, *Et Dukkehjem* (*A Doll's House*) 1879, and now, in 1882, *Gjengangere* (*Apparitions*),[1] all three dramas of singular power and artistic finish. *The Young Men's Union*[2] and *The Pillars of Society* are satirical comedies, in which the author aims his shafts at the political life in Norway, particularly as it develops in the provinces. In his last two dramas *Et Dukkehjem* and *Gjengangere* Ibsen has invaded the family, and shown, with unrelenting logic and with a cruel consistency characteristic of *Brand*, the wrongs of domestic life. In both the wife is the victim of an unhappy marriage, and in *Apparitions* she is wedded to a thoroughly immoral man, whose sins are visited upon his idiotic son. The drama seems based on Galton's work on inheritance and by *gjengangere* ('apparitions') Ibsen means the reappearance of the sins of the parents in the character and constitution of the children. The last scene in *Gjengangere* is the most thrilling passage we have ever read in any book. There is a great division of opinion in Europe, where the work has been criticised, as to whether such a theme should be treated in the form of aesthetic literature; but it is not impossible that the unveiling of these unpleasant facts on the stage is the

---

[1] I.e. *Ghosts*.
[2] I.e. *The League of Youth*.

speediest way of reform. That the author's intentions are of the very best, there can be no question, and by writing this tragedy he has staked nothing less than his whole painfully acquired reputation. The eminent critic, George Brandes, says of this book that it is 'the most noble literary act' in Ibsen's life.

7. Clemens Petersen on Ibsen and Björnson

1882

From 'An Engagement', by Clemens Petersen, *Scandinavia* (August 1882), i, 271. Petersen, a prominent Norwegian-American critic, was a regular contributor to *Scandinavia*. This article, the second to deal at some length with Ibsen in an English-language American journal, is essentially a review of George Brandes's *An Engagement*, which Petersen approaches by way of a general discussion of Norwegian literature.

Björnson and Ibsen have exercised great influence upon each other, though in the structure of genius they are very different. Björnson is a poet; Ibsen is a critic. Björnson has that power of attraction, not to say compulsion, which characterises the truly creative mind. He appeals to a feeling of responsibility in the reader. When he has spoken there must be an answer, and the answer must be a clear Yes or No. A book by him has no audience until it becomes twenty-five years old. On its appearance it has only friends and foes. Ibsen, on the contrary, stops short at the suggestion, the explanation, the instruction. He may startle the reader, but he does not force him into a decision. He may warn all passersby that the house is falling, but he does not tear it down himself. It is true that in *The Glove*[1] one of the principal arguments has been

---

[1] A play by Björnson, sometimes translated as *The Gauntlet*.

overlooked, and yet, as soon as Svava appeared she found thousands of thousands of followers. It is probable that in *A Fairy-Nest*[1] no more striking or more pointed argument could be presented and yet no one has ever dreamt of following Nora, nor ever will.

8. Henrietta Frances Lord on *A Doll's House*

1882

From Mrs H. F. Lord's introductory essay, 'The Life of Henrik Ibsen', in her translation of *Nora* (i.e. *A Doll's House*) (London: Griffith and Farran, 1882). This was the play's first English translation; as a rendering it has many limitations. (For William Archer's comments and Mrs Lord's reply see Nos 9 and 10.)

Some of the clearest light Ibsen has so far shed on marriage we get from *Nora*. The problem is set in its purest form; no unfavourable circumstances hinder the working out of marriage; nor does the temper of Nora or Helmer; both are well fitted for married life, and everything points to their being naturally suited to each other. The hindrance lies exclusively in the application of a false view of life, or—if some insist it once contained truth—a view that Western peoples have out-lived. When Helmer said he would work night and day for his wife, his were no empty words. He had done it, he meant to do it; he had been faithfully working for eight years, and there is no sign that he meant to cease. His happiness lay in Nora's being unruffled. Nor would he dream of curtailing what *he* considers her wife's freedom, *i.e.* the happy play of her imagination. He would deprive her but of one thing— reality. How could he claim to be a 'real man', he would say, if he gave it to her? And he so far succeeds in unfitting her for action, that when

[1] *A Doll's House.*

she takes upon herself to meddle in realities, she immediately commits a crime. He gives her everything but his confidence; not because he has anything to conceal, but because she is a woman. . . .

The idea in *Nora* is: the object of marriage is to make each human personality free. However incontrovertible this may be when laid down as an axiom, does that confer the power of giving it expression in real life, steering one's way among all the difficulties of deceit, inexperience, etc.? Doubtless not; but the poet's work tells us, until the relation between man and woman turns in this direction, the relation is not yet Love. This is the idea in *Nora*, freed from all side issues, and no other key will unlock it.

9. William Archer on Mrs Lord's imperfections and *An Enemy of the People*

1883

From William Archer's review of Mrs Henrietta Frances Lord's *Nora* (see No. 8) and *En Folkefiende* (Copenhagen, 1882), *Academy* (6 January 1883), xxiii, 5–6. This article, entitled 'Two Dramas by Ibsen', was Archer's first published piece on the Norwegian dramatist. William Archer (1856–1924), critic and translator, is chiefly remembered for the intelligence, vigour and persistence with which he championed Ibsen in England. His translations of Ibsen's plays (Walter Scott, 1890) were standard texts for many years.

Dr. George Brandes, in a recent masterly essay upon Henrik Ibsen, remarks that in his drama of *Ghosts*, published a year ago, he has given expression to his darkest thoughts, his most despairing moods, adding that he must strike a new key if he wishes to recover his whole popularity. The remark is perhaps the least happy in the whole essay. Ibsen has never had any true 'popularity', which implies a certain measure of affection. He has had power enough and to spare, the power which belongs to colossal strength and deadly earnestness. This power the sombre intensity of *Ghosts* could by no means diminish. But this is not popularity in the ordinary sense of the word; and in his new play, *An Enemy of the People*, he has had small thought of 'regaining' what he either never had or never lost. If a poet's popularity be measured solely by the editions of his works, then Ibsen is popular to a degree. So quinine may be said to be popular in a fever-stricken land—but the term is surely misapplied.

En Folkefiende is not so startling as its predecessor. There is no physical horror in it, and consequently it does not tell upon the nerves as did *Ghosts*. Its motive may be stated in a few words, for Ibsen has again chosen a perfectly simple theme, and forsworn all his former complexity of intrigue.

[Archer outlines the plot.]

In this play the poet has studiously avoided every effect of theatrical sensation. The whole theme and many of the individual scenes are strongly dramatic, but the thrilling situations of *The Pillars of Society* and *A Doll's House* are totally absent. In its abundance of pure humour, as well as in other respects, the play is more closely related to *The Young Men's League* than to any other of his former works. Its dialogue is perfect—not a word is thrown away, not a word is unduly brilliant, not a word is dull. Each character is clearly individualised, and Dr. Stockmann especially will one day take his place among the most masterly, as he is certainly one of the most sympathetic, of all Ibsen's creations. In none of his plays is the *technique* more exact, the welding of character and incident more thorough. Some of us would like to see the poet return to his old manner and give us another great fantastic drama in verse; but so long as he produces such plays as *En Folkefiende*, we have no valid reason to regret his adherence to realism and prose.

The difficulty of translating from Ibsen's idiomatic Norwegian into our half-Latinised tongue has proved rather too much for the lady who has attempted an English version of *Et Dukkehjem*.[1] She has neither a perfect knowledge of Norwegian nor a thorough mastery of English, so that she has perpetrated several mistranslations, while she fails throughout to reproduce the crispness and spontaneity of the dialogue. Several indications, indeed, lead one to suspect that the translation is

[1] Mrs H. F. Lord. See her retort, No. 10.

not made direct from the Norwegian, but through the Swedish. In the original, for example, Ibsen discards the foolish French fashion of marking a new 'scene' at every entrance or exit, whereas it is religiously followed in that version. It must be admitted, however, that Miss Lord has shown herself at once conscientious and courageous. She has followed the original faithfully where some might have been tempted to tone it down for the English market; and the defects of her work proceed from lack of knowledge, not from want of care or enthusiasm. A so-called 'Life of Henrik Ibsen'—being, in fact, an essay on 'Ibsen and the Marriage Question'—precedes the drama, and may assist a sympathetic reader to perceive, though it be 'through a glass darkly', some of the power of this most finished of the poet's works. It is difficult to understand why Ibsen's title, *A Doll's House*, which fits the play so perfectly, should have been discarded, in England as well as in Germany, for the meaningless and commonplace *Nora*. Even 'a public unused to Ibsen's surprises' could scarcely have failed to perceive the combined pathos and irony of the original title.

10. Mrs Lord replies

1883

A letter printed in the *Academy* (13 January 1883), xxiii, 28, referring to Archer's harsh review of the writer's translation of *A Doll's House* (see No. 9). The letter is dated 8 January, and addressed from 176 Lambeth Road, SE.

Can you give me a few lines of space to reply to the reviewer's remarks on my translation of Ibsen's *Nora*? I would merely say that I translated from the Norwegian, divided it into scenes for the practical convenience of actors, and changed certain phrases that would represent nothing to English readers: e.g. 'Sagøorer Krogstad' I called 'Government lawyer' because the Norwegian civil service is wholly different from ours. I should also like to quote (from *Temple Bar*) that Mdme. Modjeska has created a *furore* with this play in Warsaw; and we should rejoice to see it on the English stage.

11. *Kongsemnerne* (*The Pretenders*)

1884

From a long article, 'Henrik Ibsen', by the Norwegian-American critic, T. A. Schovelin, published in four successive issues of *Scandinavia* (November 1883), i, 11–18; (December 1883), i, 35–8; (January 1884), i, 66–101; and (March 1884), i, 133–7.

The article is a rambling, general exposition of Ibsen's career with some tendentious philosophical reflections thrown in for good measure and gives fairly detailed plot descriptions, up to and including *Ghosts*. Schovelin rates *The Pretenders* highest of all, however—'the greatest tragic drama in Norse Literature'— seeing in it the perfect Hegelian tragedy. The extract below is from *Scandinavia*, January 1884.

Kongs-Emnerne fulfils all the demands of the modern tragedy. The chief persons represent two contending ideas, two different views of human life. Hakon is the champion of the new era, the representative of the future, while Skule is the defender of the old *saga*, the representative of the past.

12. *Breaking a Butterfly* (*A Doll's House*)

April 1884

A signed notice by William Archer in the *Theatre* (1 April 1884), iii, 209–14, of Henry Arthur Jones's and Henry Herman's adaptation of *A Doll's House*. The play, which claimed only to be 'founded' on Ibsen's original, was called *Breaking a Butterfly*, and it was produced at the Prince's Theatre on 3 March 1884. The cast, notable for the presence of Beerbohm Tree, was as follows:

Humphrey Goddard	Mr Kyrle Bellew	Flora Goddard	Miss Lingard
Philip Dunkley ..	Mr H. Beerbohm Tree	Agnes Goddard	Miss Helen Mathews
Martin Grittle ..	Mr John Maclean	Mrs Goddard	Mrs Leigh Murray
Dan Bradbury ..	Mr G. W. Anson	Maid	Miss Annie Maclean

'A pleasant little play' or 'an unpleasant little play', 'an interesting little play' or 'a tedious little play'—these and such as these are the terms in which *Breaking a Butterfly* has been described. The one point on which all critics have agreed is that, whether good, bad, or indifferent, the play is unimportant and trifling. This judgment is undeniably just; whatever may be its merits, it is certainly not a great play. Therefore, I am prepared for general scepticism, when I assert that the play on which it is founded is a very great play, that the character of its heroine is comparable in point of sheer warm-blooded vitality to such a creation as Hetty Sorrel or Maggie Tulliver, and that some of its scenes are of unsurpassed theatrical effect. What has become of all this vitality? is the obvious question; one which I cannot quite answer even to my own satisfaction. Take a piece of music, omit all the harmonies, break up and rearrange the melodic phrases, and then play them with your forefinger on the pianoforte—do this, and you will have some idea of the process to which Messrs. Jones and Herman have subjected *A Doll's House*. The mere theatrical action of Ibsen's play bears to its social and moral significance the relation of a melody to its supporting harmonies. No one is a greater master than he of the theatrical counterpoint, so to speak, which develops every detail of plot and character from an underlying ethical 'plain-song', and so gives it symbolic generality in addition to its individual truth. It is this combination of the moralist—or 'immoralist', as some would prefer to say—with the dramatic poet which has given Ibsen his enormous influence in the three Scandinavian kingdoms; and it is this which makes his plays suffer more than any others by transportation across the Channel. For the British public will not have didactics at any price, and least of all such didactics as Ibsen's. Even a moralist like Dumas *fils* would be easier to deal with. The problems he presents are much less subtle. They turn upon absolute vice in one form or another—generally in one very definite form—and are not concerned with such intangible matters as egoism, intellectual dishonesty, conventional cowardice, repression of individuality, heredity in moral (and physical) disease, and so forth. Moreover, Dumas has not Ibsen's art of welding his didactics into his action. He preaches through the mouth of one or other of his characters, so that in many of his plays a few strokes of the pen would remove all the moralizing, and leave the action intact. Ibsen never preaches or, at least, never makes one character his mouthpiece. His moral, or rather his morals, for they are many, must be inferred from the whole structure of character and action. His didactics cannot be cut away at one stroke; they must be torn out by the roots, and are then found to have sent fibres into every scene and speech of the play. Messrs. Jones and Herman have gone about this eradication resolutely and unflinchingly, and, in so doing, have necessarily mangled and scarified their original until there is little of it left.

It is now about fifteen years since Ibsen finally deserted verse as a dramatic medium, and nine or ten since he devoted himself entirely to pictures of actual modern life. In the interval he had published his great double drama, *Emperor and Galilean*, with Julian the Apostate for its hero. It has been translated by Miss C. Ray (London 1876). Of his fantastic dramas in verse, both have been translated into German, one of them, *Brand*, as often as four or five times, but no translation into English has yet been attempted, the difficulties presented by his strong local colour and rich versification being probably insuperable. In *The Pillars of Society* (1876–7) he took his stand once for all upon the solid ground of modern life. 'I have quite given up verse', he wrote in a private letter, 'and have devoted myself to the incomparably more difficult task of fashioning my poems in simple, sincere prose.' A slightly condensed translation of *The Pillars of Society*, by the present writer, was produced at a morning performance at the Gaiety, in December, 1880, but failed to make any impression. Nevertheless the play, though not in itself such a remarkable work as *A Doll's House* is probably much better fitted for the English stage, and had I had the courage (or audacity) to adapt instead of translating it, and to transfer the action to England, the result might have been different.

In 1879 appeared *A Doll's House*. In Scandinavia its success was electrical. Edition after edition poured from the press. At the Copenhagen Royal Theatre, Fru Hennings made an almost unprecedented sensation in the part of Nora, which was repeated on a smaller scale by Fru Juul in Christiania. The character of Nora entered into the national life of the three kingdoms. Her sayings became catchwords among the frivolous, watchwords among the more serious. Continuations of the play were written, attempts to answer the mark of interrogation with which Ibsen characteristically closed his work. One amusing *jeu d'esprit* represented a discussion of the drama at a children's party, at which the little hostess (æt. six or seven) gravely maintained that Nora was quite right in leaving her husband, and asserted that had she been in her position she would have done the same thing. At last the subject had to be placed under a taboo in society, for, once brought upon the carpet, it left no chance for other themes of conversation. So strong a hold did the play take of the national mind; and the Scandinavian public is more than ordinarily critical, being familiar, on the stage, not only with its own rich dramatic literature, but with the masterpieces of the French and German drama. Clearly it must have been a very different work from *Breaking a Butterfly*.

It soon penetrated into Germany, and even into Poland. At Warsaw, Madame Modjeska scored greatly in the part of Nora, and Frau Hedwig Niemann-Rabbe positively turned the heads of the difficult Berlin public. Ibsen's conclusion, however, was found too startling. Audiences could not bear to see Nora calmly leave her husband's home, and, to his bitter regret, Ibsen was forced to make her relent on hearing the voices of her children. It was pointed out to him that if he did not make the change some one else would, and, as he had no means of preventing this, he made a virtue of necessity. The published German translation, however (in Reclam's Universal-Bibliothek), exactly follows the original, and to this I would refer any reader who wishes to gain a fair idea of the play. The English translation by Miss Frances Lord (Griffiths & Farran) is a conscientious piece of work, but heavy and not always accurate. There exists, by the way, another English translation, published in Copenhagen by some gentleman who seems to have conceived that in order to write our language he had but to procure a Danish-English dictionary, look up all the words, and take the first meaning that came to hand. The result is more humorous than 'English as She is Spoke.' The curious may consult it in the British Museum.[1]

What, then, are the differences between the Norwegian and the English play? They are so many, that it will be better to begin with the resemblances, which can be much more easily enumerated.

The events which precede the rise of the curtain are practically the same in each. A young wife, without her husband's knowledge, borrows money for a journey to Italy, which is to save her husband's life. Ignorant of the true import of the act, she writes her father's name on the back of the promissory note, he being then on his deathbed and unable to attend to business. The husband's life is saved, and through years of poverty the wife manages to keep her debt concealed from him and to pay some of it off. At length the husband is appointed to a well-paid post as manager of a bank. The man from whom the money has been borrowed is a clerk in this bank. His character is shady, and the husband's first act is to dismiss him. At this point the drama begins—and here the resemblance between the two plays may almost be said to end. In each the money-lender opens the wife's eyes to the seriousness of her position, and forces her, by the threat of a charge of forgery, to intercede for him with her husband. In each the intercession is ineffectual, and the money-lender explains the situation in a letter to the husband, which he drops into a letter-box with a glass back, visible on the stage. In each the wife makes a pretext of rehearsing a tarantella so as to distract her husband's attention from the letter box and its contents. These are, literally, the sole points of resemblance between the two plays.

Now for the differences. The easiest way, perhaps, to make them clear will be to indicate the idea of Ibsen's play.

Nora Helmer is the daughter of a thoughtlessly unprincipled though not absolutely dishonest government official. Her husband, Helmer, met her through being deputed to examine her father's accounts. He fell in love with her, and, though as a rule a man of strict probity, for her sake he winked at certain irregularities in her father's conduct of his office. Naturally of a courageous and truthful disposition, Nora has yet been brought up with no conception of the necessity for truth in the every-day affairs of life. To her nothing is 'as easy as lying'. Scarcely has the curtain risen when we find her telling small fibs in mere childish glee, and we soon learn that her life for years past has been one string of deceptions forced upon her by the necessity of paying off her debt

1 Archer later made this translation the basis for an article in *Time*. See No. 35.

without her husband's knowledge. We find Helmer, too, treating her as an irresponsible being, a child, a bird—anything, in short, but a woman—and showing clearly that he loves her as a mere plaything, not believing, or at any rate never having realized, that she too has a soul. Thus, as she herself bitterly complains when anguish has at last developed the doll into a woman, her father and her husband have conspired to keep her ignorant of the realities of life, of her rights, and of her obligations. She has all the time felt a vague longing for a higher and fuller life than this doll existence—a longing which has found partial and perverted satisfaction in her struggles to keep her priceless secret as to the money to which Helmer owes his life. She is, in short, a fine nature, warped and stunted through unfortune hereditary and educational influences, and totally misunderstood by the husband whom she, in her turn, totally misunderstands. In the English play there is nothing of all this. Flora Goddard is presented to us, once for all, as a butterfly wife, a mere Frou-Frou. The conditions which have produced her character are nowhere hinted at; it becomes at once shadowy, uninteresting, incredible.

What, then, of the husband? If all the subtlety had to be eliminated from Nora's nature, this was doubly necessary with the still more subtly conceived character of Helmer. He is, in the original, what may be called a moral sensualist, conventionally moral by reason of a sort of mild æsthetic sensibility which stands him in the stead of conscience, but, for the rest, thoroughly self-righteous, shallow, and egoistic. What English audience could be expected to take the trouble of understanding a character like this? He is Nora's hero. She endows him, in her imagination, with all the courage, strength, and unselfishness which exist, unknown and undeveloped, in her own soul. She never doubts that when the forgery is brought to light he will shield the woman who has devoted herself to him not wisely but too well, and will take the guilt upon himself. It is this which she is determined to prevent, even at the cost of her own life.

Krogstad, the holder of the forged acceptance, has dropped into the letter-box a letter telling Helmer everything; but there is a remote chance that, through the influence of a friend of Nora's whom he had once loved, Krogstad may be induced to demand his letter back unopened. The great point is to gain time. It is the afternoon of Christmas Day, and on the following evening the Helmers are going to a fancy-dress ball, where Nora, in the costume of a Capri peasant, is to dance the tarantella. Just as Helmer is about to open the letter-box, she begs him, with breathless eagerness, to play for her while she rehearses the dance. She goes through it in a wild fever of excitement, and he, seeing that she is really overwrought and ill, consents to put aside business for twenty-four hours, and devote himself entirely to her until the fancy-ball is over. Thus the crisis is deferred till the next day, and thus the tarantella is justified. In the third act, Helmer leads her in, panting and exhausted, after her brilliantly successful performance at the ball. He is in a transport of sensuous passion; she is nerving herself for suicide. The lurid intensity of the scene is heightened (after a fashion I have not space to explain) by means of the character of Dr. Rank, a very important personage, who has entirely disappeared from the English play. At last Nora insists that Helmer shall go and read his letters, intending, mean-while, to escape from the house and drown herself. Before she can do so, however, Helmer rushes from his study with Krogstad's letter in his hand. So far from having any idea of taking the guilt upon himself, he overwhelms her with selfish and brutal reproaches, and in that moment Nora's idol crumbles to dust. They are interrupted by the arrival of another letter from Krogstad, this time enclosing the forged note, and relinquishing all vindictive designs. In the reaction of relief, Helmer 'forgives' Nora all, and expects her to resume the old life of their doll's house. But Nora cannot forgive *him*. A long scene ensues, which is the most debatable point of a debatable play. I used to think it dramatically bad, however ably written, and I still believe it to be a piece of powerful dramatic logic rather than of genuine human nature. But on seeing the play in Christiania last year, I was astonished to find this scene theatri-cally effective in the highest degree. The husband and wife are face to face in their silent home at the dead of night. Calmly, relentlessly, Nora proves to him that the card-castle of their married life has irrevocably collapsed. 'He has never loved her, but only found it pleasant to be in love with her. . . . She has had no happiness with him—only amuse-ment. . . . He is a stranger to her, and she will not live in the house of a stranger.' As for her children, she is unfit to educate them until she has educated herself. She leaves her home at once and for ever. 'Can nothing bring us together again?' asks Helmer in despair. 'Only such a miracu-lous change in both of us,' she replies, 'as should make communion between us a *marriage*—farewell!'

Ibsen's drama is, in short, a plea for woman's rights—not for her right to vote and prescribe medicine, but for her right to exist as a responsible member of society, 'a being breathing thoughtful breath,' the complement and equal of man.

To make an English audience understand the spirit of the play was clearly impossible, so the adapters quite properly held that it would be equally futile to adhere to its letter. They adhered, indeed, to the letter-box, which, leading up to the tarantella, provided a novel effect for their heroine; but scarcely has Flora succeeded in diverting her husband's attention from the fatal letter when Dunkley appears to tell him the whole story by word of mouth, and all the excitement has gone for nothing. Thus the adapters have scarcely been happy in what they have retained of the original. What, then, have they cut out, and what added?

The three children are promptly suppressed, and with them disappears the supreme bitterness of the heroine's anguish, as well as one of the prettiest and most effective scenes in the play. Mrs. Linde, Nora's friend, who succeeds in getting the forged acceptance from Krogstad, is replaced by Martin Grittle, a virtuous book-keeper, who steals the fatal paper from Dunkley. One would think this a jump from the frying-pan into the fire—from unintentional forgery to intentional robbery and receiving stolen goods; but Dunkley fortunately does not take that view of the matter, and slinks off discomfited without even showing fight. The sombre figure of Dr. Rank disappears (very naturally) to make room for an ineffectual mother and sister of Goddard, and a comic personage who may be necessary for the audience, but is distinctly superfluous so far as the action is concerned. Krogstad, the cynical social pariah, becomes a much more commonplace villain in the person of Philip Dunkley. And, finally, with the change of Helmer into Humphrey Goddard, the whole meaning of the original is lost. The heroic Goddard does the very thing which Nora in her romantic imaginings had expected Helmer to do. He accuses himself of the forgery, and so makes matters a hundred times worse. A forgery committed by a thoughtless and inexperienced girl, without the smallest criminal intent and in the full belief that her father, on his recovery, would ratify the signature, is a much less serious matter than the like fault committed by an experienced man of business without the like excuses. Dunkley's accusation might have caused much unpleasantness when directed against Flora; turned against Goddard, it meant nothing less than ruin. Thus the adapters gain a sympathetic character and a telling situation by flying in the face, not only of Ibsen, but of probability and common sense.

In the word 'sympathetic' lies the key to the whole weakness of *Breaking a Butterfly*. The adapters, or more properly the authors, have felt it needful to eliminate all that was satirical or unpleasant, and in making their work sympathetic they at once made it trivial. I am the last to blame them for doing so. Ibsen on the English stage is impossible. He must be trivialized, and I believed Messrs. Jones and Herman have performed that office as well as could reasonably be expected. They have produced a little play of unusual literary finish, and with all its weak points, far from uninteresting. All I wish to point out is that the expression of the play-bill, 'founded on Ibsen's *Nora*,' indicates even more than the authors' actual obligation to their original, and would be more exact if it read 'founded on the ruins of Ibsen's *Nora*.' Let the little play be judged on its own merits, which are not few; but let it not be supposed to give the faintest idea of Ibsen's great *Et Dukkehjem*.

Not many months ago I was present at a performance of the even more extraordinary drama of *Ghosts*, which followed *A Doll's House*. The scene was an ordinary drawing-room, and the 'Ghosts,' it may be well to explain, were purely metaphorical; yet I have never experienced an intenser sensation within the walls of a theatre. It proved to me the possibility of modern tragedy in the deepest sense of the word; but it also proved the impossibility of modern tragedy on the English stage.

13. Havelock Ellis on the importance of Ibsen

1888

From Havelock Ellis's Preface to his edition of *The Pillars of Society and Other Plays* by Henrik Ibsen (London: Walter Scott, 1888). These were: *The Pillars of Society*, translated by William Archer; *An Enemy of the People*, translated by Eleanor Marx; and *Ghosts*, translated by William Archer but founded on an earlier version by Mrs H. F. Lord. Henry Havelock Ellis (1859–1939) was of course later to become a powerful and controversial campaigner against Victorian attitudes to sex and society.

He is not an aristocrat of the school of Carlyle, eager to put everything beneath the foot of a Cromwell or a Bismarck. The great task for democracy is, as Rosmer says in *Rosmersholm*, 'to make every man in the land a nobleman.' It is only by the creation of great men and women, by the enlargement to the utmost of the reasonable freedom of the individual, that the realisation of Democracy is possible. And herein, as in other fundamental matters, Ibsen is at one with the American, with whom he would appear at first sight to have little in common.

Where the men and women think lightly of the laws; . . . where the populace rise at once against the never-ending audacity of elected persons; . . . where outside authority enters always after the precedence of inside authority; where the citizen is always the head and ideal; where children are taught to be laws to themselves; . . . there the great city stands!

exclaims Walt Whitman.

In *The Pillars of Society*—which was separated from *The Young Men's League* by the appearance of *Emperor and Galilean*—Ibsen pours delicious irony on those conventional lies which are regarded as the foundations of social and domestic life. In this play also he presents us with one of the most eminent of his clergymen. Straamand in *Love's Comedy*, Manders in *Ghosts*, Rörlund here, with many minor clerical figures scattered through other plays, notwithstanding slight differences, are closely allied. The clergyman is for Ibsen the supreme representative and exponent of conventional morality. Yet the dramatist never falls into the mistake of some of his Scandinavian contemporaries, who make their clerical figures mere caricatures. Here, as always, it is because it is so reasonable and truthful that Ibsen's irony is so keen. Rörlund is honest and conscientious, but the thinnest veils of propriety are impenetrable to him; he can see nothing but the obvious and external aspects of morality; he is incapable of grasping a new idea, or of sympathising with any natural instinct or generous emotion; it is his part to give utterance, impressive with the sanction of religion, to the traditional maxims of the society he morally supports. Pastor Manders, in *Ghosts*, is less fluent than Rörlund, and of stronger character. His training and experience have fitted him to deal in all dignity with the proprieties and conventions of social morality; but when he is in the presence of the realities of life, or when a generous human thought or emotion flashes out before him, he shrinks back shocked and cowed. He is then, as Mrs. Alving says, nothing but a great child. That Ibsen is, in his clerical personages, as some have said, covertly attacking Protestantism, it is not necessary to assert. It is the traditional morality, of which the priesthood everywhere are the chief and authorised exponents, with which he is chiefly concerned. His attitude towards Christianity generally we may perhaps gather from the intensity of feeling with which Julian, in *Emperor and Galilean*, expresses his passionate repugnance to its doctrine of the evil of human nature and its policy of suppression.

You can never understand it, you [he continues] who have never been in the power of this God-Man. It is more than a doctrine which he has spread over the world; it is a charm which has fettered the senses. Whoever falls once into his hands never becomes quite free again. We are like vines planted in a foreign, unsuitable soil; plant us elsewhere and we shall develop; we degenerate in this new earth.

. . . *The Wild Duck* is, as a drama, the least remarkable of Ibsen's plays of this group. There is no central personage who absorbs our attention, and no great situation. For the first time also we detect a certain tendency to mannerism, and the dramatist's love of symbolism, here centred in the wild duck, becomes obtrusive and disturbing. Yet this play has a distinct and peculiar interest for the student of Ibsen's works. The satirist who has so keenly pursued others has never spared himself;

in the lines that he has set at the end of the charming little volume in which he has collected his poems, he declares that, 'to write poetry is to hold a doomsday over oneself.' Or, as he has elsewhere expressed it— 'All that I have written corresponds to something that I have lived through, if not actually experienced. Every new poem has served as a spiritual process of emancipation and purification.' In both *Brand* and *Peer Gynt* we may detect this process. Of late years, the chief accusation against Ibsen has been that he is an idealist making impossible claims on life; although, in face of the robust naturalism of *Ghosts*, it is not necessary to do more than point out that the charge is hardly accurate. In *The Wild Duck* Ibsen has set himself on the side of his enemies, and written, as a kind of anti-mask to *Nora* and *The Pillars of Society*, a play in which, from the standpoint to which the dramatist has accustomed us, everything is topsy-turvy. Gregory Werle is a young man possessing something of the reckless will-power of Brand who is devoted 'to the claims of the ideal,' and who is doubtless an enthusiastic student of Ibsen's social dramas. On returning home after a long absence he learns that his father has provided for a cast-off mistress by marrying her to an unsuspecting man, who is an old friend of Gregory's. He resolves at once that it is his duty at all costs to destroy the element of falsehood in this household, and to lay the foundations of a true marriage. His interference ends in disaster; the weak average human being fails to respond properly to 'the claims of the ideal;' while Werle's father, the chief pillar of conventional society in the play, spontaneously forms a true marriage, founded on mutual confessions and mutual trust. The usually drunken doctor, with whom the word of reason seems generally to rest throughout, and who regards 'ideals' and 'lies'—which, however, he elsewhere terms 'the stimulating principle in life'—as synonymous, asserts at the end that 'life would be quite good if we might be delivered from those dear fanatics who rush into our houses with their ideal claims.' That is the conclusion of a play which, while, as we have seen, it may be regarded, not quite unfairly, as a burlesque of possible deductions from the earlier plays, witnesses also, like *Ghosts*, to Ibsen's profound conviction that all vital development must be spontaneous and from within, conditioned by the nature of the individual.

In *Rosmersholm*, Ibsen's latest play, social questions have passed into the background: they are present, indeed, throughout; and to some extent they cause the tragedy of the drama, as the numberless threads that bind a man to his past, and that cut and oppress him when he strives to take a step forward. But on this grey background the passionate figure of Rebecca West forms a vivid and highly-wrought portrait. Ibsen has rarely shown such intimate interest in the development of passion. The whole life and soul of this ardent, silent woman, whom we see in the first scene quietly working at her crotchet while the house-keeper prepares the supper, are gradually revealed to us in brief flashes of light between the subsidiary episodes, until at last she ascends and disappears down the inevitable path to the mill-stream. The touches which complete this picture are too many and too subtle to allow of analysis; in the last scene Ibsen's concentrated prose reaches as high a pitch of emotional intensity as he has ever cared to attain.

The men of our own great dramatic period wrote plays which are the expression of mere gladness of heart and childlike pleasure in the splendid and various spectacle of the world. Hamlet and Falstaff, the tragic De Flores and the comic Simon Eyre—they are all merely parts of the play. It is all play. The breath of Ariosto's long song of delight, and Boccaccio's virile joy in life, was still on these men, and for the organisation of society, or even for the development and fate of the individual, save as a spectacle, they took little thought. In the modern world this is no longer possible; rather, it is only possible for an occasional individual, who is compelled to turn his back on the world. Ibsen, like Aristophanes, like Molière, and like Dumas to-day, has given all his mature art and his knowledge of life and men to the service of ideas. 'Overthrowing society means an inverted pyramid getting straight'—one of the audacious sayings of James Hinton—might be placed as a motto on the title-page of all Ibsen's later plays. His work throughout is the expression of a great soul crushed by the weight of an antagonistic social environment into utterance that has caused him to be regarded as the most revolutionary of modern writers.

An artist and thinker, whose gigantic strength has been nourished chiefly in solitude, whose works have been, as he himself says in one of his poems, 'deeds of night,' written from afar, can never be genuinely popular. Everything that he writes is received in his own country with attention and controversy: but he is mistaken for a cynic and pessimist; he is not loved in Norway as Björnson is loved, although Björnson, in the fruitful dramatic activity of his second period, has but followed in Ibsen's steps;—just as Goethe was never so well understood and appreciated as Schiller. Björnson, with his genial exuberance, his popular sympathies and hopes, never too far in advance of his fellows, invigorates and refreshes like one of the forces of nature. He represents the summer side of his country, in its bright warmth and fragrance.

Ibsen, standing alone in the darkness in front, absorbed in the problems of human life, indifferent to the aspects of external nature, has closer affinities to the stern winter-night of Norway. But there is a mighty energy in this man's work. The ideas and instincts, developed in silence, which inspire his art, are of the kind that penetrate men's minds slowly. Yet they penetrate surely, and are proclaimed at length in the market-place.

14. Gosse on Ibsen's Social Dramas

1889

'Ibsen's Social Dramas', by Edmund Gosse, appeared in the *Fortnightly Review* (1 January 1889), n.s. xlv, 107–21. This article was very well received and made a great impression on many people, including Henry James (see No. 15) and Bernard Shaw.

So long ago that the most patient chronicler of the unimportant must have forgotten the fact, I published in the pages of the *Fortnightly Review* a study of the work of the Norwegian poet, Henrik Ibsen, up to the year 1874, a study which was afterwards reprinted in enlarged form as part of a certain volume.[1] I mention this here merely to absolve myself from the duty of examining in the very briefest way the early writings of the poet. At the time the article I speak of appeared, the name of Ibsen was absolutely unrecognised in this country; it is a pleasure to me to know that it was I who first introduced it to English readers—a very poor and inadequate interpreter, but still the first. That name is now widely admired in England, and has long passed beyond any need of emphatic recommendation. All Europe admits that it is one

---

[1] 'Ibsen, the Norwegian Satirist' (No. 3). The 'certain volume' was Gosse's *Studies in the Literature of Northern Europe* (London: Kegan Paul, 1879).

of the greatest in contemporary literature, and by degrees, even here, its possessor is becoming studied and popularised.

It is the more convenient to take for granted the work of Henrik Ibsen previous to 1874, because what he has published since that year has been exclusively of a peculiar class, and that a class in which he had scarcely made any previous essays. The political comedy of *De Unges Forbund* (*The Young Men's Union*), which appeared as long ago as 1869, has a little of the character of Ibsen's later social dramas, but not very much. All the rest of his early work—his astounding *tours de force* in dramatic rhyme, his saga-tragedies, his historical dramas, his lyrics, although in all of these the careful critic traces the elements of his later and more highly developed manner—is distinguished, to a startling degree, from his social prose dramas, by a total difference of form and tone. The work by which we judge him to-day is an unbroken series of seven plays, all dealing with contemporary life in Norway, all inspired by the same intensely modern spirit, all rigorously divested of everything ideal, lyrical, or conventional, whether in form or spirit. These seven dramas are, at present, Ibsen's claim to be considered as a European imaginative writer of the first class. By the side of their strenuous originality and actuality, the lovely creations of his youth fade into comparative unimportance. These were in the tradition of poetry; those are either masterpieces of a new sort of writing or they are failures.

Ibsen, be it admitted, for the sake of the gentle reader, is not a poet to the taste of every one. The school of critics now flourishing amongst us, to whom what is serious in literature is eminently distasteful, and who claim of modern writing that it should be light, amusing, romantic, and unreal, will find Ibsen much too imposing. The critic who is bored with Tolstoi, who cannot understand what Howells is aiming at, and who sees nothing but what is 'improper' in Guy de Maupassant, will not be able to put up with Ibsen. There is no doubt that he takes his literary analysis and his moral curiosity very 'hard.' He has no conception of literature as an anodyne, and like all converts, he is a more zealous enemy of æsthetic and formal beauty in literature than those who have never been adept in touching 'the tender stops of various quills.' Ibsen's new departure was marked by the rejection of verse as a vehicle. The latest of his historical plays, his *Kejser og Galilæer* (*Emperor and Galilean*), a vast ten-act tragedy as long as Dryden's *Conquest of Granada*, was written in prose, and marks the transition. Ibsen had 'grown weary of his long-loved mistress, Rhyme,' and from that day to this he has used it only in short copies of verses. The announcement of his complete divorce reached me in a letter from which I will here translate a few words. He had told me of the preparation he was making for a new play—the same which afterwards appeared as *Samfundets Stötter*—and I ventured, with plentiful lack of judgment, as the event proved, to beg that it might be in verse. Dr. Ibsen replied—

There is one point which I must discuss with you. You think my new drama ought to be written in verse, and that it will gain an advantage if it is. Here I must simply contradict you; for the piece is, as you will find, developed in the most realistic way possible. The illusion I wish to produce is that of truth itself; I want to produce upon the reader the impression that what he is reading is actually taking place before him. If I were to use verse, I should by so doing be stultifying my own intention and the object which I placed before me. The variety of everyday and unimportant characters, which I have intentionally introduced into the piece, would be effaced (*udviskede*) and blended into one another, if I had allowed them all to converse in a rhythmic movement. We are no longer living in the time of Shakespeare, and among sculptors there is beginning to be a discussion whether statuary ought not to be painted with lively colours. Much can be said for and against such a practice. I myself would not have the Venus of Milos painted, but I would rather see a negro's head carved in black marble than in white. On the whole, my feeling is that literary form ought to be in relation to the amount of ideality which is spread over the representation. My new drama is not, indeed, a tragedy in the old-world signification of the word, but what I have tried to depict in it is human beings, and for that very reason I have not allowed them to talk 'the language of the gods.'

This severely realistic conception of what dramatic form should be, a conception which sounded oddly at first on the lips of a poet who had written impassioned five-act plays entirely in elaborate rhymed measures, was in strict harmony with the mental and moral tone of the author in this his new departure. Dr. George Brandes, in his interesting volume, *Det Moderne Gjennembruds Mænd*, has given us some valuable particulars regarding Ibsen's political and philosophical experiences at this crisis of his life. During the Franco-German war, it would seem that his sentiment with regard to life and history underwent a complete revolution. He woke up to see, or to think he saw, that we were living in the last scene of the last act of a long drama; that all which politics, morals, literature were giving us was but the last and driest crumbs swept up from under the table of eighteenth-century revolution; that 'Liberty, quality, and fraternity' was played out as a motto, and had come to mean the direct opposite of what it meant to 'the late lamented Guillotine.' He saw, or thought he saw, politicians wasting their energies on local and superficial revolutions, not perceiving that all things were making ready for a universal revolt of the spirit of men. A few months later, in the following sentences, he anticipated, with a very surprising exactitude, recent utterances of Tolstoi. Ibsen wrote thus to George Brandes:—

The State is the curse of the individual. How has the national strength of Prussia been purchased? By the sinking of the individual in a political and geographical formula. . . . The State must go! That will be a revolution which will find me on its side. Undermine the idea of the State, set up in its place spontaneous action, and the idea that spiritual relationship is the only thing that makes for unity, and you will start the elements of a liberty which will be something worth possessing.

It was in such a mood as this that Ibsen received news of the Paris Commune with extreme disgust, regarding this caricature of his ideal as likely to delay the realisation of his genuine desire through at least a generation. To await the new revolution, as religious mystics await the solemn Second Advent, was now useless. The hope of the immediate future had sunk behind the Seine, and Ibsen turned from watching the horizon to diagnose the symptoms of that mortal moral disease of which, as it appeared to him, Europe was fast advancing towards social death. The hypocrisy of society and the brutality of personal egotism—these were the principal outward signs of that inward but universal malady which he saw the world sinking beneath. It was with no thought of reforming society, with no zeal of the missionary or the philanthropist, that he started on his new series of studies. He would spend the few years left to him before the political agony of Europe in noting down, with an accuracy hitherto unparalleled, the symptoms of her disorder. But with him always, since 1870, there has remained, pre-eminent among his political convictions, this belief that the State is the natural enemy of the individual. Always an exile from his own country, he had settled in Dresden, rejoicing in the freedom of a small and uninfluential Government. But in 1875, when Saxony became more and more identified with the vaunting glory and greatness of the Empire, he fled again. In a letter to me at that time he says: 'I must go. In April I shall flit to Munich, and see if I can settle there for two or three years. I fancy that all spiritual life breathes with greater fulness and comfort there than here in North Germany, where the State and politics have drafted all the strength of the people into their service, and have arrested all genuine interests.' Always this bogey of the State, paralysing individual action, driving the poet through the cities of Europe to avoid the iron clangour of its colossal system of wheels.

Such was, briefly, the mood, as a literary artist and as a political moralist, in which Ibsen started upon the creation of his remarkable series of dramas. To enumerate them—and this must now be done—is to enumerate the entire published work of twelve years. Courted and flattered as he has been, tempted by the results of his immense prosperity to bend to slighter and less arduous work, Ibsen has never, during this long period of final maturity, resigned for a moment his idea of diagnosing, in a series of sternly realistic dramas, the disease of which this poor weary world of ours, according to his theory, is expiring. At present these plays are seven in number, issued in the winters of the years successively named. First came *Samfundets Stötter* (*The Pillars of Society*), in 1877; then *Et Dukkehjem* (*A Doll's House*), in 1879; *Gengangere* (*Ghosts*), in 1881; *En Folkefiende* (*An Enemy of the People*), in 1882; *Vildanden* (*The Wild Duck*), in 1884; *Rosmersholm* (the name of an old manor-house), in 1886; and, lastly, *Fruen fra Havet* (*The Lady from the Sea*), in 1888. Some brief description of these seven dramas, all closely related to one another, will give a rough idea, to those who do not read Danish, of a very extraordinary group of literary products.

In *The Pillars of Society* Ibsen published a play which did not at once discover to critical readers the fact that he was making a new departure. In the first place it was a drama of to-day, the scene of which was laid in a little Norwegian sea-side town, and Ibsen had already once, in *De Unges Forbund* (*The Young Men's Union*) of 1869, written a modern political comedy of life in such a part of his native country. In the second place, the piece distinctly recalled, both in form and in substance, Björnson's exceedingly successful satiric drama *En Fallit* (*A Bankruptcy*), which had attracted a great deal of attention in 1875. Looking back at the two plays, it is now difficult to understand what relation it was we thought we saw between them. The interest in Björnson's play has faded, that in Ibsen's has increased; but undoubtedly, at the first production of *The Pillars of Society*, it seemed to be less original than it now seems. Björnson, with his fresh and vivid fancy, ill-regulated zeal for moral health, and uncertain powers of technical dramatic skill, has scarcely held his own with Ibsen of late years. But it is difficult not to believe that the rivalry between these two great poets has been beneficial to the greater of the two, and if I had space, or could hope to hold the interest of the reader in such a discussion, I should like to dwell upon the relation of Björnson's *Leonora* and *The New System* to *A Doll's House*, and the possible influence of Björnson's *A Glove* on *The Wild Duck*. As far as strenuousness of purpose, depth of psychological insight, and freedom from passion are concerned, however, Ibsen appears to me to be as indisputably superior to Björnson as in grace of touch and occasional felicity of expression he is inferior.

A certain local and peculiarly Norwegian species of hypocritical respectability is the main disease treated in *The Pillars of Society*. The pathognomonic sign which attends this special malady and distinguishes it from all others, is the cautious lying silence which holds its tongue so carefully, in small social circles, and wraps around its consciousness of guilt garment after garment of false propriety, spurious indignation, and prudent hypocrisy. The hero of the play is Consul Bernick, whose ship-building business is the wealthiest and longest-established industry in the town—who is the main 'pillar,' in fact, upon which society supports itself. He not only acts as a support to the trade and the finance of the place, but by his studied morality he gives high tone to its social character. The town bristles with his charities and his improvements, and he is the very darling of its respectabilities. There are, however, two shadows, rather than spots, upon the luminous disk of this great moral sun. It is whispered that Dina Dorf, the agreeable young female to whom the consul has so condescendingly given a home in his family, is the daughter of a married woman, a strolling actress, by Johan Tönneson, Mrs. Bernick's younger brother, who was forced in consequence of this intrigue to leave for America, robbing the Bernicks of a large sum of money in the act of his departure. It is, moreover, known that Mrs. Bernick's half-sister, Lena [sic] Hessel, obstinately persisted in following her nephew to the United States, and has disgraced herself there by lecturing, and even by publishing a successful book. These misfortunes, however, are never mentioned, or mentioned only to call forth sympathy for the irreproachable Bernick.

When the curtain rises on *The Pillars of Society*, we are introduced, in a brilliant succession of scenes, and in a spirit of pure comedy, to the bustle of social and industrial life in the little seaport town. An artisan, who is foreman of the Workmen's Society, is reminded: 'You are, first and foremost, foreman in Consul Bernick's wharf. Your first and foremost duty is towards the society which calls itself Consul Bernick's firm, for that is what we all live by.' Ladies, the clergy, those townsfolk whose interest it is to get a railway opened to the town, every person, of whatever species, who exists in and on the municipality, are seen to be whirled in the current of Bernick's stupendous egotism, and the smallest critical objection to his authority is parried either by a threat or else by an appeal to do nothing to undermine so invaluable a pillar of the social edifice. Yet with the opening of the second act we learn that this splendid reputation for respectability is all based upon a structure of lies, and, strangely enough, we begin at this point to study Bernick with curiosity. What seemed an insupportable fatuity is seen to be a deep design of cunning hypocrisy, a magnificent *chef-d'œuvre* of egotistical force of purpose. We are present at the development of a moral intrigue far more serious than any of the roseate imbroglios of eighteenth-century comedy; the Scapins and the Mascarilles, whose impudence has descended, in forms always wholly conventional, to the common drama of our day, are swallowed up, are lost and buried, in this gigantic figure of a knave, before whom the Church, and the sex, and the commune, alike bow down as to a god.

Gradually the edifice of lies comes toppling down like a house of cards. In the episode of the mother of Dina Dorf, it has been Consul Bernick himself, and not Johan Tönneson, who has been the actor, while Johan has really sacrificed himself to shield the consul. The story of the theft is a pure fiction; and on Johan Tönneson's reappearance in Norway the danger breaks out again. Bernick resolves to ship him away again in an untrustworthy vessel, and as he braces himself to the committing of this murder, a torchlight procession of the townsfolk is in the act of approaching his house, to congratulate him on his support of public morality. Johan does not, as a matter of fact, start in the leaky ship, but the toils are gathering around the consul, and when the torchlight procession arrives, half in remorse, half in cynicism, he makes a clean breast of all his rogueries. The revelation comes like a thunderbolt on the deputation, and the townsfolk regard the confessions more as eccentricity than anything else. The firm of Bernick and Co. will rule the roost, we feel, as much as ever it did. The air has been cleared; that is all. There has been a moral thunderstorm. The play ends thus:—

Bernick.—There is another thing which I have learned in these last days. It is that you women are the real pillars of society.

Miss Hessel.—That's a poor lesson to have learned, brother. No! the spirits of truth and liberty, those are the pillars of society.

The whitewashing of Bernick at the end gives a somewhat conventional termination to this picturesque and powerful play, one of the most animated in action which the poet has produced. *The Pillars of*

Society was still, in measure, a well-manufactured drama, of the admired type familiar to managers. Ibsen does not recur again to this type. Henceforth he carries his realism to a much further extent, and aims at giving no more and no less than an accurate diagram of a section of life. During the two years which preceded his next public appearance, he gave great thought and attention to the question of form, and his second social tragi-comedy was a much more serious affair.

No work of Ibsen's, not even his beautiful Puritan opera of *Brand*, has excited so much controversy as *A Doll's House*. This was, no doubt, to a very great extent caused by its novel presentment of the mission of woman in modern society. In the dramas and romances of modern Scandinavia, and especially in those of Ibsen and Björnson, the function of woman had been clearly defined. She was to be the helper, the comforter, the inspirer, the guerdon of man in his struggle towards loftier forms of existence. When man fell on the upward path, woman's hand was to be stretched to raise him; when man went wandering away on ill and savage courses, woman was to wait patiently over her spinning-wheel, ready to welcome and to pardon the returning prodigal; when the eyes of man grew weary in watching for the morning-star, its rays were to flash through the crystal tears of woman.* But in *A Doll's House* he confronted his audience with a new conception. Woman was no longer to be the shadow following man, or if you will, a *skin-leka* attending man, but an independent entity, with purposes and moral functions of her own. Ibsen's favourite theory of the domination of the individual had hitherto been confined to one sex; here he carries it over boldly to the other. The heroine of *A Doll's House*, the puppet in that establishment *pour rire*, is Nora Helmar, the wife of a Christiania barrister. The character is drawn upon childish lines, which often may remind the English reader of Dora in *David Copperfield*. She has, however, passed beyond the Dora stage when the play opens. She is the mother of children, she has been a wife for half a dozen years. But the spoiling of injudicious parents has been succeeded by the spoiling of a weak and silly husband. Nora remains childish, irrational, concentrated on tiny cares and empty interests, without self-control or self-respect. Her doctor and her husband have told her not to give way to her passion for 'candy' in any of its seductive forms; but she is introduced to us greedily eating macaroons on the sly, and denying that she has touched one when suspicion is aroused.

* In his early historical tragedy of *The Pretenders* Ibsen had put it: 'To love, to sacrifice all and to be forgotten—that is woman's saga.'

Here, then, in Nora Helmar, the poet starts with the figure of a woman in whom the results of the dominant will of man, stultifying the powers and gifts of womanhood, are seen in their extreme development. Environed by selfish kindness, petted and spoiled for thirty years of dwarfed existence, this pretty, playful, amiable, and apparently happy little wife is really a tragical victim of masculine egotism. A nature exorbitantly desirous of leaning on a stronger will has been seized, condemned, absorbed by the natures of her father and her husband. She lives in them and by them, without moral instincts of her own, or any law but their pleasure. The result of this weakness—this, as Ibsen conceives, criminal subordination of the individuality—is that when Nora is suddenly placed in a responsible position, when circumstances demand from her a moral judgment, she has none to give; the safety, even the comfort, of the man she loves precede all other considerations, and with a light heart she forges a document to shield her father or to preserve her husband's name. She sacrifices honour for love, her conscience being still in too rudimentary a state to understand that there can be any honour that is distinguishable from love. Thus Dora would have acted, if we can conceive Dora as ever thrown into circumstances which would permit her to use the pens she was so patient in holding. But Nora Helmar has capacities of undeveloped character which make her far more interesting than the, to say the truth, slightly fabulous Dora. Her insipidity, her dollishness, come from the incessant repression of her family life. She is buried, as it were, in cotton-wool, swung into artificial sleep by the egotistical fondling of the men on whom she depends for emotional existence. But when once she tears the wrappings away, and leaps from the pillowed hammock of her indolence, she rapidly develops an energy of her own, and the genius of the dramatist is displayed in the rare skill with which he makes us witness the various stages of this awaking. At last, in an extraordinary scene, she declares that she can no longer live in her doll's house; husband and wife sit down at opposite ends of a table, and argue out the situation in a dialogue which covers sixteen pages, and Nora dashes out into the city, into the night; while the curtain falls as the front door bangs behind her.

The world is always ready to discuss the problem of marriage, and this very fresh and odd version of *L'Ecole des Femmes* excited the greatest possible interest throughout the north of Europe. The close of the play, in particular, was a riddle hard to be deciphered. Nora, it was said, might feel that the only way to develop her own individuality was to leave her husband, but why should she leave her children? The poet evidently held the relation he had described to be such an immoral one, in the deepest and broadest sense, that the only way out of the difficulty was to cut the Gordian knot, children or no children. In almost Nora's very last reply, moreover, there is a glimmer of relenting. The most wonderful of things may happen, she confesses; the reunion of a developed wife to a reformed husband is not, she hints, beyond the range of what is possible. We are left with the conviction that it rests with him, with Helmar, to allow himself to be led through the fires of affliction to the feet of a Nora who shall no longer be a doll.

Ibsen's dramas have a curious way of containing each the germ of the action of the next. As the relation of Bernick to his wife suggests to us the whole plot of *A Doll's House*, so the horrible incident of the diseased friend of the family, the dissipated and dying Dr. Rank, foreshadows the subject of *Ghosts*. This, or I am very much mistaken, is one of the most thrilling and amazing works in modern literature. I know nothing to compare with it for sheer moral horror except *Le Crime et le Châtiment*. The ghosts, or revenants, who give their name to this piece, are the results of self-indulgent egotism, of sensual hypocrisy, stalking through the lives of the next generation of men. These are the spectres of the pleasures of the dead, the teeth of the children set on edge by those sour grapes that their fathers ate. The warping of individuality by hereditary weakness, caused by selfish indulgence, is the tragic central idea of the dreadful play of *Ghosts*. It opens with light comedy, but the plot instantly thickens. A wealthy widow, mother of one son, an interesting delicate youth who has chiefly resided in Paris, welcomes that son on his return to be present at the opening of an asylum which had been built in honour of her husband's memory. He, the late Captain Alving, has been a 'pillar of society' and of the Church. His wife knows, and always has known, that he was a person of hopelessly dissolute conduct, but her life during their marriage was sacrificed to a skilful concealment of this fact, and since his death she has laboured no less to preserve his reputation unsullied. Some remarks of her son Oswald about the non-matrimonial but yet faithful connections entered into so often by artists and men of letters in France—remarks made to the conventional and shallow Pastor Manders—lead to a discussion in which, after her son has left the room, Mrs. Alving tears the mask from the hypocrisy of her husband's past life and the torture of her own. She relates a certain incident which finally opened her eyes to her husband's moral incapacity, and made her send her little son away, as a baby, out of such corrupting influences. She has scarcely finished telling this story, which frightens Pastor Manders half out of his wits, when through a door left ajar they hear Oswald repeating the particular offence, and, starting up, Mrs. Alving groans out the word 'Ghosts!' Her care has been in vain; the spectre of hereditary vices has revisited her swept and garnished home.

So far, no doubt, Alexander Dumas *fils* or even Sardou would go. But Ibsen, in his daring realism, goes much farther still. The only confidant of Mrs. Alving, in the dreadful guard she kept over the outward respectability of her husband, had been his physician, and the poet, with unparalleled daring, pursues the phantoms into a still lower circle of hell. In her life of long-drawn moral anguish, in the sacrifice of her individuality to hypocritical shams of every kind, the only reality which has escaped the universal taint of falseness has been the mutual love of mother and son. She has separated herself all these years from Oswald, that his young life might be untouched by the moral miasma of his home, but she has kept up close intimacy with him by correspondence, and he loves her warmly. Now he has returned, ignorant of the truth about his father, and devoted to his mother, the latter hopes to enter at last upon a period of rest and happiness, in which she need pretend nothing and endure nothing, but lie at peace watching the growth of Oswald's character. But she notices that he drinks too freely, smokes too much, and seems always restless and listless. At last he confesses to her that he is never well, that his life is physically ruined, that his nerves and body are a wreck. The evil advances with the play. His brain rapidly softens; in the long and almost intolerably affecting scene with which the play ends his reason flickers out, and the spectator, when the curtain falls, is left uncertain whether his mother will, or will not, indulge his last conscious wish, and cut his senseless second childhood short with a dose of morphia. It is hardly possible, in addressing the prudish English reader, to suggest the real meaning of the whole thing. Ghosts! ghosts! the avenging deities born of the unclean blood that spurtled from the victim of Cronos! How any human creature can see the play acted through without shrieking with mental anguish, I cannot tell. Perhaps the distraction of the scene makes it a little less terrible to witness than to read. As literature, at all events, if anything exists outside Æschylus and Shakespeare more direct in its appeal to the conscience, more solemn, more poignant, than the last act of *Ghosts*, I at least do not know where to look for it.

A storm of ill-will from the press was at first the only welcome which *Ghosts* received. It was not possible that it should be otherwise.

Conventional readers were shocked by the theme, and the drastic treatment of the theme; artistic readers could not reconcile themselves to such an outrage upon dramatic tradition. The tide soon turned; the amazing power and originality of the drama, and its place in its author's work, were presently perceived. In the meantime the wash-pot of journalism was poured over the poet. A year later he took his revenge in the interesting novelette in dialogue—for it really cannot be called a play—named *An Enemy of the People*. Björnson had been saying, with his careless vehemence, 'The majority is always right;' Ibsen sardonically answers, 'Excuse me, the majority is never right!' The hero of *An Enemy of the People* is a sort of Henrik Ibsen in practical life, a critic who is execrated because he tells the unvarnished truth to unwilling ears. The poet is, if it be possible, less optimistic in this than even in his preceding drama. The situation is this. A certain Dr. Tomas Stockmann has made the fortune of a little Norwegian seaside watering-place, by developing its natural resources, and by creating public baths, which are a centre of popular attraction. This little impoverished community has found, thanks to Dr. Stockmann, that its speculation in the baths has proved to be 'a broken hill.' Unhappily, Dr. Stockmann, who is physician and sanitary officer to the town as well as director of the baths, discovers that the drainage system of the place is defective, and that the water is full of impurities. He warns the municipality in vain. To make alterations would frighten away the public and affect, perhaps destroy, the popularity of the watering-place; and besides, there is no other outlet for the drainage of the tan-works of an influential citizen. The municipality determines nothing must be done. Dr. Stockmann then appeals to the newspapers on both sides; they are unanimous that nothing must be printed. He summons a public meeting: it hisses him down and will let nothing be said. It is at this meeting that they whom he has for so many years sustained and benefited howl at him as 'an enemy of the people.' He is boycotted, stoned, and driven from the town, merely for saying aloud what every one privately knows to be the truth.

The allegory is transparent, and the play is really a piece of rather violent personal polemic. The story would make an interesting novel; it hardly endures dramatic treatment. The work, however, remains so far dramatically true that Dr. Stockmann is in no personal degree Ibsen himself, or even a mere mouthpiece for his ideas, but represents a type, a temperament, of a very conceivable and consistent kind. He is a Radical so intense that the business of radicalism itself is as hateful to him as any other form of political jugglery. Absolute honesty, at whatever cost; absolute devotion to individuality, no matter who is offended; these are the only rules for conduct that he recognises. Accordingly, while Scandinavian criticism has been almost unanimous in holding that *An Enemy of the People* is below the level of its author's works, and has something provincial and temporary in its evolution, I cannot but hold Dr. Stockmann to be one of the most original, and to me most distinct, of Ibsen's creations. There is a great deal of Count Tolstoi in him, but whether Ibsen knew anything of the personal life and character of the great Russian so long ago as 1882 I cannot tell.

In *An Enemy of the People* the animal spirits of the poet seemed to support him on a high wave of indignant idealism. He declared the majority tame and cowardly and hypocritical, it is true, but vowed that the good man, even if quite solitary, may find his virtue his own reward, and exult like the sons of the morning. But all this physical glow of battle had faded out when he came to write *The Wild Duck*, a strange, melancholy, and pessimistic drama, almost without a ray of light from end to end. This is a very long play, by far the most extended of the series, and is, on the whole, the least interesting to read, although, like all its author's works, it possesses scenes of a thrilling vivacity. The wild duck which gives its name to the piece is an unhappy bird which is kept in captivity in a garret, and is supposed to be shot at last with a pistol by a morbid little girl. Unfortunately it is herself the little girl is found to have shot, and by no means accidentally. The hero is a most distressing Gregers Werle, a type of the new neurotic class: a weak and bloodless creature, full of half-formed aspirations and half-delirious hopes for the future of humanity. In *The Wild Duck* cynical selfishness is absolutely dominant; it has it all its own way to the end, and, if I comprehend the undercurrent of the plot at all, the ideal spirit of goodness is the untamed bird in its close and miserable garret, captive to circumstances, and with no hope of escape. There is really not a character in the book that inspires confidence or liking. I confess a preference for the merry cynic, Dr. Relling, with his monstrous set of immoral paradoxes. The photographer, Helling [Hjalmar] Ekdal, who bullies the wild duck and drives his relatives crazy with his hateful tricks and his manners, is almost beyond what a reader can bear. I read *The Wild Duck* on deck as I crossed the Atlantic in the winter of its publication, and I shall always identify its gloomy pages with the desolate environment of the dreadful ocean. *The Wild Duck* is not the kind of imaginative literature that Mr. Lang would appear to hanker after. It is not an anodyne by any means;

and if it is a medicine I do not quite understand how the dose is expected to act. There can be no doubt that it is by far the most difficult of Ibsen's dramas for a reader to comprehend. I am told, however, that it is effective enough on the stage.

In *Rosmersholm* Ibsen rose again to the height of his genius. This is no less sad a play than the most mournful of its predecessors, but it labours under no obscurity of motive or sluggishness of story. It is charged to an extraordinary degree with the explosive elements of modern thought and morals, and it is a chain of veritable ethical surprises. It closes, as we shall see, in utter darkness, but in the course of the piece so many flashing threads of hope and love have been introduced that the entire web cannot be pronounced dismal. It is a story of what the French call *une fin de race*. At the old manor-house of Rosmersholm, the family of Rosmer have lived for generation after generation, conservative, honourable, and reserved. The Rosmers have always been distinguished, they have never been amusing. No Rosmer has ever been known to laugh, and their prestige has spread a kind of anti-hilarious tradition around them. In the neighbourhood of Rosmersholm it has long been considered ungentleman-like to be merry. The last of the Rosmers, Johannes, formerly priest of the parish, remains in the house, its latest representative. His wife, Beate, who long had languished in a melancholy and distracted state, drowned herself just outside the door, in the mill-dam, a little more than a year before the play begins. Yet much earlier than that a poor but extremely clever girl from Finmark, Rebecca West, had entered the household, and gradually had obtained complete moral authority in it. Rebecca West is one of Ibsen's most admirable creations. She is an adventuress, as much as was our other friend of the name, Miss Sharp. But there is a great distinction between the two Beckies. Rebecca West thirsts for power, for influence, for independence, and she is scarcely more scrupulous than Becky Sharp, but intellectually and spiritually she is a very much finer creature. In a certain sense she is beneficent; her instincts are certainly distinguished, and even splendid; had she been completely successful, she would have been an exceptionally admired member of society. She comes into the morbid and melancholy environment of the Rosmers, with all her warmth of vitality. She is fired with a longing to save and to rehabilitate the family. She sees that Beate is past helping, and she therefore sweeps her away into the mill-dam as fast as she can; she sees that Johannes, with his beautiful mind and delicate, harmonious ideas, can be redeemed, if only Beate is got rid of. But with Beate must go the old conservative religion, the old high and dry politics. Johannes Rosmer must free himself from prejudice, as Rebecca has freed herself. After Beate's suicide, things gradually grow more hopeful in the sad old house. Rosmer and Rebecca, always on the footing of friends only, remain together, and become more and more attached to one another. Rosmer takes the colour of Rebecca in all things; accepts the radicalism that she, a nameless daughter of the people, delights in; gradually drops the Christianity that she disdains. But meanwhile a strange psychological change has taken place in her own ideas. Passionately in love with Rosmer, it has been her constant disappointment that he, with his old-world honour and his Rosmer timidity, has never suggested any closer relation between them than that of friendship. But as months pass on, she catches his sensitive distinction; Anteros takes the place of Eros in her breast, and in her new intensity of spiritualised affection, she cannot think otherwise of herself than as Rosmer's friend. Her old work as an adventuress, however, revenges itself; their fair companionship is rudely broken into from without. To prevent the scandal which idle tongues have raised, Rosmer, deeply shocked, offers instant marriage to Rebecca. But, in the meanwhile, conscience has brought up before her the spectre of Beate, persecuted to her death, and she dares not accept. Rosmer finds that the last of a venerated race cannot with impunity break all the political, moral, and religious traditions of his family. He is solitary in his freedom of mind, and even between Rebecca and himself the demon of doubt has penetrated. At last, after Rebecca has, by a full confession, sacrificed all to recover Rosmer's love, and has not regained it fully, they arrive at the determination to end their confused and hopeless relations by plunging together into the mill-dam where Beate drowned herself. Their suicide is observed, at the very close of the play, by an old woman, from the windows of the manor-house; and the house of Rosmer has fallen. The most obvious of many morals in this striking play is that new faith, modern ideas in ethics and religion, cannot with safety be put into old bottles. Opinions may perforce be altered, but the hereditary tendency remains, paralyzing the will.

Since the earlier part of this article was written, I have received Ibsen's Christmas gift to his admirers, his new drama of *The Lady from the Sea*. Perhaps the charm of novelty has biassed me, but I think not; I fancy this new work will be admitted to be one of the brightest jewels in the poet's crown. He has never been more daring in his analysis of character, never more brilliant in his evolution of it, than here; and there is thrown over the whole play a glamour of poetry, of mystery,

of landscape-beauty, which has not appeared in Ibsen's work, to anything like the same extent, since *Peer Gynt*. And, moreover, after so
many tragedies, this is a comedy. The title can scarcely be translated,
because a *havfrue* is a mermaid, a 'sea-lady', and there is an under-
meaning in this. It is the old story of the mortal who 'left lonely for ever
the kings of the sea.' In a little coast-town of Norway—very possibly
the poet's birthplace, Skien—the district physician, Dr. Wangel, being
left a widower with two daughters, thinks he will marry again. But at
the mouth of the fjord, in a lighthouse on a desolate skerry, an exquisite
girl lives with her father, the keeper. Wangel makes her acquaintance,
falls in love with her, and persuades her to marry him. He frankly tells
her of his own previous happy marriage, and she confesses it is not the
first time she has been wooed. But the alliance is a fortunate one, until
she loses her firstborn and only child. From that time she becomes
gloomy, wayward, and morbid, and though she loves her husband,
she seems divided from him. She is still to all the town 'the lady from
the sea', the sea-wife. She pines for the roaring tides, for the splendour
and resonance of the unconquerable ocean, and nothing takes the place
of the full salt breeze she has abandoned. She bathes every day in the
harbour, but she disdains these tame and spiritless waters of the fjord,
and declares that they do her no good. She has lived the very life of the
sea; her blood has tides in it, is subject to ebb and flow. She has been
transplanted too late from her ocean-rock; she pines like a sea-weed in a
tank or a petrel in a cage.

But there is more than this to afflict her spirit. The old alliance she
hinted at was a betrothal to a nameless man, a Finn, nursed, perhaps, by
some storm-gathering witch, mate of a ship, who has exercised an
absorbing influence over her. He is a creature of the sea, a sort of
impersonation of the waves. She confesses all this to her husband, and
tells him that she one day received a letter from this man, summoning
her to a rendezvous on a desolate promontory. When she got there he
told her that he had murdered his captain (a godly slaughter, by his own
account), and was now flying from justice. He took a ring from her,
tied it to one of his own, and flung it out to sea. The result of this enforced betrothal, to which her own will was never a partner, is that she
feels ever more and more the sea, embodied in this wild, seafaring Finn,
coming between her and her husband. At last, in the play, the Finn
comes back to claim her, and it is not until her husband leaves her
perfectly free to choose between the two men, and liberates her
individual responsibility, that the morbid charm is broken, and she

rapturously selects to remain with her husband, while the merman goes desperately down into his waters. It is impossible here to give the smallest idea of the imagination, subtlety, and wit concentrated in carrying out this curious story. *The Lady from the Sea* is connected with the previous plays by its emphatic defence of individuality and its statement of the imperative necessity of developing it; but the tone is quite unusually sunny, and without a tinge of pessimism. It is in some respects the reverse of *Rosmersholm*; the bitterness of restrained and baulked individuality, which ends in death, being contrasted with the sweetness of emancipated and gratified individuality, which leads to health and peace.

Here must be drawn to a close this brief and imperfect sketch of the great Norwegian poet's seven social dramas. I have spoken of them merely from the literary side; much could and should be said of them from the theatrical.★ It is easy to be led away into extravagant praise of what is comparatively little known. Perhaps better-equipped critics than myself, if they read Danish, would say that they found Ibsen occasionally provincial, sometimes obscure, often fantastic and enigmatical. Those to whom the most modern spirit in literature is distasteful, who see nothing but the stitches of the canvas in the vast pictures of Tolstoi, would reject Ibsen, or would hark back to his old sweet, flute-like lyrics. But others, who believe that literature is alive, and must progress over untrodden ground with unfamiliar steps, will recognise a singular greatness in this series of social dramas, and will not grudge a place for Henrik Ibsen among the foremost European writers of the nineteenth century.

★ Last spring I had the pleasure of attending a course of lectures on the Modern Drama, at the Royal Institution, by Mr. William Archer. In the course of the second of these he spoke in a very interesting manner of Ibsen as an acting dramatist. I regret that these valuable lectures have not been published and were not apparently reported.

15. Henry James becomes interested

January 1889

This extract from a letter to Gosse, dated 29 January 1889, contains James's earliest reference to Ibsen. He was at this time preparing to write for the stage himself (see Introduction) and subsequently became an enthusiastic admirer of Ibsen's work, speaking out repeatedly in his defence (see Nos 41, 74, 84, 96, 141, 143). The full text of this letter, and the others printed in this volume, may be consulted at the Brotherton Library, Leeds University. James's reference is obviously to Gosse's article in the *Fortnightly Review* (No. 14).

I have perused your very interesting acct. of Ibsen, as I always peruse you when I find you. You must tell me more about I. That is not in this case female-American for *me*.

16. Arthur Symons on Ibsen's modernity

April 1889

From 'Henrik Ibsen', by Arthur Symons, *Universal Review* (April 1889), iii, 567–74. This article takes as its starting-point Havelock Ellis's edition of plays published in 1888 (see No. 13). Symons (1865–1945), the well-known author and critic, was from this time counted among Ibsen's influential supporters in England.

One of the most truly notable books published in England for some time past appeared as the September issue of the 'Camelot' series. All or most of the publications of that series have been, in their way, useful and interesting; but it is after all saying little to say that the volume entitled *The Pillars of Society, and other Plays,* by Henrik Ibsen, is of quite different and quite superior value to any of the mere reprints—Swift or Lowell, Shelley or Carlyle—for which a very proper gratitude is due to editor and publisher. The book, quietly as it comes before us, is no less than a literary event, for it introduces to English readers almost for the first time, and for the first time adequately, a writer of immense genius, who is today the chief power among the Scandinavian races—'the chief figure of European significance', says Mr. Havelock Ellis, the editor of the volume, 'that has appeared in the Teutonic world of art since Goethe'.

[Symons here gives an account of Ibsen's life and career to date. He goes on:]

The art of Ibsen in his social dramas is of that essentially modern kind which is not content with holding the mirror up to nature, but desires to drive in certain reformatory ideas over and above the impression conveyed by an impartial reflection of life. Indeed, art such as Ibsen's is never impartial, and yet, if it be art at all, it is precisely in its reflection of life that almost the whole of its value lies. Ibsen is passionately in earnest; he hates the false and loves the true more warmly than a mere artist finds it needful to do; and it is with a deliberate purpose that he takes up his pen. But the power of his work—the justification, and the only artistic justification, of such a line of work—is in this, that his purpose thrusts him of itself into the very midst of humanity, forces him to know men and women as they are, to describe them as they are, and thus to base his art on the only unshifting basis. The very passion which moves him serves to sharpen the outline of the characters who move, types yet never abstractions—rather living men and women who reflect ideas—across the stage on which they appear so much at home. Ibsen's grip on his subject-matter is prodigious, and his subject-matter is modern life—life and the abuses of life. To read one of his plays is to pass an hour in a centre of existence—in a great city, where the crowds have their passions and agitations, or, better still, in some small place, a selected corner out of all this bustle, in which the action, more circum-scribed, can be concentrated, and thus strike home with a deeper intensity. The action of one of the greatest of his dramas, *Ghosts*, takes place in a country house by one of the western fjords during the hours of a single day from noon to sunset; but in its scope it embraces human-ity, and speaks to universal nature. Here again the 'purpose' with which he writes justifies itself: it is because he has a purpose—because, that is, he is a thinker who goes right down to Nature, who weighs, and finds wanting, a society which does not grow out of that one true soil—that his art becomes universal: his purpose is the life-blood of his art.

Ibsen's 'purpose' in these social dramas, is nothing narrow or fanatic; it cannot be too distinctly said that he is not a vendor of nostrums, philanthropic or other, nor that terrible being, a man of one idea. His satire plays freely on every angle of that great mass of conventions which we call society; it is now political, as in *The Young Men's League*, now purely social, as in *The Pillars of Society*; he can even seem to satirise himself, as in *The Wild Duck*. His fundamental demand is for individual liberty; he would have men live according to nature, and he can conceive of a reasonable society only as an organisation founded on the truth of things, and bound together by sincerity. 'To revolutionise people's minds', as he himself has said, 'that is the one thing that avails'. Thus his plays are no party-pamphlets, but a gospel of real light: they illuminate, they do not merely argue. Nor is Ibsen an idealist in the contemptuous sense which people often give to the word—an un-practical visionary. He is directly and steadily practical, full of common sense, shrewdness, attention to fact, to detail. He can found a play on a sanitary question; nothing is trivial, common, uninteresting to him. And he has the courage of his convictions—abundance of courage, or he would never have written *Ghosts*. What his pet ideas may be in political matters, in what is properly called party politics, the only kind of politics which the ordinary mind seems able to conceive, I neither know nor care to know. I am not aware, even after reading *A Doll's House*, in which the woman question is treated with so firm a grasp, so broad a comprehension, if he is of opinion, like Miss Cobbe, that female suffrage is the paradise of woman's progress. But I do know that for sane and suggestive treatment of social questions; for clear light upon difficult ways, straight speech on shrouded topics; for satire which is cruel and healing as the burning iron that cauterises a wound; for earnestness that is never without judgment, sincerity that is never without tact; for the qualities that make a social drama helpful and illuminating, the work of Ibsen is pre-eminent, and in these days unique.

But Ibsen is not only a great thinker, he is a great artist. Nothing shows us better than Ibsen's social dramas the true meaning of the word realism—a word which has unhappily come to be associated with pictures of life which are necessarily sordid, frequently unclean. The connection between the realistic and the abominable is a question I have never been able to fathom. Realism is a picture of life as it really is, and in life as it really is the element of grossness is only one of many elements. Ibsen's realism stifles nothing; it is daring to discuss matters over which society draws a veil, but it is never gross, never unhealthy, it 'sees life steadily, and sees it whole'. Ibsen paints ordinary life; his people are (if I may speak in terms of another nationality) the people one meets in the City, one's lawyer, one's banker, the men one hears discussing stocks and shares, business people; or, again, the officials of a country town, the clergyman, the ladies who work for charitable institutions, the doctor, the newspaper editor, the printer. All these people meet, talk over their own affairs, speak of their business, go to and fro, just as if they were really living their parts. Every character, down to the merest 'walking gentleman', is carefully finished; we get from all the same impression of reality. It is life, and yet life from a point of view which is not the point of view of the crowd. Everywhere there is a deep undercurrent of irony, and irony is the judgment of an outside observer, who is not in the throng. So cutting is the irony, that Ibsen's plays would be terrible reading for the Rörlunds and Helmers and Bernicks of society if one could only hope in them so much inner light as would suffice to show them themselves. That is what I am a little doubtful about; however, Ibsen's irony, though cutting, is so moderate, so singularly free from the exaggeration of caricature, that I have good hope it may be so. And, indeed, conventional people everywhere hate

Ibsen—because they fear him; he shocks them—because he tells the inconvenient truth. A caricaturist is never feared, but in Ibsen you never lose the lesson in the laugh. His style is precision itself; in the dialogue there is scarcely a metaphor. Energy, conciseness, and exactitude are the qualities by which his style rises through its simplicity to the finest literary art. The secret of this style lies in the precision with which every word is chosen and placed; exactly the right word is always used, and no more. Ibsen's dialogue is our everyday talk pruned of its waste— not pruned so as to lose any of the sap of life, for his art shows itself no-where keener than in a cunning use of broken sentences, interjections and interruptions, apparent trivialities and casualties. Nowhere does there seem to be any sacrifice of nature for literary effect; there is no word-brilliance, no display; and here, as always, the restraint of the true artist is justified by the finer art of the result.

In the construction of his plays, as in the management of his dialogue, Ibsen works by simplicity, rapidity, and concision. The plot is always elaborately woven, with a care which is directed to the clear present-ment of a sometimes rather complex network of action. There is often an underplot, worked into the very stuff of the main action, and contributing to its development. But in the final result all is clear and undistracted; the impression is single. In *The Young Men's League* the action centres in a political pretender, Stensgaard; he rises and falls, through the course of the vivacious comedy, steadily pushing his way onward toward the prize that will one day crown his determined seek-ing of it. Here, as elsewhere, Ibsen expresses his distrust of 'compact majorities'; his profound distrust of a sounding progress which does not begin from within. In *The Pillars of Society*, the sweep of the satire, like the course of the action, is more extensive. It falls on the conventions, small and great, which are the 'pillars' of a rotten society, touching now here, now there—the tattle of the ladies at their sewing-meeting, the barbarous inhumanity of the shipowner who sends out unworthy ships, finally and most forcibly the foundation of lies, domestic and social, on which the apparent success of Consul Bernick has been built. The play is not all gloom, for it traces the moral regeneration of a man who is manly enough to rise through confession to a spiritual victory—a regeneration brought about through the agency of a woman: in Ibsen, as in Shakespeare, in Scott, in George Meredith, the heroes are women.

A Doll's House—with *Ghosts* the finest and most impressive of Ibsen's social dramas, and certainly altogether the most charming, quite the most perfect—is an utterance on the marriage question. The portrait of Nora is the most wonderful piece of character-drawing that Ibsen has ever done, and Nora herself is the most charming creature conceivable. In the three days in which the action passes she develops from a child to a woman; a series of events—whose rapid and inevitable march, the encroaching of the fate that lies in our deeds and us, almost suspends the breath in the sympathy of pity and terror—brings her face to face with immense issues: for the first time she sees things in their true light, for the first time she speaks seriously with her husband, and the step she takes is taken with clear conviction and in full seriousness. Her story is a protest against that fatally false view of woman which turns marriage, only too often, into a bargain between a beautiful slave and a kind slave owner. In Helmer we see the man who builds a 'doll's house' for his wife, worshipping her as his idol, if you will, but with a chivalry which is but the softer side of contempt. He is the normal man, and Nora is the normal woman trained in exquisite ignorance of life, in delicate seclusion from facts, to become the dearest possession, but a possession, a property, of that superior being the normal man. When at last her awakening comes she cries to her husband, with a strange shiver of recollection: 'Torvald, in that moment it became clear to me that I had been living here all these years with a strange man, and had borne him three children'. The consciousness overwhelms her that the marriage is no marriage, that she is no fit wife for her husband, nor he a fit husband for her, that she is not fit to be the mother of her children. And she leaves him, only to return, if that should ever be, when their living together will be a true marriage.

Ghosts, with which I compared *A Doll's House* for its concentrated power, has none of the charm, none of the variety, of that play. Its subject is the most sombre of all that Ibsen has essayed, and, like *A Doll's House*, it has roused a violent opposition. It is a tragedy which encroaches as far as art can well go in the direction of physical horror, and the prolonged anguish of its action is unrelieved by even a momentary ray of really cheerful light. The play shows, in its few intense hours of crisis, the working of the relentless law of heredity. It is the final triumph of nature over conventionality, and Ibsen has not spared the morality of conventional suppression one drop of the bitter cup. The play is certainly very painful reading, but the painfulness is justified, from the moral point of view by the 'purpose', from the artistic point of view by the unquestionable power of it. I know nothing in any play so complete in its mastery over the springs of horror and sympathetic suffering as the last scene, the expected and dreaded climax—the final flowering of the latent germ of madness in the innocent Oswald. The horror of *The Cenci* is less dreadful than this.

When *Ghosts* came out, it was of course honoured with the epithet of immorality. In *An Enemy of Society*, a play which appeared in the following year, it is supposed that Ibsen alludes to his own position among his countrymen in the representation of Dr. Stockmann, the soberly heroic doctor who dares and loses all but the consciousness of duty in a fight against unconquerable prejudice. The position in which Ibsen places his hero is dramatically excellent, and the complications give the finest opportunities for social satire and that truthful exhibition of social abuses which is more deadly to them than any satire. The whole action is full of life and bustle; one scene, the scene of the public meeting, must have immense effect on the stage: never has the whole aspect, the whole movement, of such a thing been so truthfully and so brilliantly put on the boards. Here, as so often elsewhere, the demand of Ibsen is for the liberty of the individual, the 'revolutionising of people's minds'. In *The Wild Duck*, a play of inferior quality, the satire seems to turn round upon the satirist: its exposure of the unballasted idealist does but show how 'steadily' Ibsen sees life, and how he 'sees it whole'. *Rosmersholm*, the latest and not the least of Ibsen's plays, is, unlike the others, primarily a drama of passion. It has something of the individual intensity of Browning, and like one of Browning's finest works it might have been called *A Soul's Tragedy*. For a moment society is forgotten in the contemplation of a human soul.

Ibsen's art, to return to our starting-point, is the art of a renovator, a satirist; 'his work throughout', as Mr. Ellis well says in the powerful and thoughtful introduction to which I have before referred, 'is the expression of a great soul crushed by the weight of an antagonistic social environment into utterance that has caused him to be regarded as the most revolutionary of modern writers'. Such a writer is not to be weighed as we weigh the impersonal literary artist to whom all nature is a mere sketching-ground, and men and women but models. He demands of us other standards, and we must, if we would do him justice, view him as he would have himself regarded. This is what I have tried to do in the foregoing pages.

A DOLL'S HOUSE

Novelty Theatre, 7 June 1889

---

17. An unsigned notice by Clement Scott in the *Daily Telegraph*

8 June 1889, 3

Scott (1841–1904) was to become Ibsen's bitterest opponent in England. As theatre critic for the *Telegraph*, Britain's largest and most influential newspaper, his prestige was enormous: he held the post for nearly thirty years (1871–98). He was also editor of the *Theatre* between 1880 and 1889.

The original production of *A Doll's House*, starring Janet Achurch as Nora, provoked the first serious clash over Ibsen. Excepting *Quicksands* and *Breaking a Butterfly* (see Nos 5 and 12), it was the first of his plays to be performed in England. The translation was by William Archer and the cast was as follows:

Torvald Helmer	Mr Herbert Waring	Ellen	Miss Mabel K. Haynes
Dr. Rank ..	Mr Charles Charrington	Finar	Master Lionel Calhaem
Nils Krogstadt	Mr Royce Carleton	Emmy ..	Miss Amy Rayner
Porter	Mr J. Luke	Bob	Miss Ethel Rayner
Mrs. Linden ..	Miss Gertrude Warden	Nora Helmer	Miss Janet Achurch
Anna	Miss Blanche Eversleigh		

Mr. William Archer and the Ibsenites have had their grand field-day. *A Doll's House* was last night solemnly produced, peeped into, and duly discussed. No irreverent hand has dared to soil the author's master-piece, and no triviality is allowed to disfigure the amiable 'fads' of the gifted author. Word for word Mr. Archer has faithfully translated the original play and not allowed one suggestion, however objectionable, to be glossed over. The child-wife gambols like a kitten and munches her macaroons; she fibs and forges. The sensual and egotistical husband treats his Nora exactly like the spoiled baby that she is. The doctor discusses his hereditary ailments with coarse frankness, and enlarges on the virtues of truffles and oysters. The dramatic letter tumbles into the letter-box, whilst the distracted wife dances her celebrated tarantella, and, absolutely true to the original, the baby wife, who has suddenly and miraculously developed into a thinking woman, leaves her home, breaks her marriage oath, refuses to forgive her husband, abandons her innocent children, and becomes absolutely inhuman, simply because she discovers her husband is an egotist and that she has been a petted little fool. But at the present moment we have no time or opportunity to discuss Ibsen or his theories, which we might do at great length. We do not honestly believe that those theories as expressed in *The Doll's House* would ever find favour with the great body of English playgoers. How Torvald Helmer could by any possibility have treated his restless, illogical, fractious, and babyish little wife otherwise than he did; why Nora should ever adore with such abandonment and passion this conceited prig, whom she never professed to understand; and how it could ever be possible for any woman with the maternal instinct fully developed to desert her children because her pride was wounded, are points that may be very clear to the Ibsenites, but they require a considerable amount of argument in order to convince the common-sense playgoer. They are interesting points, and they will be freely discussed. In fact, we could sincerely wish that the *Doll's House* could be acted for more than one week, for the performance last night was wholly interesting. The audience—a very special one—was absorbed. Everything was well done. The translation was that of a scholar; the play was perfectly mounted; the acting was really remarkable. Not even Ibsen or Mr. Archer could have desired a better Nora than Miss Janet Achurch, who entered into her difficult task heart and soul, and whose acting requires far more analysis than can be given to it on the present occasion. The restlessness of the child wife in the first act was a trifle forced and artificial, but nothing could have been better than the scene with the doctor, who momentarily forgets the duties of a friend when the pretty wife has been discussing underclothing with him, and the whole of her share in the last long duologue was as good as it could be. Miss Achurch, who, we regret to hear, is leaving for Australia very shortly, has considerably improved her position and reputation by this most intelligent embodiment of a most difficult character. Good also in their respective lines were Mr. Herbert Waring as the priggish husband, Mr. Charles Charrington as the doctor, Mr. Royce Carleton as the savage and desperate Krogstad, and Miss Gertrude Warden as the pale-faced and neglected widow.

Mr. William Archer has done his work so admirably, and those on the stage have so ably assisted him, that it would be a pity if their devotion to their 'master' were not recognised. It is quite possible to pass a thoroughly intellectual evening in *A Doll's House* without being an immediate convert to Ibsenism. The interest was so intense last night that a pin might have been heard to drop. Miss Janet Achurch received the enthusiastic congratulations she so well deserved, and when the curtain fell there was such cheering that Mr. Charrington promised to telegraph the happy result to Henrik Ibsen. We cannot doubt that all who desire to become better acquainted with the author's new-fangled theories, and to see them put into practice in the most satisfactory manner, will crowd the Novelty Theatre for the next few evenings. If they cannot agree with the author they will, at any rate, see some admirable acting.

18. From an unsigned notice headlined 'Henrik Ibsen in English'

Daily News, 8 June 1889, 6

A play with a purpose is almost proverbially a play which affords little entertainment to the spectator. The reason of course is that the author is apt to be too intent upon the exposition of a pet theory to the neglect of dramatic art. Henry Ibsen, the Norwegian dramatist, whose reputation appears to stand so high just now in some quarters, is, we fear, no exception to this general rule. Mr. William Archer's excellent adaptation (modestly called a translation) of that author's celebrated piece, *Et Dukkehjem*, is the first attempt which has been made on our stage to present the work of that writer in a pure and unadulterated form. Unquestionably the experiment is interesting, but its success, to say the least, is doubtful. In Ibsen's opinions concerning the great problems of sociology it is not necessary at the moment to enter. All that we are concerned with just now are his views as to the place of woman in society, with which the present work treats. He thinks, with John Mill, that woman is too much subject to the caprice of the other sex. She is a dependant, a mere plaything of some man, and is allowed to develop little individuality of her own. She is brought up in ignorance of the ways of the world, and the defects of her education are apt to affect the foundation of her character. It is evident that such a starting point, whether one is disposed or not to admit its truth, has dramatic possibilities. A Sardou might conceivably turn it to excellent account on the stage. Ibsen's exposition, however, will hardly convince even the converted. Is it probable, it may reasonably be asked, that a woman, simply because she has been taught to give no serious thought to the realities of life, will therefore commit a forgery in complete ignorance of the heinousness of the offence? Such is the conduct of his heroine, Nora Helmer, who imagines that a benevolent purpose is a sufficient justification for her conduct. This is strange enough, but stranger still is the change which comes over her character and her conduct in the end in deserting her home, her husband, and above all her children, simply because she finds that her husband is angry with her, and inclined to take a selfish view of the dilemma when the exposure comes. In spite of Ibsen or any other theorist, it may be confidently asserted that no women who ever breathed would do any such thing. It is simply then as a mild picture of domestic life in Christiania that the piece has any interest at all. It is a little bit of genre painting, with here and there an effective touch. One looks at it as one looks at Teniers's rustics or tavern revellers, but then one is not obliged to gaze even at a Teniers for a whole evening; one can pass on to the next picture in the catalogue. It is peculiarly fortunate under the circumstances that the stage mounting leaves nothing to be desired. The tiled stove, with the curious gothic-looking openings, the plaques by Thorwaldsen on the walls, the very newspaper on the couch, help to present a picture of a Norwegian interior as pleasing as it is faithful.

19. From 'Flashes from the Footlights', an unsigned regular theatre column, *Licensed Victuallers' Mirror*

11 June 1889, 239

Henrik Ibsen's play at the Novelty is *the* theatrical sensation of the week.

I made the acquaintance of the now famous Norwegian poet some years ago.

When Miss Kate Ray produced the English translation of his great and powerful drama, *The Emperor and the Galilean.*

By the way I have not noticed that any of the critics have mentioned the fact that Miss Ray was the first to introduce Ibsen to the English public.

I am afraid she found that her efforts were not appreciated.

Ibsen was an unknown quantity then in this benighted land.

He will be better known after this week.

For whatever one's opinions of *A Doll's House* as a play may be, there can be no question of its startling unconventionality.

Seldom, outside a doctor's consulting room, have such candid and plain-spoken revelations been heard as to the effects of those ailments which the C.D. [sic] Acts concern themselves.

Strong meat indeed and not fit for babes—unless they be like Mr. Frank Danby's *Babe in Bohemia*—is Henrik Ibsen.

But go and see Janet Achurch before the piece is withdrawn on Friday.

Her impersonation of the heroine is the finest thing I have seen on the boards for a long time.

20. From 'Between the Acts', an unsigned regular theatre column

Queen, 15 June 1889, 825

During the week the public have had an opportunity afforded to them of studying one of those social problems which the Norwegian playwright Henrik Ibsen is so fond of treating in dramatic form. *The Doll's House* has been already adapted for the English stage, under the title of *Breaking a Butterfly*, with unsuccessful results, and there seems little reason to suppose that Mr. William Archer's clever translation of the original play would meet with more approval, even if it were possible to continue the series of performances at the Novelty Theatre beyond this week. English people may take their pleasures sadly, but they certainly do not care to go to the play to be told that everybody is bad and everything wrong, or to study matters which they would not discuss in their drawing-rooms. Ibsen's plays, it has been argued by his admirers, give their spectators much to think about. Undoubtedly they do; but they set one thinking of unpleasant topics, and depict so gloomy and disagreeable an aspect of life that they seem to reply negatively to Mr. Mallock's famous question as to the desirability of existence. . . .

The argument that woman should be treated as a human being, and not as a mere doll, is a very proper one; but the result of preaching the doctrine that every woman ought to emancipate herself, and that she is to sacrifice all rather than permit herself to be merely a pretty plaything, and, in fact, the lesser man, is a somewhat dangerous one—

> A rampant heresy, such as, if it spread,
> Would make all women kick against their lords
> Thro' all the world.

When, too, it is taken into consideration that Ibsen enforces these extravagant views by means of the most unpleasant set of people it has ever been the lot of playgoers to encounter, and, furthermore, discusses evils which we unfortunately know to exist, but which it can serve no good purpose to drag into the light of common day, it is hardly to be expected that his plays will appeal to the British public.

21. From 'Ibsen in London', a notice by Frederic Wedmore

Academy, 15 June 1889, xxxv, 419–20

This piece initiated a little battle between Wedmore (1844–1921) and Professor C. H. Herford of Aberystwyth (see No. 22); it is noteworthy that Herford subsequently replaced Wedmore as *Academy*'s Ibsen reviewer.

One is glad to have had an opportunity of seeing a play of Ibsen's—a representative piece—upon the stage in London, even though the conclusion one draws after having seen it is, that it is not particularly likely one will see it again. At all events, the stage itself—and not the closet—is the best place on which to get the question answered in regard to Ibsen. Is he a missionary, or is he an artist, or is he perchance both? So far as *The Doll's House* is concerned, we have had our answer. Mr. William Archer—who, for Mr. Walter Scott's little volume, had furnished a translation of *The Pillars of Society*, which did not read smoothly—has made what appears to me (who know nothing of the original) a much better translation of *The Doll's House*. It can hardly be, indeed, but that it is quite a good one. And Mr. Charles Charrington, Mr. Royce Carleton, Mr. Waring, and best of all, as few will doubt, Miss Achurch, have given us a performance which allowed us, as I think, to judge the play. The result of the judgment is that Henrik Ibsen must be said to be an interesting, but not a very great, artist: that he must be confessed to be a missionary into the bargain—a missionary, perhaps, before all—yet one whose mission is to some extent unnecessary, and to some extent injurious.

The Doll's House is a drama written partly to show that in a life of civilisation a woman must not be considered as man's creature alone—a ministrant or a toy. I should have thought, I confess, that, in 1889, intelligent England, and yet more assuredly intelligent America, had got beyond the need of any such teaching. To say this is not to invalidate the worth of Ibsen in Scandinavia or Germany, where conversions have yet to be made to views which France and England have accepted, off and on, for much more than a hundred years, and which America has accepted through all but the whole of her short and brilliant history. London is not the place in which the most pressing of our needs is to learn Henrik Ibsen's sapient lesson. With the lower class woman, doing as much as a man, in her own way, to earn the family loaf; with the 'young person' of the quite ordinary middle classes, presumably so much brighter, and so much fuller of initiative, than the youth with whom she condescends to consort; with the woman of the upper middle class and of the higher classes giving to society half its value and more than half its charm—nay, rising now and again to such heights of intelligence that she can voluntarily put her name to a memorial against the suffrage being ever conferred upon her: with these things so, we do not require Ibsen's tearful argument. Here he has no *locus standi*. It is as unnecessary for this thoughtful Scandinavian to inform us what a woman ought or ought not to be, as it is for us to accept from him the view that the preacher of orthodoxy must needs be a hypocrite or dullard, and that it is in the Church that conventionality most certainly and inevitably resides. He has no parson in *The Doll's House*. But, elsewhere, his parson—a study accurate enough, for all that I know, in Scandinavia—is introduced only to be ridiculed and exposed. If Ibsen were an Englishman—engaged in preaching that our women are dolls and our clergymen humbugs—I should say that he was provincial; I should say that he was suburban. And I should then pass on. But, as it is, there is no doubt little justification for being quite so hard on him. Ibsen is not suburban; he is not even provincial—he is of Scandinavia.

22. C. H. Herford's reply to Wedmore's review of *A Doll's House*

From *Letters to the Editor, Academy* (22 June 1889), xxxv, 432.
Charles Harold Herford (1853–1931), a distinguished scholar and
critic, was Professor of English at Aberystwyth (1887–1901) and
Manchester (1901–21). His letter is dated 16 June 1889, and addressed from University College, Aberystwyth. (See No. 21)

Mr. Wedmore speaks of Ibsen, with polite disdain, as a 'missionary'.
The sequel shows that this indictment includes two distinct counts; and
it remains to the end uncertain whether it is, for a dramatist, a blacker
sin to attempt to teach something, or to have—out of Scandinavia—
nothing to teach. For my own part, I attach relatively less value to this
element of Ibsen's work, as well as to the 'social' dramas, now so much
discussed, in which it mainly appears. That he has strong convictions
would be of comparatively little importance if he had not also a
faculty, unapproached in our time, of giving them dramatic form.
These convictions are in themselves mainly negative; and when, as in
the famous 'Third Kingdom' of *Kejser og Galileer*, a positive and
constructive element appears to emerge, it cannot be said that its
emergence is of very definite moment. Granting all this, however, it
still seems by no means made out that Ibsen's drastic and penetrating
pictures of social abuses are wholly superfluous for the fortunate
inhabitants of non-Scandinavian lands—or even for those of Paris and
London. It happens that the play by which Mr. Wedmore's judgment
of Ibsen has principally been determined, deals with the one social
question—the position of women—which England may fairly claim to
have brought nearer, in recent times, to its solution than any other
European people. His remarks on this head are sufficiently just—though,
by the way, to talk of Ibsen's 'tearful pleading' shows a comical misconception of one of the most masculine of modern poets. . . .

But Ibsen, as I have urged, with all his powerful advocacy, is not to
be judged simply as an advocate. His fame must rest, finally, in the

main, upon his two great and original dramatic poems. It was something more than 'interesting' art which built up, out of the fatal 'All or Nothing' of the heroic priest (an instance, by the way, for Mr. Wedmore, of a 'clergyman' who is not a 'humbug'), by the most rigidly consistent steps, the overpowering tragedy of *Brand*; and turned a study of egoism into that wonderful fantasia upon the infinite dissonances of modern life, *Peer Gynt*. These seem to me, and to not a few others, by far the most remarkable dramatic achievement of a generation which includes Browning and Swinburne, Sardou and Wildenbruch. Mr. Wedmore does not mention them; nor does it appear that they have in any way contributed to or coloured the view which he takes of Ibsen. Yet neither as a man nor as an artist can Ibsen be adequately judged without them.

23. An unsigned notice, *Spectator*

21 June 1889, lxii, 853–4

Ibsen's play, about which every one is talking, is a rather high-flown attempt to make men realise how grave a wrong it is to women to treat them as if they were mere toys made for men's pleasure, rather than for companionship in study, duty, and responsibility. That is no doubt a very wholesome and necessary lesson; but the Norwegian dramatist, whose play is by no means remarkable for either intellectual or dramatic force, has urged it in a spirit and applied it in a form which is more likely to bring it into discredit than to make sober converts to his teaching. It is hard to conceive a less ideal character than that of a wife and mother who suddenly finds all her love for her husband extinguished after eight years of tender affection, because she discovers his nature to be less generous and unselfish than she had supposed it, and who severs all the ties by which she is bound to him and her children, —pending a complete revolution in his character,—on the ground that he has treated her in the same unreal and fanciful manner in which a child makes-believe very much about her doll. Whatever the shortcoming of the husband's shallow and almost ogreish passion for his wife may be in Ibsen's play,—and no doubt it is the ordinary short-coming of a selfish and somewhat ignoble nature,—it is impossible to make it out more serious than the shortcoming in the devotion of a wife who is disenchanted in a moment of an eight years' love by the discovery that her husband's love for her is of a poorer and vulgarer type than she had imagined it. If his love for her was little more than the passion for a beautiful toy, what was hers for him? At best, the love for an illusion of her own, and anything but a deep desire to give up herself in order to make him more and more nearly what she had imagined him to be. Whatever she might properly have felt, or rather failed to feel, if the disillusion had come during the first days of betro-thal, no one who has lived happily as a wife for many years together, is worth much if her love does not survive the evidence that its object is less noble than she thought, and if she is not capable of a great self-sacrifice to make her own overflowing affection do double duty and make up for the deficiencies in that of which she is the object. In Ibsen's play, if the husband's love is the love for a toy or a source of sensuous pleasure, the wife's is the love for a dream which vanishes with the dream. Neither one nor the other has much in it of the disinterested devotion which is eager to give more than it receives. That delight in an ideal phantom which disappears when the phantom vanishes, may be and is less ignoble than the delight in a beautiful toy which pleases the senses and gratifies the instinct of ownership; but it has quite as little in it of the divine quality of love, of which it is the very essence to bestow gladly more than has been earned, and to transmute and transfigure in the very lavishness of its bestowing. Nora's complete success in getting rid of her love in the very act of getting rid of her fanciful dream, is almost more disenchanting in the reader's eyes, than Helmer's success in convincing the reader how selfish and poor his passion had been. We suppose that neither tragedy nor comedy ever before ended in a more complete clearing of the stage of everything heroic. The close is a *douche* of double disenchantment. The hero comes out a rather selfish man of the world who has found himself out; the heroine a hero-worshipper without either a hero or the magnanimity to make a hero where she had failed to find one. That slam of the door behind the heroine with which the last scene ends, leaves as complete a moral vacuum in the reader's mind as if an anti-climax were the approved literary ideal of dramatic fiction. If Ibsen's play of *A Doll's House* means anything, it means that any marriage which springs out of a poor and superficial sort of love is without significance and without sacredness, and is incapable of bearing any fruit better than the vanity or vulgar passion in which it had its origin. Indeed, his teaching is that the marriage must be wholly cancelled, and all the relations it has brought with it must be broken through, if ever the ground is to be cleared for anything better in the future. Indeed, on Ibsen's principle, every imperfect relation should be eradicated in order to make way for a better. But as every relation of life is more or less inadequate, as fathers and mothers seldom reach perfection, as brotherly and sisterly love is very seldom of the highest possible kind, as religious devotion itself is always short of what it might be, analogy would suggest that we must always be uprooting the only plants from which anything could grow, in order to put in their place some higher specimen of the same species, which, again, in its turn, must be displaced by something else. In fact, we should have to shut up our churches until we could open them for perfect worship. More thoroughgoing pessimism than Ibsen's conception of the only conceivable remedy for a marriage not founded on the highest kind of love, it would be impossible to imagine. If a man makes a toy of his wife, and the wife indulges in fanciful illusions about her husband, the only chance of reforming these false relations is, according to Ibsen's teaching, to sweep the board of them altogether, and let hearts and lives lie fallow till some nobler feeling springs up,—or fails to spring up, which would be much the more probable event.

The mistake made in the attempt to teach the useful lesson intended in Ibsen's play, is that instead of so painting the attitude of a man who makes a toy of his wife as to represent powerfully but not unfairly the distorted character of this relation between man and wife in the great majority of cases in which such distorted relations exist, Ibsen has so exaggerated both the selfishness of the feeling on the husband's side, and the mischief which it causes in dwarfing and disillusionising the wife, that it is impossible to accept the drama as suggesting any general lesson at all. That there is often a tendency, to which men and women perhaps equally contribute, to minimise the deeper sphere of co-operation and sympathy between them, and to magnify the less real and lighter aspects of the relation of husband and wife, no one who knows life will deny. But then, no one who knows life will deny that amongst Englishmen and Germans at least, and probably amongst Norwegians and Danes, to say nothing of the French, this tendency is seen very seldom indeed in such a repulsive form as that in which Ibsen paints it. In the first place, in a very unpleasant scene, Ibsen gives a relative importance to the grosser side of Helmer's nature, which is thoroughly untrue if it is to be taken as representative of the type of man who is most disposed to exaggerate the lighter and more protective, as well as the more playful aspect of the relation between husbands and wives. We venture to say that it is quite false to represent this disposition as resting chiefly on passion of that vulgar kind. It rests chiefly, we believe, on the poetical and imaginative nature, on the feeling for the delicacy, the grace, the ethereal element in women, and though often drifting into unreal sentiment of which the moral significance is very slight indeed, it is not a disposition of ignoble origin, and admits at least of very high and noble forms. The women who are so infuriated at the notion of being treated as mere toys, are, of course, perfectly in the right; but they should beware of confounding the feelings of men who look to them for nothing better than pleasant sensations and mental distraction, with the feelings of men who look to them to raise their ideal of mental and moral grace and beauty. Women who despise the sort of reverence and tenderness which this side of the feminine character inspires, are very much in the wrong indeed. The realism which would expunge this feeling from the highest relation between the sexes, would exclude a vast deal of what is best in human nature, and still more of that which leads to what is best, by refining and spiritualising what needs refining and spiritualising. Ibsen is right, of course, in resenting on behalf of women the treatment which makes playthings of them; but he is quite wrong in supposing that that treatment springs chiefly from what is coarse and frivolous in man. It is almost impossible for the ideal imagination to work at all without a certain freedom and playfulness in its movements, and if you severely frown down this freedom and playfulness of movement, the chances are that you will reduce the relation between man and woman to one of dreary and almost weary co-operation. Men are intended to find rest and refreshment in women, and women to find rest and refreshment in men; and though the rest and refreshment to be found should spring from the deepest kind of sympathy and the highest common faith, yet it should be rest and refreshment after all, and not mere laborious esteem and solid trust. The tendency of *A Doll's House* is to ignore this, and therefore we regard it as a play that is, on the whole, misleading and mischievous in drift, especially as it teaches, if it teaches anything, that the way to improve life is to root up the good wheat that has begun to grow, because there are tares intertwined with it.

24. Clement Scott on Ibsen's unlovely creed

July 1889

From 'A Doll's House', a long attack in the *Theatre* (July 1889), xiv, 19–22, by 'C.S.' (Clement Scott), who was the editor.

It is an unlovely, selfish creed—but let women hear it. Nora, when she finds her husband is not the ideal hero she imagined, determines to cap his egotism with her selfishness. It is to be an eye for an eye, a tooth for a tooth. Pardon she cannot grant, humiliation she will not recognise. The frivolous butterfly, the Swedish Frou-Frou, the spoiled plaything has mysteriously become an Ibsenite revivalist. There were no previous signs of her conversion, but she has exchanged playfulness for preaching. She, a loving, affectionate woman, forgets all about the eight years' happy married life, forgets the nest of the little bird, forgets her duty, her very instinct as a mother, forgets the three innocent children who are asleep in the next room, forgets her responsibilities, and does a thing that one of the lower animals would not do. A cat or dog would tear any one who separated it from its offspring, but the socialistic Nora, the apostle of the new creed of humanity, leaves her children almost without a pang. She has determined to leave her home. . . .

It is all self, self, self! This is the ideal woman of the new creed; not a woman who is the fountain of love and forgiveness and charity, not the pattern woman we have admired in our mothers and our sisters, not the model of unselfishness and charity, but a mass of aggregate conceit and self-sufficiency, who leaves her home and deserts her friendless children because she has *herself* to look after. The 'strange man' who is the father of her children has dared to misunderstand her; she will scorn his regrets and punish him. Why should the men have it all their own way, and why should women be bored with the love of their children when they have themselves to study? And so Nora goes out, delivers up her wedding-ring without a sigh, quits her children without a kiss, and bangs the door! And the husband cries, 'A miracle! a miracle!' and well he may. It would be a miracle if he could ever live again with so unnatural a creature.

25. William Archer on newspaper reaction to Ibsen

July 1889

'Ibsen and English Criticism', by William Archer, the *Fortnightly Review* (1 July 1889), xlvi, 30-7.

If we may measure fame by mileage of newspaper comment, Henrik Ibsen has for the past month been the most famous man in the English literary world. Since Robert Elsmere left the Church, no event in 'coëval fictive art' (to quote a modern stylist) has exercised men's, and women's, minds so much as Nora Helmer's departure from her Doll's House. Indeed the latter exit may be said to have awakened even more vibrant echoes than the former; for, while Robert made as little noise as possible, Nora slammed the door behind her. Nothing could be more trenchant than her action, unless it be her speech. Whatever its merits or defects, *A Doll's House* has certainly the property of stimulating discussion. We are at present bandying the very arguments which hurtled around it in Scandinavia and in Germany nine years ago. When the play was first produced in Copenhagen, some one wrote a charming little satire upon it in the shape of a debate as to its tendency between a party of little girls around a nursery tea-table. It ended in the hostess, aged ten, gravely declaring that had the case been hers, she would have done exactly as Nora did. I do not know whether the fame of *A Doll's House* has reached the British nursery, but I have certainly read some comments on it which might very well have emanated from that abode of innocence.

Puerilities and irrelevances apart, the adult and intelligent criticism of Ibsen as represented in *A Doll's House*, seems to run on three main lines. It is said, in the first place, that he is not an artist but a preacher; secondly, that his doctrine is neither new nor true; thirdly, that in order to enforce it, he oversteps the limits of artistic propriety. I propose to look into these three allegations. First, however, I must disclaim all right to be regarded as in any way a mouthpiece for the poet's own views. My personal intercourse with Henrik Ibsen, though to me very pleasant and memorable, has been but slight. I view his plays from the pit, not from the author's box. Very likely—nay, certainly—I often misread his meaning. My only right to take part in the discussion arises from a long and loving study of all his writings, and from the minute familiarity with *A Doll's House* in particular, acquired in the course of translating and staging it.

Is it true, then, that he is a dramatic preacher rather than a dramatic poet? or, in other words, that his art is vitiated by didacticism? Some writers have assumed that in calling him didactic they have said the last word, and dismissed him for ever from the ranks of the great artists. Of them I would fain enquire what really great art is not didactic? The true distinction is not between didactic art and 'art for art's sake,' but between primarily didactic and ultimately didactic art. Art for art's sake, properly so called, is mere decoration; and even it, in the last analysis, has its gospel to preach. By primarily didactic art I mean that in which the moral bearing is obvious, and was clearly present to the artist's mind. By ultimately didactic art I mean that which essays to teach as life itself teaches, exhibiting the fact and leaving the observer to trace and formulate the underlying law. It is the fashion of the day to regard this unconsciously didactic art, if I may call it so—its unconsciousness is sometimes a very transparent pose—as essentially higher than the art which is primarily and consciously didactic, dynamic. Well, it is useless to dispute about higher and lower. From our point of view the Australians seem to be walking head-downwards, like flies on the ceiling; from their point of view we are in the same predicament; it all depends on the point of view. Ibsen certainly belongs, at any rate in his modern prose plays, to the consciously didactic artists whom you may, if you choose, relegate to a lower plane. But how glorious the company that will have to step down along with him! What were the Greek tragic poets if not consciously didactic? What is comedy, from time immemorial, but a deliberate lesson in life? Down Plautus; down Terence; down Molière and Holberg and Beaumarchais and Dumas! Calderon and Cervantes must be kind enough to follow; so must Schiller and Goethe. If German criticism is to be believed Shakespeare was the most hardened sermonizer of all literature; but in this respect I think German criticism is to be disbelieved. Shakespeare, then, may be left in possession of the pinnacle of Parnassus; but who shall keep him company? Flaubert, perhaps, and M. Guy de Maupassant?

The despisers of Ibsen, then, have not justified their position when they have merely proved, what no one disputes, that he is a didactic writer. They must further prove that his teaching kills his art. For my part, looking at his dramatic production all round, and excepting only the two great dramas in verse, *Brand* and *Peer Gynt*, I am willing to admit that his teaching does now and then, in perfectly trifling details, affect his art for the worse. Not his direct teaching—that, as it seems to me, he always inspires with the breath of life—but his proclivity to what I may perhaps call symbolic side-issues. In the aforesaid dramas in verse this symbolism is eminently in place; not so, it seems to me, in the realistic plays. I once asked him how he justified this tendency in his art; he replied that life is one tissue of symbols. 'Certainly,' I might have answered; 'but when we have its symbolic side too persistently obtruded upon us, we lose the sense of reality, which, according to your own theory, the modern dramatist should above all things aim at.' There may be some excellent answer to this criticism; I give it for what it is worth. Apart from these symbolic details, it seems to me that Ibsen is singularly successful in vitalising his work; in reproducing the forms, the phenomena of life, as well as its deeper meanings. Let us take the example nearest at hand—*A Doll's House*. I venture to say—for this is a matter of fact rather than of opinion—that in the minds of thousands in Scandinavia and Germany, Nora Helmer lives with an intense and palpitating life such as belongs to few fictitious characters. Habitually and instinctively men pay Ibsen the compliment (so often paid to Shakespeare) of discussing her as though she were a real woman, living a life of her own, quite apart from the poet's creative intelligence. The very critics who begin by railing at her as a puppet end by denouncing her as a woman. She irritates, troubles, fascinates them as no puppet ever could. Moreover, the triumph of the actress is the dramatist's best defence. Miss Achurch might have the genius of Rachel and Desclée in one, yet she could not transmute into flesh and blood the doctrinary doll, stuffed with sawdust and sophistry, whom some people declare Nora to be. Men do not shudder at the agony or weep over the woes of an intellectual abstraction. As for Helmer, I am not aware that any one has accused him of unreality. He is too real for most people—he is commonplace, unpleasant, objectionable. The truth is, he touches us too nearly; he is the typical husband of what may be called chattel matrimony. If there are few Doll's-Houses in England, it is certainly for lack of Noras, not for lack of Helmers. I admit that in my opinion Ibsen has treated Helmer somewhat unfairly. He has not exactly disguised, but has omitted to emphasize, the fact that if Helmer helped to make

Nora a doll, Nora helped to make Helmer a prig. By giving Nora all the logic in the last scene (and she is not a scrupulous dialectician) he has left the casual observer to conclude that he lays the whole responsibility on Helmer. This conclusion is not just, but it is specious; and so far, and so far only, I grant that the play has somewhat the air of a piece of special pleading. I shall presently discuss the last scene in greater detail; but even admitting for the moment that the polemist here gets the better of the poet, can we call the poet, who has moved freely through two acts and two-thirds, nothing but a doctrinary polemist?

Let me add that *A Doll's House* is, of all Ibsen's plays, the one in which a definite thesis is most tangibly posited—the one, therefore, which is most exposed to the reproach of being a mere sociological pamphlet. His other plays may be said to scintillate with manifold ethical meanings; here the light is focussed upon one point in the social system. I do not imply that *A Doll's House* is less thoroughly vitalized than *Ghosts*, or *Rosmersholm*, or *The Lady from the Sea*. What I mean is, that the play may in some eyes acquire a false air of being merely didactic from the fortuitous circumstance that its moral can be easily formulated.

The second line of criticism is that which attacks the substance of Ibsen's so-called doctrines, on the ground that they are neither new nor true. To the former objection one is inclined to answer curtly but pertinently, 'Who said they were?' It is not the business of the creative artist to make the great generalisations which mark the stages of intellectual and social progress. Certainly Ibsen did not discover the theory of evolution or the doctrine of heredity, any more than he discovered gravitation. He was not the first to denounce the subjection of women; he was not the first to sneer at the 'compact liberal majority' of our pseudo-democracies. His function is to seize and throw into relief certain aspects of modern life. He shows us society as Kean was said to read Shakespeare—by flashes of lightning—luridly, but with intense vividness. He selects subjects which seem to him to illustrate such and such political, ethical, or sociological ideas; but he does not profess to have invented the ideas. They are common property; they are in the air. A grave injustice has been done him of late by those of his English admirers who have set him up as a social prophet, and have sometimes omitted to mention that he is a bit of a poet as well. It is so much easier to import an idea than the flesh and blood, the imagination, the passion, the style in which it is clothed. People have heard so much of the 'gospel according to Ibsen' that they have come to think of him as a mere hot-gospeller, the Boanerges of some strange social propaganda. As a matter of fact Ibsen has no gospel whatever, in the sense of a systematic body of doctrine. He is not a Schopenhauer, and still less a Comte. There never was a less systematic thinker. Truth is not, in his eyes, one and indivisible; it is many-sided, many-visaged, almost Protean. It belongs to the irony of fate that the least dogmatic of thinkers—the man who has said of himself, 'I only ask: my call is not to answer'—should figure in the imagination of so many English critics as a dour dogmatist, a vendor of social nostrums in pilule form. He is far more of a paradoxist than a dogmatist. A thinker he is most certainly, but not an inventor of brand new notions such as no one has ever before conceived. His originality lies in giving intense dramatic life to modern ideas, and often stamping them afresh, as regards mere verbal form, in the mint of his imaginative wit.

The second allegation, that his doctrines are not true, is half answered when we have insisted that they are not put forward (at any rate by Ibsen himself) as a body of inspired dogmas. No man rejects more consistently than he the idea of finality. He does not pretend to have said the last word on any subject. 'You needn't believe me unless you like,' says Dr. Stockmann in *An Enemy of the People*, 'but truths are not the tough old Methuselahs people take them to be. A normally constituted truth lives, let us say, some seventeen or eighteen years; at most twenty.' The telling of absolute truths, to put it in another way, is scarcely Ibsen's aim. He is more concerned with destroying conventional lies, and exorcising the 'ghosts' of dead truths; and most of all concerned to make people think and see for themselves. Here again we recognise the essential injustice of regarding a dramatic poet as a sort of prophet-professor, who means all his characters say and makes them say all he means. I have been asked, for example, whether Ibsen intends us to understand by the last scene of *A Doll's House* that awakened wives ought to leave their husbands and children in order to cultivate their souls in solitude. Ibsen intends nothing of the sort. He draws a picture of a typical household; he creates a man and woman with certain characteristics; he places them in a series of situations which at once develop their characters and suggest large questions of conduct; and he makes the woman, in the end, adopt a course of action which he (rightly or wrongly) believes to be consistent with her individual nature and circumstances. It is true that this course of action is so devised as to throw the principles at stake into the strongest relief; but the object of that is to make people thoroughly realise the problem, not to force upon them the particular solution arrived at in this particular case. No two life-problems were ever precisely alike, and in stating and solving one, Ibsen does not pretend to supply a ready-made solution for all the rest. He illustrates, or, rather, illumines, a general principle by a conceivable case; that is all. To treat Nora's arguments in the last scene of *A Doll's House* as though they were the ordered propositions of an essay by John Stuart Mill is to give a striking example of the strange literalness of the English mind, its inability to distinguish between drama and dogma. To me that last scene is the most moving in the play, precisely because I hold it the most dramatic. It has been called a piece of pure logic—is it not rather logic conditioned by character and saturated with emotion? Some years ago I saw *Et Dukkehjem* acted in Christiania. It was an off season; only the second-rate members of the company were engaged; and throughout two acts and a half I sat vainly striving to recapture the emotions I had so often felt in reading the play. But the moment Nora and Helmer were seated face to face, at the words, 'No, that is just it; you do not understand me; and I have never understood you—till to-night'—at that moment, much to my own surprise, the thing suddenly gripped my heart-strings; to use an expressive Americanism, I 'sat up;' and every phrase of Nora's threnody over her dead dreams, her lost illusions, thrilled me to the very marrow. Night after night I went to see that scene; night after night I have watched it in the English version; it has never lost its power over me. And why? Not because Nora's sayings are particularly wise or particularly true, but because, in her own words, they are so true *for her*, because she feels them so deeply and utters them so exquisitely. Certainly she is unfair, certainly she is one-sided, certainly she is illogical; if she were not, Ibsen would be the pamphleteer he is supposed to be, not the poet he is. 'I have never been happy here—only merry. . . . You have never loved me—you have only found it amusing to be in love with me.' Have we not in these speeches the very mingling of truth and falsehood, of justice and injustice, necessary to humanise the character and the situation? After Nora has declared her intention of leaving her home, Helmer remarks, 'Then there is only one explanation possible—You no longer love me.' 'No,' she replies, 'that is just it.' 'Nora! can you say so?' cries Helmer, looking into her eyes. '*Oh, I'm so sorry, Torvald,*' she answers, '*for you've always been so kind to me.*' Is this pamphleteering? To me it seems like the subtlest human pathos. Again, when she says 'At that moment it became clear to me that I had been living here for eight years with a strange man and had borne him three children—Oh,

I can't bear to think of it! I could tear myself to pieces'—who can possibly take this for anything but a purely dramatic utterance? It is true and touching in Nora's mouth, but it is obviously founded on a vague sentiment, that may or may not bear analysis. Nora postulates a certain transcendental community of spirit as the foundation and justification of marriage. The idea is very womanly and may also be very practical; but Ibsen would probably be the first to admit that before it can claim the validity of a social principle we must ascertain whether it be possible for any two human beings to be other than what Nora would call strangers. This further analysis the hearer must carry out for him, or her, self. The poet has stimulated thought; he has not tried to lay down a hard-and-fast rule of conduct. Again, when Helmer says, 'No man sacrifices his honour even for one he loves,' and Nora retorts, '*Millions of women have done that!*' we applaud the consummate claptrap, not on account of its abstract justice, but rather of its characteristic injustice. Logically, it is naught; dramatically, one feels it to be a masterstroke. Here, it is the right speech in the right place; in a sociological monograph it would be absurd. My position, in short, is that in Ibsen's plays, as in those of any other dramatist who keeps within the bounds of his form, we must look, not for the axioms and demonstrations of a scientific system, but simply for 'broken lights' of truth, refracted through character and circumstance.* The playwright who sends on a Chorus or a lecturer, unconnected with the dramatic action, to moralise the spectacle and put all the dots on all the i's, may fairly be taken to task for the substance of his 'doctrines.' But that playwright is Dumas, not Ibsen.

Lastly, we come to the assertion that Ibsen is a 'coarse' writer, with a morbid love for using the theatre as a physiological lecture-room. Here again I can only cry out upon the chance which has led to so grotesque a misconception. He has written some twenty plays, of which all except two might be read aloud, with only the most trivial omissions, in any young ladies' boarding-school from Tobolsk to Tangiers. The two exceptions are *A Doll's House* and *Ghosts*—the very plays which happen to have come (more or less) within the ken of English critics. In *A Doll's House* he touches upon, in *Ghosts* he frankly faces, the problem of hereditary disease, which interests him, not in itself, but simply as the physical type and symbol of so many social and ethical phenomena.

---

* It so happens that two or three formal generalisations of Ibsen's have recently been going the round of the press; but they are all taken from letters or speeches, not from his plays.

Ghosts I have not space to consider. If art is for ever debarred from entering upon certain domains of human experience, then *Ghosts* is an inartistic work. I can only say, after having read it, seen it on the stage, and translated it, that no other modern play seems to me to fulfil so entirely the Aristotelian ideal of purging the soul by means of terror and pity. In *A Doll's House*, again, there are two passages, one in the second and one in the third act, which Mr. Podsnap could not conveniently explain to the young lady in the dress-circle. Whether the young lady in the dress-circle would be any the worse for having them explained to her is a question I shall not discuss. As a matter of fact, far from being coarsely treated, they are so delicately touched that the young person suspects nothing and is in no way incommoded. It is Mr. Podsnap himself that cries out—the virtuous Podsnap who, at the French theatre, writhes in his stall with laughter at speeches and situations *à faire rougir des singes.* I have more than once been reproached, by people who had seen *A Doll's House* at the Novelty, with having cut the speeches which the first-night critics pronounced objectionable. It has cost me some trouble to persuade them that not a word had been cut, and that the text they found so innocent contained every one of the enormities denounced by the critics. Mr. Podsnap, I may add, has in this case shown his usual alacrity in putting the worst possible interpretation upon things. Dr. Rank's declaration to Nora that Helmer is not the only man who would willingly lay down his life for her, has been represented as a hideous attempt on the part of a dying debauchee to seduce his friend's wife. Nothing is further from the mind of poor Rank, who, by the way, is not a debauchee at all. He knows himself to be at death's door; Nora, in her Doll's House, has given light and warmth to his lonely, lingering existence; he has silently adored her while standing with her, as with her husband, on terms of frank comradeship; is he to leave her for ever without saying, as he puts it, 'Thanks for the light'? Surely this is a piece either of inhuman austerity or of prurient prudery; surely Mrs. Podsnap herself could not feel a suspicion of insult in such a declaration. True, it comes inaptly at that particular moment, rendering it impossible for Nora to make the request she contemplates. But essentially, and even from the most conventional point of view, I fail to see anything inadmissible in Rank's conduct to Nora. Nora's conduct to Rank, in the stocking scene, is another question; but that is merely a side-light on the relation between Nora and Helmer, preparatory, in a sense, to the scene before Rank's entrance in the last act.

In conclusion, what are the chances that Ibsen's modern plays will ever take a permanent place on the English stage? They are not great, it seems to me. The success of *A Doll's House* will naturally encourage Ibsen's admirers to further experiments in the same direction—interesting and instructive experiments I have no doubt. We shall see in course of time *The Young Men's League*, *The Pillars of Society*, *An Enemy of the People*, *Rosmersholm*, and *A Lady from the Sea*—I name them in chronological order. But none of these plays presents the double attraction that has made the success of *A Doll's House*—the distinct plea for female emancipation which appeals to the thinking public, and the overwhelming part for an actress of genius which attracts the ordinary playgoer. The other plays, I cannot but foresee, will be in a measure antiquated before the great public is ripe for a thorough appreciation of them. I should like to see an attempt made to produce one of the poet's historical plays, but that would involve an outlay for costumes and mounting not to be lightly faced. On the other hand I have not the remotest doubt that Ibsen will bulk more and more largely as years go on in the consciousness of all students of literature in general, as opposed to the stage in particular. The creator of *Brand* and *Peer Gynt* is one of the great poets of the world.

26. Janet Achurch on the difficulty of being Nora

July 1889

From 'Nora Helmer off for the Antipodes', an interview with Janet Achurch in the *Pall Mall Gazette* (5 July 1889), 1–2. The actress, who had made her name in the role, was about to leave on an Australian tour.

It is not often that any young actress achieves the phenomenal success with which Miss Janet Achurch has brought to a temporary close her dramatic career in the old country. Before *A Doll's House* was brought out at the Novelty Theatre almost every one predicted that the attempt would result in disastrous failure. Ibsen as a dramatist had never been brought before the London playgoer, and it was a somewhat daring experiment to begin with such a dish of strong meat as the drama in which the Norwegian poet laid the axe to the root of the conventional idea of matrimonial fine-ladyism. You will be fortunate, very fortunate, said sympathizing friends, if you can keep it running a week, and no doubt but for Miss Achurch's brilliant rendering of the arduous role of the heroine the play would have been numbered among the numerous failures which make up so large a part of the history of the attempts to acclimatize the higher drama on the London stage. Thanks, however, to the extraordinary fidelity with which Miss Achurch represented Ibsen's Nora, the play has had a run of three weeks, and has only been withdrawn because it was impossible to postpone any longer the departure of Miss Achurch and Mr. Charrington for Australia. They start to-day for Brindisi, where they meet the *Ballarat* and take ship for Melbourne. Seldom has any actress had a more brilliant 'send off' than that which the creation as the English Nora Helmer has supplied to Miss Achurch; and the following interview will be read with interest by many who usually regard with supreme indifference the sayings and doings of the stars of the London stage.

'Yes,' said Miss Achurch, in reply to a question from our representative, '*A Doll's House* has been a great success. But it has taken a great deal out of me, and if it had gone on much longer I should have broken down. It is the hardest part I have ever played. Nora is never off the stage for a single moment during the whole of the first and second acts, and in the third act she is only absent for five minutes. The part is heavier than that of Hamlet, and to go through it eight times a week is too great a strain.'

'Eight times a week?'

'Yes. We had a morning performance every Wednesday and Saturday, and to go through such a piece twice a day twice a week has told somewhat seriously on me. I shall be delighted to get rest on the voyage out, before beginning again on the Australian boards. As soon as we land in Melbourne we have four months' engagement before us in that city. Then we go to Adelaide and Sydney and perhaps to Brisbane. It will be eighteen months at the least, and two years at the most, before we return home.'

'But Nora, how do you like the character?'

'I like Nora better than about 200 roles I have filled since I first appeared on the stage. After Nora I think on the whole I prefer Lady

Macbeth. But Nora is a wonderful conception, into the realization of which one can throw one's whole soul.'

'Tell me, what is your reading of what Nora will do afterwards?'

'Ibsen leaves every one to form their own idea as to the sequel of his play. It is left an interrogation which every one can answer as he pleases. I think she will come back after a time and try again the experiment of living with Helmer. But it will fail. That man is impossible, utterly impossible. She did right to leave him.'

'But the children?'

'Ah! that is another matter. I don't think that was right, but you should remember that it was partly for the sake of the children she went away. She felt herself so utterly unworthy of undertaking their education, and she left them in the hands of a very good nurse.'

'At the same time don't you think it was a mistake, the last and crowning illustration of the extent to which her doll-like upbringing worked out its dismal harvest of wrongdoing? Even when she caught a glimpse of a higher ideal and aspired after a nobler life, at that very moment the impulsive weaknesses of the untrained mind asserted itself, and her frantic plunge at the last was as natural an outcome of the moral atmosphere of a doll's house as her forgery or any other of her heedless acts of impulsive ignorance.'

'Possibly you are right, but the moral is plain enough in any case. For men the play can hardly be accused of being anything but good. To open their eyes to the consequences of ignoring the moral and intellectual nature of the human being with whom they have allied themselves is surely excellent. For the women, if I may judge from the letters I have received, it has been also useful, nor do I think that it will tend, as some say, to more easy divorce and reckless abandonment of home. What it ought to do is to make them much less reckless about marrying, by showing that a plunge into matrimony in the mere fever of a passionate attachment, without any similarity of taste or common interest in the serious work of life, is to prepare for yourself a terrible awakening.'

THE PILLARS OF SOCIETY

Opéra Comique, 17 July 1889

27. From an unsigned notice in the *Daily News*

18 July 1889, 6

The performance was given for the benefit of Vera Beringer, the child actress; the *News* headlined its review: 'The Ibsenites Have a Field Day for the Benefit of Little Vera Beringer.' The play was translated by William Archer and the cast was as follows:

Consul Bernick ..	Mr W. H. Vernon	Mrs Bernick ..	Mrs Dawes
Johan Tonnesen..	Mr J. G. Grahame	Martha Bernick	Miss E. Robins
Dr Rörlund ..	Mr John Beauchamp	Dina Dorf ..	Miss Annie Irish
Hilmar Tonnesen	Mr E. Hendrie	Mrs Rummel ..	Miss Fanny Robertson
Aune	Mr A. Wood	Mrs Postmaster	
Kraft	Mr G. Canninge	Holt	Miss St Ange
Mr Rummel ..	Mr E. Smart	Mrs Dr. Tynge	Miss M. A. Giffard
Mr Vigeland ..	Mr E. Girardot	Miss Holt ..	Miss Brakstad
Mr Sanstad.. ..	Mr Branscombe	Lona Hessel ..	Miss Genevieve Ward
Olaf Bernick ..	Miss Vera Beringer		

Yesterday afternoon, at the Opera Comique, the second battle was fought in the recently inaugurated crusade of Ibsenism. *The Doll's House*, which raised such a storm in the London critical tea-cup when produced at the Novelty Theatre some time ago, undoubtedly gained for the Norwegian dramatist a good many friends in this country, and yesterday's production of *Pillars of Society* will add some more to the list. An adaptation of the play was produced at the Gaiety about seven years ago, when it met with but moderate success, the adaptor on that occasion being the translator on the present one, Mr. William Archer. For the latest English version of *Pillars of Society* sticks much more closely to the original than the former one, and benefits by its adherence to Ibsen pure and simple, undiluted with Archer. In its present form, however, or in any form that it can have whilst remaining substantially the same play, *Pillars of Society* cannot be pronounced a great play. It exhibits great gifts, of course, for no one thinks of denying that Ibsen is a writer of exceptional ability and marked individuality. But it is this very individuality which keeps the Norwegian master from touching the very highest level of dramatic art; for it is an individuality divided against itself, and can no more stand than the Scriptural house under parallel conditions. Ibsen is the oddest mixture of dramatist and preacher, and the nature of the preacher has essentially that unctuous quality which makes its perfect amalgamation with a diverse nature as impossible as the mixture of oil with alcohol. Sometimes the dramatist in Ibsen triumphs, and he is a great artist for awhile; then the preacher asserts himself and nullifies the work of his co-tenant in Ibsen. *Pillars of Society* is spoilt by just the same perfunctory mingling of adverse qualities. It has a powerfully dramatic story, magnificent snatches of dialogue, brilliant sketches of character—but the preacher will preach, and preach inopportunely.

28. From an unsigned notice by Clement Scott, the *Daily Telegraph*

18 July 1889, 4

A sensible stage manager would have made short work of Ibsen's always thoughtful, always earnest, text. It may do very well for Norway or Sweden or Berlin or Scandinavia or the Fatherland, but unfortunately it does not do unedited for England. Amidst the valuable stage material there is an intolerable deal of pedantry and mere verbiage. Had the sacred Sardou—for even he is sacred to Frenchmen—been translated as Ibsen has been translated in *The Pillars*, his *Dora* (*Diplomacy*) would not have run one week. Sardou raved, and tore his hair, and vowed vengeance on the wretched adaptors, and held them up to eternal execration; but Sardou pocketed his fees, and his excellent work was popularised in England, and thousands passed a delightful evening.

And so they might yet with *The Pillars of Society*, if only Mr. Archer and his friends would come out of the study and go on the stage, if they would learn the practical as well as the literary business of a dramatist, if they would understand that it is a foolish thing to send an audience to sleep, if they would run their pens through those tedious tirades about 'communities' and 'society,' and theories and sermons, which have nothing on earth to do with the story or development of characters, but retard the action and make the people groan inwardly. Better English literature modern play never had. In distant Scandinavia and long-winded Germany they may love this interminable talk; they may love to sit over it as they do their 'beer parliaments' and 'coffee scandals;' but here we like to come to the point; here there is no time to cut anything to waste; here we must come to Hecuba, 'cut the cackle and come to the 'osses.' It is sad that it should be so, but so it is.

Mr. William Archer is quite right when he insists that plays should be written to be read as well as acted. The poet should not be banished from the boards. Plays to please and influence, however, are not written in the solitude of the chamber, or by the light of the midnight oil, but at the prompter's desk, with a T-light illuminating the ghastly and deserted playhouse. The dramatist who shudders at these conditions will never be popular. He will not understand his business. All dramatists have had to learn this disagreeable fact, from Shakespeare to Sardou, and if Ibsen wants his 'gospel' to be heard on the highways and byways he had better get out of the study, and go on the stage to superintend a rehearsal. We arise from a perusal in the study of *The Pillars of Society* with a profound belief in its dramatic excellence. The more the dramatist talks the more we like him. He cannot talk too much in the study. He is a companion and a friend. We are attached to Lona, and admire her spirit and self-sacrifice. We can feel every beat of Consul Bernick's heart, understand his temptation, appreciate his mental agony. We picture Martha as one of the loveliest characters in dramatic fiction, a noble woman rightly planned, and so she is because the author built her so. We picture the scene, we have lived in the 'community'; every human being on the canvas is familiar to us. We arise from the book excited, impressed, our imagination tingling; the whole thing transparent, clear, convincing. But what a difference when we arise from the contemplation of the play! The whole thing is altered, deformed, misrepresented, debased, not from any fault of the actors, but simply because the literary dramatist has not thoroughly mastered the *technique* of the stage. The Lona who was such a grand study in the book is comparatively effaced. The high-minded, self sacrificing women are wearisome bores. The almost divine Martha is a youthful Mrs. Gummidge, always whining and looking out to sea. The human, pulsating Bernick is laughed at for the very sentiments that should wring tears of blood from the heart. The play that was peaceful in the study is restless on the stage. The people we loved make us yawn. The sentiments we clung to make us laugh. The scene we realised becomes paltry and trivial; the township we lived in is nothing like what we imagined; the people who were part and parcel of ourselves yesterday are dismal lay figures and dummies to-day. Why is this? Is it because Ibsen is not a dramatist? No. Is it because the acting is insufficient and incomplete? No. Is it because the translator has failed in his duty? No, for Mr. Archer's translation and his mere words must be as great a treat to speak on the stage as they are to listen to in the stalls. It is because Ibsen has not mastered the technical difficulties of his position as a dramatist, not for one country, but for all countries. It is because the Ibsenite enthusiasts will not allow their 'master' to be adapted for our amusement, but insist upon translating him for our everlasting boredom. . . .

As it was the people filed out into the wet Strand perplexed, half-weary, astonished, impressed, but as yet not wholly converted to Ibsen, even at his best. They could not quite understand the 'communities' and the society chatter, and the ceaseless allusions to the 'Indian girl,' the 'Palm Tree,' and the alliteratively-named Dina Dorf. In fact, one of the audience, earnest and anxious for conversion, was found playing with her fingers in the passages, and babbling, in memory of childhood's days:

> Ina, Dina, Dina Dorf,
> Kattler Wheeler, Wila Worf;

and even Ibsen himself would not understand this reminiscence of the British nursery!

29. From an unsigned notice, the *Daily Chronicle*

18 July 1889, 3

The theme is striking, and at points almost tragic in its intensity, but theatrical effect is, on the whole, wanting. There are too many characters in the piece, and the occasional repetition of information or of directions is wearisome. Another blemish, from the stage aspect, is the lack of variety in the principal character.

30. From an unsigned notice in the *Referee*

21 July 1889, 3

'And what do you think of *The Pillars of Society*?' was the question I heard put by one lady to another as I came through the tunnel of the Opéra Comique on Wednesday, after the matinée for the benefit of Miss Vera Beringer. 'Well,' answered the questioned one, behind her fan, 'you may think me "lapsed and lost" if you like, but I can't help saying that instead of a play it is an intolerable long jaw.' Very vulgar, very irreverent, very shocking, wasn't it? But it was exactly the truth. Ibsen is becoming a bit of a nuisance, and so, too, is his prophet, Mr. William Archer. *A Doll's House* was bad enough, but at least for a time it amused us with the doll and the naughty consumptive doctor whose father ate too much asparagus; but *The Pillars of Society* with its diffuse explanations and endless conversations and prosy dissertations, is infinitely worse; and I am quite sure that all but the Ibsenites and an elderly chatterbox who dodged about the stalls to enthuse and to give off opinions that nobody asked for, came away on Wednesday firm in the belief that, though Ibsen in the study might be exceedingly interesting, Ibsen on the stage is an abominable bore.

31. From an unsigned notice, *Lloyd's Weekly News*

21 July 1889, 5

Authors and artists possessing gifts, however fantastically and extravagantly they may apply them, soon have a number of followers—the people always ready to fall in love with novelty; and in the category must be ranked the ecstatic worshippers of the Norwegian writer. They are as much carried away by Ibsen's ethical exploits as they have been by Browning's enigmatical utterances or Rossetti's nightmares in colour. *The Pillars of Society* is a disappointing because a singularly unequal work. The earlier acts promise something dramatic, but the interest tapers off, so that towards its close it is dull, dreary and disappointing.

32. Unsigned comment in the *Hawk*

23 July 1889, 89

Ibsen is no longer the Ibscene dramatist. What angered his enemies and pleased his friends in the *Doll's House* is nowhere apparent in the *Pillars of Society*. It is merely the old story of the noble sacrifice of a man and a woman being wasted on a selfish person, who, in good old style of Scribeland, repents at the last moment. For all this, his fanatical admirers discover in it all sorts of wonderful qualities that poor Shakespeare and *bourgeois* Molière never dreamed of, and we are told with wearying reiteration that this is life at last. In it I see no attribute of greatness, but dullness, for it is dull, deadly dull, and no better and no more like life than the melodramas at the Princess's Theatre. I take no objection to the story, because it is not novel, and I do not deny that here and there there are fairly good scenes; but, like all Ibsen's plays, they go to the devil at the end. Personally, I am sorry that all the characters did not go down in the Indian Girl, and I am sorry that the hero did not cheek it out to the end. If Consul Bernick, instead of whining and repenting, and bringing the play to a happy conclusion, had simply defied his enemies, and rather patronisingly accepted the deputation with the air that it was only precisely which he deserved, the *Pillars of Society* would have been a little more like life and a less like stage land.

33. From 'Ibsen Again', a signed notice by Frederic Wedmore, the *Academy*

27 July 1889, xxxvi, 60–1

That dull first act! It leads to very little; its construction is amateurish; it is almost wholly without interest. No judge of literature could point me out in it, from its very beginning to its very end, one line in which a satire is conveyed brilliantly, or a truth conveyed potently. In it, from beginning to end, not a thing is memorable, not a thing is exquisitely said. . . .

Just as local in its application as his satire on the clergy, is Ibsen's second great point, his second great mission—the position of women. So far as I know his plays, from the beginning to the end of them there is not a moment's recognition that any place is accorded to women beyond the place of the unquestioning follower, the doll, the house-wife, or the drudge. How can a writer claim to be a 'path-breaker' for our world of Western civilisation if the world he represents lies under conditions from which this Western world has long ago been delivered? For us, Ibsen is not a discoverer; he is not an initiator; he is not a great literary artist. He is, taking him as a whole, and when we have done with his hopeless first act of *Pillars of Society*, a fairly capable and thoughtful craftsman of the second order, working, in remote regions, chiefly for the remote and the behind-hand.

But in *Pillars of Society* there is absolutely nothing to offend our insular prejudices. Ibsen, for once, has steered clear of dangerous topics, and whilst he has introduced an extremely interesting set of characters, there are none among them to shock us in any way. So much has been said and written about this play, which has also been familiarised to English readers by means of a cheap translation, that it is unnecessary now to dwell upon the details of the strong story set before us in *Pillars of Society*. It will be sufficient to recall that the play turns upon the gradual awakening of a man's conscience through the medium of one whom he has hitherto regarded as an outcast of the narrow-minded little community in which he poses as immaculate Consul. The character of this man is remarkably depicted, and his struggle between his love of popularity and adoration, and his awakened sense of unfitness to fill the position he has achieved by a life of lies, is shown with marvellous skill. We have seen nothing finer or more powerful on our stage for some time than the second act of *Pillars of Society*, which roused the enthusiasm of the whole house last week. The third is scarcely less interesting, but, unfortunately, the conventionality and slow length of the last act weakened the favourable impression created by the earlier scenes, though there is no doubt that its feebleness was accentuated by the imperfect presentation of a trial performance. It is so utterly untrue to nature as it stands, and lame and impotent a conclusion to an otherwise really fine play, that it can never be allowed to remain as it is if hopes are entertained of making *Pillars of Society* the attraction of any permanent bill. There is, indeed, every possibility, if excisions and amendments are made, that it may achieve a great success in an evening programme; for, despite the fact that it is a satire upon a people of whom we know nothing, and that it is, after all, but a study of provincial life in a small and unimportant country, it is indisputable that Ibsen deeply interests us in the story and the characters. A few more plays like this would be indeed welcome on our stage. . . . The play was enthusiastically received, though expressions of weariness at the prosiness of many of the speeches were not unfrequent.

35. William Archer on the absurdity of Mr. T. Weber

January 1890

'Ibsen as He is Translated', by William Archer, *Time* (January 1890), n.s. I.

Long ago, while as yet the recent outbreak of Ibsen-mania and Ibsen-phobia was unforeseen and undreamt of, I came across a translation of *Et Dukkehjem* which I felt to be one of the things the world would not willingly let die. At the time, however, there were probably not more than half-a-dozen people in England, to whom the name of Henrik Ibsen conveyed any meaning. Indeed, I knew of only one—Mr. Edmund Gosse. 'Henry Gibson!' said an editor to whom I proposed an article on the Norwegian dramatist. 'Who in the world is he?' I felt that the full charm of the translation would be lost upon people who had heard no rumour of the original or of its author, and for years I had almost forgotten the existence of the little book. Happening the other day to come across a copy of it, I read it with renewed enjoyment, and felt that such a masterpiece could no longer be suffered to rest in obscurity. The following extracts by no means exhaust the deep wells of the translator's humour, but they afford a fair taste of its quality.

The pamphlet bears the imprint, 'Copenhagen. Published by Weber's Academy, MDCCCLXXX,' and is dedicated,

To
Her Royal Highness
ALEXANDRA
Princess of Wales.
Your Royal Highness's
Most Humble Servant
T. Weber.

Even in the first stage-direction, Mr. Weber's mastery of English makes itself felt:

There is a ring at the bell of the corridor. It is heard a little afterwards that a door is opened. Enter Nora, humming delightfully. She is wearing over-clothing, and carrying many parcels on her arm . . . She continues laughing, and looks delightfully, while she puts off her cloak and bonnet. Then she takes out of her pocket a cornet with macaroons, and eats a few.

Here is one of the opening passages between Helmer and Nora:—

Helmer: . . . Has my thoughtless bird again dissipated money?

Nora: But, Thorvald, we must enjoy ourselves a little. It is the first Christmas we need not to spare.

Helmer: Know that we cannot dissipate.

Nora: Yes, Thorvald; we may now dissipate a little, may we not? . . .

Helmer: Nora! (*goes up to her and catches her in jest by her ear.*) Is thoughtlessness again there? Suppose that I borrowed £50 to-day, and you dissipated this sum during the Christmas week, and a tile fell down on my head New Year's eve, and I were killed—

Nora: O fy! don't speak so badly.

Helmer: Yes, suppose that such happened, what then?

Nora: If such bad were to happen, it might be indifferent to me either I had debt or no. . . .

Helmer: What do we call the birds that always dissipate money?

Nora: Gamblers, I know it, indeed.

Helmer: . . . The gambler is sweet, but it uses up excessively much money. It is incredible how expensive it is to a man to keep a gambler.

This sage reflection of Helmer's might have served as the motto to a recent autobiography.

Presently the scene continues:

Helmer: But stop, an idea strikes me. You look so—so—what am I to call it?—so suspiciously to-day.

Nora: Do I do so?

Helmer: Yes to be sure. Look hard at me.

Nora (*looking at him*): Well?

Helmer (*threatens with his finger*): Has the sweet-tooth not been prevailing in town to-day?

Nora: No, what makes you think of it?

Helmer: Has the sweet-tooth not taken a trip to the confectioner?

Nora: No, I assure you, Thorvald—

Helmer: Nor sipped a little the sweet-meat?

Nora: No, not at all.

Helmer: Not even gnawed one macaroon or two?

Nora: No, Thorvald, I assure you, indeed—

Helmer: Well, well, it is, of course, only my joke.

Mrs. Linde, an old schoolfellow of Nora's, now arrives from the country. From the scene which ensues I make the following extracts:

Nora: Yes, now I again recognise your old face. It was only at the first glance —You have turned a little paler—and perhaps a little more meagre.
Mrs. Linde: And much, much elder, Nora.
Nora. Yes, perhaps a little elder, very little; not at all much.

Nora: O, Kristine, how flighty and happy I feel! It is charming to have excessively much money and need not to give one's self any concerns, is it not?
Mrs. Linde: It must at any rate be charming to have the necessary.
Nora: No, not only the necessary, but excessively much money!

Mrs. Linde: And your husband returned completely cured?
Nora: Sound as a roach!. . . No, Thorvald has never been ill one hour since that time. And our children are well and healthy like I am (*starts up, applauding*).* Oh dear! oh dear! Kristine, it is, indeed, excessively charming to live and be happy!

Mrs. Linde: My poor mother needs me no longer, for she has died. Nor the boys; they have been employed and can shift for themselves.
Nora: How flighty you must feel—
Mrs. Linde: No, but so much abandoned.

Nora: Are you quite sure that I have *borrowed* the money . . . I may have got it from some admirer. If we look so much captivating as I do—
Mrs. Linde: You are a madman.†
Nora: You are surely very inquisitive, Kristine. . . . I don't care about neither him nor his will, for now I am sorrowless (*jumps up*). Dear me, it is charming to know, Kristine! Sorrowless! To be free from care, quite sorrowless! To play with my children and make much noise, to have a handsome and elegant home, to live just as Thorvald prizes to live.

Here is the opening conversation between Dr. Rank and Mrs. Linde:

Rank: I think I met you, madam, on the staircase, when I came.
Mrs. Linde: Yes, I mount very slowly. I cannot stand to mount.
Rank: Aha, a little inward weakness?

* In the original 'clapping her hands.'
† Mr. Weber's superiority to sex will receive further illustration towards the close.

Mrs. Linde: You might rather say overworked.

Rank: Nothing else? Thus you have come to town in order to recreate during all banquets?

Mrs. Linde: I have come here to obtain work.

Rank: Is that an infallible expedient against overworking?

Mrs. Linde: We need something for our support, Doctor Rank.

I should perhaps explain that what Mrs. Linde really says at this point is 'One must live, Dr. Rank,' and that Rank practically retorts; 'Je n'en vois pas la nécessité.' We come now to the first scene between Nora and the money-lender, Krogstad:

Krogstad: May I ask you, shortly, is Mrs. Linde to obtain a situation in the stock bank?

Nora: How dare *you* close-question *me*, Mr. Krogstad, *you*, one of my husband's subordinates?

Krogstad: Pshaw! I know your husband from the college years. I do not believe that the bank director is faster* than other husbands.

Nora: If you speak disregardingly of my husband, I'll turn you out of doors.

Krogstad: You know, of course, as well as all others, that I have been guilty of a heedlessness a lot of years ago. . . . Then I commenced the business you know. I was obliged to have a source of revenue. . . . But now I must leave all this. My sons grow. I am obliged to regain so much civic esteem as is possible for their sake. . . . And your husband is now going to kick me from my place, so that I shall again be in a nice mess. . . .

Nora: I hope that you will not tell my husband that I owe you money.

Krogstad: Hum, suppose that I told it him?

Nora: It would be badly done by you (*stifled by sobs*). He was to learn in so ugly and coarse a manner this secret, which is my joy and pride—learn it from *you*. You will expose me to the most formidable disagreeableness.

After Nora has confessed that it was she who wrote her father's name on the fatal note-of-hand, the scene proceeds:

Krogstad: I can tell you that what I once committed was neither a greater nor a worse crime than yours. I lost my civic esteem by it.

Nora: You? Will you make me believe that you have done something courageous to save your wife's life?

Krogstad: The laws do not ask of motives.

* Firmer.

Nora: Then it must be very bad laws.

Krogstad: Bad or no—if I produce this bond in court, you will be judged according to the laws.

Nora: I do not believe so at all. Was a daughter not to be allowed to exempt her old mortally-ill father from anxieties and concerns? . . . I don't exactly know the laws, but I am sure that it must somewhere be written in them that such is allowed. And you, who are a solicitor, have no knowledge about such cases. You must be a bad lawyer, Mr. Krogstad.

The translator rises to the height of his genius in the last scene of the first act, between Nora and Helmer:

Nora: I am looking forward with excessive pleasure to the fancy-dress ball at Stenborg's the day after to-morrow.

Helmer: And I am excessively inquisitive to see by which you will surprise me.

Nora: Alas, that stupid sally.

Helmer: Well?

Nora: I cannot hit upon something good. . . . Are you very busy, Thorvald?

Helmer: . . . I have received power of attorney from the retiring direction in order to take in hand the necessary innovation of the functionaries and course of business. . . .

Nora: Thus it was on that account that the poor Krogstad——

Helmer: Hum.

Nora (leaning against the back of the chair, and running slowly her fingers through his back hair): If you had not been so busy, I should have begged you for an excessively great service, Thorvald. . . . Would you not help me, and decide what person I am to represent and what dress I am to wear?

Helmer: Oh! is my little self-willed lark out in order to meet with a rescuer? . . . Well, well; I am to ponder upon the matter. We are to hit upon something, indeed.

Nora: . . . But tell me, is that which this Krogstad has been guilty of in fact so bad a thing?

Helmer: He has written counterfeit names. Have you any idea of what such means? . . . Only imagine how such a guilty man must lie, play the hypocrite, and dissemble in all ways, must be masked in presence of his nearly-related, even in presence of his wife and children. And as to the children, that is just the most terrific of all, Nora.

Nora: Why?

Helmer: Because a such atmosphere, containing lie, causes contagion and disease-substance in a home. Every breath the children draw in a such house contains germs of something ugly.

Nora (nearer behind him): Are you sure of that?

Helmer: My dear. As an advocate, I have often learned so. Almost all early depraved men have had lying mothers.

Nora: Why just—mothers?

Helmer: It is most frequently owing to the mothers, but fathers have of course the blame of it in like manner. Every solicitor knows so very well. And yet this Krogstad has poisoned his own children by lie and dissimulation. . . . Therefore, my sweet little Nora must promise me not to plead his cause. Give me your hand as an affirmation. Well, what's that? Give me your hand. Well, thus decided. I assure you, it would be impossible to me to work jointly with him. I feel literally indisposed in the presence of such men.

Mr. Weber's crowning effort, however, is reserved for the last words of the act:

Nora (pale with terror): Deprave my little children—! Poison my home? (*a short pause; she turns up her nose*). This is not true. This is in the name of wonder not true.

The stage direction so elegantly rendered, 'Turns up her nose,' means in reality, 'Tosses her head.' Picture poor Nora turning up her nose at Destiny!

Near the beginning of the second act comes the scene in which Nora explains to Mrs. Linde, Dr. Rank's position in the 'Doll's House:'

Mrs. Linde: But tell me, is doctor Rank always so despondent as yesterday?

Nora: No, but he was strangely despondent yesterday. Otherwise, he suffers from a dangerous illness! The poor being, he has dorsal consumption.

In the next scene Nora begs Helmer 'so suppliantly' not to dismiss Krogstad from the Bank.

Helmer: Oh, I understand; it is old recollections which are frightening you.

Nora: What do you mean by that?

Helmer: You remember your father, of course.

Nora: Yes, surely. Mind only how malicious men wrote in the papers of papa, and backbit him so horribly . . .

Helmer: My little Nora, there is a considerable difference between your father and me. Your father was no unassailable functionary. But so I am . . . There is one circumstance which makes Krogstad quite impossible in the bank, as long as I am the director . . . He is an early friend of mine. It is one of these precipitate acquaintances by which we are oftentimes later troubled. Yes, I may as well tell it you bluntly: we say thou to each other. And this indiscreet man does not conceal it at all, when others are present. On the contrary—he means that he has on account of that a right to speak to me in a free and easy ton (*sic*), and he trumps out every moment: thou, thou Helmer. I assure you that it influences on me in the most painful manner. He would make me my place in the bank excessively intolerable.

Here are a few speeches from the scene between Nora and Dr. Rank which has scandalized so many worthy people:

Rank: In these days I have undertaken an examination of my inner condition. Bankrupt. Within one month I am, perhaps, in my grave, and a booty for the worms.

Nora: Fy for shame, how ugly you are speaking.

Rank: The matter is also ugly, indeed . . . And to suffer for another's guilt. Is that justice? And in every family is a such inflexible retribution predominating in some way—

Nora (with her hands on the ears): Nonsense! Jolly, jolly!

Rank: All this is, indeed, but a laughing matter. My poor guiltless chine must suffer for my father during the jolly days, when he was a lieutenant.

I quote the following phrases from the closing scene of the second act lest the new and most expressive term 'exertly' should be lost to the English language. The idiomatic use of the word 'penholder' is also noteworthy:

Helmer: Rank prepared me to see a grand scene of disguise.

Rank: I understood so, but I were mistaken . . .

Helmer: But, dear Nora, you look so exertly. Have you been practising too much?

Nora: No, I have not practised at all . . . You must wholly be at my service this evening. Not work at all, no penholder in your hand. Will you not do so, dear Thorvald?

The opening scene of the third act between Mrs. Linde and her old lover Krogstad affords Mr. Weber some of his finest opportunities.

Krogstad (to Mrs. Linde): When I lost you, it seemed to me as if all solid soil left my feet. Look at me. Now I'm a shipwrecked man on a wreck . . .

Mrs. Linde: I am also sitting like a shipwrecked woman on a wreck . . . Krogstad, if we, shipwrecked men, might join.

Krogstad: What's that you are saying?

Mrs. Linde: Two on one wreck may easilier be saved than each on his.

Krogstad: Kristine!

Mrs. Linde: Do you know why I arrived at town?

Krogstad: Were you to have remembered me?

Mrs. Linde: I must work if I am to support myself. . . . But now I'm alone in the world, so excessively inane and abandoned.

We come now to the passionate scene between Helmer and Nora immediately after their return from the ball.

Helmer: I imagine that you are my clandestinely beloved, my young clandestinely betrothed, and that no one suspects that we have secrets.

Nora: Yes, yes, I know well that all your thoughts are taken up with me.

Helmer: And when we are to go, and I am laying the shawl on your tender, youthfully fresh shoulders—on this charming nape—then I imagine that you are my young bride. . . .

The grimly pathetic dialogue which precedes Rank's final exit is curiously free from extravagances; but Mr. Weber breaks out again before long. Here are a few phrases from Helmer's onslaught upon Nora after he has read Krogstad's letter.

Helmer (*being dizzy*): True. Is that which he is writing here true? Horrible! no, no; it's impossible, indeed, that this can be true.

Nora: It *is* true. I have loved you above all in the world.

Helmer: O, don't utter such stupid shuffles. . . . Doff the shawl. Doff it, I command you! . . . From this moment it depends no longer on felicity; it depends only on saving the rests, remnants and the appearance.

After Krogstad has returned the I.O.U., and Helmer's terror is over, he proceeds thus:—

Helmer: Indeed it must have been three terrific days to you, Nora.

Nora: I have been fighting a hard fight during the three last days.

Helmer: And moaned, and seen no expedient but—no, we will not call to mind all this terrific. We will only shout and repeat: it's at an end; it's at an end! . . . What does this mean—this growing* expression? . . . O, how warm and handsome our home is, Nora. Here is a shelter for you; here I am to keep you like a chased pigeon I have saved unharmed out of the talons of the hawk.

The long scene after Nora has announced her intention of leaving her home, contains many exquisite Weberisms. I have space only for the following:

Helmer: O, it's shocking. Can you flinch your holiest duties? . . . You are first of all wife and mother.

Nora: I no longer believe in that. I believe that I am first of all a man, I as well as you—or, at all events, that I am to try to become a man.

Helmer (*melancholy*): I see it, I see it. An abyss has been formed between us— O, but Nora, was it not possible that it might be filled up?

Nora: As I am now, I am no wife for you.

Helmer: I have power to grow another.

Nora: Perhaps—if the doll is taken away from you.

* Stiffening.

Helmer: Nora,—may I never more become but a stranger to you?

Nora (*takes her portmanteau.*) Alas, Thorvald, then the most wonderful must happen—

Helmer: Tell me the most wonderful.

Nora: That both you and I changed ourselves in such a manner that—O, Thorvald, I no longer believe in anything wonderful.

Helmer: But I will believe in it. Tell it me! Change ourselves in such a manner that—?

Nora: That cohabitation between you and me might become a matrimony. Good-bye.

(*Exit through the corridor.*)

Helmer: (*sinking down on a chair at the door, and concealing his face with his hands.*) Nora! Nora! (*looking about, rises.*) Empty. She is no longer here. (*Hopes are awaking in him.*) The most wonderful—?! (*It is heard that the gate is slammed*).

THE END

Mr. Weber's misadventures are, as he would say, a 'terrific' warning to the rash people who put their trust in dictionaries. It may be a piece of national vanity, but I believe that this is not an English foible. A few months ago I received a letter from a Dutch lady, with reference to this very play. She had heard that no satisfactory translation of it existed in English, and suggested that she might supply the want. Her English was painfully formal and foreign, and her qualification on the other side was that she knew—not Norwegian—but *a* Norwegian. We English, I think, are not often afflicted with this ambition to translate from a language that we are ignorant of into another that we do not know—I speak, of course, of modern languages. Mr. Weber has so far the advantage over my Amsterdam correspondent that he knows one of the languages with which he deals. His translation, indeed, is in reality singularly correct. He seldom or never mistranslates; his meaning is quite right, if only he could find the proper words. It is the fine shades that escape him; the difference, for instance, between a 'chased pigeon' and a hunted dove, between a 'portmanteau' and a hand-bag, between 'applauding' and clapping one's hands, between 'gnawing' and nibbling. If only synonyms were synonymous, how much easier language would be! But does not the beginning of wisdom for the would-be stylist lie in the recognition that synonyms do not exist, or at any rate that they are as rare as Siamese Twins?

36. C. H. Herford on *Rosmersholm* and *The Lady from the Sea*

January 1890

From 'The Two Last Plays of Ibsen', by C. H. Herford, *Academy* (January 1890), xxxvii, 38–9. The volumes under review were *Rosmersholm*, translated by Louis N. Parker (Griffith, Farren & Co., 1890)[1] and *The Lady from the Sea*, translated by Eleanor Marx (Fisher & Unwin, 1890).

The translation of the two last dramas of Ibsen adds appreciably to the materials for study, as well as to the provocatives of debate, already in the possession of his large and growing English audience. Both are highly original variations of the fundamental motive upon which Ibsen's social, and in part also his historical, drama is built—the conflict of a more or less individual nature with a false position created for it in part by its own singularity, in part by the stress of current conventions. It is only a tribute to Ibsen's dramatic genius that one might describe the fundamental motive of Shaksperean tragedy in nearly the same terms. While in Shakspere, however, we, as a rule, watch the creation of the 'false position' as well as its violent dissolution; in Ibsen the play commonly derives its initial impulse from a state of acute tension already reached at the outset. The false position is the given fact, to the significance of which the victim and the spectator gradually awake. In *Ghosts* the whole tragedy lies in this awakening, since the bondage which it reveals is riveted in the past, and cannot by any effort be annulled. Elsewhere, the issue is not in this blank and passive horror, but in action, action dominated, in general, by what has been termed the *idée mère* of Ibsen's poetry—the conception of the 'call' first definitively announced in the inexorable imperatives of *Brand*. Nora and Stockmann in their different ways obey such a call; while Lona, in the *Pillars*, is the voice through which it is obtruded upon the ears and heart of the respectable sinner Bernick. In this last case the climax is least well grounded;

---

[1] Mistakenly given as 'Louis N. Palmer' in the original article.

Bernick's repentance is not adequately justified by his past, and stands on a par with many another fifth-act conversion. Indeed, Ibsen's strength hardly lies in exhibiting gradual revolutions of character. His men and women are four-square, sharply defined, and changing (like himself) by sudden transformations if they change at all, or at least by transitions the nuances and stealing steps of which are not habitually disclosed.

As a case of 'conversion,' though hardly in any other respect, the *Pillars* may be compared with the earlier and more powerful of the two plays before us—the lurid tragedy of *Rosmersholm*.

[Herford outlines the plot.]

It is impossible to convey in a few sentences the art with which Ibsen has solved the extraordinarily difficult problem he has here set himself. We have to do, plainly, with something sufficiently unlike the ordinary 'realist' drama of crime and suicide. The climax is—like that of *Brand*, of *Peer Gynt*, of *Et Dukkehjem*—not so much an incident borrowed from actual life, as an ideal solution postulated by a set of assumed conditions. And there are touches enough which remind us that Ibsen bears within him a sleeping romantic poet, who, however resolutely lulled, will sometimess stir and cry. The fate of Rosmer, although worked out in every detail with the most masterly psychology, is permitted to gather about it a sort of half light of supernatural mystery from the bodeful legend of his house. The white horses which portend death have appeared to the old housekeeper; and in her mouth are put the terrible closing words in which the poet comments on the meaning of his catastrophe, in one sense for her, in another for his readers—'No! there's no help here! The dead wife has taken them!'

A much bolder step in this direction is represented, however, in the next, and at present the last, play of Ibsen, the *Fruen fra havet*. It is an attempt, as our readers are aware, to render in terms of modern life the beautiful myth, of which every folklore has its characteristic variant, of the mermaid wedded on land and still hungering for the sea. The transformation is accomplished with minute care, and every detail repays study.

[outlines the plot.]

The setting of this translated mermaid legend appears at first sight commonplace enough; and indeed Ibsen has scarcely ever consented to adopt with so little mitigation the bald language of ordinary middle-class discourse. But when Ibsen is commonplace it is usually with a purpose; and we easily detect how finely the atmosphere is here tempered to the subject. The course of the action required that the 'land life' should be outwardly trivial and empty, devoid of any obvious and salient interests that might capture the alien's averted sympathy. We are placed accordingly in a remote provincial town, for which its summer visitors are the great event, and untroubled by any breath of the religious and political excitement which electrifies the air of *Rosmersholm*. All the men too are landsmen of the least heroic and adventurous type. On the other hand, the action required equally that there should be roots of possible sympathy hidden under this indifferent and trivial exterior. Ellida had to be won for her family. Accordingly, we find that the two daughters, who do not 'get on' with their stepmother, have nevertheless points of sympathy with her which are gradually revealed both to them and to us. Hilde has her susceptibility to a personal spell, Bolette her vague longing for the vast unknown world. And in their love affairs, as in her's, these instincts have to do duty altogether for passion. How delicate, too, is the symbolism by which Hilde's struggling sympathy with Ellida is rendered, in the contrast (Act V. *ad init.*) between her adventurous familiarity with the sea and the timorous incapacity of Lyngstrand and Aruholm!

37. Hjalmar Boyesen presents an American view of Ibsen

March 1890

From 'Open Letters: Henrik Ibsen', by Hjalmar Hjorth Boyesen, *Century* (March 1890), xxxix, 794. H. H. Boyesen (1848–95) was born in Norway and came to America in 1868. A protégé of W. D. Howells, he was a successful novelist and taught German at Cornell (1874–80) and Columbia (1881–95). A year before he died he published his *Commentary on the Works of Henrik Ibsen* (New York, 1894) (see Introduction).

The Norwegian dramatist's fame has, at last, reached England and crossed the Atlantic. A society has even been formed in London for the purpose of furthering the study of his works and their representation upon the stage. *A Doll's House,* apart from its merits as a play, has produced a profound impression, and occasional spirited polemics between the admirers of the author and his detractors, in the press. Mr William Archer on one side and Mr Andrew Lang on the other have sustained solo parts, and more or less the discordant choruses have amplified their theme and given a multitudinous resonance to their voices. It is not necessary to take sides in the controversy. Liking or disliking Ibsen is largely a matter of temperament. The optimist, who takes life as he finds it and satisfies himself with the reflection that everything has been wisely ordained, will have no patience with the corrosive criticism to which Ibsen subjects the fundamental institutions of civilized society. A certain philosophic discontent is a prerequisite for understanding him. He persists in seeing problems of universal application where most of us see only annoyances, or, perhaps, misfortunes affecting our individual lot. To judge him as a mere playwright is absurd. Though by no means contemptible as to technique, each of his plays—with the exception of the earlier historical ones—is a dramatized piece of philosophy. Each preaches more or less incisively a moral lesson, lays bare a social canker, diagnoses a social disease. But what distinguishes Ibsen above all others who have hitherto dealt in this species of morbid anatomy is the fine surgical precision with which he handles the scalpel and the cool audacity with which he cuts.

38. W. E. Simonds on Nora's selflessness

March 1890

From 'Henrik Ibsen', by W. E. Simonds, *Dial* (March 1890), x, 300–3. This is a review of Mrs H. F. Lord's translation of *A Doll's House* which had been reissued by Appleton & Co., New York. Simonds (1841–1903) was a lawyer and, at this time, a Member of Congress.

How strange it is that so many of the critics fail to see that Nora's act is not selfishness after all! There is promise of a splendid womanliness in that 'emancipated individuality' that Ibsen's enemies are ridiculing. There will be an ideal home after the mutual chastening is accomplished: an ideal home—not ideal people necessarily, but a home, a family, where there is complete community, a perfect love.

39. E. P. Evans on Ibsen's cosmic emotion

May 1890

From 'Henrik Ibsen: His Early Career as Poet and Playwright', by
E. P. Evans, *Atlantic Monthly* (May 1890), lxv, 578–88. This article
was followed up in *Atlantic Monthly* (October 1890), lxvi, by
'Henrik Ibsen: His Life and Later Dramas'. Evans (1831–1917) was
a free-lance journalist and former Professor of Modern Languages
at the University of Michigan.

Indeed, it may be said of [Ibsen] in the language of Kant, that two things
fill his soul with ever new and increasing admiration and awe the oftener
he contemplates them: the starry heavens above him and the moral law
within him. In both cases it is the same sort of 'cosmic emotion' which
the phenomena excite; but of the two sublime and eternal revelations
of the supremacy of universal and inviolable laws, it is the microcosm,
or physical world within, that appeals to him more strongly and interests him more deeply than the macrocosm, or physical world without.
It is not the poetic or the romantic but the mystical or metaphysical
side of nature that attracts him. There is no landscape painting in his
dramas. He never introduces descriptions of scenery for their own sake,
but only as symbols of human thought and aspiration and heroic endeavour; as, for example, the allusions to the glaciers and the 'ice-
church,' the misty mountain-tops and the stormy fiord in *Brand*. He
has the love of an old Norse salt for 'the fierce, conflicting brine' but it
is the mysteriousness and unfathomableness of the restless water, type
of the seething passions of the soul (that 'sealet' within, according to
Grimm's etymology of the word), which fascinate him, and suggest
psychological problems darker than the ocean's waves 'and deeper than
did ever plummet sound' as in *The Lady of the Sea*.

40. Mrs H. F. Lord on the phases of the soul in *Ghosts*

1890

From Mrs H. F. Lord's preface to her translation of *Ghosts* (Griffith & Farran, 1890). Her translation is a revised form of an earlier version published in 1885 in the socialist periodical *Today* (v. III, pp. 29ff., 65ff., 106ff.). She takes the present opportunity to expound her views on Christian Science and suggests that Mrs Alving might have alleviated Oswald's condition if she had adopted its curative methods. Mrs Lord refers her readers to 'Christian Science and Healing', a pamphlet written by herself.

To my thinking, the disorder and hopelessness of *Ghosts* disappear, directly we read it with these deeper views of evolution. [The doctrine of the 'Twin Soul'.] Stating my philosophy of the play, I would say, part of our sense of pain and disorder arises from so many of the characters having travestied their sex; Chamberlain Alving was really a woman-soul, Mrs. Alving a man-soul; Mr. Manders is a woman; so is Oswald; Regina is a man. This leaves the arch-humbug Engstrand as the only one in a genuine position; he is a man. Some souls perform all their evolution, sub-human and human, attached to and acting through bodies of one sex; sometimes their own; sometimes the opposite;— some adopt change for selfish, some for noble reasons—education, mission, etc., Ibsen himself being a woman-soul, who has taken man's form for his work's sake. Mr. Alving took man's form for power's sake; Mrs. Alving took woman's form for a variety of good reasons, which we may sum up as 'experience.' Oswald took man's form for the sake also of experience, travel, liberty,—all good reasons in their way. Mr. Manders took man's form for power; he had been a conventual woman in a former life, and now wished the self-importance of being a male ecclesiastic. Regina took woman's form to mitigate the impact of blows in life; (change of sex always modifies the expression your harvest

149

of circumstances will take;) she had been a very bad man, and had nothing but blows to expect from Karma. . . .

The unwholesomeness of *Ghosts* consists in its mis-presenting all these transitory phases of soul history, and calling them the operation of the law of Heredity. The disorder consists in the travesty of sex; this always entails a dulling of intuitions, because it is a form of untruth. The gloom consists in there being no way out of all the difficulties; for there is none, unless it be by spiritual evolution.

Some people will say they prefer thinking *Ghosts* true in all the horror of Heredity, to accepting the interference with mortal life implied by tracing Oswald's pain to his father's mischievous and cruel efforts after death. Heredity as a *causative* principle does not exist. Relations do exist between us mortals and those who are unseen by us; these relations may be unfortunate, as between Oswald and his father, or full of beauty, truth and love. The old words about visiting the sins of the fathers upon the children unto the third and fourth generation, may be quite true, and yet not mean Heredity, not prove that Heredity is a *causative*.

41. Henry James on Ibsen's provinciality

October 1890

From a letter to Edmund Gosse, dated 17 October 1890 (Brotherton Collection, Leeds). The 'beautiful blue biography' was Jaeger's *Life of Henrik Ibsen* (Copenhagen, 1888) which Clara Bell had recently translated into English and which appeared in December 1890. The verse translations, which were a feature of the text, were undertaken by Gosse.

I have waited to thank you for the beautiful blue biography till I should have had time to master its contents. I finished it this morning & lose no time in expressing what I owe you & how skilful and resourceful you strike me as having been in your rendering of all the quotations of verse. Some of them read like Browning—I mean *du mielleurs*. How I wish there had been more of these, especially from Brand and P. Gynt. Isn't the author's account of the latter quite exasperatingly inadequate? It is indeed no account at all—only a vague descant, without illustrations, on the character of the mystic Peer. The book is interesting and earnest; but provoking throughout by its general ill-distributedness. But how respectably translated. And how provincial all these poor dear Norsefolk, including the Colossus himself. They all affect me intensely like domestic fowl clucking behind a hedge—the big bristling hedge of Germany.

42. Edmund Gosse on Ibsen and American writers

1890

From Gosse's Introduction to volume II of *Lovell's Series of Foreign Literature: The Prose Dramas of Henrik Ibsen* (New York, 1890). Gosse sent a copy of this volume to Henry James who, as an aspiring dramatist, may have been encouraged by his remarks. A substantial part of this Introduction repeats many of the points Gosse had already made in his article 'Ibsen's Social Dramas' (No. 14).

In presenting to the American public the first collected version of the works of Ibsen, it may not be uninteresting to consider in what particulars the local position of his genius, and the society out of which it springs, present a similarity with those out of which the great American dramatist, that phœnix of the future, will have to struggle to the sun. Norway, like America, but like no other country of the modern world —since the republics of South America can scarcely boast the same conditions—is a young and a vigorous people, which has broken away from an ancient power, whose population it now greatly outnumbers. In each case the parent, instead of dwindling in intellectual vitality after the secession, has rather increased in vigour and individuality; while, although developing a public spirit entirely independent, the child has preserved the paternal traditions of the race on most essential points. And more than all besides, through each political and social schism the language has remained the same, as an inseparable bond of unity. As, therefore, in considering a great American talent, we are obliged to look back and see what roots it has sent down into the earth of English literature, so, to conceive arightly how a genius like Ibsen's has become what it is, we must briefly see what it owes to its Danish as well as its Norwegian predecessors.

[Gosse sketches in the background and recounts Ibsen's career to date. He makes an interesting observation in a footnote: 'I do not know that any writer has noted the influence of Hertz's *Amors Genistreger* (1839) upon the form of Ibsen's *Love's Comedy*.']

To an American audience it would seem as though Ibsen should speak with greater certainty of a sympathetic hearing than to any other. In no European poet except himself do we find the problems of advanced democracy faced with so much courage or with so little rhetoric. The fanfarons of Victor Hugo seem old-fashioned and ineffectual, the audacities of Carducci and of Swinburne are like the sport of aristocratic children beside the gravity, the terse and stern attitude of arrest, which we meet with in Ibsen's prose dramas. The provincial atmosphere, the air of the little market-town in some country part of Norway, merely deepens the sense of strenuousness, as the earnestness of a countryman may put to shame a metropolitan frivolity. His seven plays are seven arrows in the heart of the mundane goddess of modern society. Whether it is commercial hypocrisy, as in *The Pillars of Society*; or the sacrifice of feminine individuality, as in *A Doll's House*; or the hatred of truth, as in *The Enemy of Society*; whether it is the sins of the fathers, as in *Ghosts*; or the phantom of conventional religion, as in *Rosmersholm*; or the brittle shell of humanitarian optimism, as in *The Wild Duck*; or the tenuity of the marriage tie, as in *The Lady from the Sea*, in each case a sword is driven between the bone and the marrow of modern life. Ibsen is the enemy of all convention; he takes nothing for granted. No axiom is so universally received as to be safe from his profane analysis.

Close as we are to the production of Ibsen's plays, we can hardly perhaps judge very rightly yet of the fabric which is actually being wound off the loom under our very eyes. But some things we can plainly see, and among them the absolute novelty of this new species of dramatic literature. One very interesting feature of Ibsen's work is the relation it holds to the modern novel. For the last half-century and more, the novel, in almost all countries, has been leaving the literary drama far behind it in point of interest. In France alone the drama has retained something of its old literary pre-eminence. A play of the younger Dumas holds its own by the side of a novel of the same author. A new comedy by Pailleron is read, even though a new novel by Maupassant makes its appearance. Nevertheless, in France itself, the literature of drama is less and less able to cope with the literature of fiction. In England and America, of course, the former is not in the background so much as it is positively non-existent. In Scandinavia, to a less extent, the same has been the case. Björnson's plays have not successfully competed with Björnson's novels; but Ibsen's dramas do compete successfully with their most dangerous rivals in fiction, the novels of Alexander Kjelland. The reason of this general decline of the read play, is, as all critics admit, the increased conventionality of the stage, and if Ibsen has succeeded where others have failed, it is because he is essentially less conventional than others.

Ibsen has created a new form of drama, and until he is himself superseded by some still more vivid painter of actual life, we must look upon him as the first of dramatic realists. The impression of vitality, of actuality, which his plays give us arises partly from the truth of his dialogue, which is astonishing, and partly from the alteration of plan which he has introduced. All plays before his are built on the system of climbing up the hill to a crisis and then rushing downward. The 'well-made' comedy of Scribe or of Sardou has reduced this Jack-and-Jill ideal of dramatic construction to a mechanical trick. The figures are drawn up to the apex of their intrigue with a string, and dropped down the inclined plane at a given signal. But with Ibsen the downward path has been taken before the play opens, and the velocity is cumulative from the first scene to the last.

43. *Emperor and Galilean*

December 1890

From 'Ibseniana', an unsigned review, *Saturday Review* (27 December 1890), lxx, 747–8. The books technically under discussion were: *The Life of Henrik Ibsen* by Henrik Jaeger, translated by Clara Bell (London: Heinemann, 1890); *Ghosts*, translated by Mrs H. F. Lord (Griffith, Farran & Co., 1890); *Nora*, translated by Mrs H. F. Lord (Griffith, Farran & Co., 1890); and *Henrik Ibsen's Prose Dramas*, edited by William Archer (Walter Scott, vols III and IV, 1890). The reviewer concentrates his remarks on Archer's volumes, and deals especially with *Emperor and Galilean*. Mrs Lord and Jaeger get a dismissive paragraph apiece.

The fourth volume, containing the two parts of *Emperor and Galilean* (the translation is revised or re-written by Mr. Archer, from an earlier one), affords work of very different character and merits very different treatment. There are those, we believe, who hold this vast and, to tell the truth, somewhat overgrown drama, or pair of dramas, to be the author's masterpiece, and we are not far from being of their opinion. It has, indeed, many of his defects, of those defects which it is not too much to say, from the point of view of cool and catholic criticism, will always prevent Ibsen from being accorded by such criticism a place among the greatest writers. His terrible lack of proportion, and what we have above called the mediaeval weakness of carrying on the action panorama-fashion, rather than as one carries it who deliberately composes a well-ordered picture, are observable, indeed glaring. That example of *Faust* which seems to have impressed itself so deeply on all the Northern nations is here perhaps more corruptly followed than in any other instance known to us. We have not a beginning, middle, and end of a dramatic presentation of Julian, but a series of dissolving views of Julian's soul, its atmosphere, and its companions at different periods; an interesting thing enough, no doubt, but as art (because as difficulty surmounted) a thousand miles below the great dramatic models, not merely in execution, but in conception. We have, too, that 'obsession' by a passing study, fancy, fad, or whatever it is to be called, which is another mark of inferior art. At one time or other during the many years in which *Emperor and Galilean* was a-composing, Ibsen, as any student of Schopenhauer can see, evidently came much under the influence of that amiable philosopher. And accordingly we are pestered in parts, if not throughout, with a pother of words about 'willing,' 'freedmen under necessity,' and the like. Yet, again, in parts, or rather throughout, the action is exceedingly confused, and the passion by no means extremely clear. Whether from pudibundity (which is not a usual fault of his), or from sheer inability to rise to and express the occasion, the dramatist has, at least as presented by his translator, made a complete mess of the central situation, the horrible death of Helena, and its effect of revulsion of Julian's religious and political loyalty. Not only is there a good deal of obscurity in the actual description of what happened, but the infinite talking about it and about it, the watering down of incident with dialogue which is the fault of the whole double play, is nowhere more conspicuous than here. One is perpetually struck with the thought 'Here is a man who has got a mass of the most excellent material together, but who, partly because he really does not know how to build, and partly because he has not resolution enough to discard what is not strictly necessary, has hardly achieved a building at all.'

These are grievous faults, and by no means the only ones in *Emperor and Galilean*. And yet it remains an exceedingly remarkable work. That a translated 'world-historic drama' (the tell-tale and rather damning compound adjective is in the title, filling three hundred and fifty pages, and suffering from all the defects above noted, should be yet of such interest as to make the reader read it through without any but forced pauses, must count for a good deal. The interest which secures this result is of two kinds. First, there is—as in all Ibsen's better work, and especially in his work before he became a social reformer, and when he lets social reform alone—plenty of force and vigour now and then in detached characters, scenes, and even, through the disadvantages of translation, passages. To separate a few of these for notice is not easy, considering that not only the pages but the personages of the drama or dramas count by hundreds. But the figures of Gregory Nazianzen and Basil of Cæsarea, of Basil's sister Macrina, of Libanius, of the minor sophists and parasites who crowd round Julian, are very well drawn. Helena misses, but only just misses, equal success. The Athenian student passage is lively, the incantation scene with Maximus fair, that between

Julian and the envoy of Constantius, when had the Cæsar hesitated he was lost, excellent. So also are some of the Antioch scenes, and notably that famous one with the priest of Cybele and his goose. The end suffers from Ibsen's besetting sin, and is distinctly confused; but even in its confusion it has pathos. . . .

Although he is nowhere so summed up, Julian is presented to us in effect as one who is always wanting better bread than is made of wheat, and always awaking to the fact that he has filled his mouth with chaff and ashes. He tries Christianity and stumbles at the weaknesses of Christians; he flings himself into study, and finds that study is words, and students too often men of double language and double face; he tries love with the peculiar ardour of *les cérébraux*, and loses his beloved in circumstances which make even the past possession of her a subject for gnashing of teeth. He undertakes to regenerate the world and restore the gods, only to find that the world laughs or yawns at him, and the gods apparently take no heed; he tries theurgy, and, in sure confidence of a private revelation, is juggled to death by a play of words. Whether Ibsen would himself acknowledge this Flaubertian motive as his, we do not know. Mr. Archer attempts no criticism, and Herr Jaeger, who seems rather afraid of the play, is more than usually inefficient; but we think it is the true explanation, and it certainly has given interest to our own reading.

44. An anonymous comment on the depravity of Ibsen, Edward Aveling and *Ghosts*

February 1891

From an unsigned article, *Saturday Review* (14 February 1891), lxxi, 195.

It was perhaps providential that Dr Aveling should have taken upon himself to read to the members of the Playgoers Club on Tuesday night Ibsen's *Ghosts*, or we might have been inflicted with a *matinée* performance of this unsavoury play. The 'Master' in this nasty drama deals mainly with incest and hereditary insanity; excellent subjects, no doubt, for discussion in scientific circles. But so long as young girls continue to be the chief ornaments of English theatres, *Ghosts* will, we trust, only haunt the resorts of Dr Aveling and other Ibsenites, and not thrust themselves upon wholesome-minded people in decent places of amusement.

ROSMERSHOLM

Vaudeville Theatre, 23 February 1891

---

45. An unsigned notice in the *Evening News and Post*

24 February 1891

The *News* gave its report a four-decker headline: 'Another Ibsen Play/Production of Mr Charles Archer's Version of *Rosmersholm* at the Vaudeville/'What Is This?'/Ibsenish Peculiarities and Dramatic Construction.' The translator was William Archer's brother; the cast was as follows:

Pastor Rosmer..	Mr F. R. Benson	Peter Mortensgard		Mr J. Wheatman
Rector Kroll ..	Mr Athol Forde	Madame Helseth ..		Miss May Protheroe
Ulric Brendel ..	Mr Charles Hudson	Rebecca West	..	Miss Florence Farr

---

'Henceforth,' observed Pastor Johannes Rosmer at a mystifying moment near the close of the second act, 'I can think of nothing but that one question—why?' Inconsistently enough, he wound up the act a few lines further on with a different question: (*staccato*) 'What—is—this?' It was not alone upon the stage that these two queries were put during the course of yesterday's performance of *Rosmersholm*. Everyone in the house who was not a blind believer in the Norwegian prophet found occasion to put both questions to his own intelligence and to his neighbours. 'What—is—this?' was the question which vexed them most. Mr. Ibsen, if we are to accept his translator as conveying his impressions of *Rosmersholm* accurately, had an idea that it was a play. More than that, he seems to labour under a definite delusion that it was 'a drama in four acts,' since it is thus described on the programme and in the authorised translation. Well, this is a big mistake. If there is one thing in the world that *Rosmersholm* is not, it is a drama in four acts. True, the curtain rose four times: first, on Madame Helseth and Rebecca talking about laying the table for supper; second, on Rosmer and a paper knife; third, on Madame Helseth and Rebecca discussing why Rosmer should lie in bed so late; and fourth, on Madame Helseth and Rebecca speaking of the bringing down of luggage. True, again, the curtain falls four times: first, on Madame Helseth turning down the household lamp; second, on Rosmer's very pertinent question before alluded to; third, on Madame Helseth and Rebecca speaking of a trunk; and fourth, on Madame Helseth witnessing a suicide—'off'. But there are not four acts, as we understand 'acts' in our Philistine British way, and there is no drama at all to speak of, except for a couple of brief scenes near the finish of the performance. We can see that Mr. Ibsen had a story to tell, which was not wanting in dramatic interest, but that he did not choose to make a drama of it, preferring to place it before the public in the form of 'Personal Reminiscences of Miss Rebecca West.' A little explanation may make it clear what the Norwegian dramatist, as they satirically call Mr. Ibsen, has actually done—as to what he intended or designed to do we 'can think of nothing but that one question, What?'

[outlines the events leading up to Beata's suicide.]

How far has Mr. Ibsen's drama in four acts progressed by this time? An effective story is nearly told, which would supply matter for perhaps three of the four acts, and one feels that the natural culmination of the interest, in the exposure of Rebecca and the breaking-up of the egotisical Radical philanthropist, must be impending. How much has Mr. Ibsen done? He has done nothing. He begins his drama here, a year after Beata's death, and he begins it with an act of pointless conversation about Radicalism, Beata's suicide, and things in general, in which the only lively moment is Rosmer's confession to Rector Kroll, his brother-in-law (a schoolmaster, and a pugnacious Tory), that he has changed his political and religious opinions. Two more of the Ibsen acts are devoted to Mr. Rosmer's mental stomach-aches as he gradually learns, from hints dropped by Kroll and a local Radical journalist, that his dead wife was not insane at all, and towards the close of Act III Rebecca tells Rosmer and Kroll the greater part of the yarn which we have pieced together in the light of her revelations. After this we are not surprised to learn that the flabby Rosmer allows himself to be frightened back to Conservatism and Christianity by Kroll and his friends, but there is a real surprise in the ultimate catastrophe of the play. It occurs when Rebecca confides to Rosmer her guilty passion in the past and her purely platonic admiration in the present, as a prelude to going away. He has had a good deal of the starch taken out of him, and doubts his own capacity to work such a conversion from passion to purity in such a woman. He asks her to give him proof of the reality of her faith in him by drowning herself in the convenient mill-race, and when she consents he joins her in the plunge, and both of them get a ducking. It is not explained whether they drown in the mill-race or come back to change their clothes and have hot rum, but the idea is the same.

46. From an unsigned notice, *Daily Chronicle*

24 February 1891, 5

The same paper also ran an editorial about the play (see No. 47).

Many good and clever people yesterday afternoon derived gratification from the performance, for the first time in England, of Ibsen's drama, *Rosmersholm*. Much of this play is as inexplicable as the latter portion of *A Doll's House* and some of the passages in *Pillars of Society*. To the uninitiated it is doubtless full of contradictions and wanting in the persuasive power by which an ordinary audience going to the theatre unprepared for what they will see can be interested in the motives and actions of the characters. This, however, is not the view taken by those disciples of Ibsen who regard his plays as wondrous revelations of human nature, destined to exercise a remarkable influence, not only over literature, but the men and women of the future. To them the utterances and quaint observations by which the lengthy dialogues are interspersed possess a fund of instruction scarcely to be dreamed of by the uninitiated or obtuse. They see something more in Rosmer than a melancholy being to whom our old friend the Stranger was by comparison quite rollicking, and they do not look upon Rebecca West as a faint reflection of Becky Sharp. Thackeray's type of a shrewd, far-sighted, hypocritical, and utterly unprincipled female of engaging manners might, however, have served as the model for the smooth-spoken and plotting heroine of *Rosmersholm*.

[outlines the plot.]

It should be added that the doctrine of 'Heredity' is inculcated in this work by a reference to the circumstances of Rebecca's birth.

47. Editorial comment, *Daily Chronicle*

24 February 1891, 4

(See also No. 46)

'Mr. Punch's' remark that Ibsen spells failure will have to be revised if we have many more dramatic successes of the character of yesterday's representation of *Rosmersholm* at the Vaudeville Theatre. It would be equally rash to conclude that when such a singularly mordant intelligence as Ibsen's, and such a pitilessly frank criticism of life, has once gained the ear of the play-going and the literary public in a place like London, the taste is likely to disappear. Ibsen has been read and heard under more than one guise; and he is seen to be undeniably interesting. Ibsen's plays, with their new subtle scent of life, may have the odour of the *fleurs de mal,* but they are undeniably taking root in English contemporary thought. We were going to say that if *Rosmersholm*, with its merciless gloom, its pitiless presentment of very beautiful but most unhappy types of human nature, is going down with the English public, it must be prepared to swallow the whole Ibsen-gospel without further ado. But we are not sure that *Rosmersholm* is, in fact, gloomier than the *Doll's House*, or the *Wild Duck*, or *Ghosts*. The new feature to the English student of Ibsen, as he has been at present seen on our stage, is the pathetic beauty of the dialogue. For once Ibsen has seemed to let himself go, and in the impassioned speech of the lost enthusiast and of the woman whose destiny is linked with his we get a new insight into the emotional powers of a writer who appears to dislike nothing more than mere loose sentimentalism. We are not prepared to say that the two closing acts of *Rosmersholm* will compare for pure tragedy—for insight into the abysses of the human soul—with, say, the final scenes in the *Ajax*, with *Lear*, or with *Hamlet*. But it is useless denying the peculiar power and penetration with which they probe the spiritual troubles of modern life, as well as the singularly noble and pure dramatic form in which they are cast. We may loathe Ibsen's conclusions—if we are quite sure we know what they are, for he has the slyness and subtlety of all very great writers—but the time is getting over when we can afford to laugh at his expression of them. The plain truth is that Ibsen writes for the stage as no modern English author knows how to write, or could write if he took fifty years to learn his business.

But what is precisely the root-idea of *Rosmersholm*? On the face of it, it is difficult to say. It might well be the sheer hopelessness of any attempt to live the 'ideal' life—the life of large aspirations and aims for the good of mankind. We may well ask why, if this is not the teaching of his plays, Ibsen should let a singularly fine spirit like that of Rosmer, who has worked out his own spiritual emancipation and is eager to achieve the salvation of others, flicker out into the night with that of the woman who had made him what he was, and to whom he in his turn had given a new outlook in life. It looks as if over the dead bodies of Rosmer and Rebecca Ibsen meant to write a moral of the triumph of the commonplace—of Parson Kroll dancing a solemn jig over the remains of the misguided beings who dared to think for themselves. Such we know is not the case; and it would probably be equally wide of the mark to imagine that Ibsen is anxious to moralise at the expense of the Krolls and the Helmers, and to hold them—the orthodox in life and creed—as the cause of all the social wrong and unhappiness in the modern world. Ibsen is first of all a dramatist who loves to see his men and women in free action rather than to be always crooning a moral in their and our ears. But, secondly, no doubt, with all his instinct for spiritual liberty, for realised democracy, for what has been aptly enough called 'the new spirit,' the Norwegian dramatist has a keen sense of the limitations of idealism in life. Ex-Parson Rosmer, for instance, would make all men happy and emancipated. But, while he saves others, himself he cannot save—old mental habit and tradition are too strong for him. There appears to be more hope, in Ibsen's view, in the 'emancipated woman;' but then, unlike the heroine in *A Doll's House*, Rebecca West is a very mixed character, and she, with her lover, breaks down, Hamlet-like, before the difficulty of the task before her—the too severe contrast between the new moral life which Rosmer has opened out to her and the earlier passionate strivings of the 'will to live.' All this seems to suggest that Ibsen is, after all, anxious to impress on the world the necessity of full and special preparation for any real share in human progress. His scepticism is deep, but it is not his last word. His 'much-deceived Endymions'—his Rosmers, and the like—'slip behind a tomb,' but behind them stands the veiled strong figure of the true deliverer of his kind. Rosmer and Rebecca end their sadly crossed lives in the mill-stream, but we doubt whether Ibsen means that all fine and well-directed human aspiration is meant to end that way.

48. From an unsigned notice, *The Times*

24 February 1891, 10

The literary clamour which has been raised around the name of Ibsen had the effect of crowding the Vaudeville Theatre yesterday afternoon, on which occasion one of the 'master's' dramas, *Rosmersholm*, was played for the first time in this country. It was not altogether an audience of the faithful who thus assembled, for here and there some line of the dia-logue provoked a titter, especially when the author attempted to push his theories of heredity a little too far. But there was unquestionably a keen interest displayed in the new dramatic gospel understood to be preached by the Norwegian dramatist. It was not very easily discover-able, perhaps, by the ordinary Philistine what this gospel was; and if the play held the attention of the house till the end, it is also true to say that a large number of the spectators went away in a state of some perplexity, conscious only of having witnessed the proceedings of a handful of disagreeable and somewhat enigmatical personages, who had been very seriously concerned with so ordinary a matter as a difference of opinion upon political and religious questions. Some of the faithful cheerfully admit that Ibsen is a local or provincial dramatist. There is no difficulty in conceding this point, even to the extent of saying that his sentiments and views are strongly imbued with the parochial spirit. Most assuredly it is difficult to picture such men and women as his breathing the freer air and living the larger life of great cities. They are narrow sectarians, bigoted and Quixotic, as destitute of all sense of humour as they are of the chivalrous virtues. Granted that such raw material of human nature is unduly ignored in the conventional drama, is it not equally false to dwell upon it exclusively, as the author does in *Rosmersholm*?

[the plot described.]

The question of heredity is raised in this play as in others from the same pen, though in what we cannot but regard as an unfortunate fashion. Rector Kroll investigates Rebecca's past, and discovers that her mother was unprincipled enough to have an illegitimate child, where-upon he tells her in so many words, 'Your family antecedents are detestable; the law of heredity explains your whole conduct.' Experts in physiology will be curious to know upon what grounds Ibsen or his followers justify this dictum. Unchastity may *à la rigueur* be held to result from a neuropathic, and, therefore, hereditary condition, but if there is one fact better established in heredity than another it is that the trans-mission from parent to child of physical or moral characteristics is by no means of the simple and direct kind here implied, but is governed by a complex law of variation. The point would not be worth discussing but for the importance attached by his followers to Ibsen's theories of heredity, which, in fact, are of a primitive order, long since discarded by M. Charcot and other masters of this branch of science. In *A Doll's House* the same mistaken view of the neuropathic diathesis is put for-ward, Nora Helmer's lack of moral principle being attributed without any qualification whatever to her father's dishonesty. What is really valuable in Ibsen's work, and in *Rosmersholm* as much as in any of his plays, is his incidental sketches of character, in which no scientific theories are supposed to be exemplified. The self-sufficient Rector Kroll, the bibulous agitator Ullric Brendel, and the unscrupulous Radical editor Peter Mortensgard belong to this category. In the last-named character, indeed, there is a wholesome touch of satire. But this is by no means a speciality of Ibsen's, who is at his best when he is most conventional.

49. From 'An Ibsen Service', unsigned notice, *Daily News*

24 February 1891, 6

With a courage and good faith deserving of all respect, a little company of Ibsen enthusiasts, headed by Mr. F. R. Benson and Miss Florence Farr, gave yesterday afternoon at the Vaudeville a representation of *Rosmersholm*—one of the 'modern dramas' of Ibsen, in which the Norwegian ethical Anarchist has been suspected in some quarters of a subtle design to bring ridicule at once on the extravagancies of the Spencerian Individualists and the comfortless doctrines of the disciples of Schopenhauer. The little theatre, we need hardly say, was filled with the faithful. All prominent Ibsenite men were to be seen among the gathering. There were also of prominent Ibsenite women not a few. Many sat, book in hand, and all were serious and sober-minded. Something, indeed, akin to the 'Wagnerian hush,' of which the musical devotees profess to be conscious when they enter the sacred town of Bayreuth, could be distinctly felt in the atmosphere of the place; but as the play progressed and the enraptured spectators delighting in the copious dialogue and delighting in each other, after the manner of the aesthetically elect, there was a visible increase of animation, and between the acts all the shibboleths could be heard buzzing about from lips to lips. 'Psychological insight'—which appears just now to be playing something like the part that was played by 'sensibility' in the days when Anna Matilda and Helen Maria Williams flourished, and the drama of Kotzebue was a new thing—enjoyed perhaps the most general currency. 'The great life problem' and 'the symbolic side,' however, ran it hard, together with 'ennobled from within,' 'true inwardness,' 'bitterness of baulked individuality,' 'courage to live one's own life,' 'purify the will,' 'emancipate the mind,' 'free will and spirit affinity,' and many others of the same sort. As to the imbecile Pastor Rosmer, who on discovering that his spiritual guide, Rebecca West, had driven his wife to drown herself in the millstream from an obliging desire to clear the way for the union of these twain suggests to Rebecca that she shall depart this life in the same fashion, and when she consents, finally determines to join her in that desperate and

165

foolish enterprise we can only say that without the light that has been vouchsafed to the Ibsen devotees it is very hard to take any interest in his story. If we were to complain that, after the manner of the ancient drama, though in defiance of Horatian maxims, its most dramatic details are not seen in action, but are only *demissa per aurem*, we should, we fear, be set down by the Ibsenites as hopelessly wedded to the ways of the Adelphi drama.

[comments on the acting.]

The best performance perhaps was Mr. Forde's Kroll; but no skill in the actor could impart consistency to the sketch when this incarnation of old-fashioned habits and prejudices suddenly begins to talk in good faith all the new-fangled jargon of the doctrine of heredity. As honest chroniclers, we must not forget to note that a few disbelievers had evidently got into pit and gallery, where feeble outbursts of laughter were heard when Rector Kroll, in a fashion at once indecent and absurd, began to catechise Rebecca regarding her mother's movements before her daughter's birth, as well as at some other points in the play where the sublime had a rather decided tendency to border upon the ludicrous. Pending the advent of a new and true 'Anti-Jacobin' to treat the brain-sick extravagancies of the Norwegian playwright after the manner of Canning's *Rovers*, this irreverent conduct may be regarded as at least reserving the right of protest in what seems the most appropriate fashion. This reminds us that the direction to Ruggero's song—'strikes his forehead several times against his dungeon walls, producing a visible contusion'—bears a rather close resemblance to some of Ibsen's curiously minute stage directions.

50. From an unsigned notice by Clement Scott, *Daily Telegraph*

24 February 1891, 3

Say what we will about Ibsen, he unquestionably possesses a great power of fascination. Those who most detest his theories, his doctrines, his very methods of art, confess to a strange and absorbing interest. There was a curious experiment tried yesterday afternoon. *Rosmersholm* was acted for the first time in England, and acted, on the whole, extremely well, by a young band of players of high intelligence; and, strange as the play was, unconventional and unorthodox as was the dramatic scheme, tedious and prolix as were several scenes, startling and horrifying as were some of the master's views to such as have faith in something beyond the religion of self and the creed of utter despair, still, let it honestly be confessed, there they all sat, open-mouthed, attentive, men and women alike, the believer and the agnostic, listening to one of the strangest plays ever written, and swayed by dialogue, incisive, pure, and at times unquestionably poetic. The very audience itself was a curious study.

Some there were whose hearts cried out in the words of Rosmer of Rosmersholm: 'All that is good in human nature will go to ruin if this is allowed to go on. But it shall not go on! Oh, what a joy—what a joy it would be to me to let a little light into all this gloom and ugliness!' Some there were again, whose ears and senses, confused with all this new jargon of 'emancipated' men and women, chuckled to themselves with Pastor Kroll, as he said,

Ah! I fancy it's much the same with most of what you call your 'emancipation.' You have read yourself into a number of new ideas and opinions. You have got a sort of smattering of recent discoveries in various fields—discoveries that appear to overturn certain principles that have hitherto been held impregnable and unassailable. But all this has been only a matter of the intellect—only knowledge. It has not passed into your blood.

Many there must have been who wondered what an ordinary audience of 'unemancipated' playgoers would have thought of an apostate parson recommending a double suicide to the woman who had been the direct cause of his wife's death with these astounding words, 'There is no judge over us; and therefore we must do justice upon ourselves.' And then, again, there must, even in an intelligent audience like that, have been very many who virtually wrung their hands in despair like the weak, vacillating, perplexed Rosmer, and cried out, 'I do not understand.' The new play, one of the least objectionable, most mystical, and surely the best written in the whole of the Ibsen series, is no easy one to describe. Any doubts that may have existed in the mind after reading the book again and yet again were not wholly removed by witnessing the drama in action. The old theory of playwriting was to make your story or your study as simple and direct as possible. The hitherto accepted plan of a writer for the stage was to leave no possible shadow of doubt concerning his characterisation. But Ibsen loves to mystify. He is as enigmatical as the Sphinx. Those who earnestly desire to do him justice and to understand him keep on saying to themselves, 'Granted all these people are egotists, or atheists, or agnostics, or emancipated, and what not, still I can't understand why he does this or she does that.'

Up to this hour it would surely puzzle the most philosophical Ibsenite to say clearly and decisively why Rebecca West chose such a man as Rosmer for her helpmate and soul-companion, and having got him into her toils and Mrs. Rosmer conveniently at the bottom of the pond in the garden, why she should refuse the marriage which it was her original object to attain.

[the plot described at length.]

In such a grim tragedy as this there is, of course, no chance for any relief of comedy; but ever and anon there comes on the stage an admirably-drawn character—one Ulric Brendel—who acts as the chorus in a Greek play. Mr. Charles Hudson, no doubt, did his best with the fascinating figure, but we must own we should like to have seen it read in a different fashion. In his first scene he was too obviously intoxicated; in his last he was not sufficiently sad in his cynical depression. Ulric Brendel is one of the most interesting figures in the Ibsen fiction, but he has not yet been played.

51. From 'Some Ibsenisms', unsigned comment, *Saturday Review*

28 February 1891, lxxi, 247

The dramatic critic of the *Daily News* has been at an Ibsenite play, and he is so irreverent as to style it 'an Ibsen Service.' The Faithful were there, all of them, and, as they murmured the responses in low devotional tones, this critic heard and recorded them. 'Psychological insight' was one of the catch-words, and he thinks it answers to the old 'sensibility' of Kotzebue. There were also 'ennobled from within', 'true inwardness,' 'bitterness of baulked individuality,' 'free will and spirit affinity,' and so forth. What is this all about? What is there peculiar to Ibsen in 'the bitterness of baulked individuality'? If an Ibsenite was playing his own ball against the best of two others, and if he lifted into a bunker at the hole, then he would know the bitterness of baulked individuality. But we all know it, and every dramatic poet has written on it—only, when Macbeth's ambition is defeated, and when Shylock's little game is up, no critic in his senses talks this particularly childish jargon on the subject. Why do Ibsenites talk it? Every dramatic writer worth his salt has 'psychological insight', only nobody thinks it necessary to tell him and the world that it is so. Sophocles had psychological insight; so had Molière, so had Dumas; but they were born before this chatter was invented, before the *engouement* of a narrow, ignorant, and pedantic culture. Ibsen has his qualities; nobody is denying them; what we are denying is the value of these solemn and sickly comments, which are precisely as critical as the comments of Madelon and Cathos on the madrigals of Mascarille. 'Culture,' at present, seems to be excessively short-sighted, to see nothing but the idol of the moment, to know nothing or remember nothing of poets compared to whom Ibsen is as a rushlight to the sun, to have no sympathy with humourists, because Ibsen is absolutely devoid of humour. There is not a pennyweight of it in all the tons of quartz of his translated plays, with the possible exception of *The Wild Duck*, where he seems to indulge a little in the salutary pastime of laughing at himself. Will nobody write a comedy of *The Ibsenites*, a modern variety, as has been suggested more than once, of

169

The Rovers, where Nora and Hedda Gabler may swear eternal friend-ship, and half of the characters discuss their hereditary gout, and every-body 'die beautifully,' taking great pains not to shoot themselves where the chunk of old red sandstone hit? Diversified by ballets, it would be a gay performance, and so, we presume, we shall never see Nora dancing with the pink stockings, and Hedda practising with her celebrated pistols, and all the wrong people drinking too much milk-punch. Probably there *was* lemon in that milk-punch, and lemon always dis-agreed with Mr. Lövborg. There is, we venture to think, some fun to be got out of *The Ibsenites*, who are at least as absurd as the old Sun-flower people.

52. From 'Theatrical Gossip', an unsigned regular column, *Era*

28 February 1891, 10

There is little use in arguing about a question of taste with the Ibsenites. The followers of 'the master' who would invite ladies to a reading of *Ghosts* and a discussion thereon would stick at nothing, we presume, and, if they have more hastiness to air, may snap their fingers at all authority and at those who protest in the name of decency. But there is still an Examiner of Plays, and we fancy he must have been caught nap-ping when he allowed to pass all that appears in the last act of Ibsen's *Rosmersholm*, which was presented at the Vaudeville on Monday last to a mixed assembly, that included a good many of Mr Gilbert's 'young ladies of fifteen.' If an Examiner of Plays is to examine anything, he should certainly examine this, and inquire, as Claudius did, concerning Hamlet's play, if there is any offence in it. Rebecca West and Johannes Rosmer have the scene to themselves, and this is the conversation. Rebecca—'It came over me—this wild, uncontrollable desire—oh, Rosmer!' Rosmer—'Desire? You! For what?' Rebecca—'For you.' Rosmer—'What is this?' Rebecca—'Sit still, dear; there is more to tell.'

Rosmer—'And you mean to say that you love me—in that way?' Rebecca—'I thought then that it should be called love. Yes, I thought it was love. But it was not. It was what I said. It was a wild, uncontrollable desire.' After this Mr M'Dougall may leave the comic singers alone, and turn his attention to Ibsen and his English worshippers.

53. From a pseudonymous notice by 'Momus', *Gentlewoman*

28 February 1891, 302

Let this anecdote be a testimony. It was my fate and good fortune to sit next a dramatic author and a leading actress of renown at this memorable *matinée*. I was also circled by journalistic friends. Immediately in front of us—it was in the dress circle—sat a group of openly professed Ibsenites, Socialists, and Agnostics. The group in question chattered at intervals. So did our group. Their chatter was audible and reverent. Ours was—as it turned out—also audible, but not always reverent. The Goddess of Discord descended on us, and indignant rebukes were flashed at those who could not but laugh at certain unintentionally humorous comicalities. 'There are people here who have never read the play!' 'Hush!' and so on, were fired off whenever a laugh rose, or a word said in whisper by those who sat behind the very audible praisers, Finally it came to this, that when a lady laughed at a certainly very difficult, if not dangerous, passage, another lady well, and in a sense favourably, known for her fearlessly advanced views on social and theological questions, exclaimed, 'There are some people who would laugh at the Crucifixion!' The 'retort courteous' came swiftly, 'There are some people who chatter in theatres.' Then there ensued a truce of silence, but when the curtain fell, the lady who had used the Biblical metaphor said proudly, and with evident intention, to a gentleman, 'How can you expect a work of art to succeed before such people?' It was a painful, ill-bred exhibition, of course, and I only record it to show you how

171

high party spirits runs in professional Ibsenite circles; for no discourtesy towards the play, the grim old playwright, or his proselytes, was intended by those whose excitement took a form other than that of abject adoration.

54. From an unsigned notice, *Black and White*

28 February 1891, 126

Rosmersholm has been played in London. The event marks an epoch in our modern drama, and the date, the afternoon of Monday, the 23rd of February, 1891, deserves to live in men's memories as long as that famous day which delighted the Romanticists, the day of *Hernani*. The one event is as momentous as the other. If Hugo's hot Castilian play marked most significantly the approaching triumph of a dramatic movement, Ibsen's great play proves that a new force has been brought to bear upon us, and is already exerting a very remarkable influence. The reception accorded to *Rosmersholm* on Monday afternoon, the seriousness with which the play has been considered by all critics of moment, even those who are most opposed to what is called Ibsenism, show what a hold Ibsen has already got upon the public mind. The great Norwegian dramatist has fairly taken his place among us, and we may look forward with confidence now to seeing play after play of his, from the *Wild Duck* to *Hedda Gabler*, and from *The League of Youth* to *The Lady from the Sea*, played by English actors upon a London stage. But no subsequent performance can ever be quite as interesting as was this first performance of *Rosmersholm*. The advance of what its enthusiasts call the Ibsen cause will date from it even more than from the marvellous performance of *The Doll's House* at the Novelty Theatre two years ago.

We should be inclined to say without hesitation that *Rosmersholm* was a great success. Here and there at intervals a laugh or two broke the gravity with which the audience received the strangest play that has perhaps ever been seen upon a London stage. But for the most part the most honest attention was given to the tragic story, with all its clashing theories, its merciless satire, its grim doctrines of heredity. The play is profoundly gloomy; an atmosphere of doom is about it from first to last. . . .

Many of Ibsen's plays are duels of the flesh as well as struggles of the spirit, and *Rosmersholm* shows such a duel. The motive is a foreshadowing of the motive of *Hedda Gabler*, a motive showing the fatal influence upon a passionate nature of a passionless companionship. The pedantic indifference of George Tesman is as fatal to Hedda as the almost saintly austerity of Rosmer is to Rebecca. The end of each is self-slaughter.

The intense interest which *Rosmersholm* awakened in admirers of Ibsen on Monday, the interest too which it aroused even in some of those who have shown themselves to be Ibsen's strongest antagonists, was undoubtedly due more to the play itself than to the acting. It was on the whole well acted—but it was not acted well enough. Much must be allowed for the inevitable nervousness of a first performance, a nervousness intensified naturally tenfold by the fact that the play produced was one so foreign to all the traditions of our stage, and that it was produced in the presence of an audience, many of whom were avowedly hostile, and some of whom, as a witty dramatist said, a dramatist who himself owes much to the Ibsen method, 'came to pray, and remained to scoff.'

55. Unsigned notice, *Sunday Times*

1 March 1891, 7

Ibsen is the Whistler of the drama—with a difference. Like Mr. Whistler he has provided puzzles and shocks for the multitude, because his artistic aims have been too 'new and original,' and he has been laughed at and scoffed at and abused for his pains. And they talk now of all that seems outside the traditional dramatic scheme as 'Ibsenism,' just as they call 'Whistlerism' all that which is not explained by the conventional 'canons of criticism,' and which makes for new pictorial effects. Yet Ibsen's influence on the vital dramatic art of to-day, like Whistler's on the art of painting, is insidiously potent and active, however much we may find ourselves at issue with him in respect to the selection of his subject matter, and the exposition of his ideals of life. Like the pictures of Whistler, Ibsen's plays may be 'caviare to the general,' but they, at any rate, present new points of view, and though often too obviously didactic (wherein comes the flaw in our analogy between the play-wright and the painter), they pursue a definite ideal of beauty and truth of their own, however recondite this may appear to the ordinary play-goer. No matter how unprepossessing or even ugly their parts may be, if taken separately, or how apparently incomprehensible, there is cer-tainly a unity of idea which is impressive. And if one regards Ibsen, like Mr. Whistler, as an idealist and impressionist—in the true artistic sense of the term—which he really is, and not as a 'realist,' which he is com-monly called, but certainly is not, for all his apparent delight in dissect-ing the morbidities of life, there will be found a poetry in his point of view, which transcends the ordinary experience of human nature.

It is only with this understanding that one can hope to appreciate the dramatist's ideas, and to reconcile those actual inconsistencies and moral monstrosities and improbabilities with which Ibsen's plays abound, such, for instance, as Nora unnaturally abandoning her child-ren, in *The Doll's House*, or Rebecca West, in *Rosmersholm*, unexpectedly refusing to marry Rosmer, after all her treacherous efforts to win him, and again, these two incontinently committing suicide when matrimony should, according to ordinary usage, stare them in the face. But it is not according to the logic of actual life that Ibsen's creations act; rather is it in accordance with an ideal that draws them as a magnet towards an end that may be imagined, but would scarcely occur in real life. But this is always a licence of the dramatist and poet. It is not the ordinary that makes interesting romance, but the unusual and the unexpected. *Rosmers-holm* is the play to reveal Ibsen in all his idealism, however its effects may jar upon our individual taste and senses. Therefore, in our opinion, the production of this extraordinary and absorbing, and, if you will, per-plexing tragedy at the Vaudeville on Monday afternoon was an event of far greater moment than the performances of *A Doll's House* or *The Pillars of Society*, for in *Rosmersholm* Ibsen the poet is manifest, and mystifying as some of the episodes may be, the poetry of this play ex-plains Ibsen the dramatist.

Yet, after all, what is there so mystifying about *Rosmersholm*? The

story is set in an atmosphere of supernatural suggestion, with the dark
wings of Fate hovering above, therefore, an element of mystery is
inevitable. But how does the human action appear incomprehensible in
relation to the ideal of the play, which is surely the ennobling of a
human soul through love, and the expiation of sin. A woman, lacking
in every moral sense, has, to satisfy her own ambitions and passion, with
inconceivable treachery marvellously masked, separated an ill-matched
married couple, and driven the poor wife to suicide. Then, when everything for which she has striven is within her grasp, she finds that contact with a pure man's soul has ennobled her own, and the love that has
taken the place of passion will not allow her to soil his innocence and
disturb his dreams. Conscience is twin-born with her love, and forbids
her to enjoy the spoils of her sin. It may be unusual in real life for an
adventuress to refuse marriage at the hands of the man she loves and has
schemed for; but is Rebecca West's refusal so mysterious and impossible
by the light of this ideal of love's purifying power? It may be transcendental, but if there were nothing but human nature in life, how very
commonplace it would be.

Again, with regard to the lovers' suicide. These two—the man of
broken faith and shattered ideals, the woman of vanquished vice—
could never have been happy, though married, for the shadow of the
dead wife must have always haunted him, and she would have been a
perpetual argument of reproach. Again they might have lived on and
gone their several ways to penitence, but then Rosmer would never
have felt sure that Rebecca, with her propensities, was not carrying on
with some other man. So that suicide after all was necessary if they were
ever to believe in one another again. The test might, however, have been
more pleasantly applied than through the damp definiteness of drowning. For instance, they might have taken an underdose of laudanum or
chloroform, and so enjoyed all the satisfaction of suicide without its
depressing finality. But after all, perhaps, Ibsen is right, and there is a
deeper poetry in the deadly dual dive into the millstream, whither the
hapless wife had preceded them, than in any more lively solution of the
difficulty. The story is a tragedy, not a melodrama, and so should it end
tragically. Fate has broken the lives of these three beings, and they must
all go the same way, the sinned against and the sinner. Kismet. We may
not be satisfied; we may not even have on our visiting list many persons
who would actually have behaved like this, but Ibsen, the poet and the
mystic, has worked out his ideal of sin's purification and expiation
through love and death in this way, and matter-of-fact can have no say

in the matter. In like manner he has chosen to take the unconventional artistic way of keeping secrets from his audience, just as, to return to our Whistlerian analogy, the painter only shows those details which, in his opinion, belong to the picture, omitting those which pictorial convention would include, but which he considers would be intrusive in his pictorial scheme. The question here is, how is the artistic effect of the play affected by the keeping back of certain facts until they are naturally elicited by the progress of the story? And that question must be answered by the impression conveyed to the individual temperament of the spectator. For ourselves, though we find the matter and the manner of the play weirdly morbid, we cannot share the apparently general perplexity, for the light of the author's transcendentalism illumines all the dark places. *Rosmersholm* is not a play to love and be glad with, but it is intensely interesting. Moreover, it is the key to the Ibsen puzzle. It shines with the light of the midnight sun. Let us, however, be thankful that we have still our Pineros and Joneses, our Gilberts and Grundys, to give us the brighter, happier sunshine of the day.

Rosmersholm, for its adequate interpretation, needs acting of a very high and rare order—intellectual, spiritual, and magnetic; and although the performance at the Vaudeville the other afternoon was earnest, intelligent, and creditable, it could not be said to supply all these requisites. Miss Florence Farr's Rebecca West was a most praiseworthy effort under the circumstances—well-meant and well-considered, but not a vital revelation. Mr. Benson, with all his earnestness, only succeeded in playing the transcendental Rosmer like a curate with the cholera; while Mr. Hudson, with melodramatic memories, failed to realise the grim ironic pathos of Ulric Brendel, one of the finest conceptions in modern drama. Mr. Athol Ford was successful as Kroll, the provincial prosaic, dreary schoolmaster, and Mr. Wheatman as Mortensgard, the Radical editor, and Miss Protheroe as Helseth, the superstitious old servant, were both serviceable. How much more impressive, however, would the final episode have seemed had an actress of imagination and magnetism described the tragic catastrophe. Then this might have held the audience spellbound, instead of sending the majority out of the theatre smiling or sneering. Indeed, one distinguished dramatist said that he had come to pray and had remained to scoff—which is easier. Who will read Ibsen for us by flashes of lightning?

56. From 'Flashes from the Footlights', an unsigned regular theatre column, *Licensed Victuallers' Mirror*

3 March 1891, 106

The Ibsenites had a field day last week at the Vaudeville, when *Rosmersholm* was given for the first time in England.

Shades of Anacharsis Cloots, the friend of Humanity, of Jean Paul Marat, of Tom Paine, and others of that ilk, how you will bow down before 'the master' when he visits you in Hades!

I wonder what an English audience would have thought of an *English* play the first two acts of which does not contain one single incident or situation, and is entirely occupied by a political and religious discussion between a Socialist-Atheist and a Conservative?

It is the topsy-turveydom of W. S. Gilbert, only the author of *Pinafore* is in fun; the author of *Rosmersholm* is in earnest.

A drunken reprobate, who has been expelled from his college for immorality, who has just come out of a house of correction, who sells the clothes and squanders the money a friend has just given him, behaves like a pothouse cad in his drawing-room, and insults his guest, is spoken of by the heroine as a man who has the courage to live his life in his own way, 'and that is something.'

So has the thief and the prostitute, but I never knew before that it was a merit in them to do so.

The man who has cast off all moral and social obligations, human and divine, is said to have 'emancipated' himself. Thus, according to the gospel of Ibsen, the criminal and evil liver are to be our future ideals.

A clergyman who has 'emancipated' himself exclaims, pointing upwards, 'As there is no justice there we must judge ourselves,' or words to that effect; I quote from memory. . . .

After 'emancipation', which is to make all the world joyous and happy, particularly pickpockets and ladies of loose habits, the moral of it all is—heredity. What the parent is the child must be, and, if the father or mother commit a murder, it is unjust to blame his or her offspring for doing the same; you should leave their doom to the fatal Nemesis which pursues them.

To descant upon such morbid impracticable rubbish as this would be an insult to the understanding of every reader—except an Ibsenite.

57. From 'Ibsen Up to Date', by Justin Huntley McCarthy, *Hawk*

3 March 1891, 237

Justin McCarthy (1830–1912), Irish politician and novelist, was chairman of the anti-Parnellite nationalist party from 1890 to 1896.

Rosmersholm is to my thinking a very great play. It is certainly one of the most remarkable plays that has ever been placed upon the London stage.

It is not a pleasant play, of course, but, after all, is it quite certain that the first business of a play is to be pleasant? *Hamlet* is not a pleasant play, by any means, yet it has held its own fairly well. At least, *Rosmersholm* is obedient to a new law; it does offer us events not conceived in the ordinary method of melodrama, it gives us people who are not cast in the conventional mould of drawing-room comedy. . . .

To me it seems perfectly clear that the weak, passionless Rosmer, the unhappy last-born of a house where the children never cry and the men never laugh, a house that is haunted like some old Scottish castle, is a man 'all unstrung.' To me it is clear that this Rosmer has at the end his mind, never of the strongest, quite unhinged by the sudden knowledge first of the atmosphere of terrible treachery in which he has lived, and next by the sudden revelation to his passionless nature of the fierce passion which Rebecca West had felt for him. In this aberration of the over-wrought, over-heated brain his mad proposal of purification by suicide seems natural enough. The man is almost crazed, the woman's

nature is strained to an almost unbearable tension by suppressed passion
and cheated desire; it is really logical enough that in their terrible excitement the pair over whose manhood and womanhood the blight of
the 'Rosmer View of Life' has fallen should fling their ruined lives away
together in the stream which had engulfed their victim. The sacrifice is
none the less logical because it is so futile. Indeed 'futility' seems to be
the keynote of the whole play. It is the Words of the Preacher over
again, steeped in a Scandinavian sadness instead of an Oriental Pessimism.

58. An unsigned notice, *Truth*, probably by Clement Scott

5 March 1891, 488–9

The newspapers, it seems to me, are just now doing for Ibsenism exactly
what the comic and pictorial papers did, some years ago, for æstheticism.
ism. They are steadily advertising it into undeserved importance. The
lily became a crest, the sunflower a rallying-cry, and Oscar Wilde a
prophet, merely through the misguided efforts of his journalistic friends.
It would all have died out a natural death, had it been consistently
snubbed instead of persistently puffed. And now that æstheticism is
played out, behold! we have another craze on hand. An obscure
Scandinavian dramatist and poet, a crazy fanatic, and determined socialist, is to be trumpeted into fame for the sake of the estimable gentlemen
who can translate his works, and the enterprising tradesmen who publish them. The whole thing is most amusing to those who are behind
the scenes, and the artful aid of the *réclame* is exercised with an ingenuity
worthy of the Gallic race. Meetings are held under the open pretence of
advocating the study of Ibsen, but in reality for the propagation of the
gospel of Socialism. It is inconvenient to propound the new doctrine
in the cold and foggy park or at a street corner, so the debate is transferred to a literary *séance*. The unwomanly women, the unsexed females,
and the whole army of unprepossessing cranks in petticoats who have
no opportunities just now to discuss the Contagious Diseases Act in

drawing-rooms, sit open-mouthed and without a blush on their faces whilst a Socialist orator reads aloud *Ghosts*, the most loathsome of all Ibsen's plays, that illustrates freely enough the baneful result of the abolition of the Contagious Diseases Act in Norway. The craze is here; the cranks are ready. The competition just now is for the post of the Oscar Wilde of Ibsenism. Several candidates are in the field. William Archer was first there, with his translation in his hand and his publisher at his back. But his position for prophet, priest, and king is stoutly contested by one Gosse, with more translations in his pocket, and still another enterprising publisher to support his candidature. Failing these two, a third claimant comes up in Dr. Aveling, who is conscientiously desirous of pressing the claims of Socialism, and has, moreover, a wife who also translates Ibsen and publishes his plays. And so we go on to the modern Macaronis led by young Justin Huntly McCarthy, and to other distinguished members of Edmund's staff, who seriously think that Ibsen is the Wagner of dramatic art.

If you have seen one play by Ibsen, you have seen them all. A disagreeable and nasty woman; an egotistical and preachy man; a philosophical sensualist; dull and undramatic dialogue. Already three of Ibsen's plays have been performed in London, but not one of them has as yet been submitted to a candid and unbiassed audience. They have been produced before packed houses, and played by intelligent amateurs. The few independent persons who have sat out a play by Ibsen, be it *The Doll's House* or the *Pillars of Society*, or *Rosmersholm*, have said to themselves, Put this stuff before the playgoing public, risk it at an evening theatre, remove your claque, exhaust your attendance of the socialistic and the sexless, and then see where your Ibsen will be. I have never known an audience yet that cared to pay to be bored, and the over-vaunted *Rosmersholm* bored even the Ibsenites. They turned round on the 'Master', and took exception to his best literary work. It is the old dodge. If *A Doll's House* fails, it is, 'Ah! but you should see the *Pillars of Society*;' if the *Pillars* totter, it is, 'Wait till you see *Rosmersholm*.' If the drama of suicide makes people laugh, it is, 'On the whole, I prefer *Hedda Gabler*,' and so on until the end of the chapter. The test of Ibsen's success as a dramatist for the people can only be arrived at when Ibsen is played to the people. That test has not yet been given. I am aware that one of the oldest and most conscientious Ibsenite prophets maintains that this very test was given in the case of the first production of *A Doll's House* at the Novelty. It is naïvely argued that the play would have run on, like the brook, for ever, if only it had not been necessary for Miss

Janet Achurch to go to Australia. But I have known before now Aust-ralian engagements to have been cancelled or postponed on account of declared London successes, and I must own that I should like to see the balance-sheet, after the declared success of the Novelty production. In fact, the financial success of Ibsen in London is admitted in the most curious fashion. It is proposed to transfer him and all his works to an 'independent theatre,' which is to be free of vulgar public support, and to be maintained by the contributions of the faithful!

59. From 'Between the Acts', an unsigned regular theatre column, *Queen*

7 March 1891, 386

The experiment made at the Vaudeville on Monday morning of last week by a band of young actors, who produced Ibsen's *Rosmersholm*, was fully justified by the result. This weird and gloomy play was new to the crowded audience assembled to learn more of the Scandinavian dramatist's methods, and to prove whether Miss Florence Farr, a com-paratively unknown actress, was equal to the great and difficult task she had set herself. By this time the story of this extraordinary drama has been made tolerably familiar, but only those who sat through its four unconventional and frequently prolix acts can at all realise the power and fascination of the mystical story unfolded. To understand *Rosmers-holm* is perhaps beyond even the closest student of Ibsen. There are passages in it which suggest that the great Norwegian writer is bur-lesquing himself; the motive of Rebecca West in refusing to marry the man she has sold her soul to capture in her toils is quite incomprehen-sible, and when the curtain falls on the spiritual marriage and suicide of the conscienceless Rebecca and the fate-haunted Rosmer, the spectator disparagingly cries out, like the 'emancipated' pastor, 'I do not under-stand.' Yet withal the play held the house enthralled last Monday week, and we venture to believe that many visited it a second time when the performance was repeated last Thursday.

GHOSTS

(Royalty Theatre, 13 March 1891)

60. George Moore sees *Ghosts* in Paris

From George Moore's 'Note on *Ghosts*', in his *Impressions and Opinions* (London: David Nutt, 1891), pp. 215–26. This piece marked Moore's entrance on Ibsen's side in the growing controversy.

But to return to the Théâtre Libre and Ibsen. I had read *Nora* and *Ghosts*. The first play seemed to me, in the reading, hard, dry, mechanical, and illogical. I could discover in *Nora* neither philosophy nor character-drawing. In the representation, the woodenness of Nora and Helmer came upon me with redoubled force; there were times when I felt as if I were being beaten with a mallet. Candidly, I could make nothing of it—nothing, nothing, nothing. Shortly after reading *Nora* some friends of mine begged me to come to a reading of *Ghosts*. I went, and before half the first act had been read nothing but the play existed for me. The remorseless web that life had spun, and the poor boy entangled in it, I watched, even as a child watches the fly that chance had thrown into the spider's web. I saw life represented as blind, senseless, insatiate. We had done with free will, and nature was shown working out her own ends, deaf to our appeal. The sins of the fathers shall descend upon the children even to the third and fourth generation. The Hebrew writer might have said to the hundredth, ay, and the thousandth, and what makes the play so unutterably terrible, what makes it so shocking, that is to say so human, is the intense consciousness of the boy. He knows that the sins of his father have descended upon him, and that there is no redemption. Scenes between mother and son, be what they may, scenes of forgiveness, of expostulation, of counsel, of love, are to me the most strangely pathetic that life can afford. There is something strange, mysterious, something not quite expressible in words in such confidences, and in such confidences the root of the play of *Ghosts* is set. The play abounds in these confidences, from the first act, when the boy tells the mother what the French doctor told him regarding the sinister pains he experiences in his neck, to the last, when, knowing that idiocy is nigh upon him, he begs of his mother to save him with poison from his fate.

Never in these modern years has such a scene been written as that one, nor have I ever felt so divine a horror as I did when the mother, declaring that she cannot do what is asked of her, breaks into the natural cry: 'I, who gave you life!' The son answers: 'A nice kind of life it was that you gave me.' Then the mother, overcome, rushes from the room. She is followed tumultuously by the son, and the stage is left empty—empty and not empty—for its emptiness is the symbol of the horror that we feel, the blank stage becomes at once the symbol of the blank insolvable problem which is life. And when mother and son return—their exit was no more than a brief venting of their anguish in animal movement— and continue the scene, the terror moving among the spectators becomes suddenly unbearable, and each one and every one is ready to rise to his feet and cry to them on the stage, 'Say, oh, say, that it is not true.' Many, indeed, are the great scenes that might be selected from English or French literature as perfect examples of wild passion and solemn awe, but I know of none in which the truth, the truth from which we may not escape, assails us so determinedly and conquers us so triumphantly as here.

The play acted even more grandly than it read. Céard, with whom I discussed the question, whether plays acted as they read, while waiting for the rehearsal of *Ghosts* to begin, said, that he did not think it would act as well as *Nora*. *Ghosts* had seemed to him vague and undetermined in the reading, but when the third act was over (the rehearsal was called only for the third act) I heard his voice in the tumult of praise congratulating Antoine. He confessed that he had misjudged the play; the dimness and vagueness that he feared in the reading had in the representation been changed into firmest outline.

Antoine was superb in the part of Osvalt. The nervous irritation of the sick man was faultlessly rendered. When he tells his mother of the warnings of the French doctor, at the moment when he loses his temper at her interruptions—she seeks not to hear the fearful tale—Antoine, identifying himself with the simple truth sought by Ibsen, by voice and gesture, casts upon the scene so terrible a light, so strange an air of truth, that the drama seemed to be passing not before our eyes, but deep down in our hearts in a way we had never felt before. 'Listen to me, mother.

I insist upon your listening to me,' he says, querulous already with incipient disease. And when comes the end of the first act, when the
mother, hearing the servant-girl cry out, goes to the door, and seeing
the son kissing the girl, cries, 'Ghosts, ghosts!' what shall I say, what
praise shall we bestow upon a situation so supremely awful, so shockingly true?

Owing to many new disputes, or violent continuations of former disputes, concerning cloaks and umbrellas, and seats which had been taken
possession of during temporary absences, or *strapontins* which should
exist, but did not exist or could not be found, I heard even less of the
second act than I had done the first; the entire discourse of the workman
with the wooden leg was lost to me. During the third act there was less
wrangling, and I heard nearly all. And in that half-hour I lived through
a year's emotion. It was terrible when Osvalt came in smoking, and,
puffing at his pipe, and with an air of familiar contentment, he tells his
mother how much he likes the maid-servant, and how he always wishes
her to be near him. The maid-servant is there. He calls to her, and the
distracted mother is forced to reveal the secret—the maid-servant is his
half-sister. And the scene is simple in its dire and doleful humanity.
Even the servant-girl recognises that the fatal taint inherited from their
common father has descended on her. She upbraids Mrs. Alving (Osvalt's mother) for having brought her up as a servant, and tossing her
head, and looking bitterly at the champagne, she says: 'mais cela ne
m'empêchera pas de boire du champagne avec les gens comme il faut.'
Mrs. Alving asks her where she is going, and she answers significantly
that she knows of a house where she will be welcome. *Mrs. Alving*:
'Regina, you are going to your ruin.' *Regina*: 'Oh, stuff!' (She goes out
pushing violently through the swing doors.) Then comes the awful, the
drastic, the overwhelming scene of the play, and most assuredly nothing
finer was ever written by man or god. Its blank simplicity strikes upon
the brain, until the brain reels, even as poor Osvalt's brain is reeling.

In the last moments of his sanity, before darkness comes upon him,
he calls his mother to him, and mother and son sit side by side talking.
Talking of what? Of the father whom he never knew, but who has
nevertheless laid upon him the irreparable fate of idiocy, idiocy that
even at that moment is creeping upon him, and will overtake him as
night overtakes the day. The mother calls upon him to cherish his
father's memory, and the boy answers not in tragic phrases, but in the

words so simple and so true, that listening, the heart turns to ice. And all the while they talk the dreaded malady is creeping upon him. Night is closing, and in the last moments of the twilight of the brain Osvalt shows his mother the poison, and tells her that he will not live helpless as a little child that must be dressed and fed. It is true she will always look after him. But she may die before him, he may fall into the hands of strangers. The doctors have told him he may live for years. The mother answers: 'I, who gave you life!' 'A nice kind of life it was that you gave me, and now you shall have it back again.' Startled by some incoherency in his speech, she calls in terror to him. The scream rescues him for a moment out of the night that is deepening in his brain, that is approaching blackness, and for a few moments more he speaks reasonably.

The sun has risen, the world is bright with the dawn. Mrs. Alving draws the curtains, letting the sunlight into the room. But Osvalt still sits with his back to the light, now mumbling in toneless voice, 'The sun, the sun.' Mrs. Alving stares at him in speechless terror, her hands twisted in her hair, and he still mumbles, 'The sun, the sun.'

The tragedy of fate Ibsen has taken out of the empyrean of Olympus and hexameters, substituting the empyrean of science, and in the simple language of a plain Norwegian household, we learn that though there be no gods to govern us, that nature, vast and unknown, for ever dumb to our appeal, holds us in thrall.

Out of the story the characters evolve themselves sufficiently; they are not forced into any sharp visibleness; we are merely in the presence of a mother and son; it is the idea that Ibsen seeks to express, and not special types from which the idea may be deduced; the art of Ibsen is rather that of Sophocles than that of Balzac (the exact opposite to what is generally understood, but that, of course); the mother and son could not be defined more sharply without loss to the play. But what shall be said of the parson? Who is there, I ask, who could utter one word in praise or even in mild defence of this dreary old bore, who spoils so far as it is possible the first and second acts with such intolerable sermonising as would empty the church of any nonconformist minister? I make no exception either in favour of Mr. Ibsen or Mr. Archer; neither could find a reasonable word to say in defence of his parson. Considered as *the* parson, he is an effigy, wooden in Ibsen's most wooden manner; but what is wanted is not *the* parson, but *a* parson, hard and cold if you will, but with a vein of geniality in him, not much—any too loud a note would jar the harmony of the picture. Ibsen was big enough a man to know that what was wanted was not an Abbé Constantine, 'the practical dramatist' would have rushed an Abbé Constantine into the play, sure of finding in him 'sympathetic relief'; the humanisation of the stern figure that the play demanded was not an easy task, but it was just such a one as the highest genius would have asserted itself in.

On hearing the play read, I foresaw the boredom of the parson, and my judgement was verified in the representation: the actor could do nothing with the character. Mlle Barny was excellent as the mother, and the other parts (there are only five characters in the play) were sufficiently well filled. Paris artistic and literary was in the stalls and boxes, and since the memorable night when Tolstoi's *Puissance des Ténèbres* was given, the Théâtre Libre has won a triumph either so deep or so pronounced. An evening at the Théâtre Libre is now looked forward to with the keenest interest, and instead of there being too few subscribers, Antoine is now obliged to refuse subscriptions until he can get a larger theatre. Why have we not a Théâtre Libre? Surely there should be no difficulty in finding a thousand persons interested in art and letters willing to subscribe five pounds a year for twelve representations of twelve interesting plays. I think such a number of enthusiasts exist in London. The innumerable articles which appear in the daily, the weekly, and monthly press on the London stage prove the existence of much vague discontent, and that this discontent will take definite shape sooner or later seems more than possible.

61. From an unsigned notice by Clement Scott, *Daily Telegraph*

14 March 1891, 3

The same paper also carried an editorial about the play (see No. 62). This performance constituted the first venture of J. T. Grein's Independent Theatre. The translation was by William Archer and the cast was as follows:

Mrs Alving	.. Mrs T. Wright	Jacob Engstrand	.. Mr Sydney Howard
Oswald Alving	Mr Frank Lindo	Regina ..	.. Miss Edith Kenward
Pastor Manders	Mr Leonard Outram		

Ghosts has been talked about; *Ghosts* has been advertised; *Ghosts* has been trumpeted into unnecessary and spurious notoriety; and at last *Ghosts* has been acted. The 'Independent Theatre,' as it is called, though it depends for its existence on the guineas of the faithful and the charitable mercy of the Lord Chamberlain, has been duly inaugurated by a special performance. The Ibsenites have attended in full force, full of enthusiasm, full of fervour, and tyrannical enough to cough or hush down any one prepared to laugh at the dramatic impotence and ludicrous amateurishness of the 'master.' It was a great night. Here were gathered together the faithful and the sceptical; the cynical and the curious. The audience was mainly composed of the rougher sex, who were supposed to know something of the theme that had been selected for dramatic illustration, and were entitled to discuss the licentiousness of Chamberlain Alving, his curious adventure in the dining-room with the attractive parlour-maid, and the echo of his amorous enterprise as repeated in his 'worm-eaten' son. But, strange to say, women were present in goodly numbers; women of education, women of refinement, no doubt women of curiosity, who will take away to afternoon teas and social gatherings, the news of the sensation play that deals with subjects that hitherto have been to most men horrible and to all pure women loathsome. Possibly, nay probably, they were all disappointed. They expected to find something indescribably shocking, and only met that which was deplorably dull. There was very little to offend the ear directly. On the Ibsen stage their nastiness is inferential, not actual. They call a spade a spade in a roundabout and circumlocutory fashion. Those who, actuated by curiosity, expected to find a frankness and direct exposition of fact only equalled by the sensation trials by judge and jury at the Cider Cellars in the days of Baron Nicholson, only found a dull, undramatic, verbose, tedious, and utterly uninteresting play. . . .

It is a wretched, deplorable, loathsome history, as all must admit. It might have been a tragedy had it been treated by a man of genius. Handled by an egotist and a bungler, it is only a deplorably dull play. There are ideas in *Ghosts* that would have inspired a tragic poet. They are vulgarised and debased by the suburban Ibsen. You want a Shakespeare, or a Byron, or a Browning to attack the subject-matter of *Ghosts* as it ought to be attacked. It might be a noble theme. Here it is a nasty and a vulgar one.

But out of all this mass of vulgarity, egotism, coarseness and absurdity we can at least select one character, if not for our sympathy, at least for our pity. Mrs. Alving stands out from the rest because she is human. This is the one conventional character in the play. We are attracted to her because she is not an egotist, because she is not always whining about herself, because she suffers nobly in silence and with dignity. Ibsen makes an attempt to convert Mrs. Alving to Ibsenism, but he soon gives it up. There is a wild idea of making her a mouthpiece of free-thinking, but the master thinks better of it. The others preach; Mrs. Alving acts. . . . It was Mrs. Alving, and Mrs. Alving alone, who held the audience last night, because she was a bit of human nature, and not a monstrosity.

There was a time when brilliant French dramatists such as Dumas and Augier were considered too argumentative and blamed as being talky-talky. But, ye gods! only hear Ibsen talk. He never leaves off. It is one incessant stream of talk, and not very good talk either. Suddenly he discovers that he must bring the down curtain, which he does on some ludicrous anti-climax, as with the silly remark, 'And uninsured, too!' that closes the second act. But, for the most part, it is all dull, undramatic, uninteresting verbosity—formless, objectless, pointless. It is an essay on heredity and contagious disease, and probable incest, cut into lengths—not a play at all. Acting of a very remarkable character alone saved it from speedy condemnation, which, even as matters stood, it would have received at the hands of an 'independent' audience.

62. Editorial comment, *Daily Telegraph*

14 March 1891, 5

(See also No. 61.)

Dramatic art never, in our deliberate judgement, had enemies more deadly than those who have recently clubbed together to bolster up the reputation of the Norwegian writer Henrik Ibsen, and who yesterday evening produced upon a semi-private stage his positively abominable play entitled *Ghosts*. These, beyond doubt, are strong expressions to employ, but they are adopted calmly and after due study of the works of the Scandinavian 'moralist' in question, as well as of the explanations and vindications of them freely forthcoming from his passionate admirers. A band of these strange people, deriving encouragement apparently from the licence lately accorded by the Lord Chamberlain to three previous plays by the same author, *The Pillars of Society*, *A Doll's House*, and *Rosmersholm*, have conspired—for their method is really semi-secret—to put upon a kind of surreptitious stage a further series of Ibsen's social dramas, and others of like kind. Our columns report this morning how the Royalty Theatre, which is a house licensed by the Lord Chamberlain, witnessed last night what was called a 'private invitation performance' on behalf of what is also styled 'The Independent Theatre of London.' Is it by these appellations that the promoters of the disgusting representation seen and heard yesterday at the Royalty propose to escape the reprobation due to such as aim at infecting the modern theatre with poison after desperately inoculating themselves and others? We gravely doubt whether even technically the organisers of this imitation of the French Théâtre Libre can put themselves outside the Act of Parliament governing this department of public morals. As has been already pointed out, they collect funds for the series of performances under the furtive title of 'terms of membership,' albeit no money is actually taken at the doors of their theatre. The words of the Act are clear, that

in every case in which any money, or other reward, shall be taken or charged directly or indirectly, or in which the purchase of any article is made a condition

189

for the admission of any person into any theatre to see any stage-play . . . every actor therein shall be deemed to be acting for hire;

and, if the founder of the Independent Theatre and his actors do indeed fall under this statute, the licence of the Royalty would become 'absolutely void.' Ought, then, any one who has at heart the best interests of the English stage, and who, at the same time, values a large freedom of action for its development as a moral and social teacher, as well as a recreation and delight—ought such a one, we ask, not to wish devoutly that the first representation witnessed yesterday evening of these 'sublime novelties' should also be the last? Mr. Grein, manager of the Independent Theatre, thinks the contrary, and poses altogether as a reformer and friend of high dramatic art.

Much [he says] has been done in speech and writing to misinterpret my intentions, to accuse me of a craving for the ugly. But let me assure every one that I have but one aim—to serve Art, to show the budding dramatists how powerful plays can be evolved by the simplest means. My programme will plead my cause, and I hope it will be convincing that I worship, above all, the beautiful and the artistic. *Ghosts*, I may add, is not beautiful—in the ordinary sense—but it is artistic, because it is a powerful play, written in human language, because it is as simple as a tragedy of the Greeks.

Ay! the play performed last night is 'simple' enough in plan and purpose, but simple only in the sense of an open drain; of a loathsome sore unbandaged; of a dirty act done publicly; or of a lazar-house with all its doors and windows open. It is no more 'Greek,' and can no more be called 'Greek' for its plainness of speech and candid foulness, than could a dunghill at Delphi, or a madhouse at Mitylene. It is not 'artistic' even, in the sense of the anatomical studies of the Great Masters; because they, in carefully drawing the hidden things of life and nature, did it in the single and steadfast worship of Truth and Beauty, the subtle framework and foundation of which they thus reverently endeavoured to seize. The framework theory of this Norwegian's 'inspiration,' however, is said, by his own panegyrists, to be expressed in his play, *An Enemy of the People*, where the hero, Dr. Stockmann—declared, by the way, to be the portrait of Dr. Ibsen himself—observes, 'The great discovery I have made within the last few years is the discovery that all our sources of spiritual life are poisoned, and that our whole society rests upon a pestilential basis of falsehood.' Truly, the aim and object of Ibsen's social plays seem to be to make this good by plots, situations, and dialogues about as 'Greek' as was the clout of Diogenes, and about as 'artistic' as the wrapper on a quack-medicine bottle. We do not pretend to know what graces of style may be lost to us in the Norwegian originals; but certainly, as regards the translations with which Mr. Archer, Mr. Gosse, and others have favoured the English public, there is little or nothing to redeem the dialogue from the level of the mild Kotzebue turned bestial and cynical. The passage which gives its title to the piece of offensive pessimism performed last night is couched thus: Mrs. Alving, the heroine, says,

Ghosts! when I heard Regina and Oswald in there I seemed to see ghosts before me. I almost think we're all of us ghosts, Pastor Manders, it's only what we have inherited from our fathers and mothers that 'walks' in us. It's all sorts of dead ideas and lifeless old beliefs, and so forth. They have no vitality, but they cling to us all the same, and we can't get rid of them. Whenever I take up a newspaper I seem to see ghosts gliding between the lines. There must be ghosts all the country over, as thick as the sand of the sea. And then we are, one and all, so pitifully afraid of the light!

In Ibsen's melancholy and malodorous world the ghosts that walk seem all of them, moreover, evil and miserable. He loves to make his heroes stand in the strong sun of public favour and estimation, only in order to throw beside them a dark shadow of baseness and hypocrisy which he makes out to be their real personalities. Human society itself is for him but a vile crowd of actors and actresses walking shamefully on the thin crust of a quagmire called 'Law and Order'. There is nothing new, and nothing true, and it does not signify. Until we learn at the feet, forsooth, of this Scandinavian playwright to laugh at honour, to disbelieve in love, to mock at virtue, to distrust friendship, and to deride fidelity, we have learned nothing. This new favourite of a foolish school, who is to set aside Shakespeare and Sheridan, and to teach hitherto fairly decent genius of the modern English stage a better and a darker way, seems, to our judgement, to resemble one of his own Norwegian ravens emerging from the rocks with an insatiable appetite for decayed flesh rather than any Æschylus of the North, who dares to drape with tragic splendour the Furies of Orestes, or even any new and dramatic Schopenhauer full of the sadness of human life, and blind to its gladness. Any healthy-minded critic will rise, we think, from the perusal of this so-called 'master's' works with the conclusion that Henrik Ibsen of Skien is what Zola would have been without his invention and analysis, Carlyle without his genius and piety, or the 'melancholy Jaques' without his culture and wit, if they also had been born of a seafaring family in a poor fishing village upon the Western Fiords.

Opinions may, however, very fairly differ, of course, as to the style and literary merit of any dramatic author; but there can surely be no opinion except one in sane minds as to the character of a play like *Ghosts*. There are only five characters contributing to the family drama in three acts, but within that space and with so limited a company Dr. Ibsen manages bitterly to illustrate the majority of the seven deadly sins. Of the five dramatis personae, one at most remains at the end of the play not entirely odious; the others have managed, before we arrive at the sickly and delirious conclusion, to strip off mutually pretty well every rag of truthfulness or decency which hid the corrupted hearts within. This, nevertheless, be it understood, is the real world if we will see it truly; and thus are we to be led to larger ideas and higher art, if we will consent to learn with Mr. Gosse and Mr. Archer, and the patrons of the 'Independent Theatre,' what lazar-houses of lying and sham and make-believe all our human communities are, and how everything is rotten in the State of Denmark and elsewhere. Yet all this, again, is a philosophy like another, and any author or playwriter might hold it and preach it, in much sincerity and with objects not inconsistent with such as should govern true Art. But Morality, Criticism, and Taste alike must certainly draw the line at what is absolutely loathsome and fœtid. If Medea could not, according to Horace, kill her children upon the stage, still less can Art allow what common decency forbids. Realism is one thing, but the nostrils of an audience must not be visibly held before a play can be stamped as true to nature. It is difficult to expose indecorous words—the gross, and almost putrid, indecorum of this play of *Ghosts*. Suffice it to indicate that the central situation is that of a son exposing to a mother—herself, in past days, a would-be adultress—his inheritance of a loathsome malady from a father whose memory the widow secretly execrates while she publicly honours and consecrates it. If this be Art—which word, be it remembered, is but the abbreviation of the Greek name for what is highest, most excellent, and best—then the masterpieces of English literature must be found in such vagaries as Ben Jonson's *Fleet Ditch Voyage*, Swift's mad scurrility, and Congreve's lewd coarseness. If this be 'Greek simplicity,' let us be done with Juliet, and Imogen, and Desdemona, and go to the Lock Hospital for the lovers and heroines of our English stage. Even the *Lady of the Camelias*—that hectic harlot—coughed her frail soul away with some external propriety; but Ibsen's patients expectorate, if we may venture to say so, in public, and air on the stage matters that a blind beggar would hide under his patches. In the name of outraged Art let these people—author, actors, and admirers alike—keep to themselves their clinical confessions and scenes which appertain to Mercury rather than the Muse. If their intellectual food be such literary carrion, let them devour it apart; but, in whatever measure they bring their crapulous stuff into the light of day, and within range of the senses of honest and wholesome folk, we trust that public opinion, backed, if necessary, by the law, will in that measure rebuke and restrain the novel and perilous nuisance.

63. From an unsigned notice, *Daily News*

14 March 1891, 6

The hearts of the Ibsen worshippers were made glad last night by a long-looked-for and a crowning joy. *A Doll's House*, with its empty-headed heroine, who is so suddenly metamorphosed at the last moment into something more than a Mary Woolstonecroft full blown, has made its appearance in a fitful and evanescent fashion on our stage; *The Pillars of Society*, though it has been found by English spectators dull and unsatisfying, has also had its little day or rather morning, and ex-pastor Rosmer, with the inscrutable Rebecca, have in *Rosmersholm* twice been seen going their foolish way to the mill-race in the garden. But these are moderate doses of Ibsenism compared with *Ghosts*, a drama in three acts, which, thanks to the enterprise of Mr. Grein and the device of withdrawing this unlicensable production from the cognisance of the Lord Chamberlain by calling the Royalty for the occasion 'the Independent Theatre,' and taking no money at the doors, was last night presented in all its naked loathsomeness. It is necessary to speak plainly on this matter, 'Volenti non fit injuria', says the old legal maxim. The spectators at the Royalty were for the most part members of the fanatical sect, for whose tastes apparently nothing can be too hideous, nothing too shameless for treatment before a mixed assemblage of men and women provided it can put forth the excuse that it exposes social hypocrisy and moral cowardice, and illustrates the evil results of the subjection of women, and the slavish addiction of men to outworn creeds and ethical standards. The faces that have become familiar to those whose duty it has been to attend these melancholy gatherings, were there again, and again their possessors were seen in a little playhouse 'crammed' together like the celebrated 'party in a parlour' in *Peter Bell*. When the first devout silence was broken the old catch-words and phrases—'the great life problem,' 'emancipated men and women,' and so forth—by which the true Ibsenite is made manifest to his brother and sister enthusiasts, were, we need hardly say, once more in the air. But when Mrs. Alving, in the person of Mrs. Theodore Wright, finally excused her deceased husband for having debauched his own maid servant and bequeathed to his only son an unutterable legacy of shame and physical suffering upon the ground that in the dull 'half grown' little Norwegian town 'your poor father could find no other outlet for the overpowering joy of life that was in him,' then it was that the murmurs of 'psychological insight' were heard all around, and every true devotee appeared to be agreed that at last, in the Ibsenite idiom, we had reached 'the inner truth of the situation'—at last 'the woman had the higher light.' Further discussion of the story of this most dismal and repulsive production is impossible for reasons which ought to have rendered impossible last night's performance before an audience largely composed of ladies, many of whom were of very youthful appearance. The spectators, nevertheless, bore patiently with the interminable flow of words, and sat out the play with what appeared to be intense satisfaction. The only exception was furnished by a feeble minority in the gallery, where the involuntary exclamation 'Too horrible!' at the fall of the curtain, was promptly discouraged by indignant cries of 'Order.' As to the acting of Mrs. Wright, who is, we understand, an amateur of some renown in private circles, and of Mr. Frank Lindo, Mr. Leonard Outram, Mr. Sydney Howard, and Miss Edith Kenward, we must be content with saying that the play suffered little or nothing in their hands, Under the circumstances, Mr. Grein was clearly justified in responding to the call for the manager in the few words—aptly chosen and well-spoken—in which he explained the purpose of the movement and the principles which are to guide this attempt to establish an English counterpart to the Paris 'Théâtre Libre.' It is satisfactory, at least, to know that while the young aspirant is to be welcomed, the terrible and the repulsive are not to be the staple fare of the patrons of 'the Independent Theatre.'

64. From an unsigned notice, *Daily Chronicle*

14 March 1891, 3

We have alluded to *Ghosts* as revoltingly suggestive and blasphemous. Justification of the former term would involve a more detailed explanation of the relations of three of the characters towards each other than we care to enter upon; of the second charge it is sufficient perhaps to say that a vile elderly being, as distorted in person as he is in mind, whose darling design it is to employ a young girl—supposed by some to be his daughter, though he knows to the contrary—as a decoy at a 'sailors' tavern,' where there shall be 'singing and dancing, and so forth,' is allowed to say to an extremely simple-minded clergyman, whom he is partly befooling and partly threatening, that he knows 'a man that's taken others' sins upon himself before now,' emphasising the statement by raising his right hand to heaven. *Ghosts*, however, as a play contains greater faults even than those of lack of decency or of respect for religious convictions. The characters are either contradictory in themselves, uninteresting, or abhorrent. The only really respectable individual in the piece, Pastor Manders, is nerveless just when courage is required, is an easy prey to schemers, and is rather too addicted to figuratively bringing the pulpit into private houses. To Mrs. Alving—the long-patient wife of a dissolute husband—we should by no means like to pin our faith. She has loved the pastor, and in the course of conversation with him makes one or two remarks that are certainly not in good taste respecting what might have been in the past had the clergyman succumbed to temptation when she left her drunken spouse and sought Manders's roof. Nor can we forgive her—although her life is bound up in that of her son—for not setting her face to the very end against the association of Oswald, 'worm-eaten from his birth,' with Regina. As the just and outspoken critic last night declared, 'It's too horrible!' This Regina, it should be added, is quite as artful as Rebecca West in *Rosmersholm*, though she is less constant and more self-seeking. She attempts to captivate the son of the kindly woman who has dragged her from a life of squalor and degradation, but when she learns that Oswald is ill, and that she cannot wed him, coolly throws him over, and says, with a shrug of the shoulders, 'A poor girl must make the best of her young days, or she'll be left out in the cold before she knows where she is.' This same minx, when she learns that her mother was betrayed by her employer, says, 'So mother was that kind of woman after all.' Of the reputed father of this girl and of the melancholy insane youth who persistently cries for 'the sun' as the curtain descends, after he has striven to persuade his mother to give him a fatal dose of morphia to free him from the dread by which he is possessed, we have sufficiently spoken. The one is detestable in his craft and hypocrisy, the other a pitiful, mean, and abject creature in the exposition of the doctrine of heredity.

65. From an unsigned notice, *Evening News and Post*

14 March 1891, 1

A double-decker headline: 'Ghosts/The Ingenuous Grein and the Dramatist of Hereditary Disease.' (See also No. 66.)

The dramatic critic of this paper is a conscientiously lazy man, who is always glad to have his work done for him, and the instalment of descriptive criticism supplied by Mr. Grein was very welcome, though not more so than the half-hour of club conversation which he happened on a little later in the evening, which enabled him to crystallise his ideas in a form handy for reproduction. A more or less verbatim report is appended:

SCENE: A club smoking-room.

TIME: 11.30 p.m., March 13.

INTERLOCUTORS: Our Critic and a Budding Dramatic Author.

B. D. A.: Here you are at last. How did the Ibsen show go off?

O. C.: You speak with a levity unbecoming the subject. Do you happen to know that you are speaking of *Ghosts* and of the Independent Theatre of London? Do you know that you owe a debt of gratitude to

Mr. Grein for getting up this Theatre Society and producing this play?

B. D. A.: Never! How is it?

O. C.: What do you suppose is Mr. Grein's object in promoting, founding, and managing the Independent Theatre?

B. D. A.: To exploit the Ibsenites—and Mr. J. T. Grein.

O. C.: Wrong again. He has been pained by the slowness with which we make progress in dramatic production, 'travelling by mail coach, whilst our neighbours on the Continent travel by express train,' and he wants to stimulate us by producing foreign masterpieces as a sort of liberal education to 'English dramatists in the bud.' You are an English dramatist in the bud, and it is for you that Mr. Grein has laboured.

B. D. A.: And I am to be liberally educated by Ibsen? Well, what is *Ghosts* like?

O. C.: It is like nothing in the way of drama that I have ever seen before—except other Ibsen plays.

B. D. A.: What's the plot?

O. C.: The plot? Oh, the plot is—(hesitates, and tries to recall something which a young dramatic author can be induced to accept as a plot).

B. D. A.: Go on. The plot?

O. C.: Well, the plot is that an unpleasant young man thinks he's a sort of congenital idiot, and finds out that he is.

B. D. A.: What does he do?

O. C.: He becomes an idiot.

B. D. A.: But after that?

O. C.: Nothing.

B. D. A.: But before that?

O. C.: Nothing.

B. D. A.: You're having a joke with me. I suppose he's a sort of pivot for the plot, and the other people carry on the action. Who are the other people?

O. C.: The young man's mother; a clergyman, her old friend; a superior sort of housemaid, her protégé; and a sanctimoniously hypocritical old carpenter, the reputed father of the girl. Shall I tell you what they do?

B. D. A.: Yes; fire away. Begin with the mother.

O. C.: The mother tells her ancient clerical friend that her deceased husband was a bad lot, that he played the 'gallant gay Lutheran' all round during the 18 years of their wedded life, that she had the toughest kind of work to keep up the odour of sanctity in which he lived and died, that she once heard their pretty housemaid say to him, 'Oh, don't, Mr. Alving,' and that there were 'consequences.' The consequences she explains to be the present pretty housemaid, who is reputed to be the daughter of the sanctimonious carpenter, but who isn't.

B. D. A.: But what does she *do*?

O. C.: She tells the ancient cleric that she is very sorry he made her go back to her husband when she ran away, after a year of married life, and wanted to share the clerical home. She also tells him that her son can marry his sister if he likes, or dispense with marrying her, as is sometimes done in those parts.

B. D. A.: But what does she DO?

O. C.: She tries to console her son, who is sulky and silent most part of the time before he develops pronounced idiocy, by telling him that his father was a blackguard, and that he need not reproach himself for being a fool, because Mr. Ibsen is a crank on the point of 'heredity.' She also fires off a lot of Ibsenite Social doctrine to confuse the aged cleric. She gets very near to doing something—to wit, poisoning her son—just before the curtain falls, but she is not given time to get through with it.

B. D. A.: I see. Well, what does the clergyman do?

O. C.: Oh, he doesn't do anything except talk a lot, make a background for the emotions of the mother, and generally represent conventional ideas about religion and morality so that she can knock them down with smart dialogue, like so many ninepins.

B. D. A.: What does the girl do?

O. C.: She tries to 'mash' the ancient cleric unsuccessfully. That is an incident. The rest of the time she exemplifies heredity by showing longings for an immoral life, and eventually she exits with the expressed intention of bringing her pigs to the Parisian (streets) market.

B. D. A.: And the sanctimonious carpenter—does he do anything?

O. C.: No, but he deserves credit for trying. He tries to get his daughter (she's not his daughter but believes she is) to join him in starting a 'sailor's home,' in which he explains that she is to be one of the home comforts for the mariners. Then he tries to get the parson to lend him trust money to start the 'Home' with. He is a beggar for trying, but he doesn't actually do anything except lead away the aged cleric when the latter is too shocked to listen to the mother any longer.

B. D. A.: But does nobody do anything in the play at all?

O. C.: You're an unreasonable youngster, with your cast-iron British ideas about action. Didn't I tell you that the unpleasant young man becomes an idiot? He talks a deal about it first, of course, in a vague and mournful way. Being a creation of the illustrious Norwegian dramatist he was bound to preface action with abundance of explanation. He tries to do something else, too—to marry his sister. But that is a feeble attempt, and is not persevered in after it has served its purpose of providing matter for dissertation and expectation. Then he explains that he is going to have softening of the brain, and that his idea in wanting to marry the girl was that she might be handy to poison him when the brain-softening process had continued to such a degree that he could recognise himself as an idiot. He gets his mother to promise to poison him at the right time, and then flops in a chair, rolls his eyes, drops his jaw, asks to have the sun handed to him, and waits to be poisoned. Nice boy? But there's action for you!

B. D. A.: That seems to me an attractive, moral, and lively drama. I won't ask you why was it written, because Mr. Ibsen's motives are generally obscure. But why was it produced?

O. C.: Partly because it is felt that an Independent Theatre must justify its name, I fancy. Partly also, because of the morbid charm of Ibsen's characterization. He does not do anything with his characters this time, except put them on the stage and set them to talk, but they talk so as to strip the clothes off their backs and the flesh off their bones, until you can see right down to the network of springs and wheels that make them men and women. His aged cleric is a marvellous bit of character, and so is the girl. The sanctimonious carpenter is a coarser study, and the mother, in some points, I cannot accept as a type of any conceivable mother, but it is all strong and masterful work in its way. If a play consisted in making characters reveal themselves in dialogue alone, *Ghosts* would be within measurable distance of a great play. As it is—!

B. D. A.: It is a bad one?

O. C.: More than that. It is an insult to the commonsense of all playgoers and to the sex of such of them as are female. An Independent Theatre nominally is subject to no censorship but that of public opinion, and there is all the more reason that we should denounce the dirt of a production like this, which is a theatrical equivalent of Mr. Stead's *Maiden Tribute*. It was a fatal mistake to begin with *Ghosts*.

66. An anonymous satirical poem, *Evening News and Post*

14 March 1891, 1

(See also No. 65.)

GHOSTS

Where on earth over night had I been
    Antecedent to going to bed?
For this morning I'm *ultramarine*,
    And my eyes opalescent and red!

Did I visit the clinical schools—
    The Dead House? or else had I been
Consorting in graveyards with ghouls,
    And vampires, and reptiles obscene?

Or was I with Purists, in*stead*,
    Denouncing the Spirit Unclean?
Or did I but toss in my bed
    And *dream* of the Forest of Dean?

Dean? Ah! I remember at last,
    Exactly now where I'd been,
The jokes and the jests that were passed,
    I remember thee, rollicking scene!

For I drank at the Ibsenite spring,
    At the sign of the Jolly Blue Posts;
For once in my life had my fling,
    And supped full of horrors—and Ghosts!

67. Ibsen and real life

March 1891

From a report of a murder trial in the *Evening Standard* (14 March 1891), 2.

We scent the framework of an Ibsen drama in the murder trial which concluded at Liverpool yesterday, in which there was a hero after the heart of the Norwegian dramatist. He had suffered from heart disease, rheumatism and epilepsy, had twice tried to commit suicide, and had eventually knifed his mistress as they drove in a cab together, subsequently stopping the cab to tell the driver he had done murder and to ask that a policeman might be procured. At his trial the defending council pleaded that 'there was hereditary taint in the family,' and a hardhearted jury concluded that a family with such an unpleasant tendency might benefit by losing its most active member. So he was found guilty and sentenced to death. With a heroine who had been a Scotch lassie, barmaid, and prostitute in turn before coming to her terrible end, this little drama of real life ought to work up into something essentially Ibsenish.

68. From 'Plays and Players', an anonymous theatre column, *Sunday Times*

15 March 1891, 7

Well, at any rate, *Ghosts* has been performed in a London theatre, and now surely the Lord Chamberlain must logically allow anything that has the excuse of art, however morally hideous, though Scotland Yard —or shall we say Clement Scotland Yard?—be eager for the fray.

69. An unsigned notice, *Licensed Victuallers'*
Mirror

17 March 1891, 128

The long promised 'Independent Theatre,' in imitation of the Parisian Theatre Libre, has been inaugurated at the Royalty, under the management of a Dutchman, J. T. Grein, with Ibsen's *Ghosts*.

As everybody knew it was extremely dirty, everyone connected with the new cult, especially women, was mad to enjoy it.

Seats were at a premium before the day of the performance, and on Friday night last the inhabitants of Dean Street, Soho, witnessed a sight not often seen in that dull dingy thoroughfare—crowds of people gathered round the doors of their little theatre.

And a motley crowd they were; ordinary commonplace women and girls that had come out of mere prurient curiosity were mixed up with spectacled, green complexioned, oddly-dressed females of unhealthy aspect, their bodies seemingly as diseased as their minds, who were obviously priestesses of the cult.

Young fellows who had no sympathy with Ibsen, but who liked to be 'in the know,' and who would next day be quite oracles among people who had *not* been to the Royalty;

Were mixed up with long-haired, soft-hatted, villainous or sickly-looking socialists, well-known propagandists of atheism, iconoclasts, and anarchists of every kind; journalists and literary men, sympathetic and unsympathetic.

The audience, which quickly crammed every part of the house, was drawn from all conditions of life, rich, poor, and middling, and of all ways of thinking, though, of course, the Ibsenmongers were ten to one at least.

It was curious to watch the faces of the different kinds of spectators during the performance of the most loathsome play that was ever put upon any stage.

The women, who had come out of mere curiosity, looked a little embarrassed at first as the abominations of the story were gradually unfolded.

But, observing that the spectacled and green complexioned of their sex devoured the dirty morsels with such a relish that can only be compared to that of a dog who has found some uncommonly tasty tit-bit in a gutter, they soon shook off their silly conventional modesty, which is only fashion deep, and seemed to enjoy them as well as the emancipated.

Some of the socialistic atheist school became positively ecstatic, and when a heavier lump of dirt than usual was shied at the audience, would look round with a triumphant glance, as much as to say—

'What do you say to that, ye unemancipated? Where now are your babyish Shakespeares and Sheridans, and all the other weak-kneed dramatists, past and present? This is real art; this is the new revelation, the new Scriptures.'

The unemancipated, as a body—I mean the male portion—treated the whole thing as funny, much as they would a bad story, or a packet of French pictures; and many a ferocious glance was cast upon their derisive laughter by the sinister worshipper, who, had he lived in an emancipated country, would certainly have put the blade of his knife between the ribs of the scoffer.

Actors and actresses entered thoroughly into the spirit of their task, and never attempted to gloss the meaning of the author's words; they gave them their full flavour.

The lady who played Mrs. Alving told a story of a kind which is usually reserved for the Lock Hospital, and abetted her bodily and morally diseased son in his passion for his half sister, with an entire absence of self-consciousness that was certainly artistic.

When the curtain fell upon the mother trying to make up her mind to poison her loathsome offspring, the outburst of applause from the worshippers of the goddess, Cloacina, was intermingled with some good, honest, downright hissing; and many a man's face was expressive of disgust; but, I regret to say, that I did not remark such an expression upon any woman's countenance.

But where is the Lord Chamberlain, who for years has made us the laughing stock of Europe by his silly objections to French plays that were Dr. Watts' hymns to this?

Verily he straineth at a French gnat and swalloweth a Norwegian camel. Where is the Society that attacked the Rabelais Exhibition, which was art, and has prosecuted publishers for translating Zola, who has genius, which Ibsen has not?

Where are the County Council and the McDougalls and Charringtons who groaned and turned up the whites of their eyes at Zæo's posters —and Zæo's back?

That a judicious, but not Mrs. Grundyish, censorship of the stage is necessary is amply proved by the production of *Ghosts*, which has neither wit, poetry, cleverness, nor common sense to recommend it, for it is as dull and stupid as it is dirty.

Can anyone but a crazy Ibsenite really take these things as an average picture of humanity? It may be of Norwegian humanity, but certainly it is not of English.

And if it were, what good does the author propose by laying bare this mass of corruption?

He lays the blame at the door of Society, and would destroy Society root and branch; but is it not rather the natural corruption of the human heart and the vile passions it engenders that are the cause? And yet he proposes to free those passions from every moral and religious restraint, and let them work their will.

70. From an unsigned notice, *Hawk*

17 March 1891, 291–2

(See also No. 71.)

There are three points from which you may consider *Ghosts*—as a mere play, as a study of character, or as a treatise on hereditary disease; and if it holds water in any one instance, I shall be prepared to worship with the few. Take it as a mere play, there is no story except the intrigue between the young master and the pretty slavey, which is common to every French farce. In order not to use mere generalities, I quote *The Pink Dominos*, and witness the intrigue between Henry Greenlanes and Rebecca—champagne included. Take it as a play—not founded on the old formula—we find it full of the tritest of old tricks. Name? Well, the mother telling the indiscretion of the father to Pastor Manders, and immediately hearing the incident repeated by the son. Surely no trick out of melodrama could be older? Take it as a study of character and what do we find? A mother who sacrifices all feelings to the love of her son; her son who being a prig does not consider his mother's feelings; a parson who is worldly; a carpenter who trades on his assumption of sanctity; and a slavey who sighs for satin, scent and champagne. Nothing very new in these, I fancy. As a study of hereditary disease, to my mind, it is perfectly amateurish. I am afraid I cannot discuss the subject, but if you doubt my word ask any intelligent doctor if I am not right.

What merit, therefore, has it got? To my mind, absolutely none. It has neither the merit of fine writing, the ephemeral interest of a good ghost or murder story, nor the direct truth of a chapter of forensic medicine. It has merely the suggestiveness of a virtuous pamphlet by Mr. W. T. Stead, or the lewdness of an article against girl flogging in *Truth* or *Town Talk*. As a man of the world, I saw nothing new and nothing true in it. It was merely dull dirt, long drawn out, and if Mr. Grein hopes for the success of his Independent Theatre, he must make it something but a Dispensary of Dirt.

71. 'How We Found Gibsen', an anonymous satirical story, *Hawk*

17 March 1891, 294–5

(See also No. 70.)

Our club was not an ordinary club. We were not ordinary people. We had a mission, and our mission was to expose the hollowness of life, the huge mistake of the whole scheme of creation, and the general worthlessness of everything and everybody—ourselves, of course, excepted. To conventionality in every shape we were sworn foes, and we made war upon it remorselessly in every direction. We wore strange garments; we scorned the Philistinism of linen and starch, and allowed the innovating Jaeger to claim us for his own; our hair was mostly wild and our collars limp; our whole appearance bearing witness to our unfathomable contempt of what Dr. Raveling, our president, eloquently described as the 'base Juggernaut of respectability.' We had weekly meetings and discussions, at which we shook hands with our own superior wisdom, and pitied the blindness of our unemancipated fellow-creatures, who—poor worms!—still persisted in finding some pleasure in existence. Then there was our monthly organ, the *Carrion Crow,* which teemed with the racy Hibernian eloquence of our great literary pillar, Mr. Lernard Baw. If anything could have revolutionised society, and brought the world to a due sense of its own hollowness, the *Carrion Crow* ought certainly to have done the trick. But, somehow or other, we didn't seem to make much impression on the outside public. Some laughed at us—we didn't mind that so much. But the majority took no notice of us at all—and we minded that a great deal. It is not such an easy matter as it seems, to revolutionise society. Not only is it hard to convince people that they are all wrong and all wretched without knowing it, but they have an irritating way of thinking you mad, and treating you and your theories accordingly.

At last, when we had almost despaired of accomplishing our mission, a new and great idea suddenly dawned upon us. To be strictly accurate, it dawned upon Mr. Lernard Baw, who imparted it to us at one of our weekly meetings. The stage, he declared, was now a great educational medium; we must convert it to our purpose, and bring the scent of the social cesspool over the footlights. All that was necessary was a dramatist who would not fear to depict human nature in all its existing hideousness and deformity. The suggestion was received with great enthusiasm. Then someone dubiously asked where such a dramatist could be found; and great was the excitement when Mr. Lernard Baw announced that he had already been discovered.

'Our good friend Bowman,' he said, 'has happily lighted upon a marvellous dramatic writer named Gibsen. He chanced to read one of his works, and was struck with its wonderfully accurate delineation of modern society. The leading character is an escaped leper from Molokai, and the heroine is an outpatient at the Chiropodists' Hospital. There are only five characters, four of whom commit suicide, and the fifth—the heroine—dies a violent death by the shooting of a corn, off the stage, in the last act. There are several meanings in some of the lines, and at least two in most of them. Altogether, a very remarkable work, and one that stamps Gibsen as a profound student of human nature.'

'Where is the great Gibsen to be found? has Bowman seen him?' inquired Slangwill. Slangwill is our only funny man, and, between ourselves, I have always rather doubted the sincerity of his convictions. There is no room for funny men in our club.

'Gibson is an Esquimaux,' explained Dr. Raveling, our president, rather severely. 'But our friend Bowman has translated most of his plays, including *Noah's Ark*, *Madda Jabbrer*, *Rumunsatholm*, and the *Tame Goose*, and has some hope of getting him to England if one of his dramas is produced here.'

'How about the Lord Chamberlain?' murmured Slangwill, soothingly.

'We should never allow the officials of a corrupt Government to interfere with the regeneration of the people', replied Mr. Lernard Baw, with lofty scorn. 'I propose that we start a private theatre of our own, and there produce one of these splendid works. By this means we shall familiarise the people with Gibsen's glorious theories, the effete dramatists of to-day will be pulverised, the *Daily Phonograph* will cease publication, and its dramatic critic will be driven to the workhouse, while the vile old fetish of respectability will be shattered at our feet.'

Uttered in convincing tones and a delightfully musical brogue, this sounded very inspiring, and the enthusiasm redoubled when the speaker added—'Remember, gentlemen, it is to us that the glory will belong of having discovered this great Esquimaux genius, and of having regenerated at the same time the world and the drama by his agency. We shall go down to posterity as the apostles of the glorious creed of Pessimism, of which Gibsen is the great exponent. In the meantime, we shall keep our names well before the public. What better reward could we desire?'

Needless to say, the proposal was carried by acclamation, and, after some discussion, the establishment of the Indescribable Theatre was duly effected. It was decided at a subsequent meeting that *Noah's Ark* should be the first play produced, and that free tickets should be granted to all who subscribed not less than £10 to the expenses. A few of the more enthusiastic Gibsenites voted in favour of the production of one of his more abstruse works, such as *Lady Ginger of Gostraight*, *The Imposters*, or *Vilikens at Gotoheligoland*; but ultimately *Noah's Ark* carried the day. Some little trouble was caused by our inability to find an actor willing to undertake the leading character; but the difficulty was solved by the discovery of a neglected tragedian who had been 'resting' for fifteen years, and was prepared to play all Gibsen's characters backwards, if required, for the sake of the advertisement. We didn't want him to do that, although he was foolish enough to suggest, after reading his part for the first time, that his doing so might help the audience to understand the play.

The eventful night came at last, and a thrill of excitement went round the crowded house when it was rumoured that the great Gibsen himself had come all the way from his residence near the North Pole, and was present at the back of a private box. All eyes were turned to the box, and every neck was twisted in an endeavour to catch a glimpse of 'the Master,' but all in vain. Modesty, we decided, the modesty of the truly great mind, kept him in the background. In due time the play began; but it had not proceeded far, when strange sounds of ill-suppressed chuckling made themselves heard in the auditorium. Angry sounds of 'Ss-h!' came from all parts of the house, and Mr. Brein, our courteous secretary, made some remarks in Dutch that sounded like the names of two leading cities in his native country. For a little while the sounds were subdued; but as we reached the great situation of the third act, wherein the heroine stabs her husband with a meat-skewer and goes off to efface herself in company with the clergyman of the parish, they broke out again with renewed violence. This time there could be no mistake—*they proceeded from the box supposed to be occupied by the great Gibsen*! Louder and louder they grew, until peal after peal of guttural laughter shook the Indescribable Theatre to its foundations. The curtain was hastily dropped, and a deputation, consisting of Dr. Raveling, and Messrs. Lernard Baw and Bowman, rushed up to see what was the matter. Bursting open the box-door, they found the famous Esquimaux rolling on the floor in fits of uncontrollable merriment, every now and again shouting out two words in his native tongue.

'What does he say?' asked the others to Bowman, who was the only Esquimaux scholar of the party.

'It means damned fools!' replied Bowman, in a hoarse whisper. They then retreated hastily. The audience broke up in confusion, and we adjourned to our club-room, there to discuss the situation.

Soon a note, written in the Esquimaux language, was put into Bowman's hands. He translated it to us aloud, and a great hush fell upon us all.

'My plays were written to test the depth to which the vanity and gullibility of the modern apostles of social regeneration were capable of sinking. Up to the present time I have doubted whether anyone could be found with a sufficient lack of humour and common sense to take them seriously. You, gentlemen, have satisfied me; and I thank you. My satires on your colossal dulness and conceit have not been written in vain.'

We have not yet succeeded in regenerating the world, and the *Daily Phonograph* still appears every morning.

72. '*Ghosts* and Gibberings', by William Archer, *Pall Mall Gazette*

8 April 1891, 3

This article, praised by many critics including Henry James and Bernard Shaw, marked a turning point in the history of Ibsen's reception in England (see Introduction).

'Ibsen's positively abominable play entitled *Ghosts*. . . . This disgusting representation. . . . Reprobation due to such as aim at infecting the modern theatre with poison after desperately inoculating themselves and others. . . . An open drain: a loathsome sore unbandaged; a dirty act done publicly; a lazar-house with all its doors and windows open. . . . Candid foulness. . . . Kotzebue turned bestial and cynical. . . . Offensive cynicism. . . . Ibsen's melancholy and malodorous world. . . . Absolutely loathsome and fetid. . . . Gross, almost putrid indecorum. . . . Literary carrion. . . . Crapulous stuff. . . . Novel and perilous nuisance.'—*Daily Telegraph* (leading article). 'This mess of vulgarity, egotism, coarseness, and absurdity.'—*Daily Telegraph* (criticism). 'Unutterably offensive. . . . Prosecution under Lord Campbell's Act. . . . Abominable piece. . . . Scandalous.'—*Standard*. 'Naked loathsomeness. . . . Most damned and repulsive production.' —*Daily News*. 'Revoltingly suggestive and blasphemous. . . . Characters either contradictory in themselves, uninteresting or abhorrent.'—

Daily Chronicle. 'A repulsive and degrading work'.—*Queen*. 'Morbid, unhealthy, unwholesome and disgusting story. . . . A piece to bring the stage into disrepute and dishonour with every right-thinking man and woman.'—*Lloyd's*. 'Merely dull dirt long drawn out.'—*Hawk*. 'Morbid horrors of the hideous tale. . . . Ponderous dullness of the didactic talk. . . . If any repetition of this outrage be attempted, the authorities will doubtless wake from their lethargy.'—*Sporting and Dramatic News*. 'Just a wicked nightmare.'—*The Gentlewoman*. 'Lugubrious diagnosis of sordid impropriety. . . . Characters are prigs, pedants and profligates. . . . Morbid caricatures. . . . Maunderings of nookshotten Norwegians. . . . It is no more of a play than an average Gaiety burlesque.'—W. St. Leger in *Black and White*. 'Most loathsome of all Ibsen's plays . . . Garbage and offal.'—*Truth*. 'Ibsen's putrid play called *Ghosts* . . . So loathsome an enterprise.'—*Academy*. 'As foul and filthy a concoction as has ever been allowed to disgrace the boards of an English theatre. . . . Dull and disgusting. . . . Nastiness and malodorousness laid on thickly as with a trowel'.—*Era*. 'Noisome corruption.'—*Stage*.

Henrik Ibsen.—'An egotist and a bungler.'—*Daily Telegraph*. 'A crazy fanatic and determined Socialist. . . . A crazy cranky being. . . . Not only consistently dirty but deplorably dull.'—*Truth*. 'As a dramatist, I consider the poet Calmour his superior.'—*Hawk*. 'The Norwegian pessimist in *petto*(!).'—W. St. Leger in *Black and White*. 'Ugly, nasty, discordant, and downright dull. . . . A gloomy sort of ghoul, bent on groping for horrors by night, and blinking like a stupid old owl when the warm sunlight of the best of life dances into his wrinkled eyes.' —*Gentlewoman*. 'A teacher of the aestheticism of the Lock Hospital.'— *Saturday Review*.

Ibsenites (*i.e.*, persons who omit to foam at the mouth when the name of Ibsen is mentioned).—'Lovers of prurience and dabblers in impropriety who are eager to gratify their illicit tastes under the pretence of art.'—*Evening Standard*. 'Ninety-seven per cent. [Nothing like accuracy!] of the people who go to see *Ghosts* are nasty-minded people who find the discussion of nasty subjects to their taste, in exact proportion to their nastiness.'—*Sporting and Dramatic News*. 'The socialistic and the sexless. . . . The unwomanly women, the unsexed females, the whole army of unprepossessing cranks in petticoats. . . . Educated and muck-ferretting dogs. . . . Effeminate men and male women. . . . They all of them—men and women alike—know that they are doing not only a nasty but an illegal thing. . . . The Lord Chamberlain left them alone to wallow in *Ghosts*. . . . Outside a silly clique, there is not the slightest interest in the Scandinavian humbug or all his works. . . . A wave of human folly.'—*Truth*.

These are a few extracts from a little book I am compiling—on the model of the Wagner *Schimpf-Lexicon*—to be entitled 'Ibsenoclasts: or, an Anthology of Abuse.' It will be an entertaining little work, I promise you; but the time for publication has not yet come. The materials, it is true, are already abundant; but they keep on pouring in every day, and are likely to do so for some time to come. I am anxious to make the compilation a complete and classic handbook of obloquy— a Baedeker to Billingsgate, as it were; and such is the wealth of our incomparable mother-tongue that, despite the industry of a hundred 'frumious' critics during the past month or so, I cannot suppose that the well of wormwood is as yet exhausted, or that such virtuosos in vituperation will for the future be forced ingloriously to repeat themselves. Besides, the full irony and humour of the situation cannot be quite apparent to the general reader, or to the critics themselves, until a certain time shall have elapsed. As yet, the contributors to the above florilegium can barely have recovered from the moral epilepsy into which *Ghosts*—so far, and so far only, justifying their denunciations— appears to have thrown them. By the time I publish my complete Manual of Malediction, they will have come to themselves again, and will be able to read with a smile—though perhaps a somewhat sickly one—the babble of their delirium.

For the present I would fain 'assist nature' and hasten their recovery by confronting, in one particular, the *Ghosts* of their heated imagination with the actual play as it was represented and as he who runs may read it. That the average man should abhor and resent the play, and even that he should profess himself bored by it, is only natural and proper. If it were pleasant and acceptable to the average man, it would entirely fail of its aim. The 'ghosts' of the moral world are not to be 'laid' by a single exorcism. The first effect of any disturbance of their repose is naturally to make them 'squeak and gibber in the Roman streets'. It is not even to be expected that the average man, in his exasperation, should take the slightest trouble to think out what the poet means, or to represent truthfully what he says. Yet I own I am surprised at the unanimity with which the critics have averred that the tragedy is mainly, if not exclusively, concerned with what the *Anti-Jacobin* calls the 'loathsome details of disease born of depravity.' Scarcely a paper but says the same thing, in almost the same words. The most precise of all, perhaps, is the *St. James's Gazette*:—'No detail is omitted. We see the patient before us. His symptoms are described with revolting minuteness; the quivering of an eyelid or the drooping of a lip is duly noted: the course of the disease, in its origin, development, and culmination, traced with a precision worthy of a professor of anatomy. The very theatre seems to be turned into a hospital.' Nothing can be more explicit than this statement; yet it is absolutely without foundation. Oswald tells his mother that he is suffering from softening of the brain— not a pleasant announcement, certainly, but with nothing particularly 'loathsome' about it. The only 'symptoms' mentioned are a severe headache and bodily and mental lassitude, which cannot surely be called 'revolting' phenomena. There is not a single allusion to 'quivering eyelids' or 'drooping lips'; the 'origin, development, and culmination' of Oswald's disease are not 'traced with precision,' for they are not traced at all. Instead of no detail being omitted, no detail is given. I do not for a moment suggest that the writer deliberately stated what he knew to be false. He wrote under the overpowering impression of what is undoubtedly a very terrible scene or series of scenes. The intense reality of the thing was vividly present to his mind, and he lacked time, and perhaps energy, to consider very closely how that effect of reality had been produced. In assuming that it must have been produced by 'revoltingly minute' descriptions, of which, as a matter of fact, there is no trace, he bore unconscious testimony to the subtle art of the poet. Of course it may be argued that the horror of the scene, by whatever means produced, is beyond human endurance, and consequently outside art. That is a rational position, which may be rationally discussed when the critics have quite recovered from their convulsions. But the fact remains that in Ibsen's dialogue there are none of the 'loathsome' medical details which bulk so hugely before the 'red and rolling eye' of the critical imagination.

There is a scene in *Truth*—one of those fragrant and wholesome plays beside which Ibsen, of course, seems unendurably 'fetid' and 'malodorous'—in which a party of men who have been lying egregiously to their womenfolk through two whole acts at last determine that they must tell the truth. After they have expatiated for some time on the moral elevation begotten by this resolve, one of them demurely suggests that they had better settle what the truth is to be. I would make the same suggestion to the Ibsenoclasts. Members of the same staff, at any rate, might surely arrive at a working agreement as to what is to be the truth about Ibsen. I print side by side two extracts from the *Daily Telegraph* of March 14, the first from a dramatic criticism on page 3, the second from a leading article on page 5:—

There was very little to offend the ear directly. On the Ibsen stage their nastiness is inferential, not actual. They call a spade a spade in a roundabout and circumlocutory fashion.

It can no more be called Greek for its plainness of speech and candid foulness than could a dunghill at Delphi or a madhouse at Mitylene.

What is the bewildered man in the street to make of such conflicting oracles? Is Ibsen 'candidly foul' or only 'inferentially nasty'? Where doctors (of indecorum) differ, who shall decide? Mr. Macdougall perhaps? But now we are met by a still more baffling discrepancy of judgment. When we find Mr. Clement Scott and the critic of the *Daily Telegraph* flatly contradicting each other, chaos seems to have come again. Towards the close of last month Mr. Clement Scott was invited to take part in a debate on *Ghosts* at the Playgoer's Club. He was unable to attend, but sent a letter to represent him in the discussion. In this letter, as reported in the *Detroit Free Press* of February 28, there occurs the following sentence:—'None can doubt the cleverness, the genius, the analytical power of the "Master".' After so emphatic a deliverance from so high an authority we began to take heart of grace, and to imagine that Ibsen might not be such a blockhead after all. But, alas! we reckoned without the critic of the *Daily Telegraph*. *Ghosts*, he assured us on March 14, not much more than a fortnight after the date of Mr. Scott's letter, 'might have been a tragedy had it been treated by a man of genius. Handled by an egotist (!) and a bungler, it is only a deplorably dull play. There are ideas in *Ghosts* that would have inspired a tragic poet. They are vulgarized and debased by a suburban Ibsen. You want a Shakspeare, or a Byron (!), or a Browning to attack the subject-matter of *Ghosts* as it ought to be attacked. It might be a noble theme. Here it is a nasty and a vulgar one.' Now, which are we to believe—Mr. Scott, or the literary oracle of the largest circulation, who reckons Byron among the great tragic poets? Is Ibsen a genius or merely an egotist and a bungler? I fear the weight of the evidence is in favour of the latter judgment; for I observe that a third eminent authority, the critic of *Truth*, sides with his colleague of the *Telegraph* against Mr. Scott. He writes of 'the Ibsen dust-bin,' and exclaims: 'Literature forsooth! Where is a page of literature to be found in the whole category of Ibsen's plays? It is an insult to the word.' This settles the matter! The man who can write of 'the whole category' of Ibsen's plays must be an unimpeachable authority on literature. Mr. Scott and the rest of us must e'en yield to this categorical assurance, and own Ibsen no genius but a suburban egotist.

This article, I shall be told, is purely negative, and contains no rational discussion of the merits and demerits of *Ghosts*. True; but who can carry on a rational discussion with men whose first argument is a howl for the police?

73. Ibsen speaks out

1891

'Henrik Ibsen at Vienna', an interview with the playwright ('From Our own Correspondent'), *Era* (18 April 1891), 9.

Ibsen is here, and has been superintending the production of his play *Kronprätendenten* [*The Pretenders*], which was produced this week. The first portion of the play produced a deep impression. The applause was very great, and Ibsen appeared before the curtain and thanked the public personally after the second and third acts. The last two acts, however, were very wearisome, the story collapsing in interest. The piece fell rather flat in consequence.

During his sojourn in Vienna, Ibsen has been interviewed by the correspondent of an enterprising daily paper. As Ibsen is now one of the central figures of the literary and artistic world I reproduce a portion of the interview which may interest some of your readers.

'I wish to avoid at any price,' said Ibsen, 'appearing as though I had come to Vienna with aggressive intentions, desirous of creating controversy, or propagating new principles. I cannot understand why my works have given rise to such lively differences of opinion. I have come here in compliance with a kind invitation from Direktor Burckhard, and to be present at the first performance of my play.'

'You were in Vienna once before, were you not?'—'In the year 1873, on the occasion of the Universal Exhibition. I was one of the jury in the art department. The city is charming. On that occasion I visited the Burg Theatre, and made the acquaintance of some of the artists.'

'And how long do you purpose remaining here?'—'A few days. My time is short. I am busy planning a new dramatic work, the writing of which I shall begin in the summer. I do not take work easily. Every-one of my plays is rewritten three times. I write a play straight off. When once I have decided on the plot I know no rest, and do not lay down the pen until the play is finished. Then comes the correcting, and I only allow the work to appear after the last and most careful revision.'

'In most of your dramas characters appear whom you must really have met with?'—'In a certain degree. An author is in the same position to his play as an artist is to his picture and the sculptor to his statue. An author who writes for the theatre should not photograph, but he should combine. A handsome face is the union of beautiful traits. When I bring people on the stage I have perhaps—I think I can say in most cases—met these people in real life. I have only taken note of those points about these people which interest me. I then combine the different traits of different people.'

'For example, Dr. Stockmann in the *Volksfeind* [*An Enemy of the People*]?'—'I have met this man, or, to speak more precisely, such a man.'

'Then he exists?'—'He bears a strong resemblance to somebody.'

'A lively discussion has taken place here in Vienna and in other places with respect to this drama and other of your works.' 'I have heard much about it, if I have not read all that has been said. Naturalism! What is it? I did not invent the word, and I do not know what it means. Natura-lism—Idealism! What do people understand by these words? Ideas are eminently suited to discussion. People have discovered things in my works that never occurred to me. I have often felt, and still feel, pres-sure upon me to speak out about certain things. One may have differ-ent opinions how "Truth" should be attained on the stage. I repeat again: I write dramas and comedies because writing is to me a necessity. When I begin a work I conceal my ideas from everyone. Neither my wife nor my children ever know of them. I write in the Danish language; translation is the business of others. Still, I read the translations very carefully. Whoever reads my works closely will find numerous pas-sages in them which might be written by the idealist, as he is called. I began to write at the age of nineteen. My father was a shipowner, and I was to have studied medicine. My natural bias forced me into a literary career. I wrote a tragedy, *Catilina*, my first work, and since then I have continued to write.'

74. Henry James on Ibsen's grey mediocrity

April 1891

This letter to Gosse, addressed from 34 De Vere Gardens, W, and dated 28 April 1891, was written after James saw Elizabeth Robins's *Hedda Gabler* (see No. 75), and about five weeks before he published his review 'On the Occasion of *Hedda Gabler*' (No. 84). 'The Ibsenite volume' was probably an American edition of *The Prose Dramas of Henrik Ibsen* for which Gosse had written a critical introduction (see No. 42); Andrew Lang was one of Ibsen's outspoken critics. On the envelope of this letter James scrawled: 'Your preface perfect, granting premises.'

My dear Gosse,

I return the Ibsenite volume with many thanks—especially for the opportunity to read your charming preface which is really *en somme* and between ourselves (I wdnt. say it to Lang) more interesting than Ibsen himself. That is I think you make him out a richer phenomenon than he is. The perusal of the dreary *Rosmersholm* and even the reperusal of *Ghosts* has been rather a shock to me—they have let me down, down. Surely the former isn't *good*?—any more than the tedious *Lady from the Sea* is? *Must* I think these things works of skill? If I must I will, save to you alone: to whom I confide that they seem to be of a grey mediocrity —in the case of *Rosmersholm jusqu'a en être bête*. They don't seem to me dramatic, or dramas at all—but (I am speaking of these 2 particularly) moral tales in dialogue—without the objectivity, the visibility of the drama. They suggest curious reflections as to the Scandinavian stage and audiences. Of course they have a serious—a terribly serious, 'feeling for life,' and always an idea—but they come off so little, in general, as plays; & I can't think that a man who is at odds with his form is ever a first-rate man. But I may be grossly blind, and at any rate don't *tell* it of yours tremulously,

Henry James.

HEDDA GABLER

Vaudeville Theatre, 20 April 1891

75. From an unsigned notice, *The Times*

21 April 1891, 10

The play was translated by Edmund Gosse and the cast was as follows:

George Tesman	Mr Scott Buist	Judge Brack ..	Mr Charles Sugden
Mrs Hedda	Miss Elizabeth	Ejlert Lövborg ..	Mr Arthur Elwood
Tesman ..	Robins	Bertha	Miss Patty Chapman
Miss Juliana		Mrs Elvsted ..	Miss Marion Lea
Tesman ..	Miss H. Cowen		

Ibsen does not say in so many words that he is giving us a study in *névrosité*. He allows the case to explain itself, and to do him justice it does this so effectually that in a short time we are content to resign ourselves to what is really a demonstration of the pathology of mind, such as may be found in the pages of the *Journal of Mental Science* or in the reports of the medical superintendents of lunatic asylums. To an expert, the reconstitution of the vicious hereditary influences that operate in the case of Hedda Gabler would be an easy matter. Whether Ibsen is not quite sure of his ground here, or whether he judges that a string of purely pathological facts would be tiresome to the general public, does not appear. Certain it is that the investigation of the heroine's heredity is not in this instance undertaken. The author is satisfied with bringing Hedda Gabler's insanity very plainly before us. It is suggested in her inconsequent actions, in her callous behaviour, in her aimless persecution of all around her, and it is finally proved by her motiveless suicide. That the play should be more acceptable than some of its predecessors is a necessary consequence of the very plainness of its thesis, which precludes all discussion of its heroine's actions upon ethical grounds. There is no reasoning as to a lunatic's behaviour; and Hedda Gabler is manifestly a lunatic of the epileptic class, among whom callousness to the sufferings of others and indifference to their own fate are frequently observed. . . .

If Hedda Gabler were alone in question, the play would hardly hold the attention of the house, though it might be interesting to an audience of mad doctors. Fortunately it offers other matters for consideration than the eccentricities of the title character. Hedda Gabler has a fool of a husband, a weak female friend, and a designing *cavalier servente* who is an advocate of the principle of a 'triple alliance' in affairs domestic, while on the borders of the action hovers a tiresome but well-meaning maiden aunt. Upon this group of *dramatis personæ* Ibsen exercises his analytical faculty with excellent effect. He is really admirable in the dissection of character. The subjects that he operates upon and whose vitals he lays bare for our inspection are the reverse of heroic. They are all poor creatures at bottom, with selfishness for their mainspring of action, but they are undeniably human, and to that extent interesting, if repulsive. Then the language in which the play is couched is a model of brevity, concision, and pointedness. It is as innocent of padding as it is of rodomontade; every line tells, and there is not an incident that has not some bearing upon the action, immediate or remote. These are great qualities in a play where getting on with the story is a prime consideration. They have the effect of riveting the attention of the house. The spectator can hardly afford to miss a word or a gesture on the stage, and he is thus brought into a state of constant—one might almost say painful—suspense. As a set-off to these advantages there is to be noted in the Ibsen drama a total lack of wit or humour, or of other amenities of literary style. It has neither tears not laughter in its composition, being in its essentials merely a grim, gloomy exposure of the vanity, the pettiness, and to some extent the fatalism of human life. To conceive of the Ibsen drama gaining an extensive or permanent foothold on the stage is hardly possible. Playgoing would then cease to be an amusement and become a penance; and the function of the dramatist in society would be similar to that of the skeleton at the Egyptian feast. But as a corrective to the vapid and foolish writing with which the stage is deluged, an occasional Ibsen play is not without its uses; and *Hedda Gabler* from this point of view is perhaps entitled to the place of honour.

76. 'An Ibsen Success—*Hedda Gabler* at the Vaudeville', *Pall Mall Gazette*

21 April 1891, 2

If the little Vaudeville is not fuller for the next four afternoons than it was yesterday the public is a fool. No doubt the few were also the fit. But the play was more than an artistic success. It had almost the elements of a popular one. It was a complete contrast to the last Ibsen experiment in the same walls. *Rosmersholm* was dismal to begin with, and it dragged abominably on the actor's hands. *Hedda Gabler*, though tragic enough in all conscience, is brilliant and powerful throughout; it fitted the caste like a glove, and it never hung for a moment. There is no question that the play caught hold of the audience. Some who went to curse, not inaudibly blessed; and to many who went willing to bless it was a dramatic revelation. Critics who feel that it is expected of them may pretend that they were shocked or that they were bored. But they certainly followed the play for three good hours with every outward sign of lively interest.

No, *Hedda Gabler* is *not* gloomier than *Vildanden*, in spite of its two suicides, its triumph of evil strength over good weakness, and its subtle dissection of a morbid modern type. Nor is it merely saved by the brilliant dialogue with which it sparkles in passage after passage. It conquers by the consummate art with which its plot is developed. It draws only on two successive days in the history of its characters. In that space it introduces them, exhibits them, develops them through their interaction, and hurries them to their goal. If elsewhere Ibsen stops to preach, he does not here. It must be a very perversity of cleverness which will torture a moral from this play, good or bad. If elsewhere Ibsen condescends to mystify, strews puzzles by the way as in *Rosmersholm*, or ends with a note of interrogation as in *A Doll's House*, he is kinder to his audience here. 'Why did she give him the pistol?' was a question current in the foyer yesterday. That is to overlook the complex motives of Hedda. To begin with, she suffers from that hopeless complication of maladies—anaemia of the affections, with hypertrophy of the aesthetics. In plainer English, call her an egoist-exquisite, ready to sell her soul and damn any one else's for a little poetry. *That's* simple enough. But she has also that capricious intensity which makes jealousy a stronger passion than love. *That's* not very obscure. And in these two broad clear lights everything is explained. Ennui, not passion, makes her play with Judge Brack. Passion, of jealousy not of love, either for her lover or (absurder still) her husband, makes her wreck Lövborg. The rest is plain sailing. If you are beginning to wonder what all this means—why, go and see for yourself. The acting of Miss Marion Lea and Miss Elizabeth Robins is worth the trouble even without the play. Miss Lea was justifiably nervous, but her only fault was that she sat down to write a little too composedly after Lövborg's death. Miss Robins is brilliant, no less; she is all versatility, expressiveness, and distinction. She even carries off that risky exit at the end of the first act, and she could hardly be better in the dazzling by-play with Brack, with Lövborg, and in the struggle for Lövborg's soul between the serpentine Hedda and the weak but winning Mrs. Elvsted. The two actresses are perfect foils. Mr. Charles Sugden never did better than as the Mephistophelian judge; and of the others (Miss Henrietta Cowen, Mr. Scott Buist, Mr. Arthur Elwood) not a single one did badly.

77. From a notice by Justin McCarthy, *Black and White*

25 April 1891, 382

Hedda Gabler is the name, to my mind, of Ibsen's greatest play, and of the most interesting woman that Ibsen has created. Not Nora, nor Ellida, nor Hedvig, nor Svanhild approach her for intensity of interest, for complexity of character. What is Hedda Gabler? She has something in her of Emma Bovary, a great deal of Jane de Simerose; she has kinship with Becky Sharp, and affinity with Julia. A man of genius might analyse her in an essay, or exhaust her in an epigram. She is compact with all the vices; she is instinct with all the virtues of womanhood. She is at once very possible and very terrible: portentous, and yet common-place; not inhuman, but unhuman: like the Donatello of *Transforma-tion*,[1] save that he represented the Youth of the World, and she repre-sents, not merely the *fin de siècle,* but the *fin des fins.* Under happier con-ditions she might have been a Princess de Cadignan; in more picturesque surroundings she might have been a Vittoria Corrombona; indeed, she is a 'White Devil' in the conditions and the surroundings of her meagre Norwegian life. Hers is, if not a soul, at least a body born out of due time.

Only Ibsen, of all the dramatists living, could have created such a woman as Hedda Gabler; only Ada Rehan, of all the actresses living, could have played her as she should be played. It is not very likely that we shall ever have the chance of seeing what Ada Rehan could do with this strange creation, with this ill-educated, ill-trained, over-civilised daughter of our super-civilisation. Mr. Augustin Daly does not love Ibsen, and New York audiences would scarcely be likely to applaud Ibsen's last play. But only Ada Rehan, with her infinite variety, her marvellous voice, her range of emotion, and strength of passion, could, as I think, adequately present this Sphinx of Ibsenism. It is not finding fault with Miss Elizabeth Robins to say that she does not play Hedda Gabler as Ada Rehan would play it.

78. An unsigned notice, *Saturday Review*

25 April 1891, lxxi, 498

The production of an Ibsen play impels the inquiry, What is the prov-ince of art? If it be to elevate and refine, as we have hitherto humbly supposed, most certainly it cannot be said that the works of Ibsen have the very faintest claim to be artistic. We see no ground on which his method is defensible. When Shakspeare spoke of holding the mirror up to Nature, he surely did not mean so holding it that it reflected only the

---

[1] I.e. Nathaniel Hawthorne's *The Marble Faun.*

base and strumous. An appropriate quotation to stand at the beginning of an edition of Ibsen might be culled from Shakspeare:—

> O, fie! 'tis an unweeded garden
> That grows to seed; things rank, and gross in nature,
> Possess it merely.

Things rank and gross in nature alone have place in the mean and sordid philosophy of Ibsen. Those of his characters who are not mean morally are mean intellectually—the wretched George Tesman, with his enthusiasm about the old shoes his careful aunt brings him wrapped up in a bit of newspaper, is a case in point. As for refining and elevating, can any human being, it may be asked, feel happier or better in any way from a contemplation of the two harlots at heart who do duty in *Hedda Gabler*? Ibsen has no idea of a gentleman, still less of a gentlewoman; and as for his taste, the straightforward coarseness of the Restoration plays seems to us comparatively wholesome by the side of the insidious nastiness of these photographic studies of vice and morbidity. It is an altogether minor point, perhaps, for in duologues some of the best scenes of drama are found—Macbeth and Lady Macbeth, Hamlet and Ophelia, Othello and Iago, Orlando and Rosalind, Sir Peter and Lady Teazle—but Ibsen's plays are mainly a succession of duologues; he does not possess the art of constructing a dramatic work.

That *Hedda Gabler* is the best of the series which has made its melancholy way to this country may be admitted without implying a word of commendation. It is free from the mess and nastiness of *Ghosts*, the crack-brained maunderings of *Rosmersholm*, the fantastic, short-sighted folly of *The Doll's House*, and, though it does not come into the category of pieces represented, from the crude and meaningless romanticism of *The Lady from the Sea*. *Hedda Gabler* is the study of a malicious woman of evil instincts, jealous, treacherous, cold-hearted, and, as it seems to us, wholly out of place on the stage. It is an assertion of the blusterous little band of Ibsenite idolaters that pharisaical critics object to Ibsen's characters because they are generally wicked; but, so far as we are concerned, the foolish Tesman—the chief of whose acts of folly was his marriage with such a creature as Hedda Gabler—seems to us more offensive than the wicked ones. We do not mean to say that there are not, unhappily, Hedda Gablers and George Tesmans in 'real life'. There are; but when we meet them we take the greatest pains to get out of their way, and why should they be endured on the stage? As for Lövborg, he is in truth merely the poet Bunthorne translated into prose and treated in a sombre and melodramatic fashion. Bunthorne, students of *Patience* will remember, had four and twenty female devotees; and they are here represented by Mrs. Elvsted, who has inspired him to write a book, and has helped him in the composition, thereby incurring the enmity of Hedda Gabler—Mrs. George Tesman—who wants to influence somebody, and finally gets hold of and burns the manuscript of Lövborg's latest effort. The end of Lövborg is that he shoots himself with a pistol, given him for the purpose by Hedda; she hears of it, of course, and the dialogue which follows is a perfect specimen of 'the Master':—' "At last a positive act!" she exclaims, joyously. Tesman: "God save us—Hedda, what are you saying?" Hedda: "I say there is something beautiful in this." Brack: "H'm Mrs. Tesman." Tesman: "Beautiful! No—fancy that!" Mrs. Elvsted: "O Hedda! how can you talk of beauty in such a matter?" Hedda: "Ejlert Lövborg has settled the account with himself. He has had the courage to do what—what had to be done. . . . O Judge! what a relief this is about Ejlert Lövborg." Brack: "Relief, Mrs. Hedda! Yes, indeed, it is a relief for him." Hedda: "I mean for me. A relief to know that it is still possible for an act of voluntary courage to take place in the world. Something over which there falls a veil of unintentional beauty." ' This is not burlesque—that is to say, the passage quoted is a conscientiously close translation of Ibsen. Hedda hoped that Lövborg shot himself through the heart; but Judge Brack tells her that the bullet hit him in the belly, and she cries, with an expression of disgust, 'That, too! Oh, what a curse of ridicule and of vulgarity hangs over everything that I merely touch.' Disgusted with life, she therefore shoots herself. Had Lövborg's pistol carried a few inches higher she would probably have consented to live, and would in due time have found her way to the Divorce Court, if there be such an institution in the land of Hedda Gabler. Some of the dialogue between Judge Brack and Hedda is like the work of a real dramatist, and Mr. Sugden speaks it well. Brack and Lövborg are the only male characters besides Tesman. The latter is Hedda's husband, the other two are trying to seduce her. Miss Robins plays Hedda with much misdirected talent; but Miss Marion Lea only makes Mrs. Elvsted a sort of very low-life Ophelia, depicted at the moment when her wits are going.

79. A signed review by Clement Scott, *Illustrated London News*

25 April 1891, 551–2

This piece is very similar in tone and imagery to Scott's unsigned review in the *Daily Telegraph* (21 April 1891).

A few steps out of the hospital ward, and we arrive at the dissecting-room. Down a little lower, still a few steps lower down, and we come to the dead-house. There, for the present, Ibsen has left us. From *Ghosts* to *Rosmersholm*: from *Rosmersholm* to *Hedda Gabler*—who knows where the 'master' will lead us next? Probably into the cemetery and the graveyard, among the evil spirits and the ghouls. Thanks to Miss Elizabeth Robins and to Miss Marion Lea, to Mr. Elwood and to Mr. Scott Buist, the admirers of the new school have scored what they claim to be a victory. 'We are winning! We are winning!' shouted the dramatic radicals, as with natural enthusiasm they crowded on one another's heels out of the little theatre. The jargon of the new faith had been caught up by the willing disciples and the lovers of the morbid. 'I like the play, because it is so unconventional!' 'It interests me, because the trick of the theatre is so conspicuously absent!' 'The people on the stage are so delightfully wicked, and do such extraordinary things. It is all so deliciously horrible!' These were some of the remarks that forced themselves on the attentive ear. No doubt all this was said in perfectly good faith. *Hedda Gabler* had interested an audience—a certain audience. *Hedda Gabler* had been acted as few expected it could have been acted in this country. The text had been carefully and conscientiously revised. Certain notorious passages had been suppressed. The condition of Mrs. Hedda Gabler was not too carefully inquired into. The curiosity of the maiden aunt was checked. The suggestive thoughts of Judge Brack were kept in the background. The 'master' was not allowed to talk exactly as he did at the outset. By supreme art the sense of the ludicrous, which bubbles up all over the text, was strangled at its birth. The audience was spellbound. I grant it. Those who came to laugh remained to pause, if not to pray. But, for my own part, I shall not believe that the new school has made many converts until the professors of it have the courage of their opinions. Let them put up *Hedda Gabler* for a run. Let them place it before the public and submit it to a jury of playgoers, who know no more about Ibsen than the man in the moon. The distrust of Ibsen has been compared to the distrust of Wagner. Surely it is time now to test the question whether the 'drama of the future' is a stern reality or a passing whim!

I prefer for the present to say little here about Ibsen's last play. There it is, in print. Anyone can purchase it at the nearest bookseller's shop. It is open to the enthusiast and the sceptic alike. It is well that everyone should read it for themselves. It is right that we should all have a forecast of the future. It will aid discussion and argument if the new pessimistic play is read, marked, learned, and inwardly digested; but whether those who conscientiously oppose pessimism as illuminated by art write 'fluff' or not, at least I may be permitted the honesty of owning that *Hedda Gabler*, when tackled by clever and conscientious students, acts far better than it reads.

Miss Elizabeth Robins, who has recently distinguished herself in the second rôle in Ibsen's *Doll's House*, has distinguished herself still more as the repulsive heroine of Ibsen's last work. A woman more morally repulsive has seldom been seen on the stage. She talks with conviction and acts like a lunatic. The daughter of General Gabler is what would be called in England a 'garrison hack.' She has danced till she is sick of it. Society bores her; she is threatened with the crime of being an old maid. So she marries the first fool who offers her home and sustenance. The woman has taken a false oath at the altar. She has told a lie, and intends to stick to it. Faithfulness does not enter into her creed, and she abhors maternity and its duties. She insults her husband and his relations. She falls in with the idea of a 'triple alliance' between herself, her husband, and her husband's sensual but best friend. She discovers that her old chum and school companion is under the influence of a man 'who seems in the way of improvement yet.' That alliance she determines to crush. She is the serpent with the fangs; her woman friend is the trembling rabbit. The man hovering on the brink of ruin, whom she might save and ennoble, she urges to suicide. She glories in destruction. When he is dead the only sorrow she has is that he has not killed himself artistically. He has made an ugly corpse. But she applauds his pluck in 'breaking away from the banquet of life—so early!' Her eyes brighten, and her nervous system glows when she reflects that 'Lövborg has had the courage to live his life after his own fashion!' Think only what this means. The same justification would apply to a burglar, a seducer, and a murderer. If Peace and Mrs. Pearcey had only committed suicide after their burglary and murder, they would have been justified by the propagandist of lawlessness. 'Brave man, Lövborg, to deceive three women, and then to die by your own hand!' proclaims Mrs. Hedda Gabler. And when she finds that she has made one fatal mistake in her life, and put herself into the power of her husband's best friend, the sensualist, this woman of the new school uses her last pistol on her own brain—or what is left of it—and the curtain falls. Miss Elizabeth Robins approached her task with artistic glee, and crowned it with undoubted success. The lovers of sustained art should not miss it, even if the play itself shocks them. The character grew under the influence of the actress. Her face was a study. No one could move their eyes from her. It was the morbid attraction that we have felt at the Central Criminal Court at a great murder trial. What changes of expression and of manner! What watchfulness! What a sublime study of deceit and heartlessness! It is said there are such women in the world. There may be, but thank God they are the rare exception, not the rule! And Miss Elizabeth Robins has done what no doubt she fully intended to do. She has made vice attractive by her art. She has almost ennobled crime. She has stopped the shudder that so repulsive a creature should have inspired. She has glorified an unwomanly woman. She has made a heroine out of a sublimated sinner. She has fascinated us with a savage.

And what better contrast to this sane lunatic, to this reasoning mad-woman, than the gentle, sweet-faced, almost angelic Mrs. Elvsted as played by Miss Marion Lea? We saw exactly the woman before our eyes. There she was, fair as a lily, with her glory of yellow hair and frightened eyes, weak as water, irresolute, a reed shaken by the winds, but a woman gaining courage and almost nobility under a strong in-fluence. The mere look of Mrs. Elvsted, her mild, wondering face, her pathetic voice, her intense trustfulness, almost brought tears to the eyes! Miss Marion Lea's performance is, in its way, as remarkable as that of Miss Robins. The one is the complement of the other.

And surely the Lövborg of Mr. Arthur Elwood is quite as fine a study of character. He exaggerated nothing in tone or demeanour or dress. We saw the strong intellectual man going under. We perceived the flash of power that survived the depravity. We understood how such a man, with such physical gifts, with such intellectual force, with such a face, could gain the ascendency over a trickster like Hedda Gabler, a weak fair-haired Magdalen like Mrs. Elvsted, and the dissolute red-haired actress in whose loveless arms he died! Few who saw it will forget the scene between Hedda and Lövborg over the photographs; the scene with the pistols that precedes Mr. Elwood's really fine exit to his death; the scene of the burning of the manuscript by Hedda; or the last scene at the stove between Hedda and the Judge. All credit should be given for the development of them alike to Miss Robins, to Mr. Elwood, and to Mr. Charles Sugden, who had a most difficult task, but acquitted himself admirably. The sensuality of Judge Brack was suggested, never asserted. Nor, indeed, should considerable praise be denied to Mr. Scott Buist for his impersonation of George Tesman. A kindly, affectionate nature, but a weak and foolish man. No wonder such a man bored Hedda Gabler! No wonder he jarred upon her nerves! She married him in her imperious way, and she intended to snub him for the term of his natural life. I am not likely to forget a scene in the last act, where these four characters are contrasted by Miss Robins, Miss Marion Lea, Mr. Sugden, and Mr. Scott Buist. It was a triumph of intellectual acting. Even such minor characters as the old aunt and the servant were acted to perfection by Miss Cowan and Miss Chapman.

It may be true that Ibsen can draw character, can create men and women alluring to the artist; that the very simplicity of his dialogue can fascinate the imaginative and sensitive actor or actress, and that he gives them scope for a freer use of their talent than they have hitherto enjoyed. So far as we have gone, Ibsen's lines have fallen into pleasant places. The people who have taken him up have done so devotedly and as with a religion. The play of *Hedda Gabler* is not only acted well but has been rehearsed to perfection. But if I were asked if it is a well-made play, a play for the people, a wholesome play, an instructive play, a play that amuses, or elevates, or assists the imagination or fancy, or fairly contrasts the good with the bad, the evil in life with the good, I should answer 'No.' We take it down with a gulp, and shudder afterwards. And there is no positive proof that such a dose of medicine does anybody any good whatever.

80. From an unsigned notice, *Sunday Times*

26 April 1891, 7

The production of Ibsen's latest and greatest drama, *Hedda Gabler*, at the Vaudeville this week must be accounted one of the most notable events in the history of the modern stage, for, in spite of all prejudice and opposition, it marks an epoch and clinches an influence. Miss Elizabeth Robins and Miss Marion Lea, the two venturesome young actresses who have been bold enough to introduce this remarkable play to the English stage, and confident enough to offer it for a series of afternoons, have done something more than provide a theatrical entertainment for the playgoer who takes his pleasure seriously, they have assisted a powerful artistic movement. Of course, the effect of a work of art must always depend on individual temperament, and as temperaments differ so widely, the work of art must always arouse all kinds of sentiments, and provoke widely opposing opinions. But the artistic value remains the same for those who can perceive it.

Now, to us *Hedda Gabler* appears a wonderful work of art, one that must produce a profound impression upon those who will accustom themselves to regard a stage-play from the point of view of real, living character in actual contact with the facts and sensations and possibilities of human experience, instead of gauging it by the conventional standard of playmaking, or the superficial observation of ordinary social intercourse. Ibsen has a way of going to the root of the matter, and exposing the skeleton in the cupboard, which is certainly not always a pleasant sight. But life, with its infinite subtleties and inconsistencies, is always interesting, and Ibsen shows us the wonder and the pity of it, while perhaps he only infers its loveliness by contrast. But therein he proves himself a master artist, for his point of view is definite, and the impression he produces is complete and final. In *Hedda Gabler* he gives us a typical tragedy of modern life, and in the strange, sensitive, selfish heroine, he presents one of the most wonderful and subtle conceptions of woman in the whole range of dramatic literature. But though we hate his self-centred woman, with the bored, unsatisfied life, who fights like a cunning tigress, wounding and killing without pity, to gain the emotional and sensuous food she hungers for, with what a thrilling sense of pity and terror must we regard the fatal consequences of her spoiled life. How wonderful are the contrasts of character, how artistically do they all conduce to the tragedy. And this tragedy, with its climax of the self-ending of the two marred lives that were so mysteriously and fatefully connected, is no more like a visit to the Morgue, as we have seen it described, than is *Antony and Cleopatra* with its several suicides, or *Hamlet* itself with its wholesale slaughter.

81. An unsigned notice, *Observer*

26 April 1891, 6

Hedda Gabler, the latest experiment in Norwegian drama tried before an English audience, can hardly by any stretch of critical courtesy be called a pleasant play, but it certainly came as a pleasant surprise to many of its hearers at the Vaudeville the other day. Like two, at least, of its predecessors, it is no doubt a study of insanity, and so represents yet another contribution to the drama of disease. Dr. Ibsen's emancipated heroines are nothing if they are not a trifle crazy, but there is, at any rate, a great deal more of intelligible method about the madness which impels Mrs. Hedda Tesman to blow her brains out than in the whimsical eccentricity which leads Miss Rebecca West hand in hand with Parson Rosmer into the millrace. Moreover, although there is necessarily much that is painful and ugly in the photographic delineation of a female monster like Hedda, whose crimes have not even the excuse of passion, but are committed merely to pass the weary time away, there is nothing to cause the sickening sense of revulsion with which one listened to Mrs. Alving's dull discussions concerning the advisability of forwarding her son's incestuous love affair. Hedda is about as disagreeable a product of wayward wickedness as the morbid imagination of playwright or novelist has ever conceived. But her proceedings are by no means lacking in human interest, nor is their illustration devoid—save in a few minor details of provincial coarseness—of the decency of civilised life. It is therefore possible to enjoy, almost without an *arrière pensée*, the rare skill alike of subtle analysis and of direct exposition displayed in the second and third acts of the new play. These are the acts devoted to the elucidation of the motives actuating the heartless heroine in the varying attitudes which she assumes towards the commonplace husband who bores her, the professional seducer whose cynical advances arouse only her languid curiosity, and finally the reckless lover of bygone days, whom she encourages to play with fire, partly out of jealous caprice and but still more out of idle malice. The grim comedy of these passages produces an effect which unfortunately is not sustained in the development of incident to which they lead. The serious importance attached by others as well as by Lövborg to the loss of that dissipated young author's manuscript in the course of his drunken frolic strikes one as wholly out of proportion. Hedda's melodramatic pistols and their use, first by Lövborg and then by Hedda herself, carry very little more conviction than does the fair suicide's talk about the courage and the grandeur of a self-inflicted death. We do not believe in them any more than does Judge Brack, and we recognise in them nothing more than a modernised survival of the violent expedients whereby many an old-world playwright of no philosophical or didactic pretensions whatever has deliberately set about his flesh-creeping task. The performance during the week has done full justice to a play which, though not on the whole a satisfying work of art, is yet full of artistic suggestion. Miss Elizabeth Robins has managed to endow the callous selfishness and morbid malignity of the heroine with just enough of womanly grace and inconsistent charm to make her bearable for three acts. Mr. Charles Sugden has given a really admirable rendering of Judge Brack's sardonic humour. Mr. Elwood has got over his difficulties as Lövborg with great tact, and Miss M. Lea's exaggeration of Mrs. Elvsted's affected foolishness has been readily pardoned for the sake of the intrinsic prettiness of the impersonation. It should be added that the practical result of this last Ibsen enterprise has been sufficiently encouraging to warrant its repetition this week.

82. 'Goldsmith and Ibsen/A Dramatic Contrast', an unsigned notice, *People*

26 April 1891, 6

By accident, rather than intent, playgoers have just had the opportunity of fairly judging between the truth of human nature, as characterised by Oliver Goldsmith, and its perversion and debasement, as exhibited by Henrik Ibsen—the former exemplified in Mr. Wills's *Olivia*, the revived dramatisation of *The Vicar of Wakefield* at the Lyceum; the latter in Mr. Edmund Gosse's translation of the Norwegian playwright's *Hedda Gabler*, performed on each of five afternoons of the past week at the Vaudeville. In both plays the motive lies in sin and its consequent suffering; but how oppositely treated—the one showing the wrong done under temptation, but ere long atoned for and forgiven, the other presenting crime committed heinously and in cold blood with malice prepense unextenuated either by provocation or purpose. For it is observed that, whereas the English play exemplifies the inherent goodness latent beneath the frailty of humanity, and thereby encourages hope; the Norwegian drama, utterly pessimistic in its tedious turmoil of knaves and fools, finds no result but suicide as the sole escape from despair. The sympathetic influence and attraction of Goldsmith's story, whether felt from reading or from stage presentment, is too well known to need further reference than to the fact that the average balance of good and evil is fairly kept among its characters. But in *Hedda Gabler*, not to mention other plays from the same tainted source, evil only prevails, for, whether plotters or victims, the persons of the scene are recognised as being without shame or remorse, adulterers or homicides, or both, whose sole principle of conduct is selfishness disguised under the mask of individuality. Originality the latest stage production from Ibsen's pen undoubtedly possesses, in common with all his plays, but only by contravening whatever has to be regarded through the traditions of genius endorsed by the general acceptation of mankind throughout the world as truthful, sacred, and beautiful. Starting with atheism as his first premiss, the new 'master' enunciates the dogma deduced apparently from the blighting philosophy of Schopenhauer that 'there is nothing new and nothing true, and it doesn't signify.' The only wonder is that actresses of the approved artistic intelligence and mental refinement of the Misses Robins and Marion Lea, who are responsible for the presentations of *Hedda Gabler*, should demean their quality by worshipping at the feet of such an earthy Dagon; and the marvel of his notorious influence over the feminine rather than the masculine mind becomes the greater when it is considered that his characterisations of womankind deny her the purest and highest attributes of her nature, whether as maiden, wife, or mother. Playgoers in any sort of doubt as to the truth between the two dramatic exponents of humanity here commented upon may be induced by the contrast to visit the Lyceum and Vaudeville Theatres, and, seeing the two plays, *Olivia* and *Hedda Gabler*, form their own judgment between them.

83. Henry Arthur Jones on the unfortunate depravity but enlivening influence of Ibsen

May 1891

A report in the *Era* (2 May 1891), 10. Henry Arthur Jones (1851–1929) was a popular dramatist of the day.

Mr. Henry Arthur Jones, in a letter to a correspondent in Berlin, writes: —'One of the most significant signs of the times in England is the announcement that a play of his takes the place on Monday evening of Lord Lytton's comedy of *Money*. I think Ibsen's influence has been of great value to the English stage as an emetic or liver pill. For some time past a whole army of theatricalities and conventionalities has been tottering about on the British stage only waiting for "killing truth to glare upon them." It is in the sincerity of his methods that Ibsen is of great value to the English stage just now. Our stock dummies, our regiments of falsely accused heroes, our masterpieces of impossible virtue and impossible vice, our whole apparatus of ingenious, Chinese

puzzle situation, our whole puppet show has been convicted of falsehood and unreality. All the sawdust is running out of our favourite
dolls, and in respect of much of our modern English drama the public
are rapidly adopting one of the catch phrases in *Hedda Gabler*, and are
saying, "Good God! People don't do such things!" At the same time,
one cannot help regretting that Ibsen's colossal intellectual power should
be employed in the research, not of beauty, and health, and strength,
but of disease and moral deformity, of curious and exceptional depravity, and it is amusing to see some of his worshippers cheerfully dosing
themselves with a specific for hereditary disease, and smacking their
lips over it as though it were the rarest vintage of Lachrymae Christi.
To them we must steadfastly reply that we cannot live on drugs.'

84. 'On the Occasion of *Hedda Gabler*', by Henry James, *New Review*

June 1891, iv, 519–30

Reprinted, together with James's *Master Builder* review (No. 96)
in *Essays in London and Elsewhere* (London, 1893).

Whether or no Henrik Ibsen be a master of his art, he has had a fortune
that, in the English-speaking world, falls not always even to the masters
—the fortune not only of finding himself the theme of many pens and
tongues, but the rarer privilege and honour of acting as a sort of register
of the critical atmosphere, a barometer of the intellectual weather.
Interesting or not in himself (the word on this point varies from the
fullest affirmation to the richest denial), he has sounded in our literary
life a singularly interesting hour. At any rate he himself constitutes an
episode, an event, if the sign of such action be to have left appearances
other than you found them. He has cleared up the air we breathe and
set a copy to our renouncement, has made many things wonderfully
plain and quite mapped out the prospect. Whenever such service is

rendered, the attentive spirit is the gainer; these are its moments of amplest exercise. Illusions are sweet to the dreamer, but not so to the observer, who has a horror of a fool's paradise. Henrik Ibsen will have led him inexorably into the rougher road. Such recording and illuminating agents are precious; they tell us where we are in the thickening fog of life, and we feel for them much of the grateful respect excited in us at sea, in dim weather, by the exhibition of the mysterious instrument with which the captain takes an observation. We have held *Ghosts*, or *Rosmersholm*, or *Hedda Gabler* in our hand, and *they* have been our little instrument—they have enabled us to emulate the wary mariner; the consequence of which is that we know at least on what shores we may ground or in what ports we may anchor. The author of these strange works has in short performed a function which was doubtless no part of his purpose. This was to tell us about his own people; yet what has primarily happened is that he has brought about an exhibition of ours.

It is a truly remarkable show, for as to where *nous en sommes*, as the phrase goes, in the art of criticism and the movement of curiosity, as to our accumulations of experience and our pliancy of intelligence, our maturity of judgement and our distinction of tone, our quick perception of quality and (peculiar glory of our race) our fine feeling for shades, he has been the means of our acquiring the most copious information. Whether or no we may say that as a sequel to this we know Dr. Ibsen better, we may at least say that we know more about ourselves. We glow with the sense of how we may definitely look to each other to take things, and that is an immense boon, representing in advance a wonderful economy of time, a saving of useless effort and vain appeal. The great clarifying fact has been that, with *Hedda Gabler* and *Ghosts* and all the rest, we have stood in an exceptionally agitated way in the presence of the work of art, and have gained thereby a peculiarly acute consciousness of how we tend to consider it. It has been interesting to perceive that we consider the work of art with passion, with something approaching to fury. Under its influence we sweep the whole keyboard of emotion, from frantic enjoyment to ineffable disgust. Resentment and reprobation happen to have been indeed in the case before us the notes most frequently sounded; but this is obviously an accident, not impairing the value of the illustration, the essence of which is that our critical temper remains exactly the *naïf* critical temper, the temper of the spectators in the gallery of the theatre who howl at the villain of the play.

It has been the degree in general, of the agitation, that has been remarkable in the case before us, as may conveniently be gathered from a glance at the invaluable catalogue of denouncements drawn up by Mr. William Archer after perusal of the article lately dedicated by the principal London journals to a couple of representations of Ibsen; that, if I mistake not, of *Ghosts* and that of *Rosmersholm*. This catalogue is a precious document, one of those things that the attentive spirit would not willingly let die. It is a thing, at any rate, to be kept long under one's hand, as a mine of suggestion and reference; for it illuminates, in this matter of the study of Ibsen, the second characteristic of our emotion (the first as I have mentioned, being its peculiar intensity); the fact that the emotion is conspicuously and exclusively moral, one of those cries of outraged purity which have so often and so pathetically resounded through the Anglo-Saxon world.

We have studied our author, it must be admitted, under difficulties, for it is impossible to read him without perceiving that merely book in hand we but half know him—he addresses himself so substantially to representation. This quickens immensely our consideration for him, since in proportion as we become conscious that he has mastered an exceedingly difficult form are we naturally reluctant, in honour, to judge him unaccompanied by its advantages, by the benefit of his full intention. Considering how much Ibsen has been talked about in England and America, he has been lamentably little seen and heard. Until *Hedda Gabler* was produced in London six weeks ago, there had been but one attempt to represent its predecessors that had consisted of more than a single performance. This circumstance has given a real importance to the understanding of the two courageous young actresses who have brought the most recent of the author's productions to the light and who have promptly found themselves justified in their talent as well as in their energy. It was a proof of Ibsen's force that he had made us chatter about him so profusely without the aid of the theatre; but it was even more a blessing to have the aid at last. The stage is to the prose drama (and Ibsen's later manner is the very prose of prose) what the tune is to the song or the concrete case to the general law. It immediately becomes apparent that he needs the test to show his strength and the frame to show his picture. An extraordinary process of vivification takes place; the conditions seem essentially enlarged. Those of the stage in general strike us for the most part as small enough, so that the game played in them is often not more inspiring than a successful sack-race. But Ibsen reminds us that if they do not in themselves confer life they can at least receive it when the infusion is artfully attempted. Yet how much of it they were doomed to receive from *Hedda Gabler* was not to be divined till we had seen *Hedda Gabler* in the frame. The play, on perusal, left one comparatively muddled and mystified, fascinated, but —in one's intellectual sympathy—snubbed. Acted, it leads that sympathy over the straightest of roads with all the exhilaration of a superior pace. Much more, I confess, one doesn't get from it; but an hour of refreshing exercise is a reward in itself. The sense of being moved by a scientific hand as one sits in one's stall has not been spoiled for us by satiety.

Hedda Gabler then, in the frame, is exceedingly vivid and curious, and a part of its interest is in the way it lights up in general the talent of the author. It is doubtless not the most complete of Ibsen's plays, for it owes less to its subject than to its form; but it makes good his title to the possession of a real method, and in thus putting him before us as a master it exhibits at the same time his irritating, his bewildering incongruities. He is nothing, as a literary personality, if not positive; yet there are moments when his great gift seems made up of negatives, or at any rate when the total seems a contradiction of each of the parts. I premise of course that we hear him through a medium not his own, and I remember that translation is a shameless falsification of colour. Translation, however, is probably not wholly responsible for three appearances inherent in all his prose work, as we possess it, though in slightly differing degrees, and yet quite unavailing to destroy in it the expression of life; I mean of course the absence of humour, the absence of free imagination, and the absence of style. The absence of style, both in the usual and in the larger sense of the word, is extraordinary, and all the more mystifying that its place is not usurped, as it frequently is in such cases, by vulgarity. Ibsen is massively common and 'middle-class,' but neither his spirit nor his manner is small. He is never trivial and never cheap, but he is in nothing more curious than in owing to a single source such distinction as he retains. His people are of inexpensive race; they give us essentially the *bourgeois* impression; even when they are furiously nervous and, like Hedda, more than sufficiently fastidious, we recognise that they live, with their remarkable creator, in a world in which selection has no great range. This is perhaps one reason why they none of them, neither the creator nor the creatures, appear to feel much impulse to *play* with the things of life. The impulse, when it breaks out, is humour, and in the scenic genius it usually breaks out in one place or another. We get the feeling, in Ibsen's plays, that such whims are too ultimate, too much a matter of luxury and leisure for the stage of feeling at which his characters have arrived. They are all too busy learning to live—humour will come in later, when they know how. A certain angular irony they frequently manifest, and some of his portraits are strongly satirical, like that, to give only two instances, of Tesman, in *Hedda Gabler* (a play indeed suffused with irrepressible irony), or that of Hialmar Ekdal, in *The Wild Duck*. But it is the ridicule without the smile, the dance without the music, a sort of sarcasm that is nearer to tears than to laughter. There is nothing very droll in the world, I think, to Dr. Ibsen; and nothing is more interesting than to see how he makes up his world without a joke. Innumerable are the victories of talent, and art is a legerdemain.

It is always difficult to give an example of an absent quality, and, if the romantic is even less present in Ibsen than the comic, this is best proved by the fact that everything seems to us inveterately observed. Nothing is more puzzling to the readers of his later work than the reminder that he is the great dramatic poet of his country, or that the author of *The Pillars of Society* is also the author of *Brand* and *Peer Gynt*, compositions which, we are assured, testify to an audacious imagination and abound in complicated fantasy. In his satiric studies of contemporary life, the impression that is strongest with us is that the picture is infinitely *noted*, that all the patience of the constructive pessimist is in his love of the detail of character and of conduct, in his way of accumulating the touches that illustrate them. His recurrent ugliness of surface, as it were, is a sort of proof of his fidelity to the real, in a spare, strenuous, democratic community; just as the same peculiarity is one of the sources of his charmless fascination—a touching vision of strong forces struggling with a poverty, a bare provinciality, of life. I call the fascination of Ibsen charmless (for those who feel it at all), because he holds us without bribing us; he squeezes the attention till he almost hurts it, yet with never a conciliatory stroke. He has as little as possible to say to our taste; even his large, strong form takes no account of that, gratifying it without concessions. It is the oddity of the mixture that makes him so individual—his perfect practice of a difficult and delicate art, combined with such aesthetic density. Even in such a piece as *The Lady from the Sea* (much the weakest, to my sense, of the whole series), in which he comes nearer than in others—unless indeed it be in *Hedda Gabler*—to playing with an idea from the simple instinct of sport, nothing could be less picturesque than the general effect, with every inherent incentive to have made it picturesque. The idea might have sprung from the fancy of Hawthorne, but the atmosphere is the hard light of Ibsen. One feels that the subject should have been tinted and distanced; but, in fact, one has to make an atmosphere as one reads, and one winces considerably under 'Doctor Wangel' and the pert daughters.

For readers without curiosity as to their author's point of view (and it is doubtless not a crime not to have it, though I think it is a misfortune, an open window the less), there is too much of 'Doctor Wangel' in Ibsen altogether—using the good gentleman's name for what it generally represents or connotes. It represents the ugly interior on which his curtain inexorably rises and which, to be honest, I like for the queer associations it has taught us to respect: the hideous carpet and wall-paper and curtains (one may answer for them), the conspicuous stove, the lonely centre-table, the 'lamps with green shades,' as in the sumptuous first act of *The Wild Duck*, the pervasive air of small interests and standards, the sign of limited local life. It represents the very clothes, the inferior fashions, of the figures that move before us, and the shape of their hats and the tone of their conversation and the nature of their diet. But the oddest thing happens in connection with this effect—the oddest extension of sympathy or relaxation of prejudice. What happens is that we feel that whereas, if Ibsen were weak or stupid or vulgar, this parochial or suburban stamp would only be a stick to beat him with, it acts, as the case stands, and in the light of his singular masculinity, as a sort of substitute—a little clumsy, if you like—for charm. In a word, it becomes touching, so that practically the *blasé* critical mind enjoys it as a refinement. What occurs is very analogous to what occurs in our appreciation of the dramatist's remarkable art, his admirable talent for producing an intensity of interest by means incorruptibly quiet, by that almost demure preservation of the appearance of the usual in which we see him juggle with difficulty and danger and which constitutes, as it were, his only coquetry. There are people who are indifferent to these mild prodigies; there are others for whom they will always remain the most charming privilege of art.

Hedda Gabler is doubtless as suburban as any of its companions; which is indeed a fortunate circumstance, inasmuch as if it were less so we should be deprived of a singularly complete instance of a phenomenon difficult to express, but which may perhaps be described as the operation of talent without glamour. There is notoriously no glamour over the suburbs, and yet nothing could be more vivid than Dr. Ibsen's account of the incalculable young woman into whom Miss Robins so artistically projects herself. To 'like' the play, as we phrase it, is doubtless therefore to give one of the fullest examples of our constitutional inability to control our affections. Several of the spectators who have

liked it most will probably admit even that, with themselves, this sentiment has preceded a complete comprehension. They would perhaps have
liked it better if they had understood it better—as to this they are not
sure; but they at any rate liked it well enough. Well enough for what?
the question may of course always be in such a case. To be absorbed,
assuredly, which is the highest tribute we can pay to any picture of life,
and a higher one than most pictures attempted succeed in making us
pay. Ibsen is various, and *Hedda Gabler* is probably an ironical pleasantry,
the artistic exercise of a mind saturated with the vision of human in-
firmities; saturated, above all, with a sense of the infinitude, for all its
mortal savour, of *character*, finding that an endless romance and a perpetual challenge. Can there have been at the source of such a production
a mere refinement of conscious power, an enjoyment of difficulty and
a preconceived victory over it? We are free to imagine that in this case
Dr. Ibsen chose one of the last subjects that an expert might have been
expected to choose, for the harmless pleasure of feeling and of showing
that he was in possession of a method that could make up for its
deficiencies.

The demonstration is complete and triumphant, but it does not
conceal from us—on the contrary—that his drama is essentially that
supposedly undramatic thing, the picture not of an action but of a
condition. It is the portrait of a nature, the story of what Paul Bourget
would call an *état d'âme*, and of a state of nerves as well as of soul, a
state of temper, of health, of chagrin, of despair. *Hedda Gabler* is, in
short, the study of an exasperated woman; and it may certainly be
declared that the subject was not in advance, as a theme for scenic treatment, to be pronounced promising. There could in fact, however, be no
more suggestive illustration of the folly of quarrelling with an artist over
his subject. Ibsen has had only to take hold of this one in earnest to make
it, against every presumption, live with an intensity of life. One can
doubtless imagine other ways, but it is enough to say of this one that,
put to the test, it imposes its particular spectacle. Something might have
been gained, entailing perhaps a loss in another direction, by tracing the
preliminary stages, showing the steps in Mrs. Tesman's history which
led to the spasm, as it were, on which the curtain rises and of which the
breathless duration—ending in death—is the period of the piece. But a
play is above everything a work of selection, and Ibsen, with his curious
and beautiful passion for the unity of time (carried in him to a point
which almost always implies also that of place), condemns himself to
admirable rigours. We receive Hedda ripe for her catastrophe, and if we

ask for antecedents and explanations we must simply find them in her character. Her motives are just her passions. What the four acts show us is these motives and that character—complicated, strange, irreconcilable, infernal—playing themselves out. We know too little why she married Tesman, we see too little why she ruins Lövborg; but we recognise that she is infinitely perverse, and Heaven knows that, as the drama mostly goes, the crevices we are called upon to stop are singularly few. That Mrs. Tesman is a perfectly ill-regulated person is a matter of course, and there are doubtless spectators who would fain ask whether it would not have been better to represent in her stead a person totally different. The answer to this sagacious question seems to me to be simply that no one can possibly tell. There are many things in the world that are past finding out, and one of them is whether the subject of a work had not better have been another subject. We shall always do well to leave that matter to the author (*he* may have some secret for solving the riddle); so terrible would his revenge easily become if we were to accept a responsibility for his theme.

The distinguished thing is the firm hand that weaves the web, the deep and ingenious use made of the material. What material, indeed, the dissentient spirit may exclaim, and what 'use,' worthy of the sacred name, is to be made of a wicked, diseased, disagreeable woman? That is just what Ibsen attempts to gauge, and from the moment such an attempt is resolute the case ceases to be so simple. The 'use' of Hedda Gabler is that she acts on others and that even her most disagreeable qualities have the privilege, thoroughly undeserved doubtless, but equally irresistible, of becoming a part of the history of others. And then one isn't so sure she is wicked, and by no means sure (especially when she is represented by an actress who makes the point ambiguous) that she is disagreeable. She is various and sinuous and graceful, complicated and natural; she suffers, she struggles, she is human, and by that fact exposed to a dozen interpretations, to the importunity of our suspense. Wrought with admirable closeness is the whole tissue of relations between the five people whom the author sets in motion and on whose behalf he asks of us so few concessions. That is for the most part the accomplished thing in Ibsen, the thing that converts his provincialism into artistic urbanity. He puts *us* to no expense worth speaking of— he takes all the expense himself. I mean that he thinks out our entertainment for us and shapes it of thinkable things, the passions, the idiosyncrasies, the cupidities and jealousies, the strivings and struggles, the joys and sufferings of men. The spectator's situation is different enough when what is given him is the mere dead rattle of the surface of life, into which *he* has to inject the element of thought, the 'human interest.' Ibsen kneads the soul of man like a paste, and often with a rude and indelicate hand to which the soul of man objects. Such a production as *The Pillars of Society*, with its large, dense complexity of moral cross-references and its admirable definiteness as a picture of motive and temperament (the whole canvas charged, as it were, with moral colour), such a production asks the average moral man to see too many things at once. It will never help Ibsen with the multitude that the multitude shall feel that the more they look the more intentions they shall see, for of such seeing of many intentions the multitude is but scantily desirous. It keeps indeed a positively alarmed and jealous watch in that direction; it smugly insists that intentions shall be rigidly limited.

This sufficiently answers the artless question of whether it may be hoped for the author of *The Pillars of Society* that he shall acquire popularity in this country. In what country under heaven might it have been hoped for him, or for the particular community, that he *should* acquire popularity? Is he in point of fact so established and cherished in the Norwegian theatre? Do his countrymen understand him and clamour for him and love him, or do they content themselves—a very different affair—with being proud of him when aliens abuse him? The rumour reaches us that *Hedda Gabler* has found no favour at Copenhagen, where we are compelled to infer that the play had not the happy interpretation it enjoys in London. It would doubtless have been in danger here if tact and sympathy had not interposed. We hear that it has had reverses in Germany, where of late years Ibsen has been the fashion; but, indeed, all these are matters of an order as to which we should have been grateful for more information from those who have lately had the care of introducing the formidable dramatist to the English and American public. He excites, for example, in each case, all sorts of curiosity and conjecture as to the quality and capacity of the theatre to which, originally, such a large order was addressed: we are full of unanswered questions about the audience and the school.

What, however, has most of all come out in our timid and desultory experiments is that the author of *The Pillars of Society*, and of *The Doll's House*, of *Ghosts*, of *The Wild Duck*, of *Hedda Gabler*, is destined to be adored by the 'profession.' Even in his comfortless borrowed habit he will remain intensely dear to the actor and the actress. He cuts them out work to which the artistic nature in them joyously responds—work difficult and interesting, full of stuff and opportunity. The opportunity that he gives them is almost always to do the deep and delicate thing—the sort of chance that, in proportion as they are intelligent, they are most on the look out for. He asks them to paint with a fine brush; for the subject that he gives them is ever our plastic humanity. This will surely preserve him (leaving out the question of serious competition) after our little flurry is over. It was what made the recent representation of *Hedda Gabler* so singularly interesting and refreshing. It is what gives importance to the inquiry as to how his call for 'subtlety' in his interpreters has been met in his own country. It was impossible the other day not to be conscious of a certain envy (as of a case of artistic happiness) of the representatives of the mismated Tesmans and their companions—so completely, as the phrase is, were they 'in' it and under the charm of what they had to do. In fact the series of Ibsen's 'social dramas' is a dazzling array of parts. Nora Helmer will be undertaken again and again—of a morning, no doubt, as supposedly, though oddly, the more 'earnest' hour—by young artists justly infatuated. The temptation is still greater to women than to men, as we feel in thinking, further, of the Rebecca of *Rosmersholm*, of Lona Hessel and Martha Bernick in the shapely *Pillars*, of the passionate mother and the insolent maid in the extraordinarily compact and vivid *Ghosts*—absurd and fascinating work; of Mrs. Linden, so quietly tragic, so tremulously real, in *The Doll's House*, and of that irresistibly touching image, so untainted with cheap pathos, Hedvig Ekdal, the little girl with failing eyes, in *The Wild Duck*, who pores over her story-book in the paltry photographic studio of her intensely humbugging father. Such a figure as this very Hialmar Ekdal, however, the seedy, selfish—subtly selfish and self-deceptive—photographer, in whom nothing is active but the tongue, testifies for the strong masculine side of the list. If *The League of Youth* is more nearly a complete comedy than any other of Ibsen's prose works, the comedian who should attempt to render Stensgard in that play would have a real portrait to reproduce. But the examples are numerous: Bernick and Rosmer, Oswald and Manders (Ibsen's compunctious 'pastors' are admirable), Gregers Werle, the transcendent meddler in *The Wild Duck*, Rörlund, the prudish rector in the *Pillars*, Stockmann and the Burgomaster in *The Enemy of the People*, all stand, humanly and pictorially, on their feet.

This it is that brings us back to the author's great quality, the quality that makes him so interesting in spite of his limitations, so rich in spite of his lapses—his habit of dealing essentially with the individual caught in the fact. Sometimes, no doubt, he leans too far on that side, loses sight too much of the type-quality and gives his spectators free play to say that even caught in the fact his individuals are mad. We are not at all sure, for instance, of the type-quality in Hedda. Sometimes he makes so queer a mistake as to treat a pretty motive, like that of *The Lady from the Sea*, in a poor and prosaic way. He exposes himself with complacent, with irritating indifference to the objector as well as to the scoffer, he makes his 'heredity' too short and his consequences too long, he deals with a homely and unaesthetic society, he harps on the string of conduct, and he actually talks of stockings and legs, in addition to other improprieties. He is not pleasant enough nor light enough nor casual enough; he is too far from Piccadilly and our glorious standards. Therefore his cause may be said to be lost; we shall never take him to our hearts. It was never to have been expected, indeed, that we should, for in literature religions usually grow their own gods, and *our* heaven—as every one can see—is already crowded. But for those who care in general for the form that he has practised he will always remain one of the talents that have understood it best and extracted most from it, have effected most neatly the ticklish transfusion of life. If we possessed the unattainable, an eclectic, artistic, disinterested theatre, to which we might look for alternation and variety, it would simply be a point of honour in such a temple to sacrifice sometimes to Henrik Ibsen.

THE LADY FROM THE SEA

Terry's Theatre, 11 May 1891

85. From an unsigned notice, *The Times*

12 May 1891, 12

The play was translated by Eleanor Marx and the cast was as follows:

Ellida Wangel ..	Miss Rose Meller	Hilda ..	..	Miss Edith Kenward
Dr Wangel ..	Mr Oscar Adye	Arnholm ..	..	Mr Leonard Outram
Stranger ..	Mr Charles Dalton	Lyngstrand	..	Mr Herbert Sparling
Boletta ..	.. Miss Violet Armbruster	Ballested ..	..	Mr Ernest Patterson

Another Ibsen play was acted yesterday—*The Lady from the Sea*, which has been selected as the subject of a few experimental performances at Terry's Theatre in the afternoon. There is no prospect at all that *The Lady from the Sea* will rival *Hedda Gabler* in popularity or even excite the modicum of interest that attached to *A Doll's House*. It is unquestionably the weakest of the Ibsen plays that have yet been performed in London. As enigmatical as any, it offers no opportunity for powerful acting, while its general analysis of character is shallow and its dialogue commonplace. The effect of this performance, following so close upon others of the same kind, can hardly fail to be disastrous to the Ibsen propaganda. Clearly Ibsen's best chance of being accepted as a dramatist, rather than a pathological lecturer, is that he should be administered to the public in small doses and at long intervals. Studies in morbid heredity are very well in a scientific treatise. On the stage, put forward as a public entertainment, they tend to perplex, irritate, and repel, besides being useless for any practical purpose. Ellida Wangel, the lady from the sea, is just as crazy as any of her sister heroines; her mother, we are told, died mad, and there is throughout the story a strong likelihood that she will come to the same end.

[outlines the plot.]

The case of Ellida Wangel as a victim of the insane temperament would not, *per se*, be very different from that of Hedda Gabler or Nora Helmer. Unfortunately the heroine's surroundings in the present instance are more forbidding than usual, for half the remaining *dramatis personæ* are as mad as herself. Certainly the stranger is so, and without the plea of hereditary predisposition; while the two daughters of Dr. Wangel give promise of developing into characteristically impracticable 'types' on their own account. There is, in fact, no entirely rational personage in the story from first to last—none assuredly who can attract the spectator's wandering sympathies; and one is puzzled at the end of the performance to say whether the author has been giving the rein to a morbid fancy or indulging in a joke at the expense of the disciples who sit at his feet and accept him as a revelation.

86. From an unsigned notice, *Standard*

12 May 1891, 3

The chief impression made by the performance of Ibsen's play, *The Lady from the Sea*, yesterday afternoon, was that Mr. W. S. Gilbert will have to look to his laurels. And not only Mr. Gilbert, but the most successful writers of farcical comedy would have to tax their powers to the utmost to produce a more diverting piece—regarded in its proper aspect—than the five acts of unmitigated rubbish which were presented to a scanty audience on the first bright Summer's afternoon of the season. Those who came to listen attentively remained to scoff, the ripple of laughter which was almost continuous during the fourth and fifth acts being evidently very disconcerting to the unfortunate performers. We are informed that in this play, as, indeed, in others from the same hand, the author speculates as to 'what future woman may have, if she shapes her life wholly without relation to the prerogatives of the other sex.' It is needless to add that the prerogatives in question are those which a husband is ordinarily supposed to exercise over his wife.

87. From an unsigned review by Clement Scott, *Daily Telegraph*

12 May 1891, 3

It would be distinctly unfair to blame Ibsen for the dull, lifeless, and, on the whole, unenlightened performance of his *Lady from the Sea* yesterday afternoon. It was like the water on the fjord of which the mystic Ellida Wangel complained so bitterly. 'Fresh, oh! the water here is never fresh. It is so tepid and lifeless. Ugh! the water in the fjord here is sick; yes, sick! and I believe it makes one sick, too!' Few plays by Ibsen are more interesting to read; not one has come out so badly in representation. Hour after hour passed by, and with each the same dull tirade of tedious talk. Dialogue succeeded dialogue, and despair sat on the countenances of the most devoted Ibsenites. It was not until the 'master' became absolutely conventional; it was not until the apostle of originality borrowed without blushing the stalest tricks of despised melodrama; it was not until Mr. Dalton, specially borrowed from the heretical Adelphi for the occasion, sneaked round the pasture, looked over the hedge, and demanded his 'gal' like any Jack Tar in the days of T. P. Cooke; it was not until the absolutely conventional villain, baulked in his attempt to get the faithless Ellida 'on board his lugger,' produced a pistol out of his breeches pocket to shoot the virtuous husband; it was not until Ellida, in true old-world Surrey transpontine fashion, flung herself between her spouse and the cocked revolver, that the audience woke up from its despondent lethargy, and the Ibsenites pretended not to believe that the play had been saved from insufferable boredom by a dodge of which a modern transpontine dramatist would be heartily ashamed.

But of course there is more in *The Lady from the Sea* than these purely old-world melodramatic touches. Poetry, romance, and mysticism exist in many a scene and many a character, but as ill-luck would have it the atmosphere was not charged with poetry or electricity either. It is not everyone, however earnest, however clever, however passionately attached to the Ibsen creed, who can play Ellida Wangel. It requires the strangest and strongest individuality. Ellida is a Nora who does not go out and does not bang the door. But she is a far more poetic creature than Nora. She also has lived for many years with 'a strange man.' She has borne a child to him, she has accepted the duties and responsibilities of a wife, and after six years she seems to want a change, and talks wildly of a mystic marriage with a seafaring murderer, and makes up her mind that she cannot live with a man who does not come from the sea and talk of seals, and kittewakes, and dolphins, and porpoises, and she is bored to death by a Scandinavian doctor, while anxious to elope with the man 'with the eyes'—whose eyes, by the way, have been reproduced in her dead child. The old interminable argument follows whether Ellida should or should not elope to England, whether she should or should not be emancipated, whether it would not be convenient, at any rate, to try the effect of a journey to England with the Adelphi villain, when the husband, wearied out with her wilfulness, and disinclined to try the argument of the stick, gives in, presents his wife with her freedom, tells her she may go and do precisely what she pleases, perhaps adding *sotto voce*, 'and be hanged to her,' when Ellida turns round for her husband's 'noble sake, and gives him herself indeed.'

88. From an unsigned notice, *Gentlewoman*

16 May 1891, 674

Monday's performance of this remarkable play was to me a sad disappointment. I had looked forward to it with anxiety. I had read Mrs. Eleanor Marx Aveling's apparently accurate and reliable translation, a work undertaken by this lady with the author's permission, and the romance of it caught my fancy. There was something weird, and uncanny, and mystical in this notion of the girl whose life seems so bound up with the waves and storms, who loves all the living things in the waters, and finds music in the scream of the sea-birds and sympathy in the movement of the restless ocean. Ellida Wangel, as I read her, seemed to have something of the nature of some wayward child, ever holding close to her ear some shell that breathed strange murmurings of its home in the dark depths. Twice, at all events, had I met some like her in the fiction I specially love. Once when I met Delamotte Fouqué's exquisite conception of 'Undine' in the German legend, with her fierce water-king uncle, and her passion for streams and rivers. Again, I found something like her in Hans Andersen's story of 'The Little Mermaid'—she who loved the Prince, you know, and was wont to bathe her feet in the cool water by the palace steps—and yet once more I found her in a legend of the far west of Ireland, which saw the light in an old Christmas number, under the title of 'The Story of Mrs. Peterkyne,' and was signed 'Frère Sauvage.' I was 'equipped' with sentiment to enjoy *The Lady from the Sea*, and was prepared to study the effect of the gift of freedom of individual action on Ellida, the sweeter use she put her emancipated individuality to, than that adopted by Nora, in the *Doll's House*, and I thought there would be something quaint in the ultimate pairing off of the customary six central characters. Alas for my hopes! The acting wrecked the romance. It was a crude amateurish production, brimful of errors and discords, and in more than one instance terribly disfigured by a certain harsh Cockney accent that seemed to have fallen on the performers.

89. An unsigned notice, *Referee*

17 May 1891, 2

The officious, noisy clique who, mistaking the flicker of a tändstickor for the light of the sun, profess to have discovered a great dramatist in Dr. Ibsen, were humiliated on Monday afternoon, when *The Lady from the Sea* was produced at Terry's Theatre. If the piece had been presented under any name but Ibsen's, I verily believe it would have been hissed off the stage long before the end of it. Never was a dramatist so well treated as this Norwegian; his plays are produced one after another, always with a great flourish of trumpets, and they are listened to by the faithful with the closest attention. But the most devotional of them all could not help feeling perplexed and, worse than that, bored by *The Lady from the Sea*, which is incomparably the worst of Ibsen's plays that has yet been seen in London. We have the crazy woman all over again, only crazier than ever. After a few years of married life Ellida Wangel, who is the wife of a highly respectable, devoted noodle, develops alarming symptoms of 'baulked individuality,' as the consecrated phrase is. Taking her husband tardily into her confidence, she informs him that before their marriage she had a ridiculously romantic affair with a sailor, who, as she tells her husband plainly, murdered his captain. Why the sailor murdered the captain is one of the enigmas of the play.

The sailor is so much in Ellida's mind that he drives her clean out of it, and whilst she is in that humour, what more natural than that the fellow should present himself at her garden-gate? For Ibsen does not disdain the old devices of the beginning-of-the-century dramatist. Whether she loves the sea—for which she yearns through three of the five acts—or whether she loves the sailor—for first she says she 'belongs' to one and then she says she 'belongs' to the other—there is the fact that she insists upon being 'released' by her husband, and he has no sooner given her permission to go with her sailor than she changes her mind again, and being 'free' to make her choice, elects to remain with her husband: and that's all. If she were my wife, I must say I had rather the sailor (or the sea) had taken her. What the play means Ibsen does not explain, but the mystery is variously expounded. Mrs. Eleanor Marx Aveling, who made the translation used at Terry's, has her own theory, which is simply that Ellida has been hypnotised by the sailor. Others equally ardent in their admiration for Ibsen regard Mrs. Aveling's theory of hypnotism as a story to be told to the marines—or the Psychical Research Society. My own theory is that Ibsen himself is as cranky as any one of his characters, and does not know what he means. The characters in *The Lady from the Sea* are the queerest people imaginable, and they all talk Ibsen, even to the ingenious miss Bolette, who gives unmistakable signs of growing up as 'free' as the maddest of Ibsen's heroines. They are all alike. If proofs were wanted of the disordered intellect of the writer of *The Lady from the Sea*, they are to be found in abundance in the dialogue of the piece, with its crazy images and the sudden and erratic turns in the current of ideas. It is as if the author's mind could not remain fixed upon a point for any length of time. Indeed, the whole tenour of the play is completely changed in the middle, for after the third act it is no longer a question of Ellida's nostalgia for the sea, but the same old argument about 'living one's own life' is threshed out over again in the same old way. *The Lady from the Sea* was indifferently well acted, but Miss Rose Meller's performance of the demented Ellida had none of the electric quality that gives a fascination to Miss Elizabeth Robins's impersonation of Hedda Gabler, for Miss Meller not inexcusably makes Ellida a mere congenital idiot instead of an excitable creature of maniacal tendencies.

90. From a notice by Justin McCarthy, *Hawk*

19 May 1891, 530

(See also No. 91.)

The Lady from the Sea is as delicate as a fairy tale, as poetic in its way as Hans Andersen's fancy about the little sea-maiden, as weird as the old wind-blown legend of the Flying Dutchman. The passionate realism of *Hedda Gabler* has no place here. *The Lady from the Sea* is almost what the Germans would call a 'phantasy piece.' It is to the rest of Ibsen's work what the *Peau de Chagrin* is to the rest of Balzac's work. Just as Balzac dared to introduce into modern Paris, into the Paris of Rastignac and Bianchon and Bixiou, the marvellous mystery of the ciphered skin, so Ibsen has placed in the Norway of his Wangels and his Arnholms and his Lyngstrands the mystery of the sea-woman, the creature whose every fibre moves and answers to the movement of the sea. That wild passion for the sea which is so incomprehensible to most landsfolk, that passion for the sea which finds such lyric expression in some of Mr. Swinburne's sea-songs, that is the heart of Ellida Wangel's mystery. But to act Ellida Wangel so that she shall be at once human and elfin, earth-wife and mermaid, so that she shall be intelligible and attractive, not incomprehensible and diverting, requires the genius of an Ada Rehan, a Sarah Bernhardt, or an Ellen Terry. And the lady who attempted to play Ellida at Terry's has not the gifts of these mistresses of her art.

91. From an unsigned regular theatre gossip column, *Hawk*

19 May 1891, 544

(See also No. 90.)

Ibsen is said to have invented a new slang term for intoxication. We are no longer, it is said, to have 'three sheets in the wind,' 'copped the brewer,' 'elephant's trunk,' 'half seas over,' 'a little bit on,' 'basking in the sun' and similar intelligent and elastic euphemisms. It is now to be, as quoted in *Hedda Gabler*, 'vine leaves in his hair.' It may be a more aesthetic way of describing the state, but the monosyllabic 'blind' will, I am certain, enjoy a preferential popularity which all the Norwegian dramatists in the world won't alter.

92. Ibsen parodied by J. M. Barrie

May 1891

An unsigned notice of *Ibsen's Ghost: Or, Toole Up to Date,* in *Theatre* (1 July 1891), xviii, 28–30. The play, a one-act piece, was also known as *New Hedda* and was first produced at Toole's Theatre, 30 May 1891. It was presented as an anonymous play, but the name of the author, J. M. Barrie, an unknown young writer, was soon made public. The cast was as follows:

Geo. Tesman (an artist)	Mr G. Shelton	Peter Terence (her grandpapa)	Mr J. L. Toole
Thea Tesman (his wife for the present)	Miss Irene Vanbrugh	Delia Terence (Peter's Doll)	Miss Eliza Johnstone

Although the author was not publicly announced, I believe I may thank Mr. J. M. Barrie (part author of *Richard Savage*) for twenty-five minutes' incessant laughter, and it was laughter that one did not feel shamefaced about, for one felt it had been produced by a really clever pen— the novel theories of the 'Master' are so deliciously burlesqued. Here is Thea, formerly so innocent in her platonic love, now wedded to George Tesman, and she feels she must leave him, for she cannot control her propensity for kissing every man she meets. Whence comes this mad passion she asks her grandfather. As she dilates upon her mania he responds with 'Ghosts! Ghosts!' and then he tells her it is all due to 'heredity.' He erred with the opposite sex in that way many years ago. On his wedding day he kissed a pretty bridesmaid, and so he has handed down to her the unfortunate osculatory propensity. Then it suddenly becomes dark from a heavy storm without, and when the light breaks in on us again we find Thea transformed into Hedda and Peter Terence appears as the very counterpart of Henrik Ibsen, as we know him from portraits of him. Hedda's tearing up the 'hundreds of children' (the letters) is cleverly burlesqued, and then there is a delightful satire on the emancipation of women in Delia Terence's reproach of her husband, in that he has led far too moral a life, never introduced any but the most irreproachable characters to her, and never even given her a

253

chance of being anything but the most orthodox of wives. Then comes the skit on the suicidal tendencies of Ibsen's heroes and heroines. These three characters shoot themselves with pop-guns, and to make the slaughter complete, George Tesman is shot down by his secretary. Miss Irene Vanbrugh very cleverly parodied the method of Miss Marion Lea as Thea, and in a lesser degree that of Miss Robins. Mr. G. Shelton was a second Scott Buist as George Tesman, and had caught the exact tone of his voice. Mr. J. L. Toole was very funny, and Miss Eliza Johnstone drolly caricatured the outraged feelings of the wife who has been compelled to lead such a virtuous life.

BRAND

1891

93. From 'Ibsen's *Brand*', a long article by Richard A. Armstrong, *Westminster Review*

April 1891, cxxxv, 409–28

The author was a member of the British Scandinavian Society and the original translator of *Terje Vigen* (1874).

Brand surpasses *Peer Gynt* as a work of genius. Each is occupied with the exposition of the development in inward character and outward career of a hero who bases himself on a false maxim of life. But the motto of Peer Gynt is base, while that of Brand is exalted; and it demands a higher strain of genius to portray with unswerving psychological veracity the failure involved in the pursuit of a noble though mistaken ideal, than to trace the fall of one whose theory of life is entirely ignoble. Peer Gynt's rule of self-sufficiency and self-seeking—which he confounds with self-realisation and self-reverence—leads to a career for the description of which biting irony is the poet's predominating instrument. Brand's rule, 'nothing or everything,' 'nought or all,' leads to a career full of such heroic struggle and pathetic loss and failure as only language profoundly sympathetic, tremulous with human emotion, can hope to picture.

The maxim 'nought or all,' means, on the lips and in the mind of Brand, that no half-hearted service can ever be acceptable to God. Give Him everything, or you might just as well—even better—give Him nothing. And for this perfect giving it is essential that a free and unconstrained will should always be partner in the gift. That which is rendered reluctantly is not surrendered wholly. Therefore, whatever God demands must be yielded, not only without the selfish detention of the smallest fragment, but without suffering the yearning affections to play around that which has been yielded up after the sacrifice has been made.

[Armstrong sees Brand's career as a series of terrible renunciations. Summing up his argument he says:]

Brand's successive sacrifices are ranged along an ascending scale. They are (1) his ambition, (2) his child, (3) his wife, (4) that calling itself for the sake of which the previous sacrifices had successively been made. The climax lies in the abandonment of that very post which had hitherto appeared so sacred to the priest that everything else in life must be abandoned for its sake. When affection has been irrevocably sacrificed to illusion, the acme of pathos is reached in the discovery that it is illusion.

94. From an unsigned review of William Wilson's translation of *Brand: A Dramatic Poem*, *Saturday Review*

19 December 1891, lxxii, 705

Wherever the voice of criticism proper has been allowed to make itself heard amid the roars of silly adoration and the growls of not much less silly anathema which have rolled round the name of Ibsen, it must have been felt as a misfortune that the Norwegian dramatist's work has been presented to English readers, so to speak, upside down. In hardly any case is it possible to understand a man's later work without knowing his earlier. Now the so-called 'Social' dramas are, for the most part, very late—are in all cases late—work. The very earliest of them was not written till Ibsen was past forty, and this was not immediately followed by any others. The prime of the poet's manhood, on the other hand, was occupied with quite different work, foreshadowing, it may be, to some extent, the later productions, but for that very reason all the more important for the understanding thereof. The chief pieces of this poetical work are the three plays—*Love's Comedy*, *Brand*, and *Peer Gynt*, each of which, we believe, has its champions as Ibsen's masterpiece among Ibsenites properly so called. But *Brand* has the general voice.

In choosing prose for his version Mr. Wilson may seem to have, and evidently thinks that he has, followed a prevailing taste among readers and critics. But the loss is considerable. Ibsen's verses, constructed, it may be, not without reference to Goethe and the Spanish drama, have far more influence than either the Greek trimeter, the French alexandrine, or the English heroic on the presentation of a play. Still it was probably a case of prose or nothing, and at least the substance of the drama remains intact. Brand, a Norwegian parson, pushes the self sacrifice doctrine of Christianity to its extremest possible limit. We meet him on a new 'blasted heath,' in a strange welter of the elements, and the storm, morally if not physically, continues throughout the piece. Brand is the very incarnation of the terrors of the Gospel. He does not indeed seem to see any harm in marrying Agnes, the heroine, though she is the betrothed of his friend Einar; but he would doubtless defend this on the plea that Einar is a selfish worldling, while he himself is at least trying to follow duty. But he will not visit his mother even pastorally on her deathbed, because she will not dedicate to pious uses the whole of gains which seem to him ill-gotten. He practically kills his child and his wife by keeping them in a house which he is told will be fatal to their health; and between the two deaths he martyrizes his unhappy wife by insisting that she shall not regret what the Lord has taken away, and by forcing her to give the little one's clothes to a beggar's brat. At last, when he has lost both of them and spent all his mother's money on a huge new church, he finds that the constituted authorities expect him to make his benefaction 'serve the State'. He explodes in a fit of fanatic rage, locks the doors of the church, and leads the villagers off into the moors on a sort of crusade. Their fervour lasts a short time only; they are wiled back by the Bailie and the Provost, and depart cursing and stoning him. Then the half-apocalyptic opening returns in a more apocalyptic close, and after visions of divers kinds, Brand and a mad gipsy girl, Gerd, who has acted as a sort of spasmodic chorus earlier, perish in an avalanche which the girl has brought down by firing a rifle at a supposed evil spirit.

This wild argument is not insufficiently supported by the dialogue and situations. Of course, the rendering from verse into prose accentuates the occasional eccentricity of the style; but, on the other hand, the fact of the play having been originally in verse saves its style from the vulgarity with which the later prose dramas are justly reproached. Spiritually, the piece has a place in Ibsen's theatre which the common or gutter Ibsenite will be the last to perceive. Whether the poet ever went through the spiritual state of his hero we cannot say, and it does not matter. But the exaggerated and over-strained ethics of Brand (strained still further as they are by a strong dash of Schopenhauer, which appears in all his middle period), with the underlying assumption that, short of this exaggeration, there can be nothing but the time-serving hypocrisy of the Bailie and the Provost, represent exactly the state of mind from which the next step would be, at a shorter or longer interval, the attempt to construct a new system of morality altogether, in which self-sacrifice has no place at all, but Will, retaining its predominance, turns into Self-regard only dashed with Pessimism and Necessitarianism. If we wanted a middle resting place or slipping place between, *Emperor and Galilean* very well supplies it. So much for the place of the play in that map which, when the bepraising and mouthing about Ibsen are over, will be drawn of him. As for its own merits it is, of course, avowedly extravagant; it honestly proclaims that fact in the very first lines, and keeps the promise all through. But it is of a far higher order of literature than any of the prose plays except *The Wild Duck* (for which we are glad to see that Mr. Wilson has a proper value, especially for the character of Gina Ekdal), while, however extravagant may be its pitch, it is not really more so than the topsyturvyfication of *The Doll's House* and *Rosmersholm*.

95. George Bernard Shaw on the quintessence of Ibsenism and its resemblance to Shavianism

1891

'The Moral of the Plays', from Bernard Shaw's *The Quintessence of Ibsenism* (London: Walter Scott Ltd, 1891). Shaw's study was based on a paper originally delivered before the Fabian Society. In the section reprinted below he draws together and sums up the points he has been making while discussing individual plays. Throughout the book Shaw tells us less about Ibsen than he does about himself; as Eric Bentley has acutely remarked (*Bernard Shaw*, Methuen & Co., 1947, p. 80): 'for "Ibsen," throughout *The Quintessence of Ibsenism*, we should read "Shaw" . . .'

In following this sketch of the plays written by Ibsen to illustrate his thesis that the real slavery of to-day is slavery to ideals of virtue, it may be that readers who have conned Ibsen through idealist spectacles have wondered that I could so pervert the utterances of a great poet. Indeed I know already that many of those who are most fascinated by the poetry of the plays will plead for any explanation of them rather than that given by Ibsen himself in the plainest terms through the mouths of Mrs Alving, Relling, and the rest. No great writer uses his skill to conceal his meaning. There is a tale by a famous Scotch story-teller which would have suited Ibsen exactly if he had hit on it first. Jeanie Deans sacrificing her sister's life on the scaffold to her own ideal of duty is far more horrible than the sacrifice in *Rosmersholm*; and the *deus ex machina* expedient by which Scott makes the end of his story agreeable is no solution of the moral problem raised, but only a puerile evasion of it. He undoubtedly believed that it was right that Effie should hang for the sake of Jeanie's ideals.* Consequently, if I were to pretend that Scott

---

* The common-sense solution of the moral problem has often been delivered by acclamation in the theatre. Some sixteen or seventeen years ago I witnessed a performance of a melodrama founded on this story. After the painful trial scene, in which Jeanie Deans condemns her sister to death by refusing to swear to a perfectly innocent fiction, came a

259

wrote *The Heart of Midlothian* to shew that people are led to do as mischievous, as unnatural, as murderous things by their religious and moral
ideals as by their envy and ambition, it would be easy to confute me
from the pages of the book itself. But Ibsen has made his meaning no
less plain that Scott's. If any one attempts to maintain that *Ghosts* is a
polemic in favour of indissoluble monogamic marriage, or that *The
Wild Duck* was written to inculcate that truth should be told for its
own sake, they must burn the text of the plays if their contention is to
stand. The reason that Scott's story is tolerated by those who shrink
from *Ghosts* is not that it is less terrible, but that Scott's views are familiar
to all well-brought-up ladies and gentlemen, whereas Ibsen's are for the
moment so strange as to be almost unthinkable. He is so great a poet
that the idealist finds himself in the dilemma of being unable to conceive
that such a genius should have an ignoble meaning, and yet equally
unable to conceive his real meaning as otherwise than ignoble. Consequently he misses the meaning altogether in spite of Ibsen's explicit and
circumstantial insistence on it, and proceeds to interpolate a meaning
which conforms to his own ideal of nobility. Ibsen's deep sympathy
with his idealist figures seems to countenance this method of making
confusion. Since it is on the weaknesses of the higher types of character
that idealism seizes, his examples of vanity, selfishness, folly, and failure
are not vulgar villains, but men who in an ordinary novel or melodrama would be heroes. His most tragic point is reached in the destinies
of Brand and Rosmer, who drive those whom they love to death in its
most wanton and cruel form. The ordinary Philistine commits no such
atrocities: he marries the woman he likes and lives more or less happily
ever after; but that is not because he is greater than Brand or Rosmer,
but because he is less. The idealist is a more dangerous animal than the
Philistine just as a man is a more dangerous animal than a sheep. Though
Brand virtually murdered his wife, I can understand many a woman,
comfortably married to an amiable Philistine, reading the play and envy-
ing the victim her husband. For when Brand's wife, having made the
sacrifice he has exacted, tells him that he was right; that she is happy
now; that she sees God face to face—but reminds him that 'whoso sees
Jehovah dies,' he instinctively clasps his hands over her eyes; and that
action raises him at once far above the criticism that sneers at idealism

---

scene in the prison. 'If it had been me,' said the jailor, 'I wad ha' sworn a hole through an
iron pot.' The roar of applause which burst from the pit and gallery was thoroughly
Ibsenite in sentiment. The speech, by the way, was a 'gag' of the actor's, and is not to be
found in the acting edition of the play.

from beneath, instead of surveying it from the clear ether above, which can only be reached through its mists.

If, in my account of the plays, I have myself suggested false judgments by describing the errors of the idealists in the terms of the life they had risen above rather than in that of the life they fell short of, I can only plead, with but a moderate disrespect to a large section of my readers, that if I had done otherwise I should have failed wholly to make the matter understood. Indeed the terms of the realist morality have not yet appeared in our living language; and I have already, in this very distinction between idealism and realism, been forced to insist on a sense of these terms which, had not Ibsen forced my hand, I should perhaps have conveyed otherwise, so strongly does it conflict in many of its applications with the vernacular use of the words. This, however, was a trifle compared to the difficulty which arose, when personal characters had to be described, from our inveterate habit of labelling men with the names of their moral qualities without the slightest reference to the underlying will which sets these qualities in action. At a recent anniversary celebration of the Paris Commune of 1871, I was struck by the fact that no speaker could find a eulogy for the Federals which would not have been equally appropriate to the peasants of La Vendée who fought for their tyrants against the French revolutionists, or to the Irishmen and Highlanders who fought for the Stuarts at the Boyne or Culloden. Nor could the celebrators find any other adjectives for their favourite leaders of the Commune than those which had recently been liberally applied by all the journals to an African explorer whose achievements were just then held in the liveliest abhorrence by the whole meeting. The statements that the slain members of the Commune were heroes who died for a noble ideal would have left a stranger quite as much in the dark about them as the counter statements, once common enough in middle-class newspapers, that they were incendiaries and assassins. Our obituary notices are examples of the same ambiguity. Of all the public men lately deceased, none have been made more interesting by strongly marked personal characteristics than the late Charles Bradlaugh. He was not in the least like any other notable member of the House of Commons. Yet when the obituary notices appeared, with the usual string of qualities—eloquence, determination, integrity, strong common-sense and so on, it would have been possible, by merely expunging all names and other external details from these notices, to leave the reader entirely unable to say whether the subject of them was Mr Gladstone, Mr Morley, Mr Stead, or any one else no more like Mr Bradlaugh than

Garibaldi or the late Cardinal Newman, whose obituary certificates of morality might nevertheless have been reprinted almost verbatim for the occasion without any gross incongruity. Bradlaugh had been the subject of many sorts of newspaper notice in his time. Ten years ago, when the middle classes supposed him to be a revolutionist, the string of qualities which the press hung upon him were all evil ones, great stress being laid on the fact that as he was an atheist it would be an insult to God to admit him to Parliament. When it became apparent that he was a conservative force in politics, he, without any recantation of his atheism, at once had the string of evil qualities exchanged for a rosary of good ones; but it is hardly necessary to add that neither the old badge nor the new will ever give any inquirer the least clue to the sort of man he actually was: he might have been Oliver Cromwell or Wat Tyler or Jack Cade, Penn or Wilberforce or Wellington, the late Mr. Hampden of flat-earth-theory notoriety or Proudhon or the Archbishop of Canterbury, for all the distinction that such labels could give him one way or the other. The worthlessness of these accounts of individuals is recognized in practice every day. Tax a stranger before a crowd with being a thief, a coward, and a liar; and the crowd will suspend its judgment until you answer the question, 'What's he done?' Attempt to make a collection for him on the ground that he is an upright, fearless, high-principled hero; and the same question must be answered before a penny goes into the hat.

The reader must therefore discount those partialities which I have permitted myself to express in telling the stories of the plays. They are as much beside the mark as any other example of the sort of criticism which seeks to create an impression favourable or otherwise to Ibsen by simply pasting his characters all over with good or bad conduct marks. If any person cares to describe Hedda Gabler as a modern Lucretia who preferred death to dishonour, and Thea Elvsted as an abandoned, perjured strumpet who deserted the man she had sworn before her God to love, honour, and obey until her death, the play contains conclusive evidence establishing both points. If the critic goes on to argue that as Ibsen manifestly means to recommend Thea's conduct above Hedda's by making the end happier for her, the moral of the play is a vicious one, that, again, cannot be gainsaid. If, on the other hand, *Ghosts* be defended, as the dramatic critic of *Piccadilly* lately did defend it, because it throws into divine relief the beautiful figure of the simple and pious Pastor Manders, the fatal compliment cannot be parried. When you have called Mrs Alving an 'emancipated woman' or an unprincipled one, Alving a debauchee or a 'victim of society,' Nora a fearless and noble-hearted woman or a shocking little liar and an unnatural mother, Helmer a selfish hound or a model husband and father, according to your bias, you have said something which is at once true and false, and in either case perfectly idle.

The statement that Ibsen's plays have an immoral tendency, is, in the sense in which it is used, quite true. Immorality does not necessarily imply mischievous conduct: it implies conduct, mischievous or not, which does not conform to current ideals. Since Ibsen has devoted himself almost entirely to shewing that the spirit or will of Man is constantly outgrowing his ideals, and that therefore, conformity to them is constantly producing results no less tragic than those which follow the violation of ideals which are still valid, the main effect of his plays is to keep before the public the importance of being always prepared to act immorally, to remind men that they ought to be as careful how they yield to a temptation to tell the truth as to a temptation to hold their tongues, and to urge upon women that the desirability of their preserving their chastity depends just as much on circumstances as the desirability of taking a cab instead of walking. He protests against the ordinary assumption that there are certain supreme ends which justify all means used to attain them; and insists that every end shall be challenged to shew that it justifies the means. Our ideals, like the gods of old are constantly demanding human sacrifices. Let none of them, says Ibsen, be placed above the obligation to prove that they are worth the sacrifices they demand; and let every one refuse to sacrifice himself and others from the moment he loses his faith in the reality of the ideal. Of course it will be said here by incorrigibly slipshod readers that this, so far from being immoral, is the highest morality; and so, in a sense, it is; but I really shall not waste any further explanation on those who will neither mean one thing or another by a word nor allow me to do so. In short, then, among those who are not ridden by current ideals no question as to the morality of Ibsen's plays will ever arise; and among those who are so ridden his plays will seem immoral, and cannot be defended against the accusation.

There can be no question as to the effect likely to be produced on an individual by his conversion from the ordinary acceptance of current ideals as safe standards of conduct, to the vigilant open-mindedness of Ibsen. It must at once greatly deepen the sense of moral responsibility. Before conversion the individual anticipates nothing worse in the way of examination at the judgment bar of his conscience than such questions as, Have you kept the commandments? Have you obeyed the law? Have you attended church regularly; paid your rates and taxes to Caesar; and contributed, in reason, to charitable institutions? It may be hard to do all these things; but it is still harder not to do them, as our ninety-nine moral cowards in the hundred well know. And even a scoundrel can do them all and yet live a worse life than the smuggler or prostitute who must answer No all through the catechism. Substitute for such a technical examination one in which the whole point to be settled is, Guilty or Not Guilty?—one in which there is no more and no less respect for chastity than for incontinence, for subordination than for rebellion, for legality than for illegality, for piety than for blasphemy, in short, for the standard virtues than for the standard vices, and immediately, instead of lowering the moral standard by relaxing the tests of worth, you raise it by increasing their stringency to a point at which no mere Pharisaism or moral cowardice can pass them. Naturally this does not please the Pharisee. The respectable lady of the strictest Christian principles, who has brought up her children with such relentless regard to their ideal morality that if they have any spirit left in them by the time they arrive at years of independence they use their liberty to rush deliriously to the devil—this unimpeachable woman has always felt it unjust that the respect she wins should be accompanied by deep-seated detestation, whilst the latest spiritual heiress of Nell Gwynne, whom no respectable person dare bow to in the street, is a popular idol. The reason is—though the virtuous lady does not know it—that Nell Gwynne is a better woman than she; and the abolition of the idealist test which brings her out a worse one, and its replacement by the realist test which would shew the true relation between them, would be a most desirable step forward in public morals, especially as it would act impartially, and set the good side of the Pharisee above the bad side of the Bohemian as ruthlessly as it would set the good side of the Bohemian above the bad side of the Pharisee. For as long as convention goes counter to reality in these matters, people will be led into Hedda Gabler's error of making an ideal of vice. If we maintain the convention that the distinction between Catherine of Russia and Queen Victoria, between Nell Gwynne and Mrs Proudie, is the distinction between a bad woman and a good woman, we need not be surprised when those who sympathize with Catherine and Nell conclude that it is better to be a bad woman than a good one, and go on recklessly to conceive a prejudice against teetotallism and monogamy, and a prepossession in favour of alcoholic excitement and promiscuous amours. Ibsen himself is kinder to the man who has gone his own way as a rake and a drunkard than to the man who is respectable because he dare not be otherwise. We find that the franker and healthier a boy is, the more certain is he to prefer pirates and highwaymen, or Dumas musketeers, to 'pillars of society' as his favourite heroes of romance. We have already seen both Ibsenites and anti-Ibsenites who seem to think that the cases of Nora and Mrs Elvsted are meant to establish a golden rule for women who wish to be 'emancipated,' the said golden rule being simply, Run away from your husband. But in Ibsen's view of life, that would come under the same condemnation as the conventional golden rule, Cleave to your husband until death do you part. Most people know of a case or two in which it would be wise for a wife to follow the example of Nora or even of Mrs Elvsted. But they must also know cases in which the results of such a course would be as tragi-comic as those of Gregers Werle's attempt in *The Wild Duck* to do for the Ekdal household what Lona Hessel did for the Bernick household. What Ibsen insists on is that there is no golden rule—that conduct must justify itself by its effect upon happiness and not by its conformity to any rule or ideal. And since happiness consists in the fulfilment of the will, which is constantly growing, and cannot be fulfilled to-day under the conditions which secured its fulfilment yesterday, he claims afresh the old Protestant right of private judgment in questions of conduct as against all institutions, the so-called Protestant Churches themselves included.

Here I must leave the matter, merely reminding those who may think that I have forgotten to reduce Ibsenism to a formula for them, that its quintessence is that there is no formula.

THE MASTER BUILDER

Trafalgar Square Theatre, 20 February 1893

96. 'Ibsen's New Play', by Henry James, *Pall Mall Gazette*

17 February 1893, lvi, 1–2.

This article appeared three days before the first performance of the play, and was subsequently reprinted, together with James's review of *Hedda Gabler* (No. 84) in *Essays in London and Elsewhere* (London, 1893). The translation used in the production of *The Master Builder* was by Edmund Gosse and William Archer, the first time they had collaborated in such a project, and the cast was as follows:

Hilda Wangel ..	Miss Elizabeth Robins	Dr Herdal	..	Mr John Beauchamp
		Knut Brovik	..	Mr Athol Forde
Halvard Solness	Mr Herbert Waring	Ragnar Brovik	..	Mr Philip Cuningham
Mrs Solness ..	Miss Louise Moodie	Kaia Fosli ..	..	Miss Marie Linden

In spite of its having been announced in many quarters that Ibsen would never do, we are still to have another chance, which may very well not be the last, of judging the question for ourselves. Not only has the battered Norseman had, in the evening of his career, the energy to fling yet again into the arena one of those bones of contention of which he has in an unequalled degree the secret of possessing himself, but practised London hands have been able to catch the mystic missile in its passage and are flourishing it, as they have flourished others, before our eyes. The English version of *Bygmester Solness* lately prepared by Mr. Edmund Gosse and Mr. William Archer and now, under the title of *The Master Builder*, about to appear as a volume, is, on Monday afternoon next and on the following afternoons, to be presented at the Trafalgar Square Theatre by a company of which Mr. Herbert Waring, Miss Elizabeth Robins, and Miss Louise Moodie are the principal members.

In addition to an opportunity of reading the play I have had the pleasure of seeing a rehearsal of the performance—so I already feel something of responsibility of that inward strife which is an inevitable heritage of all inquiring contact with the master. It is perhaps a consequence of this irremediable fever that one should recklessly court the further responsibility attached to uttering an impression into which the premature may partly enter. But it is impossible, in any encounter with Ibsen, to resist the influence of at least the one kind of interest that he exerts at the very outset, and to which at the present hour it may well be a point of honour promptly to confess one's subjection. This immediate kind is the general interest we owe to the refreshing circumstances that he at any rate gives us the sense of life, and the practical effect of which is ever to work a more or less irritating spell. The other kind is the interest of the particular production, a varying quantity and an agreeable source of suspense—a happy occasion in short for that play of intelligence, that acuteness of response, whether in assent or in protest, which it is the privilege of the clinging theatre-goer to look forward to as a result of the ingenious dramatist's appeal, but his sad predicament for the most part to miss yet another and another chance to achieve. With Ibsen (and that is the exceptional joy, the bribe to rapid submission) we can always count upon the chance. Our languid pulses quicken as we begin to note the particular direction taken by the attack on a curiosity inhabiting, by way of a change, the neglected region of the brain.

In *The Master Builder* this emotion is not only kindled very early in the piece—it avails itself to the full of the right that Ibsen always so liberally concedes it of being still lively after the piece is over. His independence, his perversity, his intensity, his vividness, the hard compulsion of his strangely inscrutable art, are present in full measure, together with that quality which comes almost uppermost when it is a question of seeing him on the stage, his peculiar blessedness to actors. *Their* reasons for liking him it would not be easy to overstate; and surely, if the public should ever completely renounce him, players enamoured of their art will still be found ready to interpret him for that art's sake to empty benches. No dramatist of our time has had more the secret, and has kept it better, of making their work interesting to them. The subtlety with which he puts them into relation to it eludes analysis, but operates none the less strongly as an incitement. Does it reside mainly in the way he takes hold of their imagination, or in some special affinity with their technical sense; in what he gives them or in what he leaves it to them to give; in the touches by which the moral nature of the character opens out a vista for them; or in the simple fact of connection with such a vivified whole? These are questions at any rate that Mr. Herbert Waring, Miss Robins, Miss Moodie, enviable with their several problems, doubtless freely ask themselves, or even each other, while the interest and the mystery of *The Master Builder* fold them more and more closely in. What is incontestable is the excitement, the amusement, the inspiration of dealing with material so solid and so fresh. The very difficulty of it makes a common cause, as the growing ripeness of preparation makes a common enthusiasm.

I shall not attempt to express the subject of the play more largely than to say that its three acts deal again, as Ibsen is so apt to deal, with the supremely critical hour in the life of an individual, in the history of a soul. The individual is in this case not a Hedda, nor a Nora, nor a Mrs. Alving, nor a Lady from the Sea, but a prosperous architect of Christiania, who, on reaching a robust maturity, encounters his fate all in the opening of a door. This fate—infinitely strange and terrible, as we know before the curtain falls—is foreshadowed in Miss Elizabeth Robins, who, however, in passing the threshold, lets in a great deal more than herself, represents a heroine conceived, as to her effect on the action, with that shameless originality which Ibsen's contemners call wanton and his admirers call fascinating. Hilda Wangel, a young woman whom the author may well be trusted to have made more mystifying than her curiously charmless name would suggest, is only the indirect form, the animated clock-face, as it were, of Halvard Solness's destiny; but the action, in spite of obscurities and ironies, takes its course by steps none the less irresistible. The mingled reality and symbolism of it all give us an Ibsen within an Ibsen. His subject is always, like the subjects of all first-rate men, primarily an idea; but in this case the idea is as difficult to catch as its presence is impossible to overlook. The whole thing throbs and flushes with it, and yet smiles and mocks at us through it as if in conscious supersubtlety. The action at any rate is superficially simple, more single and confined than that of most of Ibsen's other plays; practically, as it defines itself and rises to a height, it leaves the strange, doomed Solness, and the even stranger apparition of the joyous and importunate girl (the one all memories and hauntings and bondages, the other all health and curiosity and youthful insolence), face to face on unprecedented terms—terms, however, I hasten to add, that by no means prevent the play from being one to which a young lady, as they say in Paris, may properly take her mother. Of all Ibsen's heroines Hilda is indeed perhaps at once the most characteristic of the author and the most void of offence to the 'general.' If she has notes that recall Hedda, she is a Hedda dangerous precisely because she is *not* yet *blasée*—a Hedda stimulating, fully beneficent in intention; in short 'reversed,' as I believe the author defined her to his interpreters. From her encounter with Halvard Solness many remarkable things arise, but most of all perhaps the spectator's sense of the opportunity offered by the two rare parts; and in particular of the fruitful occasion (for Solness from beginning to end holds the stage), seized by Mr. Herbert Waring, who has evidently recognised one of those hours that actors sometimes wait long years for—the hour that reveals a talent to itself as well as to its friends and that makes a reputation take a bound. Whatever, besides refreshing them, *The Master Builder* does for Ibsen with London playgoers, it will render the service that the curious little Norwegian repertory has almost always rendered the performers, even to the subsidiary figures, even to the touching Kaia, the touching Ragnar, the inevitable Dr. Herdel, and the wasted wife of Solness, so carefully composed by Miss Moodie.

97. An unsigned notice by Clement Scott, *Daily Telegraph*

21 February 1893, 3

Were Ibsen's meaning always as clear as that upper atmosphere towards which the thoughts of his latest heroine—Hilda Wangel—are so constantly tending, the Scandinavian dramatist's work, it seems to us, would lose nine-tenths of the fascination which it exercises upon 'the Faithful.' Most of the magic found in these Norwegian plays by those who hold them in highest appreciation is unquestionably to be traced to that dense mist which enshrouds characters, words, actions, and motives, which shifts ever and anon for a brief moment to allow the passing of a sunbeam, but which closes in immediately afterwards in folds thicker than before, and sets the diligent enthusiasts groping for light once more and glorying in their vaporous surroundings. For such as these there is irresistible delight in searching for a signification—a delight somewhat akin, perhaps, to that experienced by the patrons of the accommodating showman who tells his audience that, having paid their money, they are at liberty to take their choice. There is, indeed, something almost intoxicating in the very vagueness of the playwright's utterances—in the feeling that each spectator can be his own interpreter, and that infinite depths in the matters of symbolism and allegory may be probed by the possessor of a sufficiently lively imagination. To go a step further, it is even possible for one who attaches neither specific weight nor definite meaning to the dramatist's scheme to summon up a certain kind of interest in the Norwegian writer's strange dramas. It may not be quite an artistic interest; indeed, one may compare it, to put an extreme case, to the sensations of a man who witnesses a play written, rehearsed, and acted by lunatics. It is the interest felt by one who asks himself, 'What are they going to do next?' If, then, there is a strong charm for the initiated in this curious emotional vagueness—and it would be idle to deny that such a charm is found in Ibsen by many—*The Master Builder*, the latest dramatic consignment from Scandinavia, is entitled to as exalted a place in the Ibsen catalogue as any of its predecessors. Its true meaning is wrapped in mystery; while the most practised playgoer would fail to make a correct forecast from scene to scene of the workings of its cloudy and word-laden plot.

And yet, with all its vagueness and lack of definite purpose, *The Master Builder*, thanks to the acting of Mr. Herbert Waring and Miss Elizabeth Robins—one excellent, and the other nothing short of remarkable—never let the attention of yesterday's audience run loose. There was curiosity to see what degree of mental stability, or the reverse, Mr. Waring would suggest in the case of Halvard Solness, architect and unconscious hypnotist; there was eagerness to note from what standpoint Miss Robins would attack the character of Hilda Wangel, a specimen of Norwegian girlhood imaginative to the point of madness. To these two personages it was possible to devote almost undivided attention, for Ibsen has given the remainder of his puppets but scanty stage-room. In what category of human beings are we to place Halvard Solness, this master builder, with his morbid fear of 'the younger generation' which is coming to supplant him in his craft, and his magnetic influence over Kaia, the damsel who keeps his books? He is a new order of man this, whose mental faculties are evidently tottering, and who is yet possessed of astounding force of will. 'Don't you agree with me,' he says presently to Hilda Wangel, 'that there exist special, chosen people who have been endowed with the power and faculty of desiring a thing, craving for a thing, willing a thing—so persistently and so—so inexorably—that at last it has to happen?' Almost without knowing it he has taken captive the very soul of Kaia Fosli, the betrothed of his assistant, young Brovik—a girl whose dog-like devotion is regarded with an air of mournful suspicion by Mrs. Solness. But Kaia is destined to serve no particular purpose in the playwright's scheme. The mist rises and the maiden fades away. Soon, heralded by an almost conventional dramatic touch, the heroine comes. Solness has just been telling a shadowy doctor, one Herdal, of his fears of rivalry from 'the younger generation,' who, sooner or later, will 'knock at his door,' when an actual knocking is heard, and there enters Hilda Wangel, clad in serviceable blue, bearing knapsack and alpenstock, and showing the dust of a long tramp on her hobnailed boots. Who is this stalwart siren? Solness knows her not until she has jogged his memory. And then the truth comes out. Exactly ten years back the master-builder superintended the completion of a church in some country district, and after the final festivities was indiscreet enough to say pretty things to the little daughter of the local doctor. In ten years, he told the white-frocked damsel, he would return and claim her for his own. She should be a princess, and a kingdom should owe her allegiance. The undertaking was sealed with several kisses, and was then promptly forgotten by its executor. But this unaccountable Hilda has a memory of her own, and for ten years she cherishes recollections of the 'strange man' who pledged himself to perform miracles, and embraced her on the strength of it. Now the hour for carrying out the contract has arrived, and the lady comes in all sober seriousness to claim fulfillment of Solness's promise. The master builder, ever susceptible to the soft influence of 'the sex,' is straightway smitten by this imaginative young lady, and their converse ranges from castles in the air to church towers, until the final catastrophe brings the play to its termination. She can hardly be sane—this Hilda Wangel—who finds unspeakable fascination in the spectacle of a man perched on the apex of a steeple, and who thinks that it must have been 'thrilling' in the old days to be carried off by Vikings. Aeromania seems as good a name as any to attach to her particular form of madness. She yearns for the upper atmosphere; she dreams of falling from a great height; she petulantly, if impracticably, bids Solness build her on the moment an airy castle. It is her mad love for altitude, indeed, which brings the master builder to his death; for she, knowing the man to be weak-headed, sends him to hang a wreath upon the topmost pinnacle of his new house. He pays the penalty of his infatuation, however, and comes tumbling to earth in the sight of his withered, neglected wife and the ethereal Hilda.

Wild and fantastic as all this may seem in the telling, there is that in the acting of Miss Elizabeth Robins which well nigh persuades us that Hilda Wangel is a real woman. The boldness and breadth of the artist's conception of this character positively baffle adequate description. One knows neither where to begin nor where to end in dealing with so remarkable a histrionic study. At the outset, perhaps, it seems difficult to harmonise the matter-of-fact masculinity which characterises so many of the woman's words and gestures with the strange imaginings which had led her to Solness a—criticism which, of course, applies rather to the playwright than to the actress. But it soon becomes evident that any looking for consistency of character is out of the question. Miss Robins achieves what, no doubt, the Scandinavian dramatist intends his Hilda to achieve, and leads us off into a region where the ruling spirit is that of pure fantasy, but where the artist has yet scope for 'natural' acting. Our stage history—at any rate, that of the present generation—furnishes no record of another such vivid combination of the realistic and the imaginative side of the histrionic art; and, if only for the purpose of witnessing Miss Robins' performance, every playgoer with an eye for acting which shows something very like a spark of genius should make it his business to see *The Master Builder*. The Halvard Solness, too, of Mr. Herbert Waring betrays infinite care and study. That a part of such inordinate length should be played in tones so well weighed and so judiciously delivered is alone no small feather in the actor's cap. Solness is not a character of great opportunities, even regarding the play from its own peculiar standpoint. Mr. Waring, however, thoughtful player as he is, contrives to indicate the various emotions that course through the breast of this inflicter of 'salutary self-torture' with a degree of discretion worthy of all praise. Many were the laughs which the actor might have drawn forth yesterday afternoon, but he dexterously avoided nearly every one.

Of the other characters in *The Master Builder* there is need to say but few words. Most important of these minor parts is the melancholy Mrs. Solness, a woman embittered both by the loss of her children and by the instability of her husband's love. Miss Louise Moodie's sound but somewhat antiquated method hardly becomes the character in question, which seems to call for modern and realistic treatment, rather than the sternness and solidity of the old school of tragedy. The Kaia of Miss Marie Linden is a tender little sketch enough. Mr. Athol Forde as Brovik, the physically broken assistant of the master builder, and Mr. Philip Cuningham as the young architect whose rivalry is so keenly dreaded by the morbid Solness, play their brief scenes with all possible point and effect; while Mr. John Beauchamp, in the character of Dr. Herdal, a mere colourless 'confidant,' makes the most of his few opportunities. In conclusion, let it be repeated that *The Master Builder*, like all Ibsen's plays, must be considered from the Ibsen point of view; otherwise it is but mere fantastic emptiness. The acting, however, of Miss Elizabeth Robins and Mr. Herbert Waring may be taken as a thing apart, and one which should engage the attention and appreciation of all who follow with any interest the progress of British histrionic art.

98. An unsigned notice, *Evening News and Post*

21 February 1893, 1

A three-decker headline: 'Ibsen's *Master Builder*/A Feast of Dull Dialogue and Acute De-/mentia at the Trafalgar Square Theatre.'

Ibsen has at last boldly entered the lists with Shakespeare, and produced a drama of insanity which his admirers can place side by side with *Hamlet*. Hitherto his characters have been only eccentric—during the operation parts of the play, though madness has in more than one case supervened in the last act [sic]. But in *The Master Builder*, produced at the Trafalgar Square Theatre yesterday afternoon, the Master has grappled with the problem of lunacy, and dealt with it in characteristic fashion. Realising the necessity of going one better than the effete Elizabethan dramatist whom a few lovers of the old order hold up as his superior, Ibsen has given himself a free hand, and instead of one mad character presents us with a trio—the hero, his wife, and the heroine. With his usual fondness for keeping an audience in the dark as to what he is driving at, the Norwegian Master tries to hide the exact mental qualifications of his principal characters during the earlier scenes of the play, but the experienced playgoers of yesterday's matinée were not puzzled for long. The chief lunatic is Halvard Solness, a gentleman who appears to have a monopoly of all the best building contracts in his native town (precise locality not indicated in the programme), and to combine method with his madness in such degree that even his operations for the local School Board have been above suspicion. In the first act Mr. Solness shows the practical quality of his insanity by devoting most of his time to making love to a pretty little girl book-keeper in his employment, and to weaving plots for keeping his talented apprentice out of business. When, however, we see him resenting certain absolutely non-existent suspicions of his wife and his doctor as to his sanity, we realise that Solness is not to be taken seriously—he is a madman under the microscope.

Later on in this act we are introduced to the lunatic second in importance, a young lady named Hilda Wangel, who drops in casually in mountaineering dress and asks to have a bed for the night. It transpires from profuse dialogue that Hilda met Solness ten years before, when she was a little girl of thirteen, and that he kissed her on the lips many times, bent back her head ever so far, and promised that in ten years time he would come back, make her a Princess, and give her a kingdom. Solness had forgotten all about the appointment, so when the ten years were up, Hilda packed a knapsack, and came to look him up. Solness is very pleased to see her. He does not take any stock in the princess and kingdom business, but Hilda is a nice, fresh, quaint sort of girl, and he undertakes to put her up in one of the three nurseries of his house, which are fully furnished with everything but children. So far, there is some slight indication of a plot in the piece, but the second act dissipates the idea that Ibsen could condescend to anything so commonplace. Hilda and Solness play about and talk at interminable length, and she makes him not only write a note to say that his clever apprentice is a really smart youngster, but dismisses the young man and his sweetheart, the pretty bookkeeper before alluded to. We gather nothing about Hilda's character except that she is subject to mania of an erotic nature, and designs to take Solness away from his wife, and bring him to live with her in a suburban villa. This programme is not clearly described, but the idea of the act is pretty well summarised by it.

In the third act Mrs. Solness gets a chance, and reveals her own special form of insanity. She is a very gloomy and limp personage, popularly supposed to be permanently crushed by sorrow for her twin baby-boys, who died years before of cold caught at the fire which burnt up the Solness establishment and enabled the Master Builder to make his name as an architect. In reality, however, the grief that weighs upon her soul is attributable to the burning of her collection of dolls in the aforesaid fire, and she confides the harrowing details to Hilda, moving the latter to a momentary hesitation as to her project of removing Solness from the domestic hearth. In the end Hilda, whose lunatic passion for Solness is largely due to her belief that he can stand on giddy heights without losing his balance, prevails upon him to climb the scaffolding round a new house he has built, and hang a wreath of flowers round the topmost pinnacle of an ornamental tower. The man is really a coward and subject to fits of dizziness, and has only once in his life ventured to a respectable distance from the ground, but his vanity induces him to yield to Hilda's persuasion. He climbs the tower, hangs the wreath, and tumbles down a hundred feet or so, killing himself comfortably and ending the play, and a good job, too.

Played with admirable discretion and much forcible expression of feeling by Mr. Herbert Waring, and Miss Elizabeth Robins in the leading parts, *The Master Builder* succeeded in holding a full audience in attentive silence during three acts of the most dreary and purposeless drivel we have ever heard in an English theatre. In his latest play Ibsen has fully demonstrated that he is a great man. No one but a great man could get a clever actor and actress to accept and produce upon the stage such a pointless, incoherent, and absolutely silly piece.

99. From an unsigned notice, *The Times*

21 February 1893, 12

Since the production at the Trafalgar-square Theatre yesterday afternoon of *The Master Builder*, the most ardent votaries of Ibsenism must be in some doubt as to whether a further prosecution of the cult is advisable. They must have left the theatre with an uneasy feeling that the master was laughing at them in his sleeve. It is only on some such hypothesis that the strange composition of the latest of Mr. Ibsen's plays can be accepted as the work of a wholly sane writer, especially a writer for the stage, where it is, above all, necessary to be clear and intelligible. The master builder is one Halvard Solness, who builds, it appears, not by contract, but in obedience to his own caprice. He began by building churches; then he took to building 'houses for human beings to live in,' but both branches of enterprise have proved unsatisfactory, though not from the commercial point of view, which indeed is never mentioned. When the play opens Solness is in two minds as to whether he will build any more, or build houses with towers. While explaining himself as best he can to the family doctor, who does not profess to understand these nebulous projects, the master builder is evidently haunted by the belief that he is not quite sane, or that his proceedings are liable to be interpreted as insanity. This view of the part, at all events, is taken by its exponent on the stage, Mr. Herbert Waring, who not only adopts something of the manner of the lunatic, but indulges from time to time in an uncanny maniacal laugh. Solness also, according to the author, believes in the transmission of will power from one person to another at indefinite distances, and credits himself with possessing the hypnotizing faculty in an exceptional degree.

[outlines the plot.]

All this, say the admirers of the Norwegian dramatist, is symbolism, and symbolism as applied to Mr. Ibsen's own work. He had begun by building churches—that is, writing orthodox plays; the houses for human beings to live in were the Ibsenite drama proper. What the castle in the air is they do not, so far as we are aware, explain, but if it should be the symbolical drama over which its author comes to grief, no impartial-minded person who witnessed this crazy performance of *The Master Builder* will be disposed to say them nay.

100. From an unsigned notice, *Standard*

21 February 1893, 3

The Ibsen controversy, which raged with such fierceness a year or two ago, is likely to be, to some extent, revived by the production, yesterday afternoon, at the Trafalgar-square Theatre, of Mr. Ibsen's last composition, *The Master Builder*. It has been ascertained, by the trustworthy test of putting Mr. Ibsen's works on the stage, that a very small number of playgoers are sufficiently interested in them to visit the houses where they are acted, but the Norwegian philosopher has a small following of ardent devotees, who have quite decided that to fail in perceiving all sorts of subtle and powerful things in his writings is an unmistakeable proof of intellectual poverty. Only those who recognise in him a great teacher and prophet are of any esteem among these frantic enthusiasts; but on the other side is arranged a gathering of equally positive opponents, who angrily maintain that Ibsenism is a sham and an imposture. Those who have not made up their minds, if they care to settle the question, have now an opportunity, for *The Master Builder* is to be given every morning this week. The method, it must be admitted, is a somewhat desperate one, and it is not for a single moment to be understood that we personally recommend any one to try it. Nor, possibly, would it be conclusive, for those who have studied this latest emanation most deeply protest that it is not in all respects a characteristic work; indeed, one of the adapters, Mr. William Archer, has frankly confessed that he does not even now quite see what it all means. Mr. Archer's mental grasp is by no means therefore to be derided. No one can tell. The suggestion that it all means nothing would be irreverent, but assuredly no one may fathom its mysteries, and those who see and read the play—so far as it can be called a play—have the privilege of putting upon it any kind of interpretation that they prefer.

[outlines the plot.]

There was one merry moment in *The Master Builder*—when Miss Wangel suddenly asked Solness, 'What is all this nonsense you are talking?' A burst of laughter suggested that the spectators also desired to be informed on this point. As regards the acting, it is impossible to criticise the incomprehensible.

The blunder has been made. *Master-Builder Solness* has been played upon the London stage. The enemies of Ibsen may well rejoice over what the friends of Ibsen must needs call a calamity. For to the friends of Ibsen— to the people, that is to say, who have from the first understood him and followed in admiration the growth of his career—*Master-Builder Solness* came as nothing less than a catastrophe. And if this 'last fruit from an old tree,' or, at all events, latest fruit from an old tree, was heart-breaking to read, it was yet more heart-breaking to see acted. There are agonies which one may endure in the study that are scarcely to be borne in a theatre. Probably no gifts of acting could have made *The Master-Builder*—to adopt the marred English title—a joy to earnest students of the work of the great northern dramatist. But it must be said at once, and without hesitation, that Miss Elizabeth Robins and Mr. Herbert Waring were not the woman and the man to cheat observers endowed with any intelligence into the belief that they were beholding a great play. To have done that would have called for a more than Egyptian glamour—a glamour denied on this occasion to the daring actor and to the daring actress.

It is the vice of enthusiasm in letters that it so speedily degenerates into partisanship, and thence into mere faction. The admiration of yesterday becomes the fanaticism of to-day and promises folly for to-morrow. This has been the case with many; it is to be hoped that it will not prove to be the case with the majority of the advocates of Henrik Ibsen. In spite of all the warfare that has raged around Ibsen's name, in spite of all the expositions, essays, and analyses, it may be asserted with truth that justice has not yet been done to his genius as a writer, as a student of man; above all, as a dramatist. The term genius is bandied about with much familiarity nowadays, till, like the assignats of a bank-rupt State, it no longer represents the value it carries on its face. But genius is the term that fits Ibsen, that belongs to the author of *Peer Gynt* and of *Hedda Gabler*, of *Fru Inger til Ostrat* and *Et Dukkehjem*. But it does not follow, unhappily, that because a man deserves to be saluted as a man of genius, therefore all his works stand upon the same level of greatness; above all, it does not follow, as faction generally would have it to follow, that the latest work is equal to the best, or is actually the best, of the author's creation. There are works that pass by the name of Shakespeare, that pass by the name of Goethe, which are the grief of the zealot. And it must, most regretfully, be admitted that *Bygmester Solness* is more unworthy of its author than anything which is unhappily associated with the name of either Shakespeare or Goethe. It would be possible for a critic wholly indifferent to sacrilege to find for himself and for his readers an infinity of sport in this wretched *Master-Builder*. At every turn it affords opportunity for the slings and arrows of the Philistines, for the flouts and jeers of those to whom the name of Ibsen has always been a hissing. But the fact that a great man has erred, has failed, has capitulated, is a fact to deplore, not a fact for mirth, for ridicule. It would be easy enough to make merry over the astonishing ineptitudes, absurdities, offences of *Master-Builder Solness*. No doubt plenty of people will be found to wax blithe over these defects. But the student of the drama, the student to whom everything in life is not a joke or the subject for a joke, can only regret in the first place that Ibsen ever wrote *Master-Builder Solness*, and, in the second place, that actors and actresses were to be found willing to exhibit this tragic error in a great career. Only the greatest acting could have made the play even temporarily attractive, could for the passing hour have cheated the beholder into the cry of Faust—the cry, 'Stay, for thou art so fair.' And great acting was not given to the service of *The Master-Builder* yesterday. Miss Robins failed to understand Hedda Gabler; she was hardly likely to understand Hilde Wangel. Mr. Waring's success as Torwald Helmer did not necessarily suggest, seemed rather to forbid, success as Halvard Solness. *Hedda Gabler* was a play of human beings, of human passions: *A Doll's Home* was a play of human passions, of human beings. But *Master-Builder Solness*, if in its mad way it is not wholly passionless, is certainly wholly unhuman. It is an allegory, so the world has been told, an allegory of the life of Ibsen and of Ibsen's works. It is curious to remember in this connection that a tower and alarm due to a tower play a part in Ibsen's earliest memories. But allegories are seldom a cause of joy, and the world has seldom seen an allegory so uncompromisingly unattractive as the allegory that is portion and parcel of the warp and woof of *Bygmester Solness*. The earnest admirer of Ibsen looked on with little less than anguish while the three grotesque acts moved at their stealthy pace. The madman Solness, the wanton Hilde, the idiot wife, jerked their way through the leaden hours only to participate in a cheap *feu de joie* in the last three minutes, after the best motive out of *Hedda Gabler* had been repeated under conditions which made the repetition laughable to the indifferent and agonizing to the serious beholder. To that serious beholder one thought dominates all others—pity for Dr. Wangel, who had such a wife as Elena Wangel, such a daughter—by an earlier marriage—as Hilde Wangel. What, such a spectator asks himself in despair, can the first Mrs. Wangel have been like to have borne such a daughter? For Hilde Wangel is perhaps the most detestable character in the drama's range. In one regard a victim of nymphomania; in another a deliberate murderess; in any aspect, mean, cheap, and hateful, Hilde Wangel stands out in dishonourable distinctness. Miss Robins can scarcely be blamed for failing to make the part attractive; but she certainly approached the part in far too burlesque a spirit. It is not persistent laughter, it is not the iteration of a jaunty attitude with hands folded behind the back, that can bring conviction to such a part. Detestable as Hilde Wangel is, she is not to be played in the spirit in which unfortunately it pleased Miss Robins to play it. And Mr. Waring, able actor though he be, was not the man for Master-Builder Solness. He failed entirely to suggest the hypnotic charm which makes woman after woman succumb to his middle-aged attractions, which makes it possible that an amorous young woman should lure him to his death for the sake of preserving her high ideal of his character. But no acting could have saved the piece from being what it is—a tragedy, though not in the sense which was intended by its author.

102. An unsigned notice, *Black and White*

25 February 1893, 224

When Socrates wanted to do what Mrs. Gamp would call a 'bold, bage thing,' he declared that he obeyed the promptings of his dæmon. What the internal dæmon was to Socrates, that the troll is to Halvard Solness, the hero, and to Hilda Wangel, the heroine, of Dr. Henrik Ibsen's new play, *The Master Builder*, as Englished by Mr. Edmund Gosse and Mr. William Archer, and produced this week at the Trafalgar Square

Theatre. Are you conscious of the troll within you? How is your troll since we last met? will supersede the weather as an afternoon-tea topic, I fancy. I regret to state that I have nothing of the troll in my composition. Hence it is, I suppose, that I miss the full significance of the new Scandinavian play. The piece passes in three acts of continuous conversation between Solness and Hilda, conversation finally terminated by a scaffold-accident, *à la Coupeau*. The accident, in Hilda's cant phrase, would be 'frightfully thrilling,' if we could only see it, but we cannot. So that on the stage itself nothing of a material external nature can be said to happen. The whole drama consists in the development of—or rather in the exposition of already developed—character. Solness and Hilda are both remarkable people. I am bound to say I never met anybody in the least like either of them. They are troll-possessed. Do you understand? No? Well, no more do I. Solness is 'a man of mature age, healthy and vigorous,' with the power of mesmerising people, especially his female book-keepers. But he has one weak point—his conscience, which, according to Hilda, is 'sickly.' Hers is, on the other hand, 'robust' and 'radiantly healthy.' Only fancy a radiant conscience! As a child, Hilda has been hypnotised by Solness, and now, grown up, she comes to hypnotise him, to impose her will upon his. In her turn, she represents the 'young generation,' of which he is afraid, and, with her full-blooded, albeit idealistic temperament, she wills that he shall give up his old-fashioned building operations,—he is a successful architect—his 'churches,' and his 'homes for human beings,' and take to building 'castles in the air,' for the two of them to inhabit. He has a wife, to be sure, a poor platitudinous creature, born to suckle fools and chronicle small beer, whose mission in life has been frustrated by the death of her twins and the desire of her husband for (figuratively speaking) more heady beverages than malt liquor. Solness wants the sparkling champagne of Hilda's presence and encouragement. Ultimately that champagne gets into his head, persuades him to ascend a high tower (as a preliminary to mounting the turrets of the 'castles in the air'), and thence he falls headlong. Hilda found his fall 'frightfully thrilling.' But what it all means the trolls only know. Why is the hypnotism dragged in? What are the 'castles in the air?' Why all the prolonged metaphor about 'churches,' and 'homes for human beings,' and 'towers pointing up, up, up'? Many commentators have come forward to explain that the whole thing is an allegory. Solness is Dr. Ibsen, the buildings are his plays, Hilda is the New Spirit, and so forth. But this is only to make darkness visible. Allegory, mysticism, and symbolism are all very well in their place, but I submit that they are not in their right place on the stage. On the stage I want lucidity, and if I don't get it I am angry. The players do their best to lighten our darkness. Miss Elizabeth Robins's Hilda is very much alive, and Mr. Herbert Waring's Solness is almost as interesting as a real human being. Some day, perhaps, I shall pierce to the true inwardness of *The Master Builder* by aid of the exegesis of some kindly troll.

103. From a pseudonymous theatre column by 'Momus', *Gentlewoman*

25 February 1893, 250

The third dramatic event of the week is of great importance. Translated by William Archer and Edmund Gosse, Ibsen's latest work *The Master Builder* is produced every afternoon at the Trafalgar. Right well have these two Norwegian scholars and artists accomplished their difficult task of the interpretation of this beautiful tragedy. Written in valuable English, acted with the finest sincerity, this work of the grim old man of the North comes on us as a veritable revelation of poetic pessimism. It is remorseless, pitiless, real, human yet monstrous, ugly but fascinating, bewildering in its witcheries, at moments innocently grotesque, a struggling bird with wounded wings, but for all that a veritable work of strongly personal art. We fought the fight of Ibsen in this column long ago, and we were against him.

We have been converted by the original *Hedda Gabler*, with Elizabeth Robins and Mr Waring, and we fearlessly tell you that Ibsen's work, acted as it is by enthusiasts, is perfectly fascinating. It is not great or good work, but it is superbly individual.

104. A poem by William Hardinge, *Observer*

26 February 1893, 6

'Failed'—say they. But the mightiest, plainest things,
  Being simple, stand as failures. Day and night
  Are daily, nightly failures, if delight
In each were meant to lift the people's wings.
And this great Daylight Play's imaginings—
  Streaked all with dawn and sunset, lurid bright—
  Fade like an hour wherein cloud-armies fight
O'ver heads bowed on smoke-wreaths and bubble rings.

So take day's failure with the day! There dwell
  Some yet for whom light shone, for whom was rung
That harp-tune up in air, who envied thee,
From that high tow'r built between heaven and hell,
  Ibsen, like thine own Master Builder, flung
After a struggle with immensity!

105. 'The Crack in the Flue', a notice by 'W.M.', *Hawk*

28 February 1893, 12–13

Ibsenites arrogate to themselves somewhat too much. There is insolence in the assumption that it is given to a few intellectual cranks to discover the hidden beauties in the works of a Master which are invisible to the multitude. You may, perhaps, appreciate some poor play of Shakespeare or admire the beauties of Homer's *Iliad*. But this man from Norway— the man who looks like a cross between Mr. Samuel Danks Waddy and the late Dr. Kenealy—that is a different matter. To understand him you must be of the Elect. Like his Master-Builder, you must stand on an Eiffel Tower. From this coign of vantage you may look down upon the houses built for human beings, and sneer at the men of narrow forehead and porcine proclivities who inhabit them. At that altitude also you will hear the sound of harps in the air, which you will find a wonderful solace. An' you be a true disciple, however, your attitude must ever be that of looking down. The human beings in the houses are mere Philistines. Ye are as gods, knowing good and evil. Within you is the animating presence of a troll, and at his bidding the helpers and the servers force you to your destiny. So that, after all, you have no feeling of moral responsibility, which must be very thrilling.

Not without a certain 'mischief-joy' do I note that the latest play of Henrik Ibsen has not been 'understanded' of the disciples themselves. The doctors differ, at length; in which case how shall the poor layman decide? Mr. William Archer, for example, regards *The Master-Builder* as a 'weird, ironic tragedy.' But Mr. Waugh sees nothing either of irony or tragedy in it. To him it is pure symbolism. This brilliant discovery, he is careful to point out, was originally made by the poet Gosse (of the Board of Trade). Waugh himself has been of late years too greatly taken up in explaining the lucid lines of Tennyson to devote much serious attention to the banalities of a Norwegian babble-monger like Ibsen. Still, he accepts Gosse as to the symbolism of the play, and further endorses the poet's opinion when he avers that the character of Solness in the play is Ibsen himself. The natural enemies of Ibsen have surely never uttered anything quite so severe as this criticism of Gosse endorsed by Waugh. These disciples could not have foreseen where this asseveration would land them. As Ibsenites cannot bear to see the Master brought to the bar of public criticism and tried by those laws which regulate the drama, let him be tried on the indictment of the poet Gosse. I ask nothing better; whether Ibsen himself will quite approve of this method of trial is quite another matter. 'SOLNESS MUST CERTAINLY BE IBSEN HIMSELF'— thus the disciples. So I take it that if I have pointed out what manner of man Solness is, I have at the same time given a description of the venerable author of the *Doll's House*. To this reasoning no objection can, I think, be taken; and at the instance of the worshippers themselves I propose to gain some insight into the character of their god by examining the creature he has made in his own image.

Halvard Solness, then, I take to be on the whole one of the most contemptible rascals of whom we have any record. He is *the* most contemptible rascal who was ever selected by an author to pose as the hero of a play. He is by profession an architect, in a large way of business. He has made his position by rising on the ruins of his former employer, and he maintains that position by adopting the plans of that ruined employer's son. One, of course, does not sympathise with this young gentleman. It is one of the peculiarities of Ibsen's works that, no matter what wrongs his characters suffer, one can never condole with them. This is your true symbolism. So while we wonder at the tame submission of this Scandinavian Tom Pinch we regard his sufferings with equanimity. Halvard Solness—who according to Gosse is Ibsen himself—does not content himself with stealing Tom Pinch's plans and elevations. He steals his sweetheart also. Solness, in a conversation with his medical adviser, explains that he has loved both much and many in his time. This sweetheart of his assistant he keeps constantly by his side, employing her as a sort of tame typewriter. She wears a green shade over her eyes when others besides Ibsen—I should have said Solness— are in the room. That the disciples have discovered some subtle symbolism in this I dare be sworn. Solness has a wife. This terrible person is a Norwegian Mrs. Gummidge. She is insanely jealous of her husband, and eternally bemoans her sterility and the loss of 'nine lovely dolls' which were destroyed in a certain fire to which I must allude more particularly by-and-by. For her jealousy Mrs. Solness had every reason. Nor was her husband very particular about the age of those to whom he offered his somewhat fly-blown attentions. In one case, at least, he had made love to a girl of thirteen. She herself tells the discreditable story in the course of the play—how that the Master-Builder, coming home from supper at the club, surprised her *alone* in a room. The salacious Ibsen italicises the 'alone'. The maiden herself, after the lapse of ten years, reminds the Master-Builder of the incident in these words, 'You took me in both your arms and bent my head back and kissed me—many times.' There comes here incidentally some vague suggestion of hypnotism; not being gifted, however, with those powers of perceiving the unseeable of which the Ibsenites boast, I shall omit this portion of the 'true inwardness' of the work, and deal with such solid facts as the Master sets before us. To whatever emotion the act of Mr. Solness may be attributed when he met the child of thirteen alone in a room after a club supper and bent her head back and kissed her many times, we are left in no doubt as to his amiable intentions with regard to her, when in answer to an invitation given ten years before, she turns up at his house as a buxom hoyden demanding a kingdom. Ibsen has apparently been studying the Marquis of Queensberry's essay on the best way to marital felicity, and he determines to establish Hilda in his house as a very intimate member of the family indeed. She on her side makes it a condition of surrender to her elderly lover that he should mount to the top of a high tower and hear 'the harps in the air.' This, as we all know, results in an accidental death which Mr. William Archer is not ashamed to describe as 'a weird, ironic tragedy.' To tumble off a scaffolding like a drunken hodman is, I think, a fitting fate for a pitiful and pitiless scoundrel. It is the one touch of dramatic truth in the play.

The turpitude of Solness is not yet told. And this brings me to the story of the Crack in the Flue, which plays a part by no means unimportant in Ibsen's 'ironic tragedy.' Solness is confessed an impostor and a seducer—he is also an incendiary. To be sure, he did not absolutely sprinkle paraffin on firewood and ignite the combustibles. He only willed that it should be so, and there being a Crack in the Flue the thing was done. He has the power—so he confesses to Hilda—'of *desiring* a thing, *craving* for a thing, *willing* a thing, so persistently and so inexorably that, at last, it *has* to happen.' I would confidently recommend this passage to members of the Junior Bar. As a defence in a case of arson it would at least have the advantage of extreme novelty. The result of the fire which Ibsen—or Solness—had contrived threw into his hands those eligible building lots the utilisation of which consolidated his fortune. The result of this conflagration, however, caused such a fright to Mrs. Solness that she was unable to afford her twin babes their natural nutriment, so they sickened and died, and Mrs. Solness, falling into the Gummidge stage could bear no other children to her husband. According to the unconventional lights of Solness it was only meet and right that he should establish such relations with the providentally discovered Hilda as should make up to him in some way for the aversion habitually manifested by the wife of his bosom. The accident on the tower prevented the fulfilment of his hopes. I never rejoiced in my life before on hearing of the death of a fellow-creature. I contemplated this decease with sentiments of the liveliest satisfaction. Whether the man suffered from vertigo, or was attacked by the troll within him, or was pushed over by the helpers and servers, or was wafted by the sound of harps in the air, I know not. It was enough that he was dead. For one brief moment I sympathised with Hilda. When it is ascertained that the Master-Builder is really killed ('the head is all crushed'), his lover waves her shawl in the air and shrieks with wild intensity: '*My—my* Master-Builder.'

I have now in a few rapid strokes given some idea of the character of

Solness as portrayed in the drama. It was never suggested by me that in painting Solness the author of *A Doll's House* was in reality depicting himself. The suggestion comes, strangely enough, from two of the disciples. I have accepted their challenge, and should like to know now what they think of their Master? To me Ibsen appears to possess all the nastiness of Sterne without any of his humour, and all the dulness of Samuel Richardson without any of that author's facility for the presentation of human character. Playwrights who cannot conform to the rules of dramatic art, and who refuse to be tried by the ordinary canons of criticism, can have no permanent success in this country. The existence of a 'troll' accepting the moral responsibility of the characters in a drama must rob a play of all its reality; and the present vogue of Ibsen is attributable solely to the arrogant insistence of certain affected critics, whose admiration for the Master is second only to their admiration for each other.

One word more. Ibsenites must never complain that their favourite author failed in his last trial because the interpretation of his play was feeble or faulty. There are really but three characters of importance in the drama, and these go through interminable lengths of dialogue. Nevertheless, the performers were letter perfect, and delivered their lines as though they were from a play of Shakespeare himself. One sympathised with an actress like Miss Louise Moodie in her attempts to give vitality to the Scandinavian Mrs. Gummidge with her nine dolls and her recurrent regrets. Mr. Herbert Waring as Ibsen (see Gosse, the poet, on this subject) did not look at all like the portraits which I have seen of the Master. And Miss Elizabeth Robins played Hilda with such humour, such spontaneity, and such evident sincerity, that once or twice I imagined I was watching the development of a beautiful human character, not that of a very shameless young woman endowed with a troll that impelled her to the pursuit and capture of another woman's husband.

106. The other Henrik Ibsen

A report in *Era*, 4 February 1893, 10

A Norwegian gentleman has just pocketed two thousand crowns by the simple expedient of passing under his own name, which happens to be Henrik Ibsen. He telegraphed to the owner of a public hall in Christiania, to secure it for a lecture he proposed to give on 'The Submission of Woman.' The hall owner promptly 'booked the date' and announced the lecture, and on the appointed day every seat was full. The manager, arrayed in his best, awaited the sturdy, bearded, bespectacled dramatist, and was just beginning to grow impatient when 'Mr Henrik Ibsen' was announced—a thin, rosy, fair-haired gentleman appeared. He *was* Henrik Ibsen; there was no mistake about it. He had even—being a far-seeing person—brought his certificate of birth to prove that he was surnamed Ibsen and Christian-named Henrik, and he duly mounted the platform and gave his lecture. The damage to the hall was estimated at three times the receipts.

107. An unsigned review, *Saturday Review*

4 March 1893, lxxv, 241–2

The Master Builder was translated by Edmund Gosse and William Archer and published in England by Heinemann in 1893.

Of the translation of *Bygmester Solness* as a translation not very much need be said. We shall all note with heartfelt pleasure that the breach is healed—that there is now no anti-pope in the English branch of the Ibsenite Church. All occasion of blasphemy is taken away by the appearance of Mr. Gosse and Mr. Archer dwelling together 'in luve and lee.' It would be invidious to attempt to discover with what particular alterations this collaboration is to be credited in contrast with the former versions. We shall only say that is seems to us to have the advantage of some—not of all—former English translations of Ibsen in not substituting positive vulgarity for the familiar vernacular of the Norwegian master. We would, indeed, that Hilda were not made to talk American —'I'll have to' for 'I shall have to,' and 'it would be lovely'—but enough of this.

It is credibly reported that the little Scandinavian world has been hard at work ever since the appearance of *Bygmester Solness*—by the way, why not keep 'Bygmester'? If 'Burgomaster,' why not 'Bygmester'?—endeavouring at mystical interpretations of the piece, and most of our English Ibsenites have followed, as in duty bound. The hoary critic—

> Mighty in his own despite,
> Miserable in his might

(or, if not exactly miserable, commiserating)—could have prophesied this beforehand and forestalled all the interpretations. When one remembers what would-be imaginative dulness made of *Peer Gynt*, which *The Master Builder* more resembles in many ways than any of Ibsen's more recent plays, it is easy to foresee what it will make of the present fantasy piece.

For a fantasy piece it is, though crossed and dashed doubtless with the social-drama strain. It fills about the same number of pages as *Hedda Gabler*, but seems—we do not know why—shorter in reading. This may be due to the fact that the personages are few and the action much concentrated. Halvard Solness is an irregularly educated architect who has become a very successful builder, though partly out of shrewdness, partly out of an arrogant humility, he will not call himself by the loftier title. He has taken captive his old master, Knut Brovik, who now serves in an inferior capacity in Solness's office, where also Ragnar Brovik, his son, is employed as a draughtsman, and Kaia Fosli, Brovik's niece, as a bookkeeper. Ragnar and Kaia are betrothed, but the latter secretly adores Solness. The Master Builder's wife, Aline, is a rather jealous, distinctly mad, and very much depressed person, who also adores her husband, but has never recovered [from] a fire which soon after her marriage has destroyed her ancestral house, with her two children indirectly, and her nine dolls directly, but which has at the same time, by clearing the estate, started Solness's fortune as builder. The artist, though generally thought a hard man in head and heart, is actually madder than his wife, entertaining crazes on the subject of church-building, and in reference to 'the younger generation' and the conflagration above mentioned, not to mention others, while he thinks himself even madder than he is. To these suddenly enters a young person (reminding us of *The Lady from the Sea*), Hilda Wangel, whom years before, as a child of twelve, Solness has kissed ('holding her head far back') and joked with, promising her all sorts of things. She, like Kaia, adores him—they all do—and soon establishes a great influence over him of a curiously mixed kind. He had caught her childish fancy by the manner in which he performed that rather uncomfortable duty of a Scandinavian Master Builder, which consists in performing the functions of a steeple-jack, and fixing a wreath on the vane of the finished building. She wants to see him do this again; and it so happens that Solness is just finishing a new house for himself which has an extraordinary high tower. But it also happens that giddiness has prevented him latterly—indeed, ever since the occasion when he captivated Hilda and kissed her holding her head far back—from performing this part of his office, whereat the 'younger generation' sneers.

This eccentrically, but not very obscurely, arranged plot works itself out pretty rapidly, and at last Solness, under Hilda's spell, outwitting his wife's alarms, mounts the new tower himself, achieves the crowning and then, the scaffold breaking, falls, to be smashed to atoms amid the horror of everybody except Hilda herself. That unconventional damsel remarks, '*as if in quiet spell-bound triumph*—'But he mounted right up to the top. And I heard harps in the air.' *Waves her shawl in the air and shouts with wild intensity*, '*My* Master Builder!' This conclusion is somewhat suggestive of two well-known passages in Dickens—that where Mr. Bagnet observes, 'With a second-hand wiolinceller. Of a good tone. For a friend,' and that where Pip and Estella waved flags while the dogs ate veal cutlet round Miss Havisham's black velvet coach. But if Dr. Ibsen could avoid these suggestions of the grotesque and *baroque* he would not be Ibsen, and as they are omnipresent in his work, we shall say no more about them nor about the inimitable stage directions which heighten their effect. The conclusion for all the oddity and bad taste, is by no means ill worked up to. The virulent and rather ignoble hate of the Broviks for Solness; the intense blind animal devotion of Kaia; the not unnatural, but, as an actual fact, unfounded jealousy of the latter entertained by Mrs. Solness (who is a thoroughly Dickensish figure; the

Nine Dolls are quite startling in their Dickensianity), and her quiet immovable despair about nothing in particular—these three are all well outlined, and fall in with the fantastic tone of the thing well enough. Of the two main characters, Solness is less interesting than Hilda. He is distinctly incomplete; there is nothing in him (even with the help of the stage directions) to justify his lady-killing; his fear of the Broviks is as ignoble as their hatred of him; and his treatment of Kaia (for whom he seems to have no sort of affection, but whom he wheedles into the belief that he is keeping young Brovik for her sake, while he is really keeping her for fear of losing the young man) is particularly repulsive. He submits to Hilda in a magnetic sort of way which, with some nonsense about thought-and-will-transmission, is the author's principal concession to his mania for incorporating pseudo-scientific crazes of the day in his work. But Hilda is much better. She is an extremely emancipated young lady—as much so as the great Hedda herself. She thinks it would have been 'fearfully thrilling' to have been carried off by a Viking; and the calmness with which, when Solness asks her to take up her abode permanently with him and his wife, she observes, 'You know it wouldn't end there, Mr. Solness,' is very refreshing. But she is less vulgar than Hedda, and though her ideals of tower-building, princess-ship, and so forth, are as cracked as they can be, they are at any rate better ideals than that of living up to the dignity of 'General Gabler's pistols.' Also the conversation between her and the Bygmester as to the 'trolls in them,' and the things the trolls do, and would like to do, has merit.

In fact, Dr. Ibsen has remounted not a few rungs of the ladder he has been descending of late (the Bygmester's imagery is contagious) by the mere fact of dipping himself once more into the fantastic. In the early scenes of this play it may look (we confess it did to us for a moment) as if the author were going to do what one of his maladroit worshippers once did, and give us the preliminary scenes of *Rosmersholm*, with Hilda for Rebecca and Aline for Beata. And there is, no doubt, considerable repetition of the situation, especially in the characters of the two wives. But, as will have been seen, the thing is worked out quite differently, and in the total impression of the piece as it stands 'modernity' of any kind has very little to say. Of course, the imaginative dulness before referred to can apply a plot and characters so fantastic and elastic to almost any theory it pleases. We are told, and can believe it, that a 'satire on the Radical party', a 'history of the author's career,' and a dozen other things have been already seen in it. We would undertake ourselves to get out of it a criticism on Mr. Gladstone's Home Rule Bill, a system of phallic worship, a refutation of evolution, and a diatribe against the Institution of British Architects, in the time requisite for writing them all out, with as many more things of the same kind as might be wished, including a theory of the man in the Iron Mask and an examination of the Casket Letters. The fact of course is, that it is of the essence of a fantasy-piece to admit of almost any number of interpretations. And it is of the essence of the intelligent reader of a fantasy-piece not to insist upon any. 'Exeunt confusedly' is the proper stage direction for such things, and though every competent reader will see in *The Master Builder* a fresh handling in allegory of the great commonplaces of life—of unsatisfied desire, of mistaken grasping, of the loss which follows gain, of the elective affinities that cannot be converted into stable connexions, and turn into something quite different—no such reader will commit the fatal folly of working out any such interpretation. Again, and always, 'The Letter killeth,' and nobody but fools will come and be killed by it.

The piece, then, shows, as literature (it is, of course, an impossible play), the better and, because slightly insane, saner side of Ibsen's genius; but it shows also the limitations of that genius, and, what is more, *des ans l'irréparable outrage*. Some of the exegetes, we doubt not, have already seen, in *Bygmester Solness*, the tower from which falls the once heaven-scaling architect of *Brand* and *Peer Gynt*. This would be worthy of them. As a matter of fact, the piece is only attractive so long as it is allowed to exercise a vague fascination. It will not stand examining. The suspicion, or rather knowledge, of his own madness with which Solness is credited may make him a more pathetic figure from the ordinary point of view, but rather detracts from his poetic interest. If Dr. Herdal, a character whom we have not yet mentioned, had done his duty after the middle of the first act, the Master Builder would have been locked up on his own confession. Hilda, as we have said, is not uninteresting—we should not altogether dislike her acquaintance. But the author takes an undue license of leaving her unexplained in detail. She reminds us a little of the sorceress Matilda in *The Monk*; and Lewis has never been considered a great artist. We make very large allowances for insanity, and are quite ready to admit that agreeable and intelligent people are often a little mad on one side. And Miss Hilda Wangel is not the only young lady who might consider it thrilling to be carried off by Vikings. But, as most of her actions and speeches show great practical shrewdness, and even some good feeling, it is not entirely intelligible why she should send her friend, if not her lover, to something like certain death, and so knock all her desires and plans on the head. She was not the person to do it for the beauty of it, like Hedda. Indeed, we very strongly suspect that Dr. Ibsen has failed to keep Hedda and Hilda as distinct in his brain as they should have been kept. However, let us not repine. There is, as we have said, next to nothing of 'modern' in *The Master Builder*, 'and sae the Lord be thankit.'

108. 'Ibsen's Last Play', an unsigned review, *Spectator*

4 March 1893, lxx, 285–6

It is useless to attempt a criticism of Ibsen's work, and at the same time ignore the fierce controversy that is waged over his merits by his admirers, and those who fail to appreciate him. One cannot remain blind to the fact that the Norwegian dramatist is regarded by a small section of the reading public as one of the greatest writers of the day, almost, indeed, as a prophet with a divine message, and by another—and rather larger section—as a half-crazed imposter, whose writings, if they have any meaning at all, can only be looked upon as the lamentable ravings of criminal lunacy; nor, unfortunately, can we remain deaf to the vehemence with which these contrary opinions are expressed, for the dramatist seems to possess the unfortunate gift of provoking both his enemies and his friends into quite unreasonable excesses of violence or civility. We, for our part, have as little wish to be over-civil as we have to be over-violent; still, we confess that we cannot quite believe in the good faith of some of the hostility that has been displayed towards Henrik Ibsen. That his critics should abhor both his matter and his method, is more than possible; but that they should fail to discover any meaning in the man at all, and can really look upon his plays as sheer drivelling rubbish, is hardly credible. It has seemed good to them to feign stupidity in answer to the preposterous claims that Ibsen's disciples have advanced on behalf of the 'Master;' and the answer is not a very happy one. Ibsen,

indeed, is intelligible enough to any one who takes the pains to understand—often quite too disagreeably intelligible—and it is not by shutting
one's own eyes that one can blind the rest of the world to his real powers.
It is useless to deny that the man is possessed of a strange dramatic force
and intensity, a weird and startling imagination, and an unrivalled power
of laying bare and dissecting the evil side of human nature, or the accidental disease of a single human soul; and not only that, but that he has also
the secret of presenting the problems of human doubt and misery in such
a form as to arrest irresistibly the attention and set to work the imagination of his readers. That much an impartial critic, who neither likes nor
admires him, is fain to concede. Unfortunately, the fanaticism of those
who do admire, demands much more. And here we may remark that
these admirers have done the object of their worship a singular dis-service
in advancing the plea of symbolism. Ibsen's plays, they say, are all more
or less symbolical; his plots, his characters, with all their horrible
incidents and occasionally grotesque absurdities—which to the ignorant
and uninitiated seem but the nonsensical dreams of a madman—are
symbols of eternal truths. Of what are his plays symbolical, and who
shall read their hidden meaning? Why, the same might be said of a
nursery-rhyme. 'Ride a cock-horse to Banbury Cross' might be called
a symbolical poem, and a hundred deeply interesting meanings attached
to it by so many different interpreters. What is the hidden meaning of
The Master-Builder? One of its translators says that it has none in particular; the other translator declares that it describes the life and aims of
the dramatist himself; and we have no doubt but that, with the help of
a little ingenuity, we could ourselves extract from it a very moving
moral for Mr. Gladstone and the Home-rule Bill. To taunt those who
are not of Ibsen's following with stupidity because they cannot fathom
a meaning upon which his followers themselves are not agreed, is a very
doubtful way of strengthening the dramatist's reputation. The Ibsen
school would do better to leave these symbolical meanings alone, and
devote their defence to those doctrines with which their master's work
is plentifully sprinkled, and of which the meaning is not obscure.

The Master-Builder, lately performed in London, is, perhaps, from
either the literary or the dramatic point of view, quite the worst play
that Ibsen has yet produced. From another point of view, it is far less
disagreeable than *Ghosts* or *Hedda Gabler*, though we are not sure if it
does not contain a moral more hopelessly wretched than even those
dreary productions. The Master-Builder, Halvard Solness, is a self-
made man; not an architect—for that he has never received sufficient

education—but a man who has forced his way up from the bottom to the top of the ladder by hard work aided by good luck. On the day that we are introduced to him, he enjoys a high position and the envy of his surroundings; and of all his little world he is the most unhappy man. His domestic life is wretched, partly through his own fault; his reputation abroad as a successful architect may crumble at any moment, because he knows that it has no stable foundation. He has risen upon the ruin of another architect, who, together with a son, is now employed in his own office; and it is upon their superior knowledge and ability that his success is founded. He is in perpetual fear of the real secret of his work being exposed, and strives to keep the Broviks, father and son, with him, and dependent upon him, by a peculiarly base manoeuvre. The opening scene between Solness and Kaia Fosli, the *fiancée* of the younger Brovik, who is employed as a book-keeper, and whose love Solness has secretly drawn to himself, serves as a keynote to the whole play. He does not love the girl, with whom he plays so treacherously, in the least; but she serves his purpose, and the wretched man has sunk so low as to find an actual pleasure in his wife's jealous suspicions, because he knows that they are unfounded, and because they seem to his perverse imagination some compensation for the real wrong that he daily does her. He has married above him; his wife has lost her two children, and with them every chance of happiness; and her devotion to her husband and her duty, in their equal combination, madden him. 'I am chained alive to a dead woman!' he cries, in a moment of agony; 'I, who cannot live without joy in life.' To this unhappy couple enters Hilda Wangel, the very embodiment of youthful joy in life,—reckless, almost insolent, in her beauty and health. At this point begins the dramatist's utter disregard for probability. We do not suppose that Solness's hypnotic powers, to which mysterious allusions are constantly made, are intended to be taken seriously; and we can only wonder at the strange ways of Norwegian society. Hilda, who as a child of twelve has met and been strongly attracted to Solness, suddenly, after the lapse of ten years, descends upon his hospitality. None of the ill-concealed misery of the *ménage* escapes her quick eyes, and she probes the wounds of Solness and his wife to the bottom. The hero of her childish imagination is no hero at all. The man who built churches, and whom she once admired standing upon the pinnacle of his own work, thinks nothing now but the low-pitched houses and the low ideals of material comfort, and is unspeakably miserable because the comfort is not for him. Such as he is, though, Hilda will take him: she has made up her mind to be a bird of prey, to take her goods wherever she can find them, and to cultivate a 'robust,' a 'radiantly healthy conscience.' The understanding between the two, after one or two false starts, is soon made. To Solness, Hilda is the younger generation which he so feared, and yet 'towards which in his heart he yearned so deeply,' all the joy and brightness of life which he seemed to have missed. And Hilda, though even her 'robust conscience' rejects the 'ugly' weapons with which Solness has hitherto fought, and quails for an instant before the chilling glimpse which she obtains into the soul of the unhappy woman she intends to rob, has made up her mind, if only her hero can mount once more to the place she assigned him her fancy, to take him as he is. He makes the attempt, but his 'dizzy conscience' plays him false. At the very moment of triumph and defiance, he falls, and lies dashed to pieces at the feet of his wife and the woman who had bade him climb for her sake. That, roughly speaking, is the outline of the strange plot, and we will freely confess that it does not do it justice. But the dramatist's habit of hiding plot within plot, and issue within issue, makes it almost impossible to give a fair idea of the main lines upon which his play is laid. Nor is it more easy to do justice to the vivid *aperçus* of character which enlighten here and there the dreary lengths of his interminable dialogues. The revelations of the self-torture to which the miserable Solness submits himself, are horribly realistic in their truth to nature; but it is that way that madness lies, and one had best draw back from exploring the dark recesses of that racked imagination. Nor is it easy to explain the secret of the rare touches of pathos in which the author sometimes indulges; we can only feel with Hilda that Mrs. Solness's lament for the nine dolls, so far from giving cause for laughter, strikes a note of such helpless sadness, that it beggars all pity.

But the moral of the whole play! If one could only fancy that the castle which Hilda and Solness contemplated building together was really a castle in the air, an ideal edifice which should harbour no earthly passion, then one might forgive much of the sordid tale that led to their resolve and its tragic ending. But the dramatist destroys all escape that way, and makes it only too clear in what spirit the two chief actors part for the last time. As Solness says of his own life, it is all 'hopeless, hopeless! Never a ray of sunlight! Not so much as a gleam of brightness to light it!' The whole play seems to us to be nothing but one desperate, raging cry of revolt against human destiny. The builder starts well in life, 'a boy from a pious home in the country,' whose one idea is to please the great Master Builder of the Universe, in whose honour his churches are built. No happiness comes to him as a reward, nothing but the emptiest vanity of success, which success, he sees to his dismay, is only gained at the expense of another's failure and his own peace of mind. His crowning victory is only won at the cost of his crowning unhappiness. Recklessly he defies the Great Builder, and becomes himself a 'Free Builder,' to shape his life after his own fashion; only to find that he is clogged by chains everywhere,—chained by marriage to a dead wife, chained to a living conscience which he cannot kill. Still, the impossible, the idea of an impossible happiness on earth, beckons him on; and in his last desperate effort to attain it, his 'dizzy conscience' once more asserts itself, and he is crushed for ever. *Vanitas vanitatum,*— one knows the text well enough, many have preached from it; but none have brought their sermons to a more hateful ending, we think, than Henrik Ibsen. There is no good on earth, he seems to say; its conventions and its morality are equally rotten and useless,—neither beyond the earth is there any happiness.

109. From an unsigned notice, *The Times*

15 June 1893, 10

The play was translated by William Archer and the cast was as follows:

Dr Thomas Stockmann	..	Mr Tree	Aslaksen ..	.. Mr E. M. Robson
Peter Stockmann		Mr Kemble	Captain Horster ..	Mr Revelle
Morten Kill	..	Mr Allan	Eilif ..	.. Master Skelly
Hovstad	..	Mr Welch	Morten ..	.. Miss Dora Barton
Billing ..	..	Mr Clark	Mrs Stockmann ..	Mrs Wright
			Petra ..	.. Miss Lily Hanbury

Those who had no previous acquaintance with Ibsen's *The Enemy of the People*, and who saw that play at this theatre yesterday afternoon, cannot have failed to experience a sensation of surprise, for the name of Ibsen in this country has hitherto been associated with work which is full of enigmas and obscurities, intelligible only to the elect, and here we have a play which everybody can understand. Whether its perfect lucidity will be recognized as a merit by the devotees who possess special gifts of insight, and for whom puzzles like *The Master Builder* are pregnant with meaning, is a question admitting of doubt. The average playgoer, however, who acknowledges that his visual powers cannot penetrate through a milestone is grateful for this total absence of obscurity. There are, in *The Enemy of the People*, no allegorical references to aerial harps, no allusions to symbolical vine-leaves; the motives of the characters are clear and their actions are those of sane people. It is not a cheerful story that the dramatist has chosen to tell, but his selection of an unpleasant theme is justified by its evident purpose, which is to show to what depths of meanness people will descend when they allow themselves to be influenced exclusively by reasons of self-interest. In another of its aspects the play is a scathing satire on the limitations of the parochial mind. . . . As the curtain falls he gives utterance to the belief that 'the strongest man on earth is he who stands alone,' which is the solitary paradox of the play. From the sketch given of the subject it will appear that the piece is more interesting than attractive. It contains nothing picturesque, and is one of the few theatrical productions from which a playwright has been bold enough to exclude what may be called the love-motive. The characterization is exceptionally good and unexaggerated, and the actions natural and convincing. In fact, so determined has the dramatist been that his play should be true to life that he has not excluded from it some dull moments.

110. From an unsigned notice by Clement Scott, *Daily Telegraph*

15 June 1893, 5

Ibsen is now no stranger in our midst. Recent years have brought forward first one enthusiast and then another to trumpet the praises of the Scandinavian dramatist, and to prove—to their own satisfaction—the transcendental beauties of a gloomy and for the most part revolting series of plays. But amid all these clamorous cries of 'Come, behold and admire!' we have hitherto heard no voice raised to direct our particular attention to *An Enemy of the People*. Mr. Grein, and the other genial spirits of the Independent Theatre Society, have given the work no place in their programmes, possibly through their failure to discover in it a sufficiency of those unpleasing qualities which they seemingly deem it their mission to thrust before their supporters. Nor has enterprise in any other quarter led hitherto to the production of the play in England. Thus, curiously enough, it has been reserved for Mr. Tree, a new interpreter of Ibsen, to introduce to our stage a drama far more interesting and convincing, as we think, than any other of the plays from 'the Master's' pen to which representation has been accorded in our theatres.

There is the familiar atmosphere of pessimism here as a matter of course. Ibsen looking on the bright side of things would not be Ibsen at all. But side by side with this invariable element there is shown in the play a truer and more direct realisation of human instincts and weaknesses than the methods of Ibsen as we know him on our stage have yet given us. It is as an 'acting play' that we must appraise *An Enemy of the People*, now that it has pleased the Haymarket manager to bring it to a public hearing; and, viewing the work from this standpoint, we can have little hesitation in declaring Mr. Tree's thought a happy one, and his taste infinitely better than that of those who have been beforehand with him in 'opening up' the arid tract of the Scandinavian drama.

'Truth is great, and will prevail,' says the classical adage. But Ibsen, in the case under discussion, elects to show us Truth crushed down and bowing her head beneath the yoke of Fraud and Deception.

[the plot described.]

To the power and virility of *An Enemy of the People*, considered as an acting play, tribute has already been paid. Let it now be added that the language of the drama falls upon the ear with a satisfying directness perpetually aimed at by Ibsen and his translators, but seldom so happily attained.

111. From an unsigned notice, *Daily Chronicle*

15 June 1893, 3

From the histrionic aspect *An Enemy of the People* is one of the very best of the Northern writer's works, but it is nevertheless a matter for congratulation that the task of stage presentation has fallen to such able hands. The loud call that summoned Mr. Tree before the curtain at the close yesterday was alike a tribute to his artistic abilities and to his judgment as a manager.

For the illustration of the firm will and undeviating conscientious-ness of Dr. Thomas Stockmann, the unselfish man of science who seeks to be a friend to the community and is howled at as a foe, Mr. Tree is, of course, particularly fitted. This was seen when *An Enemy of the People* was first talked of in connection with the Haymarket, and yesterday's performance fully realised the most favourable anticipations. In build, in manner, and in appearance he shows that the persecuted doctor is quite able, as well as willing, to fight—that he is so far from being a boaster that if given a fair field he would certainly gain the victory. Unfortunately this is just what poor Stockmann does not get. He is hounded down and becomes a martyr to the truth. Yet though brother and friends leave him, Stockmann has the inward happiness—to him inestimable—that is the reward of rectitude, and as the curtain falls, with wife by his side and children looking trustfully into his face radiant with hope, he becomes more than ever convinced that the strongest man upon earth is he who stands most alone—that is to say, remains aloof from the petty meannesses and corrupt designs of his fellow creatures.

112. A pseudonymous notice by 'Momus', *Gentlewoman*

24 June 1893, 835

It was in the hot entr'acte at this memorable *matinée* that a certain dis-tinguished actress, now playing at the Haymarket, said to me, 'This is my first Ibsen play, and I do not like it! I hate plays all about drains and water-supplies, with dirty scenery and no feminine interest in it.' She was right according to her lights, but to you, my faithful followers, I will unfold the truth the eminent actress was powerless to observe. Old hard-thinking Ibsen wrote *Ghosts*—a gruesome thing—fearfully true. In it he pointed out how the water-supplies of life and health are tainted and poisoned at their source; he wrote fearlessly, bravely. For his wisdom he was attacked by the band of critics, and the Grand Old Dramatic Man wrote this dramatic allegory concerning his own artistic position.

In the play just produced we have a doctor who discovers that the wells and waters that make his native town a 'health resort' are all infected. He calls attention to this fact, inspired, truth-loving, enthusiastic. His efforts at reformation are met with disdain and official Red-Tape-ism. He fights the good fight of truth and sincerity as long as he can. He is beaten. He declares that 'the only strong man is the man who is alone.' Loving hands and warm kisses come to aid him at the end. His mission of goodwill ends in cynicism with a redeeming touch of human love; not, indeed, the love of a woman for a man, but the love of friends and a commonplace family. His end is that of a baffled reformer. Were it not for the 'comic' framing of the play he might almost be called one who was crucified on the cross of his ideals. When you see the play you will remember that it is a legend or dream or vision of Ibsen's own life, the cynical phantom of shattered hopes, and you will not listen to those who say it is bad and foolish, because they talk as did my friend the eminent actress.

It was a brave thought of Mr. Tree's to produce it, and as a record in the new annals of the Haymarket it takes high rank. I thought him adroit and smart, but by no means great. His splendid speech at the mass meeting stood in too obvious need of the prompter, and the 'comic business' with little Mr. Robson turning on the diversity of their statures, was wholly unworthy of this resolute play. Ibsen has got to be taken seriously or not at all; Mr. Tree was not a bit like 'the Doctor' save in one particular. He made up like a young Ibsen, with horrent hair, and so far caught the allegorical spirit. The comic tone was below the high level of interpretation aimed at by the gifted lecturer on the 'Imaginative Faculty.' The play will be reproduced, and Mr. Tree will, of course, give us a more closely studied picture. All praise and congratulations to him for having had the artistic pluck to show us this most important work of art. He was ably helped in his work by Mr. Kemble and Mr. Welch, Mrs. Theodore Wright, and that remarkable rising star, Miss Lily Hanbury.

113. An unsigned notice, *Theatre*

1 July 1893, xxii, 44

It is not very often that an actor improves upon his author when the latter is a genius. But Mr. Beerbohm Tree has done it. Stockmann in Ibsen's play is a tragedian. A kind of Don Quixote, tilting at municipal windmills, he is obviously drawn as a fanatic, a single-minded iconoclast. That is good. But the tragi-comedy Mr. Tree reads into him is better. Broader, more human, and more sympathetic, the new Stockmann drives home the truth of the play with immeasurably increased force. Set, as he is, in the centre of a rather tedious play, Stockmann as an element of unrelieved seriousness would go far towards choking what interest there is in the theme by sheer overpressure of intensity. The 'suburbanism' of Ibsen, as it is called, would become the more pronounced by the vigorous application of grey earnestness. And Mr. Tree's softening of the hard high lights and toning of the deep ugly shadows, by frequent sly touches of humour, were in the nature of inspiration. So handled, the play exhales an almost exhilarating atmosphere. Stockmann becomes such a simple-hearted, big-souled fellow, that the history of his hopeless fight and inevitable downfall assumes the look of a political contest—in which when the fight is done, hands are shaken, friendships renewed, and hard words and knocks forgotten. To a certain extent, no doubt, this diminishes the tragedy of the situation. But the pathos of the honest man's defeat remains untouched, and there is wisdom in removing the problem posed from the sphere of bitter persecution. Of Mr. Tree's share as an actor in the effect achieved it would be difficult to over-estimate the value. Breezy, impulsive, vigorous, he dominated the stage. A giant among pigmies—which is exactly what Stockmann ought to be—he painted in equally glowing colours the foolishness of the great fellow and his heroism, and presented in his ill-fitting frock coat and abbreviated trousers the most engaging figure of a hot-headed, warm-hearted mixture of right-head and wrong-head —as Charles Reade might have called him—that could well be conceived. Nor was his the only emphatic success of the afternoon. Mr. E. M. Robson with his chirpy voice, quaint method, and weak manner, was Aslaksen the 'Moderate,' himself. There has been nothing on the stage more unobtrusively humourous than this leader of 'the compact majority' for many a day. Mr. Welch was a slight disappointment. His Hovstad, though conceived and played on the right lines of cringing insincerity, seemed thin and even a little mechanical. Mr. Kemble's melodramatic elder brother, a kind of unrelenting Wicked Uncle to Stockmann and his Babes, was in its way faultless. But Mr. Allan forced Kiil into too prominent a position by tricks of manner and a spluttering laugh; and Mrs. Wright also seemed to overdo Mrs. Stockmann's solicitude in her efforts to be natural. Miss Hanbury, however, restored the balance. Her simply-garbed fresh upstanding school-teacher struck precisely the right note of girlish independence.

114. William Archer sums it up

July 1893

'The Mausoleum of Ibsen', by William Archer, *Fortnightly Review* (July 1893), liv, 77–91. This article, a natural follow-up to '*Ghosts* and Gibberings' (No. 72), had an equally powerful impact.

'*The Master Builder* bids fair to raise a mausoleum in which the Ibsen craze may be conveniently buried and consigned to oblivion.'—*Illustrated Sporting and Dramatic News*, February 25, 1893.

For the past four years, ever since June 7, 1889, when *A Doll's House* was produced by Mr. Charles Charrington and Miss Janet Achurch at the Novelty Theatre, the compact majority of English theatrical critics has been assiduously, energetically, one may almost say unintermittently, occupied in building the mausoleum of Ibsen. Mausoleum, perhaps, is scarcely the word; cairn or barrow would be nearer it. Each critic has simply brought his 'chunk of old red sandstone'—his pebble of facetiousness, his 'arf-brick of abuse, his boulder of denunciation—and has added it at random to the rude pyramid under which the flattened remains of Henrik Ibsen were supposed to lie. When, at intervals, they have rested from their work, it has only been to look upon it and pronounce it very good. How often have we been informed, in tones of complacent assurance, that 'we have heard the last of Ibsen,' that 'Ibsenism' (or, if the critic be a wit, 'Ibsenity') 'has died a natural death,' that 'the cult' or 'the craze,' is 'played out,' that 'Ibsen has been tried in the balance and found wanting', that 'the public won't have Ibsen at any price,' and so forth, and so forth! There is probably not a conservative critic in London who has not announced to his readers some four or five times within the said four years that Ibsen is authentically dead at last, until even the great public, one fancies, must be beginning to regard the intelligence with suspicion. And when, after each of these announcements, it has manifestly appeared that Ibsen was not dead at all, but rather more alive than ever, the critics, with truly heroic pertinacity, have sought finally to crush him, by adding to the same old mausoleum or cairn—piling Pelion upon Ossa, Ossa upon Olympus, until the pyramid of execration has reached a magnitude almost unprecedented in literary history. Strange it should never occur to them that, since all this lapidation fails of its object, the reason can only be that Ibsen is not under that stone-heap at all, but only an effigy, a simulacrum, a 'contrapshun' as Uncle Remus would call it, compounded of their own imaginings, and bearing but the faintest resemblance to the real Ibsen. In brief, the mausoleum is a cenotaph.

My purpose in this paper is not critical but purely historical. I desire to give a few, a very few, specimens of the treatment accorded to Ibsen by the immense majority of the critics, and then to show, by means of a few facts and figures, that, despite these incessant thunders of condemnation, the works of Ibsen have met with very remarkable acceptance on the stage, and I have, in book form, attained an astounding and, so far as I know, unprecedented success.

[Archer quotes at length from the press reviews accorded *A Doll's House*, *Rosmersholm*, *Hedda Gabler* and *Ghosts*.]

We come now to the uppermost course (for the present) in the pyramid of invective. On the 20th of last February, Mr. Herbert Waring and Miss Robins produced *The Master Builder* at the Trafalgar Square Theatre, and this is how it was greeted by the Press:—

'Dense mist enshrouds characters, words, actions, and motives. . . . A certain kind of interest in the Norwegian writer's strange dramas. . . . One may compare it, to put an extreme case, to the sensations of a man who witnesses a play written, rehearsed, and acted by lunatics.'—*Daily Telegraph*.

'Assuredly no one may fathom the mysteries . . . of the play, so far as it can be called a play. . . . If it did not please, it most unquestionably puzzled. . . . It is not for a moment to be understood that we personally recommend any one to go and see it.'—*Standard*.

'Here we contemplate the actions of a set of lunatics each more hopeless than the other. . . . Platitudes and inanities. . . . The play is hopeless and in-defensible.'—*Globe*.

'People sit and make themselves think that it is great because they know it is by Ibsen. . . . The same work with an unknown name they would most assuredly ridicule and hiss.'—*Echo*.

'A feast of dull dialogue and acute dementia. . . . The most dreary and purposeless drivel we have ever heard in an English theatre. . . . A pointless, incoherent, and absolutely silly piece.'—*Evening News*.

'Rigmorale of an oracle Delphic in obscurity and Gamp-like in garrulity. . . . Pulseless and purposeless play, which has idiocy written on every linea-ment. . . . Three acts of gibberish.'—*Stage*.

'A distracting jumble of incoherent elements. There is no story; the characters are impossible, and the motives a nightmare of perverted fingerposts.'—*Saturday Review*.

'Sensuality . . . irreverence . . . unwholesome . . . simply blasphemous.'—*Morning Post*.

'Dull, mysterious, unchaste.'—*Daily Graphic*.

'A play to which even the Young Person may be taken with no more fear of harm than a severe headache. . . . Ibsen is a master of the chaotic and meaning-less epigram. . . . Thrilling moments in last act marred by bathos. The rest idle babble.'—*Figaro*.

'Presents human life in a distorted form, and is entirely without intelligible purpose.'—Mr. MOY THOMAS in the *Graphic*.

'Same old dullness prevails as was the feature of his previous prosy pratings.' —*England*.

'The blunder has been made. *Master-Builder Solness* has been played. . . . Hilde Wangel is perhaps the most detestable character in the drama's range . . . victim of nymphomania(!) . . . deliberate murderess . . . mean, cheap, hateful, stands out in dishonourable distinctness.'—*Pall Mall Gazette*.

'Ibsen has written some very vile and vulgar plays. . . . *The Master Builder* bids fair to raise a mausoleum in which the Ibsen craze may be conveniently buried and consigned to oblivion.'—*Sporting and Dramatic News*.

So much for the critical mausoleum. Was ever artist in this world denounced with greater fury, with more unwearying persistency? It must be remembered that I have only selected a few bricks from the pyramid. It would be easy to multiply such extracts twentyfold. 'This is all very well,' the reader may say, 'but how about the other side of the case?' There has, of course, been a good deal of sane and competent Ibsen criticism during these four years, and some, no doubt, extravagantly enthusiastic. But both in bulk and influence the favourable, or even the temperate, criticism, has been as nothing beside the angrily or scornfully hostile. All the great morning papers, the leading illustrated weeklies, the critical weeklies, with one exception, and the theatrical trade papers, have been bitterly denunciatory. If, now and then, I have quoted from obscure prints for the sake of preserving some delicious absurdity of criticism, the great mass of my extracts have been taken from papers of influence and position. The upshot of the whole is that the 'Scandinavian humbug,' the 'hoary-headed old Atheist,' the 'determined Socialist,'* the 'suburban Ibsen,' is dull, dreary, dirty, dismal, and dead; that no one ever did take any sort of interest in his works; and that if the English public could possibly be got to pay the smallest attention to such an incurable 'egotist and bungler,' its healthy common-sense would rise up in revolt, and it would 'hiss him off the stage.' If hard words (and foul words) could kill, in short, how very dead Ibsen would be!

Let us see, now, how dead he is—first in the book market, then on the stage.

About four years ago *The Pillars of Society, Ghosts*, and *An Enemy of the People* were published in a shilling volume, one of the Camelot Classic series. Of that volume, up to the end of 1893, Mr. Walter Scott had sold 14,367 copies. In 1890 and 1891 the same publisher issued an authorised uniform edition of Ibsen's prose dramas in five volumes, at three and sixpence each. Of these volumes, up to the end of 1892, 16,834 copies had been sold. Thus, Mr. Walter Scott alone has issued (in round numbers) thirty-one thousand volumes of the works of the man for whom nobody 'outside a silly clique' cares a brass farthing. But these figures in reality understate the case. The 'volume' is an artificial unit; the natural, the real unit, is the play; and each volume contains three plays. Thus we find that one publisher alone has placed in circulation ninety-three thousand† plays by Ibsen. Other publishers have issued single-volume editions of *A Doll's House, Ghosts, Rosmersholm, The Lady from the Sea, Hedda Gabler*, and *The Master Builder*, some of which (and especially Mr. Heinemann's copyright editions of the last two plays)

---

* He is just as much of a socialist as Mr. Herbert Spencer is—that is to say, the very reverse of a socialist. But these nice distinctions are beyond the critical intellect.

† This of course includes sales in America and the colonies; but as a matter of fact the great bulk of these editions has been sold in the United Kingdom.

must have had a very considerable sale. Thus, I think, we are well within the mark in estimating that one hundred thousand prose dramas by Ibsen have been bought by the English-speaking public in the course of the past four years. Is there a parallel in the history of publishing for such a result in the case of translated plays? Putting Shakespeare in Germany out of the question (and he has been selling, not for four years, but for a century), I doubt whether any translated dramas have ever sold in such quantities. Ibsen himself must have had a very large sale in Germany; but there his plays are to be had for threepence each, while here, on an average, they cost at least three times that sum. In English publishing, at any rate, such sales are absolutely unprecedented. The publishers to whom I proposed a collected edition of the Prose Dramas before Mr. Walter Scott undertook it, dismissed the idea as visionary, roundly declaring that no modern plays could ever 'sell' in England; and, except in the one case of Ibsen, experience justified this assertion. It will be said that the works of the French dramatists, Dumas, Augier, &c., are not translated, because people read them in the original. But do there exist in England at the present moment one hundred thousand plays by all the modern French dramatists put together—Dumas, Augier, Sardou, Meilhac, Labiche, Gondinet, and all the rest? I very much doubt it. Of course, it would be folly to deny that the very frenzies of hostility above exemplified have defeated their own ends and helped more than anything else perhaps to arouse and sustain public interest in Ibsen. But when did deserved denunciation ever secure popularity for a writer? If a book is dull, and the critics say so, people will not find it interesting out of sheer perversity. Not until criticism, in declaring a writer tedious, prosy, 'dull to the point of desperation,' contradicts itself on its very face by the eager emphasis of its invective, does the public begin to wonder whether the dullness which so potently excites the critics may not have in it some stimulus, some suggestion, in a word some interest, for the general reader as well. It is quite true, as the publishers assured me, that for fifty years or more the English public had lost the habit of reading plays, and that to many people the unaccustomed dramatic form is in itself an annoyance. Yet in spite of this drawback, in spite of the foreignness of Ibsen's subjects, his atmosphere and his point of view—in spite, too of the loss in sheer beauty of style which he necessarily suffers in translation—the fact remains that 100,000 of his plays are at this moment in the hands of the reading public. Whether the interest in his works will wax or wane no one can predict. For the present it shows no symptom of flagging. But even if it were to fall dead to-morrow, I think it will be admitted that these 40,000 volumes,* these 100,000 plays, form a tolerably handsome 'mausoleum.'

Now as to the stage—but before stating the facts of the case let me suggest a few preliminary considerations. Except in omnivorous Germany, have translated plays ever been known to take very deep root on a foreign stage? In adaptations there has been for centuries a brisk international trade—the French have borrowed from the Spaniards, we and all the world from the French, and so forth—but translations have been few and far between. In England least of all have we shown any appetite for them. Even of Molière we have made, for the stage, only crude and now almost forgotten adaptations. Since, then, Ibsen—translated, not adapted—has met with some acceptance in the English theatre, that fact is in itself practically unique. If he had indeed been 'impossible' on the English stage, he would have had as companions in impossibility Corneille, Racine, Molière, Marivaux, Hugo, Musset, Lessing, Goethe, Schiller, Lope, and Calderon;† no such despicable confraternity. As a matter of fact, and in the face of the unexampled tempest of obloquy in the Press, seven of his plays—not adapted, but faithfully translated—have been placed on the English stage. If our theatrical history presents any parallel to this, I shall be glad to hear of it; I can certainly think of none. 'This is all very fine,' cry the adversaries, 'but we do not deny that there is a "silly, noisy, &c., &c., clique of faddists" who applaud these productions. What we maintain is that the great public, the paying public, will not have Ibsen at any price.' It is undoubtedly true that the compact majority of the critics has done all that lay in its power to frighten the paying public away from any theatre where Ibsen is being played; and their invectives, though they doubtless cut both ways, have on the whole tended to diminish the chances of pecuniary success. Especially effective has been the persistent accusation of 'indecorum'—an accusation which cannot but be injurious in a country where the theatre is so largely a family institution. The cry is beginning to lose its effect, for open-minded playgoers, who have braved the warnings of the Press, have discovered for themselves that of all writers for the stage Ibsen is the farthest remote from any taint of lubricity. It is certain, as the critic of *Truth* puts it, that any one who has gone to the theatre with the view of 'gloating over' his improprieties,

---

* Mr. Scott, as aforesaid, has sold over 31,000 volumes, and we may quite safely assume a sale of 9,000 for the six single plays issued by other publishers.

† The deplorable perversions of *Faust*, and the crude melodramas made out of one or two of Hugo's plays, must certainly be reckoned as adaptations, not translations.

must have been grievously disappointed. But a superstition so adroitly implanted and sedulously fostered takes time to die, and thousands of people are doubtless kept away from Ibsen performances by the notion that they are not entertainments 'to which a daughter can safely take her mother.' Yet in spite of denunciation and misrepresentation, Ibsen's plays have by no means made the pecuniary fiasco industriously predicted and insinuated by the hostile critics. It is true that (apart from *The Master Builder** which, as I write, is still being performed, so that its balance-sheet cannot be finally made up) I know of only one instance in which any very considerable profit has been made out of an Ibsen production; but taking the others all round, he may fairly be said to have paid his way and a little more. Of the production of *The Lady from the Sea* at Terry's Theatre, I know nothing, and do not include it in my calculations. *Ghosts*, again, has never been licensed, so that no money has been taken for its two performances. As to the five remaining plays I am enabled to state with tolerable accuracy the total amount paid by the London public in order to see them on the stage, between June 7, 1889, and March 18, 1893. The public, says the critic of *Truth*, will not 'pay to be bored,' but somehow or other they have paid £4,876 to be bored (and of course bewildered, nauseated and all the rest of it) by Ibsen. Of these five plays *The Pillars of Society* was played only once and *Rosmersholm* twice to receipts amounting in all to £276. Thus it appears that for the privilege of being bored by the 'prosy prating' of *A Doll's House*, the 'Morgue inspection' of *Hedda Gabler*, and the 'unchaste drivel and gibberish' of *The Master Builder*, the London public (who 'will not have Ibsen at any price,') has paid, up to March 18, the pretty handsome price of £4,600.†

Let me not be understood to put this forward as, in itself, a very imposing result. I know that a successful production at a fashionable West-End theatre will draw as much money as this in a single month. But consider the circumstances of the case! Here are a set of foreign plays, representing society in a small and little-known country; not

---

* 'That Mr. Ibsen's fantastic balderdash has been supported during the present week by playgoers who have paid to see it, I decline to believe.' So says the indefatigable 'Rapier', of the *Sporting and Dramatic News* (March 4th). It was 'supported', and liberally supported, by the paying public. Does 'Rapier' think it a quite legitimate trick of the fence to make injurious inuendoes on matters of which he knows nothing? Another paragraphist, pursuing the same magnanimous tactics, states that to his certain knowledge the receipts have at their highest never risen to a sum to which, as a matter of fact, they have at their lowest never fallen. Such are the methods of anti-Ibsenism.

† Performances at the Crystal Palace are included in this calculation.

adapted, but translated; not produced at leading theatres with the prestige and popularity of the actor-managers to support them, but acted under all sorts of disadvantages at second-rate theatres,* by actors (in many cases) comparatively unknown to the great public; bitterly denounced and ridiculed by the vast majority of the Press; and yet, in the face of all these difficulties, making so much financial success as fairly to pay their own way, and leave a margin over! In the case of *Hedda Gabler* the margin was a very large one. The nett profit on the ten matinées, after all expenses paid, amounted to £281, or an average of £28 on each performance—a rate of profit which the most prosperous actor-manager would scarcely despise; and, when the play was put in the evening bill, it drew houses which, under ordinary circumstances, would have been fairly remunerative, though, as the manager had to pay two sets of salaries (to the *Hedda Gabler* company, and to the regular company of the theatre, who were meanwhile unemployed), he could not run it beyond a month. What becomes, then, of the assertion that 'the public will not have Ibsen at any price'? Does it not rather seem that there is a public, and not a very small one, which will have Ibsen at any price, despite such a chorus of critical anathema as was never heard before in the history of the English stage?

I am far from predicting that Ibsen will ever be really popular on the English stage, though such a prediction would seem less extravagant to-day than the prediction of the success he has actually achieved would have seemed ten years ago. It is possible, as a French critic, M. Doumic, has recently been arguing, that 'a certain mediocrity' is essential to great popular success on the stage. I have very little doubt that criticism will soon come to take a saner view of his works, and that they have a certain future before them even in the theatre. It is scarcely to be expected, however—it would contradict all experience, here and elsewhere—that they should take deep and permanent hold upon the English stage. Scarcely to be expected, and scarcely to be desired; for no theatre can for long live healthily on imported material. Each nation should produce, in its own theatre, its own criticism of its own life. Criticism of

---

* The first, and very successful, production of *A Doll's House* took place at the Novelty Theatre, a house utterly unknown to the majority of playgoers, and hidden away in a by-street on the very confines of theatrical civilization. The Vaudeville, where *Hedda Gabler* was produced, has been, and is, a popular theatre, but scarcely with the class of playgoers to whom Ibsen most directly appeals. The Trafalgar Square Theatre, where *The Master Builder* was produced, is one of the pleasantest and best-appointed houses in London, but has the disadvantage of being quite new. It takes the public a long time to discover the existence of a new theatre.

life from a foreign standpoint, and illustrated by foreign examples, may be very interesting and fascinating, but cannot, in the long run, satisfy our souls. I look forward to a time when Ibsen, having completed the work which many even of his enemies admit that he has well begun, of lifting the theatre on to a higher intellectual plane, shall himself be heard no more, or heard but rarely, upon the English stage. By that time, in a certain sense, this great Master Builder will have built his own mausoleum; but not a mausoleum of oblivion. It will tower aloft, like Hilda's castle, 'with the vane pointing upwards at a dizzy height'; and, looking up at it, we shall seem to hear *harper i luften*—'harps in the air.'

P.S. This article was in type before the recent series of Ibsen performances at the Opera Comique was so much as thought of, and while Mr. Beerbohm Tree's production of *An Enemy of the People* at the Haymarket was still in the vague future. The Opera Comique performances resulted in a clear profit, and I believe Mr. Tree has, up to the present, had every reason to be satisfied with the financial result of his experiment.

115. Mr. Gladstone as Solness

July 1893

From 'The Political Master Builder', unsigned political comment, *Saturday Review* (8 July 1893), lxxvi, 34.

We have used the phrase Master-Builder in reference to the great constructive-destructive statesman of our time and country, and the words recall to us the hero of Ibsen's drama. The true interpretation of the play so named is, we believe, as yet unascertained. His disciples dispute about it; in fact, there are as many meanings as there are disciples. Some people, among whom we are far from including ourselves, maintain that its sense cannot be discovered, because there is no sense to discover. Perhaps we may be allowed to place a conjecture at their disposal. Ibsen has, we believe, paid some attention to the contemporary life of England, including its statesmanship. May he not have designed to symbolize, in the architectural career of Mr. Halvard Solness, the political career of Mr. Gladstone? The Bygmester's constructive period, like Mr. Gladstone's, had its beginning in an act of incendiary destruction, which gave him his basis of operations. Then, again, Mr. Halvard Solness's conversion from the building of churches to the erection of secular edifices coincides with Mr. Gladstone's transition from ecclesiastical to secular politics. He does not build churches, he pulls them down or turns them, as by the application of the Irish Church Fund, into homes for the people. In Halvard Solness's dread of the young generation knocking at the door, and threatening to thrust him from his supremacy, and his advertisement of himself by startling architectural projects, a parallel perhaps may be found to Mr. Gladstone's schemes of sensational legislation. A succession of eye-opening novelties is always on hand—something frightfully thrilling. The examination into the sickliness or robustness of Mr. Solness's conscience seems vaguely to reveal things we have read about Mr. Gladstone. It is possible that in Miss Hilda Wangel, who urges Solness to build in future castles in the air, and who drives him to ascend the scaffolding from which he falls, breaking his neck, Mr. John Morley and his fatal counsels are adumbrated. There seems to be a distinct allusion to the Irish question in one of the dialogues:—Solness: 'I'm not quite clear about the plans yet.' Brovik: 'They say they're longing to get into a house of their own.' Solness: 'Yes, yes; we know all that. And so they're content with whatever is offered them.' But we must pause; and, having suggested the parallelism between the two Master-Builders, leave others to work it out in detail.

116. Hjalmar Boyesen on Ibsen's self-satire in *The Wild Duck*

September 1893

From 'Ibsen's Treatment of Self-Illusion', by Hjalmar Hjorth Boyesen, *Dial* (16 September 1893), xv, 137–40.

In no play of Ibsen's is the corrosive self-destroying character of his social criticism more apparent than in *The Wild Duck*. *A Doll-House* and *The Pillars of Society* enforced the lesson that unless there be truth in personal and social relations they cannot endure; they are built upon sand, and cannot brave the rocks of adversity. This was perhaps the first positive lesson to be derived from Ibsen's teachings. We felt that here we had at last firm ground under our feet; and Pilate's pertinent query 'What is truth?' we left preliminarily in abeyance. But no sooner have we opened *The Wild Duck* than we find the earth rocking and heaving in the most uncomfortable manner. That which we mistook for rock was after all nothing but quagmire. *The Wild Duck* teaches us that truth is by no means an unqualified boon. It takes a strong spirit to endure it. To small, commonplace men, living in mean illusions, the truth may be absolutely destructive. It is better for such people to be permitted to cherish undisturbed their little lies and self-deceptions than to be brought face to face with the terrifying truth, lacking, as they do, both the courage and the strength to grapple with it and to readjust their lives to radically altered conditions.

It appears to me as if Ibsen had undertaken to satirize himself in this play.

117. *Ghosts* in New York and Boston

January 1894

From an unsigned notice, *New York Times* (6 January 1894), 4.
Ghosts was first performed in English in America at the Berkeley
Lyceum, New York, on 5 January 1894. The cast, an English com-
pany, was as follows:

Oswald..	..	Courtenay Thorpe
Manders	..	Albert Lawrence
Engstrand	..	G. Herbert Leonard
Regina ..	..	Eleanor Lane
Mrs Alving	..	Ida Jeffreys-Goodfriend

William Dean Howells hailed the performance as 'a great theatrical
event—the very greatest I have ever known'.

The audience yesterday was very small, but what is called 'select'.
Excepting a few newspaper writers, nobody was present who is not,
presumably, of the 'cult.' Mr Howells, Mr Aldrich, Mr Brander
Matthews, Mr Lawrence Hutton and Mr Boyesen, were conspicuous . . .

The merit in Ibsen that concerns us in this young and healthful
community [i.e. America] is purely technical. His plots and the traits
of his personages are unclean; his philosophy, in spite of Archer and
Gosse and their followers in America, is vicious. If accepted it would not
make men better. In this unwholesome *Ghosts*—which shows us a
respectable man who has fought down his passions, preached wise
doctrine, bestowed alms, and lived a clean life, and then holds him up
to scorn, with a paretic, a courtesan, a procurer, and a woman, who,
having been the wife of a horribly-diseased debauchee, is prepared to
believe that all that is wrong, as his only visible associates—his morals
are at their worst. The play is bad enough in the reading, but when one
sees it acted as it was yesterday, and its horror becomes real, it makes
him wickedly yearn to see that old, gray-whiskered, canine-looking
head of the photographs on the renowned charger of the daughter of
Herodias.

118. Ibsen consigned to hell in Boston

May 1894

From 'Boston Letter', a regular column, by Charles Wingate, *Critic* (5 May 1894), xxiv, 312. The 'eminent English actor' was Mr. Courtenay Thorpe.

Ibsen's *Ghosts* has stirred up Bostonians, although it has had but one production in this city. The Rev. Isaac J. Lansing, pastor of that famous old church at the corner of Park Street, which from its conservative orthodoxy has so long gone by the name of 'Brimstone Corner,' devoted an entire service against this inroad, as he deemed it, upon public decency and morality. The theatre where this play was produced, said he, is on the same street with this church, and on its stage not long ago an eminent English actor was playing. What would be thought if in this church a clean, high-toned sermon were followed by a discourse from the vilest speaker that could be secured? An attrociously immoral production, the clergyman declared, was *Ghosts*, so attrocious that even to denounce it in public is almost degrading. Decent people, he added, should never permit themselves to endorse such plays, but should get far away from the mire of unwholesomeness and uncleanliness. The speaker made one lapse when he denounced the Governor for attending the production, because the Governor did not accept the box offered to him.

THE WILD DUCK

Royalty Theatre, 4 May 1894

119. An unsigned notice by Clement Scott, *Daily Telegraph*

5 May 1894, 7

The play was produced under the aegis of the Independent Theatre group and the cast was as follows:

Werle	.. Mr George Warde	Molvik	..	Mr Gilbert Trent
Gregers Werle..	Mr Charles Fulton	Gräberg	..	Mr Charles Legassick
Old Ekdal	.. Mr Harding Cox	Petterson	..	Mr Sydney Dark
Hialmar Ekdal..	Mr W. L. Abingdon	Jensen	..	Mr C. S. Skarratt
Gina Ekdal	.. Mrs Herbert Waring	Flor	..	Mr G. Armstrong
Hedvig	.. Miss Winifred Fraser	Balle	..	Mr Herbert Fletcher
Mrs Sörby	.. Mrs Charles Creswick	Kaspersen	..	Mr Herbert Maule
Relling	.. Mr Lawrence Irving			

A wild duck is an excellent bird, with a red, gravy-tinted breast, a judicious squeeze of lemon, and a hasty dash of cayenne pepper. Now, Ibsen's *Wild Duck* was very well cooked indeed last night. It was done to a turn. The cook had run round the kitchen with him and served him up hot, brown, and savoury. The red gravy oozed from his tender breast. The lemon and pepper were not wanting. But the poor *Wild Duck* was, as epicures would say, a trifle fishy. He had been banqueting somewhere near the sea shore. The consequence was that the most devoted Ibsenites in the audience did not know exactly what to do, to swallow the Duck or to make a wry face. Accordingly they made a not very ingenious compromise. They roared with laughter at the scenes intended to be serious, and they yawned ominously at the master's ponderous and heavy-handed wit. There is no need to enter into the details of so commonplace and suburban a story. In essence it is trivial; in effect it is bald and unconvincing. To call such an eccentricity as this

317

a masterpiece; to classify it at all as dramatic literature; or to make a fuss about so feeble a production is to insult dramatic literature and to outrage common sense. Men and women who have no sense of humour in their composition can be impressed with old Ekdal's battue of rabbits, cocks, hens, and a tame wild duck in the suburban garret, and find there a mystery and a moral; but those who can understand the meaning of the word 'bathos' will appreciate the roars of laughter that greeted the silly vapourings of the self-conscious photographer, who apparently could not make up his mind if he should represent a mild Micawber or an attenuated Harold Skimpole.

But absurd, impracticable, and indefensible as the play might be, it was interesting, as all Ibsen's plays are interesting, in that it brought to the front another young student of the stage. It was not a woman this time, but a man. The hero of last night's experiment was without a doubt Mr. Lawrence Irving, who played the commonsense Dr. Relling, who ridiculed as Ibsen ridicules and Mr. Bernard Shaw ridicules the men and women they profess to flatter, and who played a remarkably difficult character not only in an able, but a masterly manner. It looks as if in Mr. Lawrence Irving we had an actor who inherited the strong humour, the decision, and the influence on an audience that his gifted father possesses. The young man made the character tell by sheer force of will and accentuated comedy power. He was never flurried; all through he was as cool as a cucumber; but he knew the man he was playing, he lived in the part, his enunciation and style were alike excellent, and there was as much accentuated character in this Dr. Relling, as there was years ago when his father played Chevenix in *Uncle Dick's Darling*. Comedy is clearly young Mr. Lawrence Irving's line, and in comedy, if he works hard, he will one day make his mark. His Ibsenite doctor, with all its shrewdness, character, observation, and common sense, is an earnest of still better things to come.

It seemed to us, on the other hand, that Mr. W. L. Abingdon mistook the idea of the selfish, pragmatical photographer. He burlesqued what should have been from his point of view serious. He was laughing with the audience when they should have been laughing at him. No girl such as Hedrey [*sic*] could have loved or believed in such a man. He placards his character outside his coat. The suavity, the sentiment, and the charm of the man should have been convincing at least to his own household. But Mr. Abingdon was leading the laugh instead of deprecating it. It is impossible to conceive better performances than the housemaid wife, Gina Ekdal, by Mrs. Herbert Waring, and the loving girl child, by Miss Winifred Fraser. It does not seem possible that a slave woman with a past, or an intelligent girl with a too-developed mind, could be better acted. Mr. Harding Cox was also excellent, and so were the usual Ibsenite prig by Mr. Charles Fulton and the old Werle of Mr. George Warde. How far the cause has been advanced by the production of this play it would be impossible to say. Mr. Grein evidently thinks he has turned the scale with the *Wild Duck*, and said as much in his earnest and modest speech. If the *Wild Duck* were presented for a run tomorrow at a theatre where the paying public secures its seats in the ordinary fashion it would be laughed off the stage, for such eccentricities are not as yet tolerated or even recognised by a healthy and vigorous public opinion that keeps the atmosphere of the theatre free from absurdity and affectation. But if Mr. Lawrence Irving, Mrs. Herbert Waring, and Miss Winifred Fraser were to repeat the performance they gave last night for a dozen or a hundred nights they would be recognised as excellent by all good judges of acting. These three performances would never make such a play palatable or popular, but they would decidedly temper the critical wind to the shorn Ibsenite lamb. One sentence from Halmar, the photographer, must be ringing in the ears of the audience even now. 'What! Am I to drag all those rabbits with me, too?' asks the selfish photographer of his cool and complacent wife. Ibsen may be a mighty genius, but he has no sense of humour. The rabbits, the menagerie, the tipsy old Shikarry, and the dreadful Wild Duck would be enough to condemn the finest philosophical play ever written. The right thing to do is to chaff the craze, as Mr. Bernard Shaw has succeeded in doing. The sunflower has gone, and so will the Ibsenite play and the Yellow Book—in time.

120. From an unsigned notice, *Daily Chronicle*

5 May 1894, 6.

There is many a laugh to be obtained from it, particularly after the second act. It does not follow that perfect understanding of the plot or of the purpose of the author will be obtained by early attendance. Even from many members of the audience last night came the inquiry on emerging from the theatre, 'What does it all mean?'

121. From an unsigned notice, *Evening News and Post*

5 May 1894, 1

One of its gems of meaning dialogue is the remark of old Ekdal to his granddaughter that he is going into his own room 'to—wash my hands. You understand?' Pah! It is an unclean play, marked with the special Ibsen taint.

122. From an unsigned notice, *Truth*

10 May 1894, 1071

It is the most 'drunken' play, in a certain sense, that I have ever been introduced to. Nearly every character in it is either drinking or drunk. When the curtain draws up all the characters are boozing in a back parlour. They come on the stage to discuss the drink they have consumed. They top up Tokay with beer, and mix beer with punch. The women apparently drink as much as the men. When the hostess dismisses her guests, she bids her servants shove a brandy-bottle into the coat-pocket of each. Hoary-headed old men sneak into cupboards to sodden themselves with hot brandy and water, and come out half speechless to drink more beer. The parson of the parish and the doctor of the community are in a chronic state of liquor. And it is to oblige one of these semi-inebriates that a young girl of sixteen blows her brains out, preferring to die than to cause annoyance to her father, who is eaten up with vanity of the usual Norwegian pattern.

123. From a pseudonymous notice by 'Hafiz', *Black and White*

12 May 1894, 576

To pass from *King Kodak* to *The Wild Duck* is to pass from the Land of Cocayne into the Depths of the Sea. From the lightest and latest example of clowning to the grimmest and gloomiest of Ibsen's plays is a wide step, and it is only the supreme impressionist who can profess to be influenced by the two expressions of dramatic art with the same completeness. *The Wild Duck* is, in the opinion of some whose opinion is not most lightly to be neglected, the crowning mercy of Ibsen's dramatic career. It is certainly his most terrible, as it is perhaps his most faithful picture of life as it is, seen from a certain standpoint, and seen under certain conditions. In its unfailing irony, its unredeemed melancholy, its sombre acquiescence in the inexorable, it is one of the saddest and the sternest sermons that the great dramatist has ever preached disdainfully to a waning age. If it were played as it ought to be played, it might prove almost too painful an experience to endure with patience.

124. From an unsigned notice, *Era*

12 May 1894, 11

'Who would have thought the old man had so much blood in him?' asks Lady Macbeth, in somnambulistic surprise. And who could have conceived that the sage and spectacled Ibsen was a rival of Mr. W. S. Gilbert? *The Wild Duck* is an atrociously true and cruel satire. It has the rare power of appealing to that deeply buried self-consciousness of our own weaknesses which is generally suppressed, though it is always existent. But it is pitiless and pessimistic. The wretched littleness of average humanity is held up in all the nakedness of truth. The moral of the piece is—'Never rob people of their illusions.' . . .

The Wild Duck is too talky in places, and wants considerable cutting. There is too much allusion to the bird, and the symbolism in this connection is harped on even to tedium. The character of Hialmar is insisted upon too copiously, and to this part the blue pencil might lightly be applied; but otherwise the piece is theatrically effective, and is keenly satirical and by turns diverting and pathetic.

125. From an unsigned notice, *Theatre*

1 June 1894, xxiii, 329–30

Browning was obscure. So some people said, until Mr. Augustine Birrell darted piercing *obiter dicta* at their incautiously exposed intellect, and with grievous wounds enforced a shamefaced silence. But Browning at his worst is nought compared with Ibsen. When obscurity is only another word for leaps in thought, the trouble is soon past. You have only to get into your author's stride, keep his pace, and jump when he jumps, and you will never be left lagging in the rear groping for his meaning in alleged 'obscurity.' And that is the worst you have to reckon with in Browning. But Ibsen is different.

His obscurity arises from his devotion to symbolism; and a very little symbolism can, like a Will o' the Wisp, lure you a very long way. What it did with *The Master Builder* is within recent memory. It set Mr. Dawson Archer and Mr. Pythies Walkley by the ears, and for weeks was a bone of contention in peace-loving households of a (intellectually) baser sort. Why? Because it was symbolical. We could all agree that it was utterly unlike life, and curiously unlike drama; but agree upon the application of its symbolism, we could not, and *hinc multæ lachrymæ*. So with *The Wild Duck*, produced on Friday. It is obviously symbolical. But of what? Goodness—in other words Mr. Grein, as the H. M. Stanley of the exploration—only knows. And I would suggest that in future, in enterprises of this order, an official 'Digest' of the play be issued in the advertisements and programmes, much as Mr. Irving issued once when he revived *Romeo and Juliet*, to prepare us for his reading. Then we should be saved much wild speculation; we could all adopt one standard of criticism, and the poor actors who stand over-much in the pillory in these elusive plays, could at once be seen to be revealing the official idea or obscuring it.

Shorn of its symbolism, the play slowly drifts from domestic intrigue to farce tinctured with suicide, and is endurable and even interesting, mainly by reason of the living reality of the loafing egoist Hjalmar, and the pathetic truthfulness of his wife Gina and Hedvig her child. The bitterness of Ibsen's satire is as ever almost painful. That Truth is a beautiful thing he manifests in the ruin of the happiness of this family by bringing among them a staunch truth teller, and by making of this uncompromising idealist, this battler in the cause of truth, the most woefully defeated of all by the very achievement of his victory.

126. An unsigned review of *A Commentary on the Works of Henrik Ibsen, Spectator*

12 May 1894, lxxii, 652–3

Hjalmar Hjorth Boyeson's *Commentary* was published by Heinemann in 1894.

Whatever may be the future of the works of Henrik Ibsen, it can no longer be doubted that they have become one of the literary portents of the day, and that their author is now recognised throughout Europe as one of the most prominent personalities in the world of letters. In England, this recognition is as yet very imperfect, and we are therefore disposed to welcome any new light that can be thrown upon the meaning of this Continental reputation. The commentary that now lies before us is the work of a critic who is sufficiently a compatriot of Ibsen's to appreciate the forces that have been immediately at work upon that writer, and sufficiently English—or, perhaps we should say, American— to adjust his subject to the focus of English thought. As a matter of fact, Ibsen was not fortunate in his original introduction to this country. Had he been introduced to us as a poet, and had we been invited to read *Brand* or *Peer Gynt* in support of his claims, we should have been saved a good deal of idle and ignorant controversy as to his merits. But, as it was, he was presented to us as a prophet and social reformer, and we were asked to recognise his position at once from one or two grotesque translations of obscurely worded plays. No man was ever less of a social reformer than Ibsen. If he is a prophet, he is one who has no mission, no message to give us. A poet he certainly is, and perhaps the most dramatic writer of his day. To be a prophet, one should be something more than the incarnation of doubt; and to be a social reformer one must be something less than an anarchist. Ibsen's mission, if he has one at all, is purely destructive. He only puts the destroying question; never does he furnish even a hint of the saving answer. Mr. Boyesen calls him 'the wholesomely stimulating spirit that denies;' but he admits that 'social criticism, in order to be fruitful, must, as its first premise, presuppose the rationality, if not the goodness, of the universe. Otherwise it leads nowhere;' —and he adds, 'My grievance against Ibsen is that I can detect no dominant principle underlying his criticism of life. He seems to be in an ill-humour with humanity and the plan of creation in general (if, indeed, he recognises such a plan), and he devotes himself with ruthless satisfaction to showing what a paltry, contemptible lot men are, and how aimless, futile, and irrational their existence is on this earth, with its chaotic strivings and bewildered endeavours. There is no glimpse anywhere, as far as I have been able to ascertain, of Goethe's conviction that—

> A good man through obscurest aspiration
> Has still an instinct of the one true way.'

The vague belief in the coming of the 'Third Empire,' to which reference is made in the *Emperor and Galilæan*—an era which shall combine in itself the purified ideal of Paganism and Christianity—hardly finds a place in his writings, except for that one ambiguous mention. On the other hand, the whole tendency of both his poems and his plays is to pour contempt upon the cherished ideals of the day, and to prove that our civilisation is nothing but an ignoble compromise, a miserable surrender of our freedom, and of the possibility of developing our individuality, in order to obtain security for life and limb. The State is a prison, and the obligations of society are bars to protect us, the willing prisoners, from each other; as long as we cling to that cowardly shelter there is no hope for self-development. Humanity is following false ideals, believing in truths which have long ago been distorted into lies, professing a religion which is dead. In other words, it is trying to live while chained to a corpse, and until it breaks its fetters no healthy life is possible.

So long as his commentators are content to accept this as the attitude of Ibsen towards the questions of the day, they find their author perfectly consistent. But his writings are largely allegorical, and the temptation of reading a constructive philosophy of their own between the lines generally proves too much for his critics. Hence we get from his

English admirers those amazing and most contradictory appreciations of his work which have done more to render it unintelligible and displeasing to the general public than all the vehemence of his detractors. One of the chief merits of Mr. Boyesen's criticism is that it deals with the obvious drift of Ibsen's writings, and does not attempt, with misapplied ingenuity, to twist them to other meanings. Also the commentator manages to preserve throughout that perfect impartiality towards his subject which has been lamentably wanting to the writings of enthusiastic Ibsenites. Naturally, one cannot hope to understand fully the Scandinavian author without knowing something of his life and the conditions under which his plays were written.

127. Herbert Waring: an actor's view of Ibsen

October 1894

From 'Ibsen in London', *Theatre* (1 October 1894), xxxiii, 164–9. The author, Herbert Waring (1846–1909), was a well-known Ibsen actor.

On a hot evening in the early summer of 1889 I sat down to read *A Doll's House*. I shall never forget the sense of ineffable weariness with which I reached the end of the first act. It is true that Krogstad already stood out as a bold and dramatic figure. But how was it possible to feel interested in the frivolous and mendacious heroine, the commonplace and pragmatical husband—whom the author had not idealism enough to sublimate into a hero—the painfully self-abnegatory Mrs. Linden, and, above all, the morbidly amorous and hereditarily afflicted doctor? Considerably daunted, I attacked the second act with abated vigour, but with gradually awakened interest. There was a scintilla of true drama in the episode of the tarantella, and our old friend the sword of Damocles was being suspended with some skill over the unfortunate heroine's head. Still, the bald and trivial dialogue dragged its slow length along, and I incontinently resolved that wild horses should not drag me on to the stage in the unhappy and revolting person of Dr. Rank. I was half-way through the last act before I began to realise that the play was at least unconventional in design. I had confidently anticipated that the prosaic husband would wake up for a moment to a sense of his respon-sibilities as a hero, and take the onus of his wife's misdemeanour upon his shoulders; that all would be forgotten and forgiven, and that the drama would hurry to its obvious and commonplace conclusion. But when I came to the catastrophe, and the extraordinary subsequent conversation between husband and wife, I became dimly conscious that I was reading a work that was either utterly imbecile or something very great indeed. Stimulated by a new hope, I read the play through again from beginning to end, and I can honestly say that never before or since have I experienced so much pleasurable excitement in the perusal or representation of any piece. The uninteresting puppets became en-dowed with an intense vitality; the dialogue, which I had previously thought so dull and unimaginative, became the cogent and facile medium for the expression of individual and diverse character. Every word of the terse sentences seemed to have a value of its own, and to suggest some subtle *nuance* of feeling. I discovered that the character of Krogstad had impressed me on the first reading simply because it was the least complex of the group, and that Nora and Rank and Helmer were living and breathing entities, not conventionally embellished with the ordinary stock attributes of stage figures, but conceived and developed with a masterly knowledge of the intricacies of human na-ture. The whole play appeared complete and truly made, 'well diges-ted in the scenes,' and certainly free from the reproach of containing 'sallets in the lines to make the matter savoury.' Whether it is an 'hon-est method, as wholesome as sweet,' I do not pretend to determine.

Nevertheless, the play was rehearsed at the forlorn Novelty Theatre in a spirit of doubt, with frequent lapses into despondency. This was, however, felt only by the players engaged, for the managers, Mr. and Mrs. Charrington (Miss Achurch), were already keen enthusiasts on the subject. Should we ever get safely to the end of the second act, or would the audience rise in its wrath at the terribly dangerous conversa-tion between Nora and Rank, and denounce us as shameless inter-preters of a wantonly pornographic dramatist? Our fears proved groundless; the play went smoothly from start to finish, and was re-ceived at its close with quite ordinary first-night enthusiasm. Though announced for one week's representation only, the run continued for three weeks in all, and was only cut short by the prearranged departure of Mr. and Mrs. Charrington for Australia. I must confess to a keen and increasing delight, night after night, in playing Helmer. It is easier, I think, to get inside the skin of an Ibsen part than any other, for the simple reason that the characterization is so minute and elaborate, the words are so full of suggestion, that the actor has infinite scope for the exercise of his best qualities, and is able, in cricket parlance, to 'hit all round the wicket.' I feel it my painful duty to record that on the first performance of *A Doll's House* an unfortunate failure of memory caused me to omit the line, 'No man sacrifices his honour, even for one he loves,' thereby precluding Nora's immortal reply, 'Millions of women have done so.' For this momentary lapse the accomplished and erudite critic already mentioned has, I firmly believe, never quite forgiven me. I should like to add one word about the highly original conclusion of this piece. I have heard it said that the play breaks down in the last ten minutes. But the long conversation in which husband and wife seek to justify their respective attitudes, and to thrash out the possibilities of their future, seems to me more dramatic than anything which has preceded it. It is the solution of a problem of which the first two acts have been the long and elaborate enunciation.

The success of *A Doll's House*, and the recognition of Ibsen as a possible factor in the future development of English dramatic art, were responsible for the successive productions of *The Pillars of Society*, *Rosmersholm*, and *The Lady from the Sea*. But these were more or less ephemeral, and did not command the attention which such notable works deserved. The first and the last I have only read superficially, but I narrowly escaped playing Rosmer once, and may claim to have more than a casual acquaintance with *Rosmersholm*. The idea I formed on reading the play was intensified when I witnessed the production of it by Miss Florence Farr and Mr. F. R. Benson, and that is that Ibsen had for once selected a fine tragic theme, and unaccountably failed to develop it. I know nothing in Æschylus or Shakespere more weirdly impressive than the figures of the man and woman continually separated by the wraith of the dead wife, and finally united in their miserable doom by the same spiritual influence. But it seems to me that the play is top-heavy with unnecessary detail, and again and again, the magnificent intention is lost sight of through the author's insistence on the *minutiæ* of Norwegian village politics.

In 1893 Miss Elizabeth Robins and I produced, for a series of *matinées*,

The Master-Builder. Singularly enough, my recollections of this play are much less vivid than those of *A Doll's House*, although on this occasion I was more directly interested, as being one of the heads and fronts of the offending. I confess that I read the play through at least three times before I could assure myself that I comprehended the author's intention, and at least three times more before I felt that I had grasped the character of Bygmester Solness. As the work was delivered to us hot from the press, we were denied the advantage of the critical analysis and speculation as to the author's hidden meaning with which the London papers were rife for several weeks after the production. We had to disregard all considerations of allegorical significance, and simply to take the story as we found it. Solness might be the incarnation of the decadent spirit of the waning century; Hilda might be the flighty evangelist of a new humanitarian creed; and poor Mrs. Solness's nine dolls might be a type of Ibsen's nine social dramas. But with that we had nothing to do. We had simply to illustrate a plain tale of the influence of youthful ebullient womanhood on the life of a man no longer young, but still swayed by the youthful spirit of emulation; an ambitious dreamer, enduring, 'like the Turk, no rival near the throne,' half genius, half charlatan. There is no complexity in the first and third acts of this curious play. It starts with a simple and well-defined dramatic motive, and ends with a tragic catastrophe unseen by the audience, but suggested with all the technical cunning of a Sardou. But the second act presents a very difficult theatrical problem. Superficially, it is little more than an interminable conversation, carried on with more or less coherence between a man and a woman seated at opposite sides of a table, as in the final scene of *A Doll's House*. A closer study, however, reveals the fact that the apparently nugatory dialogue develops with perfect artistic gradation the painful workings of the unhappy architect's self-tortured mind; and it is in the new impetus given to this stagnating mental development by the brilliant and dominating influence of Hilda Wangel that the whole meaning of *The Master-Builder* lies. But the technical difficulties which beset the path of the actor who is doomed to play Solness might well appal the boldest histrionic spirit. The Builder is more loquacious than the Prince of Denmark himself. He is not a 'showy' part; he is throughout the second act on continually dangerous ground; and for my own part, I certainly never expected to surmount the successive obstacles of twins, fire, trolls, sagas, church towers, and second-floor windows without a heavy fall. I do not think it is possible for any actor to traject into the mind of his audience at a single sitting a full comprehension of matter which he himself has only understood after long days of laborious study. At all events, I am conscious myself of more or less complete failure in this respect. Nevertheless, as I have said, the study of this part was a labour of love to me. As one of the managers, I confess with pain that it was a labour of, or for, nothing else.

Hjalmar Ekdal, in the *Wild Duck*, is the one part in the whole range of Ibsen drama which I have hankered after, heart and soul. It was with great regret that I felt compelled to decline it when the Independent Theatre Society spoke to me about it in the spring of this year. However, it fell into the eminently capable hands of Mr. Abingdon, so the regret is mine alone. I was fortunate enough to see the dress rehearsal of the piece, and am filled with wonder that one performance of the play should have been comparatively overlooked by the critics. I have never seen a more complete incarnation of any part than the Gregers Werle of Mr. Charles Fulton. Opinions must always differ, even among experts, as to acting; but in this case there was absolutely no room for divergence. Personality, technique, intellectual grasp, and a most discreet and judicious use of the trained actor's resources were allied in this instance with the happiest results.

What, then, has been the total result of the so-called Ibsen craze? I hope I am not offending Mr. Pinero if I say that I think it has given us, first and foremost, the priceless boon of *The Second Mrs. Tanqueray*. This is only an echo of other opinions; but it is impossible to see or to read the play without feeling that the English dramatist has, unconsciously or voluntarily, recognised to a certain extent the value of the Ibsen method. One sees in places the same drastic rejection of florid embellishment in dialogue, 'the masterly pathos of designed simplicity,' as Mr. George Meredith has put it, and the same mercilessly minute analysis of human motives, which are the Norwegian's most valuable characteristics. At the same time, I hold that a drama constructed *entirely* on the Ibsen model could never find permanent favour in this or any other country. Heroism, chivalry, chastity, and self-sacrifice are not impossible or inhuman; and I think that the master misses his mark by carefully excluding these attributes from all, or nearly all, of his *personæ*. Our most facile and experienced critic has rightly said, in reviewing a play some years ago, that we must read our newspapers, and not contemporary fiction, to find our heroes and heroines of to-day. The scenic triumph of virtue over vice is, to my mind, not the mere cheap expedient of the playwright to gain the *arbitrium popularis auræ*, but a fixed and unalterable canon of dramatic art. If Ibsen could infuse into his men and women some afflatus of sweetness and light, if he could put his 'winged words' into the mouths of beings in whose nature Heaven had 'left some remnant of the angel still,' we might have a play, 'not of an age, but for all time.'

128. Ibsen on himself—I

1894

From *A Winter's Jaunt to Norway*, by Mrs Alec Tweedie (London: Bliss, Sands & Foster, 1894). Taken from Chapter IV, 'Henrik Ibsen', pp. 245–65.

'Why have you never travelled to England, when you have been such a wanderer?' [Ibsen was asked.]

'Because I do not speak the language, and I should never get at the heart of the people, and that is what I want. Yet I should like very much to go to England, because English people and English books interest me strangely; more especially I would like to see your old men. In all other countries the best work is done by men between forty and fifty years of age; in England, the best work is done by much older men, and a man of sixty or seventy is often still in his prime. I would like to see such men as Gladstone and Salisbury, Herbert Spencer and Tennyson.' . . .

Casting our eyes around, we noticed that by the side of the ink-pot on the table on which so many remarkable books have been written, there stood a little tray, and on the tray one of those small carved wooden bears so common in Switzerland. Beside it was a little black devil for holding a match, and two or three little cats and rabbits in copper, one of the former of which was playing a violin.

'What are these funny little things?' we queried.

'I never write a single line of any of my dramas unless that tray and its occupants are before me on the table. I could not write without them.

It may seem strange—perhaps it is; but I cannot write without them', he repeated; 'but why I use them is my own secret,' and he laughed quietly.

Are these little toys, these fetiches, with their strange fascination, the origin of those much discussed dolls in *The Master Builder*. Who can tell? They are Ibsen's secret.

129. Ibsen on himself—2

1896

From 'Ibsen at Home', by Edgar O. Achorn, *New England Magazine* (February 1896), xlii, 737–48. A lushly illustrated article, based on an interview, with several portraits of Ibsen, his home and his study.

[Ibsen said]: 'I am not a good English scholar. I have read very many American authors, however, as Holmes, Emerson and Howells, but mostly through German translations. So far as I have read, American literature has impressed me very favourably.' The talk turned particularly upon Howells, in whom he was interested, but he said nothing quotable. 'I never give an *opinion* of an author,' he said. 'My work in the world has not been in the line of criticism. I have not the time to criticise other's writings. Criticism requires exact study. My efforts lie in quite another direction.' . . .

He asked, speaking of the critics who say that his characters and situations are unnatural, whether I thought of any cases in point.

I ventured the opinion that in *The Lady From the Sea* the attraction of Ellida for the strange man was novel, to say the least, while *Ghosts* seems unnatural to many, and its philosophy, so far as most understand it, hard for them to approve.

'And yet both emphasize the existence of real forces at work upon humanity,' exclaimed the doctor, his face aglow with animation. 'My intention was to put Ellida under the influence of another than her husband, of such an intensity as to be at times irresistible. Such an influence has often been found, and has led many a woman astray. As for *Ghosts*, the whole drama was written to emphasize the influence of heredity. It is cruel, as is much else one finds in real life, but on that account the more to be respected.'

[on being asked which of his books he thought the best Ibsen smiled and said:]

'Today no work in particular. Each book was written in its own time, and each at the time seemed best, for it was the expression of the thought that then animated me.'

[why did he give up poetic drama?]

'I might say briefly,' he answered, 'that it followed of itself. At that time I turned to the study and treatment of modern life. Poetry could not have been used to develop my ideas. It would have been out of place.'

LITTLE EYOLF

1894

130. From an unsigned review, *Saturday Review*

15 December 1894, lxxviii, 662

Little Eyolf was translated by William Archer and published in England by Heinemann, 1894.

The event on which the drama of *Little Eyolf* is built is the death of a child. It is not a painful death. Eyolf has all the charm of thoughtful, old-fashioned childhood. He has been badly lamed by a fall, and belongs half to the other world already. Every spell that a poet can weave about death is woven round his fate. In his finest velvet dress he follows the fairylike ratwife, first cousin to the Piper of Hamelin, down to the sea; and, as she goes off in her boat, he goes to the pierhead, and past it. We see him resting for a moment in the depths, with wide-open, calm eyes, before the undertow sweeps him out. We watch him go without any wringing of the heart, except perhaps, for an almost happy pang of half longing, half curiosity, to follow him in search of the peace to which that strange old woman lures all 'little gnawing things,' children who gnaw their parents' consciences, children's own hearts, and other sorts of rats that drive people out of house and home.

One need not sign this picture with the name of Ibsen: that last stroke is itself a signature. No other hand, living or dead, draws quite in that way. In the subject we have what the commercial playwright calls an 'incident'; and such children of this world will doubtless conceive the play as leading up to it and ending with it and some slow music. One sees, on this familiar plane, the tiny form floating out to sea, like Ophelia in Ambroise Thomas's opera, with, perhaps, the bereaved mother gasping a pathetic 'tag' on the beach. But Ibsen always begins a play where other playwrights end it, being in this respect, as Peer Gynt ruefully says of God, 'not economical.' The death of little Eyolf ends, not the last act of the play, but the first.

Those who are in Ibsen's secret will not need to be told that Eyolf's death is the foundation of one of those wonderful cloud prisons which men build for themselves out of their own fears and ideals and super- stitions, with duty for the treadmill and conscience for the rack. Years ago, Bunyan, thinking ignorantly enough, but feeling surely and rightly, gave us the allegory of the pilgrim trapped in Doubting Castle, and lying there until he found that he had in his own bosom a key that fitted every lock in the castle. But in Doubting Castle there were many bones of pilgrims who did not find the key, and so perished there miserably; and Ibsen, in *Brand* and elsewhere, has told us the story of these bones oftener than that of the finder of the key. In *Little Eyolf*, however, the key is found—by a woman.

The distinction which all poets of the first rank have made between a higher and a lower love—between Tannhäuser's passion for Venus and his adoration of St. Elizabeth, and which vulgar writers can only make real to themselves and their readers by degrading Venus to the level of the streets, and then labelling a doll Elizabeth as a first-rate article without going into particulars, has hitherto taken a peculiar turn in Ibsen. We find it first in *Peer Gynt* between Solveig and Ingrid, or the Hottentot Venus Anitra, the contrast being a little forced against Venus in the vulgar manner. We have it much more subtly and origi- nally in *Rosmersholm*, where, instead of a Tannhäuser deserting Venus for St. Elizabeth, we have Venus herself attaining the higher love. But the change is one which breaks the woman's spirit; and nothing is more characteristic of Ibsen than his evident sympathy with her in a certain regret for her disablement. In *The Master Builder*, where we have the heroine in the very stage of 'free fearless will' which Rebecca West regretted, we find Ibsen still full of the same rebellious and sceptical sympathy, and still pessimistically admitting the destructive results of what he admired. But there is an utter absence of this vein in *Little Eyolf*—nay, there is something like a change of front on the question.

If this change of front is due to any external influence, it is probably due to Tolstoi's *Kreutzer Sonata*. That extraordinary tale was the first work of modern art in which it was definitely asserted that the lower love, meaning not necessarily the gross love, but the *jealous* love, is absolutely identical with hatred. The *Kreutzer Sonata* did not teach this as a lesson: it asserted it as a fact. It went further: it extended the asser- tion from the relation between husband and wife to that between parents and their children. Ibsen is one of the few men in Europe capable of feeling the staggering force of Tolstoi's assertion. And when we find in *Little Eyolf* a husband, wife, and child on exactly the *Kreutzer Sonata* terms—the man loathing the wife of whom he is enamoured, and turning with deep affection to a woman whom he supposes to be his sister, whilst the wife dotes on her husband with a jealousy that makes her hate the child and himself as well—it is difficult to avoid the guess that Tolstoi has thrown a flash on a dark spot in Ibsen's path. For whilst the other elements in *Little Eyolf* may be easily identified in the former plays, this element is quite new.

The drama will now leap to the eye of the experienced Ibsenite. The child, first lamed for life in a moment of neglect in which the husband forgets everything but his wife's beauty, is then drowned because, being thus lamed, he is the only child in the village who cannot swim. In their horror and remorse the father and mother become aware of their real feelings for one another and for the child; and there is an unspeakable 'terror and pity' in the scenes in which they turn and rend one another. These scenes will be hardly bearable on the stage until repeated performances have given the less deepsighted spectators the comfort of foreknowing that the woman has in her bosom the key that opens all the gates in Doubting Castle.

The key is the old, the only possible key. In *Little Eyolf*, as in the world's history, Venus is supplanted by the Virgin Mother. When the man, resolving to leave the wife who has become intolerable to him, bids her raze to the ground the huts on the property which shelter the fisherfolk and their brats who would not risk their lives to save his child, the woman, worn out with passion, suddenly feels the rush into her heart of the true immaculate motherhood, and declares that she will bring those brats to her house, and give them Eyolf's clothes, his toys, his books, and his mother's care. It is an exquisitely happy ending: no words can convey the tranquil joy and reassurance with which the towers of Doubting Castle are seen to be mere mist phantoms vanishing in the heavenly radiance.

When *Little Eyolf* comes into the glare of the footlights, it may prove that Ibsen the old theatrical hand has been too much for Ibsen the poet. Nine-tenths of the audience will share the apparently hopeless burden of horror which is laid so heavily on the parents; and even when the relief comes, it is likely enough that it will seem merely an ignominious retreat of the dramatist from the grimness of reality into the pretty pretence of a conventional happy ending. Whatever softness and glamour the incident of the child's death takes on when the description of it is completed in the second act, the scene in the parents' house when they are startled by the hubbub from the beach, when they learn from the outcries that a child has fallen into the water, when they miss Eyolf, whom they supposed to be playing in the garden, and, finally, when the mother hears the words, 'The crutch is floating'—all this is worked up with that frightful skill in torture described by Lamb in the well-known sentences in which he vainly tried to persuade himself and us that it was possessed as well as coveted by Webster. Then there is no sparing of our delicacy in the wife's reproach to the husband—'There stood your champagne; but you tasted it not'—and those who sigh for 'comic relief' will hardly be appeased by the grim irony of the scene in which the bereaved father, chatting happily with his beloved sister, repeatedly breaks off to blame himself for forgetting the duty of being miserable because of the boy's death. There is a passage or two which will amuse the impossible creatures who laughed at Mrs. Solness's dolls in *The Master Builder*; and there is the serious difficulty for first-night purposes that in *Little Eyolf*, as in all Ibsen's later plays, each act is fully intelligible only in the light of that which follows it; so that, unless the whole is played backwards, the unfortunate dramatic critics who do not fortify themselves by a careful study of the book before-hand are likely to blunder as helplessly as ever over it.

Mr. William Archer has translated the play as he has translated so many others by the same hand. Let those criticize him who know as much Norwegian as he.

131. From a signed review by J. T. Grein, *Sunday Times*

16 December 1894, 4

(See No. 139.) Jacob Thomas Grein (1862–1935) was the founder of the Independent Theatre.

Allmers (in suppressed desperation): Yes, that is true. (Lower) I forgot the child—in your arms.

Hark! in these few words I have sounded the key-note of Ibsen's latest tragedy. I say 'tragedy,' albeit, that the atmosphere is less sombre than in *Ghosts* or *Hedda Gabler* or *The Master Builder*. I say 'tragedy' in spite of the play ending with a ray of the light of peace breaking through the clouds; I say 'tragedy' fearless of contradiction, because now that I have closed the book and endeavour to analyse some of my impressions, my soul is full of sadness.

'I forgot the child—in your arms.' Has ever such a complaint, and such a self-accusation been framed in so terse a form. It is the world's history written in seven words. Realms have been led to perdition, thrones have fallen, might and greatness and duty have tottered and crumbled to pieces, all human responsibilities have been forgotten—in woman's arms.

[outlines the plot.]

I do not know what to admire more in this latest creation of a master mind—the men and women whom he has taken from life and condensed body and soul in the narrow frame of a three-act drama, or the language which he has put into their mouths. For I recognise Rita and Allmers and Asta and little Eyolf as my kinsmen, as beings made of the same flesh and blood as we are made of, acting as I (or you) might act, suffering as we might suffer, struggling as we might—as we do—struggle in the straits of life. I go further; I contend that Ibsen has not only copied life in thought and action. He has done more, the most difficult thing of all. He has endowed his creatures with speech such as flows from human lips. And in this respect he towers above all his

338

contemporaries. His characters speak—to use a German expression—
'as their beaks are grown.' No fine writing here, no imagery, no grandi-
loquence, no high falutin (such as is cheap and effective on the stage),
but the simple talk of ordinary people who have learned to observe and
to reflect. Hence Ibsen's power, hence the untoward effect of his sentences which will ring in our ears for ever and ever. I quote but a few
lines to illustrate what I mean. Thus the play ends: Allmers and Rita have
resolved to live a new, a higher life, and then he says:

> Allmers: Now and then, perhaps, we may still—on the way through life—
> have a little passing glimpse of them.
> Rita: Where shall we look for them, Alfred?
> Allmers (fixing his eyes upon her): Upwards.
> Rita (nods in approval): Yes, yes, upwards.
> Allmers: Upwards—towards the peaks. Towards the great stars. And
> towards the great silence.
> Rita (giving him her hand): Thanks!

Do you feel it? 'Upwards—towards the peaks. Towards the stars.
And towards the great silence.' Was ever all that is great and exalted,
and—sad, described with such simplicity, with such force, in such noble
form? I have chosen the one sentence which has moved me beyond
description in its naked beauty, but the play abounds in simple words
full of deep meaning. Read how Allmers loves his little Eyolf; read his
description of his home-coming after his travel, the end of the first act;
the scene between him and Asta in the overwhelming second act, read
it—and whether you admire Ibsen or whether you have been taught to
shun his works, you will have to bow in deference before the unaffected
greatness of his creative powers.

What impression *Little Eyolf* will produce upon the stage I cannot
say: in my own opinion it will be the most effective, the most vital of
his plays; but this I do know, in literature it will rank high among the
highest, it will live when all the detractors of the master are long gone,
buried and forgotten. And let no one henceforth venture to proclaim
that in this country Ibsen is the object of the admiration of a 'noisy
little clique.' For to-day all England is ringing with the name of the
Norwegian writer. And the publication of his latest work has been
acknowledged by the Press as an event of paramount importance.

132. Unsigned notice, *Pall Mall Gazette*

24 November 1896, 11

William Archer's translation of *Little Eyolf* was performed at the Admiralty Theatre on 23 November 1896 and the cast was as follows:

Alfred Allmers..	Mr Courtenay Thorpe
Mrs Rita Allmers	Miss Janet Achurch
Eyolf	Master Stewart Dawson
Miss Asta Allmers	Miss Elizabeth Robins
Engineer Borg-heim ..	Mr C. M. Lowne
The Rat-Wife ..	Mrs Patrick Campbell

Most of our readers have read somewhere, we fancy, the plot of *Little Eyolf*. If they have not, we are sorry, more or less; but we are constrained to assume their knowledge of it, since it is beyond our ability to give it in any summary which shall do justice to the delicate and doubtful significance of its several phases (in the measure of our small ability), and at the same time be within the possibilities of a daily journal. And before attempting to criticise it as a play for the stage, we are fain to make certain negative postulates. Nobody possessed of any knowledge regarding certain questions of medicine and biology can have seen *Little Eyolf* without perceiving that in it Dr. Ibsen suggests (we do not say as a part of his own private theory) views of those questions the truth of which is extremely disputable. We must put those questions on one side. Again, we decline to pronounce, out of hand, an opinion whether or not certain subjects of a very directly physical significance should be treated on the stage with less insistence than Dr. Ibsen treats them withal. It is ridiculous to deny the significance; nobody of average experience of life can fail to see it, and we venture to say that the significance is somewhat distressing. We believe that there are students of Dr. Ibsen who maintain that in such a play as *Little Eyolf* he treats of normal humanity, merely disclosing more ruthlessly than is common the vices and weaknesses which underlie its surface. We do not think so; we believe that *Little Eyolf* presents a picture of mental and physical disease

340

which happily is not the lot of normal humanity. But this is not to say that it is necessarily not a play to be played. You are free to go to a play, and are free to stay away from it; for our part, we were interested, and in a way impressed, and we therefore express our gratitude to Miss Elizabeth Robins for her artistic enterprise.

And now to the question of drama. Unquestionably the play is dramatic, the work of a man with an instinct for drama. But it has faults, and the greatest of these is the vagueness of its symbolism. We do not object to symbolism 'by itself,' of course. But there are conditions to be observed if it is to be artistic. Either your symbolism must be clear and determined, or, if it is to be vague, it must leave room for explanation on common grounds. This is not the case in *Little Eyolf*. The 'Rat-Wife' incident contains features inexplicable on common grounds. She stands for death: well and good, but either the incident should have been determinately symbolical, or she should have been a possible 'rat-wife' as well, and she was not. Another fault is that the patience of the audience—we do not care how thoughtful or how remote from everyday people that audience is assumed to be—is tried too severely and unnecessarily by the prolonged exposition of Allmers' egotism and weakness. A third is that the dialogue lets down the tragedy of the play into bathos too frequently—more so than the scourging of humanity really requires. But this may not be altogether Dr. Ibsen's fault. Mr. William Archer's translation reads well, but it is not altogether 'convincing'—to use a hackneyed, useful phrase—on the stage: we think he lacks a little the true dramatist's ear. All this said, the play remains, as we saw it, a powerful and interesting one.

Mrs. Patrick Campbell had the best part in the piece. The 'Rat-Wife' is on the stage for a quarter or so of one act only—but every word she has to speak impresses. Mrs. Campbell was admirable—a *tour de force* of weirdness and intensity. Miss Robins's Asta, Allmers' supposed half-sister and comforter, was excellent all through; it was a more difficult part than that she had in *The Master Builder*, and we think she played it better. Miss Achurch, as the wife, was at her best in the most tragic moments of the play, and that is high praise; in its lighter phases we think she was inclined to exaggerate the bitterness of the disappointed wife. Master Dawson is a very clever child, and had been taught not to try to do too much as Eyolf: we commend him sincerely. But we cannot, to our regret, do as much for the grown-up examples of his sex. Allmers is a terribly difficult part; its utter want of sympathy would tax the greatest actor who ever lived. But Mr. Courtenay Thorpe was not even a brilliant failure; he simply failed. And Mr. Lowne played the lover Borgheim rather in the spirit of the *jeune premier* of robust farce, not an appropriate spirit.

133. From an unsigned notice, *The Times*

24 November 1896, 4

The whole play is curiously mystic and unreal. None of the characters appear quite sane, except, indeed, the 'road-maker,' whose profession is probably symbolical, though for that we do not vouch. *Little Eyolf* interests the spectator pretty much as the other Ibsen plays interest him. He sees on the stage a set of irresponsible people, moved by unaccountable impulses and addicted to fantastic views of duty. There is no knowing what they will do next. They are not amenable to the ordinary rules of human nature. To Helmer, of *A Doll's House*, Allmers bears a family relationship, as, indeed, to most of Ibsen's husbands, in that he does not understand his wife. That, however, is not to his discredit, for we, the spectators, do not understand her either. On the other hand, she does not understand him. No more do we, except on the hypothesis of his incipient insanity. Even the supposed half-sister is a curiously enigmatical creature, although governed for the most part by sane impulses. As for the rat-wife, we can only suppose her to be symbolical, which, in the case of an Ibsen play, is an agreeable euphuism for the unintelligible. This strange medley of odds and ends of character and incident the members of the cast enact with their customary air of conviction; for there is always something suggestive of a mystic rite in the performance of an Ibsen play. This may safely be averred, that it is a terribly depressing and lugubrious society into which the author takes us. One does not breathe freely until one has escaped from the atmosphere of the theatre into the open air. Gloom, depression, and a sense of the remoteness of the action from all living human interests overcome the spectator, whose abiding impression of the play is that of having seen in a dream the patients of a madhouse exercising in their yard.

134. From an unsigned notice, *Evening Standard*

24 November 1896, 4

There had appeared good reason to hope that the English stage had seen the last of the morbid, melancholy, and unwholesome dramas of Mr. Ibsen. In ordinary circumstances this hope would have been justified. The experiment of producing these works had shown that the taste of the average English audience was far too sound and healthy to accept them. Many vulgar and pretentious plays from various sources have had their successes, it is true, but audiences emphatically drew the line at Mr. Ibsen. A little band of fanatics were loud in their praises, and, as a matter of course, declared that the failure of the world in general to tolerate Mr. Ibsen was due to lamentable lack of appreciation and perception; but the few persons who, not being fanatics, were drawn to the theatre when the plays were being given, smiled contemptuously or laughed derisively, when they were not yawning. If left to their own merits, to the ordinary theatrical laws of supply and demand, there would have been no more Ibsen in England; but some players who chanced to be out of engagements lately set themselves diligently to work to collect subscriptions towards the production of his last composition, *Little Eyolf*, and, the necessary funds having been obtained, yesterday's performance was the result. That *Little Eyolf* will do anything to create a respect or regard for Mr. Ibsen's plays is inconceivable, nor is it even likely to revive the old controversy which gave rise to such a little storm in a tea-cup when *Ghosts*, *Hedda Gabler*, and *Rosmersholm* were produced. In one or two scenes the coarseness and vulgarity which are rooted characteristics of the author are offensively perceptible in his latest composition; but *Little Eyolf* is, if possible, even vaguer and more preposterous than *The Master Builder* and its kin. It is no less full of mysticism and symbolism than its predecessors, and, as in former cases, though the disciples are convinced that the whole drama is replete with the richest significance, there is much accentuated difference of opinion among them as to what that significance is: it all means a vast deal, but they do not quite know what. Towards the end, let it be

343

freely and cordially admitted, an attempt is made to inculcate the doctrines of charity and broad humanity, and this is a very excellent lesson, of course; but one has to go through a vast deal before it is tediously reached, and even then it is very crudely expressed.

135. From an unsigned notice, *Daily News*

24 November 1896, 10

Little Eyolf has, perhaps, less of action than any other of the whole cycle of Ibsen's plays, while the motives of its personages are further removed than ever from ordinary human standards. It has been said that the 'trick of the vague' has been cultivated by the Norwegian dramatist till it has become an 'overmastering passion.' Mr. Archer, who is not only the friend and translator, but the chief expounder of Ibsen problems (though he has publicly confessed that they are occasionally a little too much for him), has told us that this play is to be regarded as an 'indictment of Nature'—a profoundly pessimistic tableau of life; but the facts that the moral law has no place in the physical universe, and that human life is apt to be a mere game of cross purposes, are and ever have been the main sources of pathetic interest. It is not because he deals with these things, but because he deals with them in an undramatic way, that Ibsen fails to fulfil the dramatic canon of Victor Hugo in his explanation of the phrase 'passioner la foule.' *Little Eyolf* comprises, certainly, more unsolved and even undefined problems than consort with the methods of the stage. Mr. and Mrs. Allmers's remorse in the thought of their erroneous training of their crippled child is, for example, clearly too recondite for dramatic treatment; nor is it clear how a different training would have saved their offspring from the Rat-Wife's fatal allurements. On the other hand the mutual recriminations of this strange couple are coarse, and, we are compelled to add, tinged with a vulgarity wholly out of keeping with the refinements and subtleties of the protracted discussion in which they at other times engage. As to the Rat-wife and the little dog in her bag, the unenlightened playgoer may well be excused if he fails to understand their precise symbolical meaning and function in the story, since the dramatist's admirers have been much at variance on these points.

136. From an unsigned notice, by Clement Scott, *Daily Telegraph*

24 November 1896, 5

If one were disposed to treat the last presented work of Ibsen, the great Scandinavian 'master,' in a light and bantering tone an alternative title might be suggested for this 'curious' work. Remembering a catch phrase—invented, we believe, by that delightful comedian, Mr. J. L. Toole—the play might be called *Little Eyolf*; *or, Not Before the Boy*; for it is by a neglect of this time-honoured precept that we are presented at once with the dramatic catastrophe and the domestic dilemma in the Allmers household. Mrs. Rita Allmers is the female echo of the Ibsenic male who wears 'vine-leaves in his hair.' Her goddess is Aphrodite, and her passion is champagne. Once put champagne on the table, and the situation, so far as Rita is concerned, becomes dangerous.

[the plot described with some distaste. Scott quotes at length from the text, especially the scenes between Rita and Allmers where the phrases 'There stood the champagne, but you tasted it not' and 'I forgot the child—in your arms' are used.]

This, then, is the domestic tragedy of the Allmers. Here is the vulgar colouring of a most unwholesome picture of real and squalid life. This is the reason that this play, alternately pathetic and nasty, rings with the fateful cry, 'The Crutch is floating. The Crutch is floating.' Grim and indefensible as are the details of the tale, the concluding moral is at least unexceptionable. Asta does not tempt Allmers into any more platonic intrigues, but disappears. The dangerous road-maker vanishes into space, and the husband and wife are left alone looking 'upwards, upwards, towards the peaks, towards the stars, and towards the great silence!'

And so the curtain falls, and the audience for a moment, unable to move, sits pale and petrified!

After the first act, which contains just one glimmer of action and a shrill, sharp-edged scream from Miss Janet Achurch, that divided 'the shuddering night,' the effect of the so-called play on the audience was sepulchral. If only Miss Achurch or somebody else could have screamed in every act, that scream would have been accepted as a godsend. But on it went, on, on, on, eternal, unbroken, never-ending talk. We are told that in this succession of dull, depressing, and suggestive duologues there is some deep, subtle, and hidden meaning, only understood or possibly revealed to the disciples of Ibsen. We have earnestly striven to attain it, and all we can gather from the theme is that moderation in marriage is to be earnestly recommended, and that the intellect is continually at war with the passions. But these things were known long ago to decent and thinking men. We did not need a seer or a prophet from Norway to tell us that, and the sermon, such as it is, cannot be preached without the running of great risks. We saw a wild, unbridled, passionate Rita turned into a dull, loveless mass of broken nerves at the instigation of a loquacious and selfish prig. We saw a good, pure woman—Asta—resisting all temptation, and going home by the boat. If there was any other deep or subtle meaning in the dreary tale it wholly escaped our notice and must have got drowned with little Eyolf in the first act.

137. From an unsigned notice, *Daily Chronicle*

24 November 1896, 8

And then how grave the subject-matter, how poignant, the treatment! Birth, death, marriage, motherhood, fate, responsibility, self-will, the right to live and enjoy, duty, revolt, submission—all these great themes run through *Little Eyolf*, and weave themselves into the thread of its simple story. Now it is pure symbolism, now again it is the direct war of human passions—'Any Wife to any Husband,' any husband to any wife. Of too easy interpretations it may be well to beware. I remember that two years ago I reviewed Mr. Archer's translation of *Little Eyolf* for *The Chronicle*, and was quite satisfied as to the meaning of the Rat-wife and her little dog, who go about the country relieving it of rats and creeping things:—

The Rat-wife (I said) is clearly Death—Death that 'lures' mankind to an end it does not seek. What is the black dog? Is it the Spirit of Doubt that Ibsen suggests in fantastic imagery, such as the Great Boyg in *Peer Gynt*, the falcon in *Brand*? And what is the dead man, lured in early youth, before the little black dog came on the scene? It may be a hint of the lost Christian ideal—the Spirit of Faith.

Whether these interpretations hold or no, certain it is that nowhere but in Ibsen have you so subtle a suggestion of 'sense and outward things' in relation to the more mysterious truths of life. Ibsen's characters are straightforward, modern enough. Their language is the simplest ever heard on the stage. But behind them walk in close attendance the shadow figures that poets use when they desire to give their deeper thoughts to the world.

138. 'Ibsen and His Interpreters', an editorial in *Era*

28 November 1896, 17

It forms a curious comment on the art of Ibsen that it seems to be tacitly allowed that much of his work is to be classed in the category of 'things no fellah can make out;' so that, even as a priest was needed to interpret the utterances of the inspired Pythoness, so the admirers of Ibsen require expounders and explainers to act as mediums of communication between the 'Master' and the devotee. The necessity for such interpreters has this evil: it saves lazy people—the majority, in fact—the trouble of reading or seeing the work thus interpreted; so that the impression made upon their minds by the account of the interpreter is substituted for a careful examination of the play itself. The result is similar to that which Don Quixote's description of Dulcinea del Toboso would have created in those who had never met that lady. This is the more to be regretted, as the points slurred over by the commentator are often exactly those which are of the greatest interest to the public. There are hundreds who, when Mr William Archer tells them, as he does, that 'beneath the marvellously-woven fabric of story and psychology of *Little Eyolf* we can discern a profoundly significant philosophical conception,' will only too gladly accept this estimate as an excuse for neither reading nor seeing the piece.

They will err in their easy acceptance, for the production of *Little Eyolf* raises a point which is of, at least, some importance to the contemporary drama—*i.e.*, whether sexual commerce in its most animal form is a fit subject for discussion in modern drama. It is all very well to draw our attention away, lapwing-like, to 'profoundly, significant philosophical conception.' What we have before us, in black and white, is the text; which at any rate is a secure rock in an ocean of foamy controversy.

Our readers may easily ascertain, by consulting the published translation of *Little Eyolf*, that we have not, below, selected a few passages which are out of the main current of the piece. On the contrary, the very source and origin of the action arises from the physical relations between the leading male personage and his wife.

Alfred Allmers, a man of letters and a tutor, has married a rich woman from mixed motives of sensuality and greed. At first he was afraid of his future wife.

RITA.—What did you feel for me first of all?
ALLMERS.—Dread.
RITA.—That I can understand. How was it, then, that I won you after all?
ALLMERS.—(*In a low voice*)—You were so entrancingly beautiful, Rita.
RITA.—(*Looks searchingly at him*)—Then that was the only reason?
ALLMERS.—(*Conquering himself*)—No; there was another as well.
RITA.—(*With an outburst*)—I can guess what it was! It was 'my gold and my green forests,' as you call it. Was it not so, Alfred?
ALLMERS.—Yes.

Since his marriage to Rita, Allmers has suffered from what we must euphoniously describe as 'loss of vitality and virile force.' Rita, unfortunately, is of an excessively amorous temperament. 'She doesn't go drowsing round with fishes' blood in her veins,' she says. Already her unbridled sexuality has caused an accident which has crippled their child, Eyolf, for life. The incident is thus plainly described in the text—

ALLMERS.—It was your fault that he became what he was. It was you who left the helpless child unwatched upon the table.

RITA.—He was lying so comfortably among the cushions, and sleeping so soundly. And you had promised to look after him.

ALLMERS.—Yes, I had. (*Lowering his voice.*) But then you came—you, you, you—and lured me to you.

RITA.—(*Looking defiantly at him*)—Oh! better own at once that you forgot the child and everything else.

ALLMERS.—(*In suppressed desperation*)—Yes, that is true. (*Lower.*) I forgot the child—in your arms.

The evening before the action commences Allmers came home utterly wearied out by a long walking tour. This is the sequel as described in dialogue—

RITA.—Then I dressed myself in white. I had let down my hair so that it flowed down my neck and shoulders. There were rose-tinted shades over both the lamps. And we were alone, we two—the only waking beings in the whole house. And there was champagne on the table.

ALLMERS.—I didn't drink any of it.

RITA—(*Looking bitterly at him*)—No, that's true. (*Laughs harshly.*) 'There stood the champagne, but you tasted it not,' as the poet says.

ALLMERS—I was so taken up with serious thoughts. I had made up my mind to talk to you of our future, Rita—and first and foremost of Eyolf.

RITA—(*Sighing*)—And so you did.

ALLMERS—No; I hadn't time to, for you began to undress.

Now, apart from any underlying symbolism or psychological meaning, we fail to see much difference, on the score of ordinary indecency, between these passages and those in a certain notorious scene in *Divorçons*—between Celestine's 'Ne tuer pas le diner par le lonch,' and Rita's 'There stood your champagne, and you did not drink it.' We find, indeed, quite appropriate to the matter the remarks made by Mr William Archer, the translator of *Little Eyolf*, respecting M. Sardou's 'spicy' play; and, with a few unimportant alterations, we take the liberty of using the critic's own phrases to describe Ibsen's play:—

There are speeches and scenes in it so suggestive that we doubt whether anything more scabrous has ever been said or done on the public stage in any civilised country. A man and a woman discussing their physical relations in the plainest terms on the public stage; the woman complaining openly of the man's backwardness—if anything much grosser than this was ever put on the stage, we have neither seen, read, or heard of it. The fact that the man is her husband does not, it seems to us, by any means purify the situation.

And we really fail to understand why a kind of licence which is forbidden to be indulged in for the diversion of a merry section of playgoers should be permitted for the delectation of the serious. No Censor who 'passed' the passages we have quoted from the translation of *Little Eyolf* can consistently object to any treatment on the stage, however naked, bold, and bare, of the sexual relationship. If our Censorship is a mere formal farce it had better be abolished and with it the office of Examiner of Plays. The translator of *Little Eyolf*, however, is in complete error in supposing that 'in every audience there are two or three persons sufficiently in earnest in the cause of good manners and decorum to take the initiative in attacking impropriety.' We can vouch for it that, during the delivery of the passages which we have quoted, the audience at the Avenue Theatre last Monday afternoon, very many of whom were women, sat in silence, eagerly drinking in every word. There was not even in them, collectively, sufficient sense of Rabelaisian humour to stimulate a solitary snigger.

139. An unsigned notice by J. T. Grein, *Sunday Times*

29 November 1896, 4

Grein refers to his review of the published play two years earlier (No. 131).

Two years ago, when *Little Eyolf* was published, I set down my opinions of it here, in the *Sunday Times*; and though indeed I have forgotten what I said as entirely as you have, that would be no excuse for saying it all over again. So I will only give you now some personal impressions of the performance of last Monday—which did but, on the whole, confirm my first feeling about the play.

For the general effect, let me say that *Little Eyolf*, when it is acted, confirms the bold contention of Mr. Robert Buchanan that the play form is altogether higher than the novel form. A novel with as much that is noble in it as this tragedy would rank among the finest; but the parts which one would skip after the first reading are fatal to the drama, for a play is a complete thing, which of its nature has to be judged as a whole. Much of the first act, nearly all the second, a little of the third, must reckon among the simplest, most beautiful, and most noble work that Ibsen has given us; but the underplot—so to call it—is mere silliness, and there are passages in the main story against which it is not prudery to protest. It is true that English criticism joyfully accepts a farce which turns on the prevention of adultery by the sickness which follows smoking, and has therefore little right to object to the most intimate details of the alcove; but there is a larger opinion than that of the professed critics of the moment, to which one may with some confidence appeal. By this time, I think, there is hardly a reader who will not—for example—blame Shakespeare for the hideous scene in which Gloucester's eyes are torn out. 'This is not for the theatre,' as one might translate M. Sarcey; and certain of the confidences of the Allmers' ménage are equally unsuited for publication on the stage.

But I must in the beginning admit that I became for the first quarter of an hour of *Little Eyolf* a rabid anti-Ibsenite. I was annoyed at the very outset by the conversation on family matters of no interest whatever which started the play—or, to be more accurate, marked time till it was ready to start. I resented this assumption which Ibsen had borrowed from Scribe—that the audience is bound to sit still and listen to some five minutes of 'explanatory' twaddle before the human interest of the story can begin.

But a much more serious matter was the revelation which came in the scene of the Rat-wife. Here, shown up by the reality of the stage, was just such a bit of shoddy—of mere convention, unfelt and therefore untrue—as one got in *The Blot on the Scutcheon*. When Browning's play was acted one saw that not Paul Merritt at the Grecian would for mere stage effect have made a lover sing a serenade as he was climbing to his mistress' window for a secret meeting at midnight. And in *Little Eyolf* one recognised at once the impossibility of the presence of the father and aunt, while the Rat-wife terrified the child with her ghastly talk; neither Allmers nor the sensible Asta would for a minute have permitted her so to frighten the nervous little fellow. Here was an 'effect', whether of the stage or of symbolism, which Ibsen wanted, and to which—from a lack either of conscience or of imagination—he sacrificed the possibility of his story: with the result that his work seemed cheap, one lost respect for it at once.

But with the scene between husband and wife, the interest of the play began and grew. I cannot altogether say that to see it acted was as good as to read it, but for this there was perhaps, in my case, a special reason. I fear I must assume that I am unlike everybody else, for to me the character of Allmers, the husband, is entirely sympathetic. It is said that he was a prig: but this is a term of abuse which suffers from the want of exact definition. M. Lemaître has translated 'priggishness' by the hybrid 'snobisme,' and in so doing has precisely defined the really objectionable prig—the blatant one. But a gentle being like Allmers, entirely inoffensive—except when he is maddened by sorrow and a rage in great part just—seems to me a person to whom the epithet is wrongly applied: he is a mere bookman, if you like, limited, ineffectual, mistaken, but quite without the obtrusive conceit, the petty arrogance, of the prig who deserves his name. He tries very hard to do what he ought to do, and, when he feels that he is bringing up his little boy in the wrong way has the courage to confess his error and change his plan. As for his treatment of that awful wife, it seems to me, until he is beside himself with anguish, to be the perfection of consideration and candour; he is always gentle, though he cannot pretend to love her—as who could?— but he treats with absolute justice her plea that she has not the 'maternal instinct.' (A plea which is entirely valid: as entirely as the contention of the thief that he was not 'born honest.')

Some critics, I see, have discovered that Allmers had more than a brother's love for Asta: which seems to me to show an entire misunderstanding of the play—surely the one thing the poor man longs for is to escape from married life, of which his experience has been so miserable, to the old quiet home-keeping of brother and sister.

On the other hand, when I first read the play I had to try very hard indeed to sympathise, even in the least, with the wife: it was as in Macbeth, where the man has always appealed to me completely, while the woman had a tendency to rub me the wrong way—a tendency so exaggerated in this Rita that it required quite a physical effort to calm down, and take her fairly, and understand her side of the question. This, as I think, I succeeded in doing, while I had the book in my hand; but with Miss Achurch before me I failed hopelessly, and from end to end.

It was not that I did not think that the actress played well: she was, indeed, almost at her best, and had conquered nearly all the mannerisms which at one time threatened to outweigh her admirable qualities. Technically, indeed, I thought that there was hardly a fault to be found with her acting, except that there was too much of it; I was reminded of Mr. Bernard Shaw's crushing sentence on Mrs. Kendal—that she acted more in ten minutes than anybody else in an entire play. (I quite believe that this was meant as honest praise; but it was very deadly.)

You see now, perhaps, why the actress put Rita quite outside my sympathetic comprehension. The woman of Ibsen seemed to me at all events simple, and strong in her simplicity: a woman misplaced, who born in the British aristocracy would have gone through her divorce-court at least with a certain sturdiness. But Miss Achurch chose another reading, and one easily to be justified; she made her—shall I say very like the picture of Charles Reade that many of us have drawn for ourselves from his books? That is to say, a being of strong and no doubt genuine passions, but an eternal 'poseur,' for ever acting to him or herself and to other people; and, therefore, an irritation rather than an interest to the onlooker, who resents being invited to look on.

Yet, with what reservation you will, all the latter part of that first act was interesting; and what was essential in the second was more than this—it was enthralling, fascinating, entirely human and right. The talk of the brother and sister at the beginning was an extraordinary and beautiful study of sorrow; the talk between husband and wife was terrible, no doubt, yet not, as I thought, horrible—it was a revelation so fine and so true that it remained art. Of course, there was the reminder of *Thérèse Raquin*, which must almost certainly have suggested this scene; but Ibsen has a redeeming beauty which Zola cannot reach.

With the beginning of the end of Act II, the scene in which the long-found sister declares that she is somebody else, comes the moment for leaving the theatre. I knew that this scene was hopeless, and I feared that the Third Act would play badly; but the dulness of it quite exceeded my warmest anticipations. For the reader, even this final act has a certain beauty; for the hearer—well, there is no hearer, because one cannot listen to it.

Yet I endured to the end, partly out of curiosity, and partly because of the actors. It is now established that one cannot criticise the playing of an Ibsen drama—the author's strength gives an interest to all his people and everybody makes a reputation in Ibsen, not always maintained out of him. As a rule, however, I think it would be not unfair to say that 'the

Master' in England has been acted carefully but not very well: and on Monday the severest criticism upon most of the other actors was the interest which Mr. Lowne always aroused as soon as he came on. He was by no means at his best, and had far and away the most difficult task in the piece; only William Morris—if he was as much superior to Garrick as an eminent critic has told us—could have made this rollicking roadmaker's optimism intelligible to an English audience. This Mr. Lowne did not do; but he avoided the fatal monotony, there was variety in his diction as there is in real life—and oh, the difference to us!

Miss Elizabeth Robins, with a very graceful modesty, took a part of second rank, and played it very sweetly; her personal charm of simple sincerity made of this Asta precisely the lovable being that readers of the play had imagined. Of Mr. Courtenay Thorpe it is really impossible to judge, after this one performance of so highly specialised a kind; but at least he thoroughly understood the lines of Ibsen—and it is no little matter—though he did not, at a first hearing, very greatly interest one. Master Stewart Dawson is the second capital stage-child the year has produced. He was very good on Monday, but not as yet in the same class with Miss Jessica Black, who is still easily the first.

Mrs. Patrick Campbell was a little too picturesque, and lacked the red umbrella on which Ibsen insists—and which, as she typifies Death, obviously symbolises the coroner who was to sit on poor little Eyolf. But she gave to this strange and difficult personage all the weirdness, all the eerie fascination, which she must have if the play is to exist at all; and it is hard to say who else on our stage could have found the character so exactly. Mrs. Patrick Campbell has imagination; and that is the beginning of things, and very nearly the end.

140. 'The Hallucinations of Mr. Clement Scott', a letter to the editor of the *Saturday Review*

26 December 1896, lxxvii

The writer, J. Warschauer, addressed his letter from Exeter College, Oxford, and dated it 24 November 1896.

Sir,—Everybody who knows Mr. Scott—and lives there the man with soul so dead, &c.?—is aware that an Ibsen performance invariably upsets that gentleman's delicate equilibrium. This is as it should be; Mr. Scott's tremendous outbursts on those occasions minister to the gaiety of nations, and for that reason alone one could wish greater fecundity to the Norwegian's slow-bearing Muse. Not unfrequently Mr. Scott's attacks after a dose of Ibsen take the shape of violent hallucinations as to matters, not of taste, but of fact; and the first performance of *Little Eyolf* at the Avenue last Monday was promptly followed by alarming symptoms. Neither in sorrow nor in anger, but merely as a modest contribution to a future psychology of Mr. Scott, I beg your permission to point out one or two of the more extraordinary of the illusions with which Mr. Scott has been recently troubled.

Allmers, the imaginative critic of the *Telegraph* tells us, in that chaste diction of which he is so accomplished a master, 'returns from a solitary scramble up the mountain . . . there to get rid of the terrible suggestion that once upon a time Mrs. Beecher Stowe tried, to the disgust of everybody, to fasten on to Lord Byron.' Will it be credited that not a line in the play lends any colour to the reason Mr. Scott assigns to Allmers's expedition, and that the 'suggestion' which he is trying, 'to the disgust of everybody,' to fasten on to the vacillating ex-tutor is entirely his own?

Further on, Mr. Scott hazards the elegant statement that Allmers and Rita were 'intimately engaged in discussing a probable successor to Little Eyolf.' Again, there is not a shadow of a warrant for this in the

355

play itself, a copy of which I believe lay in front of Mr. Scott during the performance.

But though these misrepresentations be as crimson, yet shall they appear as wool by the side of the egregious assertion that 'after the first act . . . the effect of the so-called play on the audience was sepulchral.' Those who were present at the Avenue on Monday afternoon will not soon forget the prolonged and repeated cheers which greeted the con-clusion of the play—cheers which may or may not have been in exact proportion to the merits of *Little Eyolf*; for my own part I thought them excessive. It is difficult to harmonize this fact with Mr. Scott's impres-sion. Can it be that the loud and persistent calls for Mr. Archer produced a sepulchral effect upon that part of the audience 'of which Mr. Scott was it principally himself' (*sic*)?

Toward the end of his impassioned article the good man's grammar goes the way of his temper and logic; for, speaking of Mr. Thorpe's elocution, he tells us that 'not one word of the inspired sentences were lost.' Weren't it? I lost several, and felt rather annoyed with Mr. Thorpe.

141. Henry James on Ibsen's superiority to Shakespeare

1897

From a review of Irving's *Richard III* and *Little Eyolf* under the heading 'London', by Henry James, *Harper's Weekly* (23 January 1897), xlv, no. 2092, 134–5.

If after this I say that I took, earlier in the month, a lively interest in the production, at the Avenue Theatre, by Miss Elizabeth Robins, of *Little Eyolf*, I shall be quite prepared to hear it asked if I think Ibsen, then, so superior to the Bard of Avon. I am afraid it won't take me long enough even for decency to reply that for the purpose to which he has just been so successfully applied I prefer him a hundred times. I like Shakespeare better—let me hurry to declare—'for reading;' but I like Ibsen better for—Northumberland Avenue; and Northumberland Avenue is after all but a moment's walk from that stronghold of art, the Strand. Ibsen has the merit, not vain for an author of plays, of being at his best in the theatre. He is in our chords, on our scale; he profits, up on the hilt, by the inevitable effort of our time to make the reflection of life, in the different arts, have the look and motion and sound of life. *Little Eyolf* had had to wait two years to come to the London stage; during which I dare say he has had his nine days' run in America, as these are matters in which other countries—countries other than England, I mean—are apt to be quicker on the trigger. It is true that we have at present the promise of all proper quickness in the case of *John Gabriel Borkman*, the four-act piece which embodies the very last bi-ennial revolution—a series unfailing in its regularity and as punctual to a day as the mill of fate—of the wonderful old man of Christiania. Mr. William Archer has just translated it, Mr. Heinemann is about to publish it, and it is shortly to be produced by Miss Robins, who, in England, has rendered Ibsen all the pious service of a priestess of the altar. I have read the play with the sense of a great warming of the critical heart, and I emphasize the prospect because I profess no vagueness as to the fact that it belongs to that very small group of impressions theatri-cal which—as things appear mainly to be going—denote a calculable comfort. The comfort supplied by Ibsen—I use the term in the sense of the 'higher amusement'—springs indeed from more sources than I can now attempt to enumerate, freshly opened as some of them were by the handful of performances of *Little Eyolf*. They began to operate, they always begin, within five or ten minutes of the rise of the curtain —a moment at which this special spectator becomes aware of an adjust-ment of his aesthetic sense as definite as a material 'click.' It is simply the acceptance of the small Ibsen *spell*, the surrender of the imagination to his microcosm, his confined but completely constituted world, in which, in every case, the tissue of relations between the parts and the whole is of a closeness so fascinating. The odd thing—I speak of course from the point of view of my particular stall—is that the fascination appears quite independent either of the merit of the interpretation or of the place held by the play in the Ibsen list. The place of *Little Eyolf* is not of the highest, and even in London, on other occasions, the author has had, on the whole, I think, more acting. Yet prompt to the moment the charm descended—as sharp as ever rang the little silver bell. Let me hope that I shall be able, on the production of *John Gabriel*, to express more arithmetically the mysterious force applied to it. Meanwhile there are other things to do.

JOHN GABRIEL BORKMAN

December 1896

142. An unsigned review, *Saturday Review*

19 December 1896, lxxxii, 654–5

With the regularity with which a star in some huge orrery returns to its appointed place, in the third week of December, in each alternate year Ibsen publishes a play. Friends and enemies agree that this cometary event is one of the most interesting which the two years have to offer in literature. Each time that the great Norwegian reappears there is the fear that he may have gone to pieces in the interim. Can that energy, which has supported him so long, continue, one asks, to inspire him as he approaches his seventieth year? It certainly does; *John Gabriel Borkman* is every whit as powerful a piece of composition as any one of its predecessors. It does not display, at least till its fourth act, the airy fancy of *The Master Builder* or the austere poetry of *Little Eyolf*; its relations are with an earlier section of Ibsen's work, that which began with *The Pillars of Society* and seemed to close with *Hedda Gabler*. With the former play, indeed, *John Gabriel Borkman* has a close analogy. It is a far more coherent and concentrated example of dramatic construction, and aims at a higher psychology; it is coloured by that symbolism which has become part of the bones and marrow of Ibsen. But for purposes of contrast and parallelism alike, the reader will find it agreeable to compare the new satire with *The Pillars of Society* and also with Björnson's curious *bourgeois* drama, *En Fallit (A Bankruptcy)*.

As we take it, *John Gabriel Borkman* is a tragedy of the imaginative spirit concentrated on commercial speculation. Borkman is a man who has risen by his industrial schemes to a very high social position, from which he has fallen into a penal servitude of five years, and a retirement in absolute, humiliating isolation for already eight years more. As befits a Norwegian speculator, the dream of Borkman was to exploit the physical resources of his country, and above all to bring to light its mineral wealth. He sees a Garden of the Hesperides in the bowels of the earth, if so strong an image be permissible, a garden which is longing to drop its golden fruit into the hands of man. The archaic Greek poet Pherecrates wrote a lost comedy of the *Miners*, in which mad men went down to release the spirit of gold in the heart of the world. We know not whether Ibsen ever heard of this Attic comedy, but his conception of Borkman has recalled it to us. All the slumbering spirits of gold, the shrieking millions that cry to be released, these he hears in his dreams, and he longs to free them—by their means to hold the power their mintage would give him. On the character of Borkman, the gigantic swindler, foiled, humiliated, but not wholly cast down, and on the passage of his brain through brooding disappointment to potent insanity, Ibsen has expended his highest efforts.

But this is merely the background to a vivid and almost entertaining drama. When Borkman was condemned, the half-sister of Mrs. Borkman, Ella Rentheim, whose fortune Borkman was found to have left untouched, took the one child, the boy Erhart, to live with her. When the convict left prison, penniless, Miss Rentheim lent to the family a large house of hers outside Christiania. Here, for eight years, husband and wife have contrived never to meet. He inhabits the first floor; she and her son, whom she has taken away from Miss Rentheim, occupy the rooms on the ground floor. Erhart is now twenty-three, and is the object of Mrs. Borkman's most jealous solicitude; Miss Rentheim has never once made up her mind to visit the sinister family of her sister. Borkman's only visitor is Vilhelm Foldal, a copying clerk and poetaster, a figure at once farcical and pathetic, who clings to the man whom he used to worship, although robbed by him of all his savings. Through the whole of the first act, which is played in Mrs. Borkman's drawing-room, the old financier is heard pacing up and down upon the echoing boards above. Mrs. Borkman says:—

'It sometimes seems more than I can endure—always to hear him up there, walking, walking. From the first thing in the morning to the last thing at night. And one hears every step so plainly! I have often felt as if I had a sick wolf up there, prowling up and down in a cage. Right over my head, too! Listen! there he goes. Up and down, up and down, the wolf is prowling.'

During the first act, however, though we are so ingeniously made conscious of the presence and of the disposition of the unseen Borkman, the interest is centred in the duel between the mother and the foster-mother for the love of Erhart. Each in turn has nurtured and guarded him; each fears no other danger for him than the poison of the other's presence; each has an ideal to which she desires him to rise. Mrs. Borkman sees in him the young man who will devote himself to business, will expiate in kind the sins of his father, and will recover for the family name the honour and prestige that it has lost. Ella Rentheim, whom Borkman has loved, and whom he sacrificed long ago to his financial ambition, desires another species of expiation. She thinks that her foster-son, by an infinitude of tender care, may pay back to her the affection of which his father treacherously robbed her. But the young man, so long cloistered and sheltered, will know life at last, and the appeals of his mother for obedience, and those of his foster-mother for affection, nay, even those of his awakening father for support and sympathy in rehabilitating labour, come too late. Erhart is decoyed by life in rosier and more laughing forms than these, and he departs through the snow, bound for southern lands and softer loves. No one is more skilful than Ibsen in these details, and the stage-effect by which these three old figures are left alone, gazing at one another in despair, while Erhart's silver sleigh-bells are heard, more and more distant, fading away through the winter night, should be singularly poignant and effective on the boards.

There is less in *John Gabriel Borkman* than in most of Ibsen's later works to distract the public and give his disciples mysterious airs. But one of the dramatist's old favourite themes returns here with unusual prominence. That Borkman brought vast ruin on the community and destroyed the comfort of thousands is in some measure condoned. With that, at all events, the law of his country has stringently and finally dealt, and in curious ingenuity the man himself is made the plausible defender of his own schemes. He has sailed in a war-balloon over the ranks of the enemy, and if he did not conquer, and therefore has brought calamity on his own people, he meant to conquer, and to raise them all to affluence. This is the habitual excuse of the fraudulent speculator, and Ibsen is doubtless authorized in forcing this aspect of the case upon us. But Ibsen has never seemed to care much for the sorrows of communities; he is an individualist of the purest water, and what brings about the final and spiritual chastisement of Borkman is his sin to the individual Ella. She loved him utterly and he loved her; yet, in order to gain financial power, in order to secure (as he supposed) the victory of his schemes, he abandoned her to a rival. This is the unpardonable fault, this is the 'sin against the Holy Ghost,' for which there can be no atonement made. And so, at last, when the metallic hand, the frosty, brazen fingers of Death, close upon Borkman's heart, in the thrilling final night-scene among the pine-trees and the snow-drifts, it is his peculiar punishment that Ella Rentheim, the grey and dying shadow of the joy which might have been his, confounds his expiring senses by her cruel compassion. It is not his fraudulent offences against society, it is not his ambition and his recklessness, which are the extreme ruin of Borkman; it is the coldness of his heart, his preference for the vague spectres of the hidden gold over the warm and beating bosoms of mankind.

It is announced that Mr. Archer has made arrangements for issuing a translation of this fine dramatic poem. We hope that it will not be long before we have an opportunity of seeing his version acted on the boards of a London theatre. Most of Ibsen's plays remain in part obscure to the reader until they are illuminated by the footlights; no dramatic pieces are less intended for the study. Nor do we expect to appreciate the full force and strangeness of *John Gabriel Borkman* until this opportunity is given us, although we are bound to say that it appears to us to be one of the least 'difficult' plays he has ever written. The evolution of the characters and their correlation are remarkably simple and inevitable. There are no passages—so it seems to us, at least, upon a first reading— which can be construed into having been introduced for the purpose of exciting controversy by their paradoxical effect. The little secondary figure of Frida Foldal, the infantile musical genius, is, it is true, some-what redundant; her disappearance, with Erhart and Mrs. Wilton, is explained by a single sentence which Ibsenite purism might do well, we think, to evade, since it can only be cynically interpreted. But with the exception of this solitary phrase there is not a line or an idea which the most silly person can pretend to misunderstand. *John Gabriel Borkman* ought to present no difficulty whatever to the mildest curate or even to Mr. Clement Scott.

143. From a review by Henry James, *Harper's Weekly*

6 February 1897, xlv, no. 2094, 78

I am afraid the interest of the world of native letters is not at this moment so great as to make us despise mere translation as an aid to curiosity. There is indeed no reason why we should forbear to say in advance what we are certain, every time, to say after (after the heat has cooled, I mean): namely, that nothing is easier to concede than that Ibsen—contentious name!—would be much less remarked if he were one of a dozen. It is impossible, in London at least, to shut one's eyes to the fact that if to so many ingenious minds he is a kind of pictorial monster, a grotesque on the sign of a side-show, this is at least partly because his form has a monstrous rarity. It is one of the odd things of our actual aesthetics that the more theatres multiply the less any one reads a play—the less any one cares, in a word, for the text of the adventure. That no one ever *does* read a play has long been a commonplace of the wisdom of booksellers. Ibsen, however, is a text, and Ibsen is read, and Ibsen contradicts the custom and confounds the prejudice; with the effect thereby, in an odd way, of being doubly an exotic. His violent substance imposes, as it were, his insidious form; it is not (as would have seemed more likely) the form that imposes the substance. Mr. William Archer has just published his version of *John Gabriel Borkman*, of which, moreover, French and German versions reach us at the same moment. There are therefore all the elements of a fresh breeze in the wind—one has already a sense as of a cracking of whips and a girding of loins. You may by this time be terribly tired of it all in America; but, as I mentioned a fortnight ago, we have had very recent evidence that languor here, in this connection, is by no means as yet the dominant note. It is not the dispute itself, however, that most interests me: let me pay it, for what it has been and what it still may be, the mere superficial tribute of saying that it constitutes one of the very few cases of contagious discussion of a matter not political, a question not of mere practice, of which I remember to have felt, in a heavy air, the engaging titillation. In London, generally, I think, the wandering breath of criticism is the stray guest at the big party—the shy young man whom nobody knows. In this remarkable instance the shy young man has ventured to pause and hover, has lighted on a topic, introduced himself and, after a gasp of consternation in the company, seen a little circle gather round him. I can only speak as one of the little circle, testifying to my individual glee.

The author who at the age of seventy, a provincial of provincials, turns out *John Gabriel* is frankly for me so much one of the peculiar pleasures of the day, one of the current strong sensations, that, erect as he seems still to stand, I deplore his extreme maturity and, thinking of what shall happen, look round in vain for any other possible source of the same kind of emotion. For Ibsen strikes me as an extraordinary curiosity, and every time he sounds his note the miracle, to my perception, is renewed. I call it a miracle because it is a result of so dry a view of life, so indifferent a vision of the comedy of things. His idea of the thing represented is never the comic idea, though this is evidently what it often only can be for many of his English readers and spectators. Comedy moreover is a product mainly of observation, and I scarcely know what to say of his figures except that they haven't the *signs*. The answer to that is doubtless partly that they haven't the English, but have the Norwegian. In such a case one of the Norwegian must be in truth this very lack of signs.

They have no tone but their moral tone. They are highly animated abstractions, with the extraordinary, the brilliant property of becoming when represented at once more abstract and more living. If the spirit is a lamp within us, glowing through what the world and the flesh make of us as through a ground-glass shade, then such pictures as *Little Eyolf* and *John Gabriel* are each a *chassez-croisez* of lamps burning, as in tasteless parlours, with the flame practically exposed. There are no shades in the house, or the Norwegian ground-glass is singularly clear. There is a positive odour of spiritual paraffin. The author nevertheless arrives at the dramatist's great goal—he arrives for all his meagreness at intensity. The meagreness, which is after all but an unconscious, an admirable economy, never interferes with that: it plays straight into the hands of his rare mastery of form. The contrast between this form—so difficult to have reached, so civilized, so 'evolved,'—and the bareness and bleakness of his little northern democracy is the source of half the hard frugal charm that he puts forth. In the cold fixed light of it the notes that we speak of as deficiencies take a sharp value in the picture. There is no small-talk, there are scarcely any manners. On the other hand there is so little vulgarity that this of itself has almost the effect of a deeper, a more lonely provincialism. The background at any rate is the sunset over the ice. Well in the very front of the scene lunges with extraordinary length of arm the Ego against Ego, and rocks in a rigour of passion the soul against the soul—a spectacle, a movement, as definite as the relief of silhouettes in black paper or of a train of Eskimo dogs on the snow. Down from that desolation the sturdy old symbolist comes this time with a supreme example of his method. It is a high wonder and pleasure to welcome such splendid fruit from sap that might by now have shown something of the chill of age. Never has he juggled more gallantly with difficulty and danger than in this really prodigious *John Gabriel*, in which a great span of tragedy is taken between three or four persons—a trio of the grim and grizzled—in the two or three hours of a winter's evening; in which the whole thing throbs with an actability that fairly shakes us as we read; and in which, as the very flower of his artistic triumph, he has given us for the most beautiful and touching of his heroines a sad old maid of sixty. Such 'parts,' even from the vulgarest point of view, are Borkman and Ella Rentheim! But about all this there will inevitably be much more to say when the play is produced.

144. From a notice by 'H.W.M.', *Daily Chronicle*

4 May 1897, 8

William Archer's translation of *John Gabriel Borkman* was performed at the Strand Theatre on 3 May 1897 and the cast was as follows:

John Gabriel Borkman		Mr W. H. Vernon
Mrs Borkman	..	Miss Genevieve Ward
Erhart Borkman	..	Mr Martin Harvey
Ella Rentheim	..	Miss Elizabeth Robins
Mrs Wilton	..	Mrs Beerbohm Tree
Vilhelm Foldal	..	Mr James Welch
Frida Foldal	..	Miss Dora Barton
Maid	..	Miss Marianne Caldwell

The New Century Theatre has begun its career modestly and simply enough; but it has already put to its credit perhaps the best representation of an Ibsen play which has yet been given to the English world. It has had the double good fortune of starting with a very strong cast and a very great play. I do not know that Ibsen grows into a mightier dramatist as age comes upon him; but he does certainly refine and simplify his technique until he seems to approach nearer and nearer to the classic model. *John Gabriel Borkman* is a study of life within singularly narrow limits, though it opens up the heights and goes down into the depths of most of the things that we call the nature of men and women. The Borkmans are like the Atridæ—a fate-doomed family. Within their circle move all the great passions—hate, love and self-love, pride, remorse, madness. Yet it is all modern enough. The hero is a swindling financier. The women, I suppose, will be called neurotic emblems, though they looked to me to be rather more normal than Clytemnestra or Lady Macbeth. But say what you will of Ibsen, there is one thing that not even the sternest moralists—who seem to be mainly the dramatic critics of the sporting papers—can deny about him: He shows the artist at his (or her) best. I observed Mr. Tree in the theatre, fresh from *The Seats of the Mighty*. I have not the slightest idea that Mr. Tree went to the Strand in order to sit in the seat of the scorner. But I wonder whether he, as an experienced and ambitious manager, put to himself the question why it is that everybody who plays Ibsen, straightaway becomes an actor of genius. In the cast of *John Gabriel Borkman* are included many delightful and accomplished artists; but how they play into each others' hands, how they delight in the liberal speech, how they fit themselves to the poetic atmosphere! I suppose it is because— poor untutored souls—they cannot help themselves. For it is clear that they are quite acclimatised, while their benighted critics sit shivering in their stalls. . . .

But in Ibsen no one thinks over-much of the form. It is the idea, the moving force, the intelligence working with unfailing knowledge of its medium, that affects you. And perhaps the most notable point in Ibsen's plays is that you come straight on old great thoughts presented in so new a dress that your average English audience, fed on the insipidities of modern drama, does not recognise them. I heard one or two persons titter when Ella Rentheim brings home to Borkman the nature of his sin—'You killed the love-life in me.' Did no one think of the offence against 'one of these little ones'—the offence which bars Borkman out even of the dream-kingdom that he had built up for himself? Or take that kingdom—with its 'power' and its 'glory.' Borkman is a 'criminal'; but he has done nothing more than take the 'kingdoms of the earth' for his province; a modern alchemist, he would transmute all the affections, the aspirations, the efforts of mankind, into one great material fabric, coveting for himself only the fame of architect. There is nothing mean about this castle-builder; only true Napoleonic unscrupulousness and recklessness. Truly a great and tragic figure; the tragedy of modern money-making, so presented as to sink deep into the ears of him who has ears to hear.

It is not because you see in John Gabriel a figure of great dignity, of notable power—most finely and subtly indicated by Mr. Vernon—that you miss the significance of his fall. But he is, after all, only one of a group—a family group—of victims of illusion. The Borkman-Rentheims all have their besetting passion. Their figures, even in their shadowy decline and passage into the land of shadows, are all passionately immersed in their pursuit of their own temperament, their own point of self-absorption. But note how subtly the distinctions between these characters are graded. Mrs. Borkman has her 'honourable' illusion, the restoration of the family name, disgraced by Borkman's imprisonment. And the sacrifice on her particular altar is the life of her son, Erhart.

Ella Rentheim is devoted to a milder worship, the building up again of the place in her own heart which Borkman's apostasy has left vacant. She at least has chosen the better part, which will not be altogether taken away from her. Borkman, again, hears nothing but the humming of the mill-wheels, the whirring of the bands in the factories, the tinkling of the miners' axes against the metal, which stopped when 'he died.' And all these idealists fasten on young Borkman and call on him to fulfil their broken lives for them. 'Live for me!' cries the mother. 'No, for me!' says Ella Rentheim. 'No, for me,' pleads Borkman. 'I will live for none of you—only for myself and for happiness,' answers the young man, true slip of such a tree. How exactly this dramatic idea works out; with what touches of irony, what play of diverse character and whim, you had better go to the Strand Theatre to see.

145. From an unsigned notice by Clement Scott, *Daily Telegraph*

4 May 1897, 8

It was a relief to get out of the gloomy atmosphere of Ibsen, charged to the full with the Scandinavian spirit of sublimated selfishness, and moans and groans and wrecked lives and defiant egotism! It was a treat to leave a grim and darkened theatre and to meet healthy, cheery, buoyant life again in the Strand, where it was all bustle and activity, and boys were shouting about cricket and exhibiting placards and tempting one to the study of Abel's score at the birth of the season. But the Ibsenites issuing forth in a mournful throng were not to be influenced by light of life, or air or nature. They could not forget the text of *John Gabriel Borkman*, which they had faithfully committed to memory. Said one subscriber to the New Century Theatre, 'It's true that nothing new happens; but what has happened does not repeat itself either. It's the eye that transforms the action. (Breaking off) But you don't understand this.' To which the Philistine replied, 'No, I don't understand it.'

Whereupon the disciple in true Ibsenite language permeated with egoism cut the conversation short with the curt remark, 'Ah! that's just the
curse. I have never found one single soul to understand me!'

The same remark is appropriate to the curious play under discussion.
To it may be applied the stereotyped formula that 'it reads far better
than it acts.' In reading the play there are certain scenes that are stimulating and interesting. These same scenes when acted become trivial or
commonplace, depressing or dull. The last of all, the union of the two
sad women over the dead body of their selfish hero is tragedy illumined
with poetry. It rings in the ears and haunts one like Little Eyolf's crutch.
It is a sad antiphonal wail that the reader cannot get out of his ears.

> We twin sisters—over him we both loved,
> We two shadows—over the dead man.

But in the play as acted these illumined touches come like flash lights
in such a dull morass of tedium that it requires actors of the greatest
experience and tact to make them felt or to divorce them from ridicule.
Luckily, those actors and actresses were present yesterday, and they
certainly with heroic effort gave occasional life and colour to the very
dullest and most deplorably monotonous of all the Ibsen plays yet seen
in London.

Remember, we are not discussing *John Gabriel Borkman* as a study in
literature; we make no comments on it as a book for the library or the
bed-room fireside; we are not attempting to deny that it contains many
a horrible truth and many a poem in prose. We are discussing it now as
a stage play, as a work framed for and invented for the theatre, as a
something that is to revolutionise our old-fashioned, obsolete, ridiculous, and conventional forms of dramatic art. As such we have no
hesitation in saying that it is perfectly useless, perhaps the worst possible
specimen of the master's theory, the greatest 'swashing' blow to the
disciple's faith. It fails in that important essential which the drama,
viewed in any light, imperatively demands—contrast. A play is not a
bad play because it contains one bad man or a dozen, one vile woman or
twenty; it may be a very good play in which evil overwhelms good.
But it must have contrast. Viewed as works of art, goody-goody or
ultra-sentimental plays are as indefensible as plays of pure pessimism and
mental as well as moral disease. But they cannot interest if they harp on
one string and ring eternally the old tune. Contrast and variety they
must have.

We do not suppose that Scandinavia is more prone to selfishness, or egotism, or defiant bluster than any other country on the face of the globe. And yet Dr. Ibsen would make us believe that it is. Human nature is seemingly obliterated in the land of the midnight sun. Let us take the characters in the play. John Gabriel Borkman, formerly managing director of a bank, caught red-handed in fraud, guilty of unjustifiable acts of peculation, sent to prison after having ruined the widow and orphan and beggared his own family, comes out of gaol to boast about his power, his ambition, his defiance of society, and prates about self and what he intended to do for his fellow-creatures and humanity with misery strewn before his very eyes. Pecksniff is a joke in moral obliquity and turpitude to the Danish banker. Next comes Mrs. Borkman, hard, cold, pitiless, unforgiving, unwomanly, and fiendish in most of her actions, but redeemed alone by her insane and animal love for her son, whom she would ruin and incarcerate and drive to desperation, killing the very 'love life' in him as surely as the 'love life' was slaughtered in her twin sister by the fraudulent and impudently defiant banker. She is a King Lear in petticoats. Then we have the maiden aunt who does not care how much her sister's heart bleeds, her twin sister, which makes matters worse, if she can only rob her of her whelp and cub. Wealth and power and the gift of charity are bestowed on Ella Rentheim in order that she may assert herself in a house which, as it stands, is a 'hell on earth,' and maunder over a wrecked life and a miserable existence. No one can have very much sympathy with the grey-haired maiden aunt, whose love and idolatry far more resemble vulgar revenge than any other feeling. The selfishness of Mrs. Fanny Wilton, who seduces the cub of the household, assumes a more arrogantly nasty tone. She has made up her mind to elope with the petted and passionate boy, and to provide him with a new mistress in case they do not get on together. The boy's mother, with a malignant smile, asks the seductive Fanny a very plain question—'Mrs. Wilton, do you think you are acting wisely in taking that girl with you?' Fanny is frankness itself. She returns the smile 'half ironically, half seriously,' and thus delivers herself: 'Men are so unstable, Mrs. Borkman; and women, too. When Erhart is done with me—and I with him—then it will be well for us both that he, poor fellow, should have someone to fall back upon.' But Mrs. Borkman is still unsatisfied, and asks, 'But you yourself?' Whereupon the flippant lady in the ermine tippet and jelly-bag cap replies, 'Oh! I shall know what to do, I assure you. Goodbye to you all.' So off she starts to inaugurate the *ménage a trois*. The selfishness of Erhart, when he cuts himself adrift from this hideous household, breaks his mother's heart, snubs his dying aunt, and ignores his father's claim to any consideration, is as defiant as it is unjustifiable. Even the Ibsen audience, untrue to their faith and principles, applauded him to the echo. Here we had sympathy at last when Erhart shouted out, 'I am young. I want to live for once in a way as well as other people. I want to live my own life. I don't want to work now, for I am young. That's what I never realised before, but now the knowledge is tingling through every vein in my body. I will not work! I will live, live, live!' And the audience broke out in passionate approval, not knowing or feeling that Erhart was in reality the symbol of the 'old play,' demanding to be heard once more in this desert of dreariness. Here we had commonsense and nature at last, and the first gleam of both in this dreary afternoon, save when poor old Foldal, the clerk, owned to writing plays, but acknowledged that the fact made no impression whatever on his family, and then proposed to read a five-act tragedy to the ex-convict, which proposal was rejected with the air of a Turveydrop. This was the only sign of selfishness in this mournful Ibsenite Tom Pinch. Selfishness did not even end with the maid who, aroused out of bed for an urgent mission, refused to go two steps without a covered sledge, and ended with attempting to turn poor John Gabriel and his dying Ella off their own amalgamated doorstep. It was certainly an object lesson in 'self' all round.

146. From an unsigned notice, *Era*

8 May 1897, 13

If *John Gabriel Borkman* is an example of Ibsen's latest manner, and that manner is to be his last, folks will soon come to regard the production of one of his plays with indifference. *Ghosts* would have passed quietly out of the ken of the ordinary public had not certain passages in the play excited the horrified wrath of the decent-minded critics. In *A Doll's House* there was the hotly debateable question, 'Ought Nora to have left her children?' and the indelicacy of her jokes about the stockings with Doctor Rank. Even in *Little Eyolf* there was the scandal of a man and his wife on the stage wrangling as to what we may euphemistically term 'conjugal rights.' All these things 'boomed' Ibsen exceedingly. Before *Little Eyolf* there was *The Master Builder*. Here we had the absolute incomprehensibility of many passages—appearing to the ordinary mind as drivelling foolishness; and the poor lady's distress about her dolls. More opportunity for argument. In connection with a play in which one set of critics can see nothing but folly and beastliness, and another only poetry and psychology, there is certain to be plenty of fun—for a time. But what fun is to be got out of a piece like *John Gabriel Borkman*, which was produced at the Strand Theatre last Monday afternoon? It is simply a heavy, gloomy, domestic drama, overladened with pretentiously serious dialogue, and concluding with an act of absolute absurdity. . . .

However it may strike others, this last act of *John Gabriel Borkman* simply appeared to us a tale told by a lunatic, full of words and phrases signifying nothing.

The action above described is padded out with long, tedious discussions and wordy arguments, Borkman justifying his financial swindles on the grounds that he is 'built that way', and that his dishonesty was only a proof of strong individuality; Ella denouncing Borkman for having slain her love-life, and Erhart effusively proclaiming his youth and his right to 'live.' To Erhart we are indebted for one of the rare gleams of humour which irradiated the gloomy afternoon. When, referring to Mrs. Wilton's husband, he cried 'Yes, mother, he is dead to Fanny!' the house roared.

We have recently done justice to the good points of Ibsen's works, to the vividness of some of his characterisations to the power exercised by him at times of interesting us in the souls of his personages; but no associations shall prevent our describing *John Gabriel Borkman* as a dull lifeless play. It does not move, it does not touch, it does not interest. Who can care deeply what becomes of this hard-hearted harridan, this inveterately conceited old swindler, this moribund twin-sister, this fatuous little 'bounder' with his vapourings about his youth and his determination to live his own life? We may sympathise, perhaps, with poor little Foldal, though his theories about friendship are of the most pessimistic sort; but—to speak bluntly—Borkman, Mrs. B., Ella Rentheim, and the rest are bores—solemn, portentous, oppressive bores. It was with a sense of intense thankfulness that we saw the act-drop descend for the last time at the Strand Theatre on Monday afternoon, and knew that the gloomy, wearisome performance was over and done with.

147. From an unsigned notice, *Lloyd's Weekly News*

9 May 1897, 6

In this piece Ibsen has continued his studies of the seamy side of human nature. Selfishness, egotism, uncharitableness, and obstinacy are so determinedly dwelt upon that not a gleam of sunshine is allowed to illumine the dark picture of a household the occupants of which are at cross purposes. The piece opens and ends in the gloomiest fashion. It virtually consists of a series of recriminations of an unedifying description, and a genuinely dramatic element is only conspicuous by its absence. In the title part—a cross-grained individual, who, after a lengthy imprisonment for a breach of trust that has ruined many families, considers that he is still indispensable to the welfare of the world— Mr. W. Vernon played with his accustomed strength, and Miss Genevieve Ward acted finally as a harsh, uncompromising woman, with love dead for everybody but her son. Mrs. Tree effectively represented a volatile lady, who carries off a headstrong lad, but takes the precaution to have at hand a very young girl to whom she purposes transferring her lover when she has tired of him. Miss Elizabeth Robins appeared as a long-suffering spinster, Mr. James Welch as a semi-senile old gentleman, and Mr. Martin Harvey as the infatuated youth. Except to the Ibsen worshippers, of whom there was a large muster, *John Gabriel Borkman* was dull and depressing.

148. From an unsigned notice, *People*

9 May 1897, 6

The bombastic egotist who gives its title to the piece is a defrauding bank official, who, released after serving his sentence from durance vile, returns home to pace like a Polar bear day and night to and fro in his chamber, growling at society for fettering him by his imprisonment and consequent degradation from the exercise of the stupendous genius he lays claim to, and by the free exercise of which he would become the saviour of society. This conceited monomaniac has living with him, together with the wife he worries, a sister-in-law, no less eccentric than himself—her craze finding vent in denunciation of Borkman for having married her twin sister instead of herself, thereby robbing her, as she truculently asserts, of all the precious delights of wifehood and maternity, especially maternity. The Borkmans have a son who, cub, as he shows himself to be, is at least natural in his vices. Seduced by a widow of easy virtue, his mistress in her way is as peculiar as the rest of this curious household; for, in levanting with the youth, she arranges to take with them a girl to act as a second mistress for her lover when, his lustful passion spent, he shall become tired of herself. The play closes with the suicide of Borkman, and the women, his savage wife and her salacious sister, left crooning, as they wail at the fall of the curtain over his corpse.

149. George Bernard Shaw on
A Doll's House

1897

From 'A Doll's House Again', an initialled review by George
Bernard Shaw, *Saturday Review* (15 May 1897), 539-41. The per-
formance was a revival by Janet Achurch at the Globe Theatre, 10
May 1897.

At last I am beginning to understand anti-Ibsenism. It must be that I
am growing old and weak and sentimental and foolish; for I cannot
stand up to reality as I did once. Eight years ago, when Mr. Charrington,
with *A Doll's House*, struck the decisive blow for Ibsen—perhaps the only
one that has really got home in England as yet—I rejoiced in it, and
watched the ruin and havoc it made among the idols and temples of the
idealists as a young war correspondent watches the bombardment of the
unhealthy quarters of a city. But now I understand better what it means
to the unhappy wretches who can conceive no other life as possible to
them except the Doll's House life. The master of the Doll's House may
endure and even admire himself as long as he is called King Arthur and
prodigiously flattered; but to paint a Torvald Helmer for him, and
leave his conscience and his ever-gnawing secret diffidence to whisper
'Thou art the man' when he has perhaps outlived all chance of being
any other sort of man, must be bitter and dreadful to him. Dr. Rank,
too, with his rickets and his scrofula, no longer an example, like Herod,
of the wrath of God, or a curiosity to be stared at as villagers stare at a
sheep with two heads, but a matter-of-fact completion of the typical
picture of family life by one of the inevitable congenital invalids, or
drunkards, or lunatics whose teeth are set on edge because their fathers
have eaten sour grapes: this also is a horror against which an agony of
protest may well be excused.

It will be remarked that I no longer dwell on the awakening of the
woman, which was once the central point of the controversy as it is the
central point of the drama. Why should I? The play solves that problem

just as it is being solved in real life. The woman's eyes are opened; and instantly her doll's dress is thrown off and her husband left staring at her, helpless, bound thenceforth either to do without her (an alternative which makes short work of his fancied independence) or else treat her as a human being like himself, fully recognizing that he is not a creature of one superior species, Man, living with a creature of another and inferior species, Woman, but that Mankind is male and female, like other kinds, and that the inequality of the sexes is literally a cock and bull story, certain to end in such unbearable humiliation as that which our suburban King Arthurs suffer at the hands of Ibsen. The ending of the play is not on the face of it particularly tragic: the alleged 'note of interrogation' is a sentimental fancy; for it is clear that Helmer is brought to his senses, and that Nora's departure is no claptrap 'Farewell for ever,' but a journey in search of self-respect and apprenticeship to life. Yet there is an underlying solemnity caused by a fact that the popular instinct has divined: to wit, that Nora's revolt is the end of a chapter of human history. The slam of the door behind her is more momentous than the cannon of Waterloo or Sedan, because when she comes back, it will not be to the old home; for when the patriarch no longer rules, and the 'breadwinner' acknowledges his dependence, there is an end of the old order; and an institution upon which so much human affection and suffering have been lavished, and about which so much experience of the holiest right and bitterest wrong has gathered, cannot fall without moving even its destroyers, much more those who believe that its extirpation is a mortal wound to society. This moment of awe and remorse in *A Doll's House* was at first lightened by the mere Women's Rights question. Now that this no longer distracts us, we feel the full weight of the unsolved destiny of our Helmers, our Krogstads, our Ranks and our Rank ancestors, whom we cannot, like the Heavenly Twin, dispose of by breaking their noses and saying, 'Take that, you father of a speckled toad.'

150. From an unsigned notice, *Theatre*

1 June 1897, xxix, 335–7

John Gabriel Borkman, the latest of Ibsen's plays, possesses all the characteristics of its author's work. It is dull, tedious, depressing, at times even ludicrous. The writer's views of life remain unchanged. The lightness and sweetness to be found in the world he persistently ignores; towards what is mean and ignoble he is drawn as inevitably as the needle to the pole. Now, the true dramatist is ever the first to recognise that the very essence of a play is contrast, that no picture can really offer a fair presentment of nature unless light and shade figure in it. This fact Ibsen seems determined altogether to disregard. His vocabulary begins and ends with the word 'pessimism.' The people he treats of are all touched with the same brush; they move in an atmosphere of moral degradation; their motives are selfish, their impulses evil. Of the eight characters who appear in *John Gabriel Borkman*, there is only one who has the slightest title to our sympathy, and even he is such a poor, weak fool that pity is changed into contempt. Censure, however, does not stop here. Judged merely from the standpoint of dramatic workmanship, Ibsen's last play is but an indifferent affair. The first two acts are almost entirely retrospective, and when at length the action begins to progress its development is diverted from the direct line and becomes complicated with uninteresting and puerile details. In Borkman the author has imagined a character that, adequately handled, might have formed the pivot of a great drama. Unfortunately, he has missed the opportunity thus created by himself, and, in place of a powerful, commanding figure, he gives us a querulous, impotent misanthrope, who poses with the exaggerated affectations of a Mantalini and utters the mock heroics of a Digby Grand.

151. Bernard Shaw watches Queen Victoria and the Archbishop of Canterbury watch *Ghosts*

'Ghosts at the Jubilee', initialled review by George Bernard Shaw, *Saturday Review* (3 July 1897), 12–14. This performance was a revival of the play by the Independent Theatre. It was staged at the Queen's Gate Hall, South Kensington, on 24, 25 and 26 June 1897, and is memorable for the attendance of the Queen in her Jubilee Year. The play was still banned. (See Introduction.)

The Jubilee and Ibsen's *Ghosts*! On the one hand the Queen and the Archbishop of Canterbury: on the other, Mrs. Alving and Pastor-Manders. Stupendous contrast! how far reflected in the private consciousness of those two august persons there is no means of ascertaining. For though of all the millions for the nourishment of whose loyalty the Queen must submit to be carried through the streets from time to time, not a man but is firmly persuaded that her opinions and convictions are exact facsimiles of his own, none the less she, having seen much of men and affairs, may quite possibly be a wise woman and worthy successor of Canute, and no mere butt for impertinent and senseless Jubilee odes such as their perpetrators dare not, for fear of intolerable domestic scorn and ridicule, address to their own wives or mothers. I am myself cut off by my profession from Jubilees; for loyalty in a critic is corruption. But if I am to avoid idolizing kings and queens in the ordinary human way, I must carefully realize them as fellow-creatures. And so, whilst the nation was burning war incense in a thousand cannons before the throne at Spithead, I was wondering, on my way home from *Ghosts*, how far life had brought to the Queen the lessons it brought to Mrs. Alving. For Mrs. Alving is not anybody in particular: she is a typical figure of the experienced, intelligent woman who, in passing from the first to the last quarter of the hour of history called the nineteenth century, has discovered how appallingly opportunities were wasted, morals perverted, and instincts corrupted, not only—sometimes not at all—by the vices she was taught to abhor in her youth, but by the virtues it was her pride and uprightness to maintain.

Suppose, then, the Queen were to turn upon us in the midst of our jubilation, and say, 'My Lords and Gentlemen: You have been good enough to describe at great length the changes made during the last sixty years in science, art, politics, dress, sport, locomotion, newspapers, and everything else that men chatter about. But have you not a word to say about the change that comes home most closely to me? I mean the change in the number, the character, and the intensity of the lies a woman must either believe or pretend to believe before she can graduate in polite society as a well-brought-up lady.' If Her Majesty could be persuaded to give a list of these lies, what a document it would be! Think of the young lady of seventy years ago, systematically and piously lied to by parents, governesses, clergymen, servants, everybody; and slapped, sent to bed, or locked up in the bedevilled and beghosted dark at every rebellion of her common sense and natural instinct against sham religion, sham propriety, sham decency, sham knowledge, and sham ignorance. Surely every shop-window picture of 'the girl Queen' of 1837 must tempt the Queen of 1897 to jump out of her carriage and write up under it, 'Please remember that there is not a woman earning twenty-four shillings a week as a clerk to-day who is not ten times better educated than this unfortunate girl was when the crown dropped on her head, and left her to reign by her mother wit and the advice of a parcel of men who to this day have not sense enough to manage a Jubilee, let alone an Empire, without offending everybody.' Depend on it, seventy-eight years cannot be lived through without finding out things that queens do not mention in Adelphi melodramas. Granted that the Queen's consort was not a Chamberlain Alving, and that the gaps made in a wide, numerous and robust posterity are too few for even Ibsen to see in the dissoluteness of the ancestors of the First Gentleman in Europe any great menace to the longevity of their descendants; still nineteenth-century life, however it may stage-manage itself tragically and sensationally here, or settle itself happily and domestically there, is yet all of one piece; and it is possible to have better luck than Mrs. Alving without missing all her conclusions.

Let us therefore guard ourselves against the gratuitous, but just now very common, assumption that the Queen, in her garnered wisdom and sorrow, is as silly as the noisiest of her subjects, who see in their ideal Queen the polar opposite of Mrs. Alving, and who are so far right that the spirit of *Ghosts* is unquestionably the polar opposite of the spirit of the Jubilee. The Jubilee represents the nineteenth century proud of itself. *Ghosts* represents it loathing itself. And how it *can* loathe itself when it gets tired of its money! Think of Schopenhauer and Shelley, Lassalle and Karl Marx, Ruskin and Carlyle, Morris and Wagner and Ibsen. How fiercely they rent the bosom that bore them! How they detested all the orthodoxies, and respectabilities, and ideals we have just been bejubilating! Of all their attacks, none is rasher or fiercer than *Ghosts*. And yet, like them all, it is perfectly unanswerable. Many generations have laughed at comedies like *L'Etourdi*, and repeated that hell is paved with good intentions; but never before have we had the well-brought-up, high-minded nineteenth-century lady and her excellent clergyman as the mischief-makers. With them the theme, though still in its essence comic, requires a god to laugh at it. To mortals who may die of such blundering it is tragic and ghastly.

The performance of *Ghosts* by the Independent Theatre Society left the two previous productions by the same society far behind. As in the case of *The Wild Duck*, all obscurity vanished; and Ibsen's clearness, his grip of his theme, and the rapidity, directness and intensity of the action of the piece produced the effect they can always be depended on to produce in capable hands, such as Mr. Charrington's, so far alone among those of Ibsenite stage-managers, have proved to be. Mrs. Theodore Wright's Mrs. Alving, originally an achievement quite beyond the culture of any other actress of her generation, is still hardly less peculiar to her. Mrs. Wright's technique is not in the least that of the Ibsen school. Never for a moment would you suspect her of having seen Miss Janet Achurch or any one remotely resembling her. She is unmistakably a contemporary of Miss Ellen Terry. When I first saw her act she was playing Beatrice in *Much Ado About Nothing*, with a charm and intuition that I have not seen surpassed, and should not have seen equalled if I had never seen Miss Terry wasting her gifts on Shakespeare. As it happened, Mrs. Theodore Wright, perhaps because she was so fond of acting that the stage, where there is less opportunity for it than anywhere else in England, bored her intolerably, found her way behind the scenes of the revolutionary drama of the century at a time when the happy ending now in progress had not been reached, and played Shakespeare and recited Shelley, Hood and George Eliot before Karl Marx, Morris, Bradlaugh and other volcanic makers of the difference between 1837 and 1897, as proudly as Talma played to his pit of kings. Her authors, it will be seen, were not so advanced as her audiences; but that could not be helped, as the progressive movement in England had not produced a dramatist; and nobody then dreamt of Norway, or knew that Ibsen had begun the drama of struggle and emancipation, and had declared that the really effective progressive forces of the moment were the revolt of the working classes against economic, and of the women against idealistic, slavery. Such a drama, of course, immediately found out that weak spot in the theatrical profession which Duse put her finger on the other day in Paris—the so-called stupidity of the actors and actresses. Stupidity, however, is hardly the word. Actors and actresses are clever enough on the side on which their profession cultivates them. What is the matter with them is the characteristic narrowness and ignorance of their newly conquered conventional respectability. They are now neither above the commonplaces of middle-class idealism, like the aristocrat and poet, nor below them, like the vagabond and Bohemian. The theatre has become very much what the Dissenting chapel used to be: there is not a manager in London, who in respect of liberality and enlightenment of opinion, familiarity and sympathy with current social questions, can be compared with the leaders of Nonconformity. Take Sir Henry Irving and Dr. Clifford for example. The *Dissenter* is a couple of centuries ahead of the actor: indeed, the comparison seems absurd, so grotesquely is it to the disadvantage of the institution which still imagines itself the more cultured and less prejudiced of the two. And, but for Mr. Henry Arthur Jones, the authors would cut as poor a figure from this point of view as the actors. Duse advises actors to read; but of what use is that? They *do* read—more than is good for them. They read the drama, and are eager students of criticism, though they would die rather than confess as much to a critic. (Whenever an actor tells me, as he invariably does, that he has not seen any notices of his performance, I always know that he has the *Saturday Review* in his pocket; but I respect the delicacy of an evasion which is as instinctive and involuntary as blushing.) When the drama loses its hold on life, and criticism is dragged down with it, the actor's main point of intellectual contact with the world is cut off; for he reads nothing else with serious attention. He then has to spin his culture out of his own imagination or that of the dramatist and critics, a facile but delusive process which leaves him nothing real to fall back on but his technical craft, which may make him a good workman, but nothing else.

If even technical craft became impossible at such a period—say through the long run and the still longer tour destroying the old training without replacing it by a new one—then the gaps in the actor's cultivation and the corresponding atrophied patches in his brain would call almost for a Mission for his Intellectual Reclamation. Something of this kind might have happened in our own time—I am not sure that a few cases of it did not actually happen—if Ibsen had not come to the rescue. At all events, things had gone so far that the reigning generation of actor-managers were totally incapable of understanding Ibsen: his plays were not even grammar and spelling to them, much less drama. That what they found there was the life of their own time; that its ideas had been seething round their theatres for years past; that they themselves, chivalrously 'holding up the banner of the ideal' in the fool's paradise of theatrical romance and sentiment, had served Ibsen, as they formerly served Goethe, as reductions-to-absurdity of that divorce of the imagined life from the real which is the main peril of an age in which everybody is provided with the means of substituting reading and romancing for real living: all this was quite outside their comprehension. To them the new phenomenon was literally 'the Ibsen craze,' a thing bound to disappear whilst they were rubbing their eyes to make sure that they saw the absurd monster clearly. But that was exactly Mrs. Theodore Wright's opportunity. A lady who had talked over matters with Karl Marx was not to be frightened by Pastor Manders. She created Mrs. Alving as easily, sympathetically, and intelligently as Miss Winifred Emery or Miss Kate Rorke will create the heroine of the next adaptation from the French drama of 1840 by Mr. Grundy; and by that one step she walked over the heads of the whole profession, I cannot say into the first intellectual rank as an English actress, because no such rank then existed, but into a niche in the history of the English stage the prominence of which would, if they could foresee it, very considerably astonish those who think that making history is as easy as making knights. (The point of this venomous allusion will not be missed. It is nothing to be a knight-actor now that there are two of them. When will Sir Henry Irving bid for at least a tiny memorial inscription in the neighbourhood of Mrs .Theodore Wright's niche?)

The remarkable success of Mr. Courtenay Thorpe in Ibsen parts in London lately, and the rumours as to the sensation created by his Oswald Alving in America, gave a good deal of interest to his first appearance here in that part. He has certainly succeeded in it to his heart's content, though this time his very large share of the original sin of picturesqueness and romanticism broke out so strongly that he borrowed little from realism except its pathologic horrors. Since Miss Robins's memorable exploit in *Alan's Wife* we have had nothing so harrowing on the stage; and it should be noted, for guidance in future experiments in audience torture, that in both instances the limit of the victims' susceptibility was reached before the end of the second act, at which exhaustion produced callousness. Mrs. Alving, who spared us by making the best of her sorrows instead of the worst of them, preserved our sympathy up to the last; but Oswald, who showed no mercy, might have been burnt alive in the orphanage without a throb of compassion. Mr. Leonard Outram improved prodigiously on his old impersonation of Pastor Manders. In 1891 he was still comparatively fresh from the apprenticeship as a heroic rhetorical actor which served him so well when he played Valence to Miss Alma Murray's Colombe for the Browning Society; and his stiff and cautious performance probably meant nothing but cleverly concealed bewilderment. This time Mr. Outram really achieved the character, though he would probably please a popular audience better by making more of that babyish side of him which excites the indulgent affection of Mrs. Alving, and less of the moral cowardice and futility posing as virtue and optimism which brings down on him the contemptuous judgment of Ibsen himself. Miss Kingsley's attractions, made as familiar to us by the pencil of Mr. Rothenstein as Miss Dorothy Dene's by that of Leighton, were excellently fitted to Regina; and Mr. Norreys Connell after a somewhat unpromising beginning, played Engstrand with much zest and humour.

152. *Hedda Gabler* in New York

1898

From an unsigned review in *New York Times* (31 March 1898), 5.

Moreover, there is very little to be said for the philosophy of life indicated in this drama. It is certainly not a 'nice' work. At least one of the personages is so nearly 'universal' in his fidelity to human nature as to be almost Shakespearean, and all are obviously true; but the view of society and poor humanity is harsh, bitter and uncompromising.

Hedda is a rara avis, a 'degenerate,' presumably a woman whose excessive individuality has been crushed by the petty conventions of the little society in which she is pent up. She has had repressed yearnings. She has been impelled to an evil life and restrained by fear of the consequences. She is selfish, morbid, cruel, bitter, jealous, something of a visionary, something of a wanton, something of a lunatic.

153. James Joyce, article in *Fortnightly Review*

1 April 1900, n.s., lxvii, 575–90

'Ibsen's New Drama' was written when Joyce was nineteen.

Twenty years have passed since Henrik Ibsen wrote *A Doll's House*, thereby almost marking an epoch in the history of drama. During those years his name has gone abroad through the length and breadth of two continents, and has provoked more discussion and criticism than that of any other living man. He has been upheld as a religious reformer, a social reformer, a Semitic lover of righteousness, and as a great dramatist. He has been rigorously denounced as a meddlesome intruder, a defective artist, an incomprehensible mystic, and, in the eloquent words of a certain English critic, 'a muck-ferreting dog.' Through the perplexities of such diverse criticism, the great genius of the man is day by day coming out as a hero comes out amid the earthly trials. The dissonant cries are fainter and more distant, the random praises are rising in steadier and more choral chaunt. Even to the uninterested bystander it must seem significant that the interest attached to this Norwegian has never flagged for over a quarter of a century. It may be questioned whether any man has held so firm an empire over the thinking world in modern times. Not Rousseau; not Emerson; not Carlyle; not any of those giants of whom almost all have passed out of human ken. Ibsen's power over two generations has been enhanced by his own reticence. Seldom, if at all, has he condescended to join battle with his enemies. It would appear as if the storm of fierce debate rarely broke in upon his wonderful calm. The conflicting voices have not influenced his work in the very smallest degree. His output of dramas has been regulated by the utmost order, by a clockwork routine, seldom found in the case of genius. Only once he answered his assailants after their violent attack on *Ghosts*. But from *The Wild Duck* to *John Gabriel Borkman*, his dramas have appeared almost mechanically at intervals of two years. One is apt to overlook the sustained energy which such a plan of campaign demands; but even surprise at this must give way to admiration at the gradual, irresistible advance of this extraordinary man. Eleven plays, all dealing with modern life, have been published. Here is the list: *A Doll's House, Ghosts, An Enemy of the People, The Wild Duck, Rosmersholm, The Lady from the Sea, Hedda Gabler, The Master Builder, Little Eyolf, John Gabriel Borkman*, and lastly—his new drama, published at Copenhagen, December 19th, 1899—*When We Dead Awaken*. This play is already in process of translation into almost a dozen different languages—a fact which speaks volumes for the power of its author. The drama is written in prose, and is in three acts.

To begin an account of a play of Ibsen's is surely no easy matter. The subject is, in one way, so confined, and, in another way, so vast. It is safe to predict that nine-tenths of the notices of this play will open in some such way as the following: 'Arnold Rubek and his wife, Maja, have been married for four years, at the beginning of the play. Their union is, however, unhappy. Each is discontented with the other.' So far as this goes, it is unimpeachable; but then it does not go very far. It does not convey even the most shadowy notion of the relations between Professor Rubek and his wife. It is a bald, clerkly version of countless, indefinable complexities. It is as though the history of a tragic life were to be written down rudely in two columns, one for the pros and the other for the cons. It is only saying what is literally true, to say that, in the three acts of the drama, there has been stated all that is essential to the drama. There is from first to last hardly a superfluous word or phrase. Therefore, the play itself expresses its own ideas as briefly and as concisely as they can be expressed in the dramatic form. It is manifest, then, that a notice cannot give an adequate notion of the drama. This is not the case with the common lot of plays, to which the fullest justice may be meted out in a very limited number of lines. They are for the most part reheated dishes—unoriginal compositions, cheerfully owlish as to heroic insight, living only in their own candid claptrap—in a word, stagey. The most perfunctory curtness is their fittest meed. But in dealing with the work of a man like Ibsen, the task set the reviewer is truly great enough to sink all his courage. All he can hope to do is to link some of the more salient points together in such a way as to suggest rather than to indicate, the intricacies of the plot. Ibsen has attained ere this to such mastery over his art that, with apparently easy dialogue, he presents his men and women passing through different soul-crises. His analytic method is thus made use of to the fullest extent, and into the comparatively short space of two days the life in life of all his characters is compressed. For instance, though we only see Solness during one night and up to the following evening, we have in reality watched with bated breath the whole course of his life up to the moment when Hilda Wangel enters his house. So in the play under consideration, when we see Professor Rubek first, he is sitting in a garden chair, reading his morning paper, but by degrees the whole scroll of his life is unrolled before us, and we have the pleasure not of hearing it read out to us, but of reading it for ourselves, piecing the various parts, and going closer to see wherever the writing on the parchment is fainter or less legible.

[Joyce describes the plot carefully, accurately and at great length, quoting extensively from the text. He then continues:]

Such is the plot, in a crude and incoherent way, of this new drama. Ibsen's plays do not depend for their interest on the action, or on the incidents. Even the characters, faultlessly drawn though they be, are not the first thing in his plays. But the naked drama—either the perception of a great truth, or the opening up of a great question, or a great conflict which is almost independent of the conflicting actors, and has been and is of far-reaching importance—this is what primarily rivets our attention. Ibsen has chosen the average lives in their uncompromising truth for the groundwork of all his later plays. He has abandoned the verse form, and has never sought to embellish his work after the conventional fashion. Even when his dramatic theme reached its zenith he has not sought to trick it out in gawds or tawdriness. How easy it would have been to have written *An Enemy of the People* on a speciously loftier level—to have replaced the *bourgeois* by the legitimate hero! Critics might then have extolled as grand what they have so often condemned as banal. But the surroundings are nothing to Ibsen. The play is the thing. By the force of his genius, and the indisputable skill which he brings to all his efforts, Ibsen has, for many years, engrossed the attention of the civilised world. Many years more, however, must pass before he will enter his kingdom in jubilation, although, as he stands to-day, all has been done on his part to ensure his own worthiness to enter therein. I do not propose here to examine into every detail of dramaturgy connected with this play, but merely to outline the characterisation.

In his characters Ibsen does not repeat himself. In this drama—the last of a long catalogue—he has drawn and differentiated with his customary skill. What a novel creation is Ulfheim! Surely the hand which has drawn him has not yet lost her cunning. Ulfheim is, I think, the newest character in the play. He is a kind of surprise-packet. It is as a result of his novelty that he seems to leap, at first mention, into bodily form. He is superbly wild, primitively impressive. His fierce eyes roll and glare as those of Yégof or Herne. As for Lars, we may dismiss him, for he never opens his mouth. The Sister of Mercy speaks only once in the play, but then with good effect. In silence she follows Irene like a retribution, a voiceless shadow with her own symbolic majesty.

Irene, too, is worthy of her place in the gallery of her compeers. Ibsen's knowledge of humanity is nowhere more obvious than in his portrayal of women. He amazes one by his painful introspection; he seems to know them better than they know themselves. Indeed, if one may say so of an eminently virile man, there is a curious admixture of the woman in his nature. His marvellous accuracy, his faint traces of femininity, his delicacy of swift touch, are perhaps attributable to this admixture. But that he knows women is an incontrovertible fact. He appears to have sounded them to almost unfathomable depths. Beside his portraits the psychological studies of Hardy and Turgénieff, or the exhaustive elaborations of Meredith, seem no more than sciolism. With a deft stroke, in a phrase, in a word, he does what costs them chapters, and does it better. Irene, then, has to face great comparison; but it must be acknowledged that she comes forth of it bravely. Although Ibsen's women are uniformly true, they, of course, present themselves in various lights. Thus Gina Ekdal is, before all else, a comic figure, and Hedda Gabler a tragic one—if such old-world terms may be employed without incongruity. But Irene cannot be so readily classified; the very aloofness from passion, which is not separable from her, forbids classification. She interests us strangely—magnetically, because of her inner power of character. However perfect Ibsen's former creations may be, it is questionable whether any of his women reach to the depth of soul of Irene. She holds our gaze for the sheer force of her intellectual capacity. She is, moreover, an intensely spiritual creation—in the truest and widest sense of that. At times she is liable to get beyond us, to soar above us, as she does with Rubek. It will be considered by some as a blemish that she—a woman of fine spirituality—is made an artist's model, and some may even regret that such an episode mars the harmony of the drama. I cannot altogether see the force of this contention; it seems pure irrelevancy. But whatever may be thought of the fact, there is small room for complaint as to the handling of it. Ibsen treats it, as indeed he treats all things, with large insight, artistic restraint, and sympathy. He sees it steadily and whole, as from a great height, with perfect vision and an angelic dispassionateness, with the sight of one who may look on the sun with open eyes. Ibsen is different from the clever purveyor.

Maja fulfils a certain technical function in the play, apart from her individual character. Into the sustained tension she comes as a relief. Her airy freshness is as a breath of keen air. The sense of free, almost flamboyant, life, which is her chief note, counterbalances the austerity of Irene and the dulness of Rubek. Maja has practically the same effect on this play, as Hilda Wangel has on *The Master Builder*. But she does not capture our sympathy so much as Nora Helmer. She is not meant to capture it.

Rubek himself is the chief figure in this drama, and, strangely enough, the most conventional. Certainly, when contrasted with his Napoleonic predecessor, John Gabriel Borkman, he is a mere shadow. It must be borne in mind, however, that Borkman is alive, actively, energetically, restlessly alive, all through the play to the end, when he dies; whereas Arnold Rubek is dead, almost hopelessly dead, until the end, when he comes to life. Notwithstanding this, he is supremely interesting, not because of himself, but because of his dramatic significance. Ibsen's drama, as I have said, is wholly independent of his characters. They may be bores, but the drama in which they live and move is invariably powerful. Not that Rubek is a bore by any means! He is infinitely more interesting in himself than Torvald Helmer or Tesman, both of whom possess certain strongly-marked characteristics. Arnold Rubek is, on the other hand, not intended to be a genius, as perhaps Ejlert Lovborg is. Had he been a genius like Ejlert he would have understood in a truer way the value of his life. But, as we are to suppose, the facts that he is devoted to his art and that he has attained to a degree of mastery in it—mastery of hand linked with limitation of thought—tell us that there may be lying dormant in him a capacity for greater life, which may be exercised when he, a dead man, shall have risen from among the dead.

The only character whom I have neglected is the inspector of the baths, and I hasten to do him tardy, but scant, justice. He is neither more nor less than the average inspector of baths. But he is that.

So much for the characterisation, which is at all times profound and interesting. But apart from the characters in the play, there are some noteworthy points in the frequent and extensive side-issues of the line of thought. The most salient of these is what seems, at first sight, nothing more than an accidental scenic feature. I allude to the environment of the drama. One cannot but observe in Ibsen's later work a tendency to get out of closed rooms. Since *Hedda Gabler* this tendency is most marked. The last act of *The Master Builder* and the last act of *John Gabriel Borkman* take place in the open air. But in this play the three acts are *al fresco*. To give heed to such details as these in the drama may be deemed ultra-Boswellian fanaticism. As a matter of fact it is what is barely due to the work of a great artist. And this feature, which is so prominent, does not seem to me altogether without its significance.

Again, there has not been lacking in the last few social dramas a fine pity for men—a note nowhere audible in the uncompromising rigour of the early eighties. Thus in the conversion of Rubek's views as to the girl-figure in his masterpiece, 'The Resurrection Day,' there is involved an all-embracing philosophy, a deep sympathy with the cross-purposes and contradictions of life, as they may be reconcilable with a hopeful awakening—when the manifold travail of our poor humanity may have a glorious issue. As to the drama itself, it is doubtful if any good purpose can be served by attempting to criticise it. Many things would tend to prove this. Henrik Ibsen is one of the world's great men before whom criticism can make but feeble show. Appreciation, hearkening is the only true criticism. Further, that species of criticism which calls itself dramatic criticism is a needless adjunct to his plays. When the art of a dramatist is perfect the critic is superfluous. Life is not to be criticised, but to be faced and lived. Again, if any plays demand a stage they are the plays of Ibsen. Not merely is this so because his plays have so much in common with the plays of other men that they were not written to cumber the shelves of a library, but because they are so packed with thought. At some chance expression the mind is tortured with some question, and in a flash long reaches of life are opened up in vista, yet the vision is momentary unless we stay to ponder on it. It is just to prevent excessive pondering that Ibsen requires to be acted. Finally, it is foolish to expect that a problem, which has occupied Ibsen for nearly three years, will unroll smoothly before our eyes on a first or second reading. So it is better to leave the drama to plead for itself. But this at least is clear, that in this play Ibsen has given us nearly the very best of himself. The action is neither hindered by many complexities, as in *The Pillars of Society*, nor harrowing in its simplicity, as in *Ghosts*. We have whimsicality, bordering on extravagance, in the wild Ulfheim, and subtle humour in the sly contempt which Rubek and Maja entertain for each other. But Ibsen has striven to let the drama have perfectly free action. So he has not bestowed his wonted pains on the minor characters. In many of his plays these minor characters are matchless creations. Witness Jacob Engstrand, Tönnesen, and the demonic Molvik! But in this play the minor characters are not allowed to divert our attention.

On the whole, *When We Dead Awaken* may rank with the greatest of the author's work—if, indeed, it be not the greatest. It is described as the last of the series, which began with *A Doll's House*—a grand epilogue to its ten predecessors. Than these dramas, excellent alike in dramaturgic skill, characterisation, and supreme interest, the long roll of drama, ancient or modern, has few things better to show.

154. From an unsigned notice, *Daily Telegraph*

26 January 1903, 11

Clement Scott had retired in 1898. William Archer's translation of *When We Dead Awaken* was performed at the Imperial Theatre on 25 January 1903 and the cast was as follows:

Professor Rubeck	Mr G. S. Titheradge
Ulfheim ..	Mr Lawrence Irving
Irene ..	Miss Henrietta Watson
Mrs Rubeck ..	Miss Mabel Hackney
Sister of Mercy	Miss Edith Craig
Inspector ..	Mr Morrice Seaton

'Do you think that would work?' asks poor, bewildered Professor Arnold Rubek, when it is suggested to him that since he has to live with a wife whom he does not love, and wants to live with another woman whom he does love, he had better try a 'ménage a trois.' No, comes the answer, it certainly would not help to promote ordinary human felicity —nor yet, we venture to think, does the old, old story which is thus outlined and brought before us for the thousandth time in Ibsen's last piece, serve to make a good play. *When We Dead Awaken* is not a high specimen of the Norwegian dramatist's powers for very obvious reasons. The action is even less than is usual in Ibsen; the story, such as it is, stands absolutely still throughout the second act; the hero is more uninteresting than the customary invertebrate hero of a Scandinavian piece; and 'the other woman' loses her hold upon our sympathy just in proportion as she exhibits increasing signs of patent dementia. The very presence of her keeper in the guise of 'a sister of mercy' accentuates the mock romance of the situation, for she has nothing to do except to follow about 'the stranger lady' with remorseless zeal and say 'Pax vobiscum' when the final curtain descends. On the other hand it is interesting for a student of Ibsen to watch the creation of a character like Ulfheim, a mere piece of sensuous animalism, designed to attract and tempt a mere piece of commonplace prettiness, like Rubek's wife; and also to discover, late in the dramatist's career, the inculcation of the moral that 'Art for Art's sake' is not only always and everywhere inferior to life itself, but pregnant with disaster and ruin. The figure of the professor-sculptor only gains significance if we imagine that he, by his devotion to Art for æsthetic reasons, lost his one chance of happiness in losing his beautiful model Irene. Apart from this, we have only the trite parable that if A and B are unhappily married, the intrusion of C to flirt with A and of D to flirt with B is likely to lead to tragic dénouements. We have every respect for the Stage Society's resolute endeavour to try dramatic experiments, for thus only can we hope to enlarge the area of clever and original dramatic work. But we do not for a moment believe that *When We Dead Awaken* is either a good specimen of the author's powers or a good play in itself. Except that it is more fully charged with possibly allegorical meanings, there is little or no change from, or advance on, previous work. Ulfheim we have already excepted; the other figures are familiar enough. The bright, laughing, shallow Maia is only Nora of the *Doll's House* in another guise; while as for Rubek and Irene, 'the stranger woman,' they are Rosmer and Rebecca over again, Solness and Hilda, John Gabriel Borkman, and his half-alive ghost from the tomb of past years. Irene is the eternal woman, just as the play is the 'endlessly repeated cabbage' of Scandinavian hysterics.

155. From an unsigned notice, *Daily Chronicle*

27 January 1903

Certainly life would not be worth living if the majority of humanity resembled the two principals in Ibsen's latest drama, presented yesterday afternoon by the Stage Society. Like most pieces from the same pen, *When we Dead Awaken* is deeply pessimistic in tone, and the principal characters behave and talk in a manner that makes one wonder whether they have any right to be at large. The heroine, if she may be called so, is a half-demented person who, notwithstanding that she is continually shadowed by a Sister of Mercy, is allowed to retain a dagger, day and night, for emergencies. This uncomfortable person's favourite topics of conversation are graveyards, 'cold bodies,' and shrouds, so it is not surprising that she should be without friends. Of course, much of what she says is to be regarded as symbolical of lofty purpose, and of independence of thought and action, and upon her utterances, which are occasionally of a very free and unconventional description, attentive listeners may place whatever construction they please. The realist as well as the idealist will find abundant matter for more or less serious contemplation in *When we Dead Awaken*. . . .

There is no more in the treatment of the theme than in the theme itself to recommend the piece to ordinary playgoers. Interest and curiosity lie in the unblushing frankness with which passages in the studio life of Rubek and Irene are set forth, and in the brutality displayed by 'the bear-killer' in his conquest of Maia. In other words the strength of the play is its inconsistency, combined with the air of mysticism marking nearly all the plays written by Ibsen during the past decade.

156. An unsigned notice, *The Times*

27 January 1903, 5

Nothing would be easier than to make fun of *When We Dead Awaken*. The work—we greatly fear it must be called the last dramatic work—of an old man in failing health, it has some features which rather caricature than continue the method of Ibsen in his prime. Thus Ulfheim, the bear-hunter—and bear—might be considered as an unconsciously comic personage, and we can imagine the pen of the ready parodist making fine play with the Inspector at the Baths. Nothing, again, would be easier than to expose the absurdities of the play from the rigorously matter-of-fact point of view adopted by Thomas Rymer in his examination of *Othello*. What is not so easy, and is therefore better worth doing, is to try to understand the play, to conjecture what Ibsen meant, and to measure how much of his meaning he has expressed. The proper business of criticism was never better expressed than in the words of Spinoza—*Neque flere, neque ridere, neque admirare, neque contemnere—sed intelligere.* If criticism had only minded its business over Ibsen! If it had only tried to understand him a little more, and foolishly contemned—or not less foolishly admired—him a little less! More than any modern dramatist, he has given us all 'something to break our minds upon.' And, for our own part, we find *When We Dead Awaken* a particularly hard nut to crack.

This play—or rather, to use the author's description, this dramatic epilogue—is written in Ibsen's latest or mystico-symbolical method, and, as we have said, slightly caricatures it. Even at its best that is not a method which we can think a good one for the art of the theatre. There are scores of excellent reasons why a play should, above all things, be plain-sailing, why its characters should say what they mean and mean no more than they say, why their conduct should be referable to the standards of actual life. Now this last play of Ibsen's, like its immediate predecessors, is always meaning more than it says, always saying something which is not to be taken literally, but as symbolic of something else, while the conduct of its personages, referred to the actual standards of life, would be mere midsummer madness. It is clear that when a middle-aged sculptor and a young woman in white climb a mountain in a storm and say they are going 'up to the Peak of Promise' to hold 'their marriage feast', or when the sculptor tells his wife, who has announced her intention of going off bear-hunting for some days with a strange gentleman, 'I have not the slightest objection'—it is clear when such things are said and done that more is meant than meets the eye. The fact is the people are not people, but personified ideas—embodied *états d'âme*—and their actions are not conditioned by probability, or common sense, or any external reality, but by some inner adventure-plot of ideas and soul-states. In such a case it would be absurd to find fault with the external actions on Judge Brack's ground that 'people don't do these things'. In such a case all that really matters is the inner adventure-plot. But about that the playgoer is entitled to require that it shall have some logic, some necessity, of its own; and, try as we may, we cannot see the logic of this inner adventure-plot of idea and soul-state in *When We Dead Awaken*. We say to the author, What exactly is your thesis? What conclusion would you have us draw? But the author (like Dr. Johnson when tackled by an inquisitive lady about ghosts) 'prefers to leave the subject in obscurity'. We understand, or think we understand, Rubek, the sculptor, the 'artist temperament', who has aesthetized all the flesh and blood out of life, and who thinks he has cleared his account with sin by modelling himself as a figure in a bronze group in an attitude of remorse. We understand, or think we understand, Irene, whom Rubek has 'used' as a model, and whose soul has died within her because he could never see that she was not only model, but woman. We feel reasonably sure that we understand Maia, the frivolous, excitement-loving wife, and Ulfheim, the shaggy half-human animal, the faun, who can give Maia the excitement she needs. We can understand why there should be a *chasse-croise* and exchange of partners in this quartet. But what is the logic of the avalanche which wipes out Rubek and Irene? Why should Irene be sometimes a lunatic with homicidal tendencies and sometimes only mad nor' nor' west—endowed, in fact, with remarkable powers of intellectual analysis? And what is the significance of Rubek's artistic degeneration, when he deliberately turned all his portrait-busts into malicious caricatures? All these (and some others) are to us 'puzzling questions', if 'not beyond conjecture'. We do not clearly understand the idea-plot of the play.

But there is always this to be said about Ibsen—whether you clearly understand him or not, he gives you a thrill which no one else can give you. With him you get glimpses of the strange crepuscular things of life, remote corners of the sub-consciousness—as in all the scenes wherein

Irene and Rubek review their past history—and suddenly some touch of weird poetry will bring up a 'lump' in your throat—as, at the close of Act II, when Rubek and Irene dream over the brook, throwing in leaves that turn into Lohengrin's boat. And then, after all the studies, more particularly in French literature, of the 'artist temperament', studies so numerous that it seemed there was nothing more to be said, here is Ibsen saying something more, something new. There is more illumination of the subject in a flash like Irene's half-scornful, half-pitying reference to the sculptor's statue of himself as Remorse than in all the laboured analyses of the Brothers De Goncourt. Puzzled by the play as one constantly is, one cannot resist the spell of it. It is not Ibsen at his best; perhaps it is in some respects Ibsen at his weakest. But the lees of a great mind are better than the 'first sprightly runnings' of a small one.

157. From an unsigned notice, *Sunday Times*

1 February 1903, 6

The view that Ibsen is an intense rather than a profound or an exact thinker; that there is throughout all of his work a quite discernible vein of the purely and wilfully eccentric; and that there occur during the progress of his dramas long tracts of dialogue that, owing to their lack of the essentially dramatic element, cannot truthfully be described as being anything better than tedious. In treating of a new drama by Ibsen one seems almost bound to find in him, or for him, an inner meaning. There is one meaning, easily deducible from *When We Dead Awaken*, that seems clear enough. Providence, this drama would seem to say, is long suffering, but to its patience there are limits. It does not approve of immorality, but it permits it upon occasion to go unpunished. Given the daring and strong man, who eludes, though he does not fear, the embraces of the mountain bear, he may be permitted occasionally to embrace his neighbour's wife. That wife, too, is permitted to continue in her career, seeing that she is a cheery little soul, who has a tedious husband, who is mooning, in an idealistic fashion, after someone else, whereas the little wife makes no pretensions to lofty ideas or rigid morality, but takes things just as they come. Providence, too, in its wide-reaching mercifulness, does not even otherwise punish the tedious husband for his extreme tediousness, so long as he is tedious merely; it is when he proposes to add immorality to his tedium that the patience of the powers that be wears thin, and Providence descends upon him like a thousand of bricks, with a landslip or an avalanche, or something of that sort.

[outlines the plot at length.]

The two earlier acts have a curious likeness to one another in construction; each of them opens with a scene of incompatibility between Rubek and Maia, proceeds with a very long duologue between Rubek and the Stranger Lady, and contains, incidentally, an 'episode' (I thank thee, Stranger Lady, for teaching me that word!) betwixt Maia and Ulfheim, hunter of bears. The final act has its 'locale' high in the mountains. It commences with a rather stirring scene between Maia and the bear-hunter, who is becoming very pressing in his attentions to Mrs. Rubek. She tells him that he looks like a fawn, and that he has little horns; and he describes to her his 'episode' with the lady who bestowed upon him those same horns, and, in spite of a certain crudity in his methods of wooing, she decidedly takes to him. So much so, that when Rubek and the Stranger Lady appear upon the scene, philandering, after their serious manner, she accepts the situation, and goes down to the valley with her Orson, singing, delightedly, 'I am free! I am free! I am free!' She might have added, 'and easy, both in manners and morals', without overstating the case. Rubek and the Stranger Lady resolve to devote themselves to one another, but not to go into the valley, but to ascend to heights. They depart to put this intention into practice, and the black-robed and wholly unintelligible sister of mercy comes on the scene. There is a clattering heard 'off', which is supposed to represent 'the awful avalanche' spoken of by the poet; the nun prays in Latin, and from the distant valley Maia is heard singing again, 'I am free, I am free, I am free.'

When We Dead Awaken is a play that it would take a very devoted admirer of Ibsen to accept with absolute seriousness as a definite revelation to dramatic art of what it really ought to be. It is lacking in reasonableness and in vitality; the frivolous Maia and the rough-wooing bear-hunter are conceivable, though strangely eccentric personages; but the sculptor and his model seem to be mere exercises in the Ibsen method, having no consistent relation with any conceivable view of life, either realistic or abstract. Naturally, the more definitely-drawn characters furnished the stronger acting opportunities.

158. From an unsigned notice, *Lloyd's Weekly News*

1 February 1903, 8

The utter hopelessness for the modern stage of Ibsen's latest method as a dramatist has been again displayed by two performances by the Stage Society of his three-act piece, *When We Dead Awaken*. A work more dreary in theme or more contrary to real life cannot be imagined, whilst the dialogue so often verges on the grotesque that the unprejudiced listener is once more inclined to doubt the author's earnestness. Even after allowances have been made for the differences between Norwegian and English thought, customs, and modes of expression, it is difficult to take seriously a play so far-fetched when it is not absolutely incomprehensible as *When We Dead Awaken*.

159. An unsigned notice, *Referee*

1 February 1903, 2

Balzac, in his *Contes Drolatiques*, tells a story of a little prince and princess who, after long importunity, were permitted to look upon Titian's picture representing our first parents. The story is called 'Innocence'. The King-father and the Queen-mother watched and listened with some anxiety. They were speedily reassured. 'Which is Adam and which is Eve?' inquired the young gentleman. 'Oh, you big silly!' answered the little lady: 'you can't tell that until they have their clothes on'. This reply resembled that made (under somewhat different circumstances) by a certain artist who loved Art for Art's sake, and was deaf and blind and insensible to everything else. Such an artist was Arnold Rubek, the sculptor-hero of Ibsen's three-act play, *When We Dead Awaken*, which, as translated by Mr. William Archer, was presented to the members and guests of the Stage Society at the Imperial Theatre on Sunday evening and on Monday afternoon. I call Rubek the hero because he must have some sort of a label and not because there was anything heroic about him. He was a veritable stock, and as insensible as the stone on which he worked. Once he had a beautiful model whose name was Irene. She stood to him in 'the altogether' again and again, and played so large a part in his masterpiece, 'The Resurrection Day', that when it was completed they always spoke of it as their child. Rubek, however, hardly knew she was a woman until *she put her clothes on*. 'We artists don't trouble about such things' was his remark when she reminded him of his insensibility. 'There I stood in all my undraped loveliness and you never touched me', was the lady's unblushing reproach. It was perhaps well for Rubek that he didn't touch, for had he done so she would have stabbed him with a hatpin which she wore in her hair. At least, that's what she said later on. But she was a most irritating sort of woman. There was no knowing what she would be at.

Anyway, Irene ran away from Rubek, and later on turned up at a health resort, where Rubek and his young wife, Maia, of whom he was already weary, were staying. Irene was now a Stranger Lady, who was shadowed by a nun-like keeper, and who ought to have been in a lunatic asylum. Since she last met Rubek she had (so she said) stood naked on the turntable for hundreds of men to gaze at, which, being interpreted, probably meant that she had been doing 'living-picture' business at some Continental variety show. Rubek seemed now to realise that Irene was his affinity, though she threatened to stab him, *because he called her 'an episode'*. Still, he was tired of the giddy Maia, whom he allowed to go gallivanting with the boorish, goatish Ulfheim, the bear-hunter. The Stranger Lady persuaded the gloomy artist that it would be a good thing to go up the mountains, through the mists, to the sunshine and the Peak of Promise, where they might enjoy their marriage feast, which, presumably, would consist for the most part of ice-pudding. Maia and the goatish bearhunter were also inclined for a summer night in the uplands—but a storm came on and a passing avalanche swept Rubek and his mad model away. Maia was rescued by her bearhunter, and appeared to be happy enough down below, for she was heard singing that she was free.

Ibsen worshippers and Ibsen apologists will tell you—they *have* told you—that in the Ibsen plays there is more than meets the eye; that for the believer there is a meaning which is not discoverable by the unbeliever, and that what some have condemned as unfit for publication is really symbolical of all that is pure and lofty and supremely beautiful. I don't take much stock in symbolic lobworms, Norwegian or otherwise. The difficulty is that you can't fix them with their symbols. Each of the Ibsenites interprets 'the Master' in a different way. Myself, I think no more of *When We Dead Awaken* than Uncle Toby thought of the work which was composed by the great Lipsius when he was one day old. I would do with it as Uncle Toby proposed to do with that. The dramatist who wishes to be heard, and who thinks he has a mission to fulfil, should say what he means and mean what he says. When it is impossible to find what he does mean, he may be reckoned as of small account as a dramatist, especially when, as in this case, he is not only distressingly obscure, but *deplorably dull* as well. For *When We Dead Awaken* all was done that possibly could be done by Mr. Titheradge, as the sculptor; Miss Henrietta Watson, as Irene; and Miss Mabel Hackney, as Maia. Mr. Laurence Irving played the goatish bearhunter. Mr. Henry Arthur Jones continues to clamour for the drama entirely distinct from popular entertainment. It seems to me that with Ibsen and the productions of the Stage Society there is the very thing he most desires.

160. From 'Ibsen's "Epilogue"', by 'Max' [Beerbohm], *Saturday Review*

7 February 1903, xcv, 168–9

Sir Max Beerbohm (1872–1956) was Shaw's successor as dramatic critic on the *Saturday Review* and half-brother of Sir Herbert Beerbohm Tree, the actor.

Ibsen has discovered that the great artist is always inhuman, and on this discovery his play is founded. A simple thesis, surely. Who supposed that the great artist could ever be human? All the passion of a great artist's nature goes into his work. Exactly that same energy of emotion which other men concentrate on life is in his case diverted from life into art. Unless he were absorbedly in love with it, his work could not become great. But, though he is thus detached, he cannot dispense with life. Life is a necessary means to his end. He cannot gain inspiration except through experience. He must have his human models, his human documents. Except as models, as documents, they do not interest him. But it may happen that one of them becomes very much interested in him. A human female may happen to fall in love with him. Then one of two complications is in store; and both of them are equally tragic. Perhaps he will be by the woman's love warmed to a temporary love for her. His art will seem to him a poor thing in comparison with this strange feeling. Proportionately, his work will decline, losing its strength and magic. After a time, his true nature will re-assert itself. He will cease, slowly but surely, to be human, and will return to his first love, leaving the second love forlorn. Such is the process worked out in Zola's *L'Œuvre*, and in many other more or less modern novels. The other process is worked out (retrospectively, as in Ibsen's way) in *When We Dead Awaken*. Here the artist does not respond to the passion of the woman who is his inspiring model. So soon as he has finished the great statue, she leaves him, with her heart broken by his indifference to her womanhood. He tells her that, at all events, his acquaintance with her has been for him 'a priceless episode'. So far, the process of the story has well illustrated the inhumanity of great artists in general. If such illustration had been Ibsen's one aim, then the rest of the play would have shown us merely the sculptor finding other models and creating fresh masterpieces and perhaps fresh tragedies. But Ibsen had another and dearer aim. To portray was not enough: he must also preach. And the gist of his sermon was to be that the great artist is not less pathetic a figure than his victims, in that he never knows the joy of life—a joy incomparably greater than the joy of art. In order that he might point this moral the more sharply, Ibsen manufactured a good deal of the evidence. Rubek, the sculptor, ceased to be a type, and became a peculiar example. After the withdrawal of his particular model, he ceased to care for his art, and devoted himself to pot-boilers. 'All the talk about the artist's vocation and the artist's mission, and so forth, began to strike' him 'as being very empty, and hollow, and meaningless at bottom'. What he wanted was 'life'—that 'life in sunshine and in beauty, which is a hundred times better worth while than to wear yourself out in a perpetual struggle with lumps of clay and blocks of stone'. He married a commonplace girl, and bored her and was bored by her. After a few years (and here the action of the play begins) he met again the woman who had been his model. She, through his treatment of her, had lost her reason. But, mad or sane, an Ibsen woman may always be trusted to score off an Ibsen man. Irene (for that is her name) makes very short work of Rubek's half-hearted apologies for art and for the artistic temperament. Rubek's wife has already gone up to the mountains (which are, obviously, symbols for freedom and reality of life) in the company of a full-blooded huntsman. Rubek begs that Irene will go up with him to the mountains. They go, but are overwhelmed by an avalanche, while the wife and the huntsman escape unharmed. This business of the avalanche is treated by the critics as something quite inenubilable. Yet what could be plainer than Ibsen's meaning?—that there was a time when Rubek and Irene might have lived their lives, but that now it is too late: that a man can never regain the chance he has once thrown away. The meaning may not be profound, and the symbolism may be a trifle crude; but there is no other possible objection to them. From first to last the play is as clear as it can be. If anything, it is too clear: there is too much expression of its meaning. The characters express, in varying terms, the same thoughts and the same feelings over and over again. There is not really enough in them to fill an evening bill. Nor can we wonder, remembering that this is the latest and last play of a very old man.

There is another sense in which *When We Dead Awaken* is essentially an old man's work. I have suggested that it is rather a sermon than a presentment. The great artist in his prime does not, like Rubek, hanker after 'life'. It is only when his power for art has decayed that he, looking back, realises that perhaps he has foregone the true happiness. In this 'epilogue' Ibsen speaks to us, I doubt not, of himself.

161. From a pseudonymous notice by 'Momus', *Gentlewoman*

7 February 1903, 16

The dogged determination of the greater number of English critics to take the Norwegian dramatist 'at the foot of the letter', and, placing his allegory and symbolism on one side, to write of his work *qua* human documents, expositions of the purely human drama, arises in a great measure from some such process of reasoning as the following: Here is a dramatist. Here is a theatre. Here is a play. It is our duty to report on its merits and its rendition according to our lights and to the best of our ability. But we distinctly refuse to deal in inferences, to endeavour to solve conundrums of inner meaning, and to waste ourselves in what will probably prove a futile endeavour to translate symbolic figures illustrating remote theories.

The result is a literal description of plot and occurrence which, in many cases, goes far to prove the author either a madman or the most frankly immoral writer the stage has known.

The public, the good-natured, patient, anxious-to-be-amused English public, sits bewildered, trying to hold on for dear life to the story of the play, receives petrifying shocks now and then, recovers and goes on hoping for the best.

When We Dead Awaken, which is presumably Ibsen's latest contribution to dramatic literature, is perhaps more exclusively symbolic than any other of his plays with which we are already comparatively familiar, and the characterization deals with types which are, perhaps, more difficult for an English audience to make acquaintance with than others of his creation.

In his symbols too, he seems to go further afield and their number is distracting.

The lost illusions in the shape of dolls of the Master Builder's wife are but a drop in the symbolic ocean which we breast in *When We Dead Awaken*. In the title alone we do not face the supernatural, as would seem in literal translation, but the waste of life which finds its sole and true apotheosis in death. The exposition of this is the pivot of the play.

The standing of the Stranger Lady as Professor Rubeck's model is symbolic of that denuding of the soul which can only find its salvation in the true life, i.e., death. So also Rubeck's impotence in and disgust with art. He and the Stranger Lady embody hunger and aspirations of the soul as palpably as do Maia and Ulfheim the fulfilment of the body. Ibsen may later inform us whither it leads them. It seems difficult to accept the black robed sister-of-mercy with her one utterance Pax Vobiscum after the final catastrophe in any other light than as that inevitable shadow of death which dogs human footsteps, and which according to Ibsen's allegory awakes to the true life beyond.

With no knowledge of the original, it may seem an impertinence to question Mr. Archer's use of the word 'episode', which in this connection seems at variance with our modern association, and use in the vernacular.

THE VIKINGS AT HELGELAND

Imperial Theatre, 15 April 1903

---

162. From an unsigned notice,
Daily Telegraph

16 April 1903, 7

This production caused a great stir. The sets were designed by
Gordon Craig, Ellen Terry's son, and were considered to be very
controversial. The play was translated by William Archer and the
cast was as follows:

Hiordis ..	.. Miss Ellen Terry	Dagny ..	Miss Hutin Britton
Sigurd ..	.. Mr Oscar Ashe	Gunnar ..	Mr Hubert Carter
Ornulf ..	.. Mr Holman Clark	Käre ..	Mr Mark Kinghorne
Thorolf	.. Mr Conway Tearle	Egil ..	Noel Compton

The theatrical enterprise begun last night at the Imperial Theatre was a
remarkable one for several reasons. There was the choice of play, to
begin with—'an early Ibsen', a great, rough, romantic drama, full of
loud words and replete with primitive passion. Then there was the
choice of heroine on Miss Ellen Terry's part for her first independent
dramatic venture. Hiördis, who is the main figure in *The Vikings* is a
kind of Scandinavian Lady Macbeth—a proud, vengeful, bitter-
tongued lady, who appears to possess precisely those qualities of
masculine strength in which Miss Terry is relatively deficient, and
hardly any of those tenderer, more sympathetic attributes in which Miss
Terry excels. Lastly, there was the stage-management, of which so
much has been heard, the curious lighting and scenic effects, for which
Mr. Gordon Craig is responsible, and in virtue of which his name
appears five times on the playbill. Mr. Craig will have nothing to do
with footlights, because they throw an upward shadow on the face;
but he is enamoured of toplights, which, of course, in the absence of

405

footlights, throw a downward shadow on the face. In the first act, for instance, thanks to the somewhat voluminous headgear of the characters, no single face could be accurately discerned, and therefore no play of feature was of the slightest value. Mr. Craig also likes closed scenes, with many-coloured lights thrown down from above, and gauzes—in order, apparently, to suggest a remote, imaginative, and poetic aspect to scenes laid in distant ages and far-away lands. His dresses are always striking and often picturesque; his grouping of figures is distinctly artistic and good. But we are not quite sure that the general result of this novel stage management (yet novel it can hardly be called, for, to go no further back, Professor von Herkomer tried much the same experiments at Bushey) was entirely satisfactory, except in the third act, which was quite beautiful in its atmosphere and idyllic simplicity. What Mr. Craig designed to do was to suggest a poetic background to a Scandinavian saga. What he did was to surround stirring action and virile passion with a baffling and irritating air of mystery and unreality. They could never have lived, these stout warriors and love-distracted women, we seem to say to ourselves. No such times could ever have been; it is all a dream, a piece of phantasy, in which we need not be mightily concerned. Quite appropriate to some delicate and imaginative poem, this stage-treatment hardly suited a romance of keen sword-blades and copious bloodletting. There was an obvious discord between the story told on the stage, and the atmosphere of its mise-en-scène. Nor yet can we honestly say that the play itself is throughout of any enduring and consistent dramatic nerve and power. The first two acts are admirable, the second being especially a crowning scene of heroic structure. In the two last we seem somehow to wander off the track, and the plot relaxes its grip upon our attention. It is as though the dramatist knew how to involve his leading personages in the web of destiny, and yet failed to unravel his tangled threads or give to our complete satisfaction the precise tragic solution which the story appeared to require. We ought to add, however, that, owing to the difficulties inseparable from a première, the third act went, dramatically speaking, for little or nothing last night, while the intense gloom of the final act had a most depressing effect on the spirits.

In *The Vikings at Helgeland*, we have a very different Ibsen from the dramatist with whom we associate social dramas like *The Doll's House* and *Hedda Gabler*. Before he wrote *The League of Youth*, the play which inaugurated the newer style, Ibsen had his romantic and historical period, when he was occupied with the early annals of his own country, and with those Scandinavian Sagas which have been worked up into modern forms by Messrs. Magnusson and Morris. Indeed, the best preparation for *The Vikings* is to read Mr. William Morris's *The Lovers of Gudrun*, in the third volume of *The Earthly Paradise*. The subject is much the same, albeit that instead of Gudrun with her two lovers, Kiartan and Bodli, we have as heroine Hiördis in a similar relation to Gunnar and Sigurd. But in either case, the men and women with whom we deal are of the same build. They are those who are wont to carry their lives in their hands, accustomed to danger, quick to anger, bitter in revenge, loving fiercely, hating with similar ardour, strong and un-complaining, passionate, yet full of a certain antique nobility of soul. They accept their fate without demur. They know that in their brief span of life fighting holds the chief place, with all the risks involved. Yet they find time for amorous dalliance, and are as stormy in their affections as in the existence that they have chosen for themselves. Above all, they utter no word of weak complaint. For they are the men and women whom Mr. Morris describes:

> Who, for the rest, while yet they dwelt on earth
> Wearied no God with prayers for more of mirth
> Than dying men have; nor were ill-content
> Because no God beside their sorrow went
> Turning to flowering sward the rock-strewn way,
> Weakness to strength, or darkness into day.

[the plot described.]

It is impossible, for some of the reasons already referred to, to say that the production was altogether a success, but we may call it, at all events, an interesting venture. Miss Ellen Terry, not, we venture to affirm, very happily suited with the part of Hiördis, acted, nevertheless, with both charm and strength. If neither the charm nor the strength were especially Scandinavian, or endowed in any sense with an epical quality, they were romantic with all the unfailing romance and picturesqueness which are Miss Terry's gracious privilege. Unhappily, the nervousness of a first night and a temporary loss of memory robbed the third act of much of its effectiveness, but the figure of the heroine, knotting the bow-string with her own hair, and sharpening the arrow-heads which were to be the instrument of her vengeance, and seen, by a happy exception, from Mr. Craig's customary gloom, in a clear and luminous radiance, is one which lives in the memory.

163. From a long unsigned notice, *Daily Chronicle*

16 April 1903, 8

Over three columns and with two large illustrations.

Miss Ellen Terry has no reason to regret the choice of Ibsen's tragedy, *The Vikings*, for the inauguration of her season. A grim play, the tragic strain of which is persistently maintained from beginning to end, undoubtedly satisfied an audience expectant of great things, both as regarded acting and novel pictorial effects, for the latter of which Mr. E. Gordon Craig was responsible. Miss Terry's reception on entering was enthusiastic, and after being summoned many times at the conclusion of each act, she was compelled at a quarter of an hour before midnight to lead forward Mr. Craig and to deliver a few words of thanks for the public recognition of efforts that she admitted had occasioned some anxiety.

The Vikings belongs to Ibsen's early period, and has little in common with the series of plays of social life exercising an important influence upon the work of European dramatists during the past twenty years. It is a drama of action—indeed, of fierce conflict—for might rather than right is the paramount power throughout. The characters have dramatic breadth and force, and possess the vigour that may be regarded as appropriate to an age when vital issues were left to the arbitrament of the sword. In *The Vikings* Ibsen's colouring is occasionally lurid, particularly towards the close, but the story is both clear and strong. The few reflective passages that proclaim the observation and imagination of a poet of human nature and its surroundings never retard the progress of the story. They impart to the play literary quality, and in nearly every instance shed a light upon thought and motive. On the whole, *The Vikings* is an interesting as well as stirring drama.

[lengthy description of plot follows.]

Mr. Gordon Craig again makes use of dark draped backgrounds and coloured lights, and some of the results are telling—specially so the opening scene with precipitous, sharp-pointed cliffs, on which a white ray is cast, whilst below is rocky uneven ground, and in the rear the blackness of night. Flaming torches are employed in the feast scene, all the guests, wearing robes of bright patchwork pattern, ascending to a circular and almost enclosed platform. All the lighting comes from above, and in this respect alteration is needed. Play of feature could, of course, be followed when the lantern was thrown upon the actors, but there were moments when the faces of those standing in the foreground were almost invisible.

164. From an unsigned notice, *The Times*

16 April 1903, 4

Among epidemic maladies the passion for theatrical management ranks with the influenza. It would be unfashionable not to be attacked by it; the patient's friends can only hope that the attack will be a mild one. The latest addition to the list of distinguished victims is Miss Ellen Terry, and in her case the symptoms may seem at first sight unusually alarming, for she has not only gone into management, but gone in for Ibsen. Her numerous friends may, however, be reassured. The Ibsen she has gone in for is not the Ibsen whose 'social' dramas have given several worthy gentlemen cause for much uneasiness—Ibsen Ibsenissimus—but the earlier Ibsen of the romantic period—Ibsen 'caught young'—the Ibsen, in fact, of 1858, author of *The Vikings at Helgeland*. This work is a Scandinavian saga or hodge-podge of sagas turned to dramatic uses, after (if it was not before) part of the story had been turned to musical uses by Richard Wagner.

Given the epoch—about A.D. 933 it seems—the spectator is prepared for a good deal of violence. He certainly gets his fill of it. High-tempered ladies quarrel like fish-fags about the physical prowess of their respective husbands, whom they appraise as though they were prize-fighters. If we have counted aright, at least nine persons of high social standing, not to reckon a miscellaneous crowd of retainers (or 'house-carles'), come to a violent end between the rise and fall of the curtain.

Roof-trees are burned, swords flash, axes are brandished, and arrows hurtle through the air. This is called, in the language of the piece, 'going-a-viking', which seems to have been the equivalent for going a-mafficking in A.D. 933. Domestic differences are (as usual) the cause of all the mischief. Gunnar has wedded Hiördis by fraud. The man who would win her had to slay the white bear which guarded her virgin bower; Sigurd the Strong did the deed, but his friend Gunnar, the Comparatively Weak, took the credit—by private arrangement—and the bride. Sigurd then paired off with the gentle Dagny. But in due course the truth came to light, as the truth in such matters generally does. It came to light at what should have been the festive board, had not Hiördis proved an extremely unpleasant hostess. To begin with, Hiördis so taunted young Thorolf, Dagny's brother, that, in a frenzy, he misled her into supposing that his father, Örnulf, had slain her only child, Egil. Thereupon Gunnar took an axe and clave Thorolf's skull in twain—and at the very next moment Örnulf entered with Egil, whom he had saved from some wicked peasants. Not content with this mischief, Hiördis bragged about her husband. He was the strongest man of all, for he had slain the white bear outside her virgin bower. Not so, replied Dagny; it was my husband, Sigurd, who slew the white bear. And then the feast broke up in confusion.

Hiördis now set herself to make a bow-string and to forge arrow-heads—intended, of course, for vengeance on Sigurd the Strong but Fraudulent. Sigurd, however, took a private opportunity of declaring to Hiördis that she was the only woman he had ever loved and Hiördis in return assured him that he had always had her heart. She proposed to flee with him, not as his paramour, but (if we are not mistaken) as a kind of comrade-in-arms. When he demurred, she determined that, if they would not live together, they should die together, and she planted an arrow in his heart. With his last breath he declared himself a Christian (converted, it would appear, by Æthelstan, King of England—'Æthelstan the Christian King', as Mr. Wilson Barrett would say), and Hiördis threw herself into the sea.

It is a curious play, and ought to interest students of folklore. They will find in it abundance of valuable detail about early marriages-by-capture, the etiquette of such unions, the ransom to be paid to parents, and so forth. The chief exponent of the law in primitive communities —the Sir Henry Maine of the period, so to speak—is the aged Örnulf, who, as the father of Dagny, fosterfather of Hiördis, and father-in-law of Gunnar and Sigurd is related to all the chief parties in the case. As an exponent of the law Örnulf is what the cabman called John Forster, 'a harbitrary cove', always standing upon his strict rights; indeed, he would be rather tiresome were he not ennobled by his misfortunes and the simple dignity of his grief. When he has lost all his seven sons he raises a mound over them with his own hands, and sings—for he is a bard as well as a warrior—a kind of funeral dirge, while his warriors croon a weird chorus. This is a very impressive scene, impressive by reason of Mr. Holman Clark's fine acting as well as of the scenic simplicity and severity imagined by Mr. Gordon Craig. For that matter, all Mr. Craig's scenes and costumes are good—harmonious in colouring, broad and massive in design. He has his own system of stage-lighting—all the illuminatiion, if we are not mistaken, comes from above—and the result is sometimes to leave the personages, where Dr. Johnson on a former occasion left the question of ghosts, in obscurity; but the new experiment, if not as yet a complete success, is a welcome change from the false old system of the footlights.

Miss Ellen Terry is, of course, Hiördis. She looks every inch a Viking's bride, but we do not think she is at her best as a virago. Her womanly wiles, her rippling laughter, her sense of fun have no proper chance of employment. Nor is she yet by any means perfect in her words. Mr. Oscar Asche is sufficiently burly as Sigurd the Strong, Miss Hutin Britton is an agreeable Dagny, and Young Thorolf is pleasantly played by Mr. Conway Tearle. Mr. Holman Clark's Örnulf—the happiest thing in the cast—we have already praised. An overture and incidental music supplied by Mr. M. F. Shaw were so unobtrusive as to be scarcely audible. Everybody, however, seemed highly delighted with *The Vikings*, and Miss Terry was compelled to utter a few words of thanks.

165. An unsigned notice, *Referee*

19 April 1903, 2

The most-admired actress of our time—to say so much is to name Miss Ellen Terry—has given the Scandinavian Drama one more chance in this country. On Wednesday evening the Imperial Theatre reopened, 'under the management of Miss Ellen Terry', with the production, on a very grand scale, of Dr. Henrik Ibsen's play, *The Vikings*. This is the biggest splash that has ever been made with Ibsen; and if the conflagration of the adjacent river does not ensue, then the sworn followers of the forlorn Norwegian will be hard put to it to account for the failure to set the Thames on fire by any other reason than the inherent faults of the play.

From any point of view, *The Vikings* is not a good play. If no author's name had been given in the programme, I am sure that a good many people, who will regard it as a sacred obligation to declare it a masterpiece because it is signed by Henrik Ibsen, would have looked upon it merely as an indifferent imitation of the plays of Mr. Wilson Barrett, written without Mr. Barrett's sense of the theatre or his cunning in craftsmanship. The story of *The Vikings* is mere blood and thunder, and the action indirect, heavy, and uncertain. The play, to be sure, is an early work of the author; but although the subject is highly romantic, the savagery which is so marked in his other plays, the principle that everything is for the worst in the best of all possible worlds, asserts itself in his dealings with Vikings as emphatically as it does in his observation of the narrower life of the meaner folk who figure more or less ignominiously in his later contributions to the theatre. There is nothing of *the grand manner* in his treatment of a great theme, which has been more imaginatively treated in grand opera and by an English poet. Although, once in the course of the play, Ibsen approaches an elevated dramatic position, we are not moved as we ought to be moved, and as we should be moved if the treacherous murder of the valiant son of Ornulf of the Fiords had been handled by a dramatist who designed to strike us with pity instead of with horror and disgust. Ibsen has not the gift of tears—nor of laughter either, coming to that, and it is not necessary to insist upon the limitations of a dramatist who cannot make an audience laugh or cry. Myself, I can only judge of Ibsen by the translations of his plays, which, to do him justice, have a rigidity in English which they have not in the French translations I have seen. But if the English version of *The Vikings* adopted at the Imperial is cold and bare, I feel that such an expression as 'going a-viking', which is used more than once, may be but a clumsy rendering of a perfectly acceptable Norwegian term. Some people, I know, talk of 'biking' when they speak of taking exercise on wheels; but the verb 'to bike' will not be found in the standard dictionaries, and 'to vike', as it strikes me, has no better title to a place among words of respectable origin.

When they 'go a-viking' in the play at the Imperial, they 'vike', so to say, like anything. Ornulf of the Fiords, an Icelandic Chieftain, and Sigurd the Strong, a Sea-King, visit the island of Helgeland in the tenth century, and the wife of their friend Gunnar Headman, a rich yeoman of Helgeland, intrudes so maliciously upon their domestic affairs that there is presently—to give a Viking turn to an English idiom —*Helgeland and Tommy* on the island. Hiördis, the lady in question, had married Gunnar ten years before, not because she loved him, but because she had reason to believe that he had killed the White Bear in her Bower. Now a White Bear is not exactly the kind of pet one would look for in a lady's bower, but as it is expressly stated that the bear was 'chained up' in the bower, I do not think it was such a wonderful, brave thing to have killed the brute. On the night of a feast Hiördis comes to 'vike' with the warriors, and begins to brag about her husband's great feat of killing the White Bear that was Chained Up in her Bower and challenges the others to mention any deed to equal that. Then up speaks Sigurd. He relates, with becoming modesty, how he had killed eight men at one encounter. Between you and me, I think it takes more pluck to deal with eight men than with a White Bear which is Chained Up in a Lady's Bower—and tamed, too, for all you know. Goaded to it by Hiördis, Sigurd's wife tells her bluntly that she has nothing to be so very proud of—that it was not Gunnar at all, but Sigurd himself, who had killed the White Bear which was Chained Up in the Lady's Bower, only Sigurd had agreed to let Gunnar take the credit for it—and with the credit the lady, whose favour was only to be won in that way. As soon as she hears this Hiördis is the Norwegian for 'ready to drop'. She realises, just as Ibsen's ladies will do, that she has not been 'living her own life', but somebody else's, and her affections are straightway transferred to Sigurd, who has been an exemplary husband up to this point, when he confesses, much to our surprise, that he has himself loved Hiördis all along. Under the circumstances, what is to be done next? Why, Hiördis, of course, shoots Sigurd to the heart with an arrow—just to show him how much she loves him, I suppose, and when he expires, with an utterly immaterial profession of Christian faith on his lips, Hiördis naturally flings herself into the sea, and there is an end of it.

Some novel effects of stage-lighting have been introduced by Mr. Edward Gordon Craig, by whom the 'entire production "has been" designed and directed'. Mr. Craig is an ardent reformer who has great ideas upon the subject of stage management; but his schemes, to judge by the production of *The Vikings*, are for the present better 'designed' than 'directed'. Mr. Craig, I am sure, means well. I should be very sorry to discourage an artist with lofty ideals; but Mr. Craig, who will have nothing to do with the old-fashioned footlights, has not yet perfected the means of doing without them. At the Imperial we are *all in the dark*, not only as to the author's purpose, but in a literal sense as well; for light seems to be used in *The Vikings* chiefly to show the darkness, and the effect is such that one cannot plainly see the faces of the actors. So the play of features counts practically for nothing. Mr. Craig is much too zealous a champion of the art of acting to wish to do without that. But he has yet to solve the puzzle how to preserve the mystic touch of darkness, to which he attaches so much value, without destroying the telling effects of strong light. At any rate, he gives us *a new sensation*, and we do not often get a real surprise at the theatre nowadays. It is something of a surprise, too, to see Miss Ellen Terry in such a part as that of the wicked Hiördis. I take it that Hiördis is intended to be a desperate, wicked woman, though Miss Terry makes it difficult to think so. For Miss Terry, the sunniest of her sex, has not the temperament for such a malignant character. The cares and responsibilities of management are the invariable excuse for the imperfections of a first performance, and Miss Terry, no doubt, will have acquired the complete mastery of her words since Wednesday night, when she had frequent recourse to the prompter. Mr. Holman Clark's performance of Örnulf of the Fiords is the best bit of acting in the piece; it is from beginning to end in the heroic vein, dignified without pomposity. A fine touch is his exit, with his head erect, after he has heard of the murder of his youngest son, following hard upon the death in battle of his six other sons. Mr. Oscar Asche's Sigurd the Strong is also a very good piece of acting. There is nothing of 'swagger' in the easy way in which he talks of polishing off that White Bear which was Chained Up in the Lady's Bower, and there is a world of tenderness in his scenes with his wife, Dagny, to whom he seems devoted until Hiördis turns his head. The character of Dagny is played unaffectedly and feelingly by Miss Hutin Britton, and good work is done by Mr. Hubert Carter, as the yeoman who did not kill the White Bear which was Chained Up in the Lady's Bower; by Mr. Conway Tearle, as Thorolf, the Icelandic Chief's fiery son; and by Mr. Mark Kinghorne, as a peasant who 'goes-a-viking' on what you may call 'his own'.

At the end of the performance Miss Ellen Terry expressed her thanks to the audience, who had given such frequent and exuberant expression to their friendly feeling in the course of the evening that if it were the business of a newspaper, as some profess to believe, only to record the manner in which a play is received, I should have to say that Miss Terry had achieved the greatest triumph of her career. But Miss Terry would not believe that. Nor would you. Nor do I.

Miss Ellen Terry has signalised her first venture in theatrical management by making one change for which an important class of playgoers will, I am sure, be duly grateful.

The patient pittites, who are only too little considered at some theatres in these days, have to thank Miss Terry for the substantial benefit she has conferred upon them by reducing the price of admission to the pit from half a crown to two shillings. If this puts sixpence into the pittite's pocket, I shall be surprised if the management of the Imperial do not find in this reform not a loss but a source of profit.

166. A notice by Max Beerbohm, *Saturday Review*

25 April 1903, xcv, 517–18

There is seldom the least difficulty in determining why such-and-such a play has been produced by such-and-such a manager. The reason, almost always, comes pat: the manager thought the play would draw the public, or thought it less unlikely to draw the public than any other play in his bureau. Occasionally, the motive for production seems to be the desire of an actor-manager to play a certain part at all costs. Rarelier still, the motive is that he admires the play, as a work of art, so profoundly that he must at all costs produce it. Now, Miss Ellen Terry has just initiated her management of the Imperial Theatre by producing Ibsen's *Vikings at Helgeland*. But, oddly enough, none of the aforesaid motives can be held to account for her action. The play is not, as I shall suggest, one which she in her most sanguine mood could have hoped the British public would like. Nor, as I shall suggest also, is Hiördis a part in which she could have hoped to make a personal success. Nor is it likely that she has throughout all these years been cherishing for Ibsen a secret admiration so strong as to compel her to produce, as the first-fruits of her independence, a play which is admitted (even by the straitest sect of the Ibsenites) to belong to Ibsen's immaturity. Why, then, has she done this thing? By process of exhaustion, I conclude that she did it for the sake of her son, Mr. Gordon Craig, thinking that thereby he would gain for his new ideas a wider acceptance than they had yet had. The motive is altogether to Miss Terry's credit; and I am glad that she has not been disappointed. Hitherto Mr. Craig has had to work in a hole-and-corner way, or else in a subordinate way, with the result that he has been taken less seriously than he deserves. Now, by grace of the strongest of human sentiments, he has had his chance, and has come off with flying colours. For the art of Ibsen and the art of Miss Terry our admiration has not been intensified; but the stage-manager-scene-painter-designer-of-costumes-and-all-the-rest-of-it looms up illustriously with laurels on his brow. On the first night Miss Terry led Mr. Craig before the footlights (or rather, before the place where the footlights were before Mr. Craig swept them away). It would have seemed more correct, really, if Mr. Craig, with an air of grateful acknowledgment, had led Miss Terry.

The Vikings is excellently well suited to Mr. Craig's theory of stage-arrangement. I do not mean that he is incapable of varying his methods according to the kind of work he is illustrating. On the contrary, nothing could be less like the grim mystery of his Viking effects than was the sunny and childish gaiety of the effects wrought by him for *The Triumph of Love*. But it is obvious that his method has limits to its elasticity. It could not be stretched into realism. Outside fantasy it would snap. The lighting of the stage from one place above, instead of from many places below and on either side, is, of course, a change in the direction of realism. But the abolition of ceiling or 'flies', with the effect that the people on the stage seem to be sunk in a gigantic shaft, utterly precludes any notion of realism. Decoratively, Mr. Craig wins from this system very valuable effects. But I am speaking for the moment, from the standpoint of mere drama. For a modern play, in which the aim is to produce the nearest possible illusion of actuality, Mr. Craig's system would be manifestly impossible. Further, it would be inappropriate to any poetic plays in which we are meant to accept the characters primarily as human beings. It could not be applied, for instance, to the plays of Shakespeare, except to those which Shakespeare wrote as fantasies. For his fantasies it would be as much more right than the present system as it were less right for his human plays. It would strike at once the proper keynote, reminding the audience that here they are translated from the plane of what actually does exist to the plane of what actually doesn't and couldn't. And for this very reason it is right for *The Vikings*.

I do not assert that there never actually was an actual race of Vikings. I freely admit that it existed, and that the members of it may have behaved exactly as Ibsen makes them behave. Nor do I deny that by a modern Scandinavian audience this play might not be taken as a play of human passion. But I do say that no modern English audience could regard it as anything but a wild fantasy. The difficulty is not that we are too far away from its period: we are too far away from its climate. Barbarism we can understand, if it be the kind of barbarism that flourished on our own shores or on shores adjacent to us. But the barbarism of the North strikes us as something quite beyond the pale of possibility. It strikes us as definitely inhuman. Living in a land which is never extremely cold, and on which the sun does sometimes shine, we can accept warm-blooded monsters as kindred to us. But we reject those boreal monsters whose blood has been frozen inclemently in their veins. The capacity for what we call 'passion' is the touchstone that we apply to humanity. And the kind of 'passion' that we mean depends on the action of the sun's rays. Where the barometer is always at zero, there is no 'passion' at all. That is what we miss in the modern Scandinavian drama generally. Only the intellectuality of the characters forces us to recognise them as human. Take away that intellectuality, and substitute for it the habit of mere physical violence, and the characters become, forthwith, wholly fantastic. Physical violence, without passion, is the keynote of *The Vikings*. Hiördis has no more love for Sigurd the Strong than she has for Gunnar Headman. It is only his action in killing the white bear that she loves. If the white bear had killed him instead, she would have had quite as much direct sentiment for the white bear. Conversely, we do not feel called on to pity Sigurd for that in the first instance Gunnar gets the credit for the deed, and the hand of Hiördis. We feel that it matters not in the least whom he marries. Finally, we experience no pang in the knowledge that Hiördis and Sigurd are parted after death, the one going to the Pagan Valhalla, the other to the Christian Heaven. The one will be in her element, the other will be out of his; but their disunion will detract nothing from the pleasure of the one, nor add aught to the discomfort of the other. These two characters (and the rest are like them) cannot but seem to us monstrous, impossible. The whole play cannot but seem to us a monstrous, impossible fantasy. This being so, the best way to produce it is in the extreme manner of fantasy. Hence the appropriateness of Mr. Gordon Craig. The strange, supernatural element which he casts over every scene is justified beyond all cavil. We shudder in unfathomable darknesses, in immemorial frosts. The monsters here, as monsters, become positively real to us. We are positively afraid of them. If they were presented to us in the customary realistic manner, we should merely smile at them as at animals walking on their hind-legs. It is foolish to complain, as many critics have complained, that Mr. Craig's system of lighting does not always illuminate the features of the mimes' faces. In the case of a play demanding subtle interpretation this complaint would be justified. But *The Vikings* is a play in which nothing would be lost if all the characters wore masks. Indeed, it would be all the better, if the masks were sufficiently grotesque. The muscles of the face count for nothing in it. The muscles of the arms and legs, however, really are rather important. Both Mr. Oscar Asche and Mr. Hubert Carter, who play Sigurd and Gunnar, are well developed in this respect; and, as they have, also, very strong voices, and a generally terrific manner, I do not think their respective parts could be better enacted. But it is a melancholy thing to see Miss Ellen Terry, that incarnation of our capricious English sunlight, grappling with the part of Hiördis, and trying so hard not to turn it all 'to favour and to prettiness'. Now and again, she does contrive to break away from herself, and becomes a sort of abstract figure; but, even so, she is always a pleasant, English abstraction—a genial Britannia ruling unfrozen waves.

167. W. Rothenstein on Max Beerbohm's obtuseness

May 1903

A letter to the editor of the *Saturday Review* (9 May 1903), xcv, 588. The writer, W. Rothenstein, may have been the future Sir William Rothenstein (1872–1945), a trustee of the Tate. His letter is dated 6 May 1903, and is addressed from 26 Church Row, Hampstead.

Sir,—I do not feel sure that everyone would gather from Mr. Max Beerbohm's article in the *Saturday Review* for 25 April, that there is at this moment being nightly played in London a drama, singularly grand and lofty in spirit, the interpretation of which is more remarkable than any which I have seen in this, or any other country. I refer to Mr. Gordon Craig's production of Ibsen's *Vikings*, produced under Miss Ellen Terry's management at the Imperial Theatre, in which, for the first time in the history of the stage, a whole play has been represented perfectly in every part.

A feeling against the wanton extravagance and low standard of taste which prevail in the theatre in England has been slowly gaining ground, but Mr. Craig is the first to show us that the particular qualities which excite our enthusiasm in other arts may also be brought upon the stage, and that it is possible for a play to be produced which may be judged by the same standard and enjoyed to the same degree as poetry, painting and music.

Mr. Craig's genius, his unique perception of all the qualities which go to make an atmosphere of dignity and beauty of dramatic expression, must, sooner or later, raise the standard of the theatre in England. It were a pity, however, if that active encouragement without which theatrical achievement is almost impossible in existing circumstances were not forthcoming from all those who hold that beauty is one of the essential elements of life.

168. P. T. Barnum and others cable Ibsen

June 1903

From *Current Literature* (June 1903), xxxiv, 719–20. The magazine reprinted, in the order given below, some of the telegrams which had been sent to Ibsen on his seventy-fifth birthday.

My hearty thanks for your problems, which I have faithfully sought to portray, but never succeeded in solving.

Maurice Maeterlinck

You ascend; I descend.

Maxim Gorki

How Many Thousand Dollars do you want per Evening?

P. T. Barnum

I wonder who will honour me when I am seventy-five?

George Brandes

I honour you because your name is not Björnson.

Gunnar Heiberg

My Brother: When I say 'My Brother' I raise you to the highest level I can imagine.

Björnstjerne Björnson

Congratulations and thanks because you did not become a bureaucrat.

Alexander Kielland

THE COLLECTED LETTERS OF
HENRIK IBSEN

1905

169. From 'Ibsen in His Letters', by
William Archer, *Fortnightly Review*

1 March 1905, lxxvii, 428–41

Archer reviews *The Collected Letters of Henrik Ibsen*, ed. John Laurvik and Mary Morison (London: Hodder and Stoughton, 1905).

In the first place, it is interesting to note the literary influences to which he was subjected in the impressionable years of his early manhood. We know from one or two of his immature works that the sentimental romanticism of Oehlenschlaeger must have attracted him for a time; but there is no trace of this influence in his letters. In 1852, when he was sent by the management of the Bergen Theatre to study the Danish stage in Copenhagen, he writes to his employers: 'In respect to the repertory we have been very fortunate, having seen *Hamlet* and several other plays of Shakespeare, and also several of Holberg's.' The other plays of Shakespeare which he probably saw at this time were *King Lear*, *Romeo and Juliet*, and *As You Like It*. Of these, *Lear* and *As You Like It* must greatly have impressed him, for he cites them years afterwards; but it does not appear that his acquaintance with Shakespeare was ever wide or deep. On the other hand, Holberg, the great Danish-Norwegian comedy-writer of the eighteenth century, was throughout life his favourite author. His letters abound in Holberg quotations; he declares him to be the one writer he never tires of reading; and on the only occasion when I, personally, ever saw Ibsen greatly excited, a phrase from Holberg rose to his lips.

In a former article in this *Review*, I have shown that his constant employment for several years in mounting the plays of Scribe and his school must have had a determining influence on his technique; but he clearly recognised, at an early period, that it was an influence to be outgrown. When some French critics tried, most absurdly, to class him as an imitator of Dumas *fils*, Ibsen wrote to Brandes: 'I owe absolutely nothing to Dumas in respect to dramatic form—except that I have learnt from him to avoid certain glaring errors and clumsinesses of which he is not infrequently guilty.' He could never rest satisfied with semi-realism of form; for that his sense of logic was too imperious. Before the appearance of *The League of Youth*, his first prose play of modern life, he wrote to Brandes: 'I have been very scrupulous as to form, and have, among other things, achieved the feat of working out my theme without the aid of a single soliloquy, or even aside.' This self-denying ordinance he somewhat relaxed on returning to historical drama in *Emperor and Galilean*; but when Mr. Gosse suggested that it had better have been written in verse, he energetically dissented. 'The illusion,' he said, 'which I wanted to produce was that of reality; I wanted to give the reader the impression that what he was reading had actually happened. . . . My new play is not a tragedy in the old sense of the word; I have tried to represent human beings, and therefore I have not allowed them to speak "the language of the gods."' Ten years later, when a Norwegian actress, Fru Wolf, asked him for a prologue to be spoken at her benefit, he replied to the effect that a self-respecting dramatic artist ought to be chary of reciting even a single verse upon the stage, so much harm had metre done to the art of acting. This was no doubt the utterance of a momentary fanaticism; but it harmonises with the austere repression of every lyric impulse which reached its height, just about the date of this letter, in *An Enemy of the People*. In his later plays, as we know, poetry regained the upper hand, and more and more encroached upon realism, in spirit, if not in outward form.

The making of a play meant, for Ibsen, an extraordinary effort of mental concentration. He put everything else aside, read no books, attended to no business that was not absolutely imperative, and lived for weeks and months with his characters alone. He writes in June 1884: 'I have in these days completed a play in five acts. That is to say, I have roughed it out: now comes the more delicate manipulation of it, the more energetic individualisation of the characters and their mode of expression.' This play was *The Wild Duck*. A month or two later he writes: 'The people in my new play, in spite of their manifold frailties, have through long and daily familiarity endeared themselves to me.

. . . I believe that *The Wild Duck* will perhaps lure some of our younger dramatists into new paths, and that I hold to be desirable.' In 1890, when he has finished *Hedda Gabler*, he writes to Count Prozor: 'It gives me a strange feeling of emptiness to part from a piece of work which has now, for several months, exclusively occupied my time and my thoughts. Yet it is well that it has come to an end. The incessant association with these imaginary people was beginning to make me not a little nervous.'

Of æsthetic theory, other than that which he himself constructed for his own use and behoof, Ibsen was very impatient. One of his first remarks on coming in contact with the art of antiquity and of the renaissance is that 'as yet, at any rate, I can often see only conventions where others profess to find laws.' Antique sculpture he cannot at first 'bring into relation to our time.' He misses 'the personal and individual expression, both in the artist and in his work.' 'Michael Angelo, Bernini, and his school I understand better; those fellows had the courage to play a mad prank now and then.' He afterwards saw deeper into the nature of antique art; but in 1869, after he had been five years in Italy, he wrote: 'Raphael's art has never really warmed me; his creations belong to the world before the Fall.' Yet of anything like pre-Raphaelitism, in the English sense of the term, he was entirely innocent. Florentine art, so far as we can see, had nothing to say to him. On his return to Rome in 1879 he bought a number of 'old masters,' partly from taste, partly as an investment; but he does not mention the name of a single painter. My impression is that the paintings he used to have around him would be but slightly esteemed by English connoisseurs; but, when I have visited him, I have had little attention to spare for his picture gallery. It is noteworthy, by the way, that at the Vienna Exhibition of 1873 he found the English art-section to consist 'almost exclusively of masterpieces.' In his youth, it will be remembered, he had himself given a good deal of time to painting.

This, however, is a digression: I return to his views on æsthetic theory in general. When he has been a year in Italy, he writes to Björnson that the most important result of his travels has been the elimination from his mind of the æsthetic system, 'isolated and claiming inherent validity,' which formerly had power over him. 'Æsthetics in this sense now appear to me as great a curse to poetry as theology is to religion. You,' he continues, 'have never been troubled with this sort of æstheticism, you have never gone about looking at things through your hollow hand.' Some years later, when a Danish critic, Clemens Petersen, has tried *Peer Gynt* by his æsthetic standard, and pronounced it 'not really poetry,' Ibsen retorts (in a letter to Björnson) with a splendid arrogance that Dante or Milton might have envied: 'The book *is* poetry; or if it is not, it shall become poetry. The concept "poetry" in our country, in Norway, shall refashion itself in accordance with the book.' In the same letter he continues: 'If it is to be war, so be it! If I am no poet, I have nothing to lose. I shall set up as a photographer. My contemporaries up in the north I will deal with individually, man by man. . . . Nothing shall escape me—no thought or feeling lurking behind the words in any soul that deserves the honour of being noticed.' This was written in a moment of hot indignation; but it can scarcely be said that when the indignation cooled the purpose had evaporated.

Of criticism in general Ibsen writes: 'The majority of critical strictures reduce themselves, in the last analysis, to reproaches addressed to an author because he is himself, and thinks, feels, sees, and creates like himself, instead of seeing and creating as the critic would have done—had he had the power.'

Ibsen is never tired of insisting that all his writings—even his romantic plays—stand in intimate relation to his own life. 'I have never,' he declares, 'written anything merely because, as the saying goes, I had "hit on a good subject".' He repeats again and again, to different correspondents, a distinction of which the full force escapes me. Everything he has produced, he says, has its origin in something he has not merely experienced (*oplevet*) but lived through (*gennemlevet*). Perhaps he is here repeating in another form the definition of poetry as 'emotion recollected in tranquillity'; but this seems scarcely consistent with an idea he more than once repeats, that poetic production purges the system of fermenting elements which would become poisonous if not expelled. A few examples may perhaps make his meaning clearer. *Catilina* was written in the little philistine town of Grimstad, where (as he seems to imply) he stood in very much the same relation to respectable, conservative society in which Catiline stood to the ruling oligarchy of Rome.

Lady Inger of Östraat is founded on a love-affair, hastily entered into and violently broken off. . . . *The Vikings* I wrote when I was engaged to be married. For Hiördis I employed the same model who afterwards served for Svanhild in *Love's Comedy*. . . . The fact that everyone was against me, that there was no one in the outer world who could be said to believe in me, could not but give rise to the strain of feeling which found utterance in *The Pretenders*. . . . Brand is myself in my best moments—just as, by self-dissection, I have brought to light many of the character-traits both of Peer Gynt and of Stensgaard.

In the latter character (the hero of *The League of Youth*) he was commonly accused of having drawn Björnson. Replying in advance to this accusation, he wrote: 'People in Norway will perhaps say that I have depicted real persons and circumstances. This is not the case. I have, however, used models, which are as indispensable to the writer of comedy as to the painter or sculptor.' Here again I must own that the distinction baffles me. I can only imagine the meaning to be that he takes 'composite photographs,' not individual likenesses. As a matter of fact, Stensgaard was doubtless intended rather as a warning to Björnson than as a portrait of him.

The confession that parts of Peer Gynt and Stensgaard are the result of self-dissection may be compared with Mr. Meredith's similar admission (to Stevenson) with regard to Sir Willoughby Patterne. Ibsen not infrequently insists on the sternness of his self-criticism. To a lady correspondent he writes: 'You must not think that I am so unkindly disposed towards my countrymen as many people accuse me of being. At any rate, I can assure you I am no more indulgent to myself than to others.' And, again, to Björnson: 'You may be sure that in my leisure moments I probe, and sound, and anatomise pretty searchingly in my own inward parts; and that at the points where it bites the sorest.'

On his political and social utterances I need not dwell long, for the most important of them, occurring in letters to George Brandes, have long ago been quoted by that critic, in his *Ibsen and Björnson*. It was to Brandes, for example, that he expressed his lack of interest in 'special revolutions, revolutions in externals, in the political sphere,' adding, 'What is really wanted is a revolution of the spirit of man.' Familiar, too, is his remark that 'he who possesses liberty otherwise than as an aspiration possesses it soulless, dead'; and, again, 'I confess that the only thing about liberty that I love is the fight for it; I care nothing about the possession of it.' These, and all his most noteworthy political deliverances, will be found in Brandes's invaluable essay.

A systematic political thinker Ibsen never was or could be. His views were full of incompatibilities, which he did not dream of harmonising. The one thing he consistently detested throughout life was opportunism. He was, if one may coin a word, an impossibilist. That a course of action was useless and hopeless was, in his eyes, the best reason for pursuing it. His bitter contempt for the inaction of Norway and Sweden when Denmark was crushed by Prussia was one of the forces that drove him into exile and kept him in estrangement from his country. It did not occur to him to inquire whether there would have been any use in their rushing into the quarrel. The humiliation which he then felt was, as appears from one of his letters, a main reason for his abandoning the field of national history and legend. He no longer took any pleasure in evoking the great past of his country, seeing that the men of to-day stood to the men of the sagas in the relation of a modern Levantine pirate to a hero of Homer. His impulse now was to hurl scorn at his degenerate countrymen through the mouth of Brand, and to embody in Peer Gynt their pusillanimity, their egoism, their 'halfness.' And of this feeling we find a curious echo in the very last letter included in these volumes. It is written in December, 1900, to a Dutch journalist who had upbraided him for some mildly pro-British utterance with regard to the South African War. Ibsen does not attempt to discuss the merits of the case, but answers: 'You say that the Dutch are the Boers' natural defenders in Europe: why have not your countrymen chosen a point of more strategic importance for their defensive operations? I mean South Africa. And then, this method of defending kinsmen with books, and pamphlets, and open letters! May I ask, Mr. Editor, if you could not have found more effective weapons?' 'Mr. Editor' probably thought the sneer very unreasonable; but it was precisely the reproach which in *Brand*, and in his lyrics at the time of the Danish war, the poet had flung in the teeth of his own countrymen.

One of the contradictions of Ibsen's political thinking lay (it seems to me) in the fact that he accepted the idea of definite national units, while he would fain have denied them all organisation. His hatred of 'the State' appears over and over again in these letters. He does not shrink from utterances of sheer anarchism; but he does shrink from—or rather he never attains to—the idea of internationalism or cosmopolitan-ism, without which anarchism is surely unthinkable. Ibsen is always a tribeman, though as life goes on his conception of the tribe widens. In early life he was an ardent 'Scandinavian'—a champion, that is to say, of the political union of the three northern kingdoms. 'I began,' he wrote to George Brandes in 1888, 'by feeling as a Norwegian, I developed into a Scandinavian, and have now come to rest in all-embracing Germanism. . . . I believe that national consciousness is dying out, and that it will be replaced by race-consciousness.' This course of thought is not unlike that which Mr. George Wyndham set forth in his recent Rectorial Address at Glasgow. Much earlier (1872) Ibsen had told Mr. Gosse that the introduction of his works into England was one of his 'dearest literary dreams' because 'the English people stands so near to us Scandinavians.' Without criticising the race-idea, from the point of view either of science or of expediency, one cannot but inquire how a race, any more than a nation, can maintain and assert itself in anarchic incoherence? The race-unit, no less than the nation-unit, must surely be an organism. Anarchism implies the negation of the unit, the absorption of all units in a homogeneous mass. How little Ibsen cared for consistency appears when we find him, in the 'nineties, acknowledging the benefits conferred on Germany by the drill-sergeant, and placing 'discipline' in the forefront of the ethical requirements of his countrymen.

Inconsistency of thought need not surprise us in a poet who has so strongly emphasised the relativity and consequent impermanence of truth. 'A normally constituted truth,' says Dr. Stockmann, 'lives—let us say—seventeen or eighteen years; at the outside twenty.' But this estimate is only a flourish of the worthy Doctor's. Ibsen himself would probably have been the first to admit that, on the plane of expediency at any rate, five minutes may perfectly suffice to turn a truth into a falsehood. His mind was intensive rather than extensive. He did not profess or attempt to apprehend a thing in all its relations. He saw one aspect of it vividly and stated it forcibly, without denying that there might be other aspects of equal or greater validity. He evidently believed that ideas, like organisms, must be sifted through the struggle for existence, in order that the fittest may survive. Consequently he never hesitated to throw out the thought that for the moment dominated him, and let it take its chance among the rest; well knowing, at the same time, that it might one day be swallowed up by a larger and stronger thought, perhaps emanating from his own brain.

This intensiveness is a symptom or consequence of a slow-moving, brooding habit of mind which is manifest throughout his correspondence. He is not prolific of ideas; he ruminates on one or two at a time, until they embody themselves in dramatic form, and he 'gets them off his heart.' A letter to George Brandes, dated April 1872, contains the germs of two plays, published, respectively, ten and fourteen years later. 'I hear,' he says, 'that you have founded an association. . . . How far your position is thereby strengthened, I cannot judge: it seems to me that he is strongest who stands alone.' And again, with reference to some controversy in which Brandes was engaged, he thus apostrophises him: 'Be dignified! Dignity [or, better, distinction] is the only weapon in such conflicts.' In these two utterances we have the root-ideas of *An Enemy of the People* and *Rosmersholm*; and similar germs of other plays may be discerned every here and there in his letters, at dates which indicate that he brooded over them for years. That he could, on occasion, warm into conversational brilliancy is proved by two witnesses: Professor Dietrichson, who was with him in Rome in the 'sixties, and the painter Grönvold, who saw a good deal of him in Munich in '77. But Dietrichson admits that these occasions were rare. Thoughts did not, as a rule, flash upon him as he talked; he was more apt to draw, with great deliberation, on the previously-formed ideas which were slowly revolving in his brain. I happened to be with him frequently at the time when the publication of *Ghosts* had raised a storm in Scandinavia; and I find his letters of these weeks studded with the very phrases which he used to me in conversation. . . .

Throughout his letters we find Ibsen notably free from the characteristic foibles of the literary man. Clemens Petersen's attack on *Peer Gynt* is the one criticism that stings him into what may be called personal wrath. For the rest, though he is often indignant, it is with the indignation of the exasperated satirist, not of the fretful author. George Brandes criticised *Peer Gynt* on its appearance almost as unsympathetically as did Petersen; of *Hedda Gabler*, too, he wrote in the most disparaging terms; but neither criticism made any difference in Ibsen's friendship for him. No one could ever guess from those letters that their writer had been, for ten years or so, the most furiously assailed and reprobated of European authors. He resolutely acted up to his own advice to Brandes: 'Be dignified!' It was, indeed, one of the contradictions of his nature, that while intellectually an ultra-radical he was temperamentally an aristocrat. This was the source of many of the seeming inconsistencies in his doctrine—inconsistencies which he would probably have said that it must be the task of the future to harmonise. His ideal was a democracy of aristocrats and his moods of pessimism were those in which he feared that this must for ever remain a contradiction in terms.

In 1874, he wrote to Mr. Gosse that the delicacy of his (Mr. Gosse's) lyrics ought to be specially appreciated by 'the English nation, whose practical efficiency is in such a wonderful way combined with a pure and noble habit of feeling, which makes it, as a whole, a nation of aristocrats, in the best sense of the word.' Could he have foreseen even a few of the epithets habitually attached to his name by the English Press of the early 'nineties, he might have found something to modify in this panegyric.

THE WILD DUCK

Court Theatre, October 1905

170. From a pseudonymous notice by 'Mordred', *Referee*

22 October 1905, 3

As somebody said of Racine, 'Il passera avec le café,' so it may be said of Ibsen—with more truth, I apprehend—that he has blown over. We hear and see less of him than we did a few years ago. Where to-day are the faithful who worshipped Ibsen? The altars of the Scandinavian god are deserted. In the old days the performance of an Ibsen play was a solemn rite, a religious service. The famous 'Bayreuth hush,' of which you may have heard, was nothing to the glum silence in the theatre consecrated to the Ibsen mysteries. You took your place and looked into the crown of your hat, for all the world as if you were in church. The actors who officiated, if the expression may be allowed, also cultivated the yearnest Ibsen manner. There was the Ibsen voice—a way of implying hidden meanings, as who should say 'Pass the salt' in portentous tones. Then there was the Ibsen stare. Oh, that ghastly stare! Once an actress had that she never got over it. It was very austere, very weird, very foolish; but all that is changed at the Court, where *The Wild Duck* was revived last week. Truth compels me to admit that Ibsen has always been zealously served by the actors taking part in his plays; and at the Court, where the best acting on the London stage is to be seen, the thing is, as usual, uncommonly well done. But it is done without any of the old hocus-pocus. If the character of the acting has changed, so has the character of the audience; and instead of the strong-minded women and weak-minded men, the flat-chested, flat-footed women and the men all 'sicklied o'er with the pale cast of thought,' who constituted the little sect of the old days, the audience who comes to see Ibsen at the

Court is simply a fashionable audience out for an afternoon's amusement. And a pretty dish is this *Wild Duck* to set before such an audience!

The Wild Duck is said by those who profess to know the author's purpose to be symbolical, but what it symbolises they do not tell. That remains a secret, and I confess that, although I have seen the play twice before, the meaning is to this day unrevealed to me. An ardent Ibsenite —or since there are no longer any Ibsenites, let me say a friend who was one of the first to preach the gospel according to Ibsen in this country— once told me that *The Wild Duck* was obscure to me because certain cells of my brain were not open—whatever that may mean. It did not seem to occur to my friend that I might have retorted that the opening of certain of his own brain-cells would enable him to discover that there was no meaning at all in it. I recognise that the 'wild duck,' which gives the name to the piece, is not the precious fowl which is supposed to be cooped up in Hialmar Ekdal's garret; I have an idea that the title is intended to apply to Ekdal's daughter, who is not really Ekdal's daughter; and that all the dark hints about the wild duck refer indirectly to the child Hedvig, who is a duck, in the idiomatic use of the word, as a term of endearment, if not by any means wild for a girl of her age.

It is not only when they are talking about the duck that the characters seem to be speaking metaphorically; indeed, they give you the impression, for the most part, that they always mean more than they say. It is puzzling to know what else they mean; and this sort of thing will not do for the theatre, where the materialized idea is the only thing that counts; or, to put it plainly, where seeing is believing. An audience believes what it sees, just that, and no more. Candidly, I do not believe Ibsen has any such deep design as some people pretend. My own impression is that *The Wild Duck* is only a crazy sort of play—the work of a great, unbalanced mind. The piece has fine qualities, certainly; Ibsen conducts a scene, up to a certain point, with extraordinary cunning; the dialogue is sometimes wonderfully natural and direct and dramatic, but he seems to be incapable of fixing his mind upon a plain, intelligible issue. It is genius, but it is genius 'gone wrong,' as the saying is. It is significant that Ibsen in this play, not for the first time, dwells persistently upon the idea of suicide. It is his obsession. Not for the first time, nor the second, we have a poor creature driven to suicide. And for what? I do not know. I cannot understand it. How does it further the ends of Gregers Werle, I should like to know, when the poor little Hedvig yields to his instigation to commit suicide, and the child of fourteen shoots herself? If she is mad, then so is Werle, who talks a great deal of nonsense about the 'ideal,' and seems to devote his life to making mischief with the best intentions. What does he want? I cannot say. What is his aim? I do not know. When the question is put to him point-blank at the end of the play, after the dead body of the child has been carried off, what does he answer? 'To be the thirteenth at table'—those are the last words of the play; and if you can tell me what is the sense of that remark, then you are cleverer at guessing riddles than I am.

Apart from what may be called the maniacal part of the play, there is, in the lucid intervals, matter of profound interest in *The Wild Duck*. The definition of character and the presentation of an aspect of humble life are amazingly well contrived, and a really poignant story is buried under a load of rubbish. When Hialmar Ekdal discovers that his employer had been the lover of his wife before her marriage and after, and that the little girl he adores is, for all he (or the mother) knows, the child of the older Werle, there is drama in such a position of affairs. But Hialmar's attitude towards the wife who has been a devoted helpmate to him during all the years of his married life and to the unoffending child is not even consistent with his character for selfishness and irresolution and the suicide of the child—an abominable idea—is surely no solution of the difficulty. Assuming that his affection for the child has been such as we are asked to believe it to be, the cruelty with which he turns against her is like nothing so much as an accession of madness. I can better understand his wife, the easy-going, unimaginative creature, who is prepared to bear anything and everything without complaint, but is satisfied, in her dull way, to take everything as it comes.

The representation of the character of the wife, by Miss Agnes Thomas, is the best thing in a performance which is remarkable alike for individual and collective excellence. Gina's patient endurance of a life of drudgery, her sense of love and duty to her husband and her child, and her meekness and her spiritlessness are all admirably expressed by the actress. The listless manner in which she busies herself with the household work and the ring in her voice are well in character. Indeed, the only fault I have to find is that the actress affects the accent of English low life, which is destructive at once of the illusion of a Norwegian atmosphere. For this the actress is not alone to blame, for the nameless author of the translation in use at the Court makes the same mistake in availing himself too freely of the English idiom. That the play affords an actress such opportunities—and like opportunities have been found by other actresses in other plays by the same author—shows how keen is Ibsen's sense for the theatre, but curiously perverted is that sense in the conduct of his story. We have real people always doing unreal things.

From Ibsen, I suspect, Mr. Bernard Shaw has learned the trick of self-revelation which is so marked in his plays; but, while Mr. Shaw's characters reveal themselves frankly in terms which could only occur to Mr. Shaw, Ibsen's characters are often drawn with an insight and an individuality which do not belong to the creatures of Mr. Shaw's fancy. Mr. Granville Barker endows with life the character of the self-indulgent Ekdal, though the actor has not the power to give full expression to the emotional passages in the last act of the play. It is want of feeling, not of intelligence, or perhaps I should say it is not want of feeling but merely the inability to convey all he feels to the audience. It comes to the same thing. Mr. Scott Buist distinguishes himself in the character of the enigmatic Gregers Werle, who is as Ibsen has made him, and has deliberately made him, for all I can tell, for the sane man of the play, Relling (the doctor)—played by Mr. Matheson Lang with a sense of authority and of character—seems to have no misdoubts about the state of the wretched fellow's mind. Miss Dorothy Minto is natural and unaffected as Hedvig, so very natural and unaffected that there is nothing in her composition of the part to suggest the morbid disposition of the juvenile suicide. The play is a feast of good acting, and good acting excuses a great deal. Perhaps, however, it was not only because of the acting that I enjoyed myself so much at the Court Theatre.

171. From unsigned theatre comment, *Referee*

29 October 1905, 3

A correspondent, Dr. Arthur Koelbing, who has discovered the true inwardness of Ibsen, writes at great length upon the subject of Mordred's article last week on *The Wild Duck* at the Court. This correspondent is evidently a diligent student and a sincere admirer of the

Norwegian dramatist, but he is no Ibsenite in the obsolete sense of the word. He begins, indeed, with the remark that Ibsen 'was *never appreciated or understood* in England.' What will they say to that who used to worship Ibsen in the days of the old idolatry?

You are absolutely right [says my correspondent] in making ridiculous certain so-called worshippers of the great Norwegian, who did not understand him at all, but only affected to do so, and that in a most silly way. . . . If, as you say, there is no hocus-pocus about the performance at the Court, it means only that it is a good one. In fact, I think it is one of the very best Ibsen performances I have ever seen—and I have seen a good many of them.

The opinion of such an enthusiast that 'Mr. Granville Barker's representation of the character of Hialmar Ekdal was absolutely as the dramatist intends it to be,' may not, perhaps, be accepted unreservedly by the most exacting critics, and my correspondent will no doubt be surprised to hear that Mr. Barker, who does not himself share his admirer's views altogether, has given up the part to another actor.

My correspondent will not allow that *The Wild Duck* is anything but a masterpiece, and with regard to Mordred's uncompromising description of it as 'a crazy sort of play' he says that 'it is nothing of the kind, if only one does not look for a hidden symbolic meaning it has not got.' This, I fancy, may seem flat blasphemy to the true believer. The mystery of *The Wild Duck* is perfectly clear to my correspondent. It is 'simply this' to him: 'the average man cannot face the truth.' I am bound to say that I am not converted by my correspondent's eloquent exposition of the gospel according to Ibsen, and I remain of Mordred's opinion still concerning the suicide of little Hedvig. Let us consider the case. 'As for poor little Hedvig,' says the defender of the faith, 'she has not the slightest thought of committing suicide when she leaves the room with the pistol.' Gregers Werle has suggested to her to win back her father's love by sacrificing what she loves best—that is, the 'wild duck.'

What a wild idea! As if a parent's love is to be gained in such fashion! Fancy telling children to kill their pets just to show how much they love their parents. 'When she hears Hialmar telling young Werle that he does not believe in her love, and that he felt sure she would never be willing to give her life for him, she shoots herself, overcome with grief and misery.' I find it difficult to reconcile this with my correspondent's previous statement that the child 'has not the slightest thought of committing suicide when she leaves the room with the pistol,' and the notion of instigating the child to take her own life—as Werle most assuredly does—strikes me as a monstrous, brutal, mad idea. 'That,' says my correspondent, in conclusion, 'seems to me perfectly psychological.' To me it seems perfectly idiotic, and serves only to confirm the opinion expressed with deliberation by Mordred that *The Wild Duck* is 'a crazy sort of play.'

His Majesty's Theatre, 2 November 1905

172. From an initialled notice by E. A. B[aughan], *Daily News*

3 November 1905, 8

The writer was a well-known critic. The review was headlined 'An Enemy of the People/A Drama of Individualism'.

Ibsen, it is well-known, wrote *An Enemy of the People* as an answer to the adverse criticism with which *Ghosts* was received, and not primarily as a contribution to the discussion of social and municipal ethics. Mr. Shaw will, perhaps, follow the Norwegian's example.

To the ordinary lover of the theatre the social problems suggested by this most dramatic play are not the chief point. Does the dramatist succeed in enchaining the attention of his audience and moving them? That is the aim of all drama. You may agree with Dr. Stockmann that individualism is the attitude for the strong man to take; that the minority is always right, or, at any rate, that the 'compact' majority, according to Carlyle's dictum, is certain to be wrong; you may discuss the question of whether a man's first duty is to his own family or to the larger family of the community in which he lives—all questions raised by this play; but the vitality of a drama does not rest on the ideas it may express or suggest. A tract is not drama.

I leave the answer to all these questions to abler pens than mine. All I have to deal with is the intensity of drama which Ibsen has managed to build from his material. Here I think all will agree that the play is power-ful, and that it genuinely moves, as the spectacle of a strong and brave man defying legions of moral cowards must always move. And the play has the merit of not preaching. The characters are characters in a drama and not mere abstractions or puppets in the conduct of the playwright's little tract. As I left His Majesty's Theatre I heard animated discussions, in which the opinion was freely expressed that Dr. Stockmann was a madman in making public his discoveries as to the pollution of the waters of the baths, when it meant the loss of a livelihood for himself and his family. He was mad, too, I learned, to fly in the face of the majority of his fellow-townsmen in rating them as fools, unfit to govern themselves through their representatives. An elderly gentleman of irreproachable appearance who sat behind me was strongly of opinion that if a medical officer of a watering place found that the baths were dangerous to the invalids who took them his first duty to his family was to hold his tongue. So that, after all, crude as are the ethical questions involved in Ibsen's play, they must be vital. Altruism is a sense not possessed by the majority of men, and Dr. Stockmann is obsessed by a very enthusiasm of altruism.

But I could not help feeling that he was also playing for his own bat. Partly, this was due to the self-consciousness of Mr. Tree's reading of the character. He was not naïve enough, and gave one the idea that the doctor was personally glad of having made his discovery not because it would save the lives of many invalids, but because the alteration of the water supply would furnish a test by which the Burgomaster and the municipality's altruism might be gauged and compared with his own. There is something of self-righteousness in the character which jars. May this not be the expression of Ibsen's self-exculpation as artist? He had been told that no one who loved his fellow-men could or should have written *Ghosts*; that he was an enemy of the people. The play has a certain element of giving the critics back something of their own abuse. For, after all, if Dr. Stockmann had the interests of his community as well as of the visitors to the baths so deeply at heart he might have tried what an explanation of his discovery to the authorities would bring forth. The result might have been the same, but at least the fiery altruist would have done all in his power to reform the evil without ruining his native city by an untimely public exposure. Ibsen, however, very cleverly builds up his character so that it seems natural that he should take the first opportunity of making his discovery public in the belief that the whole of his fellow-townsmen would be at his back and hail him as benefactor, but at the same time the Doctor's methods do suggest a desire to shine at the expense of every other consideration. Perhaps a simpler handling than Mr. Tree's would have had a different effect.

There is no doubt that the play held the public, especially in the big scene of the meeting at which Doctor Stockmann finds himself gagged by the wily proprietor of *The People's Messenger* and the pompous Burgomaster, both adepts at the procedure of public meetings. The characters are alive. The facing-both-ways editor, Hovstad; the printer-proprietor, Aslaksen, with his love of moderation and belief in the compact majority of the lower middle classes; the pompous Burgomaster, with his facile rhetoric and constitutional inability to seize the ethical aspects of any question which touches his pockets; the insincere, radical Billing, with his cheap, ready-made phrases; the malicious owner of the mills which are polluting the Baths, Morten Kiil, who buys up all the shares he can when the discovery is made public, and offers to leave them to Stockmann's children if he will but contradict his statements 'after due consideration,' and the practical-minded Mrs. Stockmann, who criticises her husband, but stands by his side when the storm bursts—all are alive individually, and also are types. Stockmann's daughter, Petra, is the Ibsen girl of advanced views and unfeminine courage—the future mother of altruistic citizens.

It cannot be said that the playing was quite in the picture. Mr. Robson's Aslaksen was most amusing, but the more amusing he was the less did the truth of the character come out, and it was the same with Mr. John Beauchamp's Burgomaster. The smaller parts of the editor and his 'sub.' were well played by Mr. Fisher White and Mr. Nigel Playfair. Miss Halstan was too lackadaisical as Petra, but Miss Rosina Filippi gave one of her natural and finished performances as the wife. Mr. Tree seems to have elaborated the business of his part since I saw him in it twelve years ago, and is more rhetorical. The breaking of the wine glass at the end of the first act is a piece of cheap symbolism which, I am very sure, would not meet with the approval of the author, and in the scene of the meeting Mr. Tree did not succeed in forgetting his Marc Antony. Ibsen requires rather quieter and more realistic acting. Still, the play is well done, and should prove of more than passing interest.

173. Keir Hardie on the instructiveness of Ibsen

1905

From a report, *Daily News* (3 November 1905), 8

Among the crowded audience that witnessed Mr. Beerbohm Tree's interesting revival of *An Enemy of the People* were a number of well-known politicians, County Councillors, and Churchmen interested in social reform.

From the Royal box Mr. Winston Churchill, M.P., followed with the closest attention the various phrases of Dr. Stockmann's fight against the 'confounded compact majority,' while Mr. T. P. O'Connor, M.P., in a stall at the other end of the house, seemed delighted at the realistic 'mise-en-scène' of the gagging incident in the fourth act.

'It is a grand play,' said Mr. John Burns, to a member of our staff, during the course of the matinée. 'It is superbly staged and acted, and I think that every man or woman who cares for a community ought to come and see it.'

Mr. Keir Hardie was more emphatic still in his eulogy of *An Enemy of the People*.

'A magnificent stage piece,' commented the member for Merthyr. 'And what is more, an instructive performance. Every allusion in it may be applied with equal force and truth to our municipal, not to mention our national, institutions. Unfortunately the play does not contain the whole truth. The hero will no doubt attract sympathisers in course of time, and he also will in turn become one of the "confounded compact majority."'

LADY INGER OF ÖSTRAAT

Scala Theatre, 28 January 1906

174. From an initialled notice by E. A. B[aughan], *Daily News*

30 January 1906, 9

The play was translated by William Archer and the cast was as follows:

Lady Inger	..	Miss Edyth Olive	Nils Stensson	..	Mr Harcourt William
Elina	.. ..	Miss Ellice Crawford	Biorn	.. ..	Mr W. R. Stavely
Nils Lykke	..	Mr Henry Ainley	Olaf Skaktavl	..	Mr Brydone

Ibsen's early drama produced by the Incorporated Stage Society yesterday has two qualities in common with his later work. In spite of his use of old-fashioned machinery, the young dramatist (he was only twenty-seven when he wrote the play) did attempt to make his characters explain themselves, and as far as possible he did treat his drama from the inside. A superficial critic might say there is no point at which *Lady Inger of Östraat* and, say, *Rosmersholm* touch, but if you tear away the melodramatic covering to this early play it is easy enough to see the real Ibsen beneath.

Lady Inger herself sounds a fine note of later Ibsenism. When she confesses the secret of her life, how she had had a son before she married the man she did not love, she exclaims, 'My daughters! God forgive me if I have no mother's heart towards them. My wifely duties were as serfdom to me; how then could I love my daughters? Oh, how different with my son! He was the child of my very soul!' Then there is the character of Lady Inger's third daughter, Elina. She is finely conceived in her idealism, and her distrust of a mother who had not lived up to her patriotic ideal is true Ibsen. So is the love scene between Elina and Nils Lykke, a Norwegian Don Juan of the sixteenth century.

439

As I grew up, [she confesses] your name was ever in my ears. I hated the name, for meseemed that all women were dishonoured by your life. And yet—how strange!—when I built up in my dreams the life that should be mine, you were ever my hero, though I knew it not. Now I understand it all—now know I what it was I felt. It was a foreboding, a mysterious longing for you, you only one—for you that were one day to come and glorify my life.

Nils Lykke, himself a disappointed idealist who once dreamed 'of a woman noble and stately, for whom he ever went seeking, and in vain,' is a well-drawn character—with touches of Ibsen's later insight.

But this inside of the drama is covered by its melodramatic trappings. Lady Inger herself is drawn in a wavering fashion. She has no great love for her daughters, yet she is bent on avenging the death of one of them, Lucia, who had been betrayed by Nils Lykke. She would not throw in her lot with the Norwegian Nationalist Party because a leader of the Swedes held her illegitimate son as a hostage; yet in order to avenge herself on Nils Lykke she goes far to betray her Norway into the hands of the Danes. The most melodramatically effective situation is that in which, unwittingly, she is the cause of her son's murder, thinking him the half-brother who is the rightful heir to the throne of Sweden. Then, having planned the murder on the spur of the moment, she incontinently goes mad. It is purely a theatrical scene à la *Macbeth*. But Lady Inger, as drawn earlier in the play, would not have lost her senses over such a comparative trifle as murder in Norway of the sixteenth century. Dramatically, too, it destroys the final scene, in which a ring found on the dead body proves that the murdered man is really her son. That might have sent even a Norwegian Lady Macbeth out of her senses.

175. From an unsigned notice,
Black and White

3 February 1906, 178

From the point of view of the ordinary playgoer it [*Lady Inger of Östraat*] has an exceedingly effective last act, following on four others, that fascinate or bore according to the temper of the observer; from the point of view of the serious student of theatrical history, it marks a distinct phase in the development of the greatest dramatic influence of the nineteenth century. Whatever Ibsen may or may not have done, he has revolutionised the technique of the stage, and has widened the horizon of the dramatist. Had he written none of his much-debated social dramas, how few of the plays that matter and have been born in the past twenty-five years in France, Germany, or England, would ever have been written, how few would have attained even a passing success!

176. From an unsigned obituary, *Academy*

26 May 1906, lxx, 501

The death of Ibsen, which took place at his home in Christiania on Wednesday last, came as a surprise to no one, for he may be said to have been dying for five years. It can hardly be called a loss, except, of course, to his personal friends. His work was done. He had attained an eminence all over Europe which no dramatist of his own or any age, except Shakespeare, had ever reached; and not even Shakespeare ever roused so much talk, thought, high feeling, actual animosity as Henrik Ibsen. And the eminence he won for himself is as nothing compared with the influence he exerted. He not only brought back the theatre into the number of intellectual forces; he set people thinking, questioning, searching for the truth in all countries.

[outlines Ibsen's life and career.]

His value, when all is said, lies not altogether in the actual criticisms he passed on the life of our own times, which may or may not be superseded as society changes and develops; his greatest achievement was this: that by means of the theatre, a neglected and despised instrument of education, he made people think. He knew the force of the theatre, knew that a scene or an idea conveyed by actual representation has ten times the force of one conveyed by black ink on white paper, and will reach, moreover, scores of people on whom books have little or no influence. To him we owe very largely the partial supersession on the stage of meaningless, thoughtless drama, in which old types and sentimentalities and incidents were repeated *ad nauseam*, by plays that present an idea, that set you thinking, that raise before your eyes in quite a new light your own circumstances and difficulties. It is too early yet to judge of Ibsen's influence; he has few imitators, he has left no school. Only in the general broadening of the outlook, the inculcation of ideas, the fearless pursuit and representation of truth, is it possible for us to-day to trace the effect of the works of one of the most remarkable men in all the history of literature.

177. Max Beerbohm, *Saturday Review*

26 May 1906, ci, 650–1

Sometimes, when a great man dies, it is difficult to believe that he is dead. In a sense, it is difficult to believe this of Ibsen. He was the only Norwegian who excited any interest outside Norway. He alone was 'good copy' for the journalists who supply Europe with Norwegian news. And thus, during recent years, we had read again and again that he was dying. Finding that he always lived on, we had ceased, at length, to be credulous. We had begun to think Ibsen immortal. And now, something of the incredibility of those rumours that he was dying attaches itself to the very news of his death. Those ever-recurring rumours had seemed to be so essential a feature of the modern newspaper. It is difficult to believe that there will be no more of them.

Ibsen's, however, is not one of those deaths which are in themselves hard to realise. Had he died some years ago, when he was still one of the vital forces of the world, the sudden blank would indeed have taxed our imagination. But, as it is, the force had long ago been spent. Six years have passed since Ibsen gave us *When We Dead Awaken*. And that play, interesting and valuable though it was in its significance, was the work of an evidently failing hand. It was evidently, moreover, meant to be an epilogue. The volcano was extinct. Had Ibsen died even after *John Gabriel Borkman*, we should have suffered a tragic sense of loss, knowing not of what riches we had been robbed. But to the work that he began in 1850 he wrote 'finis' in 1890. Nothing is not there that might have been. Our loss is a merely personal one.

Are we down-hearted? No. It was interesting to think of Ibsen as being still actually alive—as breathing the air that we breathed. But the thought sounded no echo in emotion. I can imagine that people must have been really touched and stirred by the thought of Walt Whitman's survival. I did not begin to read that poet till some time after he was dead. But I am old enough to have been thrilled by the fact that Robert Browning was still living, and to have felt the world emptier for me when he died. Great men may be divided into two classes: the loveable and the unloveable; and, as surely as Whitman and Browning are typical of the one class, Ibsen is typical of the other. 'Friends', he wrote, in one of his letters to George Brandes, 'are a costly luxury, and when one invests one's capital in a mission in life, one cannot afford to have friends. The expensiveness of friendship does not lie in what one does for one's friends, but in what one, out of regard for them, leaves un-done. This means the crushing of many an intellectual germ.' Ibsen had no lack of friends, so far as his genius attracted to him many men who were anxious to help him. And he used these men, unstintingly, when he had need of them. That volume of his correspondence, published not long ago, reveals him as an unabashed applicant for favours. Nor is this by any means to his discredit. The world was against him. He was poor, and a cast-away. He had to fight hard in order that he might fulfil the genius that was in him. It was well that he had no false delicacy in appealing to anyone who could be of use to him. But, throughout that correspondence, one misses in him the sense of gratitude. One misses in him the capacity for friendship. Not one 'intellectual germ' would he sacrifice on that altar. He was, indeed, a perfect type of the artist. There is something impressive, something magnificent and noble, in the spec-tacle of his absorption in himself—the impregnability of that rock on which his art was founded. But, as we know, other men, not less great than Ibsen, have managed to be human. Some 'intellectual germs' may thereby have perished. If so, they are to be mourned, duly. And yet, could we wish them preserved at the price that Ibsen paid for them? Innate in us is the desire to love those whom we venerate. To this desire, Ibsen, the very venerable, does not pander.

We need not, I think, condemn ourselves as sentimentalists, for being disappointed. I think we may fairly accuse Ibsen of a limitation. Out of strength cometh forth sweetness. The truth of this proverb is not always, I admit, obvious. The Dean of S. Patrick's, for example, was strong; and sweetness did certainly not exude from him, except in portions of his private correspondence. (Some day, perhaps, it will be found that Ibsen had a soft side to his nature. But that will not affect our general view of him as a writer, any more than Swift's private use of baby language affects our general view of *him*.) Swift's strength lay in his intellect, and in his natural gift for literature; and a gigantic strength it was. But his harshness was not symptomatic of strength. It was symptomatic of a certain radical defect in himself. He was a Titan, not an Olympian. So was Ibsen, who, without Swift's particular defect, was but a shade less harsh in his outlook on the world. He was an ardent and tender lover of ideas; but mankind he simply could not abide. Indeed, I fancy he cared less for ideas as ideas than as a scourge for his fellow-creatures. Just now I spoke of him as having been an extinct volcano after *When We Dead Awaken*; and the application of that simile was more apt than it usually is. Volcanic he had ever been, from *Catilina* onwards. His plays were a sequence of eruptions, darkening the sky, growling and sending out flashes of light more unpleasant than the darkness, and overwhelming and embedding the panic-stricken fugitives, Much has been written about his 'purpose' in this and that play. 'Purpose', in the sense of wishing to reform this or that evil, he never had. Primarily, he was an artist, pure and simple, actuated by the artist's joy in reproduction of human character as it appeared to his keen, unwandering eyes. But he had a joy within a joy: joy in the havoc he wrought. Vesuvius has no 'purpose': it does but obey some law within itself. Ibsen obeyed some similar law, and differed from Vesuvius only in the conscious pleasure that he had in the law's fulfilment. Peace was repulsive to him because the world was repulsive. The world's green pastures, smiling so smugly up at him, must be scorched black with cinders: not otherwise could any good thing ever grow out of them. And if the good thing actually grew, of what use, pray, would it be? Down with it! Eruptions, destruction: nothing else matters. Liberty! What is the use of that, except as an incentive to unrest.

Rome [he writes to Brandes, after the proclamation of the republic] was the one sanctuary in Europe, the one place that enjoyed true liberty—freedom from the political tyranny of liberty . . . The delicious longing for liberty—that is now a thing of the past. I for one am bound to confess that the only thing about liberty that I love is the fight for it; I care nothing about the possession of it.

At any rate, he cared nothing about other people's possession of it.

Because the men in his plays are mostly scored off by the women, he has often been credited with a keen sympathy for the feminine sex. 'Strong-minded' women used to regard him as their affectionate ally. It was not them he cared for, poor dears, it was only the scrimmage. Men were 'up'; so 'up' with women. Had Nature placed women in the ascendent, Ibsen would have been the first to tug them down. No dispassionate reader of his plays can fail to see that his sympathy with women is a mere reflex of his antipathy to their lords and masters. The general impression that he had tried to help the cause of their emancipation was enough to send him off at a tangent. You remember how flatly he denied, at a banquet given some years ago in his honour, that he had had any such purpose whatsoever. He had merely, he declared, portrayed certain tendencies. For his part, he considered that woman's sphere was the home. Quite feminine tears were shed, thereupon, by strong-minded women in every quarter of the globe. And to those 'droppings of moist tears' Ibsen, we may be sure, listened with grim pleasure.

It was a strange mind, this mind into which I have been peering. Posterity, too, I think, will always, from time to time, peer into it, with something of my own awe. Even when time shall have robbed the plays of the sharp savour that for us they have, Ibsen himself will be as dominant a figure as he is for us. Against his lack of love may be set the fact that he loved not even himself. Throughout his life an artist essentially, he wrote in *When We Dead Awaken* a savage attack on the artistic nature which he exemplified. And, feeble though this final play is in execution, it seems to me deadlier in intention than any of the others. Perhaps it is but another instance of Ibsen's egoism that he reserved his most vicious kick for himself.

178. From W. D. Howells's obituary in *North American Review*

July 1906, clxxxiii, 1–14

To my experience he is a dramatist of such perfection, he is a poet of such absolute simplicity and veracity, that when I read him or see him I feel nothing wanting in the aesthetic scheme. I know that there are graces and beauties abounding in other authors which are absent from him, but I do not miss them; and I perceive that he abundantly fulfils his purpose without them. I am sensible of being moved, of being made to think and feel as no other has made me think and feel, and I think that sufficient; I do not care what is left out of the means to the end. For illustration, we will say, what I believe, that *Macbeth* is the supreme play of conscience, of that spirit in us that censures conduct. The means to its end are of an opulence which renders *Ghosts* in the contrast, bare and poverty-stricken. Yet I do not miss in *Ghosts* any of the means that richly edified me in *Macbeth* and I am aware of a spirit in it that censures conscience itself. Shakespeare in Macbeth and in Lady Macbeth has made me shudder for their guilt; Ibsen in Manders and Mrs. Alving makes me tremble for their innocence. The difference measures the advance from the mediæval to the modern man, and account for the hardihood of those who have declared that Ibsen says more to them now than Shakespeare says. They are right if they mean that Shakespeare makes them question the evil, while Ibsen makes them also question the good. The time has come, apparently, when we are to ask ourselves not of the justice of our motives, so much as of the wisdom of our motives. It will no longer suffice that we have had the best motive in this or that; we must have the wisest motive, and we must examine anew the springs of action, the grounds of conviction.

That is what Ibsen invites us to do, not in *Ghosts* alone, but in most of the plays which may be called his most realistic. Some of his dramas deal typically with human, with Norwegian, life—as *Brand*, as *Peer Gynt*, as *The Lady from the Sea*; others deal personally with Norwegian, with human, life—as *Ghosts*, as *Pillars of Society*, as *The Wild Duck*, as *Hedda Gabler*, as *Little Eyolf*, and it is these last which Ibsen valued himself most upon, and which, I think, form the richest part of his legacy to literature. It has been conjectured that when they have had their full ethical effect, and the world has come more or less to the ground where they challenge conscience for its reasons, they will be of less interest and less significance than the more idealistic dramas; but if the representation of character, and the study of personality, form the highest office of art, as I believe they do, I think Ibsen will not be finally found mistaken in his preference. I am quite willing to own that I agree with him, perhaps because I like the real better than the ideal, though I find abundant reality in his idealistic dramas.

As to the ethical effect of the plays which I permit myself, in the company of their author, to like best, I have my doubts whether it is so directly and explicitly his intention as some of the highest critical intelligences have imagined. He is, first of all, not a moralist, and far less a polemicist, but an artist, and he works through instruments, as the creative force always works, in which he is himself intangible, and, as it were, absent. His instruments are of course the characters of the drama in hand, and it is not to be inferred that the end to which any of these comes is Ibsen's conclusion, any more than it is to be inferred that what any one of them says is Ibsen's opinion. You are not to take this thing or that as the point of the moral, but to consider the whole result left with you, and to use your reason, not your logic, upon it. In *Ghosts* Mrs. Alving upbraids her old lover for not letting her stay when she took refuge with him from the horror of her marriage, and for making her go back to her husband; she upbraids herself for not having sympathized with the life-lust in her husband, which mainly manifested itself in love-lust outside of their marriage; she seems willing, rather than make the same mistake again, that her son shall have his half-sister for wife, or even for mistress. But in her case, as in every other, Ibsen does not wish to teach so much as he wishes to move, to strike with that exalted terror of tragedy which has never hesitated at its means; which in Shakespeare confronts us with a son forced to bring his mother to shame for her incestuous union with his uncle, and to study the best moment for the murder to which his father's revengeful spirit urges him, and from which his own faltering temperament withholds him, though the spectator is made to feel it is his sacred duty, and shares the truculent impatience of the spectre at his delay. It would be no sillier to suppose that Shakespeare meant to inculcate such bloody deeds as that which Hamlet shrinks from doing, than to suppose that Ibsen means in Mrs. Alving's distraction to teach libertinage, or that complicity with suicide in which the play apparently ends. The moral is far back of all this, and involved by her violation of duty in marrying for the worldly ends of her family a man she does not love, for this is the wrong-doing which no after duteousness in her mismarriage can catch up. Here is the source of all the sorrow that ensues; and the lesson, so far as the play is lessoned, is that you must be true from the start, if you would not be false in the truth itself afterwards. But probably Ibsen meant nothing so explicit as that. He was writing a play, not a sermon. He was offering a bitter and poisonous flower of life as he had found it growing; not a botanical medicine that he had dried and pressed for the ethicist's herbarium.

Ghosts is the most tragical of Ibsen's plays, and it is none the less tragical because it is a tremendous effect of the author's peculiar humor.

He is a humorist in the presence of its dreadful facts not because he is a hard-hearted cynic, but because he sees that the world which a wise and merciful and perfect God has created seems full of stupidity and cruelty and out of joint to utter deformity, and he shows it as he sees it. If he is apparently inconsistent, it is because the world is really inconsistent; and if we hold him to any hard and fast rule of logic, we may indeed *have* him, but his best meaning will escape us. In *Pillars of Society*, that tragedy of his which comes nearest being a satirical comedy, or for the most part is so, the misery comes because Bernick will be a hypocrite and a liar; and the inference is, that any sort of truth, or anybody's, would be better than the falsehood in which he lives. In *The Wild Duck*, the truth is brought home from the outside to a wretched creature unable to bear it, who has existed through the lie become vital to him, and who goes to pieces at the touch of the truth, and drags those around him to ruin and death in his fall; and the inference is that the truth is not for every one always, but may sometimes be a real mischief. The two plays seem to contradict each other, but they do not; they are both true to different predicaments and situations of life, and can no more be blamed for inconsistency than God's world which they faithfully mirror. There is in fact a divine consistency running through them and through *Ghosts* where, you shall learn, if you will pay due heed, that the truth once denied avenges itself in the dire necessity of falsehood, and renders all after-truth mechanical and, of the effect of a lie. When Mrs. Alving had once been false to herself in marrying for money and position a man she did not love, while she loved another man, she never could again be true to herself without doing him harm. She lent herself to his evil as long as she could bear it, and when she could bear it no longer the worst had been done. She had borne a son on whom his father's sins must be visited, and had pledged herself to falsehood against which she revolted in vain and forever too late. If she had revolted earlier, and made known the facts of her life to all the world, still it would not have availed. People who saw in *Ghosts* merely a heredity play, based upon a questionable assumption of science, never saw it whole, and they who saw in it merely a destiny play, in which fate relentlessly brooded as in Greek tragedy, as little fathomed its meaning. This, as I think we have found, is very simple, and is not discordant with any dictate of religion or reason, and it is always Ibsen's meaning. Do not be a hypocrite, do not be a liar, do not be a humbug; but be very careful how and when you are sincere and true and single, lest being virtuous out of time you play the fool and work destruction. . . .

I do not pretend that Ibsen is a comfortable companion, or that a play of his is something to take up and while away a pleasant hour with, or that if seen upon the stage it will take a tired business man's mind off himself, or help a society woman forget the manifold vexations of the day. His plays were probably never intended to do anything of the kind, and probably they were as little meant to be seen by the inexperienced young people who go to the theatre in pairs, with or without a chaperon. But neither of these probabilities has anything to do with the question of their literary value, or their effect, though both of them have everything to do with the question of their popularity in all Anglo-Saxon countries. They will never have a great or a small popularity with our race, in any of the seven seas; and yet, for all the reasons against them, however furiously urged, we should be the better for their wide acceptance, honester and cleanlier.

It is one of the conventions of our hypocritical civilization that young people are ignorant of certain matters because they do not speak of them to their elders, and that their minds will be tainted or corrupted by others' open recognition of them. Ibsen's recognition of the fact is not, indeed, as open as it might be, but it is unmistakable, and its purport is wholly sanative. He addresses himself most terribly to those who have committed the mistakes or the misdeeds which he puts before them; but, if the hopes of reform are always with the young, he more usefully addresses himself to those who are no longer ignorant but are still innocent. I say this, not because I see any chance of his being presently suffered to do so, on the popular scale, but because I think it a pity that art should not be allowed to enforce the precepts of religion, in regard to matters of which the young drink in knowledge from the very fountain of our religion.

Such a play as *Little Eyolf* is awful, no one can deny that. It wrings the heart with grief and shame, but any one who refuses to see the hope which it holds out, that if you will do right you are safe from wrong, must be wilfully blind. It proclaims, in terms that humiliate and that almost disgrace, the truth which Tolstoy preaches in other terms when he declares that there is and can be no such thing as personal happiness. Both of these just men perceive that, in the scheme of a just God, there is no room for such happiness; and that, wherever it tries to force itself in, it pushes aside or crushes under it the happiness of some other human creature. In *Little Eyolf*, where the wife and mother vainly hopes to perpetuate the passion of her first married years, and wishes to sacrifice to that idolatry herself, her husband and her child, we have something intolerably revolting; but the lesson is, alike from Ibsen and from Tolstoy, that you must not and you cannot be happy except through the welfare of others, and that to seek your bliss outside of this is to sin against reason and righteousness both.

As for the fact involved, and put in words so plain that it can scarcely be called hinting, it is one of those things which they who shrink from such wicked and filthy things as the drama has commonly dealt with may shrink from having handled, and these will be shocked quite as much by the diabolism of Hedda Gabler as by the animalism of Rita Allmers. Obsession is an easy name for the state of such women, but if it is the true name then it is time men should study the old formulas of exorcism anew.

179. 'Ibsen as an Interpreter of American Life', by Edwin E. Slosson, *Independent*

31 May 1906, lx, 1253–5

Edwin Emery Slosson (1865–1929), chemist, educator and writer of popular works on the sciences, was literary editor of the *Independent* from 1903 to 1921.

Ibsen's chief characteristics are modernity and universality. He renounced romanticism in order that he might devote himself to present day problems, and, as a social mathematician, discover the greatest common factors of all humanity. If he had continued as he began, writing plays of Norse kings and Roman emperors, with gorgeous scenes and troops of retainers, he would have been merely a Norwegian dramatist; but when he widened his scope by narrowing his field to a half dozen middle class men and women in a cheaply furnished room of a Norwegian town, he became a world dramatist. The stage of almost every other country has been more influenced by him during the last quarter century than by any of its native writers. In Germany, Hauptmann and

Sudermann; in France, Hervieu and Brieux; in England, Pinero and Shaw, have gone to school to Ibsen, and have so far profited by their lessons as to reach a wider public than their master could.

In America, Ibsen has exerted no such influence, because there are no such dramatists to be influenced. The thought of Clyde Fitch, Augustus Thomas, or George Ade being influenced by anybody, or influencing anybody excites a smile. Our American playwrights are taken seriously neither by the public nor by themselves. We have no cause to find fault with them. They give us what we want and we pay them well for it.

An American Ibsen would starve. The Norwegian Ibsen came near it. But, as he says, thru the mouth of Dr. Stockmann, 'the strongest man in the world is he who stands most alone.' Ibsen, single handed and under the ban, conquered a place in the world's esteem which he could never have obtained if he had been hampered by a train of friends, allies and disciples. In his old age his own people received him again, and now he is dead shower upon him the praise and honor which, if he had received them in his prime, would have cheered his heart and spoiled his work. If he had come by his opinions easily he would not have believed them so strongly. If they had been accepted readily, he would not have stated them so forcibly.

Ibsen was able to break thru the barrier of language, because his characters are universal types and at the same time very definite individuals. When the scientist speaks the name of a species he does not mean the platonic ideal, perfect and non-existent; he means one particular plant, fish or fossil on a certain shelf in the British Museum or elsewhere. This is the type specimen, and it is of interest because in many parts of the world are found other specimens resembling it more or less closely in different ways. So Borkman and Stockmann, Nora and Hilda were first discovered by Ibsen in Norway, but the same species are found in all countries, and nowhere more abundantly than in America.

John Gabriel Borkman, for example, has never appeared in America on the stage, but he is well known on the street. He is the typical financier of the kind who are now being pilloried in the market place by official and unofficial investigators. He is a Napoleon of finance, but crippled in his first engagement. On the eve of success, just as he is about to carry out his gigantic schemes, he is caught in a bit of financial juggling, and sent to prison for five years. After his release he shuts himself up in the upper room of his house for eight years waiting for his vindication, pacing the floor day after day expecting those who have betrayed and wronged him to come to him there in his room and on bended knees beg him to return to the management of the bank. He thinks no one can take his place, tho in reality the business world has forgotten him.

He admits the technical illegality of his act, but cannot understand why people should make such a fuss about a little thing like that, cannot believe that they are sincere in condemning it.

I had almost reached my aim. If I had had a week more everything would have been in order. All the deposits would have been turned in. All the securities that I had boldly made use of would have been again laid in their places just as before. Not a single person would have lost a penny. And then to be struck in the back by a traitor! . . . What I could have done with the millions! All the mines that I would have opened! New shafts without end! The waterfalls! The bridges! Railroads and steamship lines thru the whole world.

He hears the ore calling to him from under the ground, singing for joy; the kobolds, guardians of the hidden treasure, waiting for the stroke of the hammer, like the midnight bell, to release them, and let them get at their work, the service of mankind.

I had the power. There lay the imprisoned millions everywhere in the depths of the mountains and called to me, cried to me for deliverance! But no one else heard. Only I, alone.

I would like to know if the others, if they had had the power, would not have done exactly as I did.

They would have if they had possessed my ability. But if they had done it they would not have done it with *my* object in view. The action would then have been a different one. In short, I have acquitted myself.

He had sacrificed his love, his family and himself to his commercial aim, but this, he insisted, was not a selfish aim. He did not want money or luxury or ease; he wanted to set the wheels going, to free the kobolds of the metals from their idle prison life. Consequently he cannot repent his act; he can only regret that the world has robbed itself of what he alone could do for it. In this we hear again the dying lament of Cecil Rhodes: 'So little time, so much to do.' He is the modern financier, with nothing extenuated and naught set down in malice.

Ibsen's *Pillars of Society* is a dramatized insurance and Slocum scandal. Consul Bernick, as he stands at the door of his home receiving the homage of his fellow townsmen and listening to the eulogy of Pastor Rörlund on the purity of his family life, the generosity he shows to his workmen, the public spirit manifested in his business enterprises, and the unselfishness and probity of his character, realizes that it is all a lie.

He knows, and he knows that there are others who know, that he has for years concealed an immoral life, that his workmen are being discharged without mercy to be replaced by machines, that he has bought up all the land along the railroad he is being praised for bringing to the town, and that the ship which is then leaving the harbor is so imperfectly repaired that it is sure to sink in a storm. He has sacrificed everything and everybody to build up a good reputation, to be called, as he is now, the ideal citizen, but at this moment he realizes the extent and meanness of his hypocrisy, he tears off the veil from his life, and exposes to the gaze of the crowd the moral rottenness of the pillars of society.

> 'But what good came of it at last?'
>   Quoth little Peterkin,
> 'Why, that I cannot tell,' said he;
> 'But 'twas a famous victory.'

This verse of Southey's might be placed as a tag to this and all the rest of Ibsen's plays. They are famous victories of self assertion over the oppression of society, and of naked truth over conventional shams, but the outcome of these outbursts of individuality and honesty Ibsen does not explain. Ibsen's curtains always fall at the most interesting point, and he does not write sequels.

According to his theory of ethics, virtue consists in daring to do what one individually believes is right, even tho the consequences be disastrous, and, in his plays, they usually are. The individual is killed or is ruined at the moment he triumphs by the assertion of his will. Ibsen offers no reward for good conduct, not even a hero medal.

Dr. Stockmann is under the common delusion that he will be greeted as a public benefactor if he exposes the faults of the society in which he lives. When he finds that the water of the Baths, on which the prosperity of his native town is built, is contaminated with disease germs and the whole system of sewer pipes must be relaid at great expense, he feels that he has deserved well of his fellow citizens, and he ingenuously suggests to his friends that he hopes they will not get up a public demonstration and a torchlight procession in his honor. When he finds that his exposé is to be suppressed by the town authorities, he turns to the Liberal press, only to find that Liberals are just as illiberal as Conservatives when their interests are touched, and, finally, when he appeals to the common people, he is ostracized and stoned. Ibsen wrote this play, *The Enemy of the People*, as a reply to the storm of denunciation which greeted his exposure of conventional shams in *The Pillars of Society*.

The present time would be a good opportunity to have *The Enemy of the People* produced upon the American stage. Possibly a company of actors for this play could be made up from those writers who have been contributing to the literature of exposure, but who now find no demand for their wares since the reaction against muck-rakers has set in. They might get as much satisfaction in playing it as Ibsen got in writing it.

The question of tainted money is treated in *Ghosts* as part of the general bad inheritance of Oswald. Mrs. Alving devotes all of Captain Alving's money to the building of an orphanage as an atonement for his sins and to free their son Oswald from their sequelæ. But 'Captain Alving's Home' burns down on the eve of its dedication, and Oswald perishes likewise from the tainted blood in his veins. Mrs. Alving, with all her courage and determination, is not able to free herself and her son from the 'ghosts' of the past.

I almost think we are all of us ghosts. It is not only what we have inherited from our father and mother that walks in us. It is all sorts of dead ideas and old lifeless beliefs, and so forth. They have no vitality, but they cling to us all the same and we can't get rid of them. Whenever I take up a newspaper I seem to see ghosts gliding between the lines. There must be ghosts all the country over, as thick as the sands of the sea. And because we are, one and all, so pitifully afraid of the light.

Ibsen is a disillusioned democrat. He is aware that tyrants do not all perish when the kings are slain. Norwegians are not afraid of kings. They discharge them and elect them at their will. But they are not a free people as Ibsen is always pointing out. The tyranny of tradition, the tyranny of conventionality, the tyranny of public opinion are the objects of his sharpest invective.

The majority has might—unhappily, but right it has not. The minority is always right. . . . I am going to revolt against the lie that truth resides with the majority. What sort of truths are those that the majority is wont to take up? Truths so full of years that they are decrepit. When a truth is as old as that it is in a fair way to become a lie. . . . You may believe me or not, but truths are by no means the wiry Methuselahs as some people think. A normally constituted truth lives—let me say—seventeen or eighteen years, at the outside twenty years, seldom longer. But truths so stricken in years are always shockingly thin.

Since *The Enemy of the People*, from which these words are quoted, was written in 1881, it might be said that all the truth it may have contained lost its validity some five years ago. But it is obvious that he applies this statute of limitation only to truths that are so far accepted as to become conventionalized. Ibsen followers are few in any land, and his doctrines will long preserve their vitality by being safely kept in hands of a very small minority.

In this country, especially, where some of the plays are never seen and rarely read, the ideas of Ibsen have the freshness and interest that they had when they first startled Europe. And nowhere is their galvanic shock more needed than here. His mission is to rouse people from self complacency and stolid satisfaction with things as they are. Even more than Norway, America lies apart from the great currents of modern thought, and there are eddies of provincialism to be found in all parts of the United States that would match anything of the kind in Scandinavia. Ibsen describes our small towns better than our own writers. The vices of the village, its narrow interests, its gossip, its exclusiveness, and its rigid control of the conduct and opinions of the individual, are the same here as in Norway, and need the same drastic exposure. We are all acquainted with Peter the pompous burgomaster, with Mortensgard, the free-thinker, who turns out to be neither free nor a thinker; Aslaksen, the moderate man, whose heart belongs to the people, but whose reason inclines to the authorities: Hovstad, the printer, whose paper is radical on questions of national politics, but observes a certain amount of caution in regard to purely local matters; Solness, the master builder, losing his grip on his work and in mortal terror of being supplanted by the younger generation; and Tesman, the professor, physically and mentally nearsighted. As for Ibsen's women, we have them all here, from Nora, the bird-woman, to Hedda, the cat-woman. There is need in America for this Ibsen, layer of ghosts and pricker of bubbles.

180. 'Playing Ibsen in the Badlands', by Joseph P. Dannenburg, *Theatre*

August 1906, vi, 219–21

This article is lavishly illustrated with photographs. (The magazine should not be confused with the British periodical of the same name.)

Strange shows find strange pastures. But never were the gods of Thespis implored to grant grace to a stranger outfit than that which left St. Paul, Minnesota, to produce Ibsen's *Ghosts* in the Bad Lands.

There are plays and players. The trail of the shekel-seeking manager extends from Maine to Calcutta. The classics mix with the tawdry, and the repertoire star does everything from rapping cocoanut shells to produce the effect of running horses to swinging forth in full tones the eloquence of Shakespeare or the memorable lines of *Uncle Tom's Cabin*. But imagine *Ghosts*, at which expert metropolitan managers shiver, being presented to farmers, cattle punchers, wheat harvesters, cowboys, Indians and gamblers! And yet the company played over fifteen months appearing nearly two hundred and twenty-five times, and covering over sixteen thousand miles of territory .

Charles A. Gay, who appeared in the Fawcett *Ghosts* company with Mary Shaw, went from New York to St. Paul, and when the company closed in the latter place a business man offered to back a company to be sent over the one-night stands through the wild and woolly section. Mr. Gay accepted the proposition and became manager. Those theatrical people who heard of the intended trip ridiculed the idea of the company staying out longer than a fortnight. Mr. Gay believed, however, that Uncle Tom and Hamlet had become mossworn in the one-night Western stands.

'One touch of Nature makes the whole world kin,' he said, and he was right. The touch of nature was found beneath the shaggy mackinaws of the Wisconsin lumbermen, the flannel-protected hunters of the

North, the Swedes in the wheat fields, the superstitious gamblers, even the rough cowboys and stolid Indians, to all of whom the grim, morbid story appealed.

True, it was not understood by many. Nearly every place, after the large cities were left behind, resolved itself into an enormous question mark with hundreds of queries as to the why and wherefore of the play. In the wilds of Wisconsin a rough lumber 'jack' elbowed his way to the doorkeeper as he entered the playhouse.

'Say, mister!' said he, 'do you really have a ghost with y'u!'?

When he was informed that the only ghost presented was the ghost of a sordid past he drew his brows to a thick frown, kicked the thin woodwork between the orchestra chairs and the cold Northern air and was ready to shoot holes in the place unless he had his money refunded. He got it.

It was in the Dakotas and the wheatlands of the North that the play found its most appreciative audiences, the population being made up largely of Norwegians and Swedes, to whom Ibsen is a household fetish. *Ghosts*! Ibsen! The very names brought the brine of their beloved fjords to their eyes, and the world seemed smaller and in closer touch. Nearly all of them had seen the production in the mother tongue. When the production reached one place in Northern Minnesota the wheat harvesters went on a strike and would not work until the play had passed on.

As to the newspaper notices they were decidedly breezy and original as regards the point of view. Here, for instance, is what the *Morning Appeal* of Carson City, Nevada, said:

Ibsen's Norwegian play of *Ghosts*, with one setting of scenery, no music and three knocks with a club on the floor to raise the curtain, was presented last evening. The play is certainly a moral hair-raiser and the stuffing is knocked out of the Decalogue at every turn. Mrs. Alving, the leading lady, who keeps her chin high in the air, has married a moral monstrosity in the shape of a spavined rake and hides it from the world. She wears a pleasant smile and gives society the glad hand and finally lets go all holds when her husband gets gay with the hired girl and gives an old tar three hundred plunks to marry her and stand the responsibility for the expected population.

Oswald, the mother's only boy, is sent to Paris to paint views for marines and takes kindly to the gay life of the capital, where the joy of living is the rage and families are reared in a section where a printer running a job office solely on marriage certificates would hit the poorhouse with a dull thud. Regina, the result of Mr. Alving's attentions to the hired girl, also works in the family and falls in love with the painter boy on his return from Paris. They vote country life too slow and plan to go to Paris and start a family. The doting mother gives her consent, and Pastor Manders, who is throwing fits all through the play, has a spasm. The boy, on being informed that the girl of his choice is his half-sister, throws another, his mamma having also thrown a few in the other act.

Engstrand, who runs a sort of sailor's and soldier's canteen, sets fire to an orphanage, and the boy, who has inherited a sort of mayonnaise dressing brain from his awful dad, tears about the stage in a spell, breaks some furniture and upsets the wine. He finally takes Rough-on-Rats and dies a gibbering idiot, with his mother slobbering over him and trying to figure out in her own mind that he was merely drunk and disorderly.

The players handled the sticky mess as well as could be expected, all being excellent actors. As a sermon on the law of heredity the play is great, but after seeing it we are glad to announce that Haverly's Minstrels will relieve the Ibsen gloom next Monday night.

The 'critics' were only on a par, however, with the theatres. Most of them were cold, cheerless halls, and at Harvey, North Dakota, the stage was erected by crossing a number of rough boards over empty beer kegs. There were no footlights and kerosene suspended from the ceiling gave out all the light by which *Ghosts* was visible. But it was sufficient for the populace.

Generally these 'theatres' had the stock scenery found in the small towns. But in Colorado an enterprising stage manager was discovered. Incidentally he owned the chief store, post office, town hall, livery, and the theatre. The assistant postmaster was call boy, property man, ticket seller and taker, bill poster and barker for the show. This individual went by the name of Bobbs. He was a product of the West and he was proud of the fact.

'I want,' said Mr. Gay, 'a hall tree for the first act.'

'Right,' said Bobbs, cheerfully.

Towards dusk Bobbs could not be found. He was needed badly, too, because he had the keys to the theatre and it was time to open up. Finally he was discovered by one of the troupe with a heavy rope around a tree which had evidently been freshly cut from the adjoining timberland.

'What's that tree for?' asked the perplexed Gay when he found Bobbs.

'Didn't you want a hull tree?' he asked. 'That's what you asked for.'

'No,' said the perplexed actor, trying hard not to laugh. 'I wanted a hall tree; something to hang clothes on.'

'Y'u said y'u wanted a hull tree,' said Bobbs doggedly, 'an' I went in the woods an' got y'u one. It took me three hours to chop it down an' drag it heah, too. So if that ain't what y'u want—well, there's nothin' else.'

That night scene 1, act 1, *Ghosts*, was without a hall tree.

From Ouray on, there was trouble. Some of the troupe wanted to blame the ill fortune on a mountain sheep which followed the troupe to the hall from the hotel. But it was later discovered this sheep had become tame through following the bands of the shows which gave street parades in Ouray. Indeed, the house manager at Ouray could not understand *Ghosts* as a traveling combination at all. Nine-tenths of the shows appearing at Ouray have a band, a street parade and travel in a red-painted car of their own, much after the fashion of the circus performers. So when Impresario Gay and his troupe of famished performers arrived at Ouray the hustling manager of the hall was the first to meet them.

'Where's your car?' he asked.

'Don't travel in one,' replied the hungry actor-manager.

'You don't?' shrieked the manager; 'where's your band?'

'Haven't any,' replied Gay; 'this isn't a minstrel show.'

'No band!' hopelessly, 'and don't you parade?'

'No,' said Gay, 'this is a legitimate attraction.'

'Legitimate be d—d,' said the manager. 'What kind of business do you expect to do? No band, no car, no parade! How'd you think people know you're alive?'

Then came the Bad Lands in earnest. En route they discovered a magnificent playhouse next the hotel in Two Harbors, Wisconsin, where two bears strolled in every evening about dark to gather their meals from the garbage box at the hotel. Imagine the joy of the feminine members of the cast when, passing to the stage entrance, they came upon Mr. and Mrs. Black Bruin sitting on their haunches licking their chops after a meal.

Crossing from St. Vincent to Pembanaux, North Dakota, the only ferryboat between the towns had become disabled and the troupe were rowed across in a small rowboat while the thermometer dallied interestingly about zero. At Pembanaux the 'town orchestra'—*i.e.*, a violin, cornet and piano—was out of commission. The cornetist was off gunning, and there was no other in the town. An enterprising agent of a pianola concern heard of the predicament and he hurriedly brought a sharp bargain to a close with the management.

'I'll send up one of my pianola machines,' said he, 'and you can use that for an orchestra. It will answer every purpose and it'll be a good "add." for us, too.'

The bargain was closed after Mr. Gay had impressed upon the merchant that only classic music should be played between acts. But when between the first and second acts for an encore the pianola worker started to grind out *The New Bully*, Mr. Gay's astonishment almost caused his wig to stand on end. Remonstrance was in vain.

'Well, th' show's purty dreary; an' we gave 'em Chopin's *Funeral March* for a first s'lection. We thought we ought to wake 'em up,' said the agent.

Crossing Iowa a twenty-nine-hour snowstorm was encountered and the bulb showed forty-two below zero for three weeks. *Ghosts* played chiefly to empty benches and cowboys who did not mind the weather. Near Dodge Center a small audience filed in to see the show. The hall was cold and dreary. As Regina, Mrs. Gay robed the part as it was played on Broadway, with a low-necked gown and short sleeves. So cold that she became almost numb, a woman in the front row noticed her condition and tapped her escort on the arm. Immediately his hand went to his hip pocket and he drew—not a gun—but a well-filled bottle containing fire water.

'Here,' said he, 'missy, drink that. It'll warm y'u up.'

Fortunately the falling curtain saved what would otherwise have been an unexpected climax.

Through West Pierre, South Dakota, on to the Black Hills, journeyed the troupe, the rowdies from Fort Pierre getting in a battle with the crowd from West Pierre because Regina had been more intently occupied on the side of the stage near the latter. Guns were drawn and for a while it looked dangerous. But the trouble was averted so far as the interior of the hall was concerned. Later it was fought out on the road.

Close by in the Black Hills was the grave of Calamity Jane, known otherwise as the Sage Hen, an intrepid guide and scout whose name is prominent in the wild annals of the West. From a national character she reached that level where, to quote her own words, she was 'slinging beer in a vulgarity shop,' meaning she was a waitress in a Western concert hall. Buried near Deadwood, her grave is within sight of the cabin she occupied where she once played seven-up with a male friend to determine what the name of her baby should be. She lost.

The gamblers in Wyoming gave *Ghosts* a wide berth. There was something in the title that made them think hard luck was near. As one expressed himself: 'It's all right, I guess, but nixie for me. I've been up against it too tough this week to take a chance on a show with a name like that.' But the cowboys, and they were plentiful, were glad to see *Ghosts* as a decided change from the *East Lynnes*, *Uncle Tomers*, and *Hamlets* that stalked in between poor burlesque entertainment for thirty-five weeks of the year.

On to Colorado was the cry after the Great American Desert was crossed, and Colorado proved formidable enough to submit to *Ghosts*. At Crede, almost the very first stop—where Bob Ford of Jesse James fame met his death—the audience entered with pistols in sight, and the way they handled them did not at all prove to the liking of the troupe. Incidentally, a half drunken cowboy formed a strong desire to ride in the theatre on his burro. He was stopped only on account of the entrance proving too small, and, fortunately, because it was up several stairs. Later 'Moonshine Mose' recovered his sanity, his good humor, and finally consented to pose the following morning for a snapshot, as being the only man who ever found sufficient nerve to attempt to ride in a theatre to see *Ghosts*.

In Crede while the men brought their guns to the playhouse the boys brought their dogs, and it was quite usual for the animals to prowl on the stage, either between acts or even during the performance. Indeed, the last scene of the play was enhanced decidedly when Oswald, seeing the rising sun, gasping for breath, pleads for it.

'The sun! The sun!' he exclaimed.

'Come here, Tige,' broke in the harsh voice of a small boy. And just in time, too, for a mangy cur, attracted by the strange light of the rising sun, was creeping stealthily to the stage. It would have been an innovation indeed for Oswald to have died with a mysterious 'purp' squatting at his feet.

Oswald drew a long breath when the curtain fell.

The trip was without incident until Fort Collins was reached. There, for the first time, financial difficulties were encountered. Money, real spendable coin of the realm, was as scarce as the proverbial hen's teeth. The section is busily engaged in raising potatoes. It is one of the great potato-raising belts of the West. But there had been an oversupply, and there were, to quote Mr. Gay, 'more potatoes in that place than I had believed could be grown in one section.' There were potatoes everywhere, and were willingly sold at the almost unbelievable price of ten cents for one hundred pounds; for that is how the product is handled out that way.

Money was so scarce, the house manager of the theatre did not want to give a performance.

'It's no use,' said he, 'nobody will come, because they haven't any money. Now, if you're willing to take potatoes for your sale of seats, well and good; but I don't think much of it; because you'd have to take five hundred pounds of potatoes for a good seat, and where would you put all your receipts if you had a crowded house? There wouldn't be room enough here to store them.'

Not over anxious to corner the visible supply of potatoes in Colorado, Mr. Gay reluctantly enough gave up the idea of giving a performance.

Into Nebraska went *Ghosts*. There the red men were encountered, and the troupe had a splendid time of it. At Genoa, however, the largest town played, *Ghosts* was booked to appear the same night the Indian Band at the College was to give a concert. Realizing the entire population would attend the concert, Mr. Gay promptly struck a bargain with the Indian Band to perform before and after the performance, and during the intermissions, and to split receipts of the double offering. There was a tremendous crowd, and the band struck some very uncanny melodies between acts that fitted excellently with the desired atmosphere.

The red men and their squaws took to Ibsen most heartily. Many of the older bucks did not understand it any better than many of their palefaced brethren in the East, but they grunted approval often, and the younger people applauded most vigorously.

Finally the tour ended. Out nearly nine months, a tired, anxious-to-rest troupe entered Chicago, almost a year after they had left St. Paul. They were not very rich as to salary, but oh, what a wealth of experiences they had collected!

APPENDIX I

IBSEN CHRONOLOGY

1828 b. 20 March, Skein, Norway.

1844 Leaves Skein for Grimstad to become apothecary's apprentice.

1855 Leaves for Christiania to prepare for university. Fails entrance. 26 September: performance of *Warrior's Barrow*.

1851 Edits *Andrhimmer* with Botten-Hansen and Vinje. 7 July: police raid—end of Ibsen's political activity. 6 November: appointed to theatre post in Bergen.

1852 Visits Copenhagen and Dresden.

1853 *St John's Night.*

1855 *Lady Inger of Östraat.*

1856 *The Feast at Solhaug.*

1857 Returns to Christiania to take up theatre post. *Olaf Liljekrans*; *The Vikings at Helgeland.*

1858 26 June: marries Susannah Thoresen.

1862 *Love's Comedy.*

1863 *The Pretenders.*

1864 Prussian-Danish war: leaves Norway for Rome.

1866 *Brand.*

1867 *Peer Gynt.*

1868 Settles in Dresden.

1869 Visits Egypt; *The League of Youth.*

1870 Visits Copenhagen.

1873 *Emperor and Galilean.*

1874 Visits Norway.

1875 Settles in Munich.

1877 *The Pillars of Society.*

1878 Returns to Rome.

1879 *A Doll's House.*

1881 *Ghosts.*

1882 *An Enemy of the People.*

1884 *The Wild Duck.*

1885 Visits Norway; settles in Munich.

1886 *Rosmersholm.*

1888 *The Lady from the Sea.*

1890 *Hedda Gabler.*

1891 Returns to Norway; settles in Christiania.

1892 *The Master Builder.*

1894 *Little Eyolf.*

1896 *John Gabriel Borkman.*

1898 Celebrations of Ibsen's seventieth birthday.

1899 Dedication of National Norwegian Theatre and Ibsen statue; *When We Dead Awaken.*

1900 Seizure and collapse.

1901 Paralytic stroke.

1906 d. 23 May.

APPENDIX II

IBSEN IN ENGLAND AND AMERICA (1872–1906)

Shortened titles and abbreviated references only are given. Articles, translations and performances originating in the United States are asterisked.

ARTICLES, REVIEWS, CRITICAL ESSAYS	TRANSLATIONS	THEATRICAL PERFORMANCES
1872 E. Gosse, 'Ibsen's Poems', *Spectator*, 16 March. E. Gosse, 'Peer Gynt', *Spectator*, 20 July. E. Gosse, 'The Pretenders', *Academy*, 2 Aug.	**1872** J. A. Dahl tr. 'Terje Vigen' in his book *Norwegian and Swedish Poems* (Bergen).	
1873 E. Gosse, 'H. Ibsen', *Fortnightly Review*, 1:74.	**1873** E. Gosse tr. some of Ibsen's poems in *On Viol and Flute* (see also art. in *Fortnightly Review*).	
	1876 Tr. of 'Terje Vigen', *Catilina* (Act 1), and three short poems in *Translations from the Norse* (A. Johnstone) (privately printed, Gloucester). *Emperor and Galilean*, tr. Catherine Ray.	
1879 E. Gosse, in 'Studies in the Literature of Northern Europe' (reprint of art. in *Fortnightly Review*, 1873). P. P. Iverslie, 'Pillars of Society', *Norden*, 2 Jan.*		**1879** *Pillars of Society* (in German), Stadttheater, Milwaukee, Feb.*
1880 Notices of *Pillars of Society* at the Gaiety Theatre in *The Times*, *Standard*, and *Athenaeum* (25 Dec.)	**1880** *A Doll's House*, tr. T. Weber (Copenhagen).	**1880** *Quicksands* (*Pillars of Society*), Gaiety Theatre (15 Dec.), tr. W. Archer.

ARTICLES, REVIEWS, CRITICAL ESSAYS	TRANSLATIONS	THEATRICAL PERFORMANCES

1880—*cont.*
P. P. Iverslie,
 'A Doll's House', *Norden*,
 25 Aug.*

1881
Anon., 'Quicksands',
 Theatre, 1 Feb.
 3:105.
W. Archer, 'H. Ibsen', *St James's Magazine*, 1:27,
 104.

1882
R. B. Anderson, 'Brand',
 Literary World, 13:325–6,
 Oct.*
R. B. Anderson, 'Ibsen',
 American, 4:8, April.*

1882
Nora, tr. Mrs. F. Lord (with Intro.).

1882
The Child Wife (*A Doll's House*), Milwaukee.*
Ghosts (world premiere, in Norwegian), Chicago.*

1883
W. Archer, 'H. Ibsen's
 Dramas', *Academy*, 1:5.
'A Dramatist at Bay',
 Saturday Review, 1:43.
E. Gosse, 'Studies in the
 Literature of Northern
 Europe' (reprint).
T. A. Schovelin, 'Ibsen',
 Scandinavia, 1:11–13,
 35–8. Nov., Dec.*

1883
Thora (*A Doll's House*),
 Louisville, Kentucky.*

1884
W. Archer, 'Breaking a
 Butterfly', *Theatre*, 1:209.
E. Aveling, 'Breaking a
 Butterfly', *To-day*, 1:473.
Athenaeum, 8 March.
Academy, 8 March.
Saturday Review, 8 March.
T. A. Schovelin, 'Ibsen',
 Scandinavia, 1:66–101,
 133–7, Jan., March.*
C. Petersen, 'Ibsen and
 Björnson', *Scandinavia*,
 1:271–2, Aug.*

1884
'The Murder of Abraham
 Lincoln' (Memorial poem),
 tr. T. A. Schovelin,
 Scandinavia, 1:259–60,
 July.*

1884
Breaking a Butterfly—
 adaptation of *A Doll's House* (by H. A. Jones
 & Henry Hermann),
 Prince's Theatre (3 March).

1885
Ghosts, tr. Mrs. Lord, in
 To-day, 1:29, 65, 105.

1885
Nora (in Mrs Lord's tr.),
 acted by amateurs.

ARTICLES, REVIEWS, CRITICAL ESSAYS	TRANSLATIONS	THEATRICAL PERFORMANCES

1886
G. Brandes, *Eminent Authors of the Nineteenth Century*, tr. R. B. Anderson.★

1887
C. H. Genung, 'Ibsen's Spectres', *Nation*, 44:116–17, Feb.★

1888
Camelot Series (ed. Havelock Ellis); *The Pillars of Society*, tr. W. Archer; *Ghosts*, tr. W. Archer; *An Enemy of the People*, tr. Mrs. E. Marx-Aveling, with Intro. by Havelock Ellis.

1889
Arthur Symons, 'H. Ibsen', *Universal Review*, April.
E. Gosse, 'Ibsen's Social Dramas', *Fortnightly Review*, Jan.
P. H. Wicksteed, 'Peer Gynt', *Contemporary Review*, 2:274.
R. K. Hervey, 'Pillars of Society', *Theatre*, 2:94.
W. Archer, 'English Criticism of Ibsen', *Fortnightly Review*, 2:30.
F. Wedmore, 'H. Ibsen', *Academy*, 1:419.
C. H. Herford, 'H. Ibsen', *Academy*, 1:432.
Clement Scott, 'A Doll's House', *Theatre*, 2:19.
R. K. Hervey, 'Doll's House', *Theatre*, 2:38.
R. F. Sharp, 'Ibsen—A Dramatic Experiment', *Theatre*, 1:73.
W. F. Lord, 'Works of Ibsen', *Nineteenth Century*, Aug.
F. Wedmore, 'H. Ibsen', *Academy*, 27 July.

1889
A Doll's House, tr. W. Archer.
Rosmersholm, tr. Louis N. Parker.
The Lady from the Sea tr. G. R. Carpenter, *Harvard Monthly*, Nov., Dec.★

1889
Nora, in W. Archer's tr., Novelty Theatre, 7 June.
Pillars of Society, a single performance, Opéra Comique, 17 July.
A Doll's House, Palmer's Theatre, 21 Dec.★

ARTICLES, REVIEWS, CRITICAL ESSAYS	TRANSLATIONS	THEATRICAL PERFORMANCES

1889—*cont.*

'A Doll's House', *Spectator*, 1:853.

'A Doll's House', *Saturday Review*, 29 June.

'H. Ibsen's Men and Women', *Westminster Review*, 1:626.

W. Archer, 'The Dying Drama', *New Review*, Sept.

Robert Buchanan, Justin McCarthy, *Daily Telegraph*, 22, 23 July.

Reviews of *A Doll's House: Evening News, Daily Telegraph, Daily News, Referee, Daily Chronicle, Queen, Observer, Lloyd's Weekly News, Era, Licensed Victuallers' Mirror, Truth, Sunday Times, Illustrated London News, Pall Mall Gazette.*

Reviews of *Pillars of Society: Daily Telegraph, Daily News, Daily Chronicle, Queen, Lloyd's Weekly News, Hawk, Era, Referee, Observer, People, Sunday Times, Evening News, Pall Mall Gazette.*

W. Archer, 'The Dying Drama', *Poet-Lore*, 1:527–30 (as *New Review*, Sept.)⋆

R. Buchanan, 'The Modern Drama and its Minor Critics', *Contemporary Review*, 56:909–25, Dec.⋆

G. R. Carpenter, 'Ibsen', *Scribner's*, 5:404–12, April.⋆

E. Gosse, 'Ibsen's Social Dramas', *Living Age*, 180: 298–307 (as *Fortnightly Review*, Jan. 1889).⋆

O. Heller, 'Ibsen', *Poet-Lore*, 1:337–42.⋆

W. F. Lord, 'Works of Ibsen', *Living Age*, 182:

ARTICLES, REVIEWS, CRITICAL ESSAYS	TRANSLATIONS	THEATRICAL PERFORMANCES
1889—*cont.* 737–46 (as *Nineteenth Century*, Aug. 1889).★ E. R. Penell, 'Ibsen in England', *Nation*, 49:7–8.★ Reviews of *A Doll's House*: *New York Times, Evening Post, Sun, World, Critic*, 15:329.★		
1890 C. H. Herford, 'H. Ibsen', *Academy*, 18 Jan. 'Ibsen's Plays', *Saturday Review*, 1:15. 'Ibsen's Dramas in Prose', *Saturday Review*, 1:352, 474. W. Archer, 'Ibsen as He is Translated', *Time*, Jan. Havelock Ellis, Essay on Ibsen in *The New Spirit*. E. Gosse, *Northern Studies* (reprint, but his essay in *Fortnightly Review*, 1889, added). H. Jaeger's *Life of Ibsen*, tr. Clara Bell. Sir Walter Besant's sequel 'The Doll's House and After', *English Illustrated Magazine*, Jan. G. B. Shaw, 'Still After the Doll's House', *Time*, Feb. H. H. Boyesen, 'Ibsen', *Century*, 39:794–6.★ H. H. Boyesen, 'Brand', *Chautauquan*, 12:207–13.★ G. E. Channing, 'Ibsen', *Overland Monthly*, n.s. 15:314–17.★ E. Cheney, *Nora's Return*.★ E. Cheney, 'A Dramatic Poem by Ibsen', *Open Court*, 4:255.★ E. P. Evans, 'Ibsen's Early Career', *Atlantic Monthly*, 65:578–88.★ E. P. Evans, 'Ibsen's Later	**1890** *The Lady from the Sea*, tr. Mrs E. Marx-Aveling (Cameo Series), with Intro. by E. Gosse. *Nora*, 2nd rev. ed. of Mrs Lord's tr., with Intro. *Ghosts*, tr. Mrs Lord, originally printed in *To-day* 1885, with Intro. *Ibsen's Prose Dramas*, authorized English edn, 5 vols., by W. Archer (also in U.S.A.★). *Rosmersholm*, tr. M. Carmichael. *Lady from the Sea*, tr. Clara Bell. *Enemy of Society*, tr. W. Archer. *Wild Duck*, tr. Mrs Marx-Aveling. *The Young Men's League*, tr. Henry Carstarphen. *Hedda Gabler*, tr. W. Archer, with Intro. by E. Gosse. *Prose Dramas of H. Ibsen* in *Lovell's Series of Foreign Literature*, with Intro. by E. Gosse.★	**1890** *Pillars of Society*, performed by amateurs, Amberg Theatre.★

ARTICLES, REVIEWS, CRITICAL ESSAYS	TRANSLATIONS	THEATRICAL PERFORMANCES

1890—*cont.*
Career', *Atlantic Monthly*, 66:457–69.*
Anon., 'A Doll's House', *Critic*, 16:89.*
E. P. Evans, 'Ibsen's Working Habits', *Critic*, 16:122.*
E. Fuller, 'Ibsen's Social Dramas', *New England Magazine*, n.s. 2:584–90.*
H. Garland, 'Ibsen as Dramatist', *Arena*, 2: 72–82.*
E. J. Harding, 'Ibsen the Iconoclast', *Critic*, 16: 131–2.*
A. N. Meyer, 'Ibsen's Attitude Towards Women', *Critic*, 16:147–8.*
E. J. Harding, 'Is Ibsen a Reformer?', *Critic*, 16: 159.*
R. C. Harrison, 'Ibsen's Individualism', *Harvard Monthly*, 11:25.*
A. H. Palmer, 'Brand', *New England and Yale Review*, 53:340–73.*
J. M. Parker, 'Prose Dramas of Ibsen', *American*, 20: 429f.*
W. E. Simonds (review of Jaeger), *Dial*, 11:146–8.*
T. Solberg, 'Ibsen and His Translators', *Nation*, 50: 67–8.*
Anon., 'Pillars of Society', *Critic*, 16:7–8.*
W. L. Cross, 'Brand', *Arena*, 3:81–90.*

1891
E. Gosse, 'Hedda Gabler', *Fortnightly Review*, Jan.
O. Crawfurd, 'H. I.', *Fortnightly Review*, 1:725.
'H. Ibsen', *Temple Bar*, 3:97.
H. A. Kennedy, 'The Drama

1891
Hedda Gabler, tr. E. Gosse (four different edns. Preface by E. Gosse to the limited edn).
Hedda Gabler, tr. W. Archer (reprint, shilling edn).

1891
Ibsen's Ghost (a burlesque), by James Matthew Barrie, Toole's Theatre, 30 May.
Rosmersholm, Vaudeville Theatre, 23 Feb.
Ghosts (single performance),

ARTICLES, REVIEWS, CRITICAL ESSAYS	TRANSLATIONS	THEATRICAL PERFORMANCES
1891—*cont.*	**1891**—*cont.*	**1891**—*cont.*
of the Moment', *Nineteenth Century*, 2:258.	*Brand*, tr. into prose, W. Wilson, with Preface.	Royalty Theatre, Soho, 13 March.
C. H. Herford, 'Brand', *Contemporary Review*, 1:407.	*Rosmersholm*, tr. C. Archer (reprint), Prefatory Note, W. Archer.	*Hedda Gabler*, Vaudeville Theatre, produced by Miss E. Robins & Miss Marion Lea, 20 April.
R. A. Armstrong, 'Brand', *Westminster Review*, 1:409.	Prose tr. of some of Ibsen's poems in P. H. Wicksteed's art. in *Contemporary Review*, 2:333.	*Lady from the Sea*, Terry's Theatre, 11 May.
'Brand', *Saturday Review*, 2:705.		*A Dolls' House*, Criterion, 2 June.

'Ghosts', *Theatre*, 1:205.

'How we Found Gibsen', *Hawk*, 17 March.

'Hedda Gabler', *Saturday Review*, 1:145, 498.

'Hedda Gabler', *Theatre*, 1:257.

Henry James, 'Hedda Gabler', *New Review*, 1:519.

'Ibsen's Ghost' (a burlesque), *Theatre*, 2:28.

'Lady from the Sea', *Theatre*, 1:306.

P. H. Wicksteed, 'Poems of Ibsen', *Contemporary Review*, 2:333.

'Rosmersholm', *Saturday Review*, 1:258.

'Rosmersholm', *Theatre*, 1:196.

'Ibsen's Social Dramas', *Quarterly Review*, 1:305.

W. Archer, 'Quintessence of Ibsenism', *New Review*, 5:463.

'Shaw on Ibsen', *Saturday Review*, 2:455.

C. E. Maurice, 'H. Ibsen', *Economic Review*, 2:348.

W. Archer, 'Ghosts and Gibberings', *Pall Mall Gazette*, 8 April.

G. B. Shaw, *Quintessence of Ibsenism*.

George Moore in *Impressions and Opinions*.

Austin Fryers, *Rosmer of Rosmersholm*, suggested by H. Ibsen's *Rosmersholm*.

Reviews of *Rosmersholm*:

ARTICLES, REVIEWS, CRITICAL ESSAYS	TRANSLATIONS	THEATRICAL PERFORMANCES

1891—*cont.*

Daily Telegraph, Standard,
Daily News, Daily Chronicle (and an editorial),
Queen, Lloyd's Weekly
News, Hawk, Gentlewoman, Black and White,
Illustrated London News,
Era, Evening Standard, The
Times, Referee, Observer.
Reviews of Ghosts: Daily
Telegraph (and an editorial),
Standard, Daily News,
Daily Chronicle, Queen,
Lloyd's Weekly News,
Truth, Gentlewoman, Black
and White, Illustrated
London News, Era, The
Times, Referee, Observer,
People, Sunday Times,
Morning Advertiser,
Evening News, Daily
Graphic, Pall Mall Gazette,
Hawk.
Reviews of Hedda Gabler:
Daily Telegraph, Daily
Chronicle, Queen, Truth,
Gentlewoman, Black and
White, Illustrated London
News, Era, The Times,
Referee, Observer, People,
Sunday Times, Morning
Advertiser, Evening News,
Pall Mall Gazette, Reynolds News, Daily Graphic.
Reviews of Barrie's parody
of Ghosts: Daily Telegraph,
Standard, Daily Chronicle,
Queen, Lloyd's Weekly
News, Licensed Victuallers'
Mirror, Gentlewoman,
Illustrated London News,
Observer, People, Morning
Advertiser, Pall Mall
Gazette, Daily Graphic.
Reviews of Lady from the
Sea: Daily Telegraph,
Standard, Queen, Hawk,
Gentlewoman, Era, The
Times, Referee, Observer,

ARTICLES, REVIEWS, CRITICAL ESSAYS	TRANSLATIONS	THEATRICAL PERFORMANCES

1891—*cont.*
*People, Sunday Times,
Morning Advertiser, Evening
News.*
Reviews of *A Doll's House*
revival: *Era, Referee,
Observer, Evening News,
Daily Graphic.*
W. Archer, 'The Quin-
tessence of Ibsenism',
New Review, 5: 463–8.*
R. Armstrong, 'Brand',
Living Age, 189:422–32 (as
Westminster Review,
1:409f.).*
W. L. Cross, 'Hedda Gabler',
*New England and Yale
Review*, 53:14–18.*
N. Hapgood, 'Reaction
against Ibsen', *Harvard
Monthly*, 13:51.*
H. A. Kennedy, 'Drama of
the Moment', *Nineteenth
Century*, 30:258–74.*
E. R. Pennell, 'Rosmer-
sholm', *Nation*, 52:216–17.
Anon., 'Ibsen's Prose
Dramas', *Critic*, 19:243–4.*

1892
C. H. Herford, 'Ibsen',
Academy, 1:247.
'Peer Gynt', *Gentleman's
Magazine*, 2:533.
'Peer Gynt', *Saturday Re-
view*, 2:417.
'Beerbohm Tree on Ibsen',
Gentleman's Magazine,
1:103.
'Ibsenism', *London
Quarterly Review*, 1:227.
P. H. Wicksteed, *Four
Lectures on Henrik Ibsen.*
W. L. Courtney in *Studies
at Leisure* (reprint from
art. in *Quarterly Review*,
1891, 1:305).
Arthur B. Walkley in *Play-
house Impressions.*

1892
Popular edn, W. Archer's
tr. *A Doll's House.*
New edn Mrs Lord's tr.
Nora.
Peer Gynt, tr. W. & C.
Archer.

1892
A Doll's House, Avenue
Theatre, 19 April.
(*Beata*, adaptation of Austin
Fryer's *Rosmer of
Rosmersholm*, 1891, Globe,
19 April).
(*A Ghost*, a parody, a spirited
sketch, not by Ibsen,
Criterion, 28 June.)

ARTICLES, REVIEWS, CRITICAL ESSAYS	TRANSLATIONS	THEATRICAL PERFORMANCES

1892—cont.

Reviews of *Beata*: *Daily Telegraph, Standard, Daily Chronicle, Queen, Lloyd's Weekly News, Truth, Black and White, Illustrated London News, Era, Evening Standard, The Times, Referee, Observer, Sunday Times, Morning Advertiser, Evening News, Reynolds News.*

Reviews of *A Doll's House*: *Pall Mall Gazette, Daily Telegraph, Standard, Daily Chronicle, Queen, Lloyd's Weekly News, Truth, Gentlewoman, Black and White, Illustrated London News, Evening Standard, The Times, Referee, Observer, People, Evening News, Reynolds News, Daily Graphic.*

C. H. Herford, 'Ibsen's Earlier Work', *Lippincott's*, 49:351–6.★

E. Tissot, 'Three Philosophical Poems', *Chautauquan*, 16:53–6.★

W. Winter, in *Shadows of the Stage*.★

1893

Mrs. Tweedie, 'Ibsen and Björnson', *Temple Bar*, 2:536.

L. Simons, 'Ibsen as an Artist', *Westminster Review*, 2:506.

Henry James, 'Master Builder', *Pall Mall Gazette*, 17 Feb.

'Masterbuilder', *Saturday Review*, 1:241.

'Masterbuilder', *Spectator*, 1:285.

W. Archer, 'Mausoleum of Ibsen', *Fortnightly Review*, 2:77.

1893

Masterbuilder, tr. E. Gosse & W. Archer. (New edn of the same with Biblio. Notes, etc.)

Reprint of Mrs Lord's tr. *Nora.*

Masterbuilder, tr. J. W. Arctander.★

1893

Ghosts, Independent Theatre, 27 Jan.

Masterbuilder, Trafalgar Square Theatre, 20 Feb.

Masterbuilder, Vaudeville Theatre, 6 March.

Hedda Gabler, Rosmersholm, The Masterbuilder, an act from *Brand*, Opéra Comique, 29 May–10 June.

An Enemy of the People, Haymarket (Herbert Beerbohm Tree), 14 June.

The Lady from the Sea (produced by Mrs & Mr Charrington).

ARTICLES, REVIEWS, CRITICAL ESSAYS	TRANSLATIONS	THEATRICAL PERFORMANCES

1893—*cont.*

A. B. Walkley, 'Master Builder', *Fortnightly Review*, 3:468–76.

Henry James in *Essays in London and Elsewhere.*

William Watson in *Excursions in Criticism.*

F. Anstey, *Mr. Punch's Pocket Ibsen.*

Reviews of *The Master Builder: Daily Telegraph, Standard, Daily Chronicle, Queen, Lloyd's Weekly News, Hawk, Gentlewoman, Black and White, Illustrated London News, The Times, Referee, Observer, People, Morning Advertiser, Evening News, Pall Mall Gazette, Daily Graphic.*

Reviews of *Hedda Gabler: Daily Telegraph, Standard, Era:* (plus *Brand, Rosmersholm*), *Observer, Pall Mall Gazette, Daily Graphic.*

Reviews of *An Enemy of the People: Daily Telegraph, Daily Chronicle, Gentlewoman, Era, The Times, Observer, Pall Mall Gazette, Daily Graphic.*

(N.B. No review of *Ghosts* except *Black and White.*)

H. H. Boyesen, 'Peer Gynt', *Chautauquan*, 17:293.*

W. M. Payne, 'Bygmester Solness', *Dial*, 14:68–71.*

H. H. Boyesen, 'Comedy of Love', *Dial*, 14:132–4.*

H. H. Boyesen, 'Ibsen's Poems', *Cosmopolitan*, 15:91–9.*

H. H. Boyesen, 'Wild Duck', *Dial*, 15:137–40.*

H. H. Boyesen, 'A Doll's House', *Cosmopolitan*, 16:84–9.*

ARTICLES, REVIEWS, CRITICAL ESSAYS	TRANSLATIONS	THEATRICAL PERFORMANCES

1893—*cont.*
W. H. Carpenter, *Ibsen as Dramatist*.★
M. F. Egan, 'Old-Fashioned View of Fiction', *Lippincott's*, 52:78–9.★
C. H. Waage, 'Notes about Ibsen', *California Illustrated Magazine*, 4:512.★

1894
'Ibsen and the Morbid Taint', *Belgravia*, 1:59.
B. Johnson, 'Books about Ibsen', *Academy*, 1:285.
'Boyesen on Ibsen', *Spectator*, 1:625.
'Boyesen on Ibsen', *Saturday Review*, 2:359.
H. Waring, 'Ibsen in London', *Theatre*, 2:164.
Sir Edward Russell, 'Ibsen', a lecture.
Mary S. Gilliland, 'Ibsen's Women', a lecture.
Mrs Alec B. Tweedie in *A Winter's Jaunt to Norway*,
Allan Monkhouse in *Books and Plays* (limited to 400 copies).
H. H. Boyesen, *A Commentary on the Works of H. Ibsen* (Heinemann).
Review of *An Enemy of the People* (Manchester): *Manchester Guardian*.
Reviews of *The Wild Duck: Daily Telegraph, Daily Chronicle, Black and White, Era, Observer, Evening News, Reynolds News, Daily Graphic.*
H. H. Boyesen, *Commentary on the Writings of H. Ibsen* (Macmillan).★
H. Garland in *Crumbling Idols*.★
A. N. Meyer, 'A prophet of the New Womanhood', *Lippincott's*, 53:575–80.★

1894
Brand, tr. into original metres, C. H. Herford, with Intro.
Brand, tr. into English verse, F. E. Garrett.
2nd edn, W. Wilson's prose tr. of *Brand*.

1894
An Enemy of the People, Manchester, 27 Jan.
The Wild Duck, Royalty Theatre, 4 May.
Hedda Gabler and *The Masterbuilder*, Manchester and other cities.
Ghosts, Berkeley Lyceum, 5 Jan.★

ARTICLES, REVIEWS, CRITICAL ESSAYS	TRANSLATIONS	THEATRICAL PERFORMANCES

1894—*cont.*

W. M. Payne, 'Boyesen's Commentary and Herford's Brand', *Dial*, 16: 236–40.★

T. R. Price, 'Ibsen's Dramatic Method', *Sewanee Review*, 2:257–81.★

M. Wergeland, 'Interpretations of Ibsen', *Dial*, 16: 262–3.★

Anon., 'Ghosts in New York', *Critic*, 24:31.★

C. Wingate 'Ghosts in Boston', *Critic*, 24:312.★

Anon., 'Boyesen's Commentary', *Critic*, 25:119.★

Anon., 'Art and Moral of Ghosts', *Poet-Lore*, 6: 356–61.★

Reviews of *Ghosts*: *New York Times, Evening Post, New York Press, World*.★

1895

Max Nordau, *Degeneration*, tr. into English.

E. J. Goodman, 'Ibsen at Christiania', *Theatre*, 2:146.

W. L. Courtney, 'Note on Little Eyolf', *Fortnightly Review*, 1:277.

Steevens, 'The New Ibsen', *New Review*, 1:39.

New ed. of F. Anstey's *Mr. Punch's Pocket Ibsen*.

Regeneration: A Reply to Max Nordau (A. E. Hake).

G. B. Shaw, *The Sanity of Art*.

W. H. Carpenter, 'Little Eyolf', *Bookman*, 1:39–40.★

W. H. Carpenter, 'Ibsen Bibliography', *Bookman*, 1:274–7.★

W. L. Courtney, 'Little Eyolf', *Living Age*, 205: 239–45 (as *Fortnightly Review*, 1:277).★

1895

Little Eyolf, tr. W. Archer.

The Master Builder, tr. E. Gosse & W. Archer, with Biblio. Notes (limited edn).

A Doll's House, tr. E. B. Ginty.★

1895

An Enemy of the People, Abbey's Theatre, 8 April.★

ARTICLES, REVIEWS, CRITICAL ESSAYS	TRANSLATIONS	THEATRICAL PERFORMANCES

1895—cont.

H. H. Boyesen, 'Drama of Revolt', *Bookman*, 1: 348–88.*

L. Monroe, 'An Enemy of the People', *Critic*, 26:208–9.*

L. Monroe, 'The Master Builder', *Critic*, 26:249.*

W. M. Payne, 'Little Eyolf', *Dial*, 18:5–6.*

W. M. Payne in *Little Leaders*.*

W. M. Payne, 'The Ibsen Legend', *Dial*, 18:259–61.*

Reviews of *An Enemy of the People: New York Times, Evening Post, New York Herald, New York Press, World*.*

1896

A. T. Quiller-Couch in *Adventures in Criticism*.

'John Gabriel Borkman', *Saturday Review*, 2:654.

'Little Eyolf', *Academy*, 2:465.

G. B. Shaw, 'Little Eyolf', *Saturday Review*, 2:563, 623.

Shaw, 'Peer Gynt', *Saturday Review*, 2:542.

Adams, 'Sarcey on Ibsen', *Theatre*, 2:19.

Reviews of *Little Eyolf: Daily Telegraph, Standard, Daily News, Daily Chronicle, Black and White, Illustrated London News, Era* (leading article), *Observer, Sunday Times, Evening News, Pall Mall Gazette, Daily Graphic*.

E. O. Achorn, 'Ibsen at Home', *New England Magazine*, n.s. 13:737–48.*

B. Björnson in 'Modern Norwegian Literature', *Forum*, 21:318–29.*

1896

Reprint of Archer's tr. of *Peer Gynt*.

Little Eyolf, tr. H. H. Boyesen.*

1896

Little Eyolf, Avenue Theatre, London, 23 Nov.

ARTICLES, REVIEWS, CRITICAL ESSAYS	TRANSLATIONS	THEATRICAL PERFORMANCES

1896—*cont.*

W. L. Cross, 'Hedda Gabler', *New Englander*, 55:14–20.*

E. Crowell, 'Shakespeare and Ibsen', *Poet-Lore*, 8:192–7.*

W. M. Hirsch, *Genius and Degeneration*.*

C. B. Wright, 'Ibsen and Shakespeare', *PMLA*, n.s. 4:31–2.*

1897

Shaw, 'John Gabriel Borkman', *Saturday Review*, 1:114.

Shaw, 'Doll's House played in 1897', *Saturday Review*, 1:539.

Shaw, 'John Gabriel Borkman in London', *Saturday Review*, 1:507.

Shaw, 'Ghosts at the Jubilee', *Saturday Review*, 2:12.

A. S. Spender, 'Little Eyolf —A Plea for Reticence', *Dublin Review*, 1:122.

Traill and McNeill, 'Ibsenism', *National Review*, 1:641.

Sir Edward Russell & P. C. Standing, *Ibsen on his Merits* (parts of it a revision of Sir Edward Russell's lecture on Ibsen, 1894).

Review of *John Gabriel Borkman: Daily Telegraph, Standard, Daily News, Daily Chronicle, Lloyd's Weekly News, Gentlewoman, Illustrated London News, Era, Observer*.

H. D. Traill, 'Ibsenism', *Living Age*, 212:317–22 (as *National Review*, 1: 122).*

1897

John Gabriel Borkman, **tr.** W. Archer. Popular edn of same.

Gleanings from Ibsen— selected and ed. E. A. Keddell & P. C. Standing, with Preface on Ibsenism.

A Doll's House, Ghosts, Lady from the Sea, The Wild Duck, Scott's shilling edn (each play one vol.).

Little Eyolf, new edn.

1897

John Gabriel Borkman, Strand, 3 May.

The Wild Duck, repeated, Globe, 22 May.

Ghosts, Independent Theatre, 24 June (attended by Queen Victoria).

John Gabriel Borkman, Hoyt's Theatre, 18 Nov.*

ARTICLES, REVIEWS, CRITICAL ESSAYS	TRANSLATIONS	THEATRICAL PERFORMANCES

1897—*cont.*

Henry James, 'Little Eyolf', *Harper's Weekly*, Jan.*

W. H. Carpenter, 'John Gabriel Borkman', *Bookman*, 5:157–60.*

W. H. Carpenter in *Warner's Library of World's Best Literature*, vol. XIV.*

W. S. McLay, 'Ibsen on his Merits', *Citizen*, 3:230–1.*

W. M. Payne, 'John Gabriel Borkman', *Dial*, 22:37–41.*

Henry James, 'John Gabriel Borkman', *Harper's Weekly*, Feb.*

C. Porter, 'John Gabriel Borkman', *Poet-Lore*, 9:302–6*.

J. Reimers, 'John Gabriel Borkman', *Overland Monthly*, 30:463–5.*

D. K. Dodge, 'Does Ibsen Write Norwegian?', *Critic*, 31:69.*

S. Sondresen, 'Ibsen Writes Norwegian', *Critic*, 31:308–9.*

Reviews of *John Gabriel Borkman: Evening Post, New York Herald, New York Press, Sunday World*.*

1898

'Brandes on Ibsen', *Saturday Review*, 1:821.

'Ibsen's Seventieth Birthday', *Academy*, 1:352.

Shaw, 'England's Compliment to Ibsen', *Saturday Review*, 1:428.

Walter Jerrold, 'Henrik Ibsen', in *Prophets of the Century*—Essays, ed. Arthur Rickett.

D. K. Dodge, 'The Language Ibsen Writes', *Critic*, 32:149.

1898

Reprint of Mrs Marx-Aveling's tr. of *An Enemy of the People* (shilling edn).

Hedda Gabler, tr. E. Gosse (new edn).

1898

Hedda Gabler, Fifth Avenue Theatre, 30 March.*

1898—*cont.*

H. Knorr, 'Ibsen and the Ethical Drama', *Poet-Lore*, 10:49–65.*

E. W. Morris, *The Drama, Its Laws and Technique*.*

W. H. Schofield, 'Ibsen and Björnson', *Atlantic*, 81:567–73.*

V. Thompson, 'John Gabriel Borkman', *National*, 8:120.*

Anon., 'Elizabeth Robins', *Critic*, 32:182.*

Anon., 'Hedda Gabler', *Critic*, 32:239, 254–5.*

Reviews of *Hedda Gabler*: *New York Times, Evening Post, New York Herald, New York Press, World*.*

1899

'H. Ibsen', *Academy*, 2:79.

Stobart, 'New Light on *Brand*', *Fortnightly Review*, 2:227.

Max Beerbohm, 'Brandes on Ibsen', *Saturday Review*, 2:101.

George Brandes, *H. Ibsen and B. Björnson*, tr. into English by Jessie Muir, intro. by W. Archer.

L. Marholm in *We Women and our Authors*.

W. M. Payne, 'Björnson and Ibsen', *Dial*, 27:314–18.*

Anon., 'Brandes, Björnson and Ibsen', *Nation*, 69:340–1.*

A. I. Coleman, 'Seventy Years of Ibsen', *Critic*, 34:34–7.*

C. Porter and H. Clarke, 'Oedipus, Lear and Borkman', *Poet-Lore*, 11:116.*

1899

New edn of Herford's tr. of *Brand*.

2nd reprint of *Peer Gynt*, tr. W. & C. Archer.

ARTICLES, REVIEWS, CRITICAL ESSAYS	TRANSLATIONS	THEATRICAL PERFORMANCES
1900	**1900**	**1900**
'Love's Comedy', *Academy*, 1:527.	*Love's Comedy*, tr. C. H. Herford, with Intro.	*The Masterbuilder*, Carnegie Lyceum, 17 Jan.*
C. H. Herford, 'Scene from Love's Comedy', *Fortnightly Review*, 1:191.	*When we Dead Awaken*, tr. W. Archer.	
Joyce, 'When we Dead Awaken', *Fortnightly Review*, 1:575.	*The Lady from the Sea*, tr. Clara Bell (reissue).*	
'When we Dead Awaken', *Academy*, 1:307.	*Rosmersholm*, tr. M. Carmichael (reissue).*	
W. L. Courtney, *The Idea of Tragedy in Ancient and Modern Drama*.	*A Doll's House*, tr. W. Archer in *Plays by Greek, Spanish, French and German Dramatists*, vol. II.*	
J. L. Ford, 'Ibsen Performance', *Munsey's*, 22:610–11.*		
C. H. Genung (review of Brandes), *Book-Buyer*, 20:140–2.*		
H. Knorr, 'The Masterbuilder in New York', *Poet-Lore*, 12:95–7.*		
W. M. Payne, 'When We Dead Awaken', *Dial*, 28:108–13.*		
Anon., 'When We Dead Awaken', *Nation*, 70–94.*		
H. Ramsdun, 'The New Mysticism', *Nineteenth Century*, 47:279–96.*		
W. L. Wendell, 'Some Modern History-Makers', *Self-Culture*, 11:304–9.*		
Reviews of *The Master Builder*: *New York Herald*, *Sun*, *New York Press*, *World*.*		
	1900–1	
	New rev. edn of *Prose Dramas of Henrik Ibsen*, ed. W. Archer: *The League of Youth*, *Pillars of Society*, *A Doll's House*, *Ghosts*, *An Enemy of the People* (each play intro. by W. Archer).	

ARTICLES, REVIEWS, CRITICAL ESSAYS	TRANSLATIONS	THEATRICAL PERFORMANCES
1901	**1901**	**1901**
Beerbohm, 'Pillars of Society', *Saturday Review*, 1:631.	3rd imp. Herford's tr. of *Brand*.	*Pillars of Society*, Strand, May.
'Ibsen's Plays in England, 1901', *Academy*, 1:244.	New edn *The Masterbuilder*, tr. E. Gosse & W. Archer.	
W. J. Clarke Miller, *H. Ibsen, a Dramatic Pioneer*.	'Memory', a poem, tr. anon. in *Current Literature*, 31:670.★	
W. Archer, 'The Real Ibsen', *International Quarterly*, 3:182–201.★	'On the Highlands' (Paa Vidderne), a poem, tr. H. Edgren in *Poet-Lore*, 13:335–48.★	
N. Hapgood, *The Stage in America*.★		
Anon., 'Spectacular in Ibsen', *Current Literature*, 31:727.★		
H. Jaeger, *Ibsen, A Critical Biography*, tr. W. M. Payne (2nd edn.★).		
Anon., 'Anent Ibsen', *Independent*, 53:2047–8.★		
C. von Klenze, 'Ibsen', *Modern Language Notes*, 16:157–8.★		
W. Leighton, 'Passing of Ibsen', *Independent*, 53:2630–3.★		
E. Limedorfer, 'Ibsen, the Man', *Theatre*, 7:8–9.★		
A. B. Walkley, 'Ibsen in England', *Living Age*, 230:789–92.★		
1902	**1902**	**1902**
A. M. Butler, 'A View of Ibsen', *Contemporary Review*, 1:709.	Streatfeild, *Lyrical Poems by Ibsen*, selected and tr.	*Lady from the Sea*, Royalty Theatre, London, 5 May.
Reviews of *Lady from the Sea: Daily Telegraph, Illustrated London News, Era, Referee, Daily Graphic*.	*An Enemy of the People*, tr. W. Archer, with Intro.	
'A Doll's House', *National Magazine*, 16:568.★	*Peer Gynt*, 3rd reprint, W. Archer's tr.	
C. Brinton, 'Ecce Ibsen!', *Critic*, 40:236–49.★	*Terje Vigen and Thirty-Six Other Poems*, tr. P. W. Shedd.★	
A. M. Butler, 'A View of Ibsen', *Living Age*, 233:769–78 (as *Contemporary Review*, 1:709)★		

ARTICLES, REVIEWS, CRITICAL ESSAYS	TRANSLATIONS	THEATRICAL PERFORMANCES

1902—*cont.*

Anon. (review of Jaeger),
  Sewanee Review, 10:127.★

W. H. Carruth (review of
  Jaeger), *Dial*, 32:16–17.★

D. K. Dodge (review of
  Jaeger), *Modern Language
  Notes*, 17:91–2.★

J. B. Halvorsen, 'Biblio-
  graphical Information of
  Ibsen', *Nation*, 74:73f.★

W. Leighton, 'Peer Gynt',
  Arena, 27:64–7.★

W. M. Payne, 'Ibsen',
  Outlook, 71:240–7.★

G. Saintsbury, 'Literary
  Prophets', *Independent*,
  54:3023–6.★

D. F. Sicker, 'Hero as
  Individualist', *Yale
  Literary Magazine*, 297–
  301, May.★

L. C. Strang in *Plays and
  Players of the Last Quarter
  Century*.★

1903

Beerbohm, 'Vikings at
  Helgeland', *Saturday Review*, 1:517.

Beerbohm, 'When we Dead
  Awaken', *Saturday Review*,
  1:168.

Reviews of *When We Dead
  Awaken*: *Daily Telegraph,
  Daily Chronicle, Lloyd's
  Weekly News, Truth,
  Gentlewoman, Illustrated
  London News, Era, The
  Times, Referee, Sunday
  Times, Pall Mall Gazette,
  Daily Graphic.*

Reviews of *Vikings at
  Helgeland: Daily Telegraph,
  Daily Chronicle, Lloyd's
  Weekly News, Gentle-
  woman, Era, The Times,
  Referee, Observer, People,
  Sunday Times, Morning
  Advertiser, Daily Graphic.*

1903

When We Dead Awaken,
  Imperial Theatre, 25 Jan.
Vikings at Helgeland,
  Imperial Theatre, London,
  15 April (Miss Ellen Terry).
Ghosts, Manhattan Theatre,
  27 Jan. (Mary Shaw).★
Hedda Gabler, Manhattan
  Theatre, 5 Oct. (Mrs
  Fiske).★

ARTICLES, REVIEWS, CRITICAL ESSAYS	TRANSLATIONS	THEATRICAL PERFORMANCES

1903—*cont.*
J. Brochner, 'A Bio-
graphical Sketch', *Book-
Lover*, 4:385–91.*
J. Brochner, 'Ibsen',
Bookman, 18:180–1.*
T. A. Brown in *History of
the New York Stage.**
E. Faguet, 'The Symbolical
Drama', *International
Quarterly*, 8:329–41.*
J. Moritzen, 'Ibsen's First
Nora', *Theatre*, 3:70–1.*
W. M. Payne, 'Ibsen',
Booklovers' Magazine,
1:575–7.*
Anon. (review of Mary
Shaw's *Ghosts*), *Theatre*,
3:100.*
Anon., 'Congratulations to
Ibsen' (telegrams),
Current Literature,
34:719–20.*

1904
'Scene from Peer Gynt',
Independent Review,
2:444.
W. Archer, 'Apprentice-
ship of Ibsen', *Fortnightly
Review*, 1:25.
New ed. of Shaw's
Quintessence of Ibsenism,
enlarged edn.
E. Goodman, 'Ibsen, the
Master Builder', *Current
Literature*, 36:551–2.*
B. Matthews in 'The Study
of the Drama',
International Quarterly,
10:92–107.*
W. Leighton (review of
Quintessence), *Nation*
79:282.*
J. N. Laurvik, 'Letters of
Ibsen', *International
Quarterly*, 10:261–7.*

1904
New edn of *Prose Dramas of
Ibsen*.

1904
Rosmersholm, Princess
Theatre, 28 March.*
Hedda Gabler (two separate
performances, Blanche
Bates & Nance O'Neill).*
When We Dead Awaken, in
New York.*

ARTICLES, REVIEWS, CRITICAL ESSAYS	TRANSLATIONS	THEATRICAL PERFORMANCES
1905	**1905**	**1905**
Archer, 'Ibsen in his Letters', *Fortnightly Review*, 2:428.	*Correspondence of H. Ibsen*, tr. Mary Morison.	*The Wild Duck*, Court Theatre, 22 Oct.
Reviews of *The Wild Duck*: *Referee* (twice).	New edn of *The Wild Duck*, tr. W. Archer, with Intro.	*An Enemy of the People*, His Majestys' Theatre, 2 Nov.
Reviews of *Enemy of the People*: *Daily Telegraph, Standard, Daily News, Daily Chronicle, Lloyd's Weekly News, Gentlewoman, Era, The Times, Referee, Observer, Sunday Times, Morning Advertiser, Evening News, Pall Mall Gazette, Reynolds News*.	New edn of *Ibsen's Prose Dramas*.	*Love's Comedy* played by amateurs, Cripplegate Theatre, 28 Nov.
W. Archer, 'Philosopher or Poet?', *Cosmopolitan*, 38:409–16.*		
W. Archer, 'Ibsen in his Letters', *Living Age*, 245:209–19 (as *Fortnightly Review*, 11:428).*		
W. M. Payne, 'Ibsen's Letters', *Dial*, 39:429–32.*		
Anon., 'Ibsen's Letters', *Current Literature*, 39:307–10.*		
H. Davidoff in *Essays in Living Dramatists*, ed. O. Hermann.*		
D. K. Dodge, 'Ibsen's Youth', *Sewanee Review*, 13:409–12.*		
A. von Ende, 'Poet, Philosopher, Revolutionist', *Craftsman*, 8:420–36.*		
M. M. Fiske 'Ibsen vs. Humpty Dumpty', *Harper's Weekly*, 49:160–1.*		
P. Harboe, 'The Real Ibsen', *Theatre*, 5:9–12.*		
A. Henderson, 'Ibsen and Social Progress', *Arena*, 33:26–30.*		
J. Huneker, *Iconoclasts. A Book of Dramatists.* *		
J. N. Laurvik, 'Letters of		

ARTICLES, REVIEWS, CRITICAL ESSAYS	TRANSLATIONS	THEATRICAL PERFORMANCES
1905—*cont.*		
Ibsen to Brandes', *Critic*, 46:157–62.*		
M. J. Moses, 'A New Femininity', *Theatre*, 5:23.*		
F. Roe, 'Ibsen', *Sewanee Review*, 13:305–18.*		
S. Whitcomb, 'Ibsen in his own Country', *Review of Reviews*, 31:365–6.*		
Anon., 'Ibsen Recital', *Theatre*, 5:49.*		
1906	**1906**	**1906**
Jones, 'Ibsen, Satirist and Poet', *Quarterly Review*, 1:71.	*The Lady from the Sea*, tr. W. Archer (new edn), with Intro.	*Lady Inger*, Scala Theatre, London, 28, 29 Jan.
Archer, 'Craftsmanship of Ibsen', *Fortnightly Review*, 2:101.	*Rosmersholm*, tr. C. & W. Archer (new edn), intro. by W. Archer.	
Archer, 'Ibsen as I Knew Him', *Monthly Review*, 2:1.	New edn of Ibsen's Prose Dramas.	
E. Dowden, 'Ibsen', *Contemporary Review*, 2:652.	*Hedda Gabler*, tr. E. Gosse (new edn).	
A. Symons, 'Ibsen', *Quarterly Review*, 2:375.	4th reprint, *Peer Gynt*, tr. W. Archer.	
Max Beerbohm, 'Ibsen', *Saturday Review*, 1:650.	2nd edn of *When we Dead Awaken*, tr. W. Archer.	
'Ibsen', *Spectator*, 1:822.		
'Ibsen', *Academy*, 1:501.	**1906–8**	
'Ibsen', *Athenaeum*, 1:647.	*The Collected Works of Henrik Ibsen*, ed. and re-vised W. Archer (11 vols.).	
E. G. Craig, A Note on *Rosmersholm*.		
Iconoclasts: A Book of Dramatists, by James Huneker.	*Brand*, tr. J. M. Olberman & A. F. Ellis.*	
Reviews of *Lady Inger of Ostraat*: *Daily News*, *Daily Chronicle*, *Era*, *Lloyd's Weekly News*, *Illustrated London News*, *The Times*, *Referee*, *Daily Graphic*.	*Brand*, tr. F. E. Garrett (reissue).*	
	Peer Gynt, The Richard Mansfield Acting Version, Abridgment of Archer's tr.*	
	Love's Comedy, tr. C. H. Herford.*	
J. L. Gilder, 'Ibsen's Letters', *Critic*, 48:280–2.*	*Little Eyolf, John Gabriel Borkman, When We Dead Awaken*, Scribner's Edn.*	
W. Archer, 'Ibsen as I Knew Him', *Reader*, 8:185–97 (as *Monthly Review*, 11:1).*	'The Sage and the Ballad', a poem, tr. E. Hearn, *Contemporary Review*, 90:318–31.*	
Anon., 'Ibsen', *Reader*, 8:324–5.*		

ARTICLES, REVIEWS, CRITICAL ESSAYS	TRANSLATIONS	THEATRICAL PERFORMANCES

1906—*cont.*

Anon., 'Ibsen and Grieg', *Reader*, 8:440–1.★

A. Clutton-Brock, 'Ibsen', *Living Age*, 249:816–18.★

G. L. Dickinson, 'Shakespeare, Ibsen, Shaw', *Living Age*, 250:437–40.★

W. D. Howells, 'Ibsen's Letters', *Harper's Weekly*, 112:958–61.★

J. A. Enander, 'Ibsen's Letters', *Outlook*, 82:321–3.★

W. O. France, 'Ibsen's Letters', *Nation*, 82:243–4.★

C. L. Due, 'Ibsen's Youth', *Critic*, 49:33–40.★

W. Archer, 'Ibsen's Craftsmanship', *Living Age*, 250:558–68 (as *Fortnightly Review*, 2:101).★

G. Brandes, 'Ibsen', *Independent*, 60:1249–50.★

E. Slosson, 'Ibsen and American Life', *Independent*, 60:1253–5.★

E. Gosse, 'Ibsen', *Atlantic Monthly*, 98:30–44.★

W. D. Howells, 'Ibsen', *North American Review*, 183:1–14.★

J. E. Olson, 'Ibsen', *Dial*, 40:351–2.★

W. M. Payne, 'Ibsen', *Harper's Weekly*, 50:816.★

Anon., 'Ibsen', *Outlook*, 83:259–61.★

Anon., 'Ibsen', *Sewanee Review*, 14:384.★

J. Hunecker, 'Ibsen', *Scribner's*, 40:351–61.★

T. Larsen, 'Ibsen', *Canadian Monthly*, 27:416–20.★

B. Matthews, 'Ibsen, the Playwright', *Bookman*, 22:568–75; 23:18–27.★

J. E. Olson, 'Ibsen In Time', *Dial*, 40:379–80.★

ARTICLES, REVIEWS, CRITICAL ESSAYS	TRANSLATIONS	THEATRICAL PERFORMANCES

1906—*cont.*

F. G. Schmidt, 'Ibsen's Influence', *Poet-Lore*, 17:112–18.*

J. D. Stone, 'Brand', *Poet-Lore*, 17:60–8.*

A. Symons, 'Ibsen', *Living Age*, 251:707–21 (as *Quarterly Review*, 2:375).*

T. Calvin, 'Ibsen', *Nation*, 82:242–4.*

J. Walsh, 'Medical Aspects of Ibsen', *Independent*, 61:444–7.*

S. Whitcomb, 'Ibsen's Influence', *Review of Reviews*, 34:37–9.*

Anon., 'Personal Traits of Ibsen', *Current Literature*, 41:62–3.*

Anon., 'Influence of Ibsen', *Current Literature*, 41:57–61.*

Anon., 'Ibsen and Shakespearean Themes', *Current Literature*, 41:304–5.*

Anon., 'New Light on Ibsen', *Current Literature*, 41:416–18.*

W. M. Payne, 'Peer Gynt in Chicago', *Dial*, 41:309–11.*

Anon., 'Mansfield's Peer Gynt', *Current Literature*, 41:654–5.*

Anon., 'Peer Gynt', *Theatre*, 6:291–4.*

Anon., 'Ibsen as World Force', *Review of Reviews*, 34:96–9.*

H. A. Jones, 'Ibsen', *Reader*, 9:105–8.*

Anon., 'Mrs. Tweedie Visits Ibsen', *Critic*, 49:1.*

BIBLIOGRAPHY

This short select bibliography is of works listing or describing Ibsen's critical reception.

Bibliographies

ANDERSEN, ANNETTE, 'Ibsen in America', *Scandinavian Studies and Notes*, vol. 14:5–6 (1937): a chronological bibliography listing all material (but not newspaper reaction) relating to Ibsen in America between 1882 and 1936. Includes summaries and quotations. Occasionally inaccurate.

FIRKINS, INA T., *Henrik Ibsen: A Bibliography of Criticism and Biography* (New York, 1921): an alphabetical bibliography listing by author all major reactions to Ibsen in America and Europe up to 1921. Does not deal with newspaper response.

HALVORSEN, J. B., *Bibliografiske oplysninger til H. Ibsens Samlede Vaerker* (Copenhagen, 1901): the standard bibliography for many years. Entries are grouped by play and list responses in all countries. Unfortunately this bibliography only goes up to 1901 and does not include *When We Dead Awaken*.

HOLLANDER, LEE M., 'A chronological bibliography of Ibsen and the interest manifested in him in the English-speaking countries', in *Speeches and New Letters by Henrik Ibsen*, ed. Arne Kildal (Boston, 1910; London, 1911): a useful working bibliography, available in most libraries. Lists chronologically with descriptive comment all major critical items, translations and performances in England and America. Occasionally inaccurate and far from complete. Does not list newspaper reactions.

PETTERSEN, HJALMAR, *Henrik Ibsen, the Norwegian Dramatist (1828–1906) in Contemporary and After-times Literature. Bibliography with selections* (Oslo, 1928): an alphabetical bibliography listing material throughout the world up to 1928. Some representative quotations included at the back.

TEDFORD, INGRID, *Ibsen Bibliography, 1928–1957* (Oslo, 1961): follows Pettersen and brings his bibliography up to 1957.

Useful accounts of Ibsen's reception in England and America

BURCHARDT, C.B., *Norwegian Life and Literature* (Oxford University Press, 1920): deals only with Ibsen in England up to 1918. Contains a useful tabulated bibliography similar to that included in this book.

DECKER, CLARENCE, 'Ibsen's Reputation and Victorian Taste', *Studies in Philology*, 32:4 (October 1935), pp. 632–45; *The Victorian Conscience* (New York: Twayne, 1952): no bibliography, but some useful references. Deals only with Ibsen in England.

FRANC, MIRIAM, *Ibsen in England* (Boston: Four Seas, 1919): with a bibliography.

HAUGEN, EINAR, 'Ibsen in America', *Norwegian-American Studies and Records*, vol. XX (1959), pp. 26–53: a valuable supplement to Paulson.

PAULSON, A. C., *The Norwegian-American Reaction to Ibsen and Björnson 1850–1900* (St Olaf College Press, 1937).

Index

The index is divided into three sections: I. Henrik Ibsen's works; II. Ibsen's life and personality, characteristics of his works and their reception; III. General (including critics, actors, contemporaries, periodicals, etc.). Ibsen is abbreviated to 'I.' in Section III.

I. HENRIK IBSEN'S WORKS

II. IBSEN'S LIFE AND CHARACTERISTICS

III. GENERAL